EXODUS FROM ROME VOLUME 1

A BIBLICAL AND HISTORICAL CRITIQUE OF ROMAN CATHOLICISM

DR. TODD D. BAKER

iUniverse LLC
Bloomington

EXODUS FROM ROME VOLUME 1
A BIBLICAL AND HISTORICAL CRITIQUE OF ROMAN CATHOLICISM

iUniverse books may be ordered through booksellers or by contacting:

iUniverse LLC
1663 Liberty Drive
Bloomington, IN 47403
www.iuniverse.com
1-800-Authors (1-800-288-4677)

Because of the dynamic nature of the Internet, any web addresses or links contained in this book may have changed since publication and may no longer be valid. The views expressed in this work are solely those of the author and do not necessarily reflect the views of the publisher, and the publisher hereby disclaims any responsibility for them.

Any people depicted in stock imagery provided by Thinkstock are models, and such images are being used for illustrative purposes only.
Certain stock imagery © Thinkstock.

ISBN: 978-1-4917-2470-5 (sc)
ISBN: 978-1-4917-2471-2 (e)

Printed in the United States of America.

iUniverse rev. date: 05/09/2014

"Have I therefore become your enemy because I tell you the truth?" (Galatians 4:16).

Special thanks goes to David Violente and Aaron Levitt for their editorial and research contributions.

CONTENTS

CHAPTER 1

EXODUS FROM ROME

The following examination of Roman Catholicism from Scripture, Church history, and reason is not designed to purposely offend, insult, or mock those who sincerely believe and follow the teachings of Roman Catholicism, but is written by a born-again Christian and former Roman Catholic deeply concerned for the perishing souls of men and women caught, entangled, and confused in the labyrinthine web of Roman Catholicism. We speak the truth from Scripture in love (Ephesians 4:11); that they might be saved by the true Gospel of grace alone (Acts 20:24) and may *"come to their senses and escape the snare of the devil, who are taken captive by him at his will"* through the manifold errors of Romanism (2 Timothy 2:26). How does Roman Catholicism differ from biblical Christianity? To answer that would take volumes to write, which many have done before us. But suffice it to say that this writer will highlight the main differences between this counterfeit religious system of salvation and the single way of salvation; between righteousness by works and the righteousness of faith; between myopic devotion to the Popes, priests, and sacraments of Rome versus salvation in the person and finished work of the Lord Jesus Christ alone.

The author is thoroughly acquainted with the religion of Roman Catholicism. He was trained, indoctrinated, and prepared for entrance into the priesthood for eighteen years, attending both seminary and parochial schools in the process. But to distill any remaining doubts in some of our readers' minds, the author will digress here and briefly give a detailed account of his personal experience and involvement with the Church of Rome. His motive and intent for doing this is the same as the Apostle Paul's in Romans 10:1. There, Paul's earnest desire and prayer to God was that Israel would find salvation in the Messiah Jesus. So too, in the same way, it is my heartfelt desire and prayer that Roman Catholics would be truly saved and born-again in Christ alone. Being raised in a moderately conservative Roman Catholic home, I naturally was taught by the priests and nuns of Rome, that if I followed the rules of the Church to the best of my ability, I would be saved from hell and probably end up in a place called purgatory after death, like most average Catholics, and, then, would undergo "temporal punishment" for the venial sins committed in this life. Only those canonized as "Saints" by the Roman Catholic Church went directly to heaven.[1]

One good thing in my training was instruction in the basic doctrines of Christian Orthodoxy—the Bible is God's word, the deity of Christ, the Trinity, the Atonement, eternal judgment, the resurrection of Christ,

---

[1] *Catechism of the Catholic Church* (New York: Image, 1995), 289-291 **[1023-031]**.

1

the Second Coming, and so on. Sadly, however, some of these fundamental truths were and are grossly superseded and eclipsed by numerous error filled, extra biblical doctrines that require faithful adherence by the observant Roman Catholic. The priests further taught me that the Roman Catholic Church was the only genuine Church Christ first established through Peter and his successors, the Popes. Outside of this Church, there was no hope of salvation. Thus, there emerged and was formed in my mind, over a period of time, the inevitable conclusion, reinforced by the clergy, that salvation in the church of Rome required an active compliance of what she commanded through the Magisterium, the decrees of the Popes, and an ongoing participation in the sacramental system. This included the weekly attendance of Mass and participating in practices like: reciting the rosary (prayers to Mary), wearing scapulars and medals, worshipping the Blessed Sacrament (wafer host), going to confession, saying prayers to the departed saints—all of which were added to gain merit and approval before God.

This all translated into the grace denying doctrine of salvation by "good" works. The more I attempted to earn divine approval through the rites and rituals of Roman Catholicism, the more I was acutely aware of my own impotence and utter depravity before a perfect, righteous, and holy God of Whom I could not consistently keep the many conflicting requirements of Rome. I was then under guilt and the fear of condemnation. Guilt, because I was not perfectly law abiding as Rome required, and fear, because if out of utter frustration I stopped practicing the rituals and rites Rome prescribes for meriting salvation, I would die in a state of mortal sin and condemnation. This moral dilemma is a common feature and experience all sincere and devout Roman Catholics seem to exhibit and walk under simply because they, and all fallible humans alike, cannot obey God's Law, or any law perfectly without fault (see Romans 3:20-23; Galatians 3:11).

The demand to keep the law perfectly, whether by the Mosaic Law, or the codified system of Rome, only intensifies the knowledge of one's inability, sinfulness, and moral weakness in not keeping the law and reinforces the sense of alienation from God (see Romans 7:7-13). Catholicism does teach nominal grace, but attaches works along with it as a precondition for final salvation. True salvation is always by God's free grace alone apart from human work or merit (Ephesians 2:8-9); and adding or subtracting from it by requiring works with it makes it a nullity. The one great work required alone from all people by God is simply to believe and trust in Jesus Christ alone for salvation (John 6:29). This truth is not the theological product of the oversimplified reductionism of Protestant "fundamentalism," as some Roman Catholic defenders would accuse, but are the very words of Christ Himself when asked by the Jews what good work one must do to have the favor of God. ***"Then they said to him, 'what shall we do, that we may work the works of God?' Jesus answered and said to them, "This is the work of God, <u>that you believe in Him</u> whom He sent"*** (John 6:27-28). No mention here of the Mass, the rosary, or the seven sacraments being required by the Lord for salvation—only faith in Jesus Christ. Saving grace is ineffectual in any religious system that demands more than this for salvation. But within any religious system that relies on works for salvation, there are those who become self-righteous. The Roman Catholic Church has its share of these types of people who see nothing wrong with themselves that think they are justified and saved before God based on what they do as practicing Roman Catholics instead of what Christ alone did for sinners on the cross two thousand years ago.

It was this same controversy of good works, as opposed to divine grace, that Paul addressed, when he sternly wrote Galatians 5:4. His words of warning there, certainly applies to those under the yoke of Rome and all other religions that stress something more is needed other than divine grace through faith in Christ alone for God's acceptance, justification, and salvation of the repentant sinner. Herein is the tragedy of many Roman Catholics: In trying to attain heaven by doing all that Rome requires, they fail to receive the salvation Christ offers that is by grace (God's unmerited favor) alone received through faith alone. Unmerited grace is the sole basis on which God sovereignly saves any of us, apart from any good and righteous deeds we do before or after becoming Christians. ***"Not by works of righteousness which we have done, but according to His mercy He saved us"*** is the emphatic declaration of the Holy Scriptures in Titus 3:5. Tragically, millions in the works-system religion of Roman Catholicism are perishing in hell, and many more will follow, because they did not properly receive salvation according to the clear teaching of Scripture, wishing, instead, to earn or merit such through their own self effort as dictated by Rome, in lieu of receiving it directly from Jesus Christ in simple faith that rests alone on the accomplished work of His cross without adding or taking away from it by assisting God in their salvation.

The plain teaching of Scripture is that good works come after faith, not as a condition or reward for salvation but, rather, as a natural consequence and practical outflow of saving faith already present and expressed (see James 2:14-20). This is the fundamental teaching in the Epistle of James and does not contradict the teaching of Paul in the book of Romans which states that faith alone justifies the sinner before God, apart from any kind of meritorious works done by the sinner (see Romans 3:26-27). James simply adds that real faith, if true and saving, will be active and therefore consequently evinced by good works (more on this will be discussed under the subject of the Roman Catholic system of salvation in contrast to the biblical teaching on salvation). Martin Luther best summed up the proper relationship between works and salvation when saying, "A man is not saved by doing good works, but a saved man does good works."

It was only after attending an all boys Catholic parochial boarding school under the supervision of Benedictine monks and priests in Arkansas, that I realized much of the Roman Catholic clergy were secretly base and immoral, albeit in the public eye they were reputed by the laity on the outside as noble, chaste, and righteous men (see Matthew 23:27-28). However, those like me, who lived with the priests and monks as a student, witnessed on a daily basis they were far from saintly and angelic, but were full of hypocrisy and iniquity within. Those sympathetic to the priesthood would say here this is an unfair appraisal, and that they were only human in the end, and being this way, had faults like anyone else. This maybe true of non-Christians, but those who profess faith in Jesus Christ will habitually exhibit a transformed lifestyle of moral purity and rectitude. True Christians will not habitually live in vice or some form of immorality as a settled lifestyle that is excused or justified (see 2 Timothy 2:19; Galatians 5:19-21; 1 Corinthians 6:9-11). This is unequivocally not the case with many of the clerics of Rome. Some, if not a considerable number of them, were given over to shameful drunkenness and had a constant supply of the intoxicating poison from the vineyards they carefully gleaned behind the Abbey. Others had not only been imbibing, but were actually involved in homosexual perversions as well.

One particular priest, who was a math instructor of the school, would frequently enter class in an inebriated state accompanied with an overpowering stench of alcohol on his person. He would customarily make arrangements to help students after school with their homework. When a student came to his office later he would motion him to come in and stand by him behind his desk. He then proceeded to help the young man with his difficult homework while he simultaneously put his hands down the front of the boy's pants pressing firmly in the area of the groin while looking up at the bewildered student with a drunken glazed over smile. The author saw and was horribly subjected to this repeated occurrence in shock and disbelief. Often times the student would be paralyzed with great fear. Later on, to cope with the traumatic experience, he would, along with his fellow students, make sport of this poor debauched soul with all sorts of verbal slurs and slang terms for the homosexual and alcoholic condition the pitiful priest was bound in. The numerous reports now coming out in the media of children being molested by priests in the last several years makes this account all the more believable.

There was another occasion were two drunken monks cast their monastic habits aside one late night and climbed the water tower together in the dark totally in the nude. Several students saw this ungodly spectacle. They could not make out what they were doing up there since there were a large cluster of trees in front of the water tower blocking their view. After waiting for an hour, the students left the scene at the strong request of a priest. They went away mocking these two unholy monks, who apparently stayed up there all night doing unspeakable acts. Nothing was said or done the next morning, or for that matter any time after that. There were also credible reports of other monks and priests engaging in acts of sodomy, bestiality, and fornication. Were these moral aberrations solely limited and confined mainly to this Abbey school, or is it merely a microcosmic indication of the moral degeneration Romanism breeds and germinates within her clerical ranks on a larger scale?

The annals of Papal Rome's sordid history among the nations she has resided in abundantly confirms this to be the case. Space does not permit us here to give a detailed account of the various Popes who raped, sodomized, murdered, and instituted mass execution campaigns all in the name of Christ, or the many of her clergy steeped in vices much too horrid to describe here for the sensitive reader. The preponderant fruit from Romanism's false doctrines is spiritual want, religious bondage, idolatry, political and religious tyranny, mass bloodshed, drunkenness, homosexuality, pedophilia, fornication, heresy, and doctrinal deception—all of which ultimately leading to damnation (for a historical review of the moral corruptions of the Roman Catholic Church see the book *Crime and Immorality in the Catholic Church* written by former Franciscan Priest Emmet McLoughlin, New York: Lyle Stuart, 1962). If the Roman Catholic or ecumenical Christian chafes at what has just been said, we appeal to the objective history of past and present. Visit Mexico, Central and South America, parts of the West Indies, Spain, France, Italy, and some of the Eastern European countries which are predominately Roman Catholic, where Rome has the preeminence and you will see these things in abundance coupled with an epidemic ignorance of biblical truth. Missionaries of biblical Christianity who are in these very countries are often shunned, silenced, threatened, and persecuted by the Roman Catholic hierarchy of bishops and priests and their fanatically devoted lay-people.

By applying the test of Scripture to this vile and wicked system, we see that Rome's conduct and content, generally speaking, can be conclusively determined to be reprobate and evil. Because the core is rotten and depraved, so will be the fruit. ***"You shall know them by their fruits. Do men gather grapes of thorns, or figs of thistles? Even so every good tree brings forth good fruit, but a corrupt tree brings forth evil fruit. A good tree cannot bring forth evil fruit; neither can a corrupt tree bring forth good fruit. <u>Every tree that does not bring forth good fruit is cut down, and cast into the fire. Therefore by their fruits you will know them</u>"*** (Matthew 7:16-20). And so in the future Tribulation period the Vatican will be engulfed in the fiery furnace of God's wrath because she stubbornly refused to bring forth fruits worthy of repentance (see Revelation 2:21-23; 17:16). Proclaiming these harsh and difficult truths is not to deny that there have been many individuals in the Roman Catholic Church—both in the past and present—who have been genuinely born-again by the Spirit of God—for even now there is at the present time a saved remnant according to the election of God's sovereign grace (Revelation 2:24-25). *However, it is important to point out that they are not saved by following the dictates of Roman Catholicism for earning salvation, but are saved in spite of them, because they wisely chose to put their trust in Jesus Christ alone for salvation and justification.* God, however, commands these very people who are His in Christ to depart from this Babylonian system of vain ritual, priest craft, sacramental magic, and idolatry (see Revelation 18:8).

After attending the parochial boarding school for two years, I was extremely disillusioned with the Roman Catholic system. Because I was taught from early childhood this was God's institution, I mistakenly equated God with it, and out of intense bitterness, embraced a militant atheism, instead. Satan had cleverly deceived me into believing God did not really exist in the face of so much immorality among those claiming to represent Him, nor was He just, moral and righteous as indicated by the moral bankruptcy of the Roman Catholic clergy. Several years past before I was to encounter the Church of Rome again on another level as a born-again Christian, who had, indeed, met the real Jesus that is revealed in Scripture. Due to limited writing space, I pass over the four years of my hellish descent into atheism and my habitual use of drugs. Rather, I will resume the narrative from the days after the Risen Christ was supernaturally revealed to me according to the Scriptures, and my subsequent entrance into a Roman Catholic seminary.

Being a spiritual babe in Christ for only a few months, I had an unquenchable love for God and a deep desire to devote the rest of my life in service to Him. Naturally, given my prior religious background, I assumed that could only be done by becoming a priest of the Roman Catholic Institution whereupon I entered a Roman Catholic seminary in Ohio. This time I reentered Romanism as a spirit-filled regenerated Christian. In addition to my discovery, a few years earlier, that the Roman Catholic institution was morally corrupt, I was to soon discover in seminary that what Roman Catholicism taught was diametrically opposed, in many cases, to what the Word of God teaches. The primary text we used in the first six months of seminary was not the Bible, but the Vatican II Council book. Not once in all that time did we ever crack open a Bible the entire semester I was there, nor was the plan of salvation clearly explained from the Scriptures! The religious man-made traditions of Rome were given the exclusive preeminence! Indeed, never once in the seminary did I hear the priests of Rome explain the clear Gospel plan of salvation; neither did I hear it during any Mass I had attended during the entire eighteen years I was in the Roman Catholic system! Jesus commands all people to first search the Scriptures that point the way to eternal life through its inerrant testimony about Him (John 5:39).

The priests in the seminary told us that what the Church taught through the Popes, Cardinals, Bishops, priests, Vatican approved theologians, ecclesiastical traditions with the voice of the Magisterium (the teaching authority of the Church), existed on an equal plane with Scripture! But this resulted, as it always does, in placing these things above the authority of Scripture. The instructors at the seminary proceeded to attack the veracity of Scripture by teaching the following blasphemies: Adam did not literally exist; the historical account of Jonah being swallowed by a whale is untrue and a mere myth or allegory to teach a moral lesson; the existence of the devil is questionable; evolution is a scientific fact; the genealogies of Christ are contradictory and historically inaccurate; Moses and the Hebrews walked through the ankle deep reed sea and not through the miraculously parted Red Sea; the creation accounts of Genesis 1 and 2 are mythical, untrue, contradictory, and irreconcilable with 'science' and evolution. Ironically, they viewed Holy Scripture through the apostate Protestant lens of the liberal theory of Form Criticism based on the anti-supernatural hermeneutic of Rudolf Bultmann and other liberal theologians, which Rome, since the Vatican II Council, has allowed to infect and permeate many of their seminaries and religious institutions. All this was just a small sample of the infidelity and heresy being taught against the truth of God-inspired Scripture in this Roman Catholic seminary I attended for a brief time.

Fortunately, by the grace of the Lord Jesus Christ, I was able to see through their falsehood and unbelief towards the Word of God. Sovereignly, the Lord was good enough to put me together with Bible believing born-again Christians outside the seminary whom a fellow seminarian, disillusioned with Rome also, introduced me to. The Bible study group lovingly and gently encouraged me to begin an in depth study of the Bible comparing its teachings with the claims of Roman Catholicism. By the Holy Spirit's ministry of illumination of the Word to me, I immediately recognized the serious errors of Romanism from my own exposure to the Word of God. The Lord was beginning to open my spiritual eyes to see the real truth about the Roman Catholic Institution. Like the great reformer, Martin Luther, I realized with profound and shocking disillusionment that the Roman Catholic Institution was a colossal counterfeit universally accepted as the one true Church of Christ for the last 1,600 years or so. But Satan sorely tried to dissuade me from this truth by whispering in my ear, "Surely all these people can't be wrong and you right; what great arrogance!" But that cunning voice of doubt was forever silenced when the appeal to the final authority for determining truth came not from myself, nor from the "Church", or from "Tradition" and the pompous papacy, but from, "Thus says the Lord" found in the inerrant Word of God that stands above all human and religious authority, church councils, Popes, creeds, and traditions.

The sufficiency of Scripture alone (taken from the great Reformation principle *Sola Scriptura*) was the supreme principle the Holy Spirit emblazoned on my mind and heart to follow and live by when following the Lord Jesus Christ. The Scriptures plainly and explicitly contradict the many traditions of Roman Catholicism, as this work will show. I cannot thank the Lord enough for opening my blind eyes to see the truth liberating me from the yoke of Roman Catholic legalism into the glorious Gospel of free grace given in the Lord Jesus Christ. Those who remain in the Roman Catholic system out a false sense of security, allegiance, fear or complacent satisfaction will no doubt take offense at what has been said in this chapter, and for the rest of this book, for that matter, and will angrily differ and smugly dispute. But in the face of Christ's finished work of redemption on Calvary obtaining eternal life and heaven for me when I believed because of what He accomplished alone for me, I say to them, ***"Let God be true and every man a liar"*** (Romans 3:4). Furthermore, to confirm the truth in my mind about this earth-shaking discovery not being self concocted or a satanic deception, the Lord gave me an admonitory vision while laying on my bed, whether awake or in a semi sleepy state, I cannot tell (See Job 33:14-17).[2] I seemed to be conscious, yet in a type of trance. In this vision God clearly warned and showed me the true spiritual state of the place and religious institution I was in and of those living there. The vision also warned me that if I did not depart from there soon great spiritual harm would come.

The vision went like this: I was in the dining hall of the seminary and around me were the priests who taught at the seminary and the students with them. They were all in a state of drunkenness and sleepiness groping as if in the dark. Their drunkenness, though, was not induced by wine or any other alcoholic beverage. I had an open Bible in my hand and went to one of the learned priests who taught philosophy and asked what the general content of the Bible means. He answered curtly, "I don't know, it is a closed Book, and I doubt God even exists." I can remember his comment striking me in an odd way. For here was a man of the Roman Catholic clergy, an avowed minister of the Church, who did not believe in the existence of God, and therefore failed to understand the basic message of God's Word! I then asked another student the same question about the meaning of Scripture. His response was that he was not educated enough to answer. After the priest's apathetic and somewhat agnostic response, I knew I had to immediately leave and get sound counsel from the Scriptures somewhere else. I was the only sober one in the group in this vision who realized what was going on. When I looked away from this ungodly sot, I saw a lighted stairway leading out of that foul place of inebriation. As I climbed up the stairs, another seminary student attempted to keep me from leaving, but I resolutely left up the lighted staircase never to return to that spiritually dark place again.

---

2   Scripture often recounts how God at critical points in history confirms or gives guidance to His people through dreams and visions (see Genesis 37:1-11; Joel 2:28; Matthew 1:20-24; 27:18). This was true in my case here when it came to leaving the Roman Catholic Institution.

The student in the vision was the same exact one who came to me several months later at the seminary and tried to convince me not to leave the Roman Catholic Institution! When I gave him Scriptural grounds for doing so he could say nothing, but instead promised me a position in his parish located in beautiful Hawaii if I finished seminary and became a priest of Rome. This was obviously a ploy of the devil to seduce me into staying in the Roman Catholic Church oppressed and frustrated by her inconsistent, anti-scriptural teachings. I realized later this vision pointed to what was to unfold several months ahead. Two weeks later, after praying for a biblical interpretation of this unusual visitation, the Lord gave me the prophetic interpretation based on Isaiah 29:9-13, which says: ***"Pause and wonder! Blind yourselves and be blind! They are drunk, but not with wine; they stagger, but not with intoxicating drink. For the LORD has poured out on you the spirit of deep sleep, and has closed your eyes, namely, the prophets; And He has covered your heads, namely, the seers. The whole vision has become to you like the words of a book that is sealed, which men deliver to one who is literate, saying, "Read this, please." and he says, "I cannot, for it is sealed." Then the book is delivered to one who is illiterate, saying, "Read this, please" and he says, "I am not literate." Therefore the Lord said: "Inasmuch as these people draw near with their mouths and honor Me with their lips, but have removed their hearts far from Me, and their fear toward Me is taught by the commandment of men."***

God was saying through the prophet Isaiah the same thing in the vision He gave me; that these religious counterfeits of the Roman Catholic clergy, and their students, were moral drunkards, spiritually blind, somnolent, and walking in darkness because they pushed aside the premium importance of knowing God's Word and practically applying it, in favor of placing the vain philosophical and religious precepts of men (as formulated in the many doctrines of Romanism) in its place. Consequently, this prevented them and their myopic followers from arriving at the correct meaning of God's Word. Though they gave verbal assent and nominal respect to the Holy Scriptures in the liturgy, the writings of the Popes, and "Church Tradition", they really treated it in the vast perspective of life as an insignificant book that is sealed, closed, and far too mysterious for the average person to understand. Their hearts had an arrogant disdain and disregard for the supreme authority, all sufficiency, and profound simplicity of the Scriptures *alone*. They, like their religious hypocritical counterparts in Isaiah's day, placed man-made tradition above the Word of God!

After this the Holy Spirit impressed on me, more than ever, that the Roman Catholic Institution was the greatest spiritual counterfeit perpetuated in the name of Christ ever to be passed off onto the hearts and minds of men. Romanism erected a vast monolithic image from the ruins of the old Roman Empire begun by the unholy fusion of church and state initiated. Such an unholy fusion began with the Roman Emperor Constantine who was devoted to political aggrandizement and power to be later clothed in the guise of the Roman Catholic Papacy.[3] This fatal compromise set in motion the rise of Papal imperialism centuries later with Roman Catholicism being the dominant religion over the civilized world by the eighth century for indeed,

> The cost of Constantine's 'conversion' to Christianity was the loss of innocence. His cynical use of Christ, in which everyone, including the Bishop of Rome, acquiesced, meant a profound falsification of the Gospel message and the injection of standards alien to it. From then on, Catholicism flourished to the detriment of Christianity and of Jesus who

---

[3] Malachi Martin, *The Decline and fall of the Roman Church* (New York: Bantam Books, 1983), 19-45. Martin was a practicing Jesuit priest until his death in 1999.

wanted no part in the world of power and politics, who preferred to be crucified rather than to impose his views on anyone. By the time Stephen III became pope, the church was thoroughly converted to the Roman Empire.[4]

In the past, we will discover that Papal Rome has destroyed those bold enough to denounce her from Scripture and expose her damnable heresies, and if given that same power today, would do so again, now, and in the future. A few months after this vision, I was bound and determined by the Spirit of the Lord to leave "Mother Church" behind to attend a Christian Bible college devoted to teaching the Bible as the supreme authority and guide for Christian faith and practice. The priests, who knew that I rightly contended and believed in the inerrancy of the Bible being literally true in its scientific, theological, and historical content, caustically labeled me a "Fundamentalist", and treated me with haughty intolerance and condescension because I had the audacity to test what they were theologically claiming by the examining light of Holy Scripture.[5]

From spending time at this Catholic seminary, I carefully deduced from the Word of God by the illumination of the Holy Spirit's guidance, that the priests and Popes of Rome were not teaching sound doctrine according to the Scriptures, but rather, they would take certain Scriptures out of context to support their false doctrine. In truth, they were not of Christ, nor did they have his light within them for the simple reason that the Scriptures were not the supreme rule and conduct for their faith (see Isaiah 8:20). Much of what they taught for Rome, at that particular seminary, was contrary to the Bible, and in fact both harmfully added and subtracted from the Word of God (i.e., the Apocrypha and Church Tradition).

The penalty for doing this will earn God's anathema and expose those who do so to be liars (see Proverbs 30:6; Revelation 22:18-19). In the following chapters of this book, we will closely and carefully examine the major doctrines that make up Roman Catholicism under the critical light of Scripture. We will demonstrate that Rome's doctrines blatantly contradict what the authors of Sacred scripture had intended for us to know and understand. In the course of this study, we will also analyze and address how the defenders of Rome typically answer from history, Scripture, and tradition to refute the factual allegation that the Bible and Romanism are contrary one to the other. This book will rebut the claims of Rome and her defenders, and demonstrate from both Scripture and church history that the grandiose claims of Roman Catholicism are spurious, anti-scriptural, and against the unmerited grace of God.

---

[4]   Peter De Rosa, *Vicars of Christ* (New York: Crown, 1988), 44-45. De Rosa was a former Catholic priest who did extensive research in the Vatican archives. He is still a practicing Catholic.

[5]   The diminutive label "Fundamentalist" is customarily used in a negative sense by most Roman Catholic apologists to unfairly categorize Protestant Christians who legitimately argue that Roman Catholicism patently contradicts biblical Christianity. Catholic apologist, Karl Keating, is infamous for this. In his book, *Catholicism and Fundamentalism* (San Francisco, CA: Ignatius Press, 1988), Keating repeatedly resorts to this name-calling tactic for anyone who dares to disagree with Rome's blasphemous claims on the basis of Holy Scripture. A person can be a fundamentalist in the sense that he or she firmly holds to the fundamental doctrines of the Christian faith, and still rightfully disagree with the anti-biblical doctrines of Rome without being dismissed as the typical 'fundamentalist' who is stereotypically portrayed to be boorish, theologically ignorant, naïve, and unlearned. Keating, and other Roman Catholic apologists, do well to remember this distinction here before dismissing the real theological concerns and problems Bible believing Protestants have with the unwarranted claims of Rome that undermine the Gospel and contradict Scripture.

CHAPTER 2

THE DOCTRINE OF THE PAPACY

The issue and subject of authority is one of great concern to both Bible believing Protestants and Roman Catholics. This is where the similarity over the issue of authority quickly begins and ends with both groups who clearly answer the issue differently. How one answers this question will determine and influence the belief system, theology, and world-view that person maintains. Where do we go to find such a reliable authority to trust in concerning matters of faith, practice, and explanation? The most important question to ask and ultimate decision to make is in which authority do we trust with our eternal destiny? For Roman Catholicism, the issue of authority in the Church is found in the Papacy and the Popes who proceed from this hierarchical institution. The Roman Catholic system stands or falls with the Papacy. Disprove the validity of it from Scripture, and the rest of the convoluted system of Romanism, collapses to the earth as an invention of men, and not from God. Rome claims that the institution of the Papacy is indeed found in the New Testament passage Matthew 16:17-19 where we read:

Simon Peter answered, "You are the Christ, the Son of the living God." Jesus replied, "Blessed are you, Simon son of Jonah, for this was not revealed to you by man, but by my Father in heaven. And I tell you that you are Peter, and on this rock I will build my church, and the gates of Hell will not overcome it. I will give you the keys of the kingdom of heaven; whatever you bind on earth will be bound in heaven, and whatever you loose on earth will be loosed in heaven."

Here in the Gospel of Matthew, the Roman Catholic Institution claims to be the one and only true Church Jesus Christ founded and built upon Peter, "the Prince of the Apostles." And this same apostolic headship over the Church has been consecutively passed on to his successors the Popes. Section 159 of the Adult Baltimore Catechism states,

> The true Church is apostolic because it is the Church Christ founded upon the Apostles, and especially upon Peter whom He called the rock on which the Church would be built. The supreme power of St. Peter in the Church has been passed down through the unbroken lives of his successors in the see of Rome.[1]

The Vatican II Council formally decreed,

---

[1]   John A. O'Brien, *Understanding the Catholic Faith* (Notre Dame, Indiana: Ave Maria Press, 1956), 119.

> The Lord made Peter alone the rock-foundation and the holder of the keys of the Church (cf. Mt. 16:18-19), and constituted him shepherd of his whole flock (cf. Jn. 21:15ff).[2]

The Catechism of the Catholic Church also reiterates the same.[3] The official name for this teaching that Christ established the Apostle Peter and his successors, the Popes, as the visible head and ruler of the Church on Earth, is called *Apostolic Succession*. It is viewed as the bedrock upon which the Papacy and the exclusive claims of the Roman Catholic Church are built. Rome has assigned various names for this teaching: The Primacy of Peter, the Petrine Confession, Apostolic Succession, the Holy See, and the Papacy. Apostolic Succession, as viewed by Rome, is one of the two great pillars upon which the whole edifice of the Papacy is built. The other pillar is *Temporal Power*. The Papacy bases Apostolic Succession on the main text of Matthew 16:17-19 and how they interpret the word "rock in verse eighteen. Roman Catholics are taught to believe by the teachings of the Vatican that Jesus proclaimed His Church would be built upon Peter "the rock"—with the living and the dead under his jurisdiction as symbolized by the keys of dominical authority given to him by Christ. All the other Apostles were therefore subject and subordinate to Peter, including the Apostle Paul. Furthermore, this delegated authority is transmitted to Peter's patrimonial successors—the Popes. The Popes are called "the Vicars of Christ on Earth" and as such act as His representatives on Earth as the visible head of the church. Official Catholic teaching affirms that,

> The Lord made Peter St. Peter the visible foundation of his Church. He entrusted the keys of the Church to him. The bishop of the Church of Rome, successor to St. Peter, "is head of the college of bishops, the Vicar of Christ and Pastor of the universal church on earth."[4]

The word "vicar" comes from the Latin word *vicarius*, from whence we derive the English word "vicarious" from. The word simply means to take the place of someone while that person is absent. According to official Roman Catholic dogma, the Pope is the "Vicar of Christ", and thus is the divinely appointed representative of Jesus Christ on Earth as the visible head of the Church while He is currently absent. The Popes in this inherited role have authority over the living and the dead. This was formally adopted as Roman Catholic Dogma by the Council of Trent, and reaffirmed by the Vatican Councils II and I. Cardinal Gibbons voices this teaching as official Roman Catholic doctrine to be believed by all faithful Catholics with unquestioning obedience. He writes:

> The Catholic Church teaches that our Lord conferred on St. Peter the first place of honor and jurisdiction in the government of his whole Church, and that same spiritual supremacy has always resided in the Popes, or bishops of Rome, as being successors of St. Peter. ***Consequently, to be true followers of Christ all Christians, both among the clergy and laity, must be in communion with the See of Rome, wherein Peter rules in the person of His successors*** (Emphasis mine).[5]

---

2   Austin Flannery, ed., *Vatican Council II* (Northport, New York: Costello Publishing Company, 1986), 375.

3   *Catechism of the Catholic Church*, 155-156 [**551-553**].

4   *Catechism of the Catholic Church*, 267 [**936**].

5   Cardinal James Gibbons, *Faith of Our Fathers* (Rockford, Ill: Tan Books, 1980), 95.

Any who deny the supremacy of the Pope as sole ruler over the entire church, and any who refuse to accept the Pope as the true successor of Peter, are brazenly placed under the eternal damnation of God, according to the Vatican Council I.

> If, then, anyone shall say that it is not by the institution of Christ the Lord, or by divine right, that blessed Peter has a perpetual line of successors in the primacy over the universal Church; or that the Roman Pontiff is not the successors of Blessed Peter in this primacy; let him be anathema.[6]

The particular term "anathema" means to invoke the curse of the eternal condemnation of God on any person who rejects and disagrees with this essential doctrine of the Papacy. The defenders of Rome, in their attempt to blunt the force of this presumptuous malediction, claim that the term is limited only to excommunication from the Roman Catholic Church and nothing more. But is that all that happens when anyone is anathematized by the Pope? We discover that in the 1913 edition of the *Catholic Encyclopedia*, when the Catholic Church anathematizes someone under the category of *major excommunication*, the Pope ritually puts curses on him or her. There is a solemn written ritual for doing this. The *Catholic Encyclopedia* article describes the ritual in detail, including extensive quotations from it. In pronouncing the anathema, the Pope wears special vestments. He is assisted by twelve priests holding lighted candles. Calling on the name of God, the Pope pronounces a solemn ecclesiastical curse. He ends by pronouncing sentence and declaring that the anathematized person is condemned to hell with Satan, his angels, and all the reprobate. The priests' reply, "Fiat" (Let it be done!), and throw down their candles![7] Pope Innocent (1198-1216), not Peter, was arguably the first Pope who claimed to be the universal "Vicar of Christ" with both apostolic and temporal powers, and during his pontificate declared on the person who disagreed with him, "We excommunicate, anathematize, curse and damn him."[8] For a lapsed Catholic, or Bible believing Protestant, to reject the Papacy is to then invite God's damnation down upon them according to the Papal Councils of Trent and Vatican I, which were both reaffirmed by Vatican II!

Upon every coronation of a Pope the following ceremonial pronouncement is said, "Take thou the tiara adorned with Triple Crown, and know that thou art the father of princes and kings, and art the governor of the world." Rome further believes and proclaims that the recognition and submission to the Papacy is essential for salvation! Roman Catholics must submit to the Pope in all matters to be saved. Not only is the Pope considered the successor of Peter, but is reputed as God sitting on St. Peter's chair in the Vatican. Pope Boniface VIII (1294-1303) declared in his Papal bull *Unam Sanctum,*

> The Roman Pontiff judges all men, but is judged by no one. We declare, assert, define, and pronounce: ***To be subject to the Roman Pontiff is to every human creature altogether necessary for salvation…. [that which was spoken of Christ, "Thou hast subdued all things under His feet, may well seem verified in me…I have the authority of the King***

---

[6] *Dogmatic Canons and Decrees* (Rockford, Ill: Tan Books, 1912), 246.

[7] *The Catholic Encyclopedia* vol. 1, Charles Herbermann, ed., (New York: Robert Appleton Company, 1907), 1913. To view this on-line go to http://www.newadvent.org/cathen/01455e.htm. I am indebted to former nun Mary Ann Collins' web site (http://www.catholicconcerns.com) for this documentation from the Catholic sources.

[8] Paul Johnson, *A History of Christianity* (New York: Simon & Schuster, 1995), 199. See also R.W. Southern, *Western Society and the Church in the Middle Ages* (Harmondsworth, 1970), 105.

of kings. I am all and above all, so that God Himself and I the Vicar of God, have but one consistory, (Church) and am able to do all that God can do. What therefore, can you make of me but God?[9]

In his encyclical, "The Reunion of Christendom" issued in 1885, Pope Leo XIII (1878-1903) pompously claimed that he "holds upon this earth the place of God Almighty." Do *some* Roman Catholics today still think the Pope is like God? When Pope John Paul II was shot in May of 1981, *Time* magazine reported a Roman Catholic bystander saying, "It's like shooting God!"[10]

The Papal claims quoted in the last few previous paragraphs from Rome's Popes and Church Councils are nothing short of rank blasphemy to the highest degree. And these claims will only be trumped by those of the future Anti-Christ of whom the Pope is a definite historical type and shadow (see 2 Thessalonians 2:3-4). Are we giving way to blind prejudicial "anti-Catholic" sensationalism or gross exaggeration as Rome's defenders routinely allege *ad nauseam* in affirming this? No, let the mouth of the Papists impugn themselves on this point. For they not only ascribe to the Pope a divine-like quality, but also the divine titles of the Trinity. The Pope is revered and addressed as, "Holy Father,"[11] This divine name belongs to God the Father alone. The name is so holy, exclusive, and reverend that the Lord Jesus Christ used it only once for His heavenly Father in John 17:11.

Christ clearly forbids His followers to call any man by the spiritual title "Father" be he Pope or priest of Rome. *"Do not call anyone on earth you father; for One is your Father, He who is in heaven"* (Matthew 23:9). Only God is truly holy in the perfect sense, for all men are sinners unholy, and unjust by nature. *"For there is not a man upon earth, that does good and sins not"* (Ecclesiastes 7:20; Romans 3:11-18). This most certainly includes the Pope, even more so than other men since he blasphemously takes to himself the names of God. Hence, he has much more in common with "the man of sin" in 2 Thessalonians 2:3 than with the divine Man of Sorrows found in the holy Gospels. Of all men, only Jesus is inherently sinless (Hebrews 7:26). At the annunciation, the angel Gabriel informed Mary that Jesus was a holy offspring begotten of the Holy Spirit of God (Luke 1:35). However, the Pope derives neither his holiness nor exaltation of office by God. The Lord will not share his divine glory with another (Isaiah 42:8). The Pope sits as "Christ" in the Vatican publicly proclaiming to be his sole representative on Earth. The following was solemnly addressed to Pope Pius IX (1846-1878) at the Vatican I Council on January 9, 1870: "The Pope is Christ in office, Christ in jurisdiction, and power...we bow down before thy voice. O Pius, as before the voice of Christ, the God

---

[9]   *The Christian Faith in The Doctrinal Documents of the Catholic Church*, eds., J. Neuner, S.J. and J Dupius, S.J. (New York: Alba House, 1982), 217-218. The brackets indicate that most Modern renditions of this Papal Bull, like the citation here, conspicuously omit the words after stating submission to the Pope is altogether necessary for salvation. No doubt the horrible megalomania of the blasphemous Pope Boniface VIII claiming attributes that belong to God alone was so shocking that even modern Catholic scholars chose to leave it off. Roman Catholic historian, Richard P. McBrien, further underscores this point noting that Boniface VIII "commissioned or permitted so many statues of himself that he was accused of encouraging idolatry. He declared that Papal authority extends over every creature in the world, and he even dressed occasionally in imperial regalia because he regarded himself as much an emperor as a pope...*Historically naïve and theologically uninformed Catholics continue to cite him today as if his exaggerated claims of papal authority, even over the political realm, are, in fact, consistent with the will of Christ*" (Emphasis mine). See Richard P. McBrien *Lives of the Popes* (San Francisco: Harper, 2000), 437.

[10]   *Time Magazine* May 25, 1981.

[11]   John A. Hardon, S.J., *Pocket Catholic Dictionary* (New York: Image, 1985), 178.

of truth, in clinging to thee, we cling to Christ." But the New Testament teaches that the presence of Jesus Christ is manifested to all born-gain believers through the indwelling presence of the Holy Spirit (see John 14:23; 2 Corinthians 6:16).

Christ said that where these true believers of His gather together, He is there spiritually present in them making them His individual and corporate representatives on Earth. *"For where two or three are gathered together in My name, I am there in the midst of them* (Matthew 18:20). *If anyone serves Me, let him follow Me; and where I am there My servant will be also. If anyone serves Me, him My Father will honor"* (John 12:26). Having the presence of the indwelling Messiah is a right and privilege given every born-again believer. This indwelling presence is not obtained through submission to the Popes of Rome, but is received by believing the Gospel. Every true Christian is therefore Christ's representative on Earth; each serves as His messenger and ambassador to preach the Gospel of salvation to all nations until He comes again. These believers collectively comprise the church of Jesus Christ, with Him as their one, true, and single Head, Who is seated at the right hand of the Father (see Matthew 28:18-20; 2 Corinthians 5:20). The Pope usurps the role of the Holy Spirit by claiming he uniquely acts or speaks for Christ in the role of His supreme Vicar while Jesus is physically absent from Earth. Roman Catholic teaching asserts that when presiding over an ecclesiastical council and pronouncing dogma or doctrine with the words, "Ex Cathedra," the Pope speaks for God in the place of the Holy Spirit.[12]

Christ promised to send the Holy Spirit to indwell and empower every Christian after He ascended to the heavenly Father. The Holy Spirit was to consequently represent, act, and minister to and through the believer for Christ in His absence (see John 14:16-18; 15:26-27). The Holy Spirit is the true Vicar of Christ representing the Lord Jesus in His stead on Earth. The Holy Spirit has been ministering in a variety of ways to every born-again Christian ever since the day of Pentecost, and will continue to do so until the Lord's physical return for His Church. Therefore, one looks in vain through the pages of the New Testament to find a human agent like the Pope solely functioning as the supreme "Vicar of Christ." However, Rome attempts to give other biblical justification for the Primacy of Peter in addition to the passage found in Matthew 16. They claim the Papacy is validated because of the following reasons: the Scriptures show the preeminence of Peter; for Peter is listed first as an Apostle of Christ throughout the Gospels (Matthew 10:1; Mark 1:16; Luke 6:14); Peter alone was first given the keys of heaven to open the way of salvation to both Jew and Gentile (Matthew 16:19; Acts 2:14-51; 10:25-48); he received his papal authority over the whole Church when Christ said to him,*" Feed My sheep"* (Luke 22:31-32; John 21:15-17); in the choosing of Matthias, Peter made the final decision (Acts 1:15-17); and lastly, it was Peter who made the opening statement at the Council of Jerusalem (Acts 15:7).

The best argument, however, against the teachings of Roman Catholicism is the simple truth of Scripture, which not only disproves the Papacy, but all their false and misleading doctrines. Former Roman Catholic priest Joseph Zacchello affirms exactly the same when writing, "The best book against Romanism was not written by a Protestant or a former priest, but by God. It is the Bible."[13] We will address the meaning of the keys later, but our main focus here is on the meaning of "Rock." The Roman Catholic interpretation of the "rock" meaning Peter in Matthew 16:18 is dead wrong for several reasons. To determine the meaning of a particular text in Scripture, the student of the Bible must first determine the context that text, verse, or passage is found in. The context of Matthew 16:13-20 concerns itself with a central, challenging question Jesus asks

---

12   *Dogmatic Canons and Decrees*, 256.
13   Joseph Zacchello, *The Secrets of Romanism* (Neptune, New Jersey: Loizeaux Brothers, 1989), vii.

His disciples at a critical point in His ministry. That question was centered on the real identity of who Jesus is. For He asks, *"Who do men say that I, the Son of Man, am?"* (Matthew16: 13).

Peter correctly gives the ultimate answer to the ultimate question all humans must answer about Jesus when the Apostle confessed of Him, *"You are the Messiah, the Son of the Living God"* (Matthew 16:16). The revelation of Jesus' identity as the Messiah was a supernatural insight Peter received from God, and would lead Jesus to use a play on words declaring, *"You are Peter, and upon this rock I will build my Church"* (Matthew 16:18). Therefore the context of this passage favors a *Christocentric* meaning on who Jesus is—the Messiah and Son of God. The answer Peter gave, argues for interpreting "this rock" as referring back to the revelation and its content. In other words, the Lord Jesus as "the Messiah, the Son of the living God" (Matthew 16:16) would be the solid rock upon which the Christian faith would rest. Every doctrine and practice of the Church would be founded upon Him. Every true believer would hold to a common conviction: Jesus is "the Christ, the Son of the living God" (Matthew 16:16).[14]

The *"rock"* of Matthew 16:17-19 is not Peter, but rather Peter's confession concerning the deity of the Lord Jesus Christ, with Jesus being the true "Rock"[15] Peter could never have been that immovable and infallible Rock, for in verse twenty-three of the same chapter Jesus rebukes him, calling him "Satan." Surely, Jesus would not address the first of his "holy Popes" as "Satan." The rock metaphor, when traced throughout the Bible, is never used symbolically of man, but always of God. To that end, the Scripture speaks of God as the only Rock there is (see Psalm18: 31). The Old Testament unanimously assigns the rock image to the God of Israel. *"There is no one holy like the Lord; Indeed, there is no one besides You, nor is there any <u>Rock</u> like our God?"* (1 Samuel 2:2). To claim otherwise would be to, in effect, proclaim a rival god, to which the word of God proclaims, *"Is there any God besides Me, or is there any other <u>Rock</u>? I know of none"* (Isaiah 44:8). King David called the Lord, *"the <u>Rock</u> of His salvation"* (2 Samuel 22:47). The Messianic prophecies of the Old Testament repeatedly call the Messiah a "Rock." (See Psalm 118:22; Isaiah 28:16; Zechariah 3:9).

In Matthew 16:18, the word "rock" appears twice in the original Greek, with two different genders indicating two different meanings. *"Peter"* (*Petros*) is in the masculine singular, and *"rock"* (*Petra*) is in the feminine singular. Therefore, when Jesus refers to Peter in Matthew 16:18 He does so in the second person, addressed as *"you"*, but when Jesus refers to *"this rock"* in the same verse, He uses the third person. In grammatical terms, the two uses of the word *"rock"* do not point to the same referent. The Greek text of Matthew 16:18 literally reads, "You are Peter" (petros or Petros as transliterated in English). Petros is in the masculine gender and actually means a small rock, or "stone that might be thrown or easily moved." "And upon this rock I will build My church"—rock, here, in the second use, is petra (Petra as transliterated in English), which is feminine in gender and denotes a massive rock, like a foundation or bedrock (as distinct from Petros).[16] The eminent Doctor William Cathcart accurately explains the true meanings these two words (petros and petra) convey in the passage of Matthew 16:18, unequivocally demonstrating that Rome's erroneous interpretation is exegetically wrong:

---

[14]   James G. McCarthy, *The Gospel According to Rome* (Eugene, Oregon: Harvest House, 1995), 240.

[15]   I see no problem with viewing "the rock", to be a synecdoche, meaning the "rock" is both Jesus and the belief (as confessed by Peter) He is the Messiah, the Son of the living God upon which the Christian Church is immovably built and secured.

[16]   W.E.Vine, Merrill Unger, and William White, Jr., *An Expository Dictionary of Biblical Words* (Nashville, TN: Thomas Nelson: 1984), 974; Henry George Liddell and Robert Scott, *A Greek-English Lexicon With A Supplement. Revised by Henry Stuart Jones* (Oxford: The Clarendon Press, 1968), 1397-1398.

The Greek word Petros, or Peter, is not the word translated rock: that word is petra. It is very manifest, that if the Savior meant Peter to be known as the rock upon which He was about to build His Church, that He would have said: "Thou art Petros, and upon this *Petros* (su ei petros kai epi toutw tw petrw) I will build My Church." But instead of that He says: "Thou art Petros, and upon this *Petra* (epi tauth th petra) I will build My Church." Petra is a noun in the *feminine* gender; the pronoun "this", in the Greek, is a noun in the feminine gender, agreeing with gender of the noun Petra; Petros, or Peter, is in the masculine gender. Petra then MUST *refer to something different from Peter.* There would have been Petros on two occasions in this verse, instead of Petros and Petra, if Peter had been the rock. Besides, Petros is a stone, a movable stone; Petra is a rock, a mass of rocks, a cliff. The one, such a stone the maidservant in the hall of judgment might upset; the other the Rock of ages—the confession that Peter made that Christ was the Son of the living God.[17]

The Lord Jesus Christ is always referred to as "the Rock" in the New Testament. The Greek word *Petra*, that is used in Matthew 16:18, is the same word used elsewhere in the New Testament for Jesus Christ. Not once, in this regard, is the term used for Peter or any other person! Thus, the writers of the New Testament, including Peter himself, understood *Petra* to mean Jesus Christ. Surely if Peter were that rock (*petra*) he would have plainly stated so in his two epistles; instead we find the Apostle Peter calling the Lord Jesus *"the rock (petra) of offence"* in 1 Peter 2:18. The Apostle Paul also states the same thing in Romans 9:33 using the Greek word *Petra* for Christ when saying, He is *"a rock (petra) of offence"* over which the unbeliever stumbles. Again, in 1 Corinthians 10:4, Paul tells us that Christ was the **rock** (*petra*) that followed the Israelites into the wilderness. Both Peter and Paul identified Christ as the Rock with the very same word for rock (petra) found in Matthew 16:18.

Roman Catholic apologists, in their vain attempts to not honestly deal with the Greek text of Matthew 16:18, traditionally deny this meaning and assert that in the Aramaic, there is only one definition for the word "rock". So by Rome's conjectural reading, Jesus simply called Peter by his Aramaic name for rock (Kepha or Cephas. See John 1:42) and therefore, Matthew 16:18 really says: "You are *Kepha*, and upon this *kepha* (Cephas) I will build My Church." But this is mere speculation without substantial support from any first century Aramaic manuscripts of a complete Gospel of Matthew. It is an historical fact of biblical paleography that the Greek texts of the New Testament precede and antedate any Aramaic text of the same by several centuries. The Greek text came first and the Aramaic and Syriac texts of the third and fourth centuries (the Peshitta) were largely translated from it. Furthermore, the Holy Spirit, who inspired the writers of Scripture to record God's Word without error, would have preserved such Aramaic manuscripts or at least import the word into the Greek text, especially since Peter's Aramaic name, Cephas, is found six times in the New Testament (John 1:42; 1 Corinthians 1:12; 3:22; 9:5; 15:5; Galatians 2:9). If the Papacy rests upon such textual proof, and if submitting to its office is necessary for salvation, why then is there no clear indication of it; and instead the opposite is found throughout the New Testament!

The Roman Catholic claim for the non-existent ancient Aramaic manuscript reading of Matthew 16:18 to mean Peter as the "rock", is simply not possible because the majority of qualified translators of the ancient Church would have most certainly noted the sameness in gender and meaning from the Aramaic into Greek. But they chose not to, and instead preserved the differences that are reflected in the extant Greek manuscripts

---

[17]   William Cathcart, *The Papal System* (Philadelphia: Griffith and Rowland Press, 1872), 76.

with regards to both meaning and gender of the word "rock." Jerome (347-420) preserved this very distinction in the Latin Vulgate—the standard Bible text of the Roman Catholic Church for over one thousand years.[18] Jesus was essentially saying in Matthew 16:17-19 that "I am the massive Rock (Petra) upon, which, you, Peter, as a little rock (Petros), by your profession of faith in Me as the Messiah, the Son of God, will be supported and built upon the foundation of Who I am." The foundation tibi of the Christian Church is built on Jesus Christ Himself, not Peter. On top of this foundation are the Apostles and Prophets, and the structure on which it supports are the "lively stones" of all true believers in Christ during the present age (see Ephesians 2:20; 1 Peter 2:5-7).

Any first century Orthodox Jew familiar with the Tenach (what Jews call the Old Testament Scriptures), like Peter or Paul, knew that the God of Israel identified Himself as the "Rock" of salvation in Israel's divine history, and would never have taken it to mean anything else (Deuteronomy 32:18; 2 Samuel 22:2, 32, 47; Psalm 31:3; 94:22). The New Testament consistently teaches that Jesus Christ alone is the foundation upon which His Church is built. There is no other as Paul writes, ***"For no other foundation can anyone lay than that which is laid, which is Jesus Christ"*** (1 Corinthians 3:11). This sure foundation does not consist solely of Peter, but is built upon God's revelation given to the Prophets and Apostles with ***"Jesus Christ Himself being the Chief Cornerstone"*** (Ephesians 2:20). Peter, the alleged first "Pope" of Rome and "Rock" of the Church, tells us that all Christians are a "spiritual house" built upon the foundation of ***"the Chief Cornerstone"*** Jesus Christ as "*lively stones*" to make up His spiritual temple (see 1 Peter 2:5-7). Every follower of Jesus Christ, like the Apostle Peter, who therefore trusts by divine revelation that Jesus is "the Christ, the Son of the living God", is being added to the Body of Christ (the spiritual house), which is His Church.

The Roman Catholic Church actually admits the teaching of Peter's primacy is not found in Scripture—the *Catholic Encyclopedia* states: ***"It (the primacy of Peter) cannot be in any way proven directly from the New Testament"*** (Emphasis mine).[19] Rome further admits that Roman supremacy in the Church was not claimed in Peter's name before the fourth century.[20] It was Pope Damasus I (366-384), not Peter, who was the first Bishop of Rome to make claims for the Roman Papacy based exclusively on a misinterpretation of Matthew 16:18, which same claims are adhered to this very day by Rome's misguided Magisterium. Damasus confirmed this belief during the Roman Synod of 381 A.D.[21] One of Rome's most famous Popes, Gregory the Great (590-604), disclaimed Peter's primacy as "Universal Bishop" over all the churches. In his epistle to the Emperor Maurice, Gregory passionately wrote:

> St. Peter is not called "Universal Apostle," the whole Church falls from its place when he who is called "Universal" falls. But far from Christian hearts be that blasphemous name. I confidently affirm that whosoever so calls himself or desires to call himself universal priest goes before Anti-Christ (Book VII, Epistle XLIII).

---

[18]   And I say to thee: That thou art Peter; and upon this rock I will build my church, and the gates of hell shall not prevail against it, which reads in Jerome's Latin text: Et ego dico tibi quia tu es ***Petrus*** et super hanc ***petram*** aedificabo ecclesiam meam et portae inferi non praevalebunt adversum eam (Emphasis mine).

[19]   *The Catholic Encyclopedia,* Vol. 7, 334.

[20]   *The Catholic Encyclopedia,* Vol. 13, 531.

[21]   J.N.D. Kelly, *The Oxford Dictionary of Popes* (Oxford: Oxford University Press, 1986), 33; Peter De Rosa, *Vicars of Christ*, 38.

Here, Gregory I is saying the Pope as Universal Bishop of the Church is a forerunner of the Anti-Christ, and yet Rome to this day claims Gregory to be this Universal Bishop as the sixty-sixth Pope! This admission by Gregory the Great—an obvious refutation of the concept of a Universal Bishop of the Church—has embarrassed Roman Catholic defenders so much that they have attempted to redefine Gregory's original statements concerning this papal issue. The most popular argument they resort to is to claim that when Gregory was writing this epistle to correct the Bishop of Constantinople John Faster, he was doing so because John claimed to be the Universal Bishop at the Synod of Constantinople in 588 A.D. Gregory, according to the Roman defenders, was thus rebuking John for holding this claim that belongs exclusively to the Pope of Rome, who at that time was Gregory himself. However, as one reads the Epistle in its entire context, Gregory never uses the title "Universal Bishop" for himself, for he goes on to say Christ alone is the Head and Bishop of the Universal Church, while the Apostles Peter, Paul, Andrew, and John were members under this Head.

The Apostles themselves were under Christ the one only Head and Universal Bishop of the Church—a title that is reserved for the Lord Jesus alone.[22] If there is any doubt of Gregory's repudiation of this title being conferred on himself, the defenders of the Roman Papacy do well to read his total rejection of such a presumptuous title after wrongly being addressed as "Universal Bishop" by Eulogius, Bishop of Alexandria, who was responding to Gregory's earlier denunciation of "Universal Bishop" as being the forerunner of the Anti-Christ. Appalled, Gregory writes back:

> *Here at the head of your letter I find the proud title of 'Universal Bishop', which I have refused. I pray your most beloved holiness not to do it again*, because what is exaggeratedly attributed to another is taken away from you. It is not in words that I would find my greatness, but in manner of life. *And I do not consider that an honour which, as I know, undermines the honour of my brothers. My honour is the honour of the universal church. My honour is the solid strength of my brothers …Away with these words which inflate vanity and wound charity* (From J.M. Tillard, *The Bishop of Rome*, (London: Health Policy Advisory Center, 1983, 52-53. Emphasis mine)

These are hardly the words of a man claiming to be, as the Popes do now, a Universal Bishop or Pope presiding over all the Church from Rome! The real framers and promoters of the Roman Primacy of Peter was not Jesus, Peter, or the Scriptures but were the early ambitious Popes themselves of the fourth and fifth centuries. They were: Pope Damasus I (366-384), Pope Siricius (384-399), Pope Innocent I (402-417), and finally Pope Leo the Great (440-461), who gave the institution of the Papacy its basic form from which the rest of the Popes after him strategically refined and utilized for political and religious power in the centuries following.[23] In the two canonical Epistles he wrote under the guiding inspiration of the Holy Spirit, the Apostle Peter negates any title or position of primacy or superiority over the other Apostles. In the opening salutation of First Peter he says he is an Apostle of Christ (1 Peter 1:1). In 1 Peter 2:4-8, Peter writes that Jesus Christ alone is the foundation of the Church. In the opening verse of chapter five, the Apostle appeals to them as a *"fellow elder"*, an equal among the other pastors of the Church, overseeing the flock of God. In verses two and three, he instructs pastors, like himself, not to "lord" their position over God's people in a domineering and overbearing way. *"Shepherd the flock of God which is among you, serving as overseers,*

---

[22]   Philip Schaff, *The Creeds of Christendom*, vol. 1 (Grand Rapids, Michigan: Baker Book House, Reprint 2007), 175.

[23]   J.N.D. Kelly, *Early Christian Doctrines* (New York: Harper & Row, 1978), 419-420.

not by compulsion but willingly, not for dishonest gain but eagerly; nor as being lords over those entrusted to you, but being examples to the flock" (1 Peter 5:2-3).

The history of the Papacy is replete with power hungry, tyrannical Popes lording over the church in an unruly, authoritarian way, (in clear violation of Peter's command in 1 Peter 5:2-3), who shed much blood, oppressed, and persecuted those who would not submit to their imperious rule out of moral conscience and scriptural objections. Surely if the Papacy is an all important doctrine "necessary for salvation," as the Councils of Trent, Vatican I and Vatican II claim, the first Pope and Universal Bishop (the Apostle Peter) would have undoubtedly recorded it in his two divinely inspired Epistles for ecclesiastical posterity to uphold, defend, perpetuate, and carry on through his successors the Popes. No such thing is even remotely hinted at in the two New Testament Epistles of Peter. Not only this, the other eleven Apostles and Paul would have unanimously accorded Peter the proper recognition and subjection merited of a Pope and supreme Vicar of Jesus Christ. None of this was explicitly taught by Christ or the other disciples, nor did it ever present itself in the sacred writings of Paul, or other writers of the New Testament. The following *facts* from the New Testament, quoted in the following paragraphs below, make this conspicuously obvious. Peter could not have been an eligible candidate for the Papacy, or, for that matter, the Roman Catholic celibate priesthood, from whom Popes are selected in accordance with Canon Law, because he had a wife (Mark 1:30)![24] She regularly accompanied Peter on his missionary journeys (1 Corinthians 9:5).

Romanists would object here, and argue instead, that Peter left his wife and family to follow Jesus and was thus able to serve as the first Pope without these domestic encumbrances. This desperate objection to save face does not agree with the New Testament qualifications given for the bishop or elder. One of those qualifications listed in 1 Timothy 3:2 and Titus 1:6 is that a bishop or elder must be *"the husband of one wife."* If Peter abdicated his responsibilities as a father and husband he would have been an apostate who had denied the faith according to New Testament teaching in 1 Timothy 5:8: *"But if anyone does not provide for his own, and especially for those of his household, he has denied the faith and is worse than an unbeliever."* God would not have entrusted Peter as a leader in the Church, much less as the first "Pope", if he did not order his family and household accordingly, but rather abandoned them to pursue a celibate priesthood and Papacy. Moreover, both a bishop and elder of the Church must first properly order the affairs in his own household before he can be given a charge over a congregation. *"For if a man know not how to rule his own house, how shall he take care of the Church of God"* (1 Timothy 3:5). These truths from the Word of God indisputably discredit the celibate priesthood, the Papacy, and the Primacy of Peter as the first Pope of Rome!

The Apostle Peter never called himself a "Pope" or "the Vicar of Christ." Nor are the Popes that supposedly followed after ever to be considered "Vicars." As we said before, it bears repeating again to Roman Catholics everywhere, that **this divine Vicar of Christ is the Third Person of the Trinity,** God the Holy Spirit. Before He left the world, the Lord Jesus told the disciples that when He would rise from the dead and ascend into heaven, He would send them another *"Comforter"*, The Holy Spirit, in His place to be with them while He is physically absent (John 14:26). The Holy Spirit is the infallible teacher about Jesus Christ on faith and morals (see John 16:7-14), and no mortal Pope can ever take His place, improve on His anointing, or usurp His didactic office as Christ's holy representative in the life of the born-again believer. The word of God agrees: *"But the anointing which you have received from Him abides in you, and you do not need that anyone teach you; but as the same anointing teaches you concerning all things, and is*

---

[24] Canon 1037 states that a candidate for the Roman Catholic priesthood must take a public vow of celibacy. (See *The Code of Canon Law*, (Grand Rapids, Michigan: Eerdmans, 1983), 185. The Canon Law is the legislative rules by which the Roman Catholic Church is governed and administered by.

true, and is not a lie, and just as it has taught you, you will abide in Him" (1 John 2:27). This verse does not deny the place of the human teacher in the New Testament Church. For the Lord Jesus gave teachers to the Church as a vital ministry in the Body of Christ (Ephesians 4:11). But that teacher is always subject to the Word of God the Holy Spirit gave the Church. John is saying, rather, that the Holy Spirit is a sufficient guide and teacher enabling every believer to discern the truth from the deceit and error false teachers propagate.

On the eve of his death, Jesus informed the disciples it was necessary for him to return to the Father in heaven so that the Holy Spirit could be sent in His place as His divine substitute leading them and us "into all truth about Jesus." Jesus promised, *"However, when He, the Spirit of truth, has come, He will guide you into all truth; for He will not speak on His own authority, but whatever He hears He will speak; and He will tell you things to come. He will glorify Me, for He will take what is mine and declare it to you"* (John 16:13-14). The Apostle John reemphasized what Jesus taught here in his first canonical Epistle. The exact purpose for this reemphasis was to warn and steer Christians away from deceitful, power hungry seducers, who sought to replace the teaching office of the Holy Spirit with themselves in the same manner the Pope of Rome unlawfully attempts to supplant the place of the Holy Spirit by proclaiming himself "The Vicar of Christ" on Earth. For this reason John writes: *"These things I have written to you concerning those that try to deceive you. But the anointing which you have received from Him abides in you, and you do not need that anyone teach you; but as the same anointing teaches you concerning all things, and is true, and is not a lie, and just as it has taught you, you will abide in Him"* (1 John 2:27-28). The Holy Spirit is the sole "Vicar of Christ" on Earth indwelling His Church and instructing them through the supernatural anointing and the counsel of His Word.

Mark the Evangelist, who was a personal aid and scribe to Peter, wrote his inspired Gospel according to the account Peter gave him. The fourth century church historian Eusebius quotes first century church leader Papias, who was told by the Apostle John, that John Mark was "Peter's interpreter" and wrote the Gospel of Mark based on Peter eyewitness account of personally following Jesus throughout His ministry in Israel.[25] This testimony is further borne out by the internal evidence of Scripture. Peter calls Mark his "son in the faith" (1 Peter 5:13). Nowhere in the Gospel of Mark do we find a clear affirmation by Christ of Peter's superiority or primacy over the other Apostles. Mark 8:27-29 is a parallel passage of Matthew 16:17-19. Here Mark omits the "Rock" passage entirely. Now surely if Peter is the "Rock", on whom the Church is built, and in that role has the preeminence as Pope and ruler over the other Apostles in the supreme role of Christ's Vicar, why didn't he tell Mark to include it here? In Mark 9:33-35 and 10:35-45 there is given two different episodes of the twelve disciples disputing among themselves about who be the greatest among them.

Mark chapter nine tells how the twelve disciples were arguing among themselves who should be first in rank among the Apostles. In Mark chapter ten, we read that James and John asked Jesus if they could have superior positions with Him at His right and left hand in the Kingdom of God. In both cases, no Apostle or disciple is named or designated by Jesus as being the greatest. If Jesus truly appointed Peter to be the greatest among the disciples by virtue of his investiture by Christ to be the Pope and Prince of the Apostles in the kingdom, Jesus would undoubtedly have reiterated this, once again, when these two issues over apostolic supremacy emerged. If Peter's supremacy had already been established by Christ earlier, why would the disciples have asked who would be the greatest among them? Instead, the Lord Jesus teaches the Twelve that greatness is demonstrated in the example of serving others and suffering for Christ. It is not achieved in an autocratic Papacy, or in an apostolic successor of Peter! *"But Jesus called them to Himself and said to them,*

---

25   Eusebius, *The History of the Church*, translated by G. A. Williamson (Middlesex, England: Penguin, 1986), 152.

"You know that those who are considered rulers over the Gentiles lord it over them, and their great ones exercise authority over them. Yet it shall not be so among you (in stark contrast to the temporal power of the sword several Popes wielded in the past)*; but whoever desires to become great among you shall be your servant. And whoever of you desires to be first shall be slave of all"* (Mark 10:42-44).

True greatness in the eyes of God is not accomplished by blind ambition for worldly power, or by exerting an overbearing show of force like rulers of nations and Popes have done in the past. Greatness to God is achieved by constantly exhibiting a child-like humility and self-effacing service towards others. The greatness of God's kingdom is not summed up in the Primacy of Peter, or his acclaimed successors the Popes presumptuously sitting in St. Peter's Basilica in Rome, but in the peerless Person of Jesus of Nazareth who came not to be served, but to serve by ultimately giving His life on the cross as a sacrificial ransom for many (Mark 10:45).

The difference between the real Christ of Scripture and the false Christ in Rome is obvious in the following contrasts: The Pope is nothing more than a self-proclaimed autocrat who comes in his own vaunted authority. Jesus came in humility under the rule and will of the heavenly Father (John 4:34). The Pope is traditionally carried aloft on men's shoulders upon the *sedia gestatoria* (portable throne) with great pomp and ceremony. But Jesus said, *"I am among you as the One who serves"* (Luke 22:27). The Pope is recognized by his subordinates with the kissing of his hand on which the fisherman's ring is worn and by prostrating before his feet. Jesus washed men's feet (John 13:5) and spread out His hands on the cross to be cruelly nailed to it (Luke 23:33). The Pope is one of the richest men in the world as head over the billions of dollars the Vatican holds in all its various assets.[26] Christ was so poor while on Earth, that He did not even own a pillow on which to rest His head (Matthew 8:20). For centuries, the Papacy has been involved with the political affairs of nations and world rulers in its attempt to establish itself as the One Universal Church of the world. Christ, however, said: *"My Kingdom is not of this world"* (John 18:36). The Pope is extravagantly crowned with a triple tiara made of gold upon his coronation while Christ was cruelly crowned with a crown of thorns.[27] The litany of contrasts is further elaborated by former Roman Catholic priest Jeremiah Crowley who boldly writes:

> Christ told his followers to keep the commandments. The Popes have methodically broken them all. Instead of practicing "Thou shall not kill", Innocent III (1198-1216) not only surpassed all his predecessors in killing, but founded the most devilish institution in history – the Inquisition, which for over five hundred years was used by his successors to maintain their power against those who did not agree with the teachings of the Romish Church. It is estimated that that Church, throughout history, has been responsible for the willful slaughter of over 100 million people. Christ preached: "Blessed are the peacemakers." Pope Julius II (1503-13) had a passion for war bordering on frenzy. His pontificate was a perpetual war, and Europe knew no peace during the period of his life. One may easily imagine the state of the Church under a Vicar of Christ who spent his time in a camp, amidst the clash of arms, and who knew no other glory than that procured in war or the pillage of a town. His successors have faithfully carried on the belligerent tradition, supporting dictators and stirring up strife to achieve their corrupt aims. Non-Roman-Catholic countries are being

---

26   See Avro Manhattan, *The Vatican Billions* (London: Paravision 1972).

27   John A. Hardon, *Pocket Catholic Dictionary*, 433-434.

brainwashed today into believing that the nature and aims of the Roman Pontiff and his Church are not what they used to be; but Rome is ever and everywhere *semper eadem*, always the same. As she was throughout past centuries, so she remains today, except that she is now playing politics more astutely than she was previously.[28]

The reason Peter is listed first in the synoptic Gospel narratives does not denote his supremacy over the other disciples, but is mentioned to indicate that Peter was one of the first disciples chosen by Jesus. If we followed the same faulty logic here that is used in Roman Catholic exegesis to justify Petrine supremacy, we could also deduce from reading John's list of the chosen disciples that Andrew must be greater than all the other disciples, because John lists Andrew ahead of Peter and the rest of the Apostles. In the Gospel of John, we do in fact find that Andrew, Simon Peter's brother, was chosen and recruited as a disciple of Jesus before Peter (John 1:38-42). This dispels the Primacy of Peter being based on the synoptic listings alone. Roman Catholic teaching also appeals to the incident in John 21:15-17 as another proof text where—

> The primacy was conferred when Christ, after His resurrection, gave the mandate to Peter, after the latter's threefold assurance of His love: "Feed my lambs! . . . Feed my lambs! . . . Feed my sheep!" (John 21, 15-17). Here, as in Mt. 16,18 et seq., the words are directed solely and immediately to Peter. The "lambs" and the "sheep" designate Christ's whole flock, that is, the whole Church (cf. 10).[29]

A closer examination of John 21:15-17 shows that it does not teach that Christ distinctly gave the primacy of papal power to Peter: ***"Then when they had eaten breakfast, Jesus said to Simon Peter, Simon, son of Jonah, do you love Me more than these? He said to Him, Yes, Lord, You know that I love You. He said to him, Feed My lambs. He said to him the second time, Simon, son of Jonah, do you love Me? He said to Him, Yes, Lord, You know that I love You. He said to him, Feed My sheep. He said to him the third time, Simon, son of Jonah, do you love Me? Peter was grieved because He said to him a third time, Do you love Me? And he said to Him, Lord, You know all things, You know that I love You. Jesus said to him, Feed My sheep."***

Peter had shamefully denied being a disciple of Jesus three times with continual curses and oaths when confronted in the courtyard of the High Priest the night Jesus was tried and condemned by the Sanhedrin (see Mark 14:66-72). Naturally, our forgiving and merciful Lord sought to reinstate the repentant Peter with the corresponding thrice-repeated question, ***"Do you love Me."*** Peter candidly answered three times in the

---

[28]   Jeremiah J. Crowley, *Romanism. A Menace to the Nation* (Aurora, Missouri: Menace Publishing Company, 1912), 203. This author was a former Roman Catholic priest and dubbed "the Martin Luther of America" at the turn of the twentieth century and was so disgusted and horrified at the utter corruption of the priests and other prelates around him that he sought to reform the Roman Catholic Church in America. After repeated letters of appeal to Rome seeking a redress of grievances, Crowley was met with fierce opposition from the Vatican and her priestly agents in America. In moral protest, Crowley resigned from the priesthood in 1908 when calls for moral reformation among the priesthood were ignored and strongly rebuffed. He later published his second book, *Romanism: A Menace To a Nation* in 1912. One wonders what this noble soul would have done in our day with the epidemic of pedophilia priests being discovered in the Roman Catholic Church and the forty year cover-up by the Vatican as CBS correspondent Vince Gonzales documented on August 6, 2003 on CBS News web site (http://www.cbsnews.com/news/sex-crimes-cover-up-by-vatican/).

[29]   Ludwig Ott, *Fundamentals of Catholic Dogma* (Rockford, Ill: Tan, 1955). 281.

affirmative that he did love the Master, which in effect, counteracted the three times he previously disavowed and denied the Lord Jesus. Christ's reinstatement of Peter brought reconciliation and a restoration of his place among the disciples as a follower and servant of the Lord Jesus. This was put into effect when the Apostle disavowed his public denial of the Lord with his public reaffirmation of love for Him in the presence of the other six Apostles. In order to demonstrate this love, Christ commanded Peter to feed His sheep, not as an expression of papal power, but as a living proof of the Apostle's love for the Lord. John the Evangelist merely recorded this restoration to remove any doubt that Christ forgave Peter and personally reinstated him to the apostleship before the presence of the other Apostles, thus demonstrating that Peter was forgiven and reappointed for service to the Lord's sheepfold. There is no mention of Peter being invested with a superior position or unique authority here as an apostolic Pope or prince ruling over the other Apostles. Nothing whatsoever is found in this text. Hence,

> Does this, after all, warrant, or even favour, the pretensions of the Pope? No indeed The Evangelist relates in what manner Peter was restored to that rank of honour from which he had fallen. The treacherous denial, which had been formerly described, had undoubtedly rendered him unworthy of the Apostleship; for how could he be capable of instructing others in the faith, who had basely revolted from it? He had been made an Apostle, but from the time that he had acted the part of a coward, he had been deprived of the honour of Apostleship. Now, therefore, the liberty, as well as the authority of teaching, is restored to him, both of which he had lost through his own fault. That the disgrace of his apostasy might not stand in the way, Christ blots it out and fully restores the erring one. Such a restoration was needed both for Peter and his hearers; for Peter, that he might the more boldly exercise himself, being assured of the calling with which Christ had again invested him; for his hearers, that the stain which attached to him might not be the occasion of despising the Gospel.[30]

Peter's reconciliation to fellowship and serve with Christ was not an investiture to become the first Universal Pope over the Church as the "chief shepherd to whom all the other shepherds are subordinate," but a restoration to follow and serve the Lord as a pastoral minister in the community of the Christian believers. Peter in no way took this to mean anything else, especially when the Apostle distinctly calls Jesus *"the Chief Shepherd"* who serves Him as a "fellow elder" among other shepherds tending and feeding God's flock with the unadulterated Word of God (1 Peter 5:1-2).[31] Indeed, to feed the Church is a New Testament activity ministers, who are not Apostles, are expected to do as well (See Acts 20:28; Ephesians 4:11-12; 1 Peter 5:1-2); it is not reserved for Peter or the Apostles alone. Renowned Roman Catholic Priest, and Bible scholar Raymond Brown, even admits that John 21:15-17 cannot of itself be used to teach the Roman Catholic doctrine of the Primacy of Peter on which the Papacy is built. Brown comments:

> Yet, if we think that only Peter is given the command to tend the flock, we do not agree with those who go to the other extremes by interpreting 15-17 to mean that Peter is explicitly made shepherd over the other disciples or over the other members of the twelve.... In our

[30] A.W. Pink quoting John Calvin in *Exposition of John* (Grand Rapids, MI: Zondervan, 1975), 1139.
[31] Andreas J. Kostenberger *John, Baker Exegetical Commentary of the New Testament* (Grand Rapids, MI: 2004), 596.

judgment, exegetes who think that Peter had authority over the other disciples cannot conclude this from John xxi 15-17 taken alone but must bring into the discussion the larger NT background of Peter's activities.[32]

The Roman Catholic Institution has historically cited Luke 22:31 to further support the concept of the Papacy with the establishment of Peter's superiority in the role of "Prince of the Apostles." *"And the Lord said, Simon, Simon! Indeed, Satan has asked for you, that he may sift you as wheat. But I have prayed for you, that your faith should not fail; and when you have returned to Me, strengthen your brethren"* (Luke 22:31).

The Vatican I Council declared this to mean with regard to the establishment of an infallible Papacy:

> And indeed all the venerable Fathers have embraced and the holy orthodox Doctors have venerated and followed their apostolic doctrine; knowing most fully that this See of Saint Peter remains ever free from all blemish of error, according to the divine promise of the Lord Our Savior made to the Prince of His disciples: "I have prayed for thee that thy faith fail not; and thou being once converted, confirm thy brethren. This gift, then, of truth and never failing faith was conferred by Heaven upon Peter and his successors in his chair, that they might perform their high office for the salvation of all.[33]

The verse in Luke twenty-one does not support, or even vaguely hint at the Roman Catholic doctrine of Peter's supremacy, but rather underscores his weakness in moment of great crisis. Christ is addressing Peter alone in the context of the passage and no one else! After his denial of Christ, the Lord instructed Peter that he would return to the faith after his fall and "confirm" to the other disciples he was truly reinstated and display the sincerity of his restored status and commitment to the Lord Jesus. As an Apostolic minister of the Gospel, Peter was to learn from this past mistake, and in turning back to faith in Christ, which he previously fell from when He denied His Master three times, the Apostle was to "strengthen" fellow Christians who had also fallen in a moment of weakness. He was to further safeguard other believers from making the same mistake he made, particularly in times of severe trial and persecution. Peter did this very thing so eloquently in both of the canonical epistles in the New Testament bearing his name (see 1 Peter 1:5-9; 5:6-10; 2 Peter 1:5-12; 2:9; 3:17-18). The Fathers of the Early Church, unlike Rome, did not unanimously agree Luke 22:31 was supportive of a Papacy, despite Vatican I's claim that *all the venerable Fathers* held to this meaning.[34]

The event in Acts 1:15-26 retells the account of the choosing of an Apostle to fill the vacancy left by Judas Iscariot. Again, the context of this procedure in no way supports or advocates the Roman Catholic doctrine of Petrine supremacy. No doubt Peter's role in this setting was a chief one, but the text itself does not indicate his was the *exclusive role* of choosing a new Apostle to replace the vacancy left by Judas the betrayer. The context of Acts 1:15-22 clearly indicates that it was not done with the thought or acquiescence of Peter arbitrating the final decision over the other Apostles. This is important to point out here, especially because the Roman Catholic teaching claims that Peter and His successors alone have the exclusive authority to appoint Bishops in the Church for the purpose of perpetuating apostolic succession.[35] But is this the ecclesial

---

[32] Raymond Brown, *The Gospel According to John XII-XXI* (Garden City, New York: Doubleday, 1970), 1116-1117.

[33] *Dogmatic Canons and Decrees*, 254-255.

[34] See George Salmon, *The Infallibility of the Church* (Grand Rapids: Baker, 1959), 343-344.

[35] *Catechism of the Catholic Church*, 254-255 **[880-883]**.

procedure followed in Acts chapter one? No, it is emphatically not! For if Peter were truly the "Universal Pope", the situation that presents itself in Acts 1:15-22 would have been an opportune moment to exercise his papal authority over the other Apostles in exclusively choosing a successor to replace the apostleship of Judas to reconstitute the Twelve.

The other Apostles do not make an appeal to Peter based on his papal authority. Peter made the stipulation, subsequently ratified with the mutual consent of the other Apostles and disciples, for replacing Judas based upon the authority of God's Word (Acts 1:15-21). Peter merely pointed out the Scriptural reason why another qualified person—one, who witnessed the ministry of Jesus Christ from His baptism until He ascension into heaven, must replace the Apostleship of Judas. After this unimpeachable qualification for choosing Judas' replacement was accepted, the eleven Apostles, along with the one hundred twenty disciples, prayed together and sought the guidance and counsel of the Holy Spirit on the matter. They collectively decided to cast lots and chose Mathias when the lot fell on him (Acts 1:26). In the casting of lots, the Apostles trusted God to intervene and overrule chance here to clearly reveal His will on the matter (Proverbs 16:33). The decision was undertaken by the whole congregation (Acts 1:24), as they prayed to God for His choice in the matter. The congregation did not acquiesce to a unilateral decree from a Papacy, or a single domineering individual like Peter in the role of Pope, but consented *together* on the matter through corporate prayer and guidance from the Holy Spirit. The choice was up to God alone, and not left to Peter or the others. The decision before the congregation in Acts 1 centered on what God thought and decided rather than on what Peter, let alone the other Apostles, preferred. Peter neither ruled here nor made the final decision.[36]

The casting of lots was a customary practice in ancient Judaism that God used to make his will known throughout the Old Testament history of Israel (Leviticus 16:8; 26:55; Numbers 26:55; Joshua 14:2; 1 Chronicles 6:54; Jonah 1:7-8) In Acts chapter I, the first century Christian Jews of Israel carried on this tradition in choosing a new Apostle, without appealing to a papal figure such as the Pope who presumes he is acting in Peter's role as supreme bishop over the entire church. The Pope still today asserts his sole prerogative to appoint bishops as apostolic successors of the Twelve. But he does so ignorant of what Scripture really teaches and without proper biblical warrant. If we apply the guidelines and the conditions for being a genuine Apostle as formulated in Acts 1:21-22 by Peter, the Popes and Bishops of Rome (who make up the Apostolic College) simply do not qualify as bona fide Apostles for the simple and obvious fact they were not personally trained by Jesus from His baptism to His ascension, nor had a personal encounter with Him after the resurrection![37]

If the Roman Catholic defender objects here on the grounds that Paul was commissioned to be an Apostle of Jesus Christ without these same conditions being met, several things must be pointed out to this lone exception. First, Paul did in fact meet one condition. He had a personal encounter with the risen and glorified Christ on the road to Damascus and was personally called into the apostolic ministry by Jesus Himself as

---

36   "The procedure followed of casting lots should not be seen as an example of congregational election, for the choice is left up to God, as is shown both by prayer and by the casting of the lots" (Quoted from Ben Witherington III, *Acts of the Apostles: A Socio-Rhetorical Commentary* (Grand Rapids, MI: Eerdmans, 1998), 125.

37   "The qualifications are two: the prospective Apostle must have been trained by Jesus from the time of Jesus' baptism to the day of his ascension; he also must be a witness of Jesus' resurrection" (Quoted from Simon J. Kistemaker, *New Testament Commentary: Acts* (Grand Rapids, MI: Baker, 2002, page 66). Obviously, the Roman Catholic understanding of apostolic succession, does not qualify here by the fact it fails to meet these two fundamental New Testament qualifications for an Apostle. Hence, Rome has no biblical grounds to stand on here for the ongoing succession of the Apostles through the Papacy!

Acts 9:1-18 dramatically testifies. Second, Paul tells his readers at Corinth that he was an Apostle "as one untimely born" (1 Corinthians 15:8) and was, therefore, the last Apostle chosen by Jesus Christ. This is further evidenced by the fact that after the death of the Apostle James in Acts 12:2, no successor was chosen to replace him by Peter or the other eleven Apostles! Third, Paul considered himself an Apostle of equal calling and authority with the other twelve Apostles. He, nevertheless, submitted his teaching and ministry to them for review (Acts 15: 2-4; Galatians 1:18; 2:9-10). Paul never included himself among the Twelve Apostles (1 Corinthians 15:5, 7-8); since it was common knowledge in the early church they were a unique group for that time and place as eyewitnesses to the earthly ministry of Jesus the Messiah in first century Israel. Thus apostolic succession began and ended with the Twelve who were chosen by Christ in the Gospels and in the book of Acts. This cannot, then, apply to any person or institution beyond that time, which most certainly disqualifies all the Popes after Peter.

The Roman Catholic Institution further adduces support for the Primacy of Peter from Acts 15:6-22 where the Jerusalem Council was convened to settle the problem of Gentile salvation and fellowship with Jewish believers. The issue hinged on whether or not Gentile Christians had to submit to the Law of Moses (as the Judaizers clamored for) to truly be saved, or was just faith in the Lord Jesus Christ alone sufficient for salvation (as the Apostles correctly affirmed). Peter was the first Apostle to formally address the Council (Acts 15:6-11). Defenders of Roman Catholicism seize upon this event to prove Peter's supremacy over the church in the same way the Popes exercise their authority today. Catholic apologist Patrick Madrid confidently affirms the following occurred at the Jerusalem Council: "While James delivers the pastoral, disciplinary teaching (cf. Acts 13-21), it was Peter who delivered the binding doctrinal teaching. His primacy was recognized by St. Paul…"[38] Is this what actually took place at the Jerusalem Council? A closer examination of what really happened at this Council will suffice to show otherwise.

At the Council of Jerusalem there was extensive debate among its constituted members (Acts 15:7). After this intense discussion was finished, Peter offers his advice as an equal member of Christ's Church on the matter of Gentile salvation, of which afterwards, the Apostle Paul and Barnabus give additional testimony (Acts 15:12). James, the head elder and pastor of the Jerusalem Church, is clearly the one presiding over the Council as its main speaker and chairman, not Peter in the role of some authoritarian Pope (Acts 15:13-21). James gives the concluding statement in verses 13-21. The decision was not left with him, who was the bishop and leading elder of the Jerusalem church, nor with Peter acting in the role of supreme ruler over the Church, but was a mutual agreement shared with the Apostles, elders, and the whole church (Acts 15:22). The authoritative basis for the Council's decision was the Old Testament Scriptures, which was the norm for the apostolic church (Acts 15:16-17).

The encyclical decree that was published in a formal letter and circulated to the churches in Antioch, Syria, and Cilicia states throughout that the Council's decision was a joint effort, (this is proven by the fact that throughout the letter given in verses 23-29 members of the whole Council are represented as *"we"* and *"us"*), and not left to a single Apostle like Peter. Finally, why is this council convened in Jerusalem where all the Apostles go to confer and allow the final statement to James? Should not the first historical council of the Christian Church have been convened in Rome with Pope Peter presiding, to whom all the other Apostles and disciples were submitted to? The fact that no such thing happens in Acts chapter fifteen, or for that matter the entire New Testament, further shows Roman Catholic claims for Peter's primacy from Rome to be utterly without biblical warrant or justification.

---

[38]   Patrick Madrid, *Where is That in the Bible* (Huntington, Indiana: Our Sunday Visitor, 2001), 34.

Throughout the council's deliberation, discussions, and final conciliar decree on Gentile salvation, there is no mention or slight hint of Peter's primacy being exercised or claimed over the other members of the Jerusalem Council as "Pope" and "Visible Head" of the Church. Yet, Rome, nevertheless, teaches the Pope alone has the exclusive authority to convene a church council and make the final authoritative decision that is binding upon the whole Church *"without the concurrence of the other bishops or of the rest of the Church"*[39]

The Roman Catholic teaching here for Peter and the Papacy does not agree with, but flatly contradicts, the very method and ecclesial procedure followed in Acts chapter fifteen, and is utterly foreign to the monarchical procedure Rome has followed for centuries in drafting their church councils. The procedure followed by the Apostles, elders, and the church in Acts 15 was that of a congregational adjudication under the guidance of the Holy Spirit using the Old Testament Scriptures to be the guide and the authoritative rule for their final decision. Another corollary to the Primacy of Peter and the establishment of the Papacy is further corroborated, Rome claims, when Jesus conferred the "keys" of God's Kingdom into Peter's hand. *"And I will give you the keys of the kingdom of heaven, and whatever you bind on earth will be bound in heaven, and whatever you loose on earth will be loosed in heaven"* (Matthew 16:19-20).

Roman Catholic tradition believes that Jesus is actually delegating a unique and exclusive authority to Peter whereby he would be given supreme authority over the other Apostles as head of the Church to grant entrance or deny access into the kingdom of God with the power to absolve sins, to pronounce doctrinal decisions, and to admit into or excommunicate members from the Church.[40] The authority Christ entrusted to Peter not only extends over the spiritual realm, but also includes the very earth itself. Vatican approved theologian, Ludwig Ott, likens this conferring of Christ's keys to Peter as the "bestowal of an empire" upon Peter and his successors the Popes have rule over. Ott explains:

> The keys of the Kingdom of Heaven mean supreme authority on earth over the Empire of God. The person who possesses the power of the keys has the full power of allowing a person to enter the Empire of God or to exclude him from it. But as it is precisely sin which hinders the entry into the empire of God in its perfection...the power to forgive sins must also be included in the power of the keys.[41]

The symbol of the keys mentioned in Matthew 16:19, taken in the context of Matthew's Gospel and the rest of the New Testament, can in no way be reasonably construed to mean the primacy of Peter's authority to include or exclude people from heaven or some ecclesiastical "Empire". In stark contrast to the Roman Catholic claim that Peter and his successors the Popes have power to admit or deny entrance into the kingdom of heaven, the Word of God emphatically declares that God Almighty, in the Person of Jesus Christ, has the sole power and authority (symbolized by the figure of the keys) over death, hell, and the grave (Revelation 1:18). Throughout the New Testament we find that Christ alone has the sovereign power to allow people access into heaven or cast them into hell fire (Matthew 7:21-23; 10:28; 25:31-45; John 5:24-30; 10:9-10; 2 Thessalonians 1:7-10; Revelation 20:11-15). Contrary to what Rome teaches, there is no mention in the New Testament of Peter, or any other human being, filling this role as Savior and Judge that only God by virtue of His perfect attributes and power can accomplish.[42]

---

[39] Ludwig Ott, *Fundamentals of Roman Catholic Dogma*, 285.
[40] *Catechism of the Catholic Church*, 153-154 **[551-553]**; 403 **[1445]**.
[41] Ludwig Ott, *Fundamentals of Catholic Dogma*, 418.
[42] Charles F. Pfeiffer, Howard F.Vos, and John Rea, eds., *Wycliffe Bible Dictionary* (Peabody, Mass: Hendrickson,

The symbol of the *key* in Scripture is used to figuratively represent power or authority. Keys ordinarily open doors to allow access and denote power by the one who holds them. Isaiah 22:22 mention ***the key of the house of David*** which refers to the royal power exercised and possessed by the Davidic monarchy. Jesus as the consummate "Son (descendant) of David" came with the full rights and privileges from Yahweh as the divine Messianic King (descended from David), who now possesses this key that provides access to God and entrance into heaven (see Revelation 3:7). The Lord Jesus censored the Scribes and Pharisees of Israel for misusing the key of biblical knowledge, and, in effect, shutting the door of heaven from the Jewish people, turning them away from accepting Him and their Messiah, who came to give them salvation (Matthew 23:13). Christ pronounced a great woe on the religious lawyers for taking away "the key of knowledge" and locking men out from God's kingdom with their innumerable man-made traditions—much like Rome does today with their "sacred tradition." The "keys" of divine authority are not found in the sole authority of Peter as "Pope", but rests in the *declaratory power of the spoken Word of God* that is best exemplified in Peter's verbal confession that Jesus is the Messiah.

The acts of ***"binding and loosing"*** are the following actions that come from the use of these keys. Binding and loosing were common rabbinic practices of first century Israel by which the Jewish Rabbis would allow or forbid certain judicial and legislative actions and decisions on religious or domestic matters pertaining to things (not persons) that affected the community. Renowned Hebraic scholar John Lightfoot provides a list of rabbinic quotations from the Talmud and other ancient Hebrew literature clearly demonstrating that the act of binding and loosing that often occurred in the Jewish culture in Jesus' day was commonly used for doctrine and judgments concerning things allowed or not allowed in the Jewish Law.[43] Rome fails to comprehend this important rabbinic practice when she assigns a non-Jewish meaning of Jesus' words of binding and loosing to instead mean *exercising Papal authority* over the souls of men on Earth; which authority also determines where men will spend eternity.

The fact that Jesus was a Torah observant Jew—the preeminent Rabbi of his day— means he also often adopted the didactic concepts of the lesser Rabbis, such as binding and loosing, to serve a greater purpose in His Church; a fact that is conveniently brushed aside when Roman Catholic teaching imposes a foreign meaning on the text. This foreign meaning would be that such acts conferred upon Peter, and his alleged successors the Popes, now give them the power, which belongs to God alone, to forgive sins and grant or bar the sinner access into God's Kingdom. The context of Scripture, and the Jewish practices of binding and loosing in first century Israel, patently militates against this forced interpretation wrongly argued by Roman Catholic theologians and apologists as a proof text for the justification of the Papacy.

The audience of Jesus' day would have never imputed this fanciful interpretation to our Lord's words, but would have naturally associated these acts with how the Rabbis commonly employed them in that day within the synagogue and community. So, in the words of John Lightfoot: "To think that Christ, when he used the common phrase, was not understood by his hearers in the common and vulgar sense, shall I call it a matter of laughter or madness?"[44] Only God has the power over men souls to assign them their eternal destiny, which ultimately hinges on whether they believe and trust in the Gospel of Jesus Christ proclaimed by the Apostles and the Church today (John 3:16-21; Mark 16:15-16). Thus, understood in its proper Jewish context, the act of binding and loosing—given first to Peter, then to the other Apostles, then to the rest

---

1998), 988-989.

[43]   John Lightfoot, *Commentary on the New Testament from the Talmud and Hebraica*, Vol. 2 (Peabody, Mass: Hendrickson, 1995), 237-240.

[44]   Ibid., 240.

of the Church—consists in forbidding (to bind) or permitting (to loose) crucial decisions that involve the proclamation of the Gospel and the consequences that follow with either an acceptance or rejection of its salvific message by those who hear it. We note later on in Matthew's Gospel that Christ bestowed the same power and authority of binding and loosing to the rest of the Apostles in Matthew 18:18. Peter was chosen first in this regard due to his confession that Jesus was the Messiah, the Son of the Living God.

The Apostles, with all other Christians, have the Christ-given power to announce and preach the good news of salvation and the acceptable terms on which God grants the free gift of eternal life to sinners who trust in Christ Jesus alone. This is called in the New Testament *"the ministry of reconciliation"* whereby the Church exhorts sinful men and women to be reconciled to a forgiving God through trust in the expiatory sacrificial death of the Lord Jesus Christ, who alone paid the price for our salvation (2 Corinthians 5:18-21). To every born-again Christian, is the this same ministry given, and is to be exercised through the declaratory power of the spoken Word of God, the Gospel, which produces life saving faith when heard by those that believe (Romans 10:17), and subsequently, have their sins *loosed* from them the moment they trust in Christ for salvation. And, conversely, the same declaratory power of God's Word pronounces condemnation on those who reject the Gospel in unbelief and have their sins still *bound* to them.[45] This is the plain meaning behind the acts of binding and loosing, and is already accomplished in heaven already determined by the foreknowledge of God, and then later exercised and confirmed on Earth by the witnessing Church in fulfilling the Great Commission of the Lord Christ during the present age of grace.

Rome's implied interpretation that Peter and his successors will be given the exclusive power in the future to bind and loose on Earth, to the extent that it will already determine what Christ decides to do in heaven, is based on a incorrect translation of Matthew 16:19 that goes back to Jerome's erroneous translation of this text in his Latin Vulgate (dated around 400 A.D.). Translations based on this manuscript tradition translate the verbs as future tenses only, when in fact the Greek construction of the verbs, "to bind" and "loose", occur in the future perfect passive periphrastic which denotes a past action already completed that continues in the present and influences the future. In light of this, Matthew 16:19 should literally read: ***"Whatever you bind on earth will have already been bound in heaven, and whatever you loose on earth will have already been loosed in heaven."*** Understood in this way, it is the decisions that have been made in heaven that will first determine what the Church on earth will do. Hence, "it is the church on earth carrying out heaven's decisions, not heaven ratifying the church's decision."[46] Christ determines the rule of discipline and doctrine for the Church. He delegates to His disciples what has already been determined and decided by the government of heaven. Peter and the Apostles then confirm and abide by this as His loyal subjects and subservient administrators—a far cry from Peter arbitrarily making these decisions as papal prince over the

---

[45]   Paul underscores this twofold aspect of binding and loosing through the proclamation of the Gospel by illustrating how believers witnessing for Christ in this fashion will be like a sweet aroma to those who are saved through the believer's Gospel witness for Christ, while the witnessing believer is an obnoxious stench of death to those who reject Christ to their condemnation (2 Corinthians 2:15-17).

[46]   Fritz Rienecker and Cleon Rogers, *Linguistic Key to the New Testament* (Grand Rapids, MI: Zondervan, 1980), 49. New Testament Greek scholar, William Chamberlain, notes that translating the phrases "shall be bound" and "shall be loosed" as simple futures is wrongly translated "seeming to make Jesus teach that the Apostles' acts will determine the policies of heaven. They should be translated "shall have been bound" and "shall have been loosed." This makes the Apostles' acts a matter of inspiration or heavenly guidance" from *Exegetical Grammar of the Greek New Testament* (Grand Rapids: Baker, 1979), 80.

other Apostles, making them unquestioning subjects to him while Christ in heaven passively accepts such imperious acts and decrees after the fact!

The act of binding and loosing, therefore, is an exercise already done in heaven determined by the foreknowledge of God and later exercised on earth by the New Testament Church in fulfilling the Great Commission of Christ during the present age. The idea that the keys signify a declaratory authority is chronologically confirmed in the book of Acts. The Early church Fathers, for the most part, understood the keys to mean the simple preaching of the Gospel which Peter and the other Apostles equally shared. William Webster provides a thorough and comprehensive review of what the Early Church Fathers taught and believed about the rock and keys of Matthew 16:16-19, and by this careful review, shows, they as a majority, did not interpret Matthew sixteen to support the Roman Catholic concept of the Papacy. Webster then irrefutably concludes from his accurate historical analysis:

> Generally speaking, the fathers viewed the rock and foundation of the Church as the person of Christ, or Peter's confession of faith which pointed to Christ. Sometimes they speak of Peter as the rock or foundation in the sense that he is the example of faith—that he exemplified faith. But they do not teach that he is representative of a papal office or that the Church was built upon him in a legalistic sense...What Christ spoke to Peter he spoke to the Church as a whole and what was given to Peter was given to all apostles and through them to the entire Church. The keys are a declarative authority to teach truth, preach the Gospel and exercise discipline in the Church.[47]

Once the door of salvation was opened by Peter's use of the keys of the Gospel, the keys are no longer needed since the door of salvation is now open through repentance and faith in Jesus Christ alone.

> Peter alone receives the keys because once the door to the kingdom of heaven is unlocked, there is no more need for keys. Once Peter opens the door to Jews, Samaritans, and Gentiles, all the disciples will continue to proclaim the gospel because all of them share the authority of "binding" and "loosing" (cf. 18:18; John 20:22b-23). People who receive the gospel are loosed from their sins so that they can enter the open door to the kingdom. People who reject the gospel message are bound in their sins, which will prevent them from entering the kingdom.[48]

Peter merely used these keys of evangelical authority of declaring the Gospel when opening the door of salvation *to the Jews first* on the day of Pentecost in Acts chapter two; and later *to the Gentiles* first when preaching to the house of Cornelius in Acts chapter ten. Peter's privilege lay in the fact that Christ chose him to be the first one to officially exercise this evangelical authority. But he was not the only one thereafter. If the Apostle Peter was indeed Pope, and submission to him was necessary for one's salvation, why did he not demand this very thing on these two occasions when he had the golden opportunities to do so? When the convicted Jews responded to Peter's sermon with the question of what they must do to be saved, Peter did not reply by telling them they were to acknowledge and submit to him as supreme Pontiff, as Rome falsely teaches. But the Apostle informed them that they were to repent and believe on the Lord Jesus Christ (Acts

---

[47]   William Webster, *The Matthew 16 Controversy* (Battle Ground, WA: Christian Resources, 1999), 156.

[48]   Michael Wilkins *The NIV Application Commentary. Matthew* (Grand Rapids, MI: Zondervan, 2004), 568.

2:38). When Cornelius, a *Roman Centurion*, sought to bow down before the Apostle Peter as some great dignitary of God, as the Pope customarily accepts and demands from clergy, laity, and all the faithful (for instance, Pope Gregory VII issued a Papal Bull entitled *Dictatus Papae* where under proposition seven it is required that only the Pope's feet are to be kissed by all princes), Peter immediately refused him saying, ***"Stand up; I myself also am a man"*** (Acts 10:25-26). Nowhere in sacred Scripture do we find Peter accepting or demanding homage and adoration from the Church or the world as Pope and Prince over the other Apostles!

Peter never stressed a papal infallibility of his own to be the guideline and ruling standard for the Christian faith. He pointed instead to the prophetic Scriptures being the ultimate criterion for truth—even above his own personal eyewitness account of being with Jesus on the Mount of Transfiguration (1 Peter 1:19)! Peter valued the writings of Paul equal in weight and authority with the Old Testament Scriptures (2 Peter 3:16-17). The Early Church Fathers and the Ecumenical Councils of the ancient Church with their ancient Creeds knew of no Primacy of Peter acting as sole head and Pope over the entire Church, rather they universally taught equality among all Bishops in the Church. Roman Catholic priest, historian, and theologian J.H. Ignaz von Dollinger honestly admits that:

> None of the ancient confessions of faith, no catechism, none of the patristic writings composed for the instruction of the people, contain a syllable about the Pope, still less any hint that all certainty of faith and doctrine depends on him.... *The Fathers could the less recognize in the power of the keys, and the power of binding and loosing, any special prerogative or lordship of the Roman bishop, inasmuch as—what is obvious to any one at first sight—they did not regard a power first given to Peter, and afterwards conferred in precisely the same words on all the Apostles, as any thing peculiar to him, or hereditary in the line of Roman bishops, and they held the symbol of the keys as meaning just the same as the figurative expression of binding and loosing....The power of the keys, or binding and loosing, was universally held to belong to the other bishops just as much as to the bishop of Rome* (Emphasis mine).[49]

The writings of the Early Church Fathers from the East and West do not give "unanimous consent" to the idea of Peter's primacy from Matthew 16:17-19. Scholar and former ex-Jesuit priest Peter Doeswyck summarizes how the Early Church Fathers basically viewed the text of Matthew 16:18:

> The Fathers differed in terminology, but not in thought. Generally speaking, the South (Egypt and Africa) explained that Peter, as the first fruit of faith, represents all believers on whom the Church is founded. *The East explained that the church was founded on faith in Christ, which Peter was privileged to confess first. The West explained that the Church is founded on Christ in whom it confesses its faith. No Father ever taught the Church was founded on Peter alone, on one man alone, or on the bishop of Rome* (Emphasis mine).[50]

Second and third century church Fathers such as Justin Martyr (100-165 A.D.), Irenaeus (140-202) and Clement of Alexandria (? -215 A.D.), never mention the church being exclusively built on Peter's supremacy. A following catena of quotes from Early Church Fathers from the East and the West will clearly demonstrate

---

[49]   J.H. Ignaz von Dollinger , *The Popes and the Council* (London, 1869), 74.

[50]   Peter Doeswyck, *Ecumenicalism and Romanism* Vol. 1 (Long Beach, California: Knights of Christ, 1961), 81.

that no such interpretation of a Petrine Papacy was found in their writings on Matthew 16:18, and that the "Rock" the Church is built on is Peter. Some of the following quotes are taken from the massive multi-volume works of the Greek and Latin Church Fathers translated and published by Roman Catholic scholar and priest Jacques Paul Migne. He still stands as one of the great scholars and organizers on Patrology (study of the Church Fathers) today even though he lived in the latter part of the nineteenth century.

Tertullian (155-230 A.D.) A prodigious writer of Christian theology, he is dubbed "the Father of Latin Christianity." His writings greatly influenced the Church Fathers that came after him. Roman Catholic apologists seize upon Tertullian's statement that the "rock" of Matthew 16: 18 is the person of Peter when he writes:

> *Was anything withheld from knowledge of Peter, who is called the 'the rock on which the church should be built'* who also obtained 'the keys of the kingdom of heaven,' with the power of 'loosing and binding in heaven and earth?'[51]

But as these defenders of Romanism and the Papacy often do, they only quote a selected portion extracted from a larger body of patristic writings to lend credence to their claims for Petrine supremacy and the Papacy.[52] However, upon further perusal of Tertullian's teaching on this matter in another section of his writings, he goes on to explain what he exactly means when he says Peter is the "rock":

> 'On thee,' He says, 'will I build My church;'...*In (Peter) himself the Church was reared; that is, through (Peter) himself: (Peter) himself essayed the key; you see what key: 'Men of Israel, let what I say sink into your ears: Jesus the Nazarene, a man destined by God for you,' and so forth. (Peter) himself, therefore, was the first to unbar, in Christ's baptism, the entrance to the heavenly kingdom, in which kingdom are 'loosed' the sins that were beforetime 'bound;' and those which have not been 'loosed' are 'bound,' in accordance with true salvation.*[53]

Tertullian clearly states that the Church is built through Peter and the Gospel of salvation he declared (partially quoting Peter's sermon from Acts 2:22, 38 as a proof). Tertullian makes no mention of any successors called the Popes that come from Peter as the "rock." Rather, Tertullian's point is that the Church is built by way of Peter's preaching the Gospel! William Webster's in his extensive scholarly examination of the Patristic exegesis of Matthew sixteen accurately and correctly elucidates that:

> When Tertullian says that Peter is the rock and the church built upon him he means that the Church is built through him as he preaches the gospel. This preaching is how Tertullian explains the meaning of the keys. They are the declarative authority for the offer of forgiveness of sins through the preaching of the gospel. If men respond to the message

---

[51]   Alexander Roberts and James Donaldson, The Ante—Nicene Church Fathers (Grand Rapids: Eerdmans, 1951), Vol. III, Tertullian, *Prescription Against Heresies* p. 22.

[52]   See Scott Butler, Norman Dahlgren, and David Hess, *Jesus, Peter, and the Keys* (Santa Barbara: Queenship, 1996), 217-218.

[53]   Alexander Roberts and James Donaldson, *The Ante—Nicene Church Fathers*, Vol. IV, Tertullian, *On Modesty* 21, p. 99.

they are loosed from their sins. If they reject it they remain bound in their sins...Tertullian explicitly denies that this promise can apply to anyone but Peter and therefore he does not in any way see a Petrine primacy in this verse with apostolic successors coming from the bishop of Rome.[54]

Origen (184-254 A.D.) He was the first Christian scholar to write an entire commentary on the Bible. He taught in Alexandria, Egypt. Origen's interpretation of Matthew 16:18 was applied to the believer's faith in Christ the Rock. Peter is a prototype of the believer's confession of Christ:

> If you suppose that *on this Peter alone the whole church is built by God, what would you say about John, the son of thunder, or about any other of the apostles? Is it at all possible to say that against Peter in particular the gates of hell shall not prevail, but that they shall prevail against the other apostles and against the elect?...Let us consider in what sense it is said to Peter and to every Peter (believer): "I will give unto thee the keys of the kingdom"...Consider how great a power the Rock has...and how great a power every one has who says: "Thou art the Christ, the Son of the living God."*[55]

Cyprian (200-258 A.D.) He was Bishop of Carthage. Cyprian was a famed orator and epistolary writer who opposed Pope Stephen over the baptism of heretics. He was later martyred in Rome. Cyprian's practical and theological treatise *On the Unity of the Church* has often been cited in the past by Roman Catholic defenders of the Papacy to support the Primacy of Peter and therefore the succession of the Papacy.[56] On the subject of apostolic authority, Cyprian writes:

> If any one considers and examines these things, there is no need for lengthened discussion and arguments. There is easy proof for faith in a short summary of the truth. *The Lord speaks to Peter, saying, "I say unto thee, that thou art Peter; and upon this rock I will build my Church, and the gates of hell shall not prevail against it. And I will give unto thee the keys of the kingdom of heaven; and whatsoever thou shalt bind on earth shall be bound also in heaven, and whatsoever thou shalt loose on earth shall be loosed in heaven." And again to the same He says, after His resurrection, "Feed My sheep." And although to all the apostles, after His resurrection, He gives an equal power, and says, "As the Father hath sent me, even so send I you: Receive ye the Holy Ghost: Whose soever sins ye remit, they shall be remitted unto him; and whose soever sins ye retain, they shall be retained;" yet, that He might set forth unity, He arranged by His authority the origin of that unity, as beginning from one. Assuredly the rest of the apostles were also the same as was Peter, endowed with a like partnership both of honour and power; but the beginning proceeds from unity. Which one Church, also, the Holy Spirit in the*

---

54 William Webster, *The Matthew 16 Controversy*, 27.
55 J.P. Migne, *The Greek Fathers* Vol. 13 (Paris, 1894), 13, 999, 1011-1015).
56 Karl Keating, *Catholicism and Fundamentalism*, 217; Stephen Ray, *Upon This Rock* (San Francisco: Ignatius, 1999), 113-145.

Song of Songs designated in the person of our Lord, and says, "My dove, my spotless one, is but one. She is the only one of her mother, elect of her that bare her." Does he who does not hold this unity of the Church think that he holds the faith? Does he who strives against and resists the Church trust that he is in the Church, when moreover the blessed Apostle Paul teaches the same thing, and sets forth the sacrament of unity saying, "There is one body and one spirit, one hope of your calling, one Lord, one faith, one baptism, one God?"[57]

Though Cyprian states that Peter is the rock, he is quick to add in the above quotation that he is not superior to the other Apostles but they share all together a unity both in leadership and ministerial authority in the Church. There is no Petrine supremacy taught here, no matter how Catholic Apologists bend and twist the Early Church Fathers like Cyprian to suit their own preconceived ideas of a Petrine Papacy; Cyprian's use of the term "the chair of Peter", which will be dealt with later under the topic of Papal infallibility, not withstanding. There is, however, an alternate version of Cyprian's treatise on *Church Unity* that explicitly states the Primacy was given to Peter. The older manuscripts (quoted above) read: *"Assuredly the rest of the apostles were also the same as was Peter, endowed with a like partnership both of honour and power"* Some two hundred years later an alternate manuscript allegedly surfaced with an interpolation that reads: *"Assuredly the rest of the apostles were also the same as was Peter, but the primacy is given to Peter, that there might be shown one Church of Christ and one see."*[58] Unfortunately, some Protestants, and most Roman Catholics, believe Cyprian wrote both versions to accommodate or modify what he wrote originally. Yet, if that were the actual case, he would be guilty of a flat contradiction and holding two mutually exclusive ideas at the same time, highly unlikely of this Early Church Father since he displays in his other writings a firm consistency that was unshakable on other theological matters. The alternate reading is a forgery falsely used to support the doctrine of Peter's primacy and the Papacy.

Indeed, *The Catholic Encyclopedia* even concedes with certain pro-Catholic qualifications that this interpolation ("conflated form") is, in fact, "spurious."[59] The great Jesuit scholar and historian Etienne Baluze (1630-1718), known by the alternate name Baluzius, (whom *The Catholic Encyclopedia* on-line says: "is to be ranked among those benefactors of literature who have employed their time and knowledge in collecting from all sources ancient manuscripts, valuable books, and state papers. He annotated them with valuable comments, being very well acquainted with profane and ecclesiastical history as well as with canon law, both ancient and modern,"), devoted his last days to studiously researching and publishing the writings of Cyprian.[60] In these studies Baluze discovered that Cyprian had been "doctored" with various mendacious interpolations. He thus rejected them outright along with the interpolation (supporting Peter's primacy and "the Chair of Peter") given above as spurious and counterfeit. But Baluze died not completing his work.

An anonymous monk was given the task to complete the job and later candidly admitted he corrupted the notes of Baluze with these various insertions justifying it with the following comments: *"It was necessary to alter not a few things in the notes of Baluzius; and more would have been altered if it could have been*

---

[57]   Alexander Roberts and James Donaldson, *The Ante—Nicene Church Fathers*, Vol. V, Cyprian, *On the Unity of the Church* 4, p. 422.

[58]   Ibid., footnote 7.

[59]   *The Catholic Encyclopedia* vol. 4, Charles Herbermann, ed., (New York: Robert Appleton Company, 1907-1913), 485. See http://www.newadvent.org/cathen/04583b.htm.

[60]   http://www.newadvent.org/cathen/02242a.htm

done conveniently"[61] Roman Catholic apologists are therefore not being honest with the facts here when they knowingly use a spurious reading of Cyprian to claim justification for the Roman Catholic Papacy. Cyprian never taught this. In fact, Cyprian dissented from Pope Stephen of Rome (254-257 A.D.) over the issue of baptizing heretics without ever acquiescing to the primacy of Rome.[62] He further presided over an African Synod that officially decreed:

> No one among us sets himself up as a bishop of bishops, or by tyranny and terror forces his colleagues to compulsory obedience, seeing that every bishop in the freedom of his liberty and power possesses the right to his own mind and can no more be judged by another than he himself can judge another. We must all await the judgment of our Lord Jesus Christ, who singly and alone has power both to appoint us to the government of his Church and to judge our acts therein.[63]

Roman Catholic scholars, who are honest, are forced to admit that the writings of Cyprian did not recognize the bishop of Rome's primacy over the other churches based on so-called Petrine supremacy. Roman Catholic historian of Patrology, Johannes Quasten, concedes the following from the decree of the African Synod and the words of Cyprian:

> From these words it is evident that **Cyprian does not recognize a primacy of jurisdiction of the bishop of Rome over his colleagues. Nor does he think Peter was given power over the other apostles.... No more did Peter claim it: 'Even Peter, whom the Lord first chose and upon whom He built His Church, when Paul later disputed with him over circumcision, did not claim insolently any prerogative for himself, nor make any arrogant assumptions nor say that he had the primacy and ought to be obeyed'** (Epist. 71, 3).[64]

Eusebius (260-340 A.D.). Considered to be "the Father of Church history" because he wrote the first history of the Christian Church that set the pattern for the many Church historians to come. Friend to the Roman Emperor Constantine, Eusebius was an influential member and delegate at the Council of Nicea in 325 A.D. He unequivocally affirms that the "rock" in Matthew 16 is Jesus Christ supporting this with corroborating passages in 1 Corinthians 10:4 and 3:11:

> Yet you will not in any way err from the scope of the truth if you suppose that 'the world' is actually the church of God, and that its 'foundation' is in first place, that unspeakably solid rock on which it is founded, as Scripture says: '**Upon this rock I will build my Church,**

---

61   Alexander Roberts and James Donaldson, *The Ante—Nicene Church Fathers*, Vol. V, p. 422; J.W. Burgon, *Letters From Rome to Friends in England* (London: 1862), 417.

62   Eminent Church historian Philip Schaff observes about Cyprian's correspondence with Stephen that: "In his correspondence he uniformly addresses the Roman bishop as "brother" and "colleague," conscious of his own equal dignity and authority. And in the controversy about heretical baptism, he opposed Pope Stephen with almost Protestant independence, accusing him of error and abuse of his power, and calling a tradition without truth an old error. Of this protest he never retracted a word" *History of the Christian Church*, Vol. 2 (Peabody, Mass: 2006), 162.

63   Johannes Quasten, *Patrology* Vol. 2 (Allen, Texas: Christian Classics, 1983), 375.

64   Ibid., 436.

and the gates of hell shall not prevail against it'; and elsewhere: The rock, moreover, was Christ' For, as the apostle indicates with these words: 'No other foundation can anyone lay than that which is laid, which is Christ Jesus.'[65]

Athanasius (296-373 A.D.) Famed Patriarch of Alexandria and stout defender of Christian Orthodoxy against the heresy of Arianism wrote that Peter's faith in Jesus the Messiah is the basis on which the Church is established:

> You are blessed who are in the Church by faith, and who dwell on the foundations of faith... For this is what is written: *"Thou art the Son of the living God", which Peter confessed by the revelation of the Father...No one, therefore, will ever prevail against your faith, most beloved brethren"*[66]

Ambrose 340-397 A.D. Considered to be one of the greatest fathers of the Western Church. Instructor to Augustine, Ambrose is one of the few Great Doctors of the Roman Catholic Church. He was the bishop of Milan. Roman Catholic apologists quote him the most when arguing for their Papal interpretation of Matthew 16:18. They smugly recite Ambrose succinct statement: "It is to Peter himself that He says: 'You are Peter, and upon this rock I will build My Church.' Where Peter is, there is the Church"[67] to support the claim that Peter and his successors are the foundation on which Christ built His church, and therefore to be in communion with Rome is to be in communion with Christ and His Church. To be out of communion with Peter and the Holy See is to be outside the Church. If this were all Ambrose wrote on Matthew 16, Roman Catholic apologists would have a legitimate case here. This is not the case, however. Ambrose made other significant comments about Peter and Matthew 16:18 throughout his writings which make it evident that such a stringent meaning assigned by Roman Catholic apologetics is not valid. Of course, more times than not, the defender of Romanism omits these other writings so as to make it appear that Ambrose taught what they claim for Peter and the Papacy in Matthew 16:18. On this very text, the revered Bishop of Milan says of Peter elsewhere:

> Faith, then, is the foundation of the Church, for it was not said of Peter's flesh, but of his faith, that 'the gates of hell shall not prevail against it...*Christ is the rock, for 'they drank of the same spiritual rock that followed them, and the rock was Christ' (1 Cor. x.4); also He denied not to His disciple the grace of this name; that he should be Peter, because he has from the rock (petra) the solidity of constancy, the firmness of faith. Make an effort, therefore to be a rock! Do not seek the rock outside of yourself! Your rock is your deed, your rock is your mind. Upon this rock your house is built. Your rock is your faith, and faith is the foundation of the Church.*[68]

---

[65]   J.P. Migne, *The Greek Fathers* Vol. 23, 176.

[66]   J.P. Migne, *The Greek Fathers* Vol. 26, 1189-1190.

[67]   Cited in W.A. Jurgens, *The Faith of the Early Fathers* (Collegeville: Liturgical, 1979), Volume 2, p. 150.

[68]   *The Fathers of the Church* (Washington D.C., Catholic University, 1963), 230-231; William Webster, *The Matthew 16 Controversy*, 64.

Taken together, Ambrose's statements on Matthew 16 do not support the Roman Catholic interpretation of the rock, since he writes that the rock is the confession of Peter's faith in Jesus the Messiah upon which the whole Church is built. A Faith that reflects Peter's confession of faith in the Lord Jesus Christ is what the Church is supported and built on. Understood in this light, Ambrose's statement, "Where Peter is, there is the Church" really means (in the overall context of what Ambrose taught concerning Matthew 16:18) where Peter's confession of faith is expressed there is the believing Church whose very faith in Jesus the Messiah is the content of Peter's faith, the Rock upon where the New Testament Church is built!

Jerome (347-420 A.D.) Jerome is known as the famed translator whose translation of the Bible (called The *Latin Vulgate*) became the authorized Bible of the Roman Catholic Church for a thousand years. He interpreted Matthew 16:18 to mean the Church was built on Christ the Rock:

> *Thou art Peter (Petrus) and upon this Rock (Petram) I will build my church….To Simon, who believed in the Rock (Petra), that is Christ, the name of Peter (Petrus) was given. The Rock is Christ who granted to His Apostles that they too should be called rock.*[69]

John Chrysostom (347-407 A.D.) Pronounced a Doctor of the Roman Catholic Church in 1568, Chrysostom, called "the golden mouthed Greek orator" and interpreter of the entire Bible, explains that Christ did not say: "Epi toi petroi" (upon this stone or upon this Peter), but "Epi tautei tei petrai (upon this rock) I will build my church. "Petros" is a stone or brick which can be handled, "Petra" is a rock foundation like Gibraltar. The two words differ in meaning and gender: *petros* is masculine, *petra* is feminine. Let no Latin theologian bluff you into believing that he knows better Greek than Chrysostom, and that the *petros-petra* argument is an old wives tale.[70] Chrysostom therefore explains

> Thou art Peter, and upon this Rock I will build my church, which means upon the faith of his confession…upon this Rock (Petram), nor upon a man, but upon his faith (fidem) He has built His Church.[71]

Augustine (354-430 A.D.) This legendary Christian stands as one of the greatest theological giants in the Christian Church. Both Protestants and Roman Catholics claim him for their own. He wrote that the "Rock" of Matthew 16: 18 was not Peter, but Christ:

> *Upon this rock I will build my church…but in order that the Church might be built upon a Rock, who was made the rock? Listen to Paul who explains…'the Rock was Christ' (1 Cor. 10:4). On Him, therefore, we (the church) have been built…Now considering that Christ is the Rock (Petra)…Therefore He said: 'Thou art Peter and upon this Rock, which thou hast confessed…that is, upon myself who am the Son of the living God, I will build My Church, I will build you upon Me, not Me on you'. The Church is not built on men but on Christ. Those who wished to be built upon men, said: I am of Paul, I am of Apollos, and I am of Cephas who is Peter (1Cor. 3:4-23). But others who did not wish to be built upon Peter, but upon the Rock, said, I am of Christ "Upon this Rock I will build*

---

[69] J.P. Migne, *The Latin Fathers* Vols. 26, p. 121; Vol. 25, p.1006 (Paris, 1894).

[70] I am indebted to former Jesuit Priest Dr. Peter Doeswyck for this observation.

[71] J.P.Migne, *Greek Fathers* Vol. 58, p. 534; Vol. 52, p. 806.

My Church: Not upon Peter (petrum) which you are, but upon the Rock (petram) which you have confessed..."The Rock upon which the church is built is Christ himself...For Christ was the Rock whom Simon confessed, even as the whole Church confesses Him.[72]

Pope Leo I (Pontificate from: 440-461 A.D.) He interpreted the Petrine text of Matthew 16:18 to mean the believer's confession of faith in Christ in this way:

The solidity of that FAITH, which was praised in the chief of the apostles, is continual...for throughout the church 'Peter' (the believer) daily says: 'Thou art the Christ, the Son of the living God'...This faith conquers the devil and loosens the bonds of the captives. It (this faith) lifts us from this earth and plants us in heaven, and the gates of hell cannot prevail against it (our faith).[73]

Pope Gregory the Great (Pontificate From: 590-604 A.D.) He is one of the most influential and prestigious Popes in Roman Catholic History. Quoted earlier in this work, as saying that any person claiming to be the Universal Bishop of the Church as Peter's successor is the forerunner of Anti-Christ, Gregory wrote that the Rock of Matthew 16:18 was Peter's faith in Jesus as the Messiah. Gregory did also view the rock pointing to Peter and his successors, the Bishops of Rome, although not as a single universal primacy but a joint authority equally shared between the patriarchates in a collegial union. Concerning the rock meaning the faith of Peter, Gregory exclaims:

Peter...Paul, Andrew, John, what were they but heads of particular communities. And yet they were all members under One Head (Christ)...Whosoever then...firmly holds the FAITH...he has laid as a foundation the same Jesus Christ, the Son of God. Moses is placed on a rock, to behold the form of God, because if any one maintains not the firmness of faith, he discerns not the Divine presence. Of which firmness the Lord says, 'Upon this rock I shall build my Church.'[74]

The Venerable Bede (673-735 A.D.) He was the ancient British Doctor of Theology and first historian of the Christian Church in England. He explained the text of Matthew 16:18 in this way:

'Thou art Peter, and upon this Rock I will build my church'. He speaks to him metaphorically: 'Upon this Rock', which means: upon the Savior whom thou hast confessed, the Church will be built.[75]

The majority of the Church Fathers from the East and West explained and understood the "Rock" of Matthew 16:18 to mean the Church was to be built on Peter's confession of faith by which he believed Christ to be the Son of the living God, or either that the "Rock" is the person of Jesus Christ upon which the Church

---

[72] J.P. Migne, *Latin Fathers* Vol. 36, p. 724; Vol. 38, p.1239, 1349; Vol. 32, p. 618.

[73] Ibid., Vol. 54, pp. 144, 146.

[74] Ibid., Vol. 77pp. 740, 980; *A Library of the Fathers of the Holy Catholic Church* (Oxford: Parker, 1850),Volume 31, p. 670.

[75] Ibid., Vol. 92, pp. 78-79.

is built and made secure. The overwhelming testimony from most of the Eastern and Western Church Fathers in the ante-Nicene, Nicene, and post-Nicene periods of church history do not substantially support, in any way, the Roman Catholic misinterpretation of Matthew 16:18. And this misinterpretation is simply a classic example of twisting the Scripture out of its context to make it fit a preconceived idea, and thus reading this misconceived idea into the text of what is simply not there. Consequently, the Roman Catholic doctrine of the Papacy, that is precariously built on such a dubious interpretation, thus flies in the face of not only the teaching of the New Testament, but also what the Church Fathers taught for almost one thousand years!

J.H. von Dollinger, a Roman Catholic Priest and recognized scholar of Church history, was forced to admit by the evidence of Patristic exegesis of Matthew 16:18 that:

> Of all the Fathers who interpret these passages in the Gospels (Matt. 16:18, John 21:17), not a single one applies them to the Roman bishops as Peter's successors. How many Fathers have busied themselves with these texts, yet not one of them whose commentaries we possess—Origen, Chrysostom, Hilary, Augustine, Cyril, Theodoret, and those whose interpretations are collected in catenas—has dropped the faintest hint that the primacy of Rome is the consequence of the commission and promise to Peter! Not one of them has explained the rock or foundation on which Christ would build His Church of the office given to Peter to be transmitted to his successors, but they understood by it either Christ Himself, or Peter's confession of faith in Christ; often both together. Or else they thought Peter was the foundation equally with all the other Apostles, the twelve being together the foundation stones of the Church (Apoc. Xxi. 14).[76]

Roman Catholic scholars have tried to bolster their claims of Petrine succession by alluding to the writings of the third century Church Father Cyprian (mentioned earlier in this chapter) in his *De Unitate Ecclesiae*. But this has been proven a forgery along with other tampered and forged writings of the Early Church Fathers: Hilary, Tertullian, Ignatius, and Origen. Indeed, it was a common practice in the Medieval Church of Rome for writings to be altered to favor their particular viewpoint.[77] The Pseudo Clementine letters and homilies were proven forgeries that were later used in the ninth century to bolster the claims of a universal Papacy over the Church.[78] The writer was allegedly Clemens Romanus who writes to James claiming that Peter appointed Clemens to succeed Peter as bishop of Rome after Peter's death. Modern scholarship has proven the Clementine documents a forgery invented by a heretic in the second century.[79] During the first millennium of Church history, no interpretation of Matthew 16:18 as explained by Rome today is found in support of a *universal* Papacy and Primacy of the bishop of Rome being Peter's successor. Such a foreign

---

[76] Von Dollinger, *The Pope and the Council*, 74.
[77] The Catholic Encyclopedia concedes: "Writers of the fourth century were prone to describe many practices as of Apostolic institution which certainly had no claim to be so regarded...Substituting of false documents and tampering, with genuine ones was quite a trade in the Middle Ages" (*Catholic Encyclopedia* Vol. III), p. 484; Vol. VI, p. 136.
[78] Alexander Roberts and James Donaldson, *The Ante—Nicene Church Fathers*, Vol. VIII, p. 601.
[79] Zachello, *The Secrets of Romanism*, pages 46-47 gives a good summary of the basic development of the Papacy based on altered or forged documents.

idea to Scripture did not surface until the early eleventh century during the reign of Pope Gregory VII with his pompous claim of universal sovereignty over the Church.[80]

Therefore, in the words of Dr. Peter Doeswyck, it can be incontrovertibly concluded:

> Of all the commentaries on Matthew 16:18, written during the first thousand years of Christianity, not one mentions the "papacy" (the Fathers would not know how to spell the word): not one mentions the "primacy" of the bishop of Rome. Such an idea and interpretation did not even exist as a heresy...Pope Hildebrand (Gregory VII) in 1073 became the first Roman bishop to openly declare himself the head of the entire world by his papal Bull, known as the "Dictatus Papae", which decreed: "(1) That the Roman Church was founded by God alone. (2) That the Roman Pontiff alone is to be called 'Universal'. (3) That he alone has the power to depose and reconcile bishops...that all princes should kiss his feet, and his alone..." etc. Bishop Anselm (d. 1086), nephew of Pope Alexander, immediately incorporated these new decrees into his Collection of Canon Laws, which since have been mutilated. Canon 10 decrees: "That upon one, that is, upon Peter the Lord God has built His church." That blessed Peter has handed down the power invested in himself to his successors" (*Migne, P.L. 149, 485-487*). Thus, in the 149th volume of Migne's Latin Fathers we find in a dubious collection the first interpretation on which Roman Catholicism is founded. It took us more than 1,000 years and more than 148 huge volumes of Latin works to find this first interpretation by a man (Hildebrand) who was the first bishop to usurp the sole title of "Pope" and "Supreme Pontiff."[81]

During the proceedings of the Vatican I Council, Roman Catholic scholar and Archbishop Peter Kenrick proved by patristic evidence that the text of Matthew 16:18 does not show the "Rock" to be built on the primacy of Peter.[82] However, in the face of this evidence, the Vatican continues to make the unsupported claim that the Papacy is validated by the presence of Peter in Rome—with Peter presiding in the office as the

---

[80] Eamon Duffy, *Saints and Sinners: A History of the Popes* (London: Yale University Press, 2006), 121-128; "The pontificate of Gregory VII, one of the most important and influential popes in the entire history of the church, marks a real watershed in the history of the papacy, from the first to the second millennium. In the first Christian millennium the papacy functioned to a great extent as a mediator of disputes, ecclesiastical and political alike. The bishop of Rome was only one of several Western patriarchs (although today there are honorary patriarchs in Lisbon, Venice, and the East and West Indies, and a Latin-rite patriarch in Jerusalem, the Pope implicitly claims to be the Church's universal patriarch, in contradiction to Pope Gregory the Great's [590-604] insistence that that the church has no universal patriarch). To be sure, individual popes of the first millennium such as Leo the Great (440-61) readily donned the mantle of the Apostle Peter and claimed a primacy of pastoral jurisdiction—but for the most part over the West alone, and even then only over key regions of the West. At the same time, there were constant tugs-of-war between Rome and Constantinople (involving both the Byzantine emperor and the patriarch), but the East never fully accepted papal primacy in the sense which it has come to be understood since Gregory VII. Gregory was the first pope effectively to claim universal jurisdiction over the whole church—laity, religious, and clergy, princes and paupers alike—and he did so on the basis of canonical and legal precedents to which no other pope before him had appealed. He is also the Pope who restricted the use of the title "pope" to the Bishop of Rome. Before that, the title was used of all bishops in the West" (Richard P. McBrien, *Lives of the Popes*, 185-186).

[81] Doeswyck, *Ecumenicalism and Romanism*, 87-88.

[82] Peter Richard Kenrick, *An Inside View of the Vatican Council* (American Trust Society), 1871.

first Pope and "Universal Bishop" of the Church until 64 or 67 A.D. Rome boldly claims that she can trace the unbroken succession of Popes from the present one all the way back to Saint Peter in order to validate the papal doctrine of Apostolic Succession and thus authenticate the papacy in history. The Vatican has compiled such lists throughout the centuries, and with each one, believed it accurately reflected the unbroken succession of Popes dating back to Peter.

The official list of the Popes issued by the Vatican is called *Liber Pontificalis* (the first complete list was compiled in the eighth century). Later, however, after an historical error was found from a forgery or chronological miscalculation, the list was revised. Popes were either added or taken off the list. Historical alterations to the Papal lists have occurred several times throughout the centuries. Both *The Catholic Encyclopedia* and *The New Catholic Encyclopedia* admit that determining which Popes ruled and when is virtually impossible; especially when the compiler(s) knowingly and unknowingly utilized some historical writings that were spurious when compiling these lists of the Popes:

> ***But it must be frankly admitted that the bias or deficiencies in the sources make it impossible to determine in certain cases whether the claimants were Popes or antiPopes.*** The compiler of the Liber Pontificalis utilized also some historical writings e.g. St. Jerome, "De Viris Illustribus"), a number of apocryphal fragments (e.g., the Pseudo-Clementine Recognitions), the "Constitutum Silvestri", the spurious Acts of the alleged Synod of 275 bishops under Silvester etc., and fifth century Roman Acts of martyrs. ***Finally the compiler distributed arbitrarily along his list of Popes a number of papal decrees taken from unauthentic sources:*** he likewise attributed to earlier Popes liturgical and disciplinary regulations of the sixth century.[83]

The exact dates assigned for the first dozen Popes are historically questionable, and whether some of them (with the exception of the Apostle Peter, of course) ever existed is debatable. The author has personally scanned several listings of Popes from different Roman Catholic publications and noticed numerous variations, deletions, and repetitions of the same names, and omissions that conflicted with each of the lists. Popes of the first century on these lists are not a settled fact of a fixed and unbroken chain of succession. Such an inconsistency caused a certain German historian of the Papacy to correctly deduce from the data:

> We are not to suppose, however, that there is any uniformity among writers, or certainty as to three or four supposed first successors of St. Peter. Says Mr. Walch, the author of a compendious but learned history of the Popes, originally published in German: " *If we may judge of the Church of Rome, by the constitution of other apostolic churches, she could have had no particular bishop, before the end of the first century. The ancient lists,*" he adds, "*are so contradictory that it would be impossible exactly to determine, either the succession of the bishops, or their chronology.* Some say that Clemens of Rome had been ordained by the apostle Peter, and was his immediate successor. Others place Linus and Cletus between them. A third set name Linus, but instead of Cletus, name ANACLETUS, DACLETUS. Lastly, a fourth party states the succession thus: Peter, Linus, Cletus, Clemens, Anacletus"...Among the early fathers, Tertullian,

---

[83]   *The New Catholic Encyclopedia* (Catholic University of America, 1967), vol. 1, p. 632.

Rufinis and Ephiphanius, say *Clement succeeded Peter*. Jerome declares that 'MOST of the Latin authors supposed the order to be Clement the successor of Peter.' But Irenaeus, Eusebius, Jerome, and Augustine, contradict the above authorities, and say Linus succeeded Peter.[84]

A press release from Vatican City in January of 1947 reported that information was changed on seventy-four Popes on the list of Popes supposedly documenting an unbroken chain of apostolic succession. Prefect of the Vatican archives, Monsignor Angelo Mercati, conducted a thorough investigation into the lists of Popes because scholars had known that the old list was inaccurate. Mercati's research confirmed just how inaccurate it was. His results were the following:

> Six Popes had to be dropped: one (Donus II) never existed; two (the supposed third and fifth Popes Cletus and Anacletus) were the same man. But three new Popes had been found: Boniface VI (for a few days in 896), and possibly, Discorus (for 22 days in 530) and Leo VIII (from 963 to 965). *In the case of no fewer than 74 Popes, changes had to be made in such matters as their names and dates.* Thirty-seven antiPopes are listed, the first of whom—Hippolytus of the 3rd century—is still considered a saint. From four legitimate pontiffs the designation of sainthood was removed. *Because of sketchy records and the questionable validity of some papal elections, Pius XII will probably never know whether he is the 256th successor to St. Peter or the 260th—or someone in between.*[85]

It is clear that the Vatican, over the course of centuries, has produced fabricated lists of Popes to support their illegitimate claim for an unbroken chain of papal successors from Peter to the current Pope, but in so doing have admittedly altered, removed, added, and in some cases, invented Popes to give this appearance of uninterrupted historical continuity. The Vatican has not produced such a list that has stood the test of time and therefore the claims of apostolic succession it makes for the papacy are historically invalidated, fraudulent, and partially fictional. Not only is this proven from the "historical" list that has repeatedly been amended and altered, but the method and manner by which some of these Popes were actually selected only reinforces the obvious truth that the Roman Catholic teaching of apostolic succession is quite simply bogus.

In the tenth century, Rome and the papacy had become so corrupted and rife with sexual immorality that this period of papal history has been graphically labeled by the Roman Catholic Cardinal Cesare Baronius as "the Papal Pornocracy."[86] During that horrendous period, several Popes were actually elected by mistresses, prostitutes, and paramours of the Popes themselves! The most notorious was the whorish mother-daughter combination of Theodora and Marozia who were mistresses to the Popes. These two women alone were directly responsible for creating and appointing nine Popes (not counting anti-pope Christopher) covering

---

[84]   John Dowling, *The History of Romanism* (New York: Crown Rights Book Company, 2002), 48

[85]   From the article "Pontifices Maximi", *Time Magazine* January 27, 1947 (find this article at: http://content.time.com/time/magazine/article/0,9171,778924,00.html). In 1961 the Vatican made other alterations to the list. Anti-pope Christopher was considered a bona fide Pope for a long time. Pope-elect Stephen was considered legitimate under the name "Stephen II" Both men were erased from the list at that time.

[86]   E.R. Chamberlin, *The Bad Popes* (New York: Dorset Press, 1986), 27.

a span of thirty-five years![87] Indeed, Pope John XI (931-935) was the illegitimate son of Marozia and Pope Sergius III (904-911)! To believe that during this particular era that nine of Christ's so-called appointed Vicars, Holy Fathers, and alleged direct successors of the Apostle Peter were legitimately chosen by adulterers and fornicators, who are excluded from the kingdom of God (see 1 Corinthians 6:9-10 and Ephesians 5:5), is blasphemous to the highest degree. And these very same nine "Popes" elected by the nefarious duo of Theodora and Marozia still remain on the Vatican's official list of legitimate Popes today! These Popes cannot possibly be genuine successors on this basis alone—there is certainly no biblical warrant here, and duly constituted authorities ordained by the Word of God did not elect them either.

Another glaring hole in the chain of Rome's apostolic succession occurred with the Great Western Schism (1378-1417) when there were three Popes at one time vying for the Chair of Saint Peter. The problem began when the Catholic Cardinals elected Pope Urban VI (1378-1389). Urban ruled with a heavy hand. His constant violent outbursts peppered with degrading insults of the Roman Curia quickly convinced the same body of Cardinals, who had elected him, to quickly depose him and elect Clement VII instead. This immediately split the Roman Catholic Church into two factions with several opposing Popes holding office at the same time for some thirty-seven years. Both Popes anathematized and ex-communicated each other. This continued with their successors until finally in 1409 a group of Cardinals at the Council of Pisa deposed both Popes Gregory XII and Benedict XIII on the grounds of schism, heresy and perjury. The council elected Pope Alexander V in their stead.

Both rival Popes (one staying in Avignon, France and the other at Rome) adamantly refused to accede and the Roman Catholic Church had three Popes instead of one! When Alexander V died suddenly on May 3, 1410, the council of Pisa then elected Cardinal Baldassare Cossa to succeed him. He took the name of Pope John XXIII. The situation became so farcical and intolerable that the Council of Constance was convened from 1414 to 1417 and elected Pope Martin V (1417-1431 A.D.) to replace the other two rival Popes (Gregory XII and John XXIII).[88]

This was to prove quite embarrassing some five centuries later when another Pope John XXIII was elected to the pontificate in 1958. Catholic officials had to rush and hurriedly remove the fifteenth century John XXIII from their chronological lists of Popes! The insoluble problem here lies in the fact that Martin V was not a direct successor of any of the other Popes, as Roman Catholic Canon law and tradition require![89] Different ecclesiastical bodies that were not united in consent with each other when it came to electing a Pope elected each Pope during the Great Western Schism. Each group, whether in Avignon or Rome, violated the binding decree of Vatican II, which states:

> *The college or body of bishops has for all that no authority unless united with the Roman*
> *Pontiff, Peter successor, as its head, whose primatial authority, let it be added, over all,*
> *whether pastors or faithful, remains in its integrity. For the Roman Pontiff, by reason of his*
> *office as Vicar of Christ, namely, and as Pastor of the entire Church, has full supreme and*
> *universal power over the whole Church, a power which he can always exercise unhindered.*

---

[87]   They were: Pope Benedict IV (900-903 A.D.), Pope Leo V (903 A.D.); Pope Sergius III (904-911 A.D.); Pope Anastasius III (911-913 A.D.); Pope Lando (913 A.D.); Pope John X (914 A.D.); Pope Leo VI (928 A.D.); Pope Stephen VII (928-931 A.D.); and Pope John XI (931-935 A.D.).

[88]   P.G. Maxwell-Stuart, *Chronicle of the Popes* (London: Thames and Hudson, 1997), 141-143.

[89]   *The Code of Canon Law*, **Canon 333**, pp.57-58.

The order of bishops is the successor to the college of the Apostles in their role as teachers and pastors, and in it the apostolic college is perpetuated. *Together with their head, the Supreme Pontiff, and never apart from him, they have supreme and full authority over the universal Church; but this power cannot be exercised without the agreement of the Roman Pontiff* (Italics mine).[90]

Furthermore, Roman Catholic Canon Law states that an ecclesiastical council decision cannot go into effect unless the Roman Pontiff first approves it.[91] The examples from Papal history in the preceding paragraphs demonstrate that any Popes who were illegitimately elected from the beginning of the tenth century through the fifteenth century could not be the genuine successors of Popes prior to that time; and therefore the supposed chain of apostolic succession is broken and no longer exists today, and thus invalidating the Papacy for the last one thousand years! For one Pope is elected and then discarded and denounced an antipope, while another, once considered an antipope, is now elected the new Pope, as in the case with Sylvester III in 1045 who was elected Pope only to be deposed some twenty-one days later by Pope Benedict IX as an imposter. And yet the *Annuario Pontificio* (the Vatican's annual directory that provides an official list of the Popes) considered Stephen II to be a Pope before his consecration until his name was removed from the official Vatican list in 1959 and all subsequent Stephen numbers were adjusted! In the same Vatican publication there is a shocking admission, after the entry of Pope Leo VII (963-965 A.D.), that to ascertain the unbroken chain of apostolic succession from the mid-tenth century until now is an impossibility and to therefore further assign successive numbers in the list of the Popes should be properly abandoned:

> At this point, as again in the mid-eleventh century, *we come across elections in which problems of harmonizing historical criteria and those of theology and canon law make it impossible to decide clearly which side possessed the legitimacy whose factual existence guarantees the unbroken lawful succession of the Successors of Saint Peter. The uncertainty that in some cases results has made it advisable to abandon the assignation of successive numbers in the list of Popes.*[92]

The Vatican's historical appeal for the Papacy, on which the doctrine of apostolic succession stands, crumbles like a house of cards in the face of such undeniable, historical facts—not only is the Papacy unbiblical, but also lacks proper historical substantiation! On the contrary, the historical evidence discounts any apostolic succession of the Roman Catholic kind. A Roman Catholic priest and former chairman of the department of theology at the University of Notre Dame categorically agrees when writing of the Apostle Peter and apostolic succession:

> Whether he actually served the church of Rome as bishop cannot be known through evidence at hand. **And from the New Testament record *alone*, we have no basis for**

---

[90]   Vatican II: *The Conciliar and Post Conciliar Documents*, 375.

[91]   *Code of Canon Law*, **Canon 38**, p. 58.

[92]   *Annuario Pontificio* 2008 (Libreria Editrice Vaticana 2008), 12. See also http://en.wikipedia.org/wiki/Anti-pope.

positing a line of succession from Peter through subsequent bishops of Rome (Author's emphasis).[93]

True apostolic succession does not come from tracing some sketchy, genealogical and dubious ecclesiastical lineage of Popes, but is obtained by preaching what the Apostles preached preserved in the canon of Scripture by every genuine servant of Jesus Christ who proclaims His Gospel.

---

[93] Richard P. McBrien, *Catholicism* (New York: Harper Collins, 1994), 753. There is now a theological movement in the more ultra conservative branch of the Roman Catholic Church called Sedevacantism—the belief that all those who have claimed to be within the Papal Succession of Pope Pius XII to the present are not even to be considered genuine Roman Catholic Popes. THERE HAVE BEEN NO LEGITIMATE POPES FOR OVER 50 YEARS TO THE PRESENT! "Sedevacantists" also reject all those professing to be priests ordained since Vatican II as "illegitimate" priests and "false" Catholics with no genuine power or authority to administer the Sacraments of the "true" Catholic Church. Apostolic succession in this system has then ceased and the unbroken chain from Peter to the present day has been broken for over the last forty-five years!

CHAPTER 3

THE PAPACY OF PETER IN ROME AND NEW TESTAMENT CHRONOLOGY

The chronology of the New Testament, according to the Acts of the Apostles, the Pauline Epistles, and the Epistles of Peter do not make allowance nor explicitly mention that Peter was in Rome before or after Paul's arrival and likely martyrdom there. Roman Catholic scholars even admit that the precise date and period of Peter's so-called papacy in Rome and the origin of the church there is unknown. Catholic historian Philip Hughes admits:

> The precise date at which the Roman Church was founded we do not know, ***nor the date at which St. Peter first went to Rome***. But it is universally the tradition of this primitive Christianity that St. Peter ruled the Roman Church and that at Rome he gave his life for Christ in the persecution of Nero...***We do not know very much about the first development of the Roman Church. The obscurity which, in these centuries, veils so much, veils this, too, very largely*** (Emphasis Mine).[1]

The presence of Peter in Rome does not rest on solid historical evidence but on unconfirmed tradition shared among most Church Fathers of the East and West. Even if Peter was in Rome, and died there, this does not prove he acted there in the role of Universal Bishop, and Supreme Pontiff. The Roman Catholic Church has long held that Peter was Pope in Rome from 41 to 67 A.D., a period of twenty-six years. But such a tradition, as we will see, has no support in Scripture. After Paul was miraculously converted by Christ and called by Him into the apostolic ministry, we read in Galatians 1:16-17: ***"Immediately I conferred not with flesh and blood. Neither did I go up to Jerusalem to them which were Apostles before me."*** Paul received his apostleship directly from Christ, ***"not of men, neither by man"*** (Galatians 1:1). Three years after this, Paul went up to Jerusalem and communed with Peter and James around the year 40 A.D. Peter remained

---

[1]   Philip Hughes, *A Popular History of the Church* (New York: MacMillan, 1962), 15-16.

in Jerusalem through 41 A.D. and was arrested that year by Herod Agrippa (Acts 12:1-19). This places the Apostle in Jerusalem, not in Rome in the role of a Pope, lording his universal bishopric over the other Apostles. Paul made his second trip to Jerusalem around 50 A.D. to attend the Jerusalem Council. While he was there, James, Peter, and John give him the right hand of fellowship. During this time no mention of Peter's supremacy as Pope over the rest is ever stated. Instead, Paul says that the same effectual work of apostleship in Peter's ministry to the Jews was equally effectual in his ministry of apostleship to the Gentiles (Galatians 2:7-8).

Both Paul and Peter were equal in apostolic rank and ministerial ability. Paul explicitly denies any sort of superiority subordinating himself as the underling of Peter. Because Peter's ministry was mainly to the Jews, and Paul's ministry to the Gentiles, Peter would have naturally gone wherever there was a large Jewish population. Jerusalem, Antioch (of Syria), and Babylon were the main cities of the ancient world that had the largest Jewish populations. In fact, Babylon is where Peter wrote his first epistle, sometime around 64 to 67 A.D.[2] Babylon, along the Euphrates River, was renowned for its Jewish influence from the time of the exile in the sixth century B.C. to the ninth century A.D. This is where the famous *Babylonian Talmud* was written and compiled in the fifth century A.D. First century Jewish historian, Flavius Josephus, writes that Babylon was a flourishing Jewish community during Peter's time "where there were Jews in great numbers."[3] It is only logical for Peter, the Apostle to the Jews, to go there and evangelize this heavily populated area of Jews in *literal* Babylon now located in present day Iraq.

We emphasize literal here because Roman Catholic exegesis has traditionally taught that the "Babylon" mentioned 1 Peter 5:13 is a code or cryptic allegorical allusion to the city of Rome from where Peter was writing at that time. But this is probably not a correct interpretation for three simple reasons: (1) Rome was not depicted as spiritual Babylon until about 96 A.D.—well after Peter died—by the Apostle John in the book of Revelation. The Babylonian Rome John writes about was a "mystery" not revealed until the time John saw it in a future vision and recorded it in the book of Revelation some thirty-two years after Peter's ministry in Babylon. "MYSTERY BABYLON THE GREAT" of Revelation 17 typifies the one world false ecclesiastical system based in Rome who aligns herself with the Anti-Christ. Many students of Bible prophecy have historically identified Babylon the Great, the Mother of Harlots to mean the apostate Papal Church of Rome, prophetically unveiled to John the Apostle, (2) Peter is probably not writing from Rome or to the believers there, but to the Jewish Christian inhabitants of Asia minor (present day Turkey) who were part of the Diaspora.

The other geographical locations mentioned in First Peter were literal places and there is good reason to suppose that when this epistle was written it was written from the actual geographical location of Babylon along the Euphrates River to other literal locations in Asia Minor, (3) Rome was mostly filled with Gentile inhabitants and would have been an ideal place for Paul's ministry to flourish. Rome had more Gentiles than Jews; hence you find Paul there as recorded in Acts 28:16. The Apostle tarried there for two years making no mention of Peter officiating as the Bishop of Rome.

In 57 A.D., when Paul wrote the epistle to the Romans, there was no recognition or mention of Peter being in Rome. Among the twenty-seven persons Paul greets, salutes, and commends in Romans chapter sixteen, the Apostle Peter is never listed. If Peter had been at Rome, Paul would have certainly sent his

---

[2]   D.Edmond Hiebert *1 Peter* (Chicago: Moody Press, 1984), 27.

[3]   *The Complete Works of Josephus, Antiquities*, Book xv, Ch 2, translated by William Whiston (Grand Rapids: Kregel, 1991), 315.

personal greetings to a Bishop of Rome and Prince of the Apostles first and foremost. Paul, not Peter, was the first Apostle directly chosen by Christ to preach the Gospel in Rome among the Gentiles. The "Apostle of the Gentiles" was looking forward to this first time experience to evangelize in Rome. As such, Paul did not publicize any primacy of Peter or his headship over the Church in the role of Pope and Bishop of Rome because Peter had never been there, and therefore Paul sought to "magnify" his apostolic office by preaching the Gospel in Rome where never an Apostle preached before (Romans 11:13). Henceforth, the more Gentiles that Paul evangelized in Rome, the greater his apostolic influence and power would be enlarged, magnified, and extended there for the greater glory of Jesus Christ (Romans 15:22-33). This reality makes it all the more conspicuous the absence of any papacy from Rome with Peter acting as the imperial head. In 62 A.D., when Paul wrote his first prison epistles sent from Rome (Colossians 4:10-14; Phil. 12), he makes no mention of Peter being there with him.

If any Apostle had reasonable justification, or grounds for apostolic supremacy from the historical record of the New Testament, it would have been Paul, not Peter. Paul's life takes up more room than any other figure next to Christ in the New Testament. Though he was certainly not greater then Peter, Paul could certainly say: ***"For I consider that I am not at all inferior to the most eminent Apostles"*** (1 Corinthians 11:5). And again, he could say by the empowerment of Jesus Christ: ***"For in nothing was I behind the most eminent Apostles"*** (2 Corinthians 12:11). This is not to minimize Peter's role in the early Church or New Testament. His role was a primary and significant one, but not to the exclusion of the other Apostles like Paul. The Roman Catholic hierarchy makes special boast of Peter being their head. From him, they say is established the Papacy with the attendant descent in order, rank, and power of Cardinals, Archbishops, Bishops, Monsignors, and Priests.[4]

The legitimacy of this power structure stands on Peter and on him is the true Church built, outside of which there is no complete salvation.[5] Thus, he who submits to Peter will submit to his successors the Popes that stand in his place and represent his person as Jesus Christ on Earth.

Does part of, or all of salvation really begin with submitting to Peter and the Popes? What says the Scriptures? The simplicity of salvation is found in the very words of Peter in Acts 4:12: ***"Neither is there salvation in any other. For there is none other name under heaven given among men whereby we must be saved."*** Salvation is not found in the Roman Catholic Church nor any other ecclesiastical organization or denomination, but is found and given directly by the Lord Jesus Christ (John 3:16-17). Anyone reading the New Testament will readily see that salvation does not include submission to Peter as "Universal Pope" over the earth, but does require trust in the Lord Jesus Christ as Savior and belief in His name and the Gospel that Peter proclaimed. Faith in Jesus Christ alone is the totality of salvation and includes nothing else. The Corinthians, like devotees of the Roman Catholic system, professed to be followers of Peter (Cephas) alone. They proudly declared: "I am of Cephas" (1 Corinthians 1:12).

Some at Corinth who gathered around the person and name of Peter only did so apparently thinking that Peter was the greatest next to Jesus Christ. They, too, believed in the "primacy" of Peter. Did this attitude among the sect that rallied around the name of Peter betoken the true Church with real spirituality focusing on the doctrinal soundness of Christ? They claimed, like Rome, that their group had the true way of salvation by which Peter was head. Did Paul commend this sect as being over and above the other sects at Corinth? Did he give unhesitating consent to the superiority of Peter (Cephas) over the other Apostles and himself as

---

4   *Vatican II: Conciliar and Post Conciliar Documents*, 369-386.

5   The Vatican still teaches that there is no salvation outside the "Church" of Rome. See *Documents of Vatican II*, General Editor Walter M. Abbot, S.J. (New York: American Press, 1966), page 222 (footnote 67).

the sole dispenser of salvation? Undoubtedly, if the truth of apostolic succession and Peter's primacy was paramount to the Church, an indispensable element for salvation and binding upon all Christians, the Apostle Paul would have given unmistakable warrant and clear explicit approval in favor and support of it since it was beginning to bud in Corinth.

If the above were true, than Paul would do everything in his power to proclaim, foster, and advance this papal claim throughout the known world of that time—both in word and letter, especially in his epistle to Corinth where this bias toward Peter being chief among the brethren first developed. But we find the opposite in First Corinthians. There we read that Paul sternly labeled these supercilious sects as sinful *"contentions"* (1 Corinthians 1:11), causing division among the body of Christian believers at Corinth (1 Corinthians 1:13). This provincial display of sectarianism on the part of the Corinthians, whether it was for Paul, **Peter**, or Apollos, really, only, betrayed a carnality and spiritual immaturity for all to see. With this being exposed, Paul exhorts the divisive and wayward Corinthian Christians to disperse with their personality sects and unify under the one banner of the crucified and risen Savior the Lord Jesus Christ where as ministerial equals Paul, Apollos, and Cephas had already gathered together as "fellow laborers together with God" (1 Corinthians 1:10; 3: 3:5-9).

The Corinthians were strongly counseled by the Apostle Paul not glorify one minister above the other. The principle applies and is true for Roman Catholics today who seek to place Peter on a higher rank than the other Apostles and ministers of Christ. *"Therefore let no man glory in men"* (1 Corinthians 3:21). Actually, God appointed the Apostles to be "last" for a spectacle to the world of men and angels. The only Apostle the Corinthians were told to follow and imitate was Paul, not Peter! They were to follow Paul just as he followed Christ (1 Corinthians 4:7-16). When the Vatican insists on Peter being the chief Apostle, even above Paul, they violate the biblical ethic of equality among other Apostles, bishops, elders, and ministers of Christ so plainly laid out in 1 Corinthians 1-3.[6] The Bible declares there is only one supreme Apostle of our Christian confession who is the Chief Shepherd over all the Church—the Lord Jesus Christ (1 Peter 5:4).

The writer of Hebrews calls Jesus *"The Apostle and High Priest of our confession"* (Hebrews 3:1), not Peter, Paul or any Pope, nor the many other alleged successors of Peter who have the presumptuous affixation of "Supreme Pontiff" attached to their man-made office. We are to look upon Peter and Paul as equal Apostles and render to them great esteem, respect, honor, and prompt submission to their apostolic writings with obedience, viewing them at the same time equal brethren with one Lord and Master over all. This is the proper order the Lord commands His Church to observe (Matthew 23:8-10). New Testament Scripture gives no precedent of exalting one Apostle over another in the form of the Papacy, *"for there is no respect of persons with God"* (Romans 2:11). In the listings of the various ministerial offices of the Church, no hierarchical structure of Priests, Monsignors, Cardinals, or a Papacy is ever named (1 Corinthians 12:28; Ephesians 4:11). The church at Rome was not apostolically founded by Peter. It had already existed before any Apostle arrived there. Paul always made it a point not to intrude into another man's ministry. He desired to preach Christ wherever He was not made know or spoken about (Romans 15:20-21). *Paul was the first Apostle ever to set foot in Rome and publicly preach Christ there* (Acts 28:30-31).

The first century church of Rome was likely established by Jews and Gentile proselytes from Rome who were present in Jerusalem on the day of Pentecost, and then relayed what happened on that miraculous day when returning to Rome (see Acts 2:10). The church could also have been conceivably started by

---

6   Ludwig Ott, *Fundamentals of Catholic Dogma*, 281-282. Pope Innocent X (1644-1655 A.D.) went so far to condemn as heretical the belief that both Paul and Peter were joint heads of the Church

Paul's converts to Christ who came from the eastern provinces of the Roman Empire, (where the Apostle evangelized Galatia, Asia Minor, and Greece), to Rome and shared their faith with the populace there.[7] With his execution imminent in Rome, Paul makes no mention of Peter being there when giving his valedictory farewell in 2 Timothy 4:6-8. All had abandoned him. Only Luke was with him in Rome (2 Timothy 4:9). This is especially significant to remember for the fact that the date for the composition of 2 Timothy was 67 A.D., the very same year Peter was supposedly martyred in Rome, yet no mention of this or Peter being there is made in this Pauline epistle or, for that matter, the rest of the New Testament corpus!

For centuries, the Roman Catholic institution has claimed that Peter was martyred in Rome. This tradition is largely based on a large body of written and oral traditions and apocryphal literature about the life of Saint Peter. There is no credible historical evidence or documentation from the New Testament Scriptures proving that Peter was ever in Rome, or that he died there. To this very day, the Vatican still insists that they house the bones of Saint Peter underneath the altar in Saint Peter's Basilica in Rome proving for them, at least, that the Apostle was indeed in Rome acting in the office of Pope when he died in 67 A.D. Two Roman Catholic priests—Bellarmino Bagatti and Josef Milik, shattered this unsupported claim in 1953. Both men were highly trained scholars of international repute in the fields of archaeology, ancient biblical manuscripts, and the ancient languages of the Middle East. Bagatti and Milik excavated a first century Jewish Christian cemetery located in Jerusalem, on the Franciscan monastery site called, "Dominus Flevit" (where Jesus was supposed to have wept over Jerusalem), on the Mount of Olives.[8] Their find was an extraordinary one! In that cemetery, they stumbled upon an ossuary with the name **"Simon Bar Jonah"** in Aramaic etched on it. Through several tests and scientific examinations, it was confirmed that this ossuary, that once housed the bones of this man named Simon Bar Jonah was, in all probability, the very same Apostle Peter with that same name mentioned in Matthew 16:17.

Both Bagatti and Milik published this finding in a scholarly monograph entitled *Gli Scavi del Dominus Flevit* printed in 1958 at the Tipografia del PP, Francescani, in Jerusalem. Researcher, F. Paul Peterson, recounts an interview with Milik who confirmed that the evidence is conclusive enough that Peter was buried in Jerusalem instead of Rome:

> I talked to priest Milik, the co-writer of this Italian book, in the presence of my friend, a Christian Arab, Mr. S. J. Mattar, who now is the warden of the Garden Tomb, where Jesus was buried and rose again. This priest, Milik, admitted that he knew that the bones of St. Peter are not in Rome. I was very much surprised that he would admit that, so to confirm his admittance, I said, to which he also agreed, ***"There is a hundred times more evidence that Peter was buried in Jerusalem than in Rome." This was something of an understatement, for he knew as I know that there is absolutely no evidence at all that Peter was buried in Rome. I have spoken on the subject to many Franciscan priests who either were or had been in Jerusalem, and they all agree that the tomb and remains of St. Peter are in Jerusalem"*** (Bold italics mine).[9]

---

[7]   *The Believer's Study Bible* (Nashville: Thomas Nelson, 1991), 1599.

[8]   The author has personally visited this sight several times on the Mount of Olives to see the actual location of this cemetery where some of these ossuaries still remain.

[9]   F. Paul Peterson, *Peter's Tomb Recently Discovered in Jerusalem* (Fort Wayne, Indiana: F.P. Peterson, 1962), 3.

The Vatican purposely suppressed and hid this embarrassing discovery. Father Bagatti went personally to Pope Pius XII in Rome with this disturbing find and presented the archaeological evidence. Pius was reported to have said the following:

> "Well, we will have to make some changes, but for the time being, keep this thing quiet'."
> In awe I asked also in a subdued voice, "So the Pope really believes that those are the bones of St. Peter?" "Yes," was his answer. "The documentary evidence is there, he could not help but believe."[10]

This momentous discovery that continues to be kept from the public view, if true, casts serious doubts on the Vatican's special claims about Peter ruling from Rome much to the private chagrin and dismay of Pope Pius XII. Surely, if the Apostle Peter understood Jesus' words recorded in Matthew 16:17-19 to mean an apostolic succession would emerge from his rule over the entire Church, then Peter would have appointed a successor for the church to acknowledge and submit to. Indeed, sensing his death was imminent, Peter neither mentions a successor to be appointed to lead the church in his place, nor to recognize him in that role, but reminds the church to follow the sure word of prophetic Scripture and the Gospel that he taught them.

> *"Of this salvation the prophets have inquired and searched carefully, who prophesied of the grace that would come to you, searching what, or what manner of time, the Spirit of Christ who was in them was indicating when He testified beforehand the sufferings of Christ and the glories that would follow. To them it was revealed that, not to themselves, but to us they were ministering the things which now have been reported to you through those who have preached the gospel to you by the Holy Spirit sent from heaven--things which angels desire to look into. For this reason I will not be negligent to remind you always of these things, though you know and are established in the present truth. Yes, I think it is right, as long as I am in this tent, to stir you up by reminding you, Knowing that shortly I must put off my tent, just as our Lord Jesus Christ showed me. Moreover I will be careful to ensure that you always have a reminder of these things after my decease. For we did not follow cunningly devised fables when we made known to you the power and coming of our Lord Jesus Christ, but were eyewitnesses of His majesty. For He received from God the Father honor and glory when such a voice came to Him from the Excellent Glory: "This is My beloved Son, in whom I am well pleased." And we heard this voice which came from heaven when we were with Him on the holy mountain. And so we have the prophetic word confirmed, which you do well to heed as a light that shines in a dark place, until the day dawns and the morning star rises in your hearts; Knowing this first, that no prophecy of Scripture is of any private interpretation, For*

---

[10]   The following dialogue was taken from an interview researcher F. Paul Peterson conducted with a Franciscan priest—a personal friend of Father Bagatti—who told the priest and friend of this personal encounter with Pius XII. For further elaboration on the paleographic and archaeological evidences see http://www.giveshare.org/churchhistory/peters-tomb-jerusalem.html. Furthermore, the present Saint Peter's Basilica in Rome, where Peter's bones are supposedly buried underneath the altar, was built on top of a first century pagan cemetery. First century Christians would not have buried the bones of a Jewish Christian, like the Apostle Peter, in such a place devoted to the false gods of Rome! Such a practice would have been unthinkable to them.

> *prophecy never came by the will of man, but holy men of God spoke as they were moved by the Holy Spirit"* (1 Peter 1:12-15; 2 Peter 1:12-21).

The reason the epistles of Peter never mention apostolic succession concerning the primacy and papacy of Peter is because they are simply not found nor taught there, or in the New Testament either. Thus, in light of this, Evangelical apologist Eric Svendsen is right to point out:

> We must not miss the point here. Peter writes these words based on certain underlying assumptions. One must ask honestly, are these words of someone who believed he was going to appoint another pope as his successor; a person supposedly infallible, who would then guide the church after his death? If so, these are strange words indeed! We must conclude that Peter missed a golden opportunity to appoint his successor. Would it not have made more sense (assuming a Roman Catholic belief in apostolic succession) to have given explicit instructions to the church to obey the new pope, such as one finds in some of the patristic writings when the author was about to be martyred?[11]

To evade the obvious here, Roman Catholic apologists will tell you that the Papacy was subject to a gradual process over a long period of time that grew from a small acorn into a mighty oak tree. For in the words of Catholic apologist Stephen Ray,

"The oak tree has grown and looks perceptibly different from the fragile sprout that cracked the original acorn, yet the organic essence remain the same. Do the words of the very first Christians contain the full-blown understanding of the Papacy as expressed in Vatican I? No, they do not."[12] The analogy of the acorn and the oak tree is related to what is called the *Doctrine of Development*, which was a term used by Cardinal John Henry Newman and other Roman Catholic theologians influenced by him to describe the way Catholic teaching has become more detailed and explicit over the centuries, while later statements of doctrine remain consistent with earlier statements. The term was introduced in Newman's 1845 book: *An Essay on the Development of Christian Doctrine.* Does this theological concept correctly reflect what the Roman Catholic Institution teaches concerning the Papacy? In fact, they teach the diametric opposite from this. The Roman Catholic Church asserts that the Papacy was a fully-grown oak tree, so to speak, from the beginning.

Rome has traditionally held that Christ directly gave it to the Church fully developed from the beginning and preserved it in the same form to this very day. Those like Stephen Ray, who appeal to gradual development, to explain away the absence of the doctrine of the Papacy in the New Testament and the Early Church, do so in apparent ignorance of what Rome teaches on this subject. To say the papacy was not an immediate and complete spiritual institution but, rather, gradually developed over time when conferred from Christ to Peter and his successors is to invoke the anathema of Rome. For, Vatican I declared:

> *At open variance with this clear doctrine of Holy Scripture, as it has ever been understood by the Catholic Church, are the perverse opinions of those who, while they distort the form of government established by Christ the Lord in His Church, deny that Peter in his simple person preferably to all the other Apostles, whether taken separately or together,*

11   Eric Svendsen, *Evangelical Answers: A Critique of Current Roman Catholic Apologists* (Lindenhurst, New York: 1999), 63.
12   Stephen Ray, *Upon This Rock* (San Francisco: Ignatius, 1999), 184.

was endowed by Christ with a true and proper primacy was not bestowed immediately and directly upon Blessed Peter himself, but upon the Church, and through the Church on Peter as her minister. If anyone, therefore, shall say that Blessed Peter the Apostle was not appointed the Prince of the Apostles and the visible head of the whole church militant, ***or that the same directly and immediately received from the same our Lord Jesus Christ a primacy of honor only, and not of true and proper jurisdiction; let him be anathema.***[13]

Defenders of the papacy, who use the Doctrine of Development, cannot have it both ways when they claim the Papacy was a institution that gradually emerged over time to explain away its apparent absence in the New Testament, when the very religious system they are blindly defending, officially teaches the papacy was immediate and direct, and those who say otherwise are forthrightly condemned. Finally, if submission to the Papacy is necessary for salvation—officially taught by Rome since the tenth century, what happened to those faithful Roman Catholics who died prior to the formulation of this doctrine during the medieval period that became binding on all who are within the Church? If indeed submission to Peter and the papacy of Rome were necessary for salvation, then Jesus, Peter, and the other Apostles in the New Testament would have unquestionably demanded it. The fact this is not even remotely the case in Scripture makes it patently obvious that the Roman Catholic Papacy is not biblical, nor was it ever endorsed or practiced in the New Testament Church!

---

[13]   *Dogmatic Canons and Decrees*, 242-243.

CHAPTER 4

THE ECUMENICAL CHURCH COUNCILS AND THE PAPACY

Having sufficiently demonstrated thus far that the Roman Catholic doctrine of the Papacy is not a normative teaching found in the New Testament, nor a teaching based on "the unanimous consent" of the Church Fathers (contra the Vatican I Council) for at least the first thousand years of Church history, the question of what do the seven major ecumenical Church Councils say about any Primacy of Rome (upon which the Roman Catholic Papacy is built) will now be addressed. The reason these seven ecumenical councils are specified here is because both Protestants and Roman Catholics generally accept them, since their theological universality applies to both in belief and practice. When a particular bishop or group of bishops convened an ecumenical council from the major regions or episcopates, representing the whole church at that time, they did so to discuss and decide on major doctrines and practices of the Christian faith.

The results of these Councils were summed up in a written confession of what those beliefs and practices were that defined and explained the basic tenets of Christianity that originated from Holy Scripture. The ecumenical Councils dealt with what the Scriptures taught about the Christian faith with the intent of clarifying, interpreting, and amplifying our understanding of the meaning of Scripture. Therefore, whatever creedal statement is made from these Councils is done with the avowed understanding that it must be founded upon Scripture and should not extend beyond it. The purpose of these Councils was not to create new doctrines, but to elucidate doctrines found already in Scripture that had been misinterpreted by heretics. Heretofore:

> The creed is simply the church's understanding of the meaning of Scripture. The creed
> says, here is how the Church reads and receives Scripture. The whole history of theology
> is the history of the interpretation of Scripture, even though the theologians do not always
> cite biblical references. In general, the victories in the great theological debates have gone
> to those who have been the most convincing interpreters of Scripture. The creeds are the
> record of the Church's interpretation of the Bible in the past and the authoritative guide to
> hermeneutics in the present…The task of the creed was to defend the Church against heresy.

The creed has the negative role of shutting the heretic out and setting the boundaries within authentic Christian theology and life can take place.[14]

With that said, if the Roman Catholic doctrine of the Papacy is correct and was practically observed from the beginning of Christianity almost two thousand years ago, then the Pope, who is the Bishop of Rome, will not only have convened and presided over each of these ecumenical councils, but his preeminent authority will have been recognized and formally observed by these same church councils. That no such thing is evinced during the course of these councils indubitably proves that the doctrine and office of the papacy was not a universal reality accepted by the church at that time for the simple fact the bishops of Rome were not accepted in this supreme role! Roman Catholic historian and priest, Ignaz Von Dollinger, defines the role and relationship that existed between the councils and bishops of Rome in the following crucial points stressing the minimal role of the alleged Popes of Rome:

> (1) The Popes took no part in convoking Councils. All Great Councils, to which bishops came from different countries were convoked by the Emperors, *nor were the Popes ever consulted about it beforehand.* (2) The Popes were not always allowed to preside, personally or by deputy, at the Great Councils, though no one denied them the first rank in the Church. At Nice, at the two Councils of Ephesus in 431 and 449, and at the Fifth Great Council in 553, others presided; only at Chalcedon in 451, and Constantinople in 680, did the Papal legates preside. *And it is clear that the Popes did not claim this as their exclusive right.* (3) *Neither the dogmatic nor the disciplinary decisions of these Councils required Papal confirmation, for their force and authority depended on the consent of the Church, as expressed in the Synod, and afterwards in the fact of its being generally received.* The confirmation of the Nicene Council by Pope Silvester was afterwards invented at Rome, because facts would not square with the newly devised theory (Italics mine).[15]

The historical evidence from the seven ecumenical Church Councils indicates that there is no admission or claim for the Bishop of Rome being the supreme head over all the other churches and bishops. The evidence shows they held to the equality of all bishops in the churches. A summary of the activities from these councils are given below relating to this truth:

The Council of Nicea 325 A.D.

The chief official who convened this Church council was not the bishop of Rome presiding in the office of Pope over all the churches but the Roman Emperor Constantine according to ancient Church historian Eusebius who was in attendance.[16] He mentions no Pope of Rome taking the lead of the council proceeding. Historian William Cathcart accurately describes what took place at Nicea:

> The Roman pontiff was not present in the council at any of its meetings. He was represented by two presbyters, named Vito and Vincentius, who took no remarkable part in its

---

[14] John Leith, ed., *Creeds of the Churches* (Louisville: John Knox Press, 1982), 8-9.

[15] Von Dollinger, *The Pope and the Council*, 63-64.

[16] Philip Schaff, *Creeds of Christendom: The Greek and Latin Creeds* (Grand Rapids: Baker, 2007), 29.

proceedings. ***There were a score of bishops there whose influence was greater than that of the aged bishop of the Eternal City.*** Constantine himself managed the Council. There is ground for doubting whether it had any other president during most of its discussions; though several persons are said to have occupied this position. He delivered exhortations to the council. He heard the propositions…reasoned with them, appealed to them…and exercised such a marvelous influence over them that ***he led the whole assembly to one mind respecting disputed Christians. And for the time became the ruler of the council, and common father of Christendom.***[17]

Canon six of the Nicean Creed confers the same authority to the bishops of the Near East that the bishop of Rome had. No Roman supremacy is asserted here. Roman Catholic defenders for an early Papacy refute this decision by asserting that the original wording of article six should read: "Rome has always had the Primacy"[18] Such a claim is made to 'prove' that the Papacy of Rome did indeed exist in the Early Church. However, the phrase about Roman primacy was summarily dismissed as inauthentic, lacking any historical validity. In fact during the proceedings of the Council of Chalcedon, the delegates from Pope Leo I sought to establish the Primacy of Rome on this reading of canon six. But they were soundly rejected on the provable grounds that such a reading was not part of the original text of canon six.[19] It was therefore rightly rejected as spurious.

The Roman Emperor Constantine confirmed the decrees of the Nicean Council. He did not defer to the Roman bishop like a Pope ruling over the entire Church for final confirmation. Eusebius, a delegate and participant at the Nicean Council writes concerning the role of Constantine, *"He confirmed and sanctioned the decrees of the council, and called on them to strive earnestly for concord, and not to distract and rend the Church, but to keep before them the thought of God's judgment. And these injunctions the emperor sent by a letter written with his own hand"* (Eusebius' *Life of Constantine*, Book III, chapter 23).[20]

The Council of First Constantinople 381 A.D.

The first Council of Constantinople was convened by the Roman Emperor Theodosius the Great. The purpose of this church council was to further expand and enlarge the Nicean confession by adding belief in the deity and Person of the Holy Spirit. Another issue brought before the council was the matter of authoritative jurisdiction within the Church. In canon three, the delegates recognized and formally elevated the see of Constantinople second in the order of primacy after Rome. The see of Rome was recognized first only in terms of *honor*, not first in the sense of exercising supreme jurisdictional authority over the other bishops of the major cities of the Empire.[21] The council hastens to affirm, however, that such an honor did

---

[17]   William Cathcart, *The Papal System*,

[18]   William Webster, *The Matthew 16 Controversy*, 166.

[19]   Catholic historian Robert Eno further elaborates that: "There was also circulating an interpolated western version of the sixth canon of Nicea which stated flatly that the Roman Church had always had the primacy. This had been presented at Chalcedon by the Roman representatives but had been rejected as inauthentic" *From the Rise of the Papacy* (Wilmington: Michael Glazier, 1990), 123.

[20]   From the Catholic web site New Advent at http://www.newadvent.org/fathers/25023.htm.

[21]   Canon three states the reason for this was because Constantinople is the "new Rome" and so, consequently, the bishop of Constantinople is to enjoy the privileges of honor after the bishop of Rome (See Norman Tanner S.J.., Ed., *Decrees of the Ecumenical Councils* (Washington D.C.: Georgetown University, 1990), Vol. II, p. 31-32.

not include allowing Rome's bishops to meddle or interfere with the jurisdictional authority of other bishops from other provinces, lest the Church be thrown into confusion. Pope Damasus did not attend this council, nor did he send any of his representatives. It was presided over by Meletius, bishop of Antioch and later by Gregory of Nazianzus, bishop of Constantinople.

The Council of Ephesus 431 A.D.

This council was not summoned by the bishop of Rome but by the Emperor Theodosius II to condemn the heresy of Nestorius. Cyril of Alexandria was given the position of President of the Council without surrendering to the authority of Pope Celestine, bishop of Rome. *The Emperor, not the Pope, assigned Cyril as Head Bishop of this council.*

The Council of Chalcedon 451 A.D.

The Council of Chalcedon was summoned by the Emperor Marcian to renounce the errors of Eutyches the monk. The bishop of Rome did not convene the council, nor was it solely ratified by his final decision. This is most evident in the 28th canon of Chalcedon where the city of Constantinople, "the New Rome", and its bishop would be awarded and recognized with "equal privileges" to the most holy throne as "the New Rome" with the city of the old Rome and the bishop of Rome.[22] The canon was ratified by the majority of the bishops with the final approval of the Emperor in response to Pope Leo the Great's attempt to assert the supremacy of the Roman See over all Christendom. He failed, and stubbornly refused to accept canon twenty-eight. The fact the council approved this measure in the face of Pope Leo's vehement opposition clearly shows that papal primacy was not universally acknowledged or approved by the church.

The Second Council of Constantinople 553 A.D.

The Emperor Justinian convened this council of 164 bishops without the consent of the Pope to condemn, among other things, the heretical writings of Theodore of Mopsuestia. Pope Vigilius, who is considered "one of the most corrupt Popes in the history of the Church", refused to attend the council or subscribe to its decrees and was, subsequently, excommunicated and banished into exile for upholding the Monophysite heresy (i.e., that Christ has only one nature). Later, he changed his mind, and gave approval to the council's deliberations. Again, we find in this council nothing of Papal supremacy, but rather a Pope submitting to the decisions of a council. *The patriarch of Constantinople occupied first place at this council.*[23] The importance here cannot be ignored. Here we have a council who believed its superiority over the Pope. The Pope was such that they believed he could be excommunicated from the Church on their authority. For during the Middle Ages, this was one of those famous histories that proved to all theologians that a *Council was superior to a pope.*[24]

---

[22] Thomas Bokenkotter, *A Concise History of the Catholic Church* (New York: Image, 2004), 91.
[23] Richard McBrien, *Lives of the Popes*, 91-93.
[24] Peter De Rosa, *Vicars of Christ*, 208.

The Third Council of Constantinople 680 A.D.

Emperor Constantine Pogonatus convened this council with 160 bishops in attendance during the later proceedings. This council was called to officially condemn Pope Honorius for the heresy of Monotheletism, the belief that Christ had one will. What happened to papal infallibility here? The delegates of the council declared of him:

> In addition to these, we acknowledge also Honorius, who was formerly pope of old Rome, *to be amongst those cast out of the holy Church of God and anathematized*, because we find from his letter to Sergius that he altogether followed his opinions, and confirmed his impious dogmas.[25]

Later, the council exclaimed, *"Anathema to the heretic Honorius!"* Popes following him denounced him with this same penalty as well. Here we see a council denouncing a pope and excommunicating him from the Church without giving respect to the primacy of Rome or papal infallibility!

The Fourth Council of Constantinople (692 A.D.).

This ecclesiastical council granted the patriarch of Constantinople *the same privileges as the church of old Rome, the same authority in ecclesiastical affairs.*[26] The decrees of this council were first signed by Emperor Basil I—not the Pope! In the first seven centuries of Church history, one looks in vain to find in the decrees of the general or ecumenical councils any jurisdictional primacy of the bishop of Rome over all the other churches. Rather, we find that an equality of Bishops were recognized and practiced by the Church in her first seven hundred years, and that a sole rulership by one bishop over the entire church, was strongly repudiated and denied by the majority of leaders in the church. Thus we reecho the unimpeachable historical fact put forth by William Cathcart in his fine work *The Papal System*:

> Neither friend or foe on earth can lay his finger on a genuine canon, decree, or resolution of any general council during the first seven hundred years after the Savior's death, giving any preeminence in legislative, judicial, or other departments in which power is accustomed to be exercised over Christendom to the Pope of Rome. There is not a scholar in the Christian world today who pretends to show such a decree, canon, or resolution. These great councils then, that are led by the Holy Spirit, for SEVEN HUNDRED YEARS KNEW NOTHING OF THE SPIRITUAL SUPREMACY OF THE BISHOPS OF ROME.[27]

The Pope's authority over any church in the East and the West did not begin to be promulgated and accepted until the early seventh century; but the East refused such a usurpation of ecclesiastical power and spilt from Rome in 1054 A.D. in what Church historians call "The Great Schism." The majority of the Church Fathers, theologians, patriarchs, and bishops of the Early Church clearly expressed in their writings that the bishops held an equal honor among themselves. Roman supremacy, along the lines of the Papacy, was foreign and repugnant to them as contrary to the Scripture and Spirit of Christ.

---

[25] For a complete copy of the Council text see http://www.fordham.edu/halsall/basis/const3.html.

[26] William Cathcart, *The Papal System*, 34-51

[27] Ibid., 51.

CHAPTER 5

THE PAPACY AND TEMPORAL POWER

The Roman Catholic doctrine of papal supremacy is actually built upon unfounded assumptions, clever forgeries, and misinterpreted Scripture passages used to prop up the faltering pillars of "Apostolic Succession" and "Temporal Power." The doctrine of Temporal Power basically states that the Pope, acting as the Universal Vicar of Christ, is the ruler over all kings and kingdoms of the earth. This autocratic "temporal" power is not found in Scripture, but particularly emerged during the Middle Ages. Pope Pius V (1566-1572) wrote, when excommunicating Queen Elizabeth I, that the Pope is "Prince over all nations, and all kingdoms, that he might pluck up, destroy, dissipate, ruin, plant, and build." Temporal Power allegedly gives the Pope complete authority over all human governments on the earth; and by virtue of his pontifical estate, can exercise supreme jurisdiction in both the religious and political spheres.

The concept of Temporal Power did not come from Christ or the Apostles, whose kingdom and citizenship is not of this world, but lies in heaven and in the future Messianic kingdom to come (John 14:1-6; 17:16; 18:36; Philippians 3:20; Revelation 19-20). Temporal power was pioneered by the ambitious Pope Innocent III (1198-1216). He craftily devised a political theory based on the metaphor of the two swords of Saint Peter, which was subsequently passed down to his successors, the Popes. The first sword is the *spiritual*, and the second is the *temporal*. This was a concept developed and defined some one hundred years earlier by Bernard of Clairvaux (1090-1153) who postulated that:

> The two swords belong to St. Peter. One, the spiritual sword, is in his hands; the other, the temporal sword, is at his command whenever it is necessary to draw it. Peter in fact was told regarding the sword which seemed the least appropriate to him, "Put thy sword back into its sheath."[1]

---

[1]   Wladimir D'Ormesson, *The Papacy* (New York: Hawthorne Books, 1959), 63-64. It is interesting to note that the imperious Pope Boniface VIII further used the two sword imagery to further enhance the Pope's dictatorial rule over Europe and the world when declaring in his Papal Bull *Unam Sanctum*: "...We are informed by the texts of the gospels that in this Church and in its power are two swords; namely, the spiritual and the temporal. For when the Apostles say: 'Behold, here are two swords' [Lk 22:38] that is to say, in the Church, since the Apostles were

Innocent III went on to write in his papal decree *Venerabilem Fratrem Nostrum that* it was the Pope who gave the right and power for the emperor or prince to rule:

> We recognize, as we must, the princes' right and power to elect the king and afterward to raise him to emperor, which is known to belong to them by law and ancient custom. This is especially true since the Apostolic See bestowed this right and power on them.... The princes should recognize as they do (and have in our presence) that the right and authority of examining the person elected king and of promoting him to the imperial office pertains to us, since we anoint, consecrate and crown him.[2]

Such an authority allowed the Popes to confer, wield, and withdraw political power from those rulers or monarchs they fitly deemed worthy, so long as these rulers of nations recognized where this power came from and were willing subjects of the Popes of Rome. Those who proved unwilling to submit to this papal power were excommunicated and subject to arrest, military action, or even death by execution. Through the use of Temporal Power the Popes customarily deposed kings and queens, excommunicated nations, governing bodies, national and religious leaders from the saving arms of "Mother Church." Rome blasphemously proclaimed that to reject the claims of the temporal power of the Popes on Earth was to reject Christ Himself! The Papal Bull *Eger Cui Levia* issued by Pope Innocent IV (1243-1253) says to this end:

> Whoever seeks to evade the authority of the Vicar of Christ... thereby impairs the authority of Christ Himself. The King of kings has established us on earth as His universal representative and had conferred full power on us; by giving to the prince of the apostles and to us the power of binding and loosing on earth not only all men whatsoever, but also all things whatsoever . . . The power of temporal government cannot be exercised outside the church, since there is no power constituted by God outside her . . . Our Lord Jesus Christ, Son of God, true man and true God . . . constituted to the benefit of the holy see a monarchy not only pontifical but royal; he committed to the blessed Peter and his successors the reins

---

speaking, the Lord did not reply that there were too many, but sufficient. Certainly the one who denies that the temporal sword is in the power of Peter has not listened well to the word of the Lord commanding: 'Put up thy sword into thy scabbard' [Mt 26:52]. Both, therefore, are in the power of the Church, that is to say, the spiritual and the material sword, but the former is to be administered for the Church but the latter by the Church; the former in the hands of the priest; the latter by the hands of kings and soldiers, but at the will and sufferance of the priest. However, one sword ought to be subordinated to the other and temporal authority, subjected to spiritual power. For since the Apostle said: 'There is no power except from God and the things that are, are ordained of God' [Rom 13:1-2], but they would not be ordained if one sword were not subordinated to the other and if the inferior one, as it were, were not led upwards by the other.... This authority, however, (though it has been given to man and is exercised by man), is not human but rather divine, granted to Peter by a divine word and reaffirmed to him (Peter) and his successors by the One Whom Peter confessed, the Lord saying to Peter himself, 'Whatsoever you shall bind on earth, shall be bound also in Heaven' etc., [Mt 16:19]. Therefore whoever resists this power thus ordained by God, resists the ordinance of God [Rom 13:2], unless he invents like Manicheus two beginnings, which is false and judged by us heretical, since according to the testimony of Moses, it is not in the beginnings but in the beginning that God created heaven and earth [Gen 1:1]. Furthermore, we declare, we proclaim, we define that it is absolutely necessary for salvation that every human creature be subject to the Roman Pontiff."

2   *Readings in Church History*, ed. Coleman J. Barry, vol. 1, (Westminster, Maryland: Newman Press, 1960), 437-438.

of the empire both earthly and celestial, as is indicated by the plurality of the keys. Vicar of Christ [the Pope] has received the power to exercise his jurisdiction by the one over the earth for temporal things, by the other in heaven for spiritual things.[3]

How was this papal sword of temporal power used, or more precisely abused? The unbiased student of history only has to look at the awful Crusades and the inexcusable inhumanities of the Inquisition to find the tragic and bloody answer. The temptation for the opportunity to assert himself, "as leader over the Eastern Emperor and Patriarch, and over the Western monarchs of Europe," prompted Pope Urban II (1088-1099) to declare at the Council of Clermont in April of 1095 that it was the duty of every responsible Christian to take part in a holy army called the "militia Christi" for the purpose of engaging in a holy war to recapture the Holy Land from the Muslim Turks. And thus, were the Crusades born. The Pope promised a full pardon for all sins to any Christian soldier who killed these pagan infidels.[4] The frenzied Crusaders of Europe, under the fanatical command of Peter the Hermit, descended upon the Holy Land in hopes of gaining wealth and papal favor by putting to death both Jews and Muslims. The First Crusade was really a papal Crusade of homicidal anti-Semitism. Jews were murdered by the tens of thousands in Europe and Jerusalem by these Crusaders of the Pope who plundered European Jews along the way to finance their lengthy expedition to the Holy Land! In Cologne Germany, some 40,000 men, women, and children, inspired by Pope Urban's decree to kill the infidel, (in this respect Medieval Catholicism is quite similar to Militant Islam), burned down the synagogue and slaughtered over 12,000 Jews.[5]

Once the armies of the Pope reached Jerusalem, Jews were butchered wherever they were found. A significant group of Jews and Rabbis were also gathered into the chief synagogue in Jerusalem and burned to death inside while the Crusaders encircled the burning structure singing, "Christ we adore Thee!"[6] Church

---

[3]   Bernard Gullieman, *The Latter Middle Ages* (New York: Hawthorne, 1959), 37-38.

[4]   Urban II was reputed to have said to the crowds at Clermont: "Although, O sons of God, you have promised more firmly than ever to keep the peace among yourselves and to preserve the rights of the church, there remains still an important work for you to do. Freshly quickened by the divine correction, you must apply the strength of your righteousness to another matter which concerns you as well as God. For your brethren who live in the east are in urgent need of your help, and you must hasten to give them the aid which has often been promised them. For, as the most of you have heard, the Turks and Arabs have attacked them and have conquered the territory of Romania [the Greek empire] as far west as the shore of the Mediterranean and the Hellespont, which is called the Arm of St. George. They have occupied more and more of the lands of those Christians, and have overcome them in seven battles. They have killed and captured many, and have destroyed the churches and devastated the empire. If you permit them to continue thus for a while with impurity, the faithful of God will be much more widely attacked by them. On this account I, or rather the Lord, beseech you as Christ's heralds to publish this everywhere and to persuade all people of whatever rank, foot-soldiers and knights, poor and rich, to carry aid promptly to those Christians and to destroy that vile race from the lands of our friends. I say this to those who are present, it meant also for those who are absent. Moreover, Christ commands it. ***All who die by the way, whether by land or by sea, or in battle against the pagans, shall have immediate remission of sins.*** This I grant them through the power of God with which I am invested. O what a disgrace if such a despised and base race, which worships demons, should conquer a people which has the faith of omnipotent God and is made glorious with the name of Christ" See http://www.fordham.edu/halsall/source/urban2-fulcher.html for the full text.

[5]   Edward H. Flannery, *The Anguish of the Jews: Twenty-Three Centuries of Anti-Semitism* (New York: MacMillan, 1965), 90.

[6]   David Rausch, *A Legacy of Hatred* (Grand Rapids: Baker, 1984), 27.

historian Philip Schaff writes that the slaughter of Jews in Jerusalem was so great that "the blood of the massacred in the temple area reached to the very knees and bridles of the horses. Such a slaughter of the pagans had never been seen or heard of. The number none but God knew.[7] All the bloody Crusades were inaugurated with solemn preaching with the approval and sanction of the Popes. The warriors made a vow and were appointed as soldiers for the papacy and Roman Catholic Church. Once sworn to fight, the Pope and his legates gave each knight a cross granted them a full pardon for their sins and immunity from civil power giving them the freedom to kill, rape, plunder and murder without any judicial punishment or prosecution.[8]

The Crusades were essentially a battle for papal dominion over the Middle East and an attempt to regain control of the East and its capital city of Constantinople. This was most evident with the Fourth Crusade (1202-1204). The tyrannical Pope Innocent III engineered this crusade by imposing a compulsory tax based on a *per capita* basis on every priest and monk of the Roman Church to fund this holy army to conquer Constantinople and force the Greek Orthodox Church back under the submission of Rome. In fact, Innocent wrote, that this Crusade was to be carried out *"in order to punish the Greek Church for its disobedience to the Roman See"*.[9] Constantinople fell and was looted and burned in 1204 by the rapacious soldiers of Innocent III. Thousands of Greek Christians who refused to submit to the supreme authority of the Pope were killed on the spot. Even the poor children of France and Germany were caught up in the Pope's delusion for glory, wealth, and power and set out for the Holy Land—eventually some thirty-thousand boys and girls with a few young adults made up the band of children Crusaders.

This was infamously known as *The Children's Crusade*. It began in 1212 A.D. when a young twelve year-old shepherd boy, Stephen of Cloyes, approached King Philip of France with letter in hand claiming it had come from Jesus Christ commanding little Stephen to gather an army of children to march on Jerusalem and liberate the holy city from the hands of the infidel. Stephen further claimed that in a vision Christ told him that the Mediterranean Sea would dry up for he and his followers to allow them to march to Jerusalem, just as God did for Moses when the Red Sea was dried up. The King told the boy to go home. But the boy went instead to the French town of Vendome where he relentlessly preached his self-appointed vision until he gathered roughly a crowd of thirty thousand young children to head south to the seas to embark on their 'miraculous journey' with the full blessing of the Church. Roman Catholic Priests held crosses in their hands and quoting Psalm 8:2 sent these poor children off to their doom doing the Pope's bidding.[10] Word reached Pope Innocent III of this brazen enterprise, and instead of preventing such a disastrous pilgrimage, or urging the parents to prohibit them from going, the Pontiff commended the children by saying, "The very children put us to shame. While they rush to the recovery of the Holy Land we sleep."[11]

Due to severe drought from a very hot summer that year in France, many of the children turned back or died along the way from hunger and thirst, leaving approximately twenty thousand children remaining by the time they arrived at the southern coast of France. When the sea did not dry up like Stephen promised,

---

[7]   Philip Schaff, *History of the Christian Church*, vol. 5, (Peabody, Massachusetts: Hendrickson, 2006), 240.

[8]   *The Catholic Encyclopedia*, Volume IV states: **All crusades were announced by preaching. After pronouncing a solemn vow, each warrior received a cross from the hands of the Pope or his legates, and was thenceforth considered a soldier of the Church. Crusaders were also granted indulgences and temporal privileges, such as exemption from civil jurisdiction, inviolability of persons or lands, etc.** See http://www.newadvent.org/cathen/04543c.htm

[9]   Henry Treece, *The Crusades* (New York: Barnes & Noble, 1962), 166.

[10]   George Gray *The Children's Crusade* (New York: William Morrow, 1972), 75.

[11]   Philip Schaff, *History of the Christian Church*, vol. 5, 268.

the large group wallowed in the misery of the heat and squalor of the port city of Marseilles for a few days until two shady merchantmen promised the naïve and gullible Stephen and his followers free passage to the Holy Land in seven ships. This was a terrible ruse. Both these men, Hugh the Iron and William the Pig, were slave traders. Two of the ships ran into a storm off the coast of Sardinia with almost a total loss of life. The five ships that survived the storm went on to Algeria where the children were sold into Muslim slavery! Most of these little children were never seen or heard from again.[12]

The Roman Catholic Institution, since that time to this day, has yet to take full responsibility or publicly apologize for this great abuse of power and corrupt influence that encouraged and allowed this terrible waste of lives to happen during the excessive violence of the Crusades that were spawned, organized, and supported directly by the Papacy. The secret and primary agenda of these eight Crusades was to convert Jews and Muslims to Roman Catholicism and to subjugate the Eastern Orthodox Church under the Pope. During the Fourth Crusade, many Greek Orthodox Christians were impaled, hacked to bits, and brutally murdered by papal decree. If both Jews and Eastern Orthodox refused conversion to the Pope at the tip of the Crusader's sword, extermination was their inescapable fate. The blind ambition for territorial and political power fueling the Popes of Rome to kill and sanction mass murder did not stop with the Crusades but increased in a far greater measure with the Inquisition.

The Inquisition is one of the great indelible blights on the Roman Catholic Institution. The simple purpose for the Inquisition was to repress and exterminate the existence of heresy in the Roman Catholic Church. The methods by which heretics were tried, tortured, and executed rivaled what would later be done by other insidious secret police organizations like the Nazi Gestapo, the KGB, and Mao Tse Tung's Red Guard police. Human rights, the dignity of the individual, and legal recourse for the accused were of course excluded from the arbitrary proceedings, persecutions, and barbaric tortures routinely practiced by the inquisitors and their sadistic henchmen. The Inquisition was a unique product of the Roman Catholic Church and the Papacy for the militant objection of the exposure and elimination of any person in Europe who held contrary beliefs to the doctrines and practices of the Roman Catholic Church and refused submission to the Pope. The history of the Roman Catholic Inquisition, in the solemn and truthful words of Church historian Philip Schaff, summarizes it at once to be one of the most blasphemous, shameful, and odious act done in the name of Jesus Christ in the last two thousand years.

> Its history presents what is probably the most revolting spectacle in the annals of civilized Europe. The representatives of the Church appear, sitting as arbiters over human destiny in this world, and in the name of religion applying torture to countless helpless victims, heretics, and reputed witches, and pronouncing upon them a sentence, which they knew, involved perpetual imprisonment or death in the flames.[13]

The Inquisition was an institution created by the Papacy and fleshed out in detail by the Popes of the thirteenth century. During the early part of the Inquisition, Bernard Gui (1261-1331) the Inquisitor of Toulouse, France, who passed sentence on 930 people, wrote an instruction manual entitled *Practica inquisitionis heretice pravitatis* (The Conduct of Inquiry Concerning Heretical Depravity) on how to effectively interrogate heretics, declared in this disturbing work that the office of the Inquisition has its

---

[12]   Steven Runciman *A History of the Crusades* Volume III: *The Kingdom of Acre and the Later Crusades* (Cambridge, 1951), pp.139-144.

[13]   Philip Schaff, *History of the Christian Church*, vol. 5, 515.

origin, authority, dignity, and commission from the Apostolic See (the Pope) itself.[14] The Inquisition received its full authority as an official Roman Catholic Institution and arm of the Papacy with full vested powers from the Synod of Tours in 1163, the Third Lateran Council of 1179, the Council of Verona in 1184, and the Fourth Lateran Council in 1215. The Council of Toulouse in 1229 formally recognized and established the office of the Inquisition to conduct the investigation and elimination of heresy. Papal decrees and bulls from Popes Gregory IX, Innocent IV, and Alexander IV expanded and enforced its terrible powers. By these means, Popes could have the property, wealth, and possessions of the accused seized by both the State and the Church for the material benefit of either. Millions upon millions of untold dollars were illegally absconded and were passed on to both the secular powers and the Vatican, whereby great wealth was accumulated over a long period of time during the seven hundred year span of the Inquisition.

This was another immoral device by which the Popes of Rome achieved wealth by ill-gotten gain. Indeed, the temptation to quickly acquire wealth greatly encouraged spying on others to accuse them of heresy before the tribunal for a fixed price. Many were falsely accused and ruined by these hired spies of the Inquisition, who both worked together in larceny to acquire material wealth through betrayal, false witness, and murder. Inquisitors became very rich by accepting bribes and fines from the wealthy that paid to avoid being tried and condemned before the Inquisition. The wealthy were prime targets for the Roman Catholic Institution who confiscated their property, land, and everything they had for generations. The Inquisition took over all of the victims' possessions upon accusation. There was very little if any chance of proving one's innocence, so this is one way the Roman Catholic Church grew very wealthy over the centuries the Inquisition lasted. Pope Nicholas III (1277-80) amassed for himself quite a fortune in this regard when serving in the capacity of Inquisitor-General. In 1231, Pope Gregory IX formally established the papal inquisition, and in April 1233 appointed the Dominican Order to be the primary inquisitors to carry out the brutal task of interrogation, torture, and execution of all heretics, with the latter being the responsibility of the secular power to carry out.[15]

The formal use of torture in the Inquisition was given full approval by the monstrous Pope Innocent IV in his papal Bull *Ad Extirpanda* issued on May 15, 1252, wherein Innocent stated that heretics should be "crushed" like venomous snakes. The papal bull also stipulated that the inquisitor and his officers were to seize the house and property of the heretic for payment in the discharge of their sacred duty! Anyone finding a heretic could seize him and take his property. The use of torture on those tried for heresy was further upheld and reinforced by Pope Alexander IV in 1255 and Pope Clement IV in 1265. The various methods and instruments of torture that were used for this horrible work of hell are disturbing and shocking. These tortures were principally designed to force a confession from the accused and to extract information leading to the arrest of other heretics. Common methods of torture included: (1) The *Stappado*. This device was used when a victim's hands were tied behind his back while his body was yanked to the ceiling by a pulley and ropes attached to the wrists or ankles Weights were attached to the limbs to increase the agonizing pain when the body was suddenly jerked up and down. (2) The use of the *Rack* was another tortuous procedure commonly employed by all inquisitors of the Roman Catholic Church. The victim was placed nude or semi nude horizontally on the ladder or rack. Ropes were tightly fastened to his arms and legs. Once secured, the victim's arms and legs were pulled in opposite direction until his bones and ligaments were torn, broken, and

---

[14] Benarddus Guidonis, *Manuel de l'inquisiteur G. Mollat* (Paris: Champion, 1926-27), 176. During Gui's administration forty-two persons were burned at the stake, sixty-nine bodies were exhumed and burned (as a post-mortem punishment for heresy against Rome), and three hundred seven were imprisoned in the grim and hopeless condition of the dungeons.

[15] Henry Charles Lea, *A History of the Inquisition of the Middle Ages*, vol. 1, (Elibron Classics, 2005), 328-329.

stretched out of their joints.[16] (3) There was the dreaded water torture (*tortura de cordeles*) used primarily in the Spanish Inquisition. The following account is a horrific description of how this torture method was used:

> The prisoner was fastened almost naked on a sort of trestle with sharp-edged rungs and kept in position with an iron band, his head lower than his feet, and his limbs bound to the side-pieces with agonizing tightness. The mouth was then forced open and a strip of linen inserted into the gullet. Through this, water was poured from a jar (*jarra*), obstructing the throat and nostrils and producing a state of semi suffocation. This process was repeated time after time, as many as eight *jarras* sometimes being applied. Meanwhile, the cords round the sufferer's limbs were continually tightened until it seemed as though every vein in his body was at bursting-point.[17]

The result left the poor helpless victim badly distended and hemorrhaging from within. Tortures continued all the way to the execution stake where the accused was to be burned. The *Heretic's fork* was a torture device used on the victim to silence him or her on the way to the burning stake, so they could not reveal what had occurred in the torture chamber or defend themselves in any way. The top prong of the instrument was pushed under the chin, and the bottom into the upper sternum, the strap fixing the device to the neck. This effectively immobilized the head at a total extension of the neck, and caused great pain preventing the accused from speaking. The inquisitors used other cruel instruments of torture such as the Judas Chair, the Iron Maiden, thumbscrews, and Spanish Boots. Though there was a rule on the books of some that torture could only be used during one session of interrogation, the inquisitors of Rome conveniently and casuistically were able to get around this to their sadistic satisfaction. In his published manual of torture procedures, *Directorum Inquisitorum,* Nicholas Eymeric (1320-1399), an inquisitor adept at torture, established a principle of continued torture circumventing the prohibition of repetition by allowing its continuation at a later time. The following guidelines for the treatment and prosecution of heretics stipulated and blessed by the Pope himself are quoted below from this *Directorium Inquisitorum,* published in Rome, October 1584, by the command of the Cardinals' Inquisitor General; dedicated to Pope Gregory XIII; translation by J.P. Callender, *Illustrations of Popery,* New York, 1838. Numbers have been added for index referencing.

1. "All believers in Christ, by the necessity of salvation, are subject to the Roman Pontiff, who carries the two swords, and judges all, but he is judged by no man. We declare, say, define, and pronounce, that subjection to the Roman Pontiff is necessary to salvation" (pp. 34,35).
2. "He is a heretic who does not believe what the Roman Hierarchy teaches. A heretic merits the pains of fire. By the Gospel, the canons, civil law, and custom, heretics must be burned" (pp. 148,169).
3. "He is a heretic who deviates from any article of faith" (p. 143).
4. "Confessors must not absolve those who keep books which are condemned. He who writes books of heresy shall be adjudged a heretic. He who retains prohibited books shall be deemed a favourer of heretics" (pp. 92,93).
5. "They who bury persons knowing them to be excommunicated, or their receivers, defenders, or favourers, shall not be absolved unless they dig up the corpse; and the place shall be deprived of the usual immunities of sepulture" (p. 104).

---

[16] Miroslav Hroch and Anna Skybova, *Ecclesia Militans: The Inquisition* (Leipzig: Dorset Press, 1988), 146.
[17] Cecil Roth, *The Spanish Inquisition* (New York: Norton, 1964), 95.

6. "A heretic may be accused and condemned after death" (p. 146).
7. "The property of heretics after their death shall be seized" (p. 151).
8. "For the suspicion alone of heresy, purgation is demanded" (p. 156).
9. "Magistrates who refuse to take the oath for defence of the faith shall be suspected of heresy. It must be required of temporal lords to expel heretics. The church may demand the aid of the secular power against both things and persons" (p. 159,176).
10. "Wars may be commenced by the authority of the church. Indulgences for the remission of all sin belong to those who are signed with the cross for the persecution of heretics" (p. 160).
11. "The Pope can enact new articles of faith. The definitions of Popes and Councils are to be received as infallible" (p. 168).
12. "Every individual may kill a heretic' (p. 175).
13. "All persons may attack any rebels to the church, and despoil them of their wealth; and slay them, and bum their houses and cities" (pp. 176,177).
14. "Persons who betray heretics shall be rewarded. But Priests who give the sacrament or burial to heretics shall be excommunicated" (p. 178).
15. "They who favour their relatives who are heretics shall not receive for that cause any milder punishment" (p. 180). "The penalty of perpetual incarceration may be mitigated by the Inquisitors" (p. 181).
16. "Those who are subject to a master or governor, or prince, who has become a heretic, are released from their fidelity. A wife may separate herself from her excommunicated or heretical husband. Children of heretics are discharged from parental authority" (p. 182).
17. "Heretics may be forced to profess the Roman faith" (p. 193),
18. "The crime of heresy is not extinguished by death" (p. 196).
19. "The testimony of a heretic is admitted on behalf of a Papist, but not against him" (p.198).
20. "A whole city must be burnt on account of the heretics who live in it. Whoever pleases may seize and kill any heretics" (p. 199).
21. "Witnesses in a cause of heresy may be forced to bear testimony, and they sin mortally if they abscond" (p. 204).
22. "A heretic, as he sins in all places, may everywhere be judged" (p. 207).
23. "A person contracting marriage with a heretic shall be punished, because it is favouring a heretic" (p. 210).
24. "Heretics must be sought after, and be corrected or exterminated. Heretics enjoy no privileges in law or equity" (p. 212).
25. "The goods of heretics are to be considered as confiscated from the perpetration of the crime. All alienations of property by heretics before their condemnation are invalid. Inquisitors are not bound to restore the price of the property which is seized in the hands of those who purchased from heretics" (p. 213).
26. "Prelates or Inquisitors may torture witnesses to obtain the truth" (p. 218).
27. "The Pope has power over infidels. The church may make war with infidels" (p. 352).
28. "Monks and Priests who contract matrimony shall be suspected of heresy" (p. 367).
29. "Those who are strongly suspected are to be reputed as heretics" (p. 376). "He who does not inform against heretics shall be deemed as suspected" (p. 383).

30. "He who marries a person unbaptized, and deserts her to marry a baptized woman, is not guilty of bigamy" (p. 383).
31. "Inquisitors are not bound to give a reason to Prelates concerning things appertaining to their office" (p. 542).
32. "An Inquisitor and his associate may mutually absolve each other from excommunication" (p. 553).
33. "An Inquisitor may force the governors of cities to swear that they will defend the church against heretics" (p. 560).
34. "An Inquisitor may proceed against temporal lords who deny the assistance required by him, or who do not obey him as they ought" (p. 562).
35. "Inquisitors, to seize heretics or their favourers, may demand the aid of the civil authority" (p. 585).
36. "Inquisitors may have a prison for the guilty, and for those who are accused to them, there to be detained or punished" (p. 585).
37. "Prelates and Inquisitors may put any persons to the question by torture" (P. 591).
38. "It is laudable to torture those of every class who are guilty of heresy. Common fame and one witness are sufficient to justify the torture. Common fame alone, or one witness alone, authorizes the torture" (pp. 594-599).
39. "Inquisitors may coerce witnesses to swear that they will testify to the truth, and should frequently examine them" (p. 600).
40. "Inquisitors may lawfully admit perjured persons to testify and act in cases concerning the faith" (p. 605).
41. "Inquisitors may lawfully receive infamous persons, and criminals, or servants against their masters, both to act and give evidence in causes respecting the faith" (p. 606).
42. "Inquisitors may allow heretics to witness against heretics, but not for them" (p. 612).
43. "Inquisitors may torture witnesses to obtain the truth; and punish them if they have given false evidence" (p. 622).
44. "Inquisitors may cite and coerce the attendance of witnesses, and also persons charged with heretical pravity in different dioceses" (p. 626).
45. "Inquisitors must not publish the names of informers, witnesses, and accusers" (p. 627).
46. "Prelates and Inquisitors are bound to force those who are suspected to abjure the heresy imputed to them" (p. 637).
47. "Penitent heretics may be condemned to perpetual imprisonment" (p. 641).
48. "Inquisitors may provide for their own expenditures, and the salaries of their officers, from the property of heretics" (p. 652).
49. "Prelates or Inquisitors may confiscate the property of all impenitent heretics, or of persons relapsed" (p. 662).
50. "Prelates and Inquisitors must deprive heretics, and all who believe, receive, defend, and favour them, and their sons to the second generation of every ecclesiastical benefice and public office" (p. 669).
51. "All persons, who are bound by any debt of homage or fidelity, or any other covenant, or contract, however strongly made, to any person who has manifestly fallen into heresy, are not held to fulfill it, but are totally absolved from it" (p. 675).
52. "Inquisitors enjoy the benefits of a plenary indulgence at all times in life, and in death" (p. 679).

Much debate has been exercised over how many deaths were caused by the evil and barbarous Roman Catholic Inquisition. Naturally, the proponents of Popery and Roman Catholicism claim that the mortality figures are sparse and negligible. In July 2004, the Vatican pitifully attempted to downgrade the Inquisition toll. They prefaced such anemic historical revisionism with an apology for the marginal excesses of a *few* Roman Catholic extremists during that time saying without proof "that torture and burning at the stake was not as widespread as commonly believed."[18] Furthermore, to self-excuse the Papacy, knowing full well the direct involvement of it in the Inquisition, Pope John Paul II presumptuously apologized in March of 2000 for such crimes the Roman Catholic Inquisition perpetrated against humanity by those misguided Roman Catholics who took their inquisitorial duties too far. But such an apology is invalid and mendacious when it was the Papacy itself that created the Holy Office of the Inquisition with the power to arrest, torture, and execute those accused of heresy against the Roman Catholic religious system. The apology should be made for what the Popes criminally did to create and continue the Inquisition for seven centuries! To do that, of course, would undermine the Pope's "infallible" authority. Pope Benedict XVI was the former head of The Congregation of the Doctrine of the Faith, which was formerly known as the Office of the Inquisition—the same office that was responsible for the torture and death of millions of Bible believers and others during the Inquisition! The Pope's 'apology' is further historically invalid when considering the fact that the victims are now dead and cannot respond; and those officials of the Roman Catholic Church responsible for such murders and mistreatment of their fellow man at that time, are no longer among the living to be held responsible for the crimes against humanity they wantonly committed. The apology needs to come directly from them against those very victims they harmed for it to be validly effective. The established facts of the Papal Inquisition clearly indicate the exact opposite: that torture and a high mortality rate from the Inquisition were high, frequent, and a normative practice and administrative standard set by the policies of Rome and the Popes of that day! They were not infrequent, as the Vatican would have us to believe. But to truly arrive at the most accurate mortality count one must go back to the very participants of this dastardly creation of Papal Rome to arrive at a more accurate mortal calculation.

Ludovicus de Paramo wrote the first comprehensive history of the Inquisition in the sixteenth century (formally entitled: *De Origine et progressu office Sanctae Inquisitionis*). His blunt record was so offensive that his book was placed on Rome's Index of Prohibited books, even though it had been printed with the approval of Roman Catholic Church theologians and by royal license. From sifting through trial documents of that time, Paramo estimated that the Inquisition killed some 10,000 souls up to his time. Roman Catholic Canon official, Juan Antonio Llorente, a secretary of the Inquisition in Madrid, Spain from 1790-1792, had personal access to the legal documents of the trial proceedings and calculated from his findings that in Spain alone, out of the more than three million people who were tried and condemned by the Inquisition, three hundred thousand were condemned and burned at the stake.[19] Former Roman Catholic priest Walter Montano deduces in his book, *Behind the Purple Curtain*, that fifty million people died for the Christian faith under the Papal Inquisition during Rome's seven hundred year reign of terror.[20] Historical researcher David A. Plaisted

18   Assoiciated Press Release from the Vatican dated June 15, 2004. See http://www.nbcnews.com/id/5218373/ns/world_news/t/vatican-downgrades-inquisition-toll/#.U2kB1i9RGxg

19   R.W. Thompson, *The Papacy and Civil Power* (New York: Harper and Brothers, 1876), 82.

20   Walter Montano, *The Purple Curtain* (Los Angeles: Cowman Publications, 1950). Over a hundred years earlier John Dowling notes: "No computation can reach the numbers who have been put to death, in different ways, on account of their maintaining the profession of the Gospel, and opposing the corruptions of the Church of Rome. A MILLION of poor Waldenses perished in France; NINE HUNDRED THOUSAND orthodox Christians were slain in less than thirty years after the inquisition of the order of the Jesuits. The Duke of Alva boasted of having put to

wrote a detailed and compelling sixty-four page study which examines the number of fatalities at the hands of the Catholic Church, citing figures from 68 million to as high as 150 million, which occurred during the long and unprecedented rule of the papacy in history.

Whatever the exact figure, he basically concludes the total number was, nevertheless, enormous. At the end of this disturbing study, Plaisted wisely admonishes us: "We need to be careful not to show hostility to Roman Catholics today because of the sins of the past. I am sure that many of us know many wonderful and loving Roman Catholic priests and church members. But it is important to know the facts of history, or else we may repeat them" (see "Estimates of the Number Killed by the Papacy in the Middle Ages and Later" at http://articbeacon.com/books/PlaistedEstimates_Number_Killed_bythe_papacy-2006.pdf). To the Roman Catholic Inquisition, failure to submit to the Pope of Rome or any of the teachings of the Church was considered heretical and needed to be stamped out and suppressed. The Inquisition especially targeted Bible-believing Christians of that time for torture and execution, who refused to trust in Mother Church, but instead put their trust in Christ alone for salvation.

Many of those martyred during this time were Bible-believing Christians. The Waldensians, Albigensians, (who have been erroneously portrayed to be from the heretical sect of the Cathari), Huguenots, and the Anabaptists were slaughtered by the hundreds of thousands and their cities were devastated and overrun in blood by the cruel machinery of the Inquisition. The method, manner, and terror of the Inquisition were consistently carried out in Europe—Spain, Italy, Holland, France, Germany, and in parts of England. Anyone, man, woman, and child, over the age of twelve, could be arrested and tried by the 'Holy' Office of the Inquisition. The trials were not conducted in a fair or democratic manner. Anyone could be arrested on mere suspicion alone. The guilt of the accused was assumed without proof from the outset of the trial. The victim was not allowed to face and answer his accusers or the witnesses.

The judges were the clergy of the Roman Catholic system operating with absolute power in cooperation with the secular arm of the State. The clergy were granted complete immunity from the Pope and from any civil prosecution or legal punishment thereby virtually giving the ecclesiastical tribunal unlimited power to arrest and torture whomever they suspected of heresy.[21] Here the hypocrisy of the Vatican is laid bare. The modern day Papacy likes to fancy itself the champion of morality, human rights, and defender of human dignity around the world. But the fact their Popes have collectively followed, supported, and endorsed the insidious evil, and immoral practices of the Inquisition for over six centuries stands to be one of the greatest violations of human rights and dignity in all history! Let the historical record unimpeachably speak for itself on this matter:

> The record of the Inquisition would be embarrassing for any organization; for the Catholic
> Church, it is devastating. Today, it prides itself, and with much justification, on being the

---

death in the Netherlands, THIRTY-SIX THOUSAND by the hand of the common executioner during the space of a few years. The Inquisition destroyed, by various tortures, ONE HUNDRED AND FIFTY THOUSAND within thirty years. These are few specimens, and but a few, of those which history has recorded; but the total amount will never be known till the earth shall disclose her blood, and no more cover her slain" (*Scott's Church History* quoted in John Dowling's *The History of Romanism*, page 542 (Book VIII). Other historians estimate the number of victims that were killed by the Inquisition to vary from five to fifteen million people (From Clyde I. Manschreck, *A History of Christianity in the World* (New York: Prentice Hall, 1964).

[21] For a detailed presentation of the trial procedures of the Inquisition see Henry Lea, *A History of The Inquisition*, vol. I, pages 399-429.

defender of natural law and the rights of man. The papacy in particular likes to see itself as the champion of morality. *What history shows is that, for more than six centuries without a break, the papacy was the sworn enemy of elementary justice. Of eighty Popes in a line from the thirteenth century on, not one of them disapproved of the theology and apparatus of Inquisition. On the contrary, one after another added his own cruel touches to the workings of this deadly machine.*[22]

Defenders of the Roman Catholic system pathetically attempt to explain away the overt atrocities of the Inquisition that were created, sustained, and sanctioned by the Papacy, while, at the same time, greatly reduce the severity and magnitude of it in order to exculpate Rome from direct guilt and universal condemnation it so rightly deserves. The ongoing desperate attempts of Rome's apologists to defend the Inquisition, even in theory apart from its gruesome historical reality, only serves to show the depths of their myopia and mindless devotion to the Papacy. Anyone who attempts, in any way, to excuse or justify the pernicious work of the Inquisition by shifting blame to a few overzealous officials of Mother Church, shows tacit support and misplaced sympathy for what was clearly a satanic attack against the Gospel and Spirit of our Lord Jesus Christ, and an utter unwillingness to admit the obvious evil of the Papacy. What is even more inexcusable is when defenders of Roman Catholicism, like Patrick Madrid, attempt to talk out of both sides of their mouths (which Roman Catholic apologists constantly do) by partially condemning, in an obvious token fashion, "some" sins of Roman Catholics during the Inquisition, while at the same time falsely claiming that such a diabolical institution was "not an invention of the Catholic Church," but God Himself.[23] To justify the Inquisition in this way makes Madrid and all defenders of the Roman Catholic Inquisition "witnesses against themselves" as guilty participants of it with their spiritual forefathers and therefore under God's righteous condemnation for the antichristian and inhuman atrocities it spawned and spread throughout Europe (see Matthew 23: 31-36).

Madrid even goes so far to justify such a Roman Catholic atrocity of the Popes by misapplying from Scripture the example of Jesus driving the moneychangers out of the Temple (Mark 11:15-17). When the Lord did this, did He ever resort to the various barbaric tortures, executions by burning at the stake, or the slow death of imprisonment in the unsanitary dungeons that characterized the ghastly Inquisition through and through? Never! The two events are different as night and day, heaven and hell, and God from Satan! Even when Jesus cleansed the Temple no harm was done, because He himself was harmless in all that He said and did; for it is written about Jesus in Hebrews 7:26 that He was "holy, *harmless*, undefiled, separate from sinners." Madrid quotes the command to stone certain offenders to death in Deuteronomy 17:2-7 to ridiculously support the death sentences carried out by the Inquisition when clearly such a Mosaic Law applied only to Israel under the Old Covenant, which is no longer valid for the Church Age now under the grace and mercy of the New Covenant.[24] In Matthew 13: 27-30, 37-40 Jesus forbids His professed followers (Christians) from destroying the tares by violent removal (counterfeit Christians and all the wicked within the Church and the world). The complete removal of the wicked within the Church, and the world at large, awaits until the end of the age, when Christ personally returns to Earth with His angels to do this with perfect exactitude, something imperfect man with his limited and flawed knowledge lacks in the present age.

---

[22]   Peter De Rosa, *The Vicars of Christ*, 175-176.

[23]   Patrick Madrid, *Where Is That In the Bible?* 160.

[24]   Ibid., 164.

To attempt such a violent effort in the present Church Age, is in clear violation of the Lord Jesus' prohibition of Matthew 13:29 and places Rome under His righteous condemnation for the Inquisition alone! Would to God had Papal Rome accurately followed this Scripture (and all Scripture, for that matter) such needless bloodshed of the Inquisition could have been easily avoided! What is even more pathetic is the invalid argument that Catholic apologists customarily resort to when saying that the Roman Catholic 'Church' was not technically guilty for the deaths of the Inquisition because the guilty were handed over to the secular arm of the State to be executed. But such a sham defense does not hold up when it was the Inquisition who first passed the death sentence on the accused and then handed them over to the State to be executed, once officials of the Roman Catholic Church passed sentence. To resort to such hypocritical, legalistic casuistry in the vain attempt to escape moral culpability for killing the innocent is reminiscent of the same tactic the Sanhedrin perfidiously used when they falsely condemned Jesus to death and then handed Him over to the secular power of Rome to be crucified in the vain attempt to evade guilt. In both instances, God found each party guilty for the murder of the innocent. Jesus revealed this to the Roman Prefect, Pontius Pilate, in John 19:11 about the Sanhedrin and prophetically to John the Apostle about Papal Rome in Revelation 17:6 for her bloody massacre of the martyrs of Jesus Christ, of whom many were killed during the Inquisition!

But surely Rome and her Popes today do not follow or endorse the savage principles and belligerencies of the Inquisition that belonged to the benighted period of the Middle Ages. In the modern world after Vatican II, where religious toleration and ecumenical brotherhood were loudly extolled by the Papacy, Rome's predilection for reverting back to the violence and destruction of the horrendous Inquisition nonetheless remains! This was evident at the thirty-first National Conference of the bishops of Brazil. Disturbed and angry over the phenomenal growth of evangelical 'sects' in Brazil, the leaders of the Roman Catholic Church threatened to launch a 'holy war' against Protestants unless they stop leading people away from the Roman Catholic Institution. A delegate at this conference, Bishop Sinesion, called evangelical Christians "a serious threat" to the Vatican's power and influence over the people in Brazil. He further made the following threat against these born-again Bible believers: *"We will declare a holy war; don't doubt it. The Catholic Church has a ponderous structure, but when we move, we'll smash anyone beneath us"* (See Arthur Noble, "Let the True Church of the Papacy Stand Up: Has Rome changed Today or Remained "Semper Eadem?" at http://www.theonemediator.com/Catholicism_Current_Online_Videos.htm) The 'Holy' Office of the Inquisition was never abolished by the Papacy but was changed to the name of the Sacred Congregation for the Doctrine of the Faith in 1965, with the name "Sacred" dropped off in 1983. The Code of Canon Law for the Roman Catholic Church still enacts the power of force and punishment in the spirit of the Inquisition on those deemed errant or who commit perceived offences against the Roman Catholic Church. **Canon 1311** states: "The Church has an innate *right to coerce with penal sanctions Christ's faithful who commit offenses*"[25]

Roman Catholic scholars admit that even today the Congregation for the Doctrine of Faith continues to operate its proceedings according to the same medieval principles of the Inquisition. Roman Catholic historian and theologian Hans Kung explains:

> The proceedings against someone who is suspected or accused are secret. No one knows who the informants are. There is no cross-examination of witnesses, nor are there any experts. The proceedings are kept closed, so that any knowledge of the preliminaries is prevented. Accusers and judges are identical. Any appeal to an independent court is ruled

---

[25]   *Code of Canon Law, Latin English Edition* (Washington, D.C.: Canon Law Society, 1999).

out or is useless, for the aim of the proceedings is not to discover the truth but to bring about unconditional submission to Roman doctrine, which is always identical with truth. In short, the goal is obedience to the church, in accordance with the formula which is still used today: *Humiliter se subiecit,* "He has humbly submitted." There is no question that such an Inquisition mocks both the gospel and the generally accepted sense of justice today, which has found expression in particular in the declarations on human rights.[26]

Because the Popes are no longer wielding political power over earthly monarchs and rulers today, as they previously did in the Medieval period, does not negate the ongoing belief of the Vatican that the Pope is still the supreme arbiter of political and temporal power; for Roman Catholic Law baldly proclaims in canons **1404-1405**:

> The First See is judged by no one; in the cases mentioned in can. 1401, the Roman Pontiff alone has the right to judge: (1) Heads of State; (2) Cardinals; (3) Legates of the Apostolic See and, in penal cases, Bishops; (4) other cases which he has reserved to himself.[27]

While it is true that some Protestant leaders shamefully resorted to the anti-Christian practice of burning declared heretics at the stake (for example when John Calvin had Michael Servetus executed in Geneva after he was already condemned by the Spanish Inquisition *in absentia*), there was, however, no sustained and systematic institution established to universally carry out such evil atrocities over the succeeding centuries. *The Roman Catholic Church infamously stands alone here, and no amount of finger pointing in the other direction or revisionist history cleverly utilized by her desperate apologists can erase this ugly, indelible fact.*

Did the Lord Jesus ever endow the New Testament Church a Temporal Power of a political and earthly nature whereby the leaders of this Church are to impose violence, force, and bloodshed to advance and defend the faith in the same manner which the Papacy has done for over one thousand years via the Crusades and the Inquisition? Comparing the Crusades and the Inquisition to the example set by Jesus Christ and His disciples is as different as night and day. Once again, the Word of God provides the answer. When one examines the mission given to the Church, found in the New Testament by the Lord Jesus Christ, it is indisputably obvious that the Vatican is not following the teachings of Christ, nor does it have the Holy Spirit indwelling and guiding it! This is made obvious by the life of Jesus and the Early Church in the New Testament. The ministry of Jesus was one of service, gentleness and meek demonstration of divine power in the face of inveterate opposition and hatred. The Messiah's ministry would not be coercive, violent, or destructive (Isaiah 42: 1-4; Matthew 12: 18-21). Those who opposed Christ were lovingly confronted, chided, and exhorted by Him to repent and believe upon Him for salvation (Matthew 23; Luke 13:1-5; John 5-7, et al.)

When beaten, whipped, and crucified He lovingly prayed that God would forgive His enemies and murderers (Luke 23:34). He eschewed violence against His enemies at every turn (Matthew 5: 43-48) and sharply remonstrated His disciples, James and John, who wanted to start the first "Inquisition" when they sought to have fire come down from heaven to destroy the Samaritans who opposed Jesus' ministry. Christ countered this by declaring His stated mission: ***"For the Son of Man did not come to destroy men's lives but to save them"*** (See Luke 9:51-56). Should not the Roman Catholic Papacy have followed His example? Here are godly virtues that were the diametric opposite of the militant and megalomaniacal Popes claiming to be

---

26   Hans Kung, *The Catholic Church: A Short History* (New York: Modern Library, 2003), 97.
27   *Code of Canon Law,* 250.

Christ's unique Vicars on Earth when carrying out the murderous policies of the Crusades and Inquisition against perceived heretics and enemies of 'Mother Church.' If we assume, for the sake of argument, that Peter was the first Pope of the Roman Catholic system, then he would have the initial right to first make use of the sword of temporal power when the opportunity presented itself. Since Christ supposedly gave this power exclusively to the Apostle, such a power would be approved when the cause of Christ needed to be defended when threatened by those very enemies who would seek to destroy it. And this is the exact scenario we find when Jesus was in agony in the garden of Gethsemane with his life and just cause being threatened by those who came to unjustly apprehend Him in the stealth of night.

When the Temple guard came to arrest Jesus, the Apostle Peter unsheathed his sword to defend the rights of Christ and His Church, (represented by Peter and the other ten Apostles), and cut off the right ear of Malchus, servant of the High Priest. Instead of commending Peter for the use of the sword, Christ forcefully reprimanded Peter to ***"put your sword in its place, for all who take the sword will perish by the sword"*** (John 18:10-11; Matthew 26:52). Jesus did not need the protection of the temporal sword of Peter, for the Lord could have easily requested twelve legions (72,000) of angels from the heavenly Father to defend and destroy the enemies of Christ (Matthew 26:53). Here we have a clear rebuke by Christ of any use of force or violence by the temporal sword of Peter, the alleged first Pope, who holds the temporal power of the sword, against the enemies of God. Furthermore, such a prohibition of violence is also given in other passages of the New Testament to Christians when dealing with heretics and those who oppose the Gospel.

An obstinate heretic is to be sharply rebuked by the counsel of God's Word (2 Timothy 3:16-17; Titus 3:10) twice and is then to be rejected by the Church, not hunted down, tortured, or put to death in the manner apostate Rome did for centuries. Christians are not to resort to the physical weapons of war and torture like those used in the Crusades and Inquisition when combating the unbeliever, heresy, and error, but are to use the spiritual sword of God's Word to refute and bring every contrary thought, idea, and belief captive to the obedience of the Gospel of Jesus Christ (2 Corinthians 10:4-5). No command is given in Scripture for the New Testament Church to take up arms and force conversion by the sword or to use torture on the heretic. ***"For the wrath of man does not produce the righteousness of God"*** (James 1:20).

The Apostle Peter instructs the believer in Christ to defend the faith with gentleness and respect in 1 Peter 3:15: ***"But sanctify the Lord God in your hearts, and always be ready to give a defense to everyone who asks you a reason for the hope that is in you with gentleness and respect."*** The bellicose policies of the Roman Catholic Institution carried out in the barbaric and bloody Crusades and Inquisition for the "defense" of the Papacy against the infidel and heretic are decidedly unbiblical, and in stark contrast to the Spirit of Christ. A behavior of this bloody nature shows, at once, that Rome cannot be the true Church of Jesus Christ because she sanctioned murder—and the murderer of his fellow man neither knows God, nor has His Spirit living within him (See 1 John 2:11; 3:15; 4: 20-21).

What is the real motive behind the papal doctrine of "Temporal Power"—was it evangelical? Was it humanitarian? Was it promoting peace? On all three counts the answer is *absolutely not*. The only motives for this Pope exalting, Christ dishonoring doctrine are greed for wealth and lust for political power and nothing more. This is readily seen by tracing the authoritative documents on which the temporal power of the Pope is based. As with many of the other forged documents papal Rome uses to deceitfully authenticate its claims, the doctrine of the temporal power of the Pope is likewise based on forged historical documents of the eighth century called *The Donation of Constantine* and *The Donation of Pepin*. During that pivotal period of time, the Holy See was losing vast tracts of land to the invading Muslim hordes in Western Europe,

North Africa, and the Middle East. Italy was being invaded and ransacked by the Germanic Lombards from the north. Rome was soon to be conquered and pillaged by these rapacious invaders.

The papal empire was on the verge of total collapse. Realizing the dire straits and desperate situation the Church of Rome was in, Pope Stephen II (752-757 A.D.) devised a clever plan to induce King Pepin of the Franks (714-768 A.D.) to defend Rome and save the Holy See. Under the strategic guidance of the Pope, papal prelates composed a letter written in gold on expensive parchment. Stephen II claimed that the message was so important that Saint Peter himself hand delivered it from heaven to him. The forged letter besought the military aid of King Pepin to save Rome. An elaborate papal delegation escorting the Pope with impressive regal pomp and circumstance came to King Pepin with letter in hand. The king was taken in by the *deception* of Pope Stephen II, and overwhelmed that Saint Peter personally knew him to make such an important request. Pepin immediately gathered his armies together to defend Rome.[28] The Lombards were defeated and Pepin gave Rome and the surrounding area to the Pope.

After Pepin died, Pope Adrian I (772-795 A.D.), not content with this limited land grant, in his thirst for more power and wealth, appealed to another forged document that claimed Pepin had given the papacy all of Italy; Pepin's son and regal successor, Charlemagne (742-814 A.D.), was hoodwinked by it. This falsified document was called *The Donation of Pepin*, which laid the groundwork for the papal claim of temporal power over all nations. Later, under the cunning of Pope Leo III (795-816 A.D.), another spurious document was deceptively used for the same purpose. It was called *The Donation of Constantine,* which was actually composed earlier than *The Donation of Pepin. The Donation of Constantine* alleged by its name, that the Emperor Constantine had made the Popes his successors to the Roman Empire. Gradually, the whole of Europe's monarchies bought this grandiose lie and submitted to the Pope in Rome as God's sovereign on Earth.[29]

This document was later to be proven an absolute fraud, thanks to the papal aide, Lorenzo Valla, who scrutinized the document line by line and proved it was indeed a great fraud in his treatise *De falso credita et ementita Constantini donatione* published in 1440 at great risk to his own life.[30] Despite Valla's findings, Rome stubbornly continued insisting on the historical validity of the document for centuries to come.

The Donation of Constantine was part of a larger collection of spurious documents called *The Isidorian Decretals,* an extensive collection of approximately 100 forged papal letters, most of which were purportedly written by the Roman bishops of the first three centuries of the Church. These false documents would supposedly give historical justification for the papacy's powers that would essentially subject all religious authorities to the final (and absolute) authority of the Pope, and these documents helped form the emergence of the Holy Roman Empire—which would crumble in pieces centuries later. Since the political claims of the Papacy for universal power rests on these documents, the fact they are false means by logical extension that the Pope's claim for temporal power is illegitimate and rests on pure fiction instead of scriptural support and historic fact! William Webster notes the undermining consequence of this:

> In the middle of the ninth century, a radical change began in the Western Church, which
> dramatically altered the Constitution of the Church, and laid the groundwork for the full
> development of the papacy. The papacy could never have emerged without a fundamental

---

[28] Edward Gibbon, *The History of the Decline and Fall of the Roman Empire* Volume III, (London: Penguin, 1994), 108-109.

[29] See William Berry, *Papal Monarchy* (Kessinger Publishing, 2003).

[30] Peter DeRosa, *Vicars of Christ*, 40-42.

restructuring of the Constitution of the Church and of men's perceptions of the history of that Constitution. As long as the true facts of Church history were well known, it would serve as a buffer against any unlawful ambitions. However, in the 9th century, a literary forgery occurred which completely revolutionized the ancient government of the Church in the West. This forgery is known as the "Pseudo-Isidorian Decretals," written around 845 A.D. The "Decretals" are a complete fabrication of Church history. They set forth precedents for the exercise of sovereign authority of the Popes over the universal Church prior to the fourth century and make it appear that the Popes had always exercised sovereign dominion and had ultimate authority even over Church Councils.... In addition to the "Pseudo Isidorian Decretals" there were other forgeries which were successfully used for the promotion of the doctrine of papal primacy.

One famous instance is that of Thomas Aquinas. In 1264 A.D. Thomas authored a work entitled 'Against the Errors of the Greeks'. This work deals with the issues of theological debate between the Greek and Roman Churches in that day on such subjects as the Trinity, the Procession of the Holy Spirit, Purgatory and the Papacy. In his defense of the papacy Thomas bases practically his entire argument on forged quotations of Church fathers.... These spurious quotations had enormous influence on many Western theologians in succeeding centuries. The authority claims of Roman Catholicism ultimately devolve upon the institution of the papacy. The papacy is the center and source from which all authority flows for Roman Catholicism. Rome has long claimed that this institution was established by Christ and has been in force in the Church from the very beginning. But the historical record gives a very different picture. This institution was promoted primarily through the falsification of historical fact through the extensive use of forgeries as Thomas Aquinas' apologetic for the papacy demonstrates. Forgery is its foundation."[31]

If the real truth were told, the Vatican to this day still hopes in the future to regain the temporal power she once had over the world. The Pope would ideally like to be the central leader of religious and secular power through the working of Concordats with various nations mixed with political maneuvering done in undercover fashion by manipulating the nations and world religions to go Rome's way.[32] To woo the Catholic vote, leaders of nations have always considered it politically expedient to court the Vatican's favor in order to gain support and approval from her that could ensure possible votes from the Roman Catholic population of these nations the leaders represent.

By courting papal favor in some measure, this would potentially assure large Catholic votes that could keep these world leaders in power. Therefore, to establish and maintain diplomatic relations with the Vatican is always politically expedient. Since Roman Catholicism claims over one billion members, the political leaders of the world, hungry to stay in power, will do whatever it takes within reasonable limits to have the approval of the Vatican. This of course is a prophetic fulfillment of Revelation 17:2. The Vatican is "the

---

[31]   William Webster, "Forgeries and the Papacy: The Historical Use of Forgeries in Promotion of the Doctrine of the Papacy" at http://www.christiantruth.com/articles/forgeries.html.

[32]   A *concordat* is an agreement between the Pope and a government or sovereign on religious matters. This often included both recognition and privileges for the Catholic Church in a particular country.

whore that sits upon many waters (nations)" and still has a considerable political influence over the nations—though today it is subtler in administration. The visit of former Soviet Union leader, Michael Gorbachev in December of 1990 with Pope John Paul II is amazing proof of this. The Soviet leader praised John Paul II *as "the highest religious authority in the world."* This statement is all the more amazing coming from a former leader of an atheistic country!

The forged documents of Constantine and Pepin manifestly prove the claims of the papacy are based on **sheer lies**, rather than the solid historical realities that are clearly present and endorsed with God's biblical approval for a normative practice of the New Testament Church. Up to this point, we have examined the man-made institution of the Papacy in the revealing light of Holy Scripture and unbiased history and found it to be utterly contrary and antithetical to the teachings of Christ and the Apostles. We have also adequately demonstrated that the papal claim of temporal power rests on fabricated historical documents upon which the Popes committed the most savage atrocities against mankind and the true Church of Jesus Christ. In the future an apostate Pope will endeavor to use temporal power again for universal rule by enticing the world to follow and worship the coming Anti-Christ whom he will aide in his world wide rule. It is the writer's studied opinion that this future Pope will act as the False Prophet of Revelation 13:11-13 aping the real Christ. If the roots of the papacy are not found explicitly in the Scriptures, or truly verified by genuine historical documentation, and recognized by the majority of the Early Church Fathers, then from whence did such a tyrannical concept come from? Spiritually, all that is false, deceitful, and counterfeits the true Christ comes from the devil—the father of all lies (John 8:44).

CHAPTER 6

THE PAGAN ORIGIN OF THE PAPACY

The official title for the head of the Roman Catholic Church has its direct origins from pagan Rome. The main ecclesiastical title for the Pope is "Supreme Pontiff"—in Latin it is *Pontifex Maximus*.[1] History bears out that this religious title did not begin with Christianity or the Roman Catholic Church, but was an religious title first used by the Roman emperor Julius Caesar in 63 B.C. and his imperial successors until the fourth century A.D.[2] During this time, the emperor was the Pontifex Maximus and ruled over all the pagan priesthoods of Rome. Archaeologists recovered several ancient coins minted during Augustus Caesar's reign from 27 B.C. to 14 A.D. The coins show the head of Augustus with the words "Pontifex Maximus" embossed around it. This title is repeatedly inscribed throughout the Vatican and is seen on various papal medallions struck by different Popes to commemorate their particular pontificate. Nowhere is such a foreign and pagan term used for Peter and the other leaders of the New Testament Church. The term *Pontiff* used for the Popes of Rome is derived from the pagan title *Pontifex Maximus*. *The Catholic Encyclopedia* explains where the concept of Pontiff originally came from:

> This term, *borrowed from the vocabulary of pagan religion in Rome*, early made its way into Christian discourse. Lexicographers derive it, though with clear misgivings, from the Latin words *pons* (bridge) and *facere* (to make, build). If this derivation be accepted, it is easy to see how readily it applies to those who build a bridge, make a way for men to God. In any case it designated in Roman religion members of the council of priests (pagan.. ed.) forming the **"Pontifical College"**, which ranked as the highest priestly organization at Rome and was presided over by the **"Pontifex Maximus."** It is not clear when it first made its appearance as a designation for Christian religious leaders, or whether Tertullian's ironic use of the designation **"Pontifex Maximus"** (in his *De pudicitia*, c. A.D. 220) for a Catholic bishop represents current terminology or not. In the Vulgate Pontifex is used in Hebrews for the Greek ἀρχιερεύς (chief priest, high priest). In present ecclesiastical usage

---

[1] Richard P. McBrien, ed., *The Harper Collins Encyclopedia of Catholicism* (New York: Harper/Collins, 1995). This volume readily admits that the title *Pontifex Maximus* "was originally a pagan title given the emperor as head of the college of priests in Rome" (page 1010).

[2] Matthew Bunson, *A Dictionary of the Roman Empire* (Oxford: Oxford University Press, 1991), 338.

the term **"Pontiff"** (with its derivatives, "Pontifical" and the verb "Pontificate") <u>is applied to bishops and **especially to the Pope**</u>. Though we still for the sake of clarity prefix supreme (sovereign) or Roman to the word Pontiff <u>in designating the Pope</u>, it is generally <u>to him that there is reference when we speak of **"the Pontiff**</u> (Emphasis mine).[3]

Pontifex Maximus meant that the Roman Emperor was the High Priest of all the State approved pagan deities of Rome. He governed both the religious and secular affairs of the Empire. As High Priest of the Empire, he presided over all the pagan priests (*Pontifices*) of the various polytheistic and pagan religions of Rome.[4] The pagan title *Pontifex Maximus* continued to be ascribed to every Roman Emperor up to the first so called "Christian" Emperor Constantine (280-337 A.D.) in the fourth century after Christ. He was the first to successfully integrate the mystery pagan religions of Rome with a perverted form of Christianity that later evolved into what is called today Roman Catholicism. Constantine used his fabricated conversion story to unify both the Roman State and the Church under his imperial rule. Though still a pagan sun worshipper at heart, Constantine was acclaimed the "Pontifex Maximus" of both the Christian and pagan religions of Rome.[5] This began what was later to develop into Roman Catholicism. Of this Catholic writer Peter De Rosa writes:

> So began the fatal alliance between Caesar and Pope, Throne and Altar. In time, ***it was to be a part of Catholic orthodoxy***. Emperor Constantine never relinquished his title Pontifex Maximus, head of the pagan state cult. When, in the year of 315, his victory arch was completed, he attributed his victory to 'the inspiration of the deity', unspecified. His coinage still depicted the sun-god...He sponsored Christianity because it proved itself useful in winning him a decisive battle.[6]

The first *de facto* Popes were not Peter, Linus, or the other alleged papal successors. Constantine was the first **official** Pope of the Roman Church both by title and action. Roman Catholic Canon Law states that only the Pope can convene and preside over a church council (**Canon 338**).[7] Constantine was the first, and did this several times—the most famous being the Council of Nicea in 325 A.D. He utilized his bishops as political advisors (early church historian, Eusebius being one of the most famous). The Popes do the very same thing with their Cardinals, Prelates, and Nuncios—all serving as political advisors to him today. The Church or State could not act independently on any crucial matter or important decision until Constantine made the final decision to do so. The Roman hierarchy, under the rule of the Pope, must follow and depend on him for religious and political guidance as well.[8]

The Bible expressly forbids Christians to mix with any religious system that is pagan in name and practice. This prohibition would certainly include applying the pagan title *Pontifex Maximus* to a man as

---

[3] *The Catholic Encyclopedia,* Volume 11, 549.

[4] Fergus Millar, *The Emperor in the Roman World* (Ithaca, New York: Cornell, 1992), 357-361.

[5] Will Durant, *The Story of Civilization. Caesar and Christ,* vol. 3 (New York: Simon and Shuster, 1980), 656; Michael Grant, *Constantine the Great: The Man and His Times* (New York: Barnes & Noble, 1998), 131-132.

[6] Peter De Rosa, *Vicars of Christ,* 36.

[7]   *The Code of Canon Law,* 58.

[8] For further historical proof that Constantine was the first **real** Pope see *The Story of Civilization, Vol. III: Caesar and Christ*, pages 656-657.

supreme ruler over the Church. To the Apostles and Christians of the first two centuries of the Christian Church, acknowledging and submitting to anyone called *Pontifex Maximus* as head of Christ's Church would have been tantamount to participation in the idolatrous worship of the Roman Emperors and other pagan practices of that time. The early Christians would have preferred martyrdom than to submit to such blasphemous paganism. Scripture commands us, that as the called out body of believers in Jesus Christ, we are not to adopt the pagan observances of heathen religions. ***"Thus says the Lord, learn not they way of the heathen"*** (Jeremiah 10:2). True Bible believing Christians will not mix the holy with the unholy, and the sacred with the profane. Whenever there is a danger in doing this, the conscientious born-again Christian will act in the manner of 2 Corinthians 6:14-17 and separate from that which can defile. The whole concept of the high priesthood of the Papacy with his College of Cardinals comprising the *Pontifical College* originated from ancient Babylon—whose pagan council of priests was headed by the high priest of the mysteries:

> From the Pope downwards, all can be shown to be now radically Babylonian. The College of Cardinals, with Pope at its head, is just the counterpart of the Pagan College of Pontiffs, with its "Pontifex Maximus," or "Sovereign Pontiff," which had existed in Rome from the earliest times, and which is known to have been framed on the model of the grand original Council of Pontiffs at Babylon.[9]

This should not surprise the enlightened student of Scripture. It has been frequently proven and documented elsewhere that the whole system of Romanism originally came from the mystery religions of ancient Babylon and Rome and was later adopted and assimilated with faint embellishments of Christianity into what we now call Roman Catholicism. Roman Catholic theologians are fond of using the term mystery when speaking about *the mystery of faith*, *the mystery of the sacraments*, *the mystery of the Eucharist*, and *the mysteries of the Rosary*. The Word of God condemns this false religious system calling it, instead, MYSTERY BABYLON THE GREAT (Revelation 17:5), for its roots come directly from ancient pagan Babylon. Hence:

> ...Though Babylon as a city had long been but a memory, her mysteries had not died with her. When the city and temples were destroyed, the high-priest fled with a company of initiates and their sacred vessels and images to Pergamos, where the symbol of the serpent was set up as the emblem of the hidden wisdom. From there, they afterwards crossed the sea and emigrated to Italy.... There the ancient cult was propagated under the name of the Eustruscan Mysteries, and eventually Rome became the headquarters of Babylonianism. The chief priests wore mitres shaped like the head of a fish in honor of Dagon, the fish god, the Lord of life....The chief priest when established in Rome took the title Pontifex Maximus and this was imprinted on his mitre. When Julius Caesar (who like all young Romans of good family, was an initiate) had become the head of the state, he was elected Pontifex Maximum, and this title was held henceforth by all the Roman emperors down to Constantine the Great, who was, at one and the same time, head of the church and high

---

[9] Alexander Hislop, *The Two Babylons* (Neptune, N.J.: Loizeaux Brothers, 1959), 206. This classic work is a detailed historical account documenting how the papal, clerical aspects of Roman Catholicism directly descended from the ancient pagan mystery religions of ancient Babylon. Though assaulted by many Roman Catholic apologists over the years, the historical observations of this classic book have withstood the test of time and still remain largely valid today.

priest of the heathen! The title was afterwards conferred upon the bishops of Rome, and is borne by the Pope today, who is thus declared to be, not the successor of the fisherman-apostle Peter, but the direct successor of the high priest of the Babylonian mysteries, and the servant of the fish-god Dagon, for whom he wears, like his idolatrous predecessors, the fisherman's ring. During the early centuries of the church's history, the mystery of iniquity had wrought with such astounding effect, and Babylonian practices and teachings had been so largely absorbed by that which bore the name of the church of Christ, that the truth of the Holy Scriptures on many points had been wholly obscured, while idolatrous practices had been foisted upon the people as Christian sacraments, and heathen philosophies took the place of Gospel instruction. Thus was developed that amazing system which for a thousand years dominated Europe and trafficked in the bodies and souls of men, until the great Reformation of the 16th century brought a measure of deliverance.[10]

Noted secular historian Will Durant wrote, "the vestments of the clergy were legacies from pagan Rome." The very mitre and papal robes worn by the Pope are directly descended from the same crown and robe worn by the high priest of the Babylonian fertility and fish god Dagon (Judges 16:23; 1 Samuel 5:2). Catholic scholars readily admit the mixture of paganism with their religion as the mark of victory over the pagan practices of heathendom by way of accommodation and assimilation. Concerning certain pagan rites the Catholic Encyclopedia states: "But the Church from a very early period took them into their service, just as she adopted many other things...which were not identified with any idolatrous cult, *they were common to almost all cults*".[11] Even today, Roman Catholic missionaries in Africa and Central and South America encourage the fusing of Animism and Voodooism (in what is known as Santeria) with Catholicism in worship. The author remembers, a while back, observing in the grocery store religious candles with various Roman Catholic themes on them. One candle, in particular, had a crucifix on it with a prayer recitation to the "Seven Spirits of Africa." Native occultists from these geographical places mentioned above have no theological problems incorporating the ritual of Roman Catholicism into their voodoo practices. Famous monastic writer Thomas Merton had no qualms either with merging the eastern mystic concepts of Hinduism and Buddhism with Roman Catholicism. From her origins up until the present time, the Roman Catholic institution has always practiced the eclectic approach of blending the unholy elements of pagan religions with the distinct and supreme revelation of Christianity. The Word of God clearly informs us that mixing the one true religion of God with false pagan religions is a mark of apostasy and spiritual harlotry (see Hosea 3-4).

The Lord will bring swift and devastating judgment on those who participate in it (see Ezekiel 8-9). Over and over again, we read in the Old Testament of God's sweeping judgment on Israel for their apostate mixture of paganism with the true worship of the Lord. The New Testament carries the same stern message of judgment. The Lord warns those caught in the syncretistic web of Romanism to come out of it before His judgment falls on the headquarters of it in fiery destruction (Revelation 17:16). Those Roman Catholics who are truly saved and born-again by the Spirit of God should remove themselves from this pagan, wicked, and anti-Christian institution known in Scripture as spiritual Babylon the great. This is not an option but a command from God. *"And I heard another voice from heaven saying, come out of her My people, that you be not partaker of her sins and that you receive not of your plagues"* (Revelation 18: 4). Roman Catholics

---

[10] H.A. Ironside, *Lectures on the Revelation* (Neptune, NJ: Loizeaux Brothers, 1967), 287, 295.
[11] *The Catholic Encyclopedia*, Vol. 3, 246.

claiming to have a born-again experience by faith alone in Jesus Christ, yet justify following and staying within the Roman Catholic system by claiming they must win others to Christ within the Roman Church do well to heed Jeremiah 51:9: *"We would have healed Babylon, but she is not healed. Forsake her and let us go every one into his own country. For her judgment reaches to heaven and is lifted up even to the skies."*

Throughout the centuries, the Vatican has continued to be obstinate by refusing correction from the Word of God. Indeed, great and brave men like Jerome Savonarola, John Huss, Hugh Latimer, Thomas Cranmer, John Wycliffe, and Martin Luther, who sincerely sought to reform the Roman Catholic Church from within by the holy standards of God's Word, were rebuffed, excommunicated, and in some instances killed. This has proved the Great Whore to be by nature unrepentant, apostate, reprobate, and beyond the correction of God's Word! Instead of putting away the statues, images, wafer gods, rosaries, relics, medals and Scapulars all used to earn or merit salvation, and the many other articles of idolatrous worship, the Vatican tenaciously clings to them in apostate defiance, claiming to do so in the hallowed name of Jesus Christ, much like the idolatrous Israelites did who *"feared the Lord, yet served their own gods"* while disregarding the clear teaching of God's Word (2 Kings 17: 32-41). The Lord Jesus has given the Roman Catholic Institution space to repent of her spiritual harlotries for over 1,700 years; but she brazenly refuses to do so. Therefore, in anticipation of this, Bible prophecy has foretold that she will be cast into the Great Tribulation with all those who blindly follow her (Revelation 2:21-22).

To assert the Pope is the Pontifex Maximus in the ecclesiastical role of high priest over the whole Church is a blasphemous usurpation of the unique high priesthood that belongs to the Lord Jesus Christ alone! Scripture proclaims that He alone is rightly qualified to be *"the High Priest of our confession"* (Hebrews 3:1); *"For no man takes this honor to himself"* (just like the Popes of Rome presumptuously do), *"but He that is called of God"* (Hebrews 5:4). Jesus Christ was called and ordained of God after the singular order of the Melchizedek priesthood. This high priesthood exclusively belongs to the eternal Christ and is an untransferable priesthood that cannot be passed on or transmitted down to fallible, mortal, and sinful men such as the papal pretenders of Rome are. For it is written in Hebrews 7:23-24: *"Also there were many priests, because they were prevented by death from continuing. But He, because He continues forever, has an unchangeable priesthood."*

The New Testament Greek word for "unchangeable" is απαραβατος (*pronounced: aparabatos*) which literally means, "not able to be passed on to another, inviolable, nontransferable." This obviously implies that the priesthood of Jesus Christ does not pass to a successor, like a pope or Roman Catholic priest, because it is an unceasing, eternal priesthood belonging to Christ alone by virtue of His resurrection from the dead.[12] In light of this exegetical reality, the Roman Catholic clergy, or any other earthly religious order, cannot be heirs of this priesthood. The observation of Puritan divine John Owen is warranted here:

> The expositors of the Roman church are greatly perplexed in the reconciling of this passage of the apostle unto the present priesthood of their church. And they may well be so, seeing they are undoubtedly irreconcilable...This is directly contrary unto the words and design of the apostle. For the reason he assigns why the priesthood of Christ doth not pass from him unto any other is, because he abides himself forever to discharge the office of it. Now this excludes all subordination and conjunction, all vicars as well as successors; unless we

---

12   Fritz Rienecker and Cleon Roger, *Linguistic Key to the New Testament*, 688.

shall suppose, that although he doth thus abide, yet is he one way or other disenabled to discharge his office.[13]

Only Jesus Christ can efficaciously intercede as the great High Priest accepted before God who is able to save to the uttermost all that come to God directly through Him. By giving His life, a sacrificial ransom for many, and being a divine sinless substitute for sinners, Christ uniquely qualifies Himself to be our redeeming High Priest. When He shed His blood on the cross, He cleansed us from sin and forever removed the penalty of eternal damnation thereby saving us who trust in Him. This was permanently accomplished on the cross when Jesus took upon Himself the full penalty of our sins, and by virtue of its perfect content, never needs to be repeated again. Currently, our High Priest is interceding for us before God the Father in heaven as our divine Mediator resurrected from the dead (Hebrews 7:25-27). The Scriptures tell us that Jesus Christ alone is our great High Priest who has passed into the heavens and now stands before the resplendent presence of God on our behalf (Hebrews 9:24). The Pope in the capacity of Pontifex Maximus can in no way qualify himself in the same manner Christ did in the role of High Priest. To the fervent papists I ask: Can the Pope offer himself a sinless sacrifice to God to take away sin? Furthermore, can the Pope of his own volition ascend to heaven to be the redeeming Mediator before God in the place of man? Is the Pope divine, eternal, and sinless in being so that his propitiatory sacrifice remains forever? Was he crucified for you and risen from the dead? To be High Priest according to the specifications of the book of Hebrews under the New Testament era the candidate must possess these qualifications (see Hebrews 8-10). With mortal man this is impossible.

I speak foolishly in this way to point out the absurd and ludicrous position of the papists when claiming that the bishop of Rome is somehow given the title "High Priest" that the New Testament says belongs to Jesus Christ alone and no other. If Roman Catholics, after knowing the obvious answers to these simple hypothetical questions, still stubbornly maintain their position the Pope is the *Pontifex Maximus* of the Church, in light of the fact that the New Testament is squarely against such a blasphemous claim, then one can truthfully and sadly conclude that the ***"god of this world has blinded the minds of them that believe not, lest the light of the glorious Gospel of Christ, who is the image of God, should shine in them"*** (2 Corinthians 4:4). For the Pope to be the Pontifex Maximus (High Priest) he must be so in no other way than in the manner prescribed under the New Covenant—and only one Person in history fits that qualification—Jesus Christ. To claim the Pope is the High Priest of the entire Church in the face of what the book of Hebrews reveals about the one, perfect, and untransferable priesthood of Jesus Christ merits the response of Romans 3:4: ***"God forbid, yes, let God be true, but every man a liar."***

---

[13]   John Owens, *Hebrews*, Vol. 5, (Carlisle, PA: Banner of Truth, 1991), 518-519.

CHAPTER 7

THE INFALLIBILITY OF THE POPE

Papal infallibility is the central doctrine of the Papacy that officially makes the Pope an ecclesiastical Despot both in theory and practice. William Cathcart rightly prognosticates what the great, harmful repercussions will be that naturally follow from the audacious claim of Papal infallibility:

> The Popes never relinquish anything. Their coral rocks always grow. The claims of their infallibility would lead them, had they the power, to dethrone modern kings; to burn the successors of John Huss and Jerome of Prague; to dig up and consign to the flames the bones of our modern Wycliffes; to cast the bible into the fire; to destroy the liberty of the press; the freedom of conscience, the worship of Protestants, and every other obstacle to the triumph of priestly despotism. Infallibility means an unparalleled *mental, moral, material and universal tyranny…*[1]

The doctrine of Papal infallibility dangerously sets a man above the rule and law of Scripture and places into the hands of the Popes supreme authority in the Church which properly belongs to Jesus Christ alone on Earth and in heaven. The word of man is placed above the Word of God here paving the way for more deception and papal dictatorship in the future. The despotic claims of the Pope do not stop with ascribing the names and offices of God and Christ to him. The Roman Catholic institution audaciously asserts that the Popes are infallible on "faith and morals" when speaking the Latin phrase, "Ex Cathedra", literally meaning, "from the chair". *Webster's Dictionary* defines the word infallible with the following definitions: **(1)** Incapable of error, never wrong, **(2)** Not liable to fail, go wrong, or make a mistake. Therefore, when the Pope speaks in his official capacity, he is incapable of speaking error in setting forth and proclaiming doctrine on faith and morals with the pronouncement of "Ex Cathedra." When infallibly speaking in this way, the Pope can neither deceive nor be deceived.[2] Outside of this stipulated condition both Roman Catholic theologians and apologists alike freely admit the Pope is capable of error and sin.

---

[1]   *The Papal System*, 349.

[2]   The Pope's infallibility assures immunity from error that guarantees protection against either "passive or active error" see Avery Dulles, "Infallibility: The Terminology," in *Teaching Authority and Infallibility in the Church*, Paul C. Empie, ed. (Minneapolis: Augsburg, 1979), 71.

The First Vatican Council in 1870 gave a detailed formulation on the doctrine of papal infallibility. The Council defined it in the following words:

> We teach and define that it is a dogma divinely revealed that the Roman Pontiff when he speaks *ex cathedra*, that is, when in discharge of the office of Pastor and Doctor *of all Christians*, by virtue of his supreme Apostolic authority, he defines a doctrine regarding faith and morals to be held by the Universal Church, by the divine assistance promised him in blessed Peter, is possessed of that infallibility with which the divine Redeemer willed that His Church should be endowed for defining doctrines of the Roman Pontiff of themselves—and not by virtue of the consent of the Church—are irreformable.[3]

The doctrine of papal infallibility is not an option for Roman Catholics to accept or reject. This doctrine, according to Rome, is binding on all Catholics and is necessary for salvation in the Roman Catholic system. The Vatican I Council invoked an anathema on both non-Catholics and Catholics alike who dare disagree, contradict, or reject the doctrine of papal infallibility when dogmatically declaring: "But if *anyone* which may God, forbid, contradict this our definition, *let him be anathema*" (i.e., under the eternal curse of God Almighty).[4] The Second Vatican Council reaffirmed all that Vatican I pronounced on the Pope's infallibility:

> The Roman Pontiff, head of the college of bishops, enjoys this infallibility in virtue of his office, when, as supreme pastor and teacher of all the faithful—who confirms his brethren in the faith (cf. Lk. 22:32)—he proclaims in an absolute decision a doctrine pertaining to faith or morals. For that reason his definition are rightly said to be irreformable by their very nature and not by reason of the assent of the Church in as much as they were made with the assistance of the Holy Spirit promised to him in the person of blessed Peter himself; and as a consequence they are in no way in need of the approval of others, and do not admit of appeal to any other tribunal. For in such case the Roman Pontiff does not utter a pronouncement as a private person, but rather does he expound and defend the teaching of the Catholic faith as the supreme teacher of the universal Church, in whom the Church's charism of infallibility is present in a singular way.[5]

Converts to Roman Catholicism must recite the oath of faith in which they are to affirm their unquestioned allegiance to "the Roman Pontiff, and his infallible teaching authority." However, there are stipulated limitations to Papal infallibility. During one of the sessions of the First Vatican Council, the general council of bishops in concurrence with the Pope, gave three conditions for declaring a teaching infallible followed with the pronouncement "ex cathedra": (1) The Pope must be seated in the actual chair of Saint Peter and speak in his official capacity as Universal Bishop of the Church. (2) The infallible declaration must be binding on the entire Church. (3) The pronouncements must involve matters concerning faith and morals. All three conditions for alleged papal infallibility, when examined closely, are proved to be false, inaccurate, and without *proper* biblical warrant.

---

[3]   *Dogmatic Canons and Decrees*, 256.

[4]   Ibid, 257.

[5]   *Vatican Council II: The Conciliar and Post Conciliar Documents*, 380.

For centuries, the Vatican claimed that they possessed the actual Chair where Saint Peter and his successors carried out the responsibilities of the papacy. But this reputed Chair of Saint Peter, where Popes traditionally pontificate and infallibly proclaim, "ex cathedra", was scientifically disproved to be the authentic chair Saint Peter supposedly ruled from as the first bishop of Rome. In July of 1968, Pope Paul VI appointed a special group of qualified scientists to evaluate and determine the approximate date for "the Chair of Saint Peter". The results of the findings were published in an official report released in 1969. By using the scientific method of Radio Carbon dating and other age finding techniques, the commission stated in their official report that the Chair dates back to the late ninth century, and is of French origin. There is some evidence that it might have been the coronation chair of Charles II, the King of France (823-877 A.D.). The scientists definitely concluded the Chair to be no older than the ninth century and on the Ivory panels in the front are scenes of Greek pagan mythology from the storied life of Hercules! Concerning this shocking truth, The Catholic Encyclopedia says:

> For the adornment of the front of the seat eighteen small panels of ivory have been used, on which the labours of Hercules, also fabulous animals, have been engraved; in like manner it was common at this period to ornament the covers of books and reliquaries with ivory panels or carved stones representing mythological scenes.[6]

To claim that Papal infallibility is binding upon the whole Church blatantly ignores the history of the Christian Church prior to 1870. When Vatican I suddenly and arbitrarily decided that belief in Papal infallibility was now incumbent upon faithful Roman Catholics for salvation, the obvious question that must be posed to the papal infallibilists is: "What about the uncounted millions of sincere, devoted Roman Catholics who did not believe or know about the infallibility of the Pope before 1870?" Further, are we to suppose God overlooked them when he finally enlightened the Vatican I Council about its all importance two thousand years later? Nowhere does the Roman Catholic find in the last 1,600 years of Church history, prior to the Vatican I council of 1870, any man-made doctrine of Papal Infallibility declared indispensable for salvation with the clear pronouncement of ex cathedra attached to it in the sense that Vatican I defined it. Indeed, the members of the Council pushing for infallibility did not base this doctrine on Church history, but what the Church and Pope taught in the nineteenth century. The key phrase and concept for this blasphemous pretense was "ex cathedra". Proponents of papal infallibility at Vatican I anachronistically assumed from this premise, and then read back into history what was clearly not there, and therefore obfuscated the facts and refused to substantially answer the historical and biblical proofs marshaled against this unsupported doctrine presented by the anti-Infallibilists. Roman Catholic Arch Bishop August Bernhard Hasler, who worked in the Vatican for several years as the Vatican Secretariat for Christian Unity, had access to the secret archives of the Vatican, disturbingly discovered in his extensive research on the proceedings of the Vatican I Council that it was a sinister proceeding built on lies, obfuscation, threats, and strong arm tactics. He produced his shocking find in his book *How the Pope Became Infallible*. On the all-important claim of *ex cathedra*, Hasler discovered that:

> The magic word that sweeps away all the problems here is *ex cathedra*. Only *ex cathedra* pronouncements are to be infallible. Since this concept did not even exist before the sixteenth century, it cannot be said with certainty of any papal declaration from the first fifteen

---

[6]   *The Catholic Encyclopedia*, Vol. 3, 554.

hundred years that it was made *ex cathedra*. This did away with all sorts of unpleasantness, such as the condemnation of Pope Honorius I as a heretic by three ecumenical councils. Furthermore, papal proclamations endorsing murder and manslaughter could tarnish the luster of infallibility: By classifying them as not *ex cathedra* the situation was saved…At this point it is clear, at least, that the Infallibilists did not ground their proofs in history and the findings of historical research. Their arguments were essentially based on what the Church, and still more the Pope, taught and preached at that point in the nineteenth century. Since prevailing opinion within the Church supported the thesis of papal infallibility, it had to be true…The Infallibilists went to great lengths to obscure the real foundation of their proofs. They trotted out hundreds of historical arguments, leaving the crucial elements in their thinking out of sight. Hence, they cannot escape the charge of having misused history to push through the definition of infallibility. They erected a façade of serious historical reasoning and arranged to have an inconsequential "ritual discussion," with the (mostly unconscious) intention of glossing over their own dogmatism.

A very large number of majority bishops had barely an inkling of these contrivances. Still, one cannot overlook the carelessness, frivolousness, and ignorance they displayed in presenting their historical arguments. Many of them may have been acting in good faith, aided and abetted by intellectual laziness and lack of critical sense. Others were probably urged on by fear of sanctions or calculating opportunism. But even then it was possible to know better—the minority bishops are proof of that.[7]

Shortly after the release of his expose, Hasler met an "untimely death" in July of 1980. A considerable contingent made up of both laity and high-ranking clergy who opposed papal infallibility at the First Vatican Council admirably did so on the firm, reasonable grounds that Church history, Popes, and former ecclesiastical councils opposed it in principle. The Popes of the past disavowed the attribute of infallibility. Pope Hadrian VI (1522-23) disclaimed any sort of infallibility in the area of faith where Vatican I claims such exists. Hadrian VI exclaimed: "If by the Roman church you mean its head or Pontiff, *it is beyond question that he (the Pope) can err even in matters touching the faith. He does this when he teaches heresy by his own judgment or decretal. In truth many Roman Pontiffs were heretics*." Pope Innocent III (1198-1216) declared, "I can be *judged by the church for a sin concerning matters of faith*." Pope Innocent IV (1243-54) candidly admitted, "*Of course a Pope can err in matters of faith*. Therefore, no one ought to say, I believe that because the Pope believes it, but because the Church believes it. *If he follows the Church he will not err*."[8] Several Popes disqualified themselves in the past from being infallible when it came to the matters of faith since they were heretics.

On July 13, 1870, during one of the sessions of Vatican I, eighteen bishops supported and voted in favor of an argument that was raised on the floor citing well-known historical occasions that strongly militated against papal infallibility. One brave delegate declared:

Well venerable brethren, *history raises its voice to assure us that Popes have erred*. You may protest against it or deny it as you please, I'll prove it. Pope Victor in 192 first

---

7   August Bernhard Hasler, *How the Pope Became Infallible*, (Garden City, New York: Doubleday, 1981), 183-184
8   Peter De Rosa, *Vicars of Christ*, 204.

approved of Montanism and then condemned it. Marcellinus was an idolater; he entered the temple Vesta and offered incense to the goddess. You'll say that it was an act of weakness, but I answer *a Vicar of Jesus dies rather than become an apostate*. Liberius consented to the condemnation of Athanasius and made a profession of Arianism that he might be recalled from his exile and reinstated in the Holy See. Honorius adhered to monothelitism. Father Gratry has proved that to demonstration. Gregory I conceded a reinstitution of the chalice to the church of Bohemia, Pius II revoked the concession. Hadrian II declared civil marriages to be valid, Pius VII condemned them. Sixtus V published an edition of the Bible and a bull recommended it to be read. Pius VII condemned the reading of it. Clement XIV abolished the order of the Jesuits, but it was permitted again by Paul III and Pius VII. Pope Vigilius purchased the papacy from Bilesarius, Lieutenant of the Emperor Justinian. Eugenius III imitated Vigilius. Bernard, the bright star of the Reformation says, 'Can you show me in this great city of Rome anyone who would receive you as pope that they had not received gold or silver for it?' You know the history of Formosus too well for me to add to it. But you will tell me these are fables! Go, Monsignori to the Vatican library and read Platina, the historian of the papacy and the annals of Baronius. There are facts which for the honor of the Holy See we would wish to ignore.[9]

Yet despite this, and many other laudable protestations from the most revered and able scholars of the Roman Church, papal infallibility was decreed a dogma of the Church in spite of the obvious contradictions to it presented from history, tradition, and most importantly the Holy Scriptures. If defenders of papal infallibility object here by pointing out that the infallibility of the Pope was implicitly believed and expressed well before 1870, we must say in return, that salvation, as it is revealed in the Word of God, is not based on inferences or implicit hints, but is openly and explicitly revealed to leave no doubt of how a person can truly be saved (see John 1:14; 12:32; Acts 26:26; 1 John 1:1-3). The one and only binding obligation on every soul is to believe what the Bible testifies about the Person and work of Jesus Christ. Once trust is put in Christ alone, salvation is immediately given (see John 5:24; 6:47; Acts 16:31; Romans 10:9-10). In this light, papal infallibility is irrelevant, heretical, and contrary to Scripture and diametrically opposes the biblical way of salvation!

Papal infallibility never once plays into the scheme of salvation as it is carefully and clearly set out in the Scriptures by God. The two areas papal infallibility extends to are: the faith and morals of the

---

[9] Quoted from a television debate between Father Mitchell Pacwa and Dr. Walter Martin on *The John Ankerberg Show*—1986 edition. Another recent example of such documented truth from church history comes from Roman Catholic priest and German theologian Hans Kung, who was stripped of his license to teach as a Roman Catholic theologian by the disgruntled Pope John Paul II in 1979 for his scholarly critique of Papal Infallibility in *Infallible? An Inquiry* published in 1971. In this book, Kung documents that his extensive research found one result among others to be true: (1) "The existence of propositions which are infallible in principle has not been convincingly substantiated either by Vatican I or Vatican II in its statements on infallibility is obviously completely dependent on Vatican I and is on very shaky ground when, for its own part, it attempts to broaden the conception of Vatican I with the aid of an unhistorical theory of an exclusive apostolic succession of bishops. But Vatican I cites neither Scriptural testimonies which show the need for infallible propositions nor testimonies of a universal, ecumenical tradition which might substantiate an infallibility of propositions." From *Infallible? An Inquiry* (New York: Doubleday, 1971), 151.To this day Kung remains a persistent critic of papal authority, which he claims is man-made (and thus reversible) rather than instituted by God.

Christian religion. These two areas are very broad indeed within the perimeters of Christianity. In fact, the Christian religion is basically divided into two elementary categories: (1) Faith—which is what we believe about Christ and is defined within biblical theology. (2) Morals—this is composed of ethics and personal behavior exhibited by the saved members of the church who act out and obey the Word of God. The whole of Christianity could be summed up and constituted in these two categories. The Vatican consciously exploits this rudimentary truth in her insatiable desire to control and manipulate. Surely the Pope knows full well that faith and morals are very broad and extensive to the degree that almost anything having to do with secular or religious affairs can be conveniently molded and subordinated under the categories of "faith and morals." This of course allows the Vatican more room to dominate and tighten the grip on the mass following and blind allegiance she already receives from the faithful.

This absolute and unconditional submission to the Pope could be a preparatory prelude for the total submission the Anti-Christ will demand from his followers during the Great Tribulation. When the future apostate Pope endorses and approves of the Anti-Christ, this will certainly assure the submission of many Roman Catholics who consider the Pope's word to be irrefutable and trustworthy. This politico-religious compact between the papacy and the leader of the revived Roman Empire in Daniel 2:42-44; 7:24-25 and Revelation 13:1; 17:3 will be a greater reenactment of the Emperor Charlemagne's achievement of joining the papacy and the Roman Empire into one political entity in 800 A.D. Papal infallibility further affords the Vatican unlimited control over any area of the Catholic's life, now and in the future, whenever deemed expedient for the self serving interests of the papal agenda. The Vatican II Council made it quite clear that the unconditional submission implied in the infallibility of the Pope when saying, "ex cathedra" is to extend far beyond that into other areas than just faith and morals. The Council decreed:

> This loyal submission of the will and intellect must be given in a special way, to the authentic teaching authority of the Roman Pontiff, even when he does not speak ex cathedra...that his supreme teaching authority be acknowledged with respect, and that one sincerely adhere to decisions made by him conformably with his manifest mind and intention..."[10]

One of the distinctive traits of a cult is the demand for unconditional surrender of the individual's will and intellect to an authoritarian figure that is given a (quasi) divine status holding supreme power over the group. The blasphemous demands of the papacy for the total surrender of the conscience and will do indeed fit under this particular descriptive trait of a cult. Founder of the ambitious Jesuit order, Ignatius of Loyola (1491-1556), taught in his *Constitutions* that Jesuits are not only to blindly follow the Pope but are to slavishly and fanatically obey their superiors. The original text in paragraph of Rule 36 reads: "The inferior is as a cadaver in the hands of his superior."[11] The analogy is clear. Roman Catholics are supposed to yield themselves to the Pope's disposal like lifeless corpses without independent thoughts or actions of their own. The Pope is to direct and move them about like puppets under the direction of his autocratic whim. Carried to its logical conclusion, this is where the tyrannical implications of papal infallibility ultimately lead the

---

[10]   *Second Vatican Council*, 379. Roman Catholic Canon Law demands a cultish obedience to the Pope in **Canon 752**: "While the assent of faith is required, *a religious submission of intellect and will is to be given to any doctrine which either the Supreme Pontiff or the College of Bishops, exercising their authentic Magisterium, declare upon a matter of faith and morals, even though they do not intend to proclaim that doctrine by definitive act* (Emphasis mine).

[11]   Manfred Barthel, *The Jesuits* (New York: Quill, 1984), 66.

unstable and fearful soul caught in the despotic grip of Roman Catholicism. On the other hand, experiencing true surrender to the Lord Jesus Christ is a life giving, transforming freedom that brings rest, joy, assurance, peace, and spiritual fulfillment to the believing heart (see John 8:36; 10:10; 14:27; 1 John 5:13).

Scripture reveals to us that the only person Christians are commanded to yield unconditional and absolute surrender to is the Lord Jesus Christ, not the Holy See of Rome. ***"Therefore submit to God"*** (James 4:7; see also Proverbs 3:5-6). It is to Christ alone we wholeheartedly present our bodies as a "living sacrifice" for the holy and acceptable service of God (Romans 12:1). Our minds are to be totally subordinate to His Word only and held captive by it (2Corinthians 10:4-5). The Popes should take the clear advice of Peter whom they revere to be the first "infallible Pope." When confronted with the dilemma of obeying a religious institution of man versus Jesus Christ and His Gospel, Peter invariably replied, ***"We ought to obey God rather than man"*** (Acts 5:29). This timely principle practiced by the humble fisherman of Galilee does indeed provide a stinging rebuke to a religious system that demands unconditional obedience to it in the name of papal infallibility—even when it is obviously contrary to the teaching of Scripture—and that from Peter himself! Author Dave Hunt in his controversial book, *A Woman Rides the Beast*, accurately describes the tragic results existing among many of the one billion members of the Roman Catholic institution who enthusiastically accept the doctrine of papal infallibility without a critical and correct examination from Holy Scripture:

> To see the devastating effect of ascribing such supreme authority to a mere man, one need only to watch the obsequious reaction of those who find themselves fortunate enough to meet the Pope in person, to shake his hand or reach out and touch him. Observe the wild enthusiasm of the tens of thousands who gather when the Pope makes a personal appearance. In their fawning acknowledgment of infallibility there is an unwholesome identification which breeds even among common church members a binding and destructive pride at belonging to "oldest and largest...the one true Church, outside of which there is no salvation." That conceit makes devout Catholics insensitive to what would be otherwise failings in their Church, and keeps them in its power. The Church has become the Savior in the place of Christ, leading to the seductive and appealing belief that no matter what happens, that the institution with the good offices of the Pope, the saints, and especially Mary will eventually get one to heaven if surviving relatives pay enough for Masses to be said in one's name. It is a deadly delusion which is promoted in catechisms taught from childhood to all Catholics. Such destructive deceit is made plausible by the teaching that although Christ paid for our sins on the cross, the Church is the dispenser of the "graces and merits" He won. Add to that the ruinous conceit that subtly ensnares members of a Church whose head is infallible," and one has the elements to create craven superstition and, finally tragedy.[12]

The Lord Jesus prophetically warned that in the "last days" of this present age many false prophets would come in the name of Christ, acting as His sole representative on Earth, presumptuously saying what Christ would say and doing what Christ would do. The end result will be mass deception. ***"Take heed that no man deceive you. For many shall come in My name, saying I am Christ, and shall deceive many"*** (Matthew 24:4-5). The long dynasty of Popes claiming to be the visible, infallible Vicars of Christ on Earth accurately

---

[12]   Dave Hunt, *A Woman Rides the Beast* (Eugene, Oregon: Harvest House), 142.

fulfills and ominously parallels the above quoted prophecy of the Lord Jesus Christ in New Testament Scripture for the last days. Sadly, millions of sincere Catholics have been terribly deluded by the blasphemous anti-Christian claims of the papacy. The Popes down through the centuries are directly responsible for leading multitudes of Roman Catholics away from the Christ of Scripture to embrace one of Romish invention in the office and person of the Pope. This is shockingly confirmed in the encyclical letters of Pope Leo XII wherein he brazenly claims the Popes *"hold upon this earth the place of God Almighty."* Eminent theologian of the Roman Catholic Church, Cardinal Bellarmine wrote, *"All the names which are given in the Scriptures to Christ—even these same names are given to the Pope—whence it appears he is superior to the Church."*

Thus, when the Pope sits in the chair of Saint Peter and acts in official capacity, he does so claiming to be Christ on Earth in his absence. But what does the Word of God have to say about men claiming to be infallible instructors acting for God and Christ on Earth? In the opening verses of Ezekiel 28 we read of a certain King of Tyre, whom historians believe to be the ancient King of Phoenicia, Ithobalus, who like the Popes of Rome seated in Saint Peter's chair, boasted of being a universal ruler over all nations enthroned and seated thinking himself like God. For this insane aspiration, the Lord promises to do the following to the King of Tyre and the pretentious Popes who proclaim they are acting in the place of Almighty God: *"Therefore thus says the Lord God: "Because you have set your heart as the heart of a god, Behold, therefore, I will bring strangers against you, the most terrible of the nations, and they shall draw their swords against the beauty of your wisdom, and they shall defile your splendor. They shall bring you down to the pit, and you shall die the deaths of the slain in the midst of the seas. Will you yet say before him that slays you, 'I am God'? But you shall be a man, and no God, in the hand of him that slays you. You shall die the deaths of the uncircumcised"* (Ezekiel 28:6-10).

Ultimately, the judgment of God on the anti-Christian papacy will be fulfilled during the seven-year tribulation period in the future when the Anti-Christ and the ten nation confederacy with him breaks the concordat with the Vatican when he destroys Vatican City in a nuclear ball of fire (see Revelation 17:16). The Pope is nothing more than an erring mortal dressed up in a white religious costume flatulently claiming to be something he most certainly is not! Is there anything else in Scripture that further identifies the real spiritual identity of someone like the Pope who sits ruling as God in Christ's place within the monolithic structure of Saint Peter's Basilica? The Bible definitely speaks about a great religious figure sitting in a temple devoted to God parading himself about like God. Second Thessalonians says the following: "Let no man deceive you by any means. For that day shall not come except there come a falling away first, *and that man of sin be revealed the son of perdition who opposes and exalts himself above all that is called God, or that is worshipped so that he as God sits in the temple of God showing himself that he is God."* Many Bible teachers today have traditionally interpreted these passages to refer to the coming future Anti-Christ who will go into a rebuilt Jewish temple at Jerusalem and desecrate it by proclaiming himself God in there. How then does the passage in Second Thessalonians chapter two specifically apply to the Popes of Rome? To answer this question properly we must first define the meaning of anti-Christ.

Scripture gives two definitions for the word. The first definition of anti-Christ is one who denies that Jesus is the true Christ who came in the flesh (see 1 John 2:22-23; 4:1-3). This kind of anti-Christ denies that Jesus of Nazareth is God Almighty in human form. The Pope *in no way* belongs under this theological category of being an anti-Christ. Throughout the centuries the papacy has long upheld and declared the incarnation and deity of Jesus Christ. The second definition describes an anti-Christ as any person who takes the place of Christ by falsely claiming to be Him or like Him as His sole representative on Earth (see Matthew 24:5, 24-26; Mark 13:6; Luke 21:8). All the passages cited above from the prophetic portions of the

Gospels warn believers not to give credence to these many Christ pretenders, but rather to keep away from them! The Pope undoubtedly fulfills the second description of being an anti-Christ when claiming to be Christ's unique representative on Earth in His physical absence as the "Vicar of Christ." A former Roman Catholic bishop of Orleans, France historically referred to Popes John XII, Boniface VII, and Leo VIII as "monsters of guilt, reeking in blood and filth," and as *"Anti-Christ sitting in the temple of God."* Pope John XXII was condemned and excommunicated from the Catholic Church by the Council of Avignon in 1327. He was burned in effigy as *"Anti-Christ"*.[13] Pope Gregory the Great, while Bishop of Rome, warned the Emperor not to create a papacy because any bishop who assumes jurisdiction over other bishops is *"the forerunner of Anti-Christ."*[14]

At his coronation, Pope Innocent IV declared himself to *"the bodily presence of Christ on earth,"* and called anyone who disagreed with this a heretic. The Apostle John warned of many anti-Christs that would precede the final Anti-Christ to come. *"Little children, it is the last time, and as you have heard that Anti-Christ shall come. Even now there are many anti-christs whereby we know that it is the last time"* (1 John 2:18). Therefore the Pope is *an* anti-Christ, but not *the final* Anti-Christ. He, like many other historical figures, is a prophetic foreshadowing of the one who will be the supreme and final Anti-Christ to come. The long successive list of official Popes from Constantine to the present aptly portray the many anti-Christs of 1 John 2:18. Christ did not appoint Peter alone and the Popes to rule and guide the Church in His absence. The Word of God teaches otherwise. Our Lord sent the Holy Spirit to guide, counsel, teach, and comfort the Church by personally indwelling the heart of every born-again Christian. He alone is the infallible and authoritative guide for the Christian. Jesus promised this to every believer:

"And I will pray the Father, and He will give you another Helper that He may abide with you forever— the Spirit of truth, whom the world cannot receive, because it neither sees Him nor knows Him; but you know Him, for He dwells with you and will be with you. I will not leave you orphans: I will come to you… But the Helper, the Holy Spirit, whom the Father will send in My name, He will teach you all things, and bring to your remembrance all things that I said to you…Nevertheless I tell you the truth. It is to your advantage that I go away; for if I do not go away, the Helper will not come to you; but if I depart, I will send Him to you. And when He has come, He will convict the world of sin, and of righteousness, and of judgment: of sin, because they do not believe Me; of righteousness, because I go to My Father and you see Me no more; of judgment because the ruler of this world is judged…However when He, the Spirit of truth, has come: for He will not speak on His own authority, but whatever He hears He will speak; and will tell you things to come" (John 14:16-18, 26, 16:7-13).

For anyone to assign this place for himself in the role of "Visible head of the Church" commits a gross act of blasphemy by attempting to misappropriate the places of Christ and the Holy Spirit from their co-regent positions. The Holy Scriptures unanimously testify that Christ alone is the Head of the Church and ministers to her through the personal agency of the Holy Spirit and the cleansing power of the Word. *"And [Christ] is the head of the body, the church: who is the beginning, the firstborn from the dead; that in all things he might have the preeminence"* (Colossians 1:18; see also 1 Corinthians 11:3; 12:12-27; Ephesians 5:23). The whole concept of papal infallibility is just another manifold expression of humanism (couched in a religious pretext), that is, the anthropocentric viewpoint that believes man is the measure and sum of all things, and from that, assumes to be the supreme arbiter and interpreter of right and wrong. Although Rome's papal

---

[13]   Peter Doeswyck, *Ecumenicalism and Romanism*, Vol. 1, p. 58.

[14]   Ibid., 63-64.

humanism is cleverly masqueraded behind a shallow façade of Christianity, it is humanism, nonetheless. The inevitable result from this is that a man is virtually worshipped (in the person of the Pope) instead of God alone. This is the philosophy behind humanism. Roman Catholicism is an ecclesiastical humanism with shallow Christian embellishments. Christ is merely a crucial rung on the ladder for the papacy to unlawfully climb to the top and amass for itself secular and religious power that haughtily demands universal submission from all. Instead of the preeminence of the Lord Jesus Christ and His Word being the absolute and *infallible* rule and measure for Christian faith and morals, the Pope supplants such by stating, instead, that all Christians must unconditionally accept the doctrine of papal infallibility under the pain of eternal damnation according to the imperious decrees of Vatican I and II—even if such a foreign concept is diametrically opposed to the clear teaching of Scripture.

Fortunately, the emergence of the Reformation brought the Scriptures to the masses and reestablished the primary importance of biblical thinking that proclaimed God and His Word to be the supreme authority to which all Christians must unconditionally obey and surrender to instead of the papal Church of Rome! Anything else is nothing more than tyranny and enslavement of the conscience. It is certainly not coincidental that the Dark Ages (500 to 1500 A.D.) were exactly concurrent with the one thousand year period the Roman Catholic Church held sway over the known world, until the emancipating light of the Reformation brilliantly shone through the terrible darkness of papal tyranny which kept the European masses in bondage for centuries. With the invention of the movable printing press by Johannes Gutenburg (1400-1468 A.D.), the Holy Scriptures could now be published and widely distributed among the common people, allowing them to read the Bible for themselves and come to a saving knowledge of Jesus Christ without the trammeling effects of superstition and the endless extra biblical traditions of Romanism fostered by the papacy to keep Europe biblically illiterate and utterly dependent on Rome's sacramental system. Worse yet, a man claiming to be God's sole representative on Earth, or claiming to be divine or embodying the divine, is not merely imitative of the earthly king of Tyre, a false Christ, or an anti-Christ, *but the devil himself*!

This valid deduction is not the mere ravings of an alleged, rabid anti-Catholic author, but was declared by a Pope himself! In 1280 Franciscan priest and theologian, Peter Olivi was the first one to publicly impute infallibility to the Pope on matters of faith and morals when attempting to uphold for all time a decision made by Pope Nicholas III (1270-1280 A.D.) in favor of the Franciscan doctrine that renunciation of material possessions was a way to salvation. Some forty years later Pope John XXII thought otherwise on this point and forthrightly condemned the arrogant notion of papal infallibility as "the work of the devil" in his papal bull *Qui quorundam* issued in 1324.[15] These are all different children begotten from the same supernatural father. The Bible calls him Satan, the Devil. He was the very first being to revolt against God by insanely trying to become like God in attempting to usurp His place of supreme authority. Satan, an angelic creature of the highest order, sought to be superior to the Creator. Isaiah 14:13-14 describes the revolt of Satan against God. Satan wanted to become God, and within his foolish and blasphemous heart declared: ***"I will exalt my throne above the stars of God. I will also sit upon the mount of the congregation in the sides of the north. I will ascend above the heights of the clouds; I will be like the Most High."*** In the end, Satan was easily defeated and overthrown by the omnipotent hand of the Lord. All who aspire to be their own god or presumptuously proclaim to be God's exclusive and supreme representative of the Godhead on Earth, like the Popes do, are therefore reflecting the sinister image of their real spiritual father—the devil. *Hence, the specious claim of papal infallibility is another satanic grasp at what belongs to the Triune God alone.*

---

[15]   August Hasler, *How the Pope Became Infallible*, 36-37.

When papal infallibility was ratified in 1870 by the Vatican I Council, it was initially met with strong opposition from many of the Bishops and Cardinals who immediately saw the potential abuse and multiple dangers inherent in such a dangerous proposition. Among the leading opponents of papal infallibility was the learned Bishop Georg Strossmayer. He publicly repudiated the concept of papal infallibility before the council in a famous speech. The sagacious bishop discovered from his exhaustive studies of Scripture, Church history, and tradition that the papacy, along with the infallibility of its office, is *totally absent* from the New Testament and the early history of the Church. He boldly declared to the Vatican I delegation:

> I have set myself to study with the most serious attention the Old and New Testaments, and I have asked these venerable monuments of truth to make known to me if the holy pontiff, who presides here, is the true successor of St. Peter, vicar of Christ, and the infallible doctor of the church. I find in the apostolic days *no question of a Pope, successor to Saint Peter, the Vicar of Jesus Christ*, anymore than a Mohammed who did not exist. Now having read the whole New Testament, I declare before God, with my hand raised to that great crucifix *that I have found no trace of the papacy as it exists at this moment.*

The Bishop goes on to say:

> I have established: (1) That Jesus gave to His apostles the same power that He gave to St. Peter. (2) That apostles never recognized in St. Peter the vicar of Jesus. (3) That Peter never thought of being pope, and never acted as if he were pope. (4) That the councils of the first four centuries, while they recognized the high position which the bishop of Rome occupied on account of Rome, only accorded to him the preeminence of honor, never power of jurisdiction. (5) That the holy fathers in the famous passage, 'Thou art Peter and upon this rock I will build my church,' never understood that the church was built on Peter (super Petrum) but on the rock (super petram). That is, on the confession of the faith of the apostle. *I conclude victoriously, with history, with reason, with logic, with good sense, and with a Christian conscience, that Jesus Christ did not confer any supremacy on St. Peter, and that the bishops of Rome did not become sovereigns of the church, but only by confiscating one all the rights of the episcopate.*[16]

Bishops from the democratic countries of the United States, Canada, and England naturally had strong misgivings about ratifying the infallibility dogma. There was strong opposition to convene Vatican I Council that would consider ratifying papal infallibility as an official dogma of the Roman Catholic Church. A secret session which was held in the Vatican among influential prelates before the Council revealed that eighty-eight delegates opposed the Council and dogma, eighty abstained, and only sixty-five favored passing it. Many Roman Catholics are led to believe that papal infallibility was a dogma always taught and accepted by Rome without dissent or controversy among the clergy. History records otherwise with the real inner workings of Vatican I. A strong group of Cardinals and bishops vociferously objected to the absolutist claims of Pope Pius IX for papal infallibility in the face of dangerous opposition from the Pope and his militant coterie. This courageous group comprised the anti-infallibilists minority and were unremittingly threatened, blackmailed, and maliciously treated with censure and excommunication by Pius IX and his strong-arm

---

[16]   Richard Knolls, *Roman Catholicism: Issues and Evidences* (Chattanooga, TN: John Ankerberg Show, n.d.), 37.

group led by the powerful Jesuits of the semiofficial organization of the Vatican, *La Civilta Cattolica*. Their fanatical devotion to seeing the Pope made "infallible" reached such a toxic level that these Jesuits sought to convince certain bishops and priests close to the Vatican I Council proceedings to take a vow to ardently fight for the ratification of papal infallibility "to the point of bloodshed." They spearheaded the radical group of infallibilists that successfully forced this doctrine through to official acceptance in the Roman Catholic Church.[17] Rules were changed during the course of Vatican I so that free and open debate and dialogue was suppressed and curtailed so as to eliminate any legitimate dissent or opposition. Any who dared to justly and intelligently object, were regularly decried in the vilest of terms by the antipathetic advocates of infallibility. Bishop Georg Strossmayer was a prominent target of this vile, verbal abuse:

> The greatest storm broke out on March 22, 1870, when Bishop Joseph Georg Strossmayer affirmed in the great hall of the Council that even among Protestants there were many individuals who loved Jesus. When he went on to dispute the feasibility of deciding dogmatic questions by majority rule, the majority shouted him down. Many cried out, "Lucifer! Anathema, anathema!" all the infallibilists loudly demanded, "Down with him, down with him!" Complaints were heard everywhere about the lack of debate. According to Bishop Dupanloup, the bishops had the freedom to speak but not to discuss. He noted in his diary that the bishops' tongues had not been cut out, only caught in a vise—so the bishops couldn't use them to explain themselves. Bishop Maret considered the Council an acclamation disguised as a discussion.[18]

Pius IX, and the infallibilists group fighting for him, even resorted to various tactics of intimidation both individually and collectively to force the opposition into submission. Financial pressure was brought to bear on bishops who signed a particular document during the Council opposing papal infallibility. If they did not recant, financial support for themselves and their respective parishes would be summarily removed. Such effective browbeating worked and many signatories withdrew their names.[19] Formidable opponent and Roman Catholic prelate, John Stephanian, refused to recant and the papal police attempted to arrest him in the streets of Rome! When he resisted, a great riot ensued. Other Bishops from Armenia attending the Council in opposition to papal infallibility were denied exit visas, threatened with imprisonment, and feared for their lives.[20] Pius IX personally harangued, insulted, and intimidated various members of the Council to vote for papal infallibility. Chaldean patriarch of Babylon, Joseph Audu, was summoned to the private papal chambers of Pius IX for a speech Audu gave the prior day calling for a limitation of papal powers. When Audu arrived, the Pope bolted from behind the door, trembling with rage and seething with anger, sternly warned and threatened the aged Patriarch that he would not leave the room until he had given his written consent. Given the choice of complying or resigning, Audu chose the latter. Due to further conflicts that arose between the two, Pius IX later removed the Patriarch from office.[21]

The elections were a sham because free exchange and the right of dissent through democratic process were suppressed and stifled. The outcome to ratify papal infallibility was already predetermined by the Pope

---

[17] August Hasler, *How the Pope Became Infallible*, 57.
[18] Ibid., 80-81.
[19] Ibid., 96-97.
[20] Ibid., 97-98.
[21] Ibid., 89-90.

and his lackeys before the Council began. Pope Pius IX exhibited despotic traits in his personality which logically corresponds and is disturbingly reflected in his fanatical and overbearing insistence upon the dogmatization of papal infallibility during the Vatican One Council. One member of this Council observed:

> Along with his sense of possessing a divine mission, Pius IX had a strongly authoritarian character. The Pope is the object of the most intense flattery… and therefore his situation is the most distorted … no one dares to say a word… This secular and spiritual omnipotence destroys the mind and heart of a man… and everything around him.[22]

Pius IX could not be dissuaded from pursuing absolute power for himself through the new dogma of papal infallibility. It fitted his autocratic personality perfectly well. There was no stopping him from achieving this totalitarian goal.

> Pius IX *wanted the new dogma at any cost*. Not only did he make use of rather dubious methods, he was also blind to the dangers which might arise from a definition… Bishop de Las Cases described the Pope as an authority subject to no other control than his own whims and preferences. The new dogma, he felt, must lead to despotism. *To others the Pope was already acting the despot by applying massive pressures to dominate the Council.* Every now and then Pius tried to pretend impartiality, but before long he would squelch any remaining doubts that everything depended upon him. Several bishops reported that the people closest to him were saying, *"Don't count either the majority or the minority. The Pope is everything"*… *Pius IX felt that discussing his opponent's arguments was a waste of time. He knew that he would triumph thanks to the power of his office…* More distressing than all this are the many abusive terms which Pius IX heaped on the bishops of the minority in private conversations and on public occasions. They covered the gamut from "crazy" to "ass," all the way down to "traitor" and "chief of the sectarians." The Pope deeply injured the bishops with his biting remarks (Emphasis mine).[23]

It was during the Council, after much pressuring, coercion, and intimidation coupled with threats of anathemas and excommunication, that the dogma of papal infallibility passed with a majority vote by the Jesuit controlled Council under the manipulating hand of the power driven Pope Pius IX. He was guilty of committing the logical fallacy of begging the question, and affirmed himself to be infallible in 1870, which the church never universally recognized before. Pius IX said: "I am the successor of Peter, I am the infallible teacher," and the council said why, and he answered: "Because I said so." The courageous Bishop Joseph Ignaz Dollinger from Germany vigorously opposed the dogma at Vatican I to the bitter end. Unwilling to concede to the new dogma as true and worthy of his unconditional surrender, the Pope excommunicated the aged scholar who had faithfully devoted forty-seven years of his life as a theological instructor of the Roman Catholic Church. The Holy Office of the Inquisition placed his book, *The Pope and the Council* on The Index of Forbidden Books because of its factual and compelling arguments against papal infallibility. Dollinger was unfairly punished by the Vatican for telling the truth by showing that the fiction of papal infallibility was against Scripture and Church history!

---

22 Bishop Felix Dupanloup wrote these words in his personal diary on December 17, 1869.
23 Ibid., 116-118.

Papal infallibility has practically turned the papacy into a full-blown autocracy without proper checks and balances of a moral and doctrinal accountability that is reinforced with disciplinary regulation. In the future, no doubt, when (not if) the Pope should morally and doctrinally err when arrogantly speaking "ex cathedra" before the Roman Catholic Church, her clergy and laymen will be powerless to curb and correct such erroneous excesses with the corrective of Scripture, since his decrees would assume to be infallible and guided by the Holy Spirit by their very nature. Realizing this serious predicament prompted eminent Catholic historian Lord John Emerich Edward Acton (1834-1902) to write the famous adage warning against the unbridled tyranny of papal infallibility: ***"Power tends to corrupt, and absolute power corrupts absolutely."*** Acton's well reasoned opposition to the dogma of infallibility at the Council nearly got him excommunicated from Rome. The infallibility clause actually gives the papacy unlimited dictatorial rule free of democratic interposition from any civil or religious power. Fallen human nature, being self centered and sinful as it is, needs a moral restraint implemented by outside governmental restraint from the Church and State to prevent abuse, anarchy, and despotism. The Framers of the U.S. Constitution knew full well the peccable and corrupt inclination of human nature when installing the system of checks and balances for each branch of the United States government to prevent a tyrant from unlawfully seizing the reins of the government.

Vatican I far exceeded those moral limitations and rational boundaries when ratifying 'papal infallibility.' It is only a matter of time when a Pope of "fierce countenance" arises and rules with an iron fisted hand doing whatever he criminally pleases under the pretext of "ex cathedra." Both clergy and laity will loudly protest and rebel in vain because Vatican I foolishly gave the awful precedent for such a thing to happen. It is therefore not a question of **if** this will happen, but **when** it will happen. If the Pope is supposedly infallible in office concerning faith and morals, why doesn't he use some of his inerrant magic to solve the many moral problems plaguing our world and the theological difficulties that the Christian Church has grappled with for centuries? Since 1870, the Popes seem very reluctant to speak "ex cathedra" in a broad scope knowing full well they are quite capable of error even when speaking from the chair—though not ever publicly admitting this. In fact to underscore this very point, the Pope has declared only one teaching to be an infallible pronouncement since 1870—the unscriptural teaching of Mary's Assumption into heaven by Pope Pius XII in 1950. The Pope's reliance on the Roman Curia for political and religious counsel is a practical denial of the immediate presence of infallibility. If Popes had possessed this infallibility by virtue of their office prior to 1870, why is there no clear, consistent affirmation of this in the historical records!

Indeed, papal infallibility is proven to be patently false both in doctrine and morals by examining and comparing the decrees, pronouncements, and shameful lives of the Popes throughout the history of the Roman Catholic institution. The Popes by their actions in the past have shown to be anything but infallible when it comes to Christian doctrine and morals. When examining the various statements the Popes made on faith and morals, we discover that they often contradicted and denounced each other as heretics and anti-Popes—thus invalidating and disproving the legitimacy of papal infallibility. In the fourth century, Pope Liberius (352-366 A.D.) sided with Arius in his Christological heresies and condemned Athanasius for his orthodox views on Jesus Christ and the Trinity.[24] Rome's interpretation of Matthew 16:18-19 that Jesus would protect the Church from heresy through papal infallibility obviously fails here if such an interpretation was correct from the start. Pope Vigilius (537-555 A.D.) called "one of the most corrupt Popes in the history of the Church" by a Roman Catholic priest and author, embraced the Monophysite heresy (the belief that Christ had only one nature) and refused to condemn those who taught it as heretics. Later, when threatened with

---

[24]   J.N.D. Kelly, *The Oxford Dictionary of the Popes*, 30-31.

excommunication by the Council of Constantinople in 553 A.D., he submitted to their united condemnation of the Monophysite heresy confessing that he was used as a "tool of Satan."

Pope Gregory I (590-604 A.D.) denounced the papal title "Universal Bishop" to be the "precursor of Antichrist."[25] After his pontificate, the Popes resumed the title of "Universal Bishop", and still do to this day. Pope Honorius (625-638 A.D.) was condemned after his death as a heretic for his monothelite belief (the doctrine that Christ had only one will) by the Third Council of Constantinople held in 680 A.D. This council declared of him: "...that he was altogether alien from the Apostolic dogmas" "anathema to Honorius, the heretic" "a tool in the hands of the devil," and guilty of "unholy betrayal."[26] During the thirteenth session of the Council this same Pope was anathematized and excommunicated from the Catholic Church! Both Popes Agatho (678-678 A.D.) and Leo II (682-683 A.D.) condemned Pope Honorius as a heretic. Here, we have one infallible Pope condemning another infallible Pope. One of them has to be in error for this to occur. Embarrassed by this lapse in papal infallibility, even Roman Catholic sources are force to admit by this: "*A pope is not infallible in such proceedings as those of Honorius* who contributed unintentionally to the increase of heresy."[27] In their vain attempt to uphold the integrity of papal infallibility, defenders of Rome claim Honorius did not teach in his official capacity as the Pope speaking ex cathedra from the chair of Saint Peter, but was privately giving his own opinion on the matter. The Council was therefore remonstrating him for expressing his personal opinion. However, the facts surrounding this situation clearly reveal that Honorius was speaking in his capacity as Pope and that he was condemned by both Popes and church councils shortly thereafter with that explicit understanding. William Webster explains further concerning the written text of the Third Church Council of Constantinople:

> However, the text of the official decrees of the sixth Ecumenical Council proves that it thought otherwise. It condemns Honorius as a heretic in his official capacity as pope, not as a private individual, for being used by Satan for actively disseminating a heresy which would be a stumbling block for all orthodox people. In other words, it condemns the Pope as a heretic on the basis of pronouncements which the Church would later define as meeting the conditions of *ex cathedra* statements.[28]

Other Popes that were declared heretics by the Roman Catholic Church are Gregory XII, John XXII, Paul V, Marcellus, Benedict XIII, and Formosus. If any Pope is to be found guilty of heresy he is no longer a Christian, much less an infallible Pope, or even a good standing member of the Roman Catholic Church. Furthermore, if a Pope is a heretic, he is no longer a legitimate successor of Saint Peter, and the supposed unbroken chain of apostolic succession is severed. Today, these heretical Popes are still found on the official list of Popes published by the Vatican! During the ninth century, Adrian II declared civil marriages to be valid. Pope Pius VII pronounced them to be invalid in the nineteenth century. This presents a puzzling contradiction if Popes are infallible in office while making these contrary moral pronouncements. Pope Sixtus V (1585-1590 A.D.) translated and edited a Latin version of the Bible and prefaced it with a papal Bull declaring an excommunication on anyone altering the text while copying or republishing it. Two years later in 1592, the infallible Pope Clement VIII declared that Sixtus' translation was filled with numerous errors

---

25 Gregory the Great, *Epistles of St. Gregory the Great*, Book VII, *Epistle 33* (Grand Rapids: Eerdmans, 1956), 226.

26 Addis and Arnold, *Catholic Dictionary* (New York: Catholic Publication Society, 1887), 409.

27 Conway, *Question Box* (New York: Paulist Press, 1929), 173.

28 William Webster, *The Church of Rome At the Bar of History* (Carlisle, PA: Banner of Truth, 1995), 67-68.

and had it replaced with another Latin translation with a significant number of alterations made. To cover up this fallible mistake of the previous "infallible" pope, Clement VII, who believed Sixtus V ruined the Bible, had Cardinal Robert Bellarmine secretly issue a revised edition of the Scriptures, lest the blunder of the infallible Sixtus V was discovered. Apparently, Clement VII was more "infallible" than his predecessor who was obviously less infallible. Why are there so much ignorance, uncertainty, and blatant error associated with the premium importance of determining the canon and meaning of Scripture if these Popes are truly infallible in office?

Pope Eugene IV (1431-1447 A.D.) condemned Joan of Arc as a heretic in 1431 and had her burned at the stake for supposedly being a witch. Five centuries later, Pope Benedict XV (1914-1922) canonized her a saint in 1920. What one infallible pope believes to be heretical another infallible pope believes to be saintly! In 1378, the Great Schism in the Roman Catholic Church occurred, and lasted until 1417. During this period, Italian Cardinals elected as their pope, Urban VI, while at the same time the French Cardinals elected Clement VII to be their pope. Both Popes condemned and excommunicated each other. Later, they were both deposed and another Pope (Boniface IX) was elected in their place. How could Pope Paul V (1605-1621 A.D.) and Pope Urban VIII (1623-1644 A.D.) be infallible when they both publicly condemned Galileo's heliocentric theory (the idea that the earth revolves around the sun) to be heretical and contrary to Scripture? In 1633, Galileo was threatened with torture and placed under house arrest by the inquisition for several years because of his empirical belief that the earth revolves around the sun, which Copernicus, the Roman Catholic priest, expounded on earlier. The Vatican had already placed Copernicus' book, *De Revolutionibus orbium coelstium* (*On the Revolution of the Celestial Spheres*), on the list of forbidden books in 1616. All of this changed in 1829 when Pope Leo XII removed the writings of Copernicus from the list of forbidden books and allowed Catholics to read them. Thus, what one Pope declares to be *heretical*, another Pope declares this to be truth! Both Popes cannot obviously be infallible here. Was Pope Leo XIII (1878-1903) doctrinally infallible when he condemned free thought and free speech in his various encyclical letters?[29]

This further points out that if the Lord Jesus Christ really endowed the Popes with infallibility, it would have been demonstrated in the course of Church history and the proof of such a sacred deposit would have been evinced by the Popes in uninterrupted succession to the present day. But the verdict of papal history decidedly manifests the utter falsity of papal infallibility simply because the Popes committed error, heresy, and lived the most foul and immoral lives imaginable! Roman Catholic apologists seeking to defend the fallacious doctrine of papal infallibility at all costs, would reject these observations on the premise that the Popes involved were not seated in the Chair of Saint Peter, nor did they speak ex cathedra. This is neither intellectually honest nor consistent with the facts at hand, but is anachronistic and refuted by the facts of history. These symbolic gestures are non sequitur to the larger implications of real infallibility. If the Pope indeed has *real* infallibility, why does he not effectively exercise it more often to do good and relieve humanity of the manifold evils in the world that desperately need perfect solutions? Why does he not arrive at a proper and accurate translation of the Holy Scriptures to dispel all doubt of its credibility and proper interpretation for the entire Church? To refrain from using this for the evangelization of the lost, for the common good, and most importantly for the sole exaltation of Jesus Christ because it does not serve the particular interests of the papacy, or further advance the specious doctrines of the Roman Catholic Institution, is self serving, criminal, and leaves the Pope morally liable for not using this spiritual endowment more effectively and extensively abroad. ***"Therefore to him that knows to do good, and does it not, to him it is sin"*** (James 4:17).

---

[29]   See *The Great Encyclical Letters of Pope Leo XII* (Rockford, IL: Tan Books, 1995).

In the clear area of morals, a good majority of the Popes down through history have habitually proven themselves anything but infallible Vicars of Christ in the most graphic and disgusting ways. Many of the Popes were guilty of the most vile sins of every kind: adultery, murder, lying, fornication, simony, drunkenness, homosexuality, pedophilia, extortion, heresy, deception, concubinage, thievery, mass bloodshed and a host of other evils to go with these! And in the ugly face of this horrible litany of vice and immorality, we are supposed to naively presuppose that such papal profligates possessed infallibility on morals in some measure or another! But God's moral law on this matter is inviolate: nothing morally pure can originate or emanate from something or someone that is by nature morally impure. For Holy Scripture decrees: ***"Who can bring a clean thing out of an unclean? No one!"*** (Job 14:4). The infamous accounts of papal depravity distinctly demonstrate moral *fallibility* through and through on the grounds of their heinous immorality. No church historian can easily forget the horrific account of how Pope Stephen VI insanely brought his dead predecessor Pope Formosus to trial in March of 896 A.D. at the *Synod of Horrenda*, which is also called *The Cadaver Synod*. Stephen had the dead body of Formosus exhumed, whom already been dead for eight months. The rotting and stinking corpse was ceremoniously placed on the papal throne dressed up in the elaborate vestments of the papacy with the mitre placed upon its decaying head. The ghastly sight, accompanied by the overwhelming stench of the body, shocked and revolted the council of Bishops and Cardinals Pope Stephen called forth to witness the mock trial.

Stephen angrily questioned the accused while a frightened young deacon of eighteen years of age stood by as Formosos' legal counsel. The young man wisely said nothing during the maniacal proceedings. When the lifeless corpse naturally did not give a response in his defense, Stephen pronounced him guilty and summarily removed the crown and papal garments from the rotting corpse of Formosus and cut his fingers off. His body was then dragged in the streets of Rome and later thrown into the Tiber River.[30] By this atrocious act, are we seriously expected to believe Pope Stephen VI possessed moral infallibility whenever speaking *ex cathedra*. Absolutely not! To assert otherwise in the inflexible and blind manner Rome and their apologists would surely do here is an insult to moral conscience, basic reason and intelligence; most importantly, however, it is also an egregious violation of the Judeo-Christian ethic laid down in Scripture. Pope Sergius III (904-911 A.D.) acquired the papacy by murder. This Pope was a notorious womanizer and was "the slave of every vice and the most wicked of men" committing "infinite abominations amongst light women."[31] His most infamous trysts were with the Jezebel- like women Morazia and her mother, Theodora, mentioned earlier in this book. Pope John X (914-928 A.D.) obtained the papacy by the conniving of Theodora. Roman Catholic historian Bishop Liuprand of Cremona states the reason why: "Theodora supported John's election in order to cover more easily her illicit relations with him."[32] Later, Marozia smothered him to death so that her newfound paramour Pope Leo VI (928-929 A.D.) could reign in John's place. She killed Leo VI less than a year later because he gave his vile affections to another woman more base than herself!

Both these scandalous women helped turn the papacy and the papal court into a brothel with a licentiousness and greed that goes beyond any decent description. The period Marozia and Theodora ruled and slept with various Popes, lasting for fifty-nine years from 904 to 963 A.D., has been called, "the rule of Harlots." Pope Sergius III was the father of twenty-year-old Pope John XI (931-935 A.D.) through his

---

[30] For a full account of the *Synod Horrenda* see E.R. Chamberlin, *The Bad Popes*, pages 19-21; *The Catholic Encyclopedia*, Volume IV, 141.

[31] Nigel Cawthorne, *Sex Lives of the Popes* (London: Prion, 2004), 65.

[32] Liudprand of Cremona, *Works: Antapodosis; de Rebus Gestis Ottonis; Relatio de Legationes Constantinopolitana*, trans by F.A. Wright, (London: 1930), chapter xlviii.

adulterous affair with Marozia. The worst and most corrupt of Marozia's debauched offspring was, no doubt, her grandson, who became Pope John XII in 955 A.D. He became involved in every type of vice and immorality imaginable. A Roman Synod that sought to depose John indicted him for acts of fornication, incest, simony, sacrilege, murder, adultery, theft, and perjury. His profligate lifestyle turned the Lateran Palace into a sordid brothel and school of prostitution filled with papal whores and paramours of his choosing. No married or unmarried woman was safe from this insatiable whoremonger. Bishop Liudprand, a contemporary of Pope John XII, scathingly notes: "No honest lady dared show herself in public, for Pope John had no respect either for single girls, married women, or widows—they were sure to be defiled by him, even on the tombs of the holy Apostles, Peter and Paul."[33] John was later smitten by paralysis while in the very act of adultery and died eight days later on May 14, 964. The avaricious Pope Benedict IX (1033-1045 A.D.) sold the papal office for fifteen hundred pounds plus the tribute from the church to England for life (after he already wantonly committed acts of murder and adultery) to his godfather, Robert Gratian who assumed the pontifical name Gregory VI. Benedict sought to be released from this 'holy office' so that he could be free to marry his cousin. So apparently, the office of the Pope with its gift and function of infallibility given by Christ, can be bought and paid for at a whim. Will the Roman Catholic apologists deem this an infallible transfer regardless of the simony involved?

By far the greatest of the Popes who committed murder was Pope Innocent III. He gave legal sanction for the Inquisition at the Fourth Lateran Council (convened in 1215 A.D.). It was during this period, great numbers of innocent people were murdered under such a reign of terror propagated by Innocent III under the Crusades and the Inquisition he supervised. The Waldensians, who were non-Catholic Bible-believing Christians, were put to the sword. He also decreed at this Council that Jews were to wear a distinguished badge for means of identification. Adolph Hitler (a Roman Catholic) and his Nazi Germany took their cue from this rank anti-Semite when he also required the Jews of Europe to wear the yellow Star of David to mark them out for abuse and mistreatment! The issue of being morally infallible, or being moral at all, for that matter, was of no concern to an egomaniac like Innocent III:

> Innocent was not really interested in moral law. He favoured gold and jewels. He had a special tiara made from white peacock feathers, covered in jewels and topped by a sapphire. He also insisted on having his feet kissed by one and all and aspired to be ruler of the world. In May 1204 he oversaw the sacking of Constantinople during the Fourth Crusade.[34]

Innocent met an end worthy of his abominable and wicked character. Seven months after the Fourth Lateran Council concluded on June 16, 1216, his nude corpse was found abandoned in the cathedral of Perugia and stripped of its costly vestments.[35] In 1252, Pope Innocent IV enjoined the secular powers of the State to arrest, convict, and crush heretics "like venomous snakes" in the papal Bull *Ad Extirpanda*. These two murderous Popes were anything but innocent! Pope Nicholas III (1270-1280 A.D.) grew extremely wealthy by the Inquisition, while hypocritically extolling the virtue of monastic poverty in the Bull *Exiit qui seminat*. Medieval Italian historian Gregorovius observes that Nicholas was "avid in amassing treasure, completely dedicated to worldly interests."[36] Pope Boniface VIII (1294-1303 A.D.) ranks high in the infamous exploits

---

[33]   Ibid., 471-476.

[34]   NigelCawthorne, *Sex Live of the Popes*, 99-100.

[35]   Hans Kung, *The Catholic Church: A Short History*, 100.

[36]   Quoted in *The Popes: Histories and Secrets*, 345.

of papal corruption. He freely engaged in simony, sorcery, sexual indulgence, homosexuality, treachery, idolatry, blasphemy, murder, and heresy. Steeped in sexual perversion, he was reputed to have publicly said: "Why it is no more a sin to enjoy oneself sexually with women and boys than rubbing one's hands together."[37] Of the resurrection of the dead, he mockingly commented: "A man has as much hope of survival after death as that roast fowl on the dining table there."[38]

The libertine Pope Clement VI (1342-1352 A.D), known for his indiscreet relations with women, called his numerous, illicit affairs, "Sessions of plenary indulgence." The poet laureate Petrarch (1304-1374 A.D.), a contemporary of Clement VI, anonymously described (for fear of being burned at the stake) the papal court of Clement VI as:

> The shame of mankind, a sink of vice, a sewer where is gathered all the filth of mankind. There God is held in contempt, money alone is worshipped and the laws of God and men are trampled underfoot. Everything there breathes a lie: the air, the earth, the houses and above all the bedrooms."[39]

Indeed, while the papal headquarters was located in Avignon, France from 1309-1377, Petrarch censured both Papacy and Roman Curia of "rape, adultery, and all manner of fornication." Pope Pius II (1458-1464) was a homosexual and allegedly died of a heart attack while being sodomized by one of his selected catamites.

The fifteenth century saw the papacy descend into *even greater* depths of moral perversity! Pope Alexander VI (1492-1503 A.D.) is renowned in ecclesiastical history for being one of the most morally corrupt of the Renaissance Popes. His vile escapades were recently made famous by the television series, *The Borgias* starring actor Jeremy Irons as Pope Alexander VI. As an Archbishop, he had four illegitimate children by one of his mistresses, Vannoza. When Alexander was fifty-eight years old he resorted to pedophilia when he took another mistress—fifteen-year-old Giulia Farnese. Both were mistresses of this impious fraud! As Pope, this vile monster openly lived in incest with two of his sisters and allegedly with his own daughter, Lucretia! He was notorious for having sexual orgies and drunken revelries within the walls of the Vatican. Pope Leo X (1513-1521 A.D.) became the epitome of papal extravagance, gluttony, and self indulgence no matter what the cost. He was fully given over to the hedonistic amusements and epicurean pleasures that would have made the wealthiest blush. Leo's dinners consisted of sixty-five courses. Naked girls served the papal court of his day at supper and nude little boys jumped out of rich puddings at dessert. Exotic dancing and entertainment was a lavish regularity in the papal court.

It was during the reign of Leo X that the young priest, Martin Luther, made an eventful pilgrimage to Rome. Secular historian, Will Durant recounts what happened to the great Reformer when approaching "the City of Seven Hills":

> As he caught the first glimpse of the seven-hilled city, he fell to the ground and said: "Holy Rome I salute thee." He had not spent much time there, however, until he saw that Rome was anything but a holy city. Iniquity existed among all classes of the clergy. Priests told indecent jokes and used awful profanity, even during Mass. No one can imagine what sins

---

[37] E.R. Chamberlin, *The Bad Popes*, 111.
[38] Ibid.
[39] Quoted in *Vicars of Christ: The Dark Side of the Papacy*, 85.

and infamous actions are committed in Rome. They must be seen and heard to be believed. Thus they are in the habit of saying, "If there is a hell, Rome is built over it.[40]

This factual description sounds more like a typical day in the cities of Sodom and Gomorrah rather than a city where the "holy Vicar of Christ" presumably dwells. Though history does record Popes who were relatively good, moral, and beneficent, these continual and frequent examples of papal immorality expose the fallacy of the Pope's moral infallibility. One cannot be infallibly moral in any sense if his conduct is habitually immoral; nor can an unclean thing produce something pure and morally clean. This is an utter impossibility (See Job 14:4; Matthew 7:16-20). A person's essential nature invariably defines and determines his conduct and character. *Thus, what you do by habit on the outside is, first, based on what you are on the inside.* Therefore, the Popes of Rome have unequivocally proven by their own conflicting decrees and iniquitous conduct that they do indeed constantly make mistakes and gravely err in matters pertaining to faith and morals. These are ineffaceable traits that irrefutably disprove papal infallibility. Even a small child could correctly deduce that the long train of moral transgressions and grotesque scandals of the papacy, with or without the said conditions for infallibility ratified by Vatican I, clearly militate against any type of papal infallibility. Again, this is not to deny there were several kind and humane Popes, as there were indeed; but in the words of William Cathcart we concur that:

> Of all the vain delusions ever darting through the disordered minds of lunatics, or the sober intellects of wise men, nothing quite equals the insane doctrine of papal infallibility... There have been good and kind men Popes of Rome; but there have been many of another sort; men whose company would be an insult to Judas, and whose infallibility in faith and morals is too ridiculous to discuss.[41]

A true representative of Jesus Christ will depart from any sort of immoral practice and exercise himself with self-control and sexual purity. *"Let everyone who names the name of Christ depart from iniquity"* (2 Timothy 2:19). *"For this is the will of God, your sanctification: that you should abstain from sexual immorality; that each of you should know how to possess his own vessel in sanctification and honor, not in passion of lust, like the Gentiles who do not know God...For God did not call us to uncleanness, but in holiness"* (1 Thessalonians 4:3-5, 7). A genuine follower of Jesus Christ will neither seek honor and glory for himself. *"Let us not become conceited, provoking one another, envying one another"* (Galatians 5:26). *"Let nothing be done in selfish ambition or conceit, but in lowliness of mind let each esteem others better than himself"* (Philippians 2:3). The true servant and minister of Jesus Christ will not be covetous for wealth and riches either (1 Timothy 3:3; 6:10-11). The majority of the Popes in history egregiously behaved otherwise, and could not have possibly been true representatives of Jesus Christ. Far from their lives resembling the holy and humble lives of Jesus and His Apostles, the moral turpitude of the Popes is more likened to the lives of pimps, whoremongers, drunkards, infidels, blasphemers, murderers, pedophiles, homosexuals, ruffians, thieves, rapists, adulterers, fornicators, and brutal dictators. What does the word of God promise to those who practice these things? *"For this you know, that no whoremonger, no unclean person, nor covetous man who is an idolater has any inheritance in the kingdom of Christ and of God. Let no man deceive you*

---

[40]   Will Durant, *The Story of Civilization: The Reformation, Volume Six* (New York: Simon & Schuster, 1965), 344.

[41]   William Cathcart, *The Papal System*, 341-342.

with vain words. For because of these things the wrath of God comes on the children of disobedience" (Ephesians 5:5-6; See also 1 Corinthians 6:9-10; Galatians 5:19-21; Revelation 21:8).

For Roman Catholic apologists to defend and affirm papal infallibility in the face of these apostate and abominable practices of certain pagan and unsaved Popes means that they are either intellectually dishonest, obstinate, or just plain deceived, perhaps all three. And that is all there is to that! The Apostle Peter never once claimed infallibility, but rather, pointed to the Holy Scriptures being the only source of inerrant and infallible counsel that brings eternal salvation (see 1 Peter 1:23-25; 2 Peter 1:19-21). Peter erred fallibly even after he met and followed Jesus Christ in the very areas of faith and morals. Never once did he conjure up an *ex cathedra* formula or proclamation to bolster an infallible claim. Peter was woefully wrong when he attempted to dissuade Jesus from going to the cross. Consequently, Jesus sternly rebuked him, saying: ***"Get behind Me Satan"*** (Matthew 16:22-23). This event immediately happened after the Petrine confession of verses sixteen and seventeen where Roman Catholic doctrine erroneously teaches that Jesus founded and built the Church on the infallible rock of Peter (see chapter two for the biblical refutation of this) and his successors, the Popes. Peter never displayed or exercised the kind of papal infallibility, as defined by Rome and the Vatican I Council. Peter committed a moral wrong when he cut off the ear of Malchus with a sword in the garden of Gethsemane. Jesus immediately upbraided Peter for this impetuous act (John 18:10).

Peter further failed miserably when he denied the Lord three times. Catholic theologians have quibbled with Protestants on these points because they claim these mistakes were committed while Christ was on Earth, *before* Peter became the Vicar of Christ until the Lord ascended to heaven so that Peter could take His place in His absence as the "Visible head of the Church". However, after Christ ascended to heaven, Peter still made mistakes. Morally, he thought God could only save Torah observant Jews. In Acts chapter ten, Peter is corrected by the Lord for this moral error. The Apostle thought, that according to Jewish tradition, the Gentiles were unclean by nature and therefore unworthy of God's salvation. God then gives Peter a heavenly vision showing this to be untrue. As a result of this supernatural revelation, Peter preaches salvation to the Gentile house of Cornelius resulting in the salvation of Gentiles in the same manner Jews were saved—a salvation that is by faith alone in the Lord Jesus Christ (Acts 10:1-48). Unlike the unscriptural heresy of Vatican I, Peter never mentions a belief in his infallibility as a prerequisite for salvation. This free gift of salvation is offered to whoever believes on the Lord Jesus Christ for the forgiveness of sins (Acts 10:43).

Indeed, one searches in vain throughout the canonical writings of the Apostle Peter in the Holy Scriptures to find it necessary to believe in the infallibility of 'Pope' Peter and his successors for salvation. This is because it is an invention of men and has absolutely nothing to do with the great plan of salvation revealed by God through the Gospel of Jesus Christ. Peter not only morally erred after Christ ascended into heaven, but also doctrinally strayed away from the faith and temporarily embraced false doctrine that undermined the Gospel! This necessitated a corrective rebuke from the Apostle Paul. Peter was vacillating from the truth of the Gospel: that salvation by faith was equally available to both Jews and Gentiles alike. This episode happened in the region of Galatia where the Judaizers were deceiving the churches. This pseudo Jewish Christian sect taught that salvation was a combination of faith plus the works of the Mosaic Law (circumcision and obedience to the moral injunctions and ceremonial demands of the Law). For a time, Peter freely fellowshipped among the converted Gentiles, until a delegation of Judaizers came to the region from Jerusalem. In order not to offend the Jewish delegation, Peter refrained from further fellowship with the Gentile Christians of Galatia, giving the impression that only Jews who subscribed to the Law of Moses were saved and worthy of fellowship.

This course of action, taken by what is supposed to be the infallible Pope of the Roman Catholic Church, jeopardized the very lifeblood of the Gospel—namely, that a man is not justified by the works of the Law but by *faith alone* in Jesus Christ (Galatians 2:16). Peter's dangerous diversion away from this paramount truth harmfully influenced other believing Jews, including Barnabus, to do the same. Paul therefore rightly charged Peter with hypocrisy in claiming one thing, but turning right around and doing the exact opposite (see Galatians 2:11-14). Peter failed in this incident to walk uprightly according to the truth of the Gospel (Galatians 2:14). If Peter was infallible, this severe correction by Paul was unnecessary, and worse yet—an act of infidelity, if as the Roman Catholic Church claims, Peter is the infallible teacher of faith and morals, like all the Popes that followed after him. Moreover, if Peter was infallible according to the definition of the Vatican Council I, Paul could not have justifiably corrected him in the area of Christian faith, since by virtue of his papal office, Peter could remain infallible even though Paul was defending the faith and disagreed with Peter over this most important doctrinal issue. If this were true under the theological rubric of papal infallibility, then Paul's rebuke (in accordance with what the Scriptures teach) would have been deemed *out of order*. Yet the Vatican would have us to believe so—if submission to papal infallibility, as they define it, is a necessary truth for salvation. Surely if Peter possessed the divine attribute of infallibility, he would have used it to solve the Galatian heresy which strikes at the very heart of the Christian faith.

The truth of the matter is Peter was not infallible, but was a flawed individual like all of us. Nevertheless, the Apostle was redeemed by Christ and mightily used of God, despite the obvious flaws he had. Papal infallibility rests upon an irreconcilable contradiction that cannot be harmonized with the Vatican I decree of 1870 and the conciliar decrees of the Councils of Constance (1414), Basle (1431), and Florence (1439). All three of these fifteenth century councils ratified the general consensus of the Roman Church: that the Roman Pontiff is subject to the actions and decisions enacted by a council at any given time *and all three of these councils unreservedly confirmed this important historical fact.*[42] All these Councils unreservedly declared that a council is to be superior to the Pope. During the fifth and sixth sessions of the Council of Constance, delegates unanimously issued a formal decree of faith stating:

> The Holy Synod of Constance… declares first that it is lawfully assembled in the Holy Spirit,
> that it constitutes a general council representing the Catholic Church, and that therefore,
> it has its authority immediately from Christ; and that all men of every rank and condition,
> ***including the Pope himself***, are bound to obey it in matters of faith, the ending of schism
> and the reformation of the Church of God in its head and members (Emphasis mine).

The chief abbreviator of the Council of Basle, Aeneas Silvio, who was to later become Pope Pius II, candidly wrote later: "Hardly anyone doubts that a council is above a Pope." The Council of Basle declared seventeen years after Constance that "even the Pope is bound to obey the Councils." To further reinforce a Church council's power above the Pope, the Council of Constance indicted and deposed three Popes for

---

[42]   For instance, Sessions five and six of the Council of Constance declared: "*that anyone of whatever condition, state or dignity, <u>even the Pope</u>, who contumaciously refuses to obey the past or future mandates, statutes, ordinances or precepts of this sacred council or of any other legitimately assembled general council, regarding the aforesaid things or matters pertaining to them, shall be subjected to well-deserved penance, unless he repents, and shall be duly punished, even by having recourse, if necessary, to other supports of the law.*" Sessions five and six are famously called the *Haec Sancta* and are commonly known for contradicting Vatican 1 on papal infallibility (Emphasis mine).

abusing and misusing the papal office with disorderly and immoral conduct. The Council elected another Pope (Martin V) in their place. After 1870, Vatican I changed all that, and in effect, stated the Pope was now above the Church and its councils—even if they should disagree with him on moral and theological issues. Present-day Roman Catholic Canon Law readjusted to this change and now dictates that a Pope must approve the decisions of a council for final ratification.[43]

The contradiction is clear and obvious here. If Popes were truly infallible from the time of Peter the Apostle to the present day, what about the Popes who submitted to Church Councils (as opposed to *ruling* them) before1870? In doing so, they were not aware of being infallible—over and above councils—according to the definition of Vatican I, or else they would have wielded their superior power over them; and since this was the case, they were fallible Popes, thus negating the decree of infallibility, reducing it to an unworkable paradox at best. A further contradiction is seen in the fact that if a Pope is infallible by virtue of his office and is above Church Councils, why then did Pope Pius IX solely rely on the ratification of the Vatican I Council for his infallibility, especially if the infallibility of the Pope does not depend on the electoral consent of the church or its councils, as it was stipulated by Vatican I.[44] Since the absolutism of Papal Infallibility was dependent on the majority vote of the Vatican I Council, its existence could not be antecedent to that Council.

This historical and logical fact destroys the whole premise of papal infallibility paradoxically proposed by the Vatican I Council, essentially claiming that papal infallibility can be inferred to overrule the consent of an ecclesiastical body when it actually required the very concession and confirmation of a church council in 1870 to authorize it. And here is where the paradox begins and ends. **Papal Infallibility is nothing more than a *reductio ad absurdum*—a self-contained argument trapped within an inexorable contradiction.** Indeed, there are only two infallible sources that Christians are exhorted to refer to for doctrinal instruction and moral guidance; and most certainly not the Popes of Rome! No, they are rather, God and His inerrant Word.[45] In the Scriptures, God has perfectly revealed His infallible Word to men. Nowhere in its sacred and flawless pages do we ever find a teaching that espouses a Pope having limited, or for that matter, unlimited infallibility that Bible believing Christians must unconditionally submit to.

The defenders of Rome systematically resort to obscurantism over when and when not the Popes are infallible to evade the obvious fact they have fallibly erred in the past over the very areas of faith and morals. One way they accommodate this is by creating the artificial distinction between "official" and "unofficial" statements. Naturally, those statements made by past Popes that contain error on some doctrine or moral instruction are automatically deemed "unofficial", and those that agree best with the doctrine of papal infallibility are deemed "official" statements. Another common tactic defenders of Rome use is to deliberately regulate the definition of papal infallibility to the vague and nebulous realm in order to avoid any real culpability for the Popes when they do in fact commit a fallible act. In so doing, they commit the

---

[43]   **Canon 338** states: It is the prerogative of the Roman Pontiff alone to summon an Ecumenical Council, to preside over it personally or through others, to transfer, suspend or dissolve the Council, and to approve its decrees. It is also the prerogative of the Roman Pontiff to determine the matters to be dealt with in the Council, and to establish the order to be observed. The Fathers of the Council may add other matters to those proposed by the Roman Pontiff, but these must be approved by the Roman Pontiff. *The Code of Canon Law*, page 58.

[44]   *Dogmatic Canons and Decrees*, 256.

[45]   By inerrant or biblical inerrancy this means "that when all facts are known, the Scriptures in their original autographs and properly interpreted will be shown to be wholly true in everything that they affirm whether that has to do with doctrine or morality or with the social, physical, or life sciences" (From Norman Geisler, ed., *Inerrancy* (Grand Rapids: Zondervan, 1980), 294.

logical fallacy of ambiguity. A double standard is seen here when Rome's apologists dogmatically claim that papal infallibility has only been "officially" exercised twice, and yet they still appeal to this very same doctrine on other issues favorable to their cause, while they are quick to deny it in other instances that would undermine it. The inconsistency and hypocrisy with such a self-serving, dishonest apologetic is glaring. The objective of using such a double standard here is obvious in the words of evangelical apologist Jason Engwer:

> Nobody knows just when the Pope supposedly is speaking infallibly and when he isn't, and he's to be obeyed even when he isn't speaking infallibly. This reasoning allows the Roman Catholic Church to derive all of the *benefits* of claiming infallibility, such as having hundreds of millions of people obey it, while avoiding the responsibilities of claiming infallibility. Even the Catholic apologists who claim that papal infallibility has only been used twice often cite papal infallibility on other issues. They're inconsistent. To avoid the implications of papal errors such as Liberius's support of Arianism and Honorius' support of Monotheletism, Catholics will argue that papal infallibility is defined so narrowly that those papal errors aren't part of that definition. However, when Catholics are discussing the canon of scripture, for example, they'll claim that a Pope such as Damasus or Innocent infallibly declared what the cannon of scripture is. Or when discussing an issue such as the deity of Christ or the Trinity, they'll claim that Popes *infallibly* settled those matters.[46]

But the irrefutable examples given in the pages above, culled from the many scandalous events in Papal history, have been further conveniently dismissed by Roman Catholic apologists who explain them away by creating a false dichotomy between infallibility and impeccability. The thinking goes that a Pope's moral condition (whether moral or immoral) is separate from the office of infallibility and therefore is irrelevant one to another. The former does not guarantee the latter, so infallibility can remain while the vilest and most immoral Popes occupies the Holy See of Rome. The Scriptures and the teaching of the early church fathers clearly believed that no such artificial separation existed. Both generally held that a person's doctrine influenced their moral conduct. So, right doctrine generally produced right conduct, and false doctrine produced immoral conduct (See the Epistle of Jude and the Second Epistle of Peter for this particular theme).

The moral qualifications to be a bishop in the Church enumerated in the New Testament would clearly forbid a considerable number of past Popes from holding that office without giving due regard for the fine distinction between the terms "infallible" and "impeccable", which Roman Catholic apologists typically use to ridiculously explain away how an infallible pope can be immoral while still holding the office of "Universal Bishop." First Timothy 3:1-7 and Titus 1:7-9 denies the Roman Catholic concept that a bishop of Rome can be a murderer, rapist, fornicator, heretic, drunkard, greedy and so forth, yet still be a legitimate bishop. Popes who were guilty of these offenses in the past should have been immediately removed from office, barred from any bishopric, and denied the claim of infallibility in the process!

Since Catholic apologists cannot rationally reconcile these passages of Scripture with the Roman Catholic dogma of papal infallibility, they either ignore them or simply claim they have a different interpretation without further explanation. The false separation between infallibility and impeccability is just another clever and elusive way to escape the obvious fact that the notion of papal infallibility is made incoherent by the death of a thousand qualifications through constant equivocation. Therefore, whenever a Pope commits an

---

[46]   Jason Engwer, "The Fallibility of Infallibility" at http://www.inplainsite.org/html/fallibility_papal_infallibilit.html

error in the past or future, whether by an immoral act, or holding to wrong doctrine, the dishonest defender of popery will manage to object, and then go on to explain that "extenuating circumstances" disallow the application of the standard, so the Pope was not really acting or speaking "officially," or was not speaking in conjunction with the bishops, or some other qualification".[47] The truth of the matter is that the whole idea of the infallibility of the Pope cannot be epistemologically verified or empirically justified, because, when logically reduced in the end, one demonstrable error by the Pope alone demolishes this absurd claim; it is a circular argument Rome has speciously fashioned.

So in this circular spin, the Roman Catholic typically responds in the face of the previous objections, that the Pope is still infallible because the Pope says so by virtue of his infallible office, and the 'Church' following his lead, has decreed it to be so, while citing fallacious misreading of Scripture passages to serve as proof texts, notwithstanding. The error and danger of Papal infallibility is that it simply makes members of the Roman Catholic Institution beholden to the word of a Pope instead of the Word of God. It rests upon human authority and man-made religious tradition that supplants the supreme authority of God and His Word. The only two times papal infallibility was officially exercised occurred in 1854 by Pope Pius IX with the Immaculate Conception decree of Mary, and in 1950 by Pope Pius XII with the decree on the Assumption of Mary.

Even in these two instances there are numerous theological errors that blatantly contradict the Word of God. For example, in the Immaculate Conception decree, Pope Pius IX referred to Mary as the one who has crushed the head of Satan—based on a gross mistranslation of Genesis 3:15 in the Latin Vulgate—the standard Bible of the Roman Catholic Church for centuries![48] The person who will crush the head of Satan

---

[47] Eric Svendsen, *Evangelical Answers* (Lindenhurst, New York: 1999), 34. Svendsen goes on to conclude in his cogent dismantling of infallibility that to spill much ink on such an endeavor will not convince the obstinate defender of Rome. "It is simply a no-win situation. It is abundantly clear by reading the Catholic apologists that they will not accept any evidence that overturns papal infallibility. No matter how badly a pope has erred—morally, doctrinally, or otherwise—no charge against papal infallibility will ever stick. It would save us a lot of time if Catholic apologists will simply admit this. In reality, this is nothing short of historical gymnastics and wishful reconstructions at best—and blatant dishonesty at worst. There were no distinctions between "official" and "unofficial" statements made by popes of antiquity—they simply meant what they said and said what they meant. It is only the desire somehow to vindicate papal infallibility that the modern Catholic apologist has introduced the terms "official" and "unofficial" (page 35). I could not agree more; and so this book is primarily written with sincere Catholics in mind who are seeking truth from God's Word and freedom from the bondage of religious man-made tradition!

[48] The text reads: *"I will put enmities between thee and the woman, and thy seed and her seed: she shall crush thy head, and thou shalt lie in wait for her heel."* The correct translation from the accepted Hebrew text should read: *"And I will put enmity between you and the woman, and between your seed and her seed. He shall crush your head, and you shall bruise his heel."* Pius IX's decree, formally entitled *Ineffabilis Deus*, states in paragraphs thirteen and fourteen the following: "The Fathers and writers of the Church, well versed in the heavenly Scriptures, had nothing more at heart than to vie with one another in preaching and teaching in many wonderful ways the Virgin's supreme sanctity, dignity, and immunity from all stain of sin, and her renowned victory over the most foul enemy of the human race. This they did in the books they wrote to explain the Scriptures, to vindicate the dogmas, and to instruct the faithful. *These ecclesiastical writers in quoting the words by which at the beginning of the world God announced his merciful remedies prepared for the regeneration of mankind -- words by which he crushed the audacity of the deceitful serpent and wondrously raised up the hope of our race, saying, "I will put enmities between you and the woman, between your seed and her seed"[13] -- taught that by this divine prophecy the merciful Redeemer of mankind, Jesus Christ, the only begotten Son of God, was clearly foretold:*

in this verse is actually masculine in gender, not feminine, and points directly to the Messiah, not to His mother! But Roman Catholics must adhere to this doctrine under pain of Rome's anathema since it is an infallible decree of the Pope and therefore binding on all Roman Catholics to believe for salvation! To believe otherwise is to call down the damnation of God.[49] Thus, the Pope allegedly made an infallible decree based on an error in translation, thereby proving at once his decree to be utterly fallible. The argument for necessity that an infallible Pope is needed to guarantee the safety of the Church from irreparably falling into error will be examined and refuted later in this book when dealing with the corporate idea of the Magisterium.

The Lord never once told his followers to inquire after Pope Peter's infallible pronouncements, but instead admonished them to study the Scriptures that reveal the infallible God in the impeccable Person of Jesus Christ. It is with the Lord Jesus Christ preeminently in mind that we are commended to diligently *"search the Scriptures"* to learn and understand how to receive eternal life through belief in Him by the infallible testimony of Sacred Writ (See John 5:39). After His resurrection from the dead, Jesus systematically taught the disciples from the Scriptures all the prophesied events concerning Him (Luke 24:44-46). The only infallible humans to ever exist, apart from the Lord Jesus Christ, were the divinely inspired authors of the sixty-six books of the Bible. This infallibility extended from God Almighty to the human writers of Scripture *only when they wrote those Scriptures* so as to prevent them from committing any type of error when composing the Word of God—Who is the supreme impeccable Author of Scripture.

God superintended the human authors to miraculously write the Scriptures in such a way so as to prevent them from committing any error in the process of writing while under the inspiration of God the Holy Spirit (See 2 Peter 1:21). Once the Canon of Scripture was completed with the book of Revelation, this supernatural and miraculous endowment of infallibility to write divine Scripture ceased and now resides only within the Triune Godhead, and no other person. For, the Lord alone is infallible. *"As for God, **His way is perfect;** The Word of the Lord is proven; He is shield to all to all who trust in Him"* (2 Samuel 22:31). The New Testament records that there were "many infallible proofs" presented for the risen Messiah (Acts 1:3). The Holy Scriptures are all sufficient in themselves to instruct the Christian completely in the areas of Christian faith and morals equipping Him fully to accomplish the task at hand (2 Timothy 3:16-17).

Furthermore, if we are lacking in theological wisdom and moral instruction, we are not exhorted to look or seek papal Rome for the answers, but Scripture instructs us that we are to confidently ask our heavenly Father for wisdom with the prayer of faith. *"If you any lacks wisdom, let him ask God, who gives to all liberally and without reproach, and it will be given to him. But let him ask in faith, with no doubting, for he who doubts is like a wave of the sea driven and tossed by the wind"* (James 1:5-6). The Lord Jesus

---

That his most Blessed Mother, the Virgin Mary, was prophetically indicated; and, at the same time, the very enmity of both against the evil one was significantly expressed. Hence, just as Christ, the Mediator between God and man, assumed human nature, blotted the handwriting of the decree that stood against us, and fastened it triumphantly to the cross, so the most holy Virgin, united with him by a most intimate and indissoluble bond, was, with him and through him, eternally at enmity with the evil serpent, and most completely triumphed over him, and thus crushed his head with her immaculate foot"[14] (Emphasis mine).

49 The papal decree concludes by declaring: "Therefore, if some should presume to think in their hearts otherwise than we have defined (which God forbid), they shall know and thoroughly understand that they are by their own judgment condemned, have made shipwreck concerning the Faith, and fallen away from the unity of the Church; and, moreover, that they by this very act subject themselves to the penalties ordained by law, if by word, or writing, or any other external means, they dare to signify what they think in their hearts" (*Dogmatic Canons and Decrees*, page 184).

Christ and the Apostles appealed to the Scriptures alone as the infallibly supreme and all sufficient guide to knowing God and the way of salvation (Luke 24:27; 44-46; 2 Timothy 3:15; 2 Peter 2:2). Never once in the New Testament is the 'infallibility' of Peter invoked or looked to as the ultimate source of authority by Jesus or His disciples. The only reliable source giving infallible guidance, counsel, historical and scientific information is the Bible. Though the Bible is not a scientific or historical textbook, *per se*, it nevertheless, contains factual data that is in harmony with both science and history when correctly interpreted. The Old and New Testament Scriptures verify their own infallibility. We must urgently look to them instead of the contradictions and heresies put forth by the Popes of Rome blasphemously claiming to be infallible.

The Word of God is perfect—error free, and absolutely truthful in content. It alone has the transforming power to save and convert. *"As for God, His way is <u>perfect</u>: the Word of the Lord is tried: He is a buckler to all those that trust Him"* (Psalm 18:30). The Word of God alone has the transforming power to save and convert the lost sinner making him wise in the ways of God. *"The Law of the Lord is perfect, converting the soul. The testimony of the Lord is sure making wise the simple"* (Psalm 19:7). The Word of God is perfectly capable of steering and guiding the obedient with divine certainty and enlightenment during the dark and unsure periods of this life. *"Thy Word is lamp unto my feet, and a light unto my path"* (Psalm 119:105). The Word of God is free of any blemish or error. When honestly scrutinized, the Scriptures are found to be inherently pure from any sort of imperfection now and forever. *"The words of the Lord are pure words, like silver tried in a furnace of earth, purified seven times. You shall keep them, O Lord, you shall preserve them from this generation forever"* (Psalm 12:6-7). The Word of God is sufficient in itself to teach us how to mature and grow spiritually (Hebrews 5:12-14; 1 Peter 2:2). The Holy Scriptures wonderfully provide complete and reliable information on the redemption of God revealed fully through Jesus Christ. The divine revelation recorded in Scripture is given so that people may believe Jesus is the Son of God, and the Savior of the world—one receives eternal life exclusively by believing in Him (John 20:31).

The Holy Scriptures are the authoritative norm of the Christian faith. All genuine Christian doctrine and morality emanate from it; it is the warp and woof of Christianity giving it a complete picture and full explanation. The Bible alone serves as the divine plumb line by which all other beliefs, doctrines, and traditions are measured. The Word of God is the objective criterion of truth allowing the born-again believer to determine with certainty what is right or wrong, true or false, Christian or non-Christian. We do not sit in judgment upon the Bible, but let the Bible sit in judgment upon us regardless of rank and file. Popes priests, laymen, and the ordinary person are equally alike to be judged by the Word of God. If they teach, or do contrary to it, they are to be rejected. The Popes and all the church councils are not above the teaching authority of the Bible but rather are subordinate to the scrutiny of Scripture by which the believer is informed. When humbly received with faith, the Scriptures are able to save the sinner and are an active agent in the salvation of the human soul (James 1:18, 21).

The Scriptures adequately provide spiritual comfort and instill within the heart and mind of the saved sinner the assurance and sure hope of salvation. *"For whatever things were written before were written for our learning, that we through the patience and comfort of the Scriptures might have hope"* (Romans 15:4). The Word of God only is able to make a person *"wise to salvation through faith in Jesus Christ"* (2 Timothy 3:15). This saving faith comes by hearing the Word of God (Romans 10:17). The revelation of Jesus Christ is solely disclosed through the enlightening words of Holy Writ (John 5:39; Acts 28:23; 1 Corinthians 15:1-8). The Catholic's ultimate confidence should not be placed in a Pope's fictional infallibility, or any other mortal man in particular. *"Give us help from trouble, for the help of man is vain"* (Psalm 60:11). *"Do not trust in princes, in mortal man, in whom there is no salvation"* (Psalm 146:3). For, *"Cursed is the one who trusts in man...but blessed is the man who trusts in the Lord"* (Jeremiah 17:5-7). The Catholic should rather turn away from the vain wrangling and contradictory statements of the papacy and look to the unchangeable Rock of Ages and His inerrant Word of truth—The Bible alone, for doctrine moral instruction, edification, and knowledge of the divine. Lastly, if defenders of Roman Catholicism still insist that to omit papal infallibility is to remove the "Visible Head of the Church" and his necessity to function in this indispensable office, the Bible believer can rightfully reply with the poignant words of Jesus: *"You do err, not knowing the Scriptures, nor the power of God"* (Matthew 22:29).

The New Testament only knows and declares that there is One Head of the Church, while Romanists would have us believe in two heads—the Pope being the visible head and Christ its invisible head. But Scripture knows of no such two-headed monstrosity! Jesus Christ is the only One referred to in the New Testament as the Head of the Church and rules her with divine omnipotence and guides, instructs, and moves within her through the indwelling presence of the Holy Spirit that lives in each member (See Matthew 28:18-20; 1 Corinthians 12:12-31; Ephesians 1:22-23; 5:23-31; Colossians 1:18; 2:10). Christ alone (*Sola Christi*) is the Head of the Church and does not need the 'infallible' assistance of frail mortal, fallible man. True biblical faith recognizes this spiritual reality and does not defer to a carnal and inferior substitute claiming to be the "visible head of the whole church" (see the *Catechism of the Catholic Church*, paragraphs **669**, **882, 936**) for the wandering eye to see masquerading around in the dazzling white costume of a Pope. For *"we look not at the things which are seen, but at the things which are not seen. For the things which are seen are temporary, but the things which are not seen are eternal"* (2 Corinthians 4:18). Indeed, it has been sufficiently shown that Scripture, history, and the conflicting decrees and erroneous teachings of the Popes themselves legitimately disqualify and invalidate the doctrine of papal infallibility. But this infallibility does not end with the papacy. Roman Catholic dogma teaches that it also extends to all the bishops in union with the Pope to collectively comprise the Magisterium of the Roman Catholic Church. In the following chapter, we will extend our critical analysis of papal infallibility further to include this important element.

CHAPTER 8

THE POPE AND THE MAGISTERIUM

Roman Catholics are not only taught that the Pope holds the supreme authority as the visible infallible head of Christ's Church, and in that capacity they are to render complete submission to him, but that the bishops also collectively share the same authority under him. The Pope, and the bishops in union with him, comprises the teaching authority of the Roman Catholic Church called the *Magisterium*. The word Magisterium comes from the Latin word for "teacher" or "master." The teaching authority of the Roman Catholic Church fully resides in the Magisterium. The *Catechism of the Catholic Church* defines the Magisterium in the following terms:

> The task of giving an authentic interpretation of the Word of God, whether in its written form or in the form of Tradition, has been entrusted to the living, teaching office of the Church alone. Its authority in this matter is exercised in the name of Jesus Christ. This means that the task of interpretation has been entrusted to the bishops in communion with the successor Peter, the Bishop of Rome.[1]

The Magisterium is the supreme authoritative teacher of the Church, and by that presumed right, is the only legitimate interpreter of Holy Scripture on Earth for the faithful to believe and follow. The task of interpreting Scripture has thus been *solely* entrusted to the Magisterium made up of the Pope and the bishops of Rome in communion with him. The Documents of Vatican II teach: "The task of authentically interpreting the word of God, whether written or handed on, has been *entrusted exclusively* to the living teaching office the Church ..."[2] The Magisterium alone performs the supreme role of being the authoritative teacher of the Church on doctrinal matters of the faith. And so faithful Catholics must unreservedly believe what this group declares the Scriptures to mean. They are also forbidden to interpret it for themselves apart from or outside the teaching authority of the Magisterium. This would also mean that there is no room for disagreement or dissent from concerned Roman Catholics if that teaching authority were to teach or proclaim a particular doctrine, tradition, or dogma that was contrary to the Scriptures, which, it has repeatedly done in the past! The Second Vatican Council denies this very thing has happened, dismissing it to be "purely imaginary" through the use of circular reasoning—based on the assumption that the Holy Spirit *directs the Pope in*

---

[1] *Catechism of Catholic Church*, 32 [**85**].
[2] Walter Abbott, *The Documents of Vatican II*, 117-118.

every instance—yet without demonstrating this from the historical evidence which has proven otherwise (see Walter Abbott, *The Documents of Vatican II*, page 49, footnote 125). Furthermore, if the claims of the Roman Catholic Magisterium were true, both Catholics and non-Catholics alike would then be prohibited from interpreting the Bible correctly on their own. In order to know and understand the Scriptures, Catholics must look without question to the Magisterium alone for ultimate guidance and interpretation. The official teaching of Vatican II mandates that the Catholic's submission to the Pope and bishops in this manner is to be the same quality of unconditional obedience any Christian would show toward the Lord Jesus Christ.[3]

The Magisterium, like the Pope, is also infused with the gift of infallibility concerning faith and morals; and when speaking together with one voice under the care and headship of the Pope, they act in the exclusive role of the infallible teacher of the Church. Vatican II defines it in this way:

> The infallibility promised to the Church resides also in the body of bishops when that body exercises supreme teaching authority with the successor of Peter. To the resultant definitions the assent of the Church can never be wanting, on account of the activity of that same Holy Spirit, whereby the whole flock of Christ is preserved and progresses in unity of faith. But when either the Roman Pontiff or the body of bishops together with him defines a judgment, they pronounce it in accord with revelation itself. All are obliged to maintain and be ruled by this revelation, which, as written or preserved by tradition, is transmitted in its entirety through the legitimate succession of bishops and especially through the care of the Roman Pontiff himself.[4]

The Roman Catholic concept of spiritual authority, as defined by the concept of a Magisterium, is simply without proper biblical warrant. There is no explicit mention of this kind of ecclesiastical infallibility found anywhere in the New Testament. The Holy Scriptures in no way lends credence or support to this authoritarian structure of a Pope and group of bishops wielding a unilateral rule over the Church in the New Testament; nor was there ever a select ecclesiastical body of men arbitrarily interpreting the Scriptures for the local congregations that were established by the Apostles and their disciples during the first century. We do not find the Apostles in the book of Acts demanding their converts to unconditionally submit their minds and understanding to "the living teaching authority of the Church." Once again, Rome greatly errs here on the matter of what comprises the spiritual authority in the life of the Bible believing Christian. The Bible teaches that the supreme authority for Christian doctrine and faith was not Peter, or the other Apostles, but the Holy Scriptures. The Bible does not admonish believers in Christ to uncritically submit their understanding to any so called Magisterium in order to understand what Scripture means for the Christian.

The Apostle Paul, who never admitted to a conferred infallibility he supposedly shared with Pope Peter and other apostolic members of a Magisterium, exhorts Christians to individually examine all things taught and hold fast to what is good (1 Thessalonians 5:21). It is, therefore, the responsibility of every Christian to critically analyze what the leaders and teachers in the Church are teaching. The Apostle John commands every Christian to "test" the spirit of every person claiming to be teachers of God (1 John 4:1-3). Scripture alone is the infallible rule of faith. The lay people of Berea were commended for testing the Apostle Paul's authority and teaching by examining and comparing it with the Scriptures (Acts 17:11). The New Testament believer has the responsibility of testing the teaching of any person claiming to be an Apostle, pastor, or

---

3   Ibid,. 40.
4   Ibid., 49.

teacher in the Church with the Word of God. It is the believer's God given right and responsibility to interpret Scripture, as he or she is aided by the Holy Spirit, who alone reveals the meaning of the spiritual truths of Scripture to the mind and heart of the believer (see 1 Corinthians 2:12-16). We read in Second Corinthians 4: 2 that Paul purposely appealed to each person's conscience to decide for themselves if what he was preaching to them was true. The Apostle humbly exclaims: *"But we have renounced the hidden things of shame, not walking in craftiness nor handling the word of God deceitfully, but by manifestation of the truth commending ourselves to every man's conscience in the sight of God."*

The Bible teaches that the supreme standard to be used by which teachers within or outside the Church are to be tested and examined is the Word of God. *"To the Law and testimony! If they do not speak according to this Word, it is because there is no light in them"* (Isaiah 8:20). Concerning this crucial truth from the passage in Isaiah, *The New Treasury of Scripture Knowledge* comments:

> Here we learn the absolute importance of basing every doctrine, every belief, on the written word of God. No error is more fundamental, nor more disastrous, than depending upon some external source of authority, whether extra-biblical writings, or an organization claiming to dispense God's truth. The only source of authority is the written Word of God.[5]

The meaning is plain here: the Word of God is the absolute and supreme standard to be used and compared when testing the doctrines of religious organizations like the Roman Catholic Magisterium, or the claims of the Papacy. When this is done with reason, intelligence, and insight from Scripture illumined by the Holy Spirit, it is obvious that what Rome teaches in many areas runs totally contrary to the infallible teachings of the Holy Scriptures. This is because the Roman Catholic Church habitually deemphasizes the centrality of the Word of God having the preeminence in teaching and formulating Christian doctrine and practice. The Apostles of Christ, themselves, submitted their authority and teaching to the greater authority of Scripture. Peter affirmed the authenticity of the prophetic Scripture to be more certain and authoritative than his own eyewitness account of Christ's transfiguration (2 Peter 1:15-19). In 2 Peter 1:19, the Apostle is saying, "The Holy Scriptures are more certain than experience. He is saying, "If you don't believe me, go to the scriptures."[6] The Apostles who were present at the Jerusalem Council based their decision not on their own apostolic position or authority in the Church, but on the supreme authority of Scripture alone (Acts 15:15-19).

The Apostle Paul instructed the Galatian Christians that if any Apostle or angel from heaven should teach or preach contrary to the Gospel they would fall under God's anathema. *"But even if we, or an angel from heaven, preach any other gospel to you than what we have preached to you, let him be accursed. As we have said before, so now I say again, if anyone preaches any other gospel to you than what you have received, let him be accursed"* (Galatians 1:8-9). The salient point here is that no appeal to apostolic authority, or a collective infallibility of bishops, is placed above Scripture, rather it is Scripture itself, having the superlative role, which determines the authenticity of the message or messenger, regardless of office or rank held in the Church. Therefore, it is the transcendent teaching of Scripture that stands above the leaders and members of the Church as the final arbiter for right or wrong.

The apologists of Rome further argue from the concept of moral necessity that the Church needs such an infallible interpreter to preserve and safeguard it from falling into error. This is the primary function of

---

[5]   Jerome H.Smith, ed., *The New Treasury of Scripture Knowledge* (Nashville: Thomas Nelson, 1992), 753.

[6]   Michael Green, *2 Peter and Jude* (Grand Rapids: Eerdmans, 1989), 98.

the Roman Catholic Magisterium. Roman Catholic apologist, John Salza argues for such a necessity when writing:

> Infallibility means the Holy Spirit prevents the Church from teaching error on matters relevant to our salvation. Thus, whenever the successor of Peter, either in his capacity as the chief shepherd of the Church (*ex cathedra* teaching) or together with the bishops throughout the world united to him in a gathering called a council (conciliar teaching), definitively teaches a matter on faith and morals to be believed by the universal Church, the teaching is free from error. God protects His Church from going "of the rails."[7]

Amazingly, Salza goes on to say in the next paragraph that "the Church, not Scripture, is the final arbiter on matters of the Christian faith" with the official seal and approval of the Roman Catholic Church (both the *Nihil Obstat* and *Imprimatur* are given for this book). He assumes this based on the authority Christ gives the Church for matters of discipline in Matthew 18:17-18. Had he read the passage in question more closely, and in its correct context, he would have seen quite the opposite. The Church is acting under the infallible instructions of its head Jesus Christ. The instructions Jesus gave to the Apostles here found their way into Scripture for the Church to follow and submit to. Thus, the New Testament Church is to follow and submit to these biblical guidelines for discipline and restoration in the church. Pastors and leaders of the Church are forbidden to act on their own authority, but are to conform to those very stipulations Christ gave in Matthew 18:15-20, which are now a part of the authoritative Scriptures and the New Testament Canon. If Salza's interpretation were correct—that the Church is the final arbiter above and beyond the Word of God—then he would still be basing that teaching on Scripture first because he appeals to Matthew 18:17-18 for this claim, and would therefore contradict his own premise. Scripture is still the final arbiter and authority here on Earth for the Church to follow when "binding and loosing". Scripture is not subservient to the Church, but the Church is subservient to the Scripture.

The necessity for the infallibility of the Pope and bishops together is not an essential ingredient to protect the true Church from error. The universal presence and power of the Lord Jesus Christ dwelling within the Church protects her from permanently falling into irrecoverable error. When giving the Great Commission to the Church, Christ promised the protection of His presence to every believer in the Church throughout the duration of the present age, ***"All authority has been given to Me in heaven and on earth. Go therefore and make disciples of all the nations, baptizing them in the Name of the Father and of the Son and of the Holy Spirit, teaching them to observe all things I have commanded you; and lo, I am with you always, even to the end of this age"*** (Matthew 28:18-20). In this promise, Christ affirms the ongoing *indestructibility* of the Church down through the ages; He does not guarantee that it would remain infallible in a closed institutional organization like the Roman Catholic Church. The Holy Spirit's role in the formation of the Church is composed of those spiritually regenerated by repentance and faith in the Lord Jesus Christ. The Spirit of God regenerates and resides in the hearts of all Christians, and moves freely like the wind wherever He chooses, responding to all who believe the Gospel, regardless of their denomination. He is not primarily contained in the religious system of Roman Catholicism. It is the sovereign Lord who teaches us in the way of His truth and thus keeps us walking in it so that we may not fall into error. ***"Teach me Your way, O Lord; and I will walk in Your truth. Give me an undivided heart to fear Your Name"*** (Psalm 86:11). Jesus prayed

---

[7] John Salza, *The Biblical Basis for the Catholic Faith* (Huntington, IN: Our Sunday Visitor, 2005), 61.

to the Father, ***"Sanctify them through Your truth: Your Word is truth"*** (John 17:17). The Holy Spirit through the written Word of God, not the Popes, bishops, or a Magisterium, is the authoritative and infallible teacher of the Church. Christ Jesus sent Him to indwell, teach, and lead the believer into the truth about God found in Scripture whom the Holy Spirit authored and inspired as the "Spirit of truth" (John 14:16-21, 26; 16:13-15). The Holy Spirit anoints and appoints teachers and elders in the Church to equip, edify, and empower believers in Christ to know the truth, function in ministry, and protect oneself from error (1 Corinthians 12:28; Ephesians 4: 11-12). These teachers are to teach only what God's Word contains and are not to go beyond what is written therein (2 Corinthians 4:6). Submission to leadership in the Church is conditioned and based on the fact they are abiding in God's Word and following Christ (1 Corinthians 11:1; Philippians 3:17; 2 Thessalonians 2:4-13; 2 Timothy 1:13).

The Christian faith is squarely based upon the written documents of the Bible originally written for and delivered into the hands of common and ordinary Christians to be studied, interpreted, obeyed, and passed down to future generations of believers (2 Timothy 2:2). It was not given to a select hierarchy in the Church to be kept in reserve out of the reach of the common man as Rome customarily did all throughout its dominance in the Middle Ages. God has entrusted the Christian faith to all the "saints" to receive and promulgate (Jude 3). It is every Christian's right and privilege to read, comment, and expound on the Scriptures. But this right does not guarantee that every person's own interpretation will be always correct. In many of the books of the New Testament, the Holy Spirit addresses all believers as "saints" (Romans 1:7; 1 Corinthians 1:2; 2 Corinthians 2:1; Galatians 1:3; Philippians 1:1; Colossians 1:1); no hierarchical distinction is made or preference given to a Pope, bishop, or Magisterium! The testimony of the New Testament does not teach that the leaders of the Church, whether Apostles, bishops, elders, or teachers are supernaturally endowed with infallibility to safeguard the Church from error. Nor does it ever suggest they were immune from error or committing a moral mistake. The Apostle Peter proved fallible when he was carried away with the heresy at Galatia and Paul had to remonstrate him for it (Galatians 2:11-15). Paul also warned the chief leaders of the Church at Ephesus that savage wolves would come in "among you" to harm the flock (Acts 20:29).

Indeed, throughout the New Testament, we are warned that false teachers, false prophets, and bogus Apostles would emerge from the leadership of the Church, especially in the "last days" to lead the child of God astray (2 Corinthians 11:13-15; 1 Timothy 4:1-3; 2 Timothy 3:1-13 2 Peter 21-3; 1 John 2:18-19; 3 John 9-10; Jude 3-13). *It is by abiding in the Word of Christ that the Church is kept safe and free from false teaching and deception, not by blindly trusting in an ecclesiastical hierarchy to interpret for us what the Scriptures mean.* Jesus promises, ***"If you abide in My word, you are my disciples indeed. And you shall know the truth and the truth shall make you free"*** (see also John 15:4-10). This is the exclusive job of the Holy Spirit leading and guiding the Christian into all truth. ***"But you have an anointing from the Holy One, and you know all things. I have written to you because you do not know the truth, but because you know it, and that no lie is of the truth"*** (1 John 2:20-21). From this, a former Roman Catholic priest provides an excellent summary of the material covered in this chapter; he poses a question concerning the teaching authority in the Church, and where ultimate truth is found for the Christian.

> Finally, can we place the teaching authority of the church on the same plane with the Bible? Certainly we should listen to and respect Christian teachers. Pastors (also known as bishops and elders) are God's gift to His church. They are appointed by God to teach and lead the churches, and Christians are commanded to submit to them. The leaders' responsibility is to study and teach God's Word as it is, without additions or change. They

should study the Word carefully for they are liable to make mistakes (2 Timothy 2:15). And since they are not infallible, the apostle Paul advises us to 'test all things; hold fast what is good' (1 Thessalonians 5:21), while James warns us: 'My brethren, let not many of you become teachers, knowing that we shall receive a stricter judgment. For we all stumble in many things' (James 3:1). In short, the Bible is the Word of God and there is nothing of equal authority. Hence the Christian's commitment is to the Bible alone as the ultimate and absolute authority.[8]

The unresolved dilemma for the Roman Catholic consists in the fact that if the Magisterium were really the infallible interpreter of faith, morals, and Scripture for the Church, then it would entail a corresponding infallible interpretation from those subject to their teaching authority. For an infallible teacher would automatically need an infallible student, or follower to interpret such teaching correctly, and thus formally confirm that professed infallibility to be valid. But what makes this interpretation correct from the latter to the former infallibly correct without a further infallible interpretation of the infallible interpretation of the interpreter's interpretation, until it regresses into an infinite series of open ended and unresolved conundrums? And who is the person to interpret the infallible interpretation from the infallible interpreter? In the end, each person along the chain of interpretation would need to be infallible. If this were so, what need then would one have for an infallible Magisterium to begin with if their subjects were already capable of making infallible interpretations on their own?[9] The proposition of an infallible Magisterium suffers from the problem of *infinite regress* that cannot be logically resolved.[10] This is especially evident when there are a variety of conflicting interpretations and viewpoints crying out for a final infallible resolution within the Roman the Catholic Church today and in her past over topics such as: the nature of papal infallibility, debate over proper biblical exegesis between the liberal, moderate, and conservative Catholics, differing interpretations over the papal decrees and encyclicals, and the reconciliation between the Tridentine brand of Catholicism versus the more modernized version of Vatican II. These conflicts only enhance the indecisiveness and ineffective nature of an infallible teaching Magisterium as Evangelical scholars, Norman Geisler and Ralph Mackenzie, point out:

> If an infallible teaching Magisterium is needed to overcome the conflicting interpretations of Scripture, why is it that even these supposedly infallibly decisive declarations of the

[8] http://whateverycatholicshouldknow.com/wecsk/commonQ.htm

[9] See Eric Svendsen, *Evangelical Answers: A Critique of Current Roman Catholic Apologists*, 40.

[10] An **infinite regress** in a series of propositions arises if the truth of proposition P_1 requires the support of proposition P_2, and for any proposition in the series P_n, the truth of P_n requires the support of the truth of P_{n+1}. There would never be adequate support for P_1, because the infinite series needed to provide such support could not be completed. Thus in the present scenario: The truth of the infallibility of the Magisterium requires the support of a corresponding infallible interpreter with an infallible interpretation which requires the further support of an infallible interpretation of that infallible interpretation and so on, *ad infinitum*. In refuting Catholic apologist Tim Staples' argument, that unless you have an infallible means of interpretation (i.e., the teaching Magisterium of the Church), you cannot teach with authority, Evangelical scholar, James White, underscores the incoherence of Rome's justification for the teaching authority of the Magisterium when commenting: "First, the Roman Catholic has no infallible way of knowing Rome is in fact the authority she claims to be. Secondly, he has also no way of infallibly interpreting the interpretations of the infallible interpreter, and as is readily proven, Roman Catholic theologians often disagree about what was meant by this Council or that dogmatic decree" (*The Roman Catholic Controversy*, 234).

Magisterium are subject to conflicting interpretations? There are many hotly disputed differences among Catholic scholars on just what *ex cathedra* statements mean, including those on Scripture, tradition, Mary, and justification. Even though there may be future clarifications on some of these, the problem remains for two reasons. It shows the indecisive nature of supposedly infallible pronouncements, and, judging by past experience, even these future declarations will not settle all matters completely.[11]

Another problematic area with the idea of an infallible Magisterium is that it commits the formal fallacy in logic called *affirming the consequent*. This fallacy occurs when one affirms the consequent of a conditional statement without evidentiary justification, and then infers the affirmation of the antecedent. In this situation, the Roman Catholic assumes the consequent by affirming the leadership of his Church is already the infallible teacher of Scripture, because God prevents the Church from falling into error by imbuing its leaders with infallibility; yet the Roman Catholic is unable to provide any evidence of this. The underlying assumption made by Rome is that God's sole way to prevent the Church from falling into error is by giving it an infallible Magisterium. However, God has given His Word and the indwelling Holy Spirit to be His infallible interpreter as the means by which every Christian is personally safeguarded from moral transgression and doctrinal apostasy (Psalm 51:10-12; 119:11; John 16:13). The New Testament Scriptures and the Septuagint (Greek translation of the Old Testament, circa 270 B.C.) were originally written in Koine Greek, the universal dialect of the ancient world and the *lingua franca* of the Roman Empire. They were written with the intent of reaching the common man—so all would have access to them for their own personal benefit. The exhortation and command given in II Timothy 2:15 is for all Christians, not just a clergy or a select group of elite scholars, to study the Scriptures and interpret them correctly. ***"Study to show yourself approved to God, a workman that does not need to be ashamed, rightly dividing the word of truth."***

How does one meet the moral and spiritual qualifications for being an interpreter of God's Word? The Bible mentions nothing about serving as Pope or bishop in a collective Magisterium in order to do so. A cursory review of these qualifications from God's Word will irrefutably demonstrate this. The true interpreter of Holy Scripture must be spiritually born again by the Holy Spirit and the Word of God (John 3:1-12; 1 Peter 1:23). The Bible is a spiritual book inspired and produced by the Holy Spirit. For the individual to decipher what Scripture means, he or she must have its Divine Author living within them speaking to their minds during the interpretation process. To understand Scripture, the Christian must go to the source—the very Author Himself to know what it really means. Hence, the believer in Christ is to go to the Lord first (and not passively defer this crucial responsibility on to a Pope and bishops) in prayer asking Him to grant the ability to rightly interpret Scripture. In this most sacred endeavor, the born-again Christian should exclusively turn to the Lord and earnestly pray: ***"Open my eyes, that I may see wondrous things from Your law"*** (Psalm 118:18). The true interpreter of Scripture will have an insatiable hunger for the Word of God.

Those who have been born again through faith in Jesus Christ will evince their spiritual rebirth by an intense desire to study and know God's Word. They will not seek to blend church tradition, speculation, or religious opinion with it; since it is true spiritual meat and drink indeed to be more valued than physical food (Deuteronomy 8:3; Job 23:12). They will let the Scriptures speak for themselves, and reject any thought, doctrine, or path that contradicts its tenets—including the numerous false doctrines and traditions taught in the name of "Christ" according to the Church of Rome.

---

[11]   Norman Geisler and Ralph MacKenzie, *Roman Catholics and Evangelicals*, 215-216.

The true interpreter must come to the bar of Scripture with a heart of humility and a humble mind. ***"God resists the proud but gives grace to the humble"*** (1 Peter 5:5). The student of Scripture will seek to ***"receive with meekness the implanted word"***, which is able to save the soul (James 1:21). He will let the Scripture judge his life and correct the errors of his way. This attitude of humility is a far cry from the pompous claims of the Papacy and Magisterium today—who, both claim together, the incommunicable divine attribute of infallibility –an attribute that belongs to God alone (Numbers 23:19)—and demand unquestioned obedience from Roman Catholics. In this rank arrogance, Rome has no way of correcting her errors since the Pope is the ultimate authority in the Catholic Church and is above correction from those bishops beneath him! The true interpreter of Scripture will depend on the Holy Spirit, first and foremost. The Holy Spirit is not only the sacred Author, but is the only true expositor of what the Scripture means. When He leads and guides the interpretation process, the enlightened follower will abide in truth and eschew any error or misinterpretation. Guidance implies our obedience to the Word with child-like humility and a willingness to be led by the didactic authority of the Holy Spirit.

The true interpreter of Scripture must believe in the totality of its divine inspiration. He must hold to the firm conviction that the contents of Sacred Writ from Genesis to Revelation are directly inspired by God, are inerrant in all aspects of their original composition, and throughout its recording ***"holy men of God spoke as they were moved by the Holy Spirit"*** (2 Peter 1:21). In this regard, the Bible is peerless and preeminently unique. If it is not viewed in this light, esteemed to be the Book of all books, those reading it will fail to greatly appreciate it, and also fail to interpret it correctly. Rome has failed miserably here for the simple fact they proudly place their traditions of the "Fathers, Popes, and the Church" on an equal plane with the Word of God, and thereby nullify its full authoritative power when claiming that Scripture can only be understood according to Roman Catholic tradition placed along side of it.

The true interpreter of the Bible will not look to an institutional hierarchy or religious organization to understand Scripture, but will look rather to the *Holy Spirit Himself,* whose illumination is indispensable to rightly dividing the Word of Truth. The Holy Spirit inspired Scripture, and it is He who must disclose it's meaning as well. This is what is meant by illumination. By this illumination, God reveals His nature, acts, character, attributes, and being. So "all that may be known of God in this life is founded in and upon the Scriptures. They are the only inspired and infallible authority for all Christian faith and practice."[12]

The Bible is a book of divine revelation and revelation is imparted truth from God that cannot be understood by the natural reasoning of man (2 Corinthians 2:14). It must be spiritually understood (1 Corinthians 2:7-16). Divine inspiration is the supernatural process by which this revelation was recorded in the Bible. God miraculously communicated this infallibly through the instrumentality of fallible men without violating their personalities or wills (2 Timothy 3:16; 2 Peter 1:20).

Revelation is the substance of God's message, and inspiration is the process by which that message was communicated to man. Illumination is that supernatural ability given by God to understand the meaning and message of the Scriptures. Revelation and inspiration are both the infallible acts of God in the content and communication of His inerrant Word. However, attempting to understand the Word without illumination from the Holy Spirit can result in a fallible, improper interpretation of the Bible. This is because, as authors Kevin Connor and Ken Malmin rightfully point out: "the Holy Spirit knows what He meant when He inspired the Word; we, therefore, need His illumination. We must be sensitive to the Spirit, for it is His ministry to lead us

---

[12]   Kevin J. Conner and Ken Malmin, *Interpreting the Scriptures* (Portland: Bible Press, 1983), 11.

into all truth *(John 15:26; 16:12, 13)*."[13] The true interpreter of Scripture must be morally and intellectually honest. We are to be judged by Scripture and subject to its exposure of our sins. When studying God's Word, our prayer to the Lord should be, *"Search me, O God, and know my heart. Try me and know my thoughts, and see if there is any wicked way in me, and lead me in the way everlasting"* (Psalm 139:23-24).

Rome would have the misguided soul believe he must first come to their bishops and Popes to understand what the Bible means so that they can have a monopoly on the Bible and dictate how it should be interpreted—even if that interpretation is wrong with Scripture itself on many points. Jesus said that it was in a good and honest heart that the seed of His Word sprouts up and bares much fruit (Luke 8:15). Conversely, a false teacher with a dishonest heart will twist and bend the Scriptures to fit any false doctrine that supports their belief or religious system. Every cult within and without the pale of Christendom uses both a fallacious exegesis and hermeneutic to provide proof texts for their "damnable heresies"; and in the deadly process, deceive and destroy countless souls who fail to study the Scriptures for themselves to confirm and authenticate if these things are so (2 Corinthians 4:2; 2 Peter 3:15-16). As we proceed on in our critique of Roman Catholicism, it will become more apparent that the Roman Catholic teachers and apologists routinely take the Scriptures out of context to cleverly fit and accommodate the aberrant teachings and practices of Rome. Rather than let Scripture alone determine Christian doctrine and belief, they impose their colored, sectarian bias, and dogmatic presuppositions on the biblical text, giving the facile appearance that the text actually supports their outlandish claims, while showing themselves to be intellectually dishonest in the process.

One example of this, which ties in well with the current discussion in this chapter, is the passage in 1 Timothy 3:15. There, the Apostle Paul tells the young pastor, Timothy: *"...I write so that you may know how you ought to conduct yourself in the house of God, <u>which is the church of the living God, the pillar and ground of the truth</u>."* Roman Catholic apologists quickly seize upon this verse to prove the infallible teaching authority of the Roman Catholic Church to act and arbitrate on matters of truth, doctrine, and belief in exercising its rule over the canon of Scripture itself (See Ludwig Ott, *Fundamentals of Catholic Dogma*, page 298). They use this verse to allege that the Church is the final authority in Christianity. A certain Catholic apologist is so sure of this interpretation that he assumes it has confounded Protestants to the degree that they cannot successfully argue against it and provide a better meaning that is more in keeping with the context of First Timothy.[14] But a careful exegesis of First Timothy 3:15 has been done by conservative Bible scholarship to successfully refute and answer such an unfounded assumption!

Paul uses two images to describe the role and function of the New Testament Church here—a pillar and foundation. Both terms can variously be translated "pillar", "column", "pedestal", "foundation", "ground", or "bulwark" (see George W. Knight III, *The Pastoral Epistles: The New International Greek Testament Commentary* (Grand Rapids: Eerdmans, 1992), 181). Paul is speaking in the context of chapter three about the proper conduct the Christian should have in the Church, illustrated by the analogies of a family and a household of God under His watchful care (verses 5 and 15). As dutiful and responsive children in this ecclesial family, Christ has entrusted the members of His Church with the stewardship of disseminating and defending the truth of the Gospel and God's Word, with truth being used as a synonym for the Gospel in the

---

[13]   Ibid.

[14]   Dave Armstrong, *The Catholic Verses: 95 Passages That Confound Protestants* (Manchester, New Hampshire: Sophia Press, 2004), 3. This book, an obvious counterwork and poor imitation of Luther's stellar ninety-five theses, is the standard attempt to defend Catholicism with half-truths, selective conclusions, historical inaccuracies, revisionism, and blatant eisegesis. Reformed apologist James White gives a devastating critique of this book at Alpha and Omega Ministries web site: http://www.aomin.org.

Pastoral Epistles (cf. 1 Timothy 2:4). The metaphor of the pillar speaks of support and proclamation. The pillar is specifically designed to support the superstructure of a building. Pillars and columns were common support mechanisms erected in the pagan temples of Greece, Rome, and the Jewish Temple at Jerusalem.[15] In public squares and agoras of the first century Greco-Roman world, the freestanding pillar was especially used as a post on which legal decrees, treaties, public agreements, or a ruler's acts were made known to the masses.[16] In the New Testament, the term pillar is used as a metaphor to symbolize both Apostles and victorious believers. Paul referred to James, Cephas, and John as reputed *pillars* of the Church. When addressing the Church at Philadelphia, Jesus promises to make every Christian that overcomes *"a pillar in the temple of My God"* (Revelation 3:12).

The Church is called to support the truth of God by public proclamation of His Word, and to be a living witness of the Gospel. The support or bulwark picture (vaguely translated "ground" in English) is one of setting up a defense against the assault of an invading enemy. The Greek Word for ground or foundation is εδραιωμα (*pronounced: edraioma*), and connotes the idea of *protection*.[17] Therefore, the Church acting as a support and pillar of truth is called to protect and uphold the deposit of divine revelation from attacks, and to be a public witness of that revelation in word and deed. The Church is to carry out this most solemn and sacred task of sharing and upholding this infallible word of God's truth, which is the Holy Scripture, with evangelism (preaching the Gospel as stipulated in 2 Timothy 4:2) and apologetics (defending the Gospel as stipulated in 1 Peter 3:15). In carrying out the great commission, those in the Church are to be *servants* to God's truth and not *sovereigns* over it. The syntax construction in the Greek text of 1 Timothy 3:15 is anarthrous, meaning that the definite article is absent and literally should read: *"a pillar and ground of truth,"* not *"the pillar and ground for truth."* This is an important linguistic distinction. The definite article would set that thing or person apart to be singular or unique from the rest. But the fact it is missing here means that the Church is not the only pillar and support for God's truth. This would undermine the teaching that Rome's Magisterium acts as the sole teaching authority, which leads to the deduction that there are others (e.g., Christ, the Holy Spirit, and the Scriptures) that also fulfill this office or function. New Testament Greek scholar William Mounce concurs in principle, and concludes from the exegetical piece of evidence from 1Timothy 3:15 that:

> Identifying the pillar and support with the church also best explains the fact that the construction is anarthrous. The Church is not ο στυλος και εδραιωμα, "the pillar and support," but is rather στυλος και εδραιωμα, "a pillar and support." This could mean that the Ephesian church is one of many supporting churches, or it could mean that the church is only one of several entities that support the Gospel, another support possibly being Scripture. Even if the church fails in its task, the Gospel will continue (2 Tim. 2:9).[18]

The idea that the deposit of divine revelation contained in both Scripture and "Sacred Tradition" is *subordinate* to the authority of the Roman Catholic Church is not supported in any way from the text of 1

[15]   Jerome D. Quinn and William C. Wacker, *The First and Second Letters to Timothy* (Grand Rapids: Eerdmans, 2000), 312-313. This is a Roman Catholic commentary and quite good on historical and exegetical details from the Greek text.

[16]   Ibid., 314.

[17]   William Mounce, *Pastoral Epistles: Word Biblical Commentary*, vol. 46 (Nashville: Thomas Nelson, 2000), 222-223.

[18]   Ibid., 224.

Timothy 3:15, or anywhere else in the Pastoral Epistles; neither is the idea that the church is the *foundation* for the Gospel. Once again such ideas, are man-made traditions of the Magisterium that were developed centuries later, which were simply read back into the biblical text without any contextual support from the panoply of Scripture. The New Testament teaches that the Church is built upon the foundation of Jesus Christ (1 Corinthians 3:10-11; Ephesians 2:20; 1 Peter 2:6-8), "the chief cornerstone." Through Him, with Him, and in Him does the Church proclaim, defend, and uphold the truth of the Gospel to a lost world.[19]

The Roman Catholic Church claims that the Magisterium alone has the authority to infallibly interpret Scripture; this infallibility from God is corroborated in accordance with the "unanimous consent of the fathers." Both the Councils of Trent and Vatican I decreed that it was unlawful to interpret Scripture on one's own private judgment. The only authorized interpretation was the one established by the hierarchical leaders of the Roman Catholic Church. Those who presume to do so would be subject to censure and punishment. During its Fourth session, the Council of Trent decreed:

> Furthermore, to check unbridled spirits, it decrees that no one relying on his own judgment shall, in matters of faith and morals pertaining to the edification of Christian doctrine, distorting the Holy Scriptures in accordance with his own conceptions, presume to interpret them contrary to that sense which holy mother Church, to whom it belongs to judge of their true sense and interpretation, has held and holds, or even contrary to the unanimous teaching of the Fathers, even though such interpretations should never at any time be published. Those who act contrary to this shall be made known by the ordinaries and punished in accordance with the penalties prescribed by the law.[20]

The Vatican I Council later reaffirmed this decree in 1870.[21] Both Councils decreed the Roman Catholic Church has the sole right to interpret Scripture correctly, with the *unanimous consent* of the early Church fathers who received this interpretation from the Apostles, who in turn received it directly from Jesus Christ. Rome claims its body of tradition has preserved this long line of teaching that is still proclaimed by the Popes and bishops today. The Roman Catholic body of tradition and teaching is the preservation of this long line of teaching and interpretation that is still proclaimed by the Pope and the bishops today.

The "unanimous consent" factor does not mean that every church Father had to agree on every facet of Christian doctrine, but is understood in terms of holding a consensus by the majority. For, indeed, the Church Fathers held to different and divergent views on a wide variety of subjects. So if the majority of the Church Fathers held to the same interpretation on a particular issue of faith or a moral subject, such a consensus view was considered to be the official teaching of the Church. But concerning what the

---

[19] "Nothing in the PE supports the idea that the gospel is subordinate to the church (i.e., that the church is the foundation of the gospel) as developed in later centuries...It is the gospel that takes preeminence...The church is a protector and a helper in the proclamation of the gospel. In the debate over the interpretation of the role of the church in this text, some refer to 1 Cor. 3:10-11,where Paul says, "According to the grace of God given to me, like a skilled master builder I laid a foundation, and another man is building upon it. Let each man take care how he builds upon it. For no other foundation can anyone lay than that which is laid, which is Jesus Christ" (cf. Eph 2:20). It is argued that if εδραιωμα in 1 Tim 3:15 means "foundation," then the author of the PE is saying that the church is the foundation of the gospel, which would contradict 1 Cor. 3:10-11"(William Mounce, *Pastoral Epistles*, 223).

[20] *The Canons and Decrees of the Council Trent*, 18-19.

[21] See *Dogmatic Canons and Decrees of Vatican I Council*, 222-223.

Vatican defines to be essential doctrines of the Catholic faith for salvation—the infallibility of the Pope, the Immaculate Conception and Assumption of Mary, and Peter being "the Rock" upon which the Church is built—Christian history conclusively shows there is no majority or "unanimous consent" of interpretation by the Church Fathers on these things. This is especially true concerning the interpretation of who and what "the Rock" is in Matthew 16:18. It was documented earlier in this book (see chapter two) that the Roman Catholic interpretation of the rock, which became the standard interpretation of Rome almost one thousand years after the Christian Church was born, stood in direct contrast to the majority consensus of the Church Fathers spanning the first millennium of Christianity. Most of them interpreted the rock to mean Christ or Peter's confession that Jesus is the Messiah, the Son of the Living God. Here then is a manifest contradiction between what the Roman Catholic Church of later centuries taught (the Magisterium) with what the majority of the Church Fathers taught earlier before. And so, the claim of the Magisterium as the infallible teaching authority of Scripture is falsified and thus historically disproven by this fact alone, not to mention the many other examples that could be cited here as well. William Webster's observations on this unassailable truth are worth mentioning here:

> It is clear that the Roman Catholic Church of later centuries interprets the rock of Matthew 16 differently from the overall patristic consensus, so how can it claim to be an infallible interpreter of Scripture? The Magisterium of a later age contradicts that of the patristic age on an issue of interpretation. The claims and assertions of unanimous consent are utterly false. None of the Church's teaching in its tradition, based on the interpretation of Scripture, can claim a unanimous consent of the Fathers to support its teachings. In fact, there are a number of major passages which Rome interprets in a peculiarly Roman way, such as the papal passages, which actually contradicts the unanimous interpretation given by those very Fathers.[22]

Another reason that the infallibility of the Magisterium is proven false is the fact Rome has not materially produced an infallible commentary on the Bible containing an infallible interpretation of every verse. Roman Catholic scholars readily admit that only a small handful of biblical texts have been 'infallibly interpreted.' An official Roman Catholic Bible Commentary candidly admits:

> Very few texts have in fact been authoritatively determined and there consequently remain many important matters in the explanation of which sagacity and ingenuity of Catholic interpreters can and should be freely exercised...The numbers of texts infallibly interpreted is small...It has been estimated indeed that the total of such texts is under twenty, though there are of course many other indirectly determined (From Dom Bernard Orchard, M.A., ed., *A Catholic Commentary on Holy Scripture* (London: Thomas Nelson, 1953, 223-224).

The proud assertion of Rome's apologists that the Catholic Church alone has the authority to interpret Scripture is an empty claim by virtue of this indisputable fact. Rome has yet to publish this infallible interpretation of the Bible; they certainly cannot start now from a clean slate especially when the Magisterium has already incorrectly interpreted several key passages in Scripture (e.g., Matthew 16:16-18; John 3:5;

---

[22]   William Webster, *Roman Catholic Tradition: Claims and Contradictions* (Battle Ground, WA: Christian Resources, 1999), 37-38.

6:32-65; 1 Corinthians 3:12-23). This infallible interpretation is supposedly based on "the unanimous consent of the fathers"; however, when studying Church history, one finds no monolithic or uniform structure of patristic interpretation based on an alleged *unanimity* of the church Fathers from either the East or West! Many of them use the allegorical method of interpretation, or the historical/grammatical method of interpretation. Known for his excellent Bible scholarship in Catholic and Protestant circles, Roman Catholic priest and professor of biblical exegesis, Joseph Fitzmyer S.J., reinforces this by affirming:

> When one hears today the call for a return to a patristic interpretation of Scripture, there is often latent in a recollection of Church documents that spoke at times of 'the unanimous consent of the Fathers' as a guide for biblical interpretation (thus the Council of Trent in its decree of 1546 on the Latin Vulgate and the mode of interpreting Scripture…and in its profession of faith). But just what this would entail is far from clear. For…there were Church Fathers who did use a form of the historical critical method, suited to their own day, and advanced a literal interpretation of Scripture, not the allegorical. But not all did so. Yet there was no uniform or monolithic patristic interpretation, either in the Greek Church of the East, Alexandrian or Antiochene, or in the Latin Church of the West.[23]

When it came to using a particular hermeneutic (mode of interpretation) for a certain book of the Bible, namely, the book of Revelation, some of the Church Fathers interpreted most of these prophecies as already fulfilled in history (Preterism), while a great many others taught that the bulk of the Apocalypse was yet to be fulfilled in the future (Futurism), and still other Fathers viewed these prophecies symbolically fulfilled during the present age. There was no single, fixed interpretation for this book. And so, the claim that the Roman Catholic Magisterium has the sole right and power to alone infallibly interpret Scripture, according to the unanimous consent of the Church Fathers, is disproven from the history of patristic hermeneutics, and also, more importantly, contradicts the clear teaching of Scripture. Catholics are encouraged to study and read the Bible, but only insofar as these Bible studies are approved and sanctioned by the Magisterium with the appropriate study notes reinforcing Roman Catholicism. They are not free to determine what Scripture means apart from the authoritative teachings of the Magisterium.[24] Roman Catholic Scholars and theologians of the Church are similarly enjoined with the same disclaimer and must conduct their scholarly studies "under the watchful care of the sacred Magisterium" for the avowed purpose that a greater fidelity to Rome is fostered.[25]

Here the Vatican's real objective for encouraging Bible study is exposed. The purpose is not for the student of Scripture to discover the intended and original meaning of the biblical text, but rather to subject him to the way the Roman Catholic Church arbitrarily interprets it. The faithful Catholic must submit unquestioningly to that end. This is nothing more than a form of mind control. Each individual has a God-given privilege to read and understand the Scriptures for himself—with prayer, obedience, and dedication to the Lord Jesus Christ. To abdicate that freedom *in Christ*, and replace it with submission to the *Magisterium* as the ultimate authority, results in the enslavement of the mind and conscience to the religious tyranny of Rome. Former Catholic Nun, Mary Ann Collins has some choice words of warning for both Roman Catholics and non-Catholics to heed and follow:

---

[23] Joseph Fitzmyer, S.J., *Scripture, the Soul of Theology* (New York: Paulist Press, 1994), 70.

[24] *Catechism of the Catholic Church*, 38-39 **[113, 119, 891, 2051]**.

[25] Walter Abbott, *The Documents of Vatican II*, 126.

We should never put our conscience in someone else's hands. This is a foundational problem with Catholicism. For obedient Catholics, their primary source of moral guidance is the Catholic hierarchy, rather than the Bible. No person is good enough, or holy enough, or wise enough, to give our conscience to. We have to discern things for ourselves. We have to get to know the Bible, so that we can have God's perspective about things. The Bible says that we cannot afford to be like children, whose beliefs are at the mercy of other people. (Ephesians 4:14) We need to grow up and take responsibility for our own beliefs, and for having our consciences be based on biblical principles. We need to be like the Bereans, and test everything against the Bible. An old hymn says: "On Christ the solid rock I stand. All other ground is sinking sand." The traditions of the Catholic Church are sinking sand. We need to take our stand on Jesus Christ and the Bible.[26]

The whole idea of a Roman Catholic Magisterium should be thoroughly rejected on these grounds by the Bible-believing Christian, and more importantly by the simple truth that such a dangerous doctrine utterly circumvents the primacy of Scripture and the preeminent role of the Holy Spirit being the One and only infallible teacher of the Scripture for the inquiring Christian.

---

[26]   Catholic Concerns at: http://www.catholicconcerns.com/MindControl.html

CHAPTER 9

THE ROMAN CATHOLIC PRIESTHOOD

Have you ever noticed that when the world at large attempts to favorably represent Christianity to mainstream society through the media or cinema it is almost always universally done in the person of the Roman Catholic priest? Hollywood, early on, gave this favorable impression with endearing movies like *Boy's Town*, *The Keys of the Kingdom*, *Going My Way*, and *The Bells of St. Mary*. These movies painted the Roman Catholic priest in the brightest and most positive of colors, as if to say this is what true authentic Christianity is. Each week for eleven straight years, millions of viewers tuned into the long running, successful television series *M*A*S*H* and became endeared with the winsome character of Father Mulcahy. In more recent times, there is the inimitable Father Jonathan Morris on *Fox News* television giving his weekly insights on contemporary, social, moral, and religious issues on the *Fox and Friends* segment. The overall image presented in these dramatizations is designed to give the viewer the distinct impression that the Roman Catholic priest is the best and most accurate expression of the Christian religion and faith in the world today. But is such a popular representation true to biblical Christianity? This chapter will seek to honestly answer that question from the Word of God and the unvarnished history of the Roman Catholic Institution.

The Catholic priest is an indispensable person and authority in the Roman Catholic religion, for he is the one appointed mediator who stands between God and the Roman Catholic faithful (See C.P. Bennett, *The New Saint Joseph Baltimore Catechism* (New York: Catholic Book Publishing CO., 1969, page 211). In this role, he is supposedly given the power to offer the sacrifice of the Mass, and the authority to forgive sins. The priest is thus the central figure in the Roman Catholic system of salvation. Without him, that salvation cannot be duly administered and offered to the Catholic faithful. Holy Orders are the sacrament through which men are ordained to the Catholic priesthood.[1] Without the ordained priest, there can be no administering of

---

[1] Properly explained, Holy Orders are defined in the following manner: "The sacrament through which men become priests by receiving from the bishop the power to offer sacrifices and to forgive sins." (Ibid, page 247). *The Catechism of the Catholic Church* also states concerning this, "Christ, whom the Father hallowed and sent into the world, has, through his apostles, made their successors, the bishops namely, sharers in his consecration and mission; and these, in turn, duly entrusted in varying degrees various members of the Church with the office of their ministry. The function of the bishops' ministry was handed over in a subordinate degree to priests so that

the sacraments, including the sacrifice of the Mass for the forgiveness of sins, the sacrament of penance for continued forgiveness; and the sacrament of Extreme Unction for the final forgiveness of sins. The priesthood is built on a hierarchical system and is open only to men (see *Catechism of the Catholic Church*, paragraphs **1577** and **1598**). The priest is God's chosen representative to administer sacraments to Catholics, which they receive at birth, during life, and finally at death, with the ultimate hope of attaining salvation. Celebrating the sacraments for salvation is the primary of role of the priest. The Council of Trent argues for the necessity of the Roman Catholic priesthood in these sacramental matters when it decreed:

> Sacrifice and priesthood are by the ordinance of God so united that both have existed in every law. Since therefore in the New Testament the Catholic Church has received from the institution of Christ the holy, visible sacrifice of the Eucharist, it must also be confessed that there is in that Church a new visible and external priesthood, into which the old has been translated. That this was instituted by the same Lord our Savior, and that to the Apostles and their successors in the priesthood was given the power of consecrating, offering and administering His body and blood, as also of forgiving and retaining sins, is shown by the Sacred Scriptures and has always been taught by the traditions of the Catholic Church.[2]

The Council of Trent went on to openly condemn anyone who denied the whole concept of the Roman Catholic priesthood:

> If anyone says that there is not in the New Testament a visible and external priesthood, or that there is no power of consecrating and offering the true body and blood of the Lord and of forgiving and retaining sins, but only the office and bare ministry of preaching the Gospel; or that those who do not preach are not priests at all, let him be anathema.[3]

The Catholic priest is unique and set apart in the Roman Catholic system to an elevated status placed above all the lay people. He is held in high esteem by virtue of his office and the power that is conferred on him. The position and power he holds is said to be greater than the President of the United States or any other power an earthly potentate wields.[4] That power enables the Catholic priest to administer the sacraments,

---

they might be appointed in the order of the priesthood and be co-workers of the Episcopal order for the proper fulfillment of the apostolic mission that had been entrusted to it by Christ...Hence the priesthood of priests, while presupposing the sacraments of initiation, is nevertheless conferred by its own particular sacrament. Through that sacrament priests by the anointing of the Holy Spirit are signed with a special character and so are configured to Christ the priest in such way that they are to act in the person of Christ the head...Through the sacrament of Holy Orders priests share in the universal dimensions of the mission that Christ entrusted to the apostles" pages 437-438 **[1563, 1565]**.

[2] *The Canons and Decrees of the Council Trent*, 160. This primary function of the Priest administering the sacraments for salvation is still maintained in Modern Catholicism with equal vigor. Catholic Priest, Donald B. Cozzens candidly asserts: "*Saving souls through pastoral care and the celebration of the sacraments is the primary function of the priest* from the perspective of the cultic model" (Emphasis mine). See Donald Cozzens, *The Changing Face of the Priesthood* (Collegeville, MN: The Liturgical Press, 2000), 8.

[3] Ibid, 162-163.

[4] "Not only Catholics, but most people show reverence for a priest. They realize that he is dedicated to Almighty God in a very special way. The dignity of the priest is higher than any earthly dignity; he has powers that not even

which includes performing the act of transubstantiation during the Mass whereby the elements of bread and wine are actually changed into the physical body and blood of Jesus Christ, so that the recipients may receive the forgiveness of sins (see the *Catechism of the Catholic Church* Paragraphs **1411, 1461, 1566**). The Catholic priest acts in the very person of Christ continuing His sacrificial work through the offering of the Mass. The *Catechism of the Catholic Church* explains it this way:

> It is the same priest, Christ Jesus, whose sacred person his minister truly represents. Now the minister, by reason of the sacerdotal consecration which he has received, is truly made like to the high priest and possesses the authority to act in the power and place of Christ himself (*virtute ac persons ipsius Christi*). Christ is the source of all priesthood: the priest of the old law was a figure of Christ, and the priest of the new law acts in the person of Christ.[5]

Catholic doctrine teaches that Jesus Christ supposedly established the institution of the Roman Catholic priesthood at the Last Supper. When consecrating the bread and wine, He told the disciples to take, eat and drink in remembrance of His death. From that moment on, the Apostles and their successors, the Roman Catholic priests—those who share in His eternal priesthood—have had the power to offer the selfsame sacrifice Christ made on Calvary through the Mass *in an unbloody manner*. To reflect this belief, new priests at the time of their ordination will recite the New Testament passage from Hebrews 7:17: *"You are a priest forever according to the order of Melchizedek."* The priest is therefore not only a mediator for Christ, acting in His person, but is also an *Alter Christus* (which from Latin to English literally means, "Another Christ") in the sense that he continues Christ's ministry of sacrifice through the Mass, and Christ's mediatorial work of absolution through the Sacrament of Penance, granted to the penitent Catholic.[6]

Jesus Christ has therefore transmitted His mediatorial and sacrificial priesthood to the Roman Catholic clergy of priests, bishops and Popes. The purpose and intent of this priesthood is to grant salvation to compliant Roman Catholics through the sacraments. Without the institution of this priesthood, the sacraments,

---

the President of the United States has." From the Catholic Catechism, *Instructions in the Catholic Faith*, cited in *Roman Catholicism: Issues & Evidences*, page 81.

[5]   *Catechism of the Catholic Church*, 431 **[1548]**

[6]   "The priest has rightly been called '*another Christ*' – not that he shares in Christ's divine nature and human perfection, but because he has been appointed by God to continue Christ's mission in the world, and must consequently, within the limits of his power, try to live the life of Christ on earth. Like Jesus on the cross, he stands at the altar as a mediator between God and man, lifting up to heaven his hands filled with Christ's merits and prayers, and offering the redeeming Blood of the Divine Victim, the price of our salvation. Thus he sends up to God the infinite tribute of adoration, thanks and reparation due to Him, which Christ alone can pay for us; thus he brings down upon men a shower of divine grace and precious blessings. He is the merciful Jesus who forgives sinners, purifies their souls and directs them towards heaven, through the Sacrament of Penance." From the web site of Saint Thomas Aquinas Seminary: www.**sspxseminary.org**. There is only one indivisible Jesus Christ, born of the Virgin Mary, who was fully God and Man in one Person who died once for our sins, was buried, and raised from death and ascended to heaven from whence He will return to establish His reign over all the earth from Jerusalem at the conclusion of the present age. Paul warns believers about the danger of accepting another "Jesus" contrary to the biblical revelation given of Him that is a counterfeit to the true and only Christ (2 Corinthians 11:4). Since the Roman Catholic priest cannot be the true representation of the peerless one of a kind Jesus Christ, as described according to Scripture, he is simply "another Christ" who is not genuine to the true pattern given in the Word of God.

by which the saving power of God's grace is conveyed, cannot be rightly administered to Roman Catholics. Without the priest to give these sacraments, there would be no salvation in the Roman Catholic system. The administering of the sacraments by the priest is a necessary element in Roman Catholic Soteriology. This is called *Sacerdotalism* (from Latin *sacerdos*, priest, literally one who presents sacred offerings, *sacer*, sacred, and *dare*, to give). Sacerdotalism is the belief in an intermediary system in which the priest has been given the special authority to act as a spiritual mediator between God and mankind. The Roman Catholic, Eastern Orthodox, and High Anglican traditions are all sacerdotal. However, in all of these traditions, the sacerdotal system finds its fullest expression within Roman Catholicism, which fully depends upon this sacrificial and mediatorial priesthood.

> The sacerdotal principle finds very complete expression in the thoroughly developed and logically compacted system of the Church of Rome. According to this system God the Lord does nothing looking to the salvation of men directly and immediately: all that he does for the salvation of men he does through the mediation of the Church, to which having endowed it with powers adequate to the task, he has committed the whole work of salvation.[7]

Is the mediatorial and sacrificial concept of the Roman Catholic priesthood found in the New Testament? The answer is an emphatic *no*! The Roman Catholic priesthood is rightfully considered by many to be an unbiblical institution, as it is not mentioned anywhere in the New Testament! The inspired writers of the New Testament never define the role of ministers as "priests who mediate and offer up the ongoing sacrifice of Christ for the Church." Nowhere in the New Testament Scriptures are the terms "priest" and "priesthood" as defined by Rome found; nor is such sacerdotal terms applied to an individual Christian minister, with the understanding that he is offering the sacrifices of the body and blood of Christ for sin. The first time anyone associated Christian ministry with a sacerdotal priesthood was not until the third century with Cyprian, (200-258 A.D.), the Bishop of Carthage, more than two hundred years after Christ. Cyprian claimed that the role and function of the New Testament ministers (priests) should be patterned after the Old Testament Aaronic priesthood, with its numerous sacrifices, rites and ordinances. Such a claim, later to be used by Roman Catholic exegetes in an attempt to justify the priesthood of Rome, flies in the face of the central truth of the book of Hebrews. The Aaronic priesthood of the Old Testament was abolished and replaced by the permanent priesthood of the Lord Jesus Christ, whom God now recognizes as the only mediator and High Priest of the New Covenant.

The next prominent Church Father that attempted to make the same type of analogy by calling New Testament ministers "priests" was Chrysostom (349-407 A.D.), about one hundred years after Cyprian in his treatise entitled *On the Priesthood*.[8] Both church fathers apparently failed to comprehend the grand truth that

---

[7]   Benjamin Warfield, *The Plan of Salvation* (Grand Rapids, MI: Eerdmans, 1984), 53.

[8]   John Chrysostom, *Treatise on the Priesthood and Six Books on the Priesthood* (Kessinger, 2005). Near the beginning of the second century, Clement of Rome makes a similar analogy in his epistles to the Corinthians where he too suggests a parallel between ordained ministers of the Christian Church and the priests of the Old Testament. Several centuries later, this inference gave way to the recapitulation of the Old Testament priesthood--partially revived under the guise of the Roman Catholic priesthood which repeatedly offers up the body and blood of Jesus Christ for an expiatory sacrifice for sins. But as Pastor P.J. Mathew rightly points out, such an unbiblical concept of Christ's sacrifice and a New Testament sacrificial priesthood under the rubric of Roman Catholic Sacerdotalism is particularly refuted in the New Testament book of *Hebrews*: "The sacrificial death of Jesus Christ annulled

resounds throughout the Epistle to the Hebrews and the Apostolic writings of the New Testament: The only High Priest who has made the final sacrifice for sin which cannot be repeated ever again is the Lord Jesus Christ, whom God set forth to be the propitiation for our sins (Romans 3:25; Hebrews 2:17; 1 John 2:2; 4:10). This sacrifice took place *exclusively* at Calvary's cross, and cannot be replaced anywhere else, including in the Mass. The main reason why there is no need for a sacrificial priesthood in the New Testament Church is that the once for all, perfect sacrifice of Jesus Christ (the great High Priest) put an end to both the sacrifices of the Old Testament and its Levitical priesthood. This is one of the prominent themes in the book of Hebrews, wherein it mentions *six times* in the book of Hebrews how Christ's perfect sacrifice for sin was offered *"once for all"* and therefore abolished the need for a repetitious sacrifice of sin, and a priesthood required to offer such a sacrifice (Hebrews 7:27; 9:26, 28 10:10,12,14).

Moreover, the eternal priesthood of Christ, patterned after the unique order of Melchizedek, cannot be transferred to anyone else, particularly to Roman Catholic priests, because it rests alone upon the *impeccability* and *eternal existence* of Jesus Christ. These two attributes belong exclusively to *Him alone* and cannot be found in any imperfect, mortal, and incomplete priesthood that characterized the priests and animal sacrifices of the Old Covenant. For these reasons, the writer of Hebrews tells us that the perfect priesthood of Christ Jesus is untransferable and cannot have any successor (Hebrews 7:23-25). *"Also there were many priests, because they were prevented by death from continuing. But He, because He continues forever, has an untransferable priesthood. Therefore He is also able to save completely those who come to God through Him, since He always lives to make intercession for them"* (Hebrews 7:23-25). Therefore, no Roman Catholic priest or any other earthly clergy can claim to perpetuate it or assume a priestly, mediatorial role in doing so.

The Roman Catholic priesthood with its sacrifice of the Mass collapses on this truth alone. Surely if the Roman Catholic priesthood needed biblical justification for its existence, we would certainly find it in the book of Hebrews where the dominant emphasis is on the comparisons and contrasts between the Levitical priests and their repetitive animal sacrifices of the Old Testament with the singular priesthood and the once for all perfect sacrifice of Jesus Christ Himself under the New Testament. Hebrews chapter ten unequivocally teaches that Christ's supreme sacrifice has abolished any further need of an ongoing sacrifice for sin, and thus eliminating any more need for a human priesthood to offer those sacrifices. The whole idea of a priesthood offering a continual sacrifice of Christ is contradictory to the Word of God. William Webster in his excellent book, *Salvation, the Bible, and Roman Catholicism* accurately understands this most serious heresy of Rome and is quite correct to point out the following from the pages of the New Testament:

---

the Aaronic priesthood, as we read in the Epistle to the Hebrews. There is no need to continue offering up literal expiatory sacrifices. As the perfect Son of God and High Priest, Jesus established a new covenant (Heb. 9:15-22) with better promises (Heb. 8:6) when he offered himself (Heb 9:27) as the perfect victim once for all (Heb 7:27) as our substitute (Heb 7:27) and ransom (Heb. 9:15). By his death he took away our sins (Heb. 9:28), made us perfect (Heb. 10:14), obtained for us eternal redemption (Heb. 9:12). He now invites every believer with a clean conscience (Heb. 9:14) to enter the Most Holy Place by the blood of Jesus (Heb. 10:19) to offer continually spiritual sacrifices (Heb. 13:15, 16) as priests in Christ. In our one mediator between God and man, Christ Jesus, Christians come immediately and directly to God. They have no further need for any fallible priest, whether Roman Catholic or evangelical"— J.P. Mathew, "The Priesthood of All Believers" at http://www.gracevalley.org/articles/Priesthood. html. We shall revisit this same truth in more detail when dealing with the Mass and the Eucharist in chapter ten of this book.

Does the Bible teach that the Lord Jesus Christ instituted a special class of men in the church known as priests who would be given the authority to reconcile men with God through the Mass and through confession and penance? The answer to that question, as we shall see, is quite simply no. First of all, as we noted in the previous chapter, the whole concept of continuing sacrifices is completely contradictory to the teaching of the Word of God. The Lord Jesus did not commission or institute a human priesthood, beginning with the apostles, who would continue the offering of sacrifices in a Mass. All sacrifices have now been abolished because the 'once for all' sacrifice of Jesus Christ is complete. Since the sacrifices have been abolished (Heb 10) there is no longer any need for a priesthood. Whatever it was the Lord Jesus was commissioning his apostles to do, it was not to authorize them to become priests who would continue his sacrifice in the offering of the Mass...The old system, the old human priesthood, has been set aside and replaced by the eternal priesthood of Jesus Christ. Because he abides forever, he holds his priesthood *permanently (Heb.7: 24)*. The word 'permanently' is the Greek word *aparabatos* which means 'unchangeable, not liable to pass to a successor' (*Thayer's Greek-English Lexicon*). Jesus Christ could not have instituted a human priesthood through the disciples, for the Bible teaches that he exercises an exclusive priesthood forever. It cannot be shared by or transferred to anyone else .The Mosaic system in the Old Testament foreshadowed the person and work of the Lord Jesus Christ. Now that He has come, the old system has been abolished.[9]

One of the leading biblical scholars of the Roman Catholic Church, Raymond Brown, admits to the striking absence of a Christian priesthood in the New Testament in his book, *Priest and Bishop: Biblical Reflections*:

> When we move from the OT to the NT, it is striking that while pagan priests and Jewish priests are on the scene, no individual Christian is ever specifically identified as a priest. The Epistle to the Hebrews speaks of the high priesthood of Jesus by comparing his death and entry into heaven with the actions of the Jewish high priest who went into the Holy of Holies in the Tabernacle once a year with a blood offering for himself and for the sins of the people (Heb 9:6-7). *But it is noteworthy that the author of Hebrews does not associate the priesthood of Jesus with the Eucharist or the Last Supper; neither does he suggest that other Christians are priests in the likeness of Jesus. In fact, the once-for-all atmosphere that surrounds the priesthood of Jesus in Hebrews (10:12-14) has been offered as an explanation of why there are no Christian priests in the NT period* (Emphasis mine).[10]

In the book of Hebrews, a very priestly book, and in the rest of the New Testament, no hint or even slight allusion is made of a Christian priesthood that reoffers Christ's sacrifice over and over again in an "unbloody manner" through the Mass. Indeed, quite the opposite is taught from Scripture, as we have noted above. Scripture mandates that there can be no efficacious sacrifice or atonement for sin without the shedding of blood. *"Without shedding of blood there is no remission"* (Hebrews 9:22; Leviticus 17:11). Therefore

---

9   William Webster, *Salvation, The Bible, and Roman Catholicism* (Carlisle, PA: Banner of Truth, 1990), 29-30, 33.

10   Raymond Brown, *Priest and Bishop: Biblical Reflections* (Eugene, Oregon: Wipf and Stock Publishers, 1999), 13.

the sacrifice of the Mass cannot truly be expiatory for sin, since no blood is actually shed! If the Catholic priesthood were a legitimate institution of the New Testament Church, and necessary for one's salvation, then Christ and the Apostles would have prominently placed it in the forefront of their teaching in *bold relief.* The collective silence of them on this matter is deafening. In fact, the New Testament teaches quite the contrary: God has ordained His Son, Jesus Christ to be the only legitimate Priest to stand as a Mediator between sinful man and God (1 Timothy 2:5; Hebrews 9:11-15). His atoning death on the cross two thousand years ago is the only sacrifice for sins that God legitimately recognizes to this day. We have no need for a human priesthood, since Christ in His divine priesthood grants us full remission of sins through His perfect sacrifice. He also allows us full and immediate access to the throne of God. It is Christ who acts as the sole, priestly mediator between the forgiven sinner and the reconciling God.

This was supernaturally manifested when Jesus died on the cross. At the hour of Christ's sacrificial death on Calvary, the great veil (or curtain) in the Temple that separated the Holy Place from the Holy of Holies was torn in two, from top to bottom (indicating this was the hand of God at work, and not man), signifying that the law of Moses had been fulfilled (Matthew 27:51-53). God tore the veil Himself, making it known to all that direct access into His presence is now possible through the death of His Son, Jesus Christ, our Great High Priest. This final, *one-time* sacrifice for sin has eliminated the need for any human priesthood that offers *continual* sacrifices for sin. The assertion of a Roman Catholic priesthood offering up a continual reenactment of Christ's sacrifice on Calvary—through the unbloody repetition of the Mass—is a profane attempt at patching up that torn veil!

Without any sanction or approval from the Word of God, Rome imposes other priests and sacerdotal mediators to arbitrarily stand in front of the open entrance into the Holy of holies, truly barring the way. The Roman Catholic priesthood is guilty here of doing the very same thing Jesus condemned the Pharisees for doing in Matthew 23:13—shutting up and obstructing the kingdom of heaven from men with their unscriptural doctrines and practices. ***"But woe to you, scribes and Pharisees, hypocrites! For you shut up the kingdom of heaven against men; for you neither go in yourselves, nor do you allow those who are entering to go in."*** The comments of Presbyterian theologian Lorraine Boettner are quite enlightening on this particular point:

> The sacrifice of Christ was therefore a "once-for-all" sacrifice which only He could make, and which cannot be repeated. By its very nature it was final and complete. It was a work of Deity, and so cannot be repeated by any man any more than can the work of creation. By that one sacrifice the utmost demands of God's justice were fully and forever satisfied. Final atonement has been accomplished! No further order of priests is needed to offer additional sacrifices or to perpetuate that one. His was the one sacrifice to end all sacrifices. Let all men now look to that one sacrifice on Calvary! Any continuing priesthood and any "unbloody repetition of the Mass," which professes to offer the same sacrifice that Christ offered on Calvary, is in reality merely a sham and a recrudescence of Judaism within the Christian Church.

> The abolition of the priestly caste which through the old dispensation stood between God and man was dramatically illustrated at the very moment Christ died on the cross. When He cried, "It is finished" a strange sound filled the temple as the veil that separated the sanctuary from the holy of holies was torn from top to bottom. The ministering priests

found themselves gazing at the torn veil with wondering eyes, for God's own hand had removed the curtain and had opened the way into the holy of holies, symbolizing by that act that no longer did man have to approach Him through the mediation of a priest, but that the way of access to Him is now open to all.

But the veil which had been torn by the hand of God was patched up again by priestly hands, and forty years, until the fall of Jerusalem, sacrifices continued to be offered in a restored temple service, and in Judaism the veil continued to stand between God and men. In our day the Roman priesthood has again patched up the veil. Through the use of spurious sacraments, the sacrifice of the Mass, the confessional, indulgences, and other such priestly instruments it insists on keeping in place the curtain that God Himself has removed.[11]

The sinner can now come directly to God through the Person and work of Jesus Christ alone. He does not need the mediatorial aid of a Roman Catholic priest with his magic bag of sacraments in tow because Christ is *the Perfect Priest* and *the final Sacrifice* through which His mediatorial intercession grants every Christian believer complete, irrevocable redemption and immediate entrance into the holy presence of God, where reconciled sinners are joyously welcomed as sons and daughter of the Most High (John 10:7, 9; 14:6). There is no longer any need for sacramental priests and sacerdotal mediators. With Christ's atoning sacrifice and ongoing mediatorial intercession for us before God, the need for human priests to interpose between the redeemed sinner and God has been rendered obsolete with the abolition of the Old Testament priesthood by the eternal priesthood of Jesus the Messiah. In this light, the Roman Catholic priest who still seeks to act as mediator and sacrificial priest for Christ thus repudiates the full efficacy, and supreme finality of Christ's unrepeatable sacrifice on the cross. He also usurps the authority of the one and only priestly Mediator whom God has established between man and Himself, in whom the believer has direct access to the power, presence, and Person of God, the Father. To this, the Scripture in Hebrews 10:19-22 testifies: ***"Therefore, brethren, having boldness to enter the Holiest by the blood of Jesus, by a new and living way which He consecrated for us, through the veil, that is, His flesh and having a High Priest over the house of God, let us draw near with a true heart in full assurance of faith."***

The New Testament teaches that every true believer in Jesus Christ is a priest before God, who now having gained access to the presence of God through the atoning death of Christ is able to "boldly" approach the throne of grace to intercede for themselves and others (Hebrews 4:14-16). This is a universal priesthood shared by all Christians from every tribe, kindred, tongue, and nation that includes both men and women; it is not reserved for a few select celibate men dressed in black clerical garb (Revelation 1:6; 5:9). God's priestly redeemed will be dressed in *white* robes that have been purified in the atoning blood of Jesus, ***"the Lamb slain before the foundation of the world"*** (Revelation 3: 4, 5, 18; 19:8). In this universal priesthood of all genuine Christians, there is no difference among believers. All have equal share in this priestly ministry. For, ***"there is neither Jew nor Greek, slave nor free, male nor female, for you are all one in Christ Jesus. If you belong to Christ, then you are Abraham's seed, and heirs according to the promise"*** (Galatians 3:28-29).

The universal priesthood of the Church will be visibly evident during the millennial reign of Christ on Earth (Revelation 20:6). Twice in his epistles, the Apostle Peter writes that God has chosen and set apart all Christians in the universal church to be a "royal" and "holy" priesthood offering up spiritual sacrifices

---

[11] Lorraine Boettner, *Roman Catholicism* (Phillipsburg: P&R Publishing, 1980), 49.

acceptable to God (1 Peter 2:5; 9). These spiritual sacrifices the New Testament believer is exhorted and commanded to offer up to God through Jesus, the Great High Priest, in no way correspond to the continuation, re-presentation, and perpetuation of Christ's sacrifice on the cross through the sacramental rite of the Mass. The Bible informs us just what these "spiritual sacrifices" are, and they are decidedly different and altogether foreign to the Roman Catholic Mass.

The first and most important spiritual sacrifice is self-consecration to the Lord which entails the complete surrender of one's body, soul, and mind to the Lord. Romans 12:1 exhorts the Christian to present his body *"a living sacrifice, holy acceptable to God."* The disciple of Christ is to therefore dedicate His entire life to the service of Jesus Christ in a self-sacrificial way, preferring the Lord's will to his own in all things. The Christian's mind and thoughts should be submitted and conformed to God's Word. He is to think God's thoughts after Him, do His will, and act, as He would have us to act.

Contrition, humility, and a brokenness of heart are more types of spiritual sacrifices of the New Testament believer. *"The Sacrifices of God are a broken spirit; a broken and contrite heart, O God, you will not despise"* (Psalm 51:17). We offer the sacrifices of brokenness and contrition by confessing our sins daily to the Lord in prayer and asking for His forgiveness. Prayer and praise are also important spiritual sacrifices involved in the life of the universal priesthood of the Church. As believer-priests of the Lord Jesus Christ, we are to praise God for the great salvation He has brought us. *"Therefore by Him let us continually offer the sacrifice of praise to God, that is the fruit of our lips, giving thanks to His name"* (Hebrews 13:15). We are to thank God continually for the benefits of His unmerited kindness and marvelous works shown to us with "sacrifices of thanksgiving" (Psalm 107:22).

The prayers of believers are likened to incense that goes up before God during the evening sacrifice in the Temple. They too constitute a spiritual sacrifice offered to the Lord. The prayer of the New Testament believer-priest should be like that of King David who prayed in Psalm 141:2, *"Let my prayer be set before You as incense, the lifting up of my hands as the evening sacrifice"* (Psalm 141:2). Helping the poor, distributing material goods to the needy and the giving of alms is performing the service of a New Testament priest. The writer of Hebrews 13:16 instructs the New Testament Church, *"not to forget to do good and to share with others, for with such sacrifices God is well pleased"* (Hebrews 13:16). Sacrificial support for Christian ministries and missionaries by the Church is another expression of priestly service and sacrifice. When the Philippian Church sacrificially gave their material goods to the Apostle Paul, he exclaimed that their financial gifts were, *"a sweet smelling aroma, an acceptable sacrifice, well pleasing to God"* (Philippians 4:18).

Every born-again Christian, is a son or daughter of God, forgiven of all sins past, present and future, and is clothed with the imputed righteousness of Christ secure in His saving hands forever (John 10:28-29; Romans 5:12-21; 8:35-39; Colossians 1:14; 2:14). Belonging to a holy priesthood, every Christian is set apart by Christ as a royal priest and king. He trusts in Jesus Christ alone as his sole Mediator and High Priest who died once on the cross for the salvation of the sinner so that the forgiven believer is brought into the presence of God through the redemption and intercession of Jesus Christ alone. Catholics are taught to look to the priest and the rituals of the sacraments for salvation instead of *"looking unto Jesus, the Author and finisher of our faith"* (Hebrews 12:2).

There is therefore no need of a hierarchical system of Roman Catholic priests or papal mediators performing the re-sacrifice of Christ in the Mass, which keeps souls in blind bondage and dependency to this religious system. The New Testament militates against such an ill-conceived and unfounded practice. It does not teach or affirm that the Church leadership is to consist of a priestly hierarchy. Scripture does not describe the ministry and offices of the Church in the recurring role of priests performing sacramental rites.

Whenever Church leaders are mentioned in the New Testament two distinct words are used—"bishop" and "elder." The writers of the New Testament never use the Greek word for priest when referring to a bishop or elder.[12] They are distinct and never confused one for the other.

The Bible teaches there are three separate offices that define the order of the leadership in the New Testament Church; the offices of bishop, elder and deacon. In the New Testament the term "priest" or "priesthood" are nowhere applied or used for the minister or ministry of the Christian Church in these three offices. The word for *bishop* in the Greek New Testament is *episkopos* (ἐπίσκοπος) which is literally translated *overseer*, and means "to look or watch" over.[13] The bishop or overseer in the Church looks after the care of God's people and is to diligently protect and watch over them with love, care, and sound teaching from the Word of God. This term bishop (*Episkopos*) is used several times in the New Testament with this function and purpose in mind (see Acts 20:28; Philippians 1:1; 1 Timothy 3:2; Titus 1:7; 1 Peter 2:25). A bishop must hold firm to the sure Word, so that he may be able by sound doctrine to both exhort and convince those who are contrary to the faith (Titus 1:7,9). A bishop must have the aptitude to teach and attend to reading and teaching from Scripture (1 Timothy 4:13), and must rebuke those in sin before all (1 Timothy 5:20). He is to be married to one wife and must able to lead and rule his family accordingly (1 Timothy 3:2,5). A requirement of this nature certainly precludes a Roman Catholic priest from becoming a bishop under these terms, since he is an unmarried celibate. It is obvious to the reader that the New Testament does not teach that a bishop must be celibate. Elder, the other term used to describe the Christian overseer, is translated from the Greek word *presbyteros* (πρεσβυτερος), where the English word "Presbyter" comes from. The word elder denotes a person who is mature, well experienced, and tempered in the Christian faith

An examination of this word in the New Testament shows that both *elder* and *bishop* describe the selfsame person and office of *overseer*. Paul uses elder and bishop interchangeably in Acts 20:17-28 to mean one and the same office with the same ministry duties in the Church. Here, Paul called for the elders (presbyters) whom the Holy Spirit appointed to be overseers (bishops) to shepherd (pastor) the church of God, and exhorted them to faithfully tend to the needs of the flock. By calling the leaders of the Church at Ephesus both elders and bishops, Paul equates the elder and the overseer to be of the same ecclesiastical office and ministry. Therefore bishops are over oversees, and overseers are elders. The two are interchangeable in the Bible. This is further verified by the fact that Scripture gives the same qualifications for both elder and bishop indicating they occupy one and same church office and function of ministry (compare 1 Timothy 3:1-7 with Titus 1:5-9).

No mention of priests is made in these critical passages on defining leaders and their respective roles and duties in the Church! The duties of the bishop/elder in the church are administrative and pastoral. The overseer is to lead the church by being a servant of God's people, not in a dictatorial sense, but with an attitude of humility (Titus 1:7). This is contrary to the tyrannical history of the papacy with its claim that the Pope is the "Universal Bishop" of the entire church, demanding her unconditional submission (1 Peter 5:2-3). The duty of a bishop/elder is to be educational. He is to teach the Word of God so that the Church can grow and mature spiritually in the faith. He is to rebuke those who are in sin and strengthen the weak (1 Timothy 3:2;

---

[12] This is especially borne out by the observation that the New Testament Greek word for priest, which is *hiereus* (ἱερεύς), is never used for a bishop or elder; nor is *hiereus* ever mentioned in the sense of the Roman Catholic understanding where the priest is set apart in an office or ministry of a select group of male celibate candidates; who are placed above other believers in the church for the purpose of offering up the sacrifice of Christ over and over again.

[13] W.E.Vine, *An Expository Dictionary of Biblical Words*, 121.

Titus 1:9). The role of the elder is also pastoral. He is to meet the spiritual needs of the flock and administer care when needed (Acts 20:28; 1 Peter 5:2).

In the pertinent New Testament passages dealing with the responsibilities and duties of an overseer and elder there is no teaching or command given that he is to act in a priestly role, performing a sacrifice of the Mass, or dispensing saving grace through sacraments. Such an artificial construct of a priestly hierarchy is altogether foreign and antithetical to the ecclesiology of the New Testament. Having a plurality of elders was the norm for each local church in the New Testament. There was no centralized, monarchical episcopate established in the apostolic church; such an idea would not emerge until some six centuries later with the rise of the papacy. Every Church founded by the Apostles and their followers was governed by a plurality of bishops and elders selected carefully by each congregation (1 Timothy 5:17; Hebrews 13:17).

The right to act, make decisions of discipline, and appoint leaders was a joint effort equally shared amongst the leaders and the congregations they pastored in the first century church. This would tend to favor a democratic structure of sorts within the Christian Church contra the hierarchical monarchy of the Roman Catholic Institution. Reinforcing this point further, the valid observation can be made that the epistles of Paul and Peter were written for all Christians to read, rather than just a select bishop or a group of ecclesiastical leaders. Paul's letters to Timothy, Titus, and Philemon were addressed to individual leaders in the churches who were to share the written instructions and apostolic teaching with the rest of the congregation.

The third distinct office and ministry in the Christian Church that is mentioned in Scripture is the deacon. The Greek word for deacon is *diakonos* (διακονος) and has various meanings in the New Testament. The word can mean, *minister* (Ephesians 3:7); *servant* (Matthew 23:11; John 2:5); and *deacon* (Philippians 1:1; 1 Timothy 3:9). Deacons are those who serve in the church. Their primary responsibilities include helping the poor (Acts 6:1-6) and relieving the elders of certain duties so that these men can continue to teach the Word of God. Women could also hold the office of deacon in the Church and were known as deaconesses (e.g., Phoebe in Romans 16:1). The qualifications listed for a deacon are specified in First Timothy 3:8-12 and include the same moral qualifications that are stipulated for the office of bishop.[14] The New Testament description of the Christian minister whether elder, overseer, pastor, or deacon in no way fits with the Roman Catholic idea of an exclusive circle of priests. The New Testament does not endorse the whole idea of a mediating and expiatory priesthood. From the beginning of the Church, the earliest generations of Christian believers lived and died without calling any man a priest, nor did they seek the assistance of a sacrificial priesthood. Historians of every religious persuasion admit this.[15]

Rome's explanation for the absence of a sacerdotal priesthood in the New Testament is to posit that such an absence and glaring omission is due to the fact that the Apostles who presided over the "Eucharist" were already known to be priests in every way except in name only. According to Rome, the Apostles and Christian ministers of that time were not explicitly called "priests" because the Jewish priests, after the Aaronic order, were still offering animal sacrifices in the temple at Jerusalem, and any rival priesthood would be immediately crushed and their followers disbanded. Hence, to protect the fledging Church, the Apostles

---

[14]   For a good overview of the three offices of the Christian Church see H. Wayne House, *Charts of Christian Theology and Doctrine* (Grand Rapids: Zondervan, 1992), 118-121.

[15]   James White made this unassailable fact known in the same way during his debate with Jesuit priest, Mitchell Pacwa in *The Great Debate 2003*: "Is the Roman Catholic Priesthood Biblical and Ancient?" DVD or CD recording available through Alpha & Omega Ministries.

and their followers did not openly proclaim this newly established priesthood, but tacitly acknowledged it among themselves.[16]

However, in view of what we know from Scripture, this explanation given by Roman Catholic apologists as to why there be no mention of priests is completely untenable for several important reasons. First, the reason there is no mention in the New Testament of a sacrificing priesthood is clearly answered by the writer of Hebrews. His main thesis provides the reason why for this silence: the eternal priesthood of Christ with His once for all sacrifice for sin put an end to the Old Testament priesthood with its ongoing animal sacrifices. This abolishment practically applies to any and all contrived needs for a human priesthood and system of sacrifices so that they are no longer necessary and valid. By virtue of their superior quality, nature, and unrivaled efficacy, the priesthood and sacrifice of Jesus Christ has permanently removed any need for human priests offering their own physical sacrifices for sin.

The early church knew this and saw no need to repeat Christ's sacrifice in any way, whether with the elements of the Lord's Supper, or in some other prescribed manner. That is why there is no mention of an ongoing priesthood and sacrificial system of the New Testament Church. Secondly, the first believers in the early Christian Church were exclusively Jewish. These Jewish Christians did not regard Christianity as a new religion with new priests and sacrifices, but rather saw their faith in the Messiah as a fulfillment of biblical Judaism. They knew that Christ was the only sacrificial priest of the New Testament. They did not view the Eucharist and the Lord's Supper to be continuation of the Messiah's sacrifice. They viewed the Temple and its animal sacrifices to be types and shadows pointing to the atoning Messiah Jesus and His final sacrifice for sin (Hebrews 10:1). Indeed, as proof of this, we read in Acts 2:46 that the disciples broke bread in their homes, yet they still went to pray and worship in the Temple. The Apostle Paul presented offerings in the Temple as well. These examples clearly demonstrate that the early first century church did not assume that the Old Testament Jewish priests had been replaced by a new and special order of Christian priests.

Whenever the New Testament speaks of their celebrating the Lord's Supper, the Eucharistic bread and wine are never referred to as a continuation of Christ's sacrifice on the cross, offered exclusively by New Testament priests, but rather as a fellowship meal among worshipping Christians which symbolically commemorates the great salvation event of the cross (1 Corinthians 11:24-26). This subject will be dealt with in greater detail later in this book when discussing the Roman Catholic Mass. The concept of the Roman Catholic priesthood was an idea that gradually developed centuries after the New Testament period, culminating, finally, in the latter part of the eleventh century. To attempt to read the Roman Catholic priesthood back into the New Testament is simply unjustified and a gross oversimplification about apostolic teaching and practice in the first century Christian Church. Even Roman Catholic scholars admit the existence of their priests have no biblical warrant or justification. Again, Roman Catholic scholar and priest, Raymond Brown, is honest enough to concede this very thing when admitting that:

> A more traditional Catholic explanation of why individual Christians are not specifically designated as priests in the NT is that the apostles who presided at the Eucharist were priests in everything but name, for the name was too closely associated with the Jewish priests of the Temple. But this explanation is based on serious over simplification about apostles in the NT...and suffers from the added difficulty of unwarrantedly supposing

---

[16]   Ibid. Jesuit Priest, Mitchell Pacwa, offered this argument in defense of the Roman Catholic priesthood in his debate with Reformed Evangelical scholar, James White

that in NT times the Eucharist was thought of as a sacrifice and therefore associated with priesthood.[17]

Brown must later appeal to tradition for the establishment of the Roman Catholic priesthood after admitting its total absence in the New Testament. Third, the Apostles would not have shunned announcing that the Christian priest's re-presentation of Christ's sacrifice in the Eucharist was necessary for the forgiveness of sins—if it was central to the salvation of the sinner. The chief reason being, that their message was directly oriented around what Jesus Christ alone accomplished in His death and resurrection for the salvation of man. If, indeed, a sacramental priesthood was necessary for the forgiveness of sins, and an integral channel through which God's saving grace flows to the recipient, why were the apostles utterly silent in their teaching, preaching, and witnessing of this in the New Testament? They had already incurred the injurious wrath of the religious leaders of Jerusalem comprised of the Scribes, Priests Pharisees, Elders, and the High Priest for publicly proclaiming that salvation was in Jesus Christ alone (Acts 4:31). They were repeatedly arrested, beaten, and interrogated for this (Acts 4:13-21; 5:12-42 9:23-29; 12:1-10; 22-26). The willingness to suffer in these adverse ways for preaching that Jesus is the Messiah would not have further prevented them from proclaiming a new order of Christian priests, especially if their repetitious Eucharistic sacrifice of Christ given in the Mass was indispensable for salvation. To omit this crucial act from the central message of salvation would be unthinkable to the apostolic band that courageously faced martyrdom and severe persecution for their unshakable conviction and public confession that salvation can only be found in the crucified and risen Christ.

If there were a New Testament order of sacrificing priests that replaced the Aaronic priests of Old Testament Judaism, the Apostles would have fearlessly and repeatedly affirmed this vital truth in their teachings, speeches, sermons, and acts that were recorded in Sacred Scripture, just as they did when uncompromisingly preaching the Gospel. The fact that there is no such apostolic declaration of an ongoing Christian priesthood in the likeness of Jesus Christ, argues that there were no Christian priests cast in the mold of Roman Catholicism extant at that time due to the universal understanding in the Church that the "once for all" nature of Christ's sacrifice for sin, and the singular priesthood He occupies, effectively eliminated any further need for priests and sacrifices. The Roman Catholic priesthood is nothing more than a product of man-made religious tradition that began to evolve some two centuries after the birth of the New Testament Church.

There is no precedent or justification for the existence of the Roman Catholic priest in the writings of the New Testament. The Lord Jesus Christ is the one true Priest of the Christian and His saving death on the cross two thousand years ago is His sole saving sacrifice. When the New Testament does give extensive lists of the various ministries and gifts Christ Jesus gave to His Church *there is no mention of priests in any of these vital lists.* There are in fact five of these ministry/gift lists given in the New Testament (Ephesians 4:11; 1 Corinthians 12:4 -11, 28-30, Romans 12:6-8; 1 Peter 4:9-11). A brief review of these lists will patently show that neither a priest, nor a papacy is found among them. This is hard to believe if in fact both of these ecclesiastical ministries and offices are the bedrock of the New Testament Church, according to the hierarchical construct of Roman Catholicism. Both the papacy and the priesthood should head the New Testament lists of gifts and ministries of the Church, if, as Rome believes, they are the ground and pillar of the Church.

---

[17]   Raymond E. Brown, *Priest and Bishop*, 16.

In his epistle to the Ephesians, the Apostle Paul lists five ministerial gifts that Christ bestowed on the church for the mutual edification and maturation of it. *"And He Himself gave some to be apostles, some prophets, some evangelists, and some pastors and teachers for the equipping of the saints for the work of the ministry, for the edification of the body of Christ"* (Ephesians 4:11-12). The fivefold ministerial office is given here in the following order: (1) Apostles; (2) Prophets; (3) Evangelists; (4) Pastors and (5) Teachers. No mention of "Priests" is recoded in Ephesians 4:11, a place where their crucial sacramental ministry would surely be enumerated and clearly demonstrated, since Rome teaches its priesthood is essential for the spiritual welfare of the Church and Roman Catholic salvation. The omission from Paul is deliberate here because he, and the Christians he was writing to, already knew that Christ put an end to the sacrificial priesthood of men. We find the same is true in the two other New Testament passages where the ministries and gifts of the Church are also mentioned and explained. Paul gives an extensive list of spiritual gifts and ministerial offices in 1 Corinthians 12:4-11, 28-30, respectively. Here, Paul lists nine miraculous gifts of the Holy Spirit and three offices of the church. Not once does he mention the two miraculous "gifts" of the Roman Catholic papacy and priesthood with their power to forgive sins. Later, in the same chapter, Paul speaks of the appointed offices God has given ministers of the Church, that are similar to the list in Ephesians chapter four. They are apostles, prophets, teachers, miracles, healing, helping, administration, tongues, and interpretation of tongues.

The fourth list of spiritual gifts given in Romans 12:6-8 include prophecy, serving, teaching, exhortation, giving, leading, and showing mercy. The fifth and final list of spiritual gifts given in the New Testament is found in 1 Peter 4:9-11. Peter lists two distinct gifts for the Christian minister in this passage—speaking (primarily used in teaching and evangelizing), and *serving*. Thus, in all five New Testament lists of the ministries and spiritual gifts of the Church, there is no obvious mention, hint, or even vague inference of New Testament priests with a ministry of re-sacrificing Christ, or a papacy derived from the Apostle Peter! This is an embarrassing omission from the New Testament for the Dogmatists of Rome, especially in light of the fact they are sentimentally fond of saying that both the papacy and the sacramental priesthood are "gifts" to the Church from Christ. If so, why are not such vital and indispensable gifts supposedly given to the New Testament Church explicitly mentioned in the forefront of these five lists? Brilliant Lutheran theologian, Martin Chemnitz provides, the obvious answer with the following astute observation from Scripture:

> For it is worthy of note that although the Scriptures of the New Testament apply various terms to the ministry, yet in no passage of the New Testament are the ministers of the Word and the sacraments called priests. Nevertheless it is wholly that, by reason of their ministry, certain things belong to the ministers of the church which the rest of the faithful are not commanded to perform. But the question is which and what kind these are. It is not sufficient if one says that in the Old Testament the act of sacrificing made the distinction between priests and laity; therefore it should be the same also in the New Testament. For, first of all, the teaching about the abrogation of the Levitical priesthood of the Old Testament must be noted. Second, the term "priest" is nowhere in the New Testament applied to the ministers of the Word and of the sacraments. Third, in the Old Testament the priests did not sketch out for themselves on their own authority what they wanted to have belong to their ministry, but they had a prescribed Word and command of God which they followed in the actions of their ministry. Let us not fight about the question whether the term "priest" may be applied to the ministers of the New Testament on the basis of the Word, prescription, and command which has been handed down about the ministry in the

New Testament Scriptures...In all these passages there is found no discourse, no word, no syllable, nor even a letter to the effect that the ministers of the New Testament should by a theatrical representation in the Mass offer the body and blood of Christ to God the Father as a propitiatory sacrifice for the sins of the living and the dead; yes, this is in conflict with the statement of the Word of God in the Epistle to the Hebrews.[18]

The whole idea of a clerical hierarchy ruling over the rest of the Church, typical of the Roman Catholic clergy presiding over their "laity", is another alien concept that is not favorably supported or found in the New Testament. On the contrary, Jesus personally condemns this false distinction between a "clergy" and "laity" twice in the book of Revelation! Indeed the whole idea of an ecclesiastical or priestly class exercising control over the common people in the Church began to emerge at the close of the first century when the Apostle John was writing the book of Revelation while banished on the small Mediterranean island of Patmos by the Roman Emperor Domitian (51-96 A.D.). The risen and glorified Christ appeared to John on the island to reveal the prophetic events that would conclude the present age with the Second Coming. In chapter two of the book, the Lord Jesus twice makes a cryptic allusion to the teaching and doctrine of the "Nicolaitans," which is a striking precursor to the priestly clergy of the Roman Catholic institution. Apparently, the Nicolaitans were a heretical sect that brought destructive teachings into the churches of Ephesus and Pergamos (Revelation 2:6, 15). But who and what was this religious sect that posed a serious threat to the moral welfare and doctrinal integrity of Christ's Church? Bible commentators and New Testament scholars have spent much time attempting to identify who these Nicolaitans were, and what they believed. The early church fathers Irenaeus, Tertullian, and Hippolytus believed that the sect was founded by Nicolaus of Antioch, one of the seven original deacons selected by the Apostles in Acts 6:5, who later apostatized from the faith and formed this heretical sect.[19]

A second theory postulates that the Nicolaitans were a Gnostic antinomian group that denied the sinfulness of the human body, and by that negation, taught that a person was free to habitually indulge in licentious vices of the flesh.[20] Both of these theories rest on speculation and tradition but lack clear historical documentation connecting the Nicolaus of Acts chapter six with the incipient Gnosticism of a late first century religious sect identified to be the Nicolaitans.[21] Perhaps ascertaining the identity of this heretical group lies within the etymology of the word of "Nicolaitan" itself. The two Greek words that make up this compound word are *nikos* (νικος) meaning, "victory" or "conqueror", and *laos*, (λαός) meaning, "people". The word Nicolaitan thus means, "conquering of the people."

The word "laity" comes from the Greek word *laos* and is commonly used to refer to the faithful lay people of a Roman Catholic parish. With its applied meaning of *conquerors* or *rulers over the* people, the name Nicolaitans strongly suggests that they were an esoteric religious party that arose in the first century church (they first appeared in Ephesus and then Pergamos), and attempted to impose a religious hierarchy within the church to rule over the *common* people, who later came to be universally referred to with the diminutive term of the "laity".[22] The Nicolaitans attempted to make their congregations dependent upon their

18   Martin Chemnitz, *Examination of the Council of Trent, Part II*, (St. Louis: Concordia, 1978), 468.
19   See Robert Thomas, *Revelation 1-7: An Exegetical Commentary* (Chicago: Moody, 1992), 148.
20   John Peter Lange, *Revelation* (Grand Rapids: Zondervan, 1956), 116.
21   David Aune, *Word Biblical Commentary 52A: Revelation 1-5* (Nashville: Thomas Nelson, 1997), 148-149.
22   The Roman Catholic priesthood eventually used the word laity to mean the "nonclergy, distinguishing them as the common, uneducated dependents of the clerical governing elite"(*Encyclopedia of Catholicism*, page 746). Today, over 98 percent of the members in the Roman Catholic Church are laity.

vaunted spiritual authority and subordinate to their false doctrines, as well. The control and domination of other Christians was done through the establishment of an elitist hierarchy. They attempted to set themselves up as a priestly order in the role of the clergy, and those outside of the pale were deemed to be on a lower order called the laity whereby the people were to be subjugated to the Nicolaitan clergy's aberrant teachings and overbearing authority.

Nicolaitanism was most probably the forerunner to the clerical hierarchy of Romanism, which was later arbitrarily forced upon the ignorant masses, enslaving them to a sacramental system of rituals in place of a simple child-like trust in the finished work of Christ and the sure promises of God's Word. Loyalty to the church hierarchy replaced loyalty to Jesus Christ, which was falsely assumed to be the same. This resulted in church members placing their complete trust in a small select group of men for spiritual instruction and the prescribed rituals they performed in order to "dispense" salvation. This ecclesiastical hierarchy replaced the preeminence of Christ, the primacy of Scripture, and the leading of Holy Spirit in the lives of the laypeople. The heresies of Sacerdotalism, clericalism, and a priestly hierarchy found there way into Roman Catholicism, with its false class distinction of "clergy" and "laity", an idea which originated with the doctrine of Nicolaitanism, a doctrine which Jesus condemns twice when addressing the churches at Ephesus and Pergamos (Revelation 2:6, 15). The Roman Catholic priesthood and clergy, with its false class distinction of "clergy" and "laity, is a direct descendant of the doctrine of the Nicolaitans that Jesus strongly condemned in Revelation chapter two. Noted Bible author Tim LaHaye, in his commentary *Revelation Unveiled*, accurately describes the dangerous and harmful consequences that inevitably followed when Nicolaitanism was adopted and practiced by the Roman Catholic hierarchy of priests, monsignors, bishops, archbishops, cardinals, and Popes:

> This is a most dangerous principle indeed, since every human being is dependent on an abiding relationship with the Lord Jesus Christ to maintain spiritual vitality. "Holy men" may cease "abiding" after taking office, to the great detriment of the church. Another evil of this practice is that it causes the local church to look to human beings for the solution to their problems rather than to the Holy Spirit. The Lord Jesus said that He would send the Holy Spirit, who "will guide you into all truth" (John 16:13). Nicolaitanism, which is synonymous with modern day ecclesiasticism, is a concept about which Jesus Christ said, "I also hate." Would to God that the Church of Jesus Christ could learn the valuable lesson that it is not by ecclesiasticism or organization or promotion or administration, but "by my Spirit says the Lord." The greatest single curse in modern Christendom is ecclesiasticism. When human beings get control of the spiritual teaching of other people and are in a position to dominate the church, their theological position will eventually dominate that church.[23]

Eventually, the establishment of an ecclesiastical clergy, that usurped the universal priesthood of all believers, became so firmly ensconced in the church by the seventh century A.D. that members of the church were not allowed to read and comment upon the Scriptures for themselves. They were told what to believe and were indoctrinated to rely upon the rites and rituals of the priesthood to mediate between the person and God. Gradually, the sole headship of Christ was practically set aside in favor of the ecclesiastical hierarchy

---

[23] Tim LaHaye, *Revelation Unveiled* (Grand Rapids: Zondervan, 1999), 46.

of Popes and priests who arrogated to themselves titles and actions that belong to Jesus Christ alone, many of which the author has already addressed in this work. This all happened because the Church left its first love in the same manner the church of Ephesus did. Whenever this occurs, the Nicolaitan error, so prominently evident in the Roman Catholic system, will soon follow when the truth and authority of Christ and Scripture are supplanted and substituted with man-centered doctrines and human leadership.

> When a church leaves its first love, it begins to turn attention to ecclesiastical power and influence. When its leaders talk about "church loyalty" they are actually demanding loyalty to themselves, while they are leading the people from the Bible. The movements of the churches to enhance their political power and social prestige by union, federation, and worldly alliances are the deeds of the Nicolaitans. It is the effort of the church to restore by its own method what it has lost by forsaking God's method.[24]

There simply is no support or proof for a clerical hierarchy in the New Testament. When it first arose some two centuries after Christ, hierarchical clericalism gradually evolved into the unscriptural and abusive system of the Roman Catholic priesthood, which later took shape at the close of the fifth century.[25] Since Catholic scholars admit they cannot find this priesthood anywhere in the New Testament, they must bolster their arguments for it on church dogma and spurious tradition based on forgeries such as the Pseudo-Dionysus writings of the fifth century.

> *The divine institution of the threefold hierarchy cannot of course be derived from our text; in fact it cannot in anyway be proved directly from the New Testament*; it is a Catholic dogma by virtue of the dogmatic tradition, i.e., in a later period of ecclesiastical history the general belief in the divine institution of the episcopate, presbyteriate, and diaconate can be verified and thence followed on through the centuries. But the dogmatic truth cannot be traced back to Christ himself by analysis of strict historical testimony (Emphasis mine).[26]

The old Catholic Dictionary goes on to further add:

> The Word (hierarchy) first occurs in the work Pseudo-Dionysius on Celestial and Ecclesiastical Hierarchies. The signification was gradually modified until it came to be what it is at the present. A hierarchy now signifies a body of officials disposed organically in ranks and orders, each subordinate to the one above it.[27]

Another disturbing feature of the Roman Catholic priesthood is the mandatory celibacy required for all priests. Candidates who will be admitted into the priesthood are to be unmarried for the entire duration of their priestly service to the Roman Catholic institution.[28] Thus, one cannot be married if he is to be a priest

---

[24]   Arthur Bloomfield quoted in Gordon Lindsay's *The Seven Churches of Prophecy: Revelation Series, Volume 2* (Dallas, Texas: Christ for the Nations, 1982), 38

[25]   *Catholic Encyclopedia,* Volume IX, 61.

[26]   *Catholic Encyclopedia,* Volume VII, 334.

[27]   Addis and Arnold, *Catholic Dictionary* (New York: Catholic Publication Society, 1887), 402.

[28]   *The Code of Canon Law* **[Canon 1037]**, 185.

in this organization. To endorse the marriage of clergy is forbidden, and to allow them to exercise this right from the creation mandate of God is flatly condemned by the infamous Council of Trent during the twenty-fourth session:

> If anyone says that clerics who are in sacred orders, or persons in a monastic order, who have solemnly professed chastity, are able to contract matrimony, and that the contracted marriage is valid, ecclesiastical law or vow notwithstanding, and that the contrary is nothing else than to condemn marriage, and that all who do not think that they have the gift of chastity (even though they have vowed it) can contract matrimony, let him be anathema, since God does not deny this those who rightly ask, neither suffers us to be tempted above our strength.[29]

Was celibacy a normative requirement for the Christian minister according to the Lord Jesus Christ, His Apostles, and the New Testament Scriptures? When the honest inquirer reads the New Testament, he or she will plainly see there is neither a mandatory requirement for the celibacy of a Christian pastor, bishop, and deacon, nor any rule that prohibits the Christian minister from getting married, if he so chooses. Most of the Apostles, including Peter, were married and took their wives with them on their missionary travels—which would contradict Rome's insistence that her ministers remain celibate, from priest to the Pope himself. Though the Apostle Paul was unmarried, he could have lawfully taken a wife in marriage just like Cephas (Peter) and the other Apostles did (1 Corinthians 9:5). Marriage for the Christian minister was a norm in the first century for bishops, elders, and deacons. Each one was to be married to one woman—***"the husband of one wife"*** according to the stipulations laid out by the Apostle Paul in 1 Timothy 3:2, and Titus 1:6. Roman Catholic defenders pause here and try to escape the obvious by arguing that the marriage clause for bishops was not a necessary qualification for that office, but an admission of the conditions of the first century church before the church tradition of a celibate priesthood took firm root. However, the Greek words used in the syntax of 1 Timothy 3:2 and Titus 1:6 suggest that this is more than a mere accommodation or permission for that particular time period, but rather a general necessity for holding the office of bishop in the New Testament Church. The Greek text in 1Timothy 3:2 is δει ουν τον επισκοπον μιας γυναικος ανδρα ειναι, which is literally translated to read: "It is necessary that a bishop must be the husband of one wife."

The key Greek word used here and in Titus 1:6 is the impersonal verb dei (δει), denoting the necessity of the circumstance or the qualification of what is needed.[30] The verb carries the idea that all the domestic, social, and moral qualities listed for the office of a bishop are indeed necessary for a man to be a leader in Christ's church. Bishops, then, *must*, or *ought*, to be the husband of one wife.[31] There is no requirement or stipulation that a bishop must be celibate in these two New Testament passages. Both passages in the Greek text clearly

---

[29] *The Canons and Decrees of the Council of Trent*, 182.

[30] George W. Wright, *The International Greek Testament Commentary: The Pastoral Epistles* (Grand Rapids: Eerdmans, 1992), 155.

[31] This, of course, is not to say that a bishop, elder, or deacon has to be married in every case. He can be unmarried or widowed. The general rule for this in the New Testament, however, is that a qualified male leader in the church is to be married to one wife in order to demonstrate that just as he is capable of maintaining a wife and family, he then is able to faithfully take care of the Lord's church in similar fashion. The logic of the Apostle is clear here: If a man does not know now how to rule his family well, then he proves himself unfit to assume a governing role in the church.

teach that a bishop should be married—exactly opposite of what Roman Catholic doctrine demands of her unmarried bishops and priests! Dr. C Elliott further elaborates:

> The terms made use of in these passages mean more than a bare *permission* to marry, or a bare *tolerance* in office to those who are married. The words used denote *duty* or *necessity*…. The expression of the apostle (1 Tim. iii. 2) is δει ουν τον επισκοπον μιας γυναικος ανδρα ειναι, for a *bishop* MUST OR OUGHT *to be the husband of one wife.* And, in the Epistle to Titus (ch. i., verse 7), the expression is similar, and means a bishop *must* or *ought* to be blameless. The married state is here presented as that which is *most becoming, proper* or indeed *necessary* for a man who presides over the flock of Christ. And it is considered as needful a qualification as temperance, blamelessness, aptitude to teach, and the like. And though a minister may be a good one who is not married; yet he is not *so good*, in general, as those who have pious and intelligent wives and walk worthy their vocation. We do not hear the apostle say, "Although bishops and deacons are not to be prohibited from marrying, yet, whenever it can be done, it is well to prefer those who have professed virginity." No such language escapes the apostle. He represents a bishop to be one who has a wife and children, and who, rules his house.[32]

Not one word is found in 1 Timothy 3:2 or Titus 1:7 that advocates an exclusive celibacy for the minister, leader, or clergy in the church. The ideal bishop in view of Scripture is not one who maintains an unreasonable and enforced celibacy but a man who has a wife and children whom he serves and provides for as the head and leader of the home. The reader of the New Testament will search in vain for a mandatory celibacy required for the ministers and leaders of the Church. No such thing existed in the form that Rome teaches and demands from its "clergy" today. Roman Catholic scholars even admit there was no obligatory celibacy in apostolic times and that such a historical fact proves detrimental to their prohibition of marriage for the clergy. Concerning 1Timothy 3:2, 12 and Titus 1:6, the *Catholic Encyclopedia* concedes: "These passages seem fatal to any contention that celibacy was made obligatory upon the clergy from the beginning."[33] The Word of God says a bishop "must" be the husband of one wife, and Rome blatantly contradicts Scripture by demanding their bishops and priests must be unmarried celibates.

When you peruse a book written by a defender of Rome's priesthood, he will typically refer to Paul's preference for celibacy in 1 Corinthians 7 and the statement of Jesus concerning eunuchs in Matthew 19:11-12. First Corinthians chapter seven covers important topics that pertain to marriage, divorce, celibacy, and singlehood, yet we do not find the Apostle dogmatically insisting that every ordained minister has to remain celibate. Paul teaches that celibacy was good, and wishes that everyone could see the spiritual benefits of remaining single for Christ, but to remain single or to marry was not weighed in terms of compulsory necessity, as each is a gift of God. God individually calls every Christian servant to either be married or unmarried. This naturally begs the question of how the Christian is to know whether or not he or she is to remain celibate or not. The simple and practical answer Paul gives is if one lacks sexual control, then he or she does not have the gift of celibacy and should therefore marry (verses 7-8). Paul never demeans marriage for the believer or Christian minister. He never eschews marriage for those called to it.

---

[32]   Dr. C Elliott, *Romanism, Volume 1* in *The History of Romanism*, page 69-70.
[33]   *Catholic Encyclopedia*, Volume III, 483.

Paul goes on to say that being single and unmarried like he was, can afford the servant of Christ a better opportunity of undistracted service for Christ, whereas the married Christian's (verses 32-35) devotion would naturally be divided between the domestic needs of family and his ministerial responsibilities to Christ and His church. In saying this, however, Paul never categorically states that the condition of celibacy is a superior state of spirituality compared to married life, nor is this idea found anywhere else in Scripture. Rome's proof text for a celibate priesthood is not justified here and is a case of simply reading their own presuppostional biases into the text of First Corinthians chapter seven to illegitimately support compulsory celibacy for the "clergy." Jesus' commentary on celibacy in Matthew 19:11-12 was given within the context of divorce and remarriage, not a requirement for being a Christian priest or minister. The strict prohibition Jesus lays down for marriage and divorce prompted His disciples to cynically ask him, ***"If such is the case of the man with his wife, it is better not to marry"*** (Matthew 19:10). Jesus responded by saying those who wish to remain celibate do so only if they willingly choose to accept it as a vocation and calling by God. ***"But He said to them, all cannot accept this saying, but only those to whom it has been given. For there are eunuchs who were born thus from their mother's womb, and there eunuchs who were made eunuchs by men, and there are eunuchs who have made themselves eunuchs for the kingdom of heaven's sake. He who is able to accept it, let him accept it*** (Matthew 19:12).*"* Notice in this passage Jesus says there are three kinds of celibacy. The first kind is *congenital celibacy*. This occurs when a person is physically born without the necessary sexual organs to have marital relations. The second kind is *compulsory celibacy* where men are forced by society or individuals to be celibate. In the ancient Near East, compulsory celibacy was practiced on those males chosen to serve in king's harems. These men were emasculated to prevent any sexual scandal among a king's wives and concubines and were thus "made Eunuchs by men."

The third kind of celibacy Christ names in Matthew 19 is a *celibacy of personal conviction*. It is a celibacy that is voluntarily chosen by a person who deliberately forgoes the married life to remain single in order to better serve the Lord Jesus Christ without the incumbent distractions of supporting the needs of a wife and family. Christ allows celibacy on a voluntary and volitional level, if that person believes he has the gift of celibacy, but it is personal matter left to the individual and God.[34] It is in the context of marriage that Jesus speaks about celibacy in Matthew 19. Jesus Christ did not establish a religious institution in which single men were required to be celibate in order to form a priesthood or monastic order, nor did He make compulsory celibacy a prerequisite when choosing the twelve Apostles. Nor did the Apostles demand obligatory celibacy for any prospective minister to hold a governing office or leadership role in the early Church. Rome admits that both Scripture and early church tradition deny this requirement, and are thus forced to appeal to later church tradition to support this unbiblical doctrine![35] In 1967, Pope Paul VI released a papal encyclical entitled *Sacerdotalis Caelibatus*, and readily admitted the following:

> Let us look openly at the principle objections against the law that links ecclesiastical celibacy with the priesthood. The first seems to come from the most authoritative source, the New Testament which preserves the teaching of Christ and the Apostles. It does not demand celibacy of sacred ministers but proposes it rather as a free act of obedience to a special vocation or to a special spiritual gift. Jesus himself did not make it a prerequisite in his choice of the Twelve, nor did the Apostles for those who presided over the first

---

[34]   John Phillips, *Exploring the Gospel of Matthew* (Grand Rapids: Kregel, 1999), 380.
[35]   Walter Abbott, *The Documents of Vatican II*, 565.

Christian communities (Vatican Council II Documents No. 95, *Sacerdotalis Caelibatus*, 24 June 1967, Vol. II Sec.5, p. 286).

The Vatican admits the New Testament is "the most authoritative source" on the issue of celibacy, and yet she ignores what the Scriptures says, as she does regarding so many other doctrines and practices; but, nonetheless, she made celibacy a "canon law" making it a mandatory requirement for its priesthood! Clearly such an example in this case merits the rebuke of the Lord Jesus Christ who censured the Pharisees for doing exactly what the Roman Catholic Institution does here with regard to mandatory celibacy and its utter absence in the New Testament: *"Well did Isaiah prophesy of you hypocrites, as it is written: 'This people honors Me with their lips, but their heart is far from Me, and in vain they worship Me, teaching as doctrines the commandments of men'...All too well you reject the commandment of God that you may keep your tradition"* (Mark 7:6-9).

A most startling revelation is made known when the prophetic Scriptures of the New Testament accurately foretold the prohibition of marriage that would exist in apostate Christendom during "the last days". This telling prophecy is found in 1Timothy 4:1-3, where Paul warns Timothy that in the time leading up to the return of Christ (denoted by the phrase "in the latter times") false doctrines, inspired by deceiving spirits, will be introduced and circulated throughout the church. The Apostle then lists several examples of these demonic doctrines when forewarning the young Timothy: *"Now the Spirit explicitly says that in the latter times some will depart from the faith, giving heed to deceiving spirits and doctrines of demons, speaking lies in hypocrisy, having their own conscience seared with a hot iron; <u>forbidding to marry</u>..."* (1Timothy 4:1-3). Paul informs Timothy that for anyone to forbid or prohibit marriage in the Christian church is one indication that a person or group within the Church is apostate and promulgating a doctrine of demons! Rome thus fulfills this latter times prophecy with her obstinate insistence on having an unmarried priesthood. According to 1 Timothy 4:3, the Roman Catholic teaching that forbids their priest from marrying is a *doctrine of demons*, and is therefore clearly unbiblical.

In their vain attempt to explain this away, Catholic theologians and apologists claim Paul was instructing Timothy about those who viewed marriage itself as bad or evil.[36] They claim this was particularly fulfilled by the rise of Gnosticism in the second century A.D. Gnostics typically held a disdain for the physical body along with its sensual aspects associated with it and therefore prescribed an ascetic prohibition against it. Therefore, Rome teaches that Paul's warning and prophecy is directed towards these Gnostic sects, but such a narrow interpretation is not the full scope of Paul's discourse to Timothy.

Undoubtedly, Paul had these groups in mind, but his warning is against *all prohibition of marriage in general for whatever reason*. To prohibit legitimate marriage *for any reason* in the church is inherently wrong and goes against the creation mandate God universally designed for a man and woman in marriage (Genesis 1:27; 2:24; Matthew 19:4-6). The prophecy of 1 Timothy 4:3 applies to any person or institution that would arise within the Church to prohibit marriage on any level.

The establishment of mandatory celibacy in the Roman Catholic Church is a major fulfillment of this prophecy, and a doctrine of demons as well. Proponents of Roman Catholicism routinely deny this by arguing that the Catholic Church forbids no one to marry, and those who choose to join the priesthood do so voluntarily without compulsion by the Church, and that any Catholic is free to marry if he so chooses.[37]

---

[36] John Salza, *The Biblical Basis for the Catholic Faith*, 122; Karl Keating, *What Catholics Really Believe—Setting the Record Straight* (Ann Arbor: Servant Publications, 1992), 134-135.

[37] A typical case here is the explanation provided by apologist Karl Keating's Catholic Answers web site at www.

Though this disavowal may appear to be true on the surface, the practical effect remains the same. Roman Catholics can marry if laity, but if they seek to take the full role and responsibilities of a clerical minister in the Catholic Church they must enter the priesthood which forbids marriage to all candidates who are single. The Roman Catholic Canon Law states they are "obliged" to remain unmarried once they become priests. Marriage is forbidden for them.[38] Catholics cannot attain to the highest level of ministry in their religious system unless they submit to the prohibition of marriage in order to become ordained priests with the full authority to administer all seven sacraments.

The issue here is not whether Rome prohibits marriage individually or corporately; the fact is, she does prohibit it for all single males who desire to pursue a vocation in the Roman Catholic priesthood. They are not allowed to become priests until they surrender to the Vatican's arbitrary demand for celibacy. The assumption for mandatory celibacy is that a priest can better devote Himself to Christ, when in reality the priest becomes more enslaved to the papacy and its man-made rules and traditions instead. And so, this apostate religious body violates 1Timothy 4:3 repeatedly when forbidding their celibate priest to marry!

Priests who would simply exercise their God given right from Scripture to take a wife in the honorable state of marriage are subject to severe punishment and dismissal from the clerical state. For Roman Catholic Canon Law dictates in **Canon 1395**: "A cleric who attempts marriage, even if only civilly, incurs a *latae sententiae* suspension. Once warned, if he has not reformed, and continues to give scandal, he can progressively be punished by deprivations, or even by dismissal from the clerical state."[39] Scripture teaches that he who finds a wife finds a good thing and obtains favor from the Lord (Proverbs 18:22). Marriage is esteemed "honorable among all" in Hebrews 13:4. Despite the fact God's Word declares marriage good and honorable for all (including ministers of Christ), the Roman Catholic Church punishes and excommunicates those priests who would receive this gift of marriage, denigrating it to be a scandal and a punishable offense by their Canon Law.

The sexual turpitude and scandals currently plaguing the Roman Catholic Church have come from the unnatural repudiation of marriage which is demanded of her priests. Enforced celibacy is the main reason for the sexual abuse atrocities that have shaken the Catholic hierarchy to its very foundations. The proof for this is so widespread; not only in the modern day, but also in the Church's past, that to fully document them could possibly fill enough volumes to take up the space of several floors in a public library! Former Dominican priest, Richard Bennett corroborates this tragic fact of Romish apostasy when commenting:

> The agony, misery, and morality of thousands of Roman Catholic priests notwithstanding, the Roman Catholic Church continues to enforce its own law on its followers. As Scripture says, those who teach such things have departed from the faith in order to propagate their demonic doctrine. Rome has departed from the faith commending and enjoining celibacy and virginity to the office of a Pastor that God has never commanded. What they consider 'Holy' turns out to be unholy, and what is in fact 'Holy', Rome absolutely prohibits. The

---

catholic.com/library/celibacyandthepriesthood.asp. The one lone exception in the Latin rite of the Catholic Church is if a married priest from the Anglican Church decides to "convert" and become a priest of Rome, he can remain married. Those priests who follow the Eastern Rite are allowed to marry before ordination, but not after it. However, celibacy is strongly encouraged from the outset.

[38] **Canon 277** states, "Clerics are obliged to observe perfect and perpetual continence for the sake of the Kingdom of heaven, and therefore bound to celibacy

[39] *The Code of Canon Law*, 247.

present crisis of the Roman Catholic Church show what a disaster may come when the Bible is set aside as the basis of all truth. And in its place is set the inane Tradition of fallible man.[40]

While there have been some sincere priests who have kept their vow of celibacy intact, the imposition of an unnatural and unbiblical burden placed upon the Roman Catholic clergy has historically created a dysfunctional atmosphere that has engendered sexual immorality and perversion of every kind. Pedophilia, homosexuality, adultery, and fornication are the recurrent fruits of the Pope's dictatorial imposition of celibacy upon his deluded clerical subjects. A religious system that demands the unrealistic and unbiblical yoke of mandatory celibacy among a large number of men for the last 1000 years, or so, have created a pathological environment where sexual deviance and immorality naturally follow and now run amok in the Catholic clergy. The history of her Popes and priests are replete with this ugly fact. The reason for this is simple: to deny the act of marriage to a minister of the Christian church for any reason, as Rome has done, is contrary to God's natural order for procreation and only intensifies, enflames and exacerbates the natural tendency for sexual intimacy within a heterosexual man. And since the Roman Catholic priest cannot legitimately express his sexuality in marriage, he is therefore tempted to seek out other ways to fulfill it.

Most males within the Roman Catholic priesthood, who cannot endure the unreasonable restraint of imposed celibacy, and there is a significant number of them, that have a heterosexual inclination, usually resort either to the sin of fornication or adultery. Those who are afflicted with the perversity of homosexuality will find an all male society like the Roman Catholic priesthood an ideal place to surreptitiously engage in their terrible immorality under the respectable guise of being a priest, which the Roman Catholic Church unwittingly affords them. Indeed, the priesthood is rife with a pervasive homosexuality to the disturbing extent that sincere heterosexual candidates leave the seminary and abandon their religious vocations because of the gay subculture they were forced to endure. Many of them were propositioned or harassed, and in some cases, molested by these clerical sodomites.[41] Recently, an unidentified priest from the archdiocese of Boston, Massachusetts, anonymously revealed to a reporter with the *Boston Herald* that such deviant occurrences

---

[40]   Richard Bennett, "Better To Marry Than To Burn: Boston and the Catholic Troubles", page 5 (Article from http://www.bereanbeacon.org). Another former priest who lived in the mid-nineteenth century, who was aghast at the pervasive sexual immorality of Roman Catholic priests, sorrowfully wrote without exaggeration, "I am sorry to say, from my knowledge of Roman Catholic priests...that there is not a more corrupt, licentious body of men in the world" (William Hogan, *Popery As it Was and As It Is* (Hartford: 1854). Kessinger Publications republished this monograph in 2004.

[41]   Michael Rose, *Goodbye! Good Men* (Cincinnati, Ohio: Aquinas, 2002), 93. Rose, a Roman Catholic author, goes on his chapter entitled, *The Gay Subculture*, to disturbingly document how the pervasive homosexual subculture in Roman Catholic seminaries among students and faculty is so widespread that the homosexual politics that govern them routinely discriminate against healthy, heterosexual men from entering the priesthood, (see pages 90-133 of the aforementioned book). While attending a Roman Catholic seminary, the author was propositioned by a homosexual seminarian and forthrightly rejected his unwanted advances. As recounted earlier in chapter one, the author was also horribly aware of homosexual priests and monks who went morally unchecked among each other and the student body where he attended an all boys Catholic parochial boarding school. He was unable to go to anyone in authority because they were covering it up and threatened anyone who exposed (no pun intended) this scandalous debauchery, or they were also homosexual themselves and would naturally do nothing to correct and censure such depravity, but only encouraged it.

were commonplace among the gay subculture existing within Roman Catholic seminaries and priests; of which he himself was shamefully subjected to. He gives the following personal account:

> "The problem is," said the priest, "there's a subculture of gay priests and everyone knows it. I went through seminary *with a lot of them and got hit on.* And when I reported it, I was harassed to a point where, emotionally, it was very difficult to get ordained. I'm not the only one who had to fight to get through it; I know guys who left because of it. It was clear there was a cabal tacitly saying, 'Don't bother reporting this stuff.' You wouldn't believe the self-justifications, like, 'Well, celibacy only applies to not getting married we can do whatever we want.' It was horrible, with a lot of intimidation..."[42]

The problem of homosexuality in the Catholic seminaries and priesthood is so rampant that gay seminarians feel quite comfortable with being open about their homosexuality without fear of discipline or removal. An atmosphere that welcomes and nurtures this kind of sexual perversion has no doubt created a tolerance and tacit approval throughout the hierarchical ranks of the clergy, to the extent that many homosexuals feel comfortable in this all-male environment where marriage and interaction with women are strongly prohibited and discouraged. An unhealthy atmosphere of this kind can only breed and nurture the aberrant phenomenon of homosexuality, along with other forms of sexual immorality. Roman Catholic priest and rector of Saint Mary Seminary, Donald Cozzens, in his best selling book, *The Changing Face of the Priesthood*, describes the sociological elements that have led to this in the Catholic clergy and seminaries when pointing out:

> Gay seminarians are likely to feel at home and at ease in a seminary with a significant gay population. They feel they belong and their need for meaningful, deep relationships with other gay men is easily met, and because they instinctively recognize other gay seminarians, circles of support and camaraderie are quickly formed. Their nurturing community provides engaging conversation reflecting their common interests in spirituality and performing arts. Not infrequently, however, the sexual contacts and romantic unions among gay seminarians creates intense and complicated webs of intrigue and jealousy leading to considerable inner conflict.[43]

The fact that this same observation is often made amongst Catholic priests themselves indicates that this problem is quite common. Defenders of Rome would quickly object by claiming the percentage of homosexual in her priesthood is no higher that the normal percentage of homosexuals within the adult male population. Rome claims this number is perhaps five to ten percent of the clerical population, but they fail to cite valid statistics supporting their assertion. The data that is available to determine what percentage of 'celibate' priests are homosexual actually proves that this is not a random occurrence, or rare anomaly, but a fairly common trait. Though no researcher or statistician can provide an exact percentage of how many priests are homosexual, extensive research suggests the number is significantly higher than in society. Recent

---

[42]   Joe Fitzgerald, "Priests fears gays in ranks pose threat to Church," from the March 6, 2002 edition of the *Boston Herald*.

[43]   Donald B. Cozzens, *The Changing Face of the Priesthood* (Collegeville, Minnesota: 2000), 135.

research and surveys indicate that as many as half of the Roman Catholic clergy are homosexuals. From his book, Donald Cozzens shockingly reveals:

> Vicars of priests and seminary administrators who have been around awhile speak among themselves of the disproportionate number of gay men that populate our seminaries and presbytereates. They know that a proportionate number of gay priests and seminarians would fall between 5 and 10 percent. An NBC report on celibacy and the clergy found that 'anywhere from 20 percent to 58 percent of Catholic clergy have a homosexual orientation. Other studies find that approximately half of American priests and seminarians are homosexually oriented. Sociologist James G. Wolf in his book *Gay Priests* concluded that 48.5 percent of priests and 55.1 percent of seminarians were gay. The percentage appears to be highest among priests under forty years of age. Moreover, the percentage of gay men among religious congregations of priests is believed to be even higher.[44]

The truth is that the strong homosexual presence within the Catholic clergy is due to the unsettling fact that you have an unbiblical system where only celibate men are allowed in its priesthood, thus opening up the very real possibility that a higher percentage of homosexual men are going to be attracted to such a profession where the environment is exclusively male![45] In her stubborn adherence to man-made tradition, Rome refuses to make the obvious connection between enforced celibacy and the widespread sexual immorality in the priesthood that has existed for over one thousand years. When men in the Roman Catholic priesthood are forced to live with each other within the closed confines of an insular monastery or Rectory, where women are not allowed, the need for sexual expression, whether in a heterosexual or homosexual manner, is supposed to be absent. But the opposite often occurs, and the urge for sexual expression is only magnified to an unbearable level—hence the sexual scandals of pedophilia, homosexuality, adultery, and fornication abound and continue among a morally corrupt 'celibate priesthood.' Author Kendrick Kendall gives a most frightening and accurate assessment of why this keeps happening:

> When a man is immersed in a closed culture in which relationships with women are expressly forbidden, they are not at the same time stripped of their libido (be it hetero- or homosexual). Yes, they do 'sign-up' for celibacy because it is required to attain a truly admirable goal: to become a priest who serves the people. But more often than not it is merely a means to an end that denies and ignores the nature of the man himself - unless, of course, that man is a homosexual or pedophile to begin with. All too often the result is what most researchers term "arrested psychosexual development." That is to say that for many priests, their ability to face, to deal with their natural sexuality, remains at an immature, juvenile level. Also, the Catholic tradition that considers celibacy a higher state than marriage, not only denigrates both marriage and women, but fosters intimate bonds

---

[44]   Ibid., 99. See also Timothy Unsworth, *The Last Priest in America* (New York: Crossroad, 1991), 248; James Wolf, ed., *Gay Priests* (San Francisco: Harper and Row, 1989), 59-60.

[45]   Jason Berry, *Lead Us Not Into Temptation: Catholic Priests and the Sexual Abuse of Children* (Garden City, New York: Image Books, 1992), 185.

between people of the same sex - men. Is it any wonder that the seminaries are producing an increasing number of sexually deviant priests?[46]

The blatant hypocrisy of Rome is never more evident than when they tolerate this homosexual subculture within their own ranks, yet would immediately remove a priest who would chose to marry. But if the priest is gay, he is quietly tolerated by his superiors and permitted to discreetly carry on. God unequivocally condemns the homosexual lifestyle throughout the pages of Scripture in both the Old and New Testaments. To engage in the homosexual act is morally detestable to a holy God. Twice in Holy Scripture it is labeled an *abomination* in the Lord's sight (Leviticus 18:22; 20:13). A primary reason God overthrew the twin cities of Sodom and Gomorrah was because of homosexuality (Genesis 19). Both depraved cities were notorious for their public practice and approval of this sin. The perverted inhabitants of Sodom and Gomorrah were *"exceedingly wicked and sinful against the Lord"* (Genesis 13:13). Homosexuality is one dreadful result of rejecting the one true God; it twists and perverts what God has intended for a man and a woman in the natural order of creation (Romans 1:26-32). Those who habitually engage in the unnatural act of homosexuality will not inherit the Kingdom of God (1 Corinthians 6:9-10), and if they refuse to repent (turn from their sin) and trust in the Lord Jesus Christ, they are destined for the lake of fire (Revelation 21:8).

If the Vatican were truly committed to upholding and following the moral precepts, teachings, and commandments of Scripture—which clearly condemn the awful sin of homosexuality—it certainly would not allowed a thriving, gay subculture to be firmly ensconced within its priesthood. They know that the homosexual lifestyle is decidedly unbiblical and have stated this so in the past, in public decrees and documents issued from the Popes and bishops; yet they refuse to carry out a sustained policy to ferret out and remove active homosexuals from the priesthood. There are several reasons for the Vatican's reticence do this. First, Rome knows full well that if she removed all known homosexual priests from their ranks, the shortage of priests that now exists, and this is a serious problem, would cause the whole hierarchical infrastructure to collapse, since there is a significant number of priests who are homosexual. In his revealing book, *The Power and the Glory*, author David Yallop relates how an influential figure in Rome told him why the Vatican would not adopt a zero tolerance policy regarding sex abusers and homosexuals:

> Recently a Rome based prelate observed to me, 'There will not be, either in the short or medium term, a policy of zero tolerance with regard to the sex abusers. *If such a policy existed and was applied across the board, irrespective of position, there are many bishops who would be forced to resign ... many cardinals who would have to take early retirement ... As for zero tolerance towards homosexuals, we already have that. It just happens to be confined to the laity.* **If it were applied to the priesthood, the infrastructure would collapse'** (Emphasis mine).[47]

Secondly, if Rome carried out a systematic purge to remove incorrigible homosexuals from the priesthood, she would be continually portrayed by a liberal media as a militant, homophobic institution carrying out a witch-hunt against "innocent victims" rivaling that of the medieval inquisition. In a politically correct world, Rome cannot afford such a costly misstep, if she is to continue as a great religious authority that champions

---

46 Kendrick A. Kendall, *Blow the Trumpets* (Bloomington, IN: Trafford Publishers, 2005), 29.
47 David Yallop, *The Power and the Glory: Inside the Dark Heart of John Paul II's Vatican* (New York: Carroll & Graf, 2007), 353.

human rights and the just treatment of man. But in order to save moral face among religious and social conservatives, the Vatican verbally disapproves of homosexuality in the world at large, while tolerating it among their clergy under a sanctimonious façade of celibacy.

Pedophilia (having sexual contact with children) is another rotten and sinister fruit of enforced celibacy, particularly for those priests who already have a secret penchant for this heinous habit. Hiding behind the mask of sexual and moral purity (under the guise of celibacy), is the perfect cover for these predatory priests to molest unsuspecting children. Unsuspecting Catholic parents are routinely caught off guard with the pious front the molester priest cleverly maintains, and once he has won the confidence of the parents with the trust of their children, the trap is horribly set for sexual abuse to begin. Recent studies have been conducted on the causes of the pedophilia scandal currently engulfing the Roman Catholic Church. One significant study, conducted by the Center for the Study of Religious Issues, under the research division of CITI Ministries, carried out extensive quantitative studies during a five-year period from 1999 to 2004.[48] The evidence accumulated from this determinative study shows that an obvious connection exists between enforced celibacy and sexual abuse. Author of *The Bingo Report*, Louise Haggett concludes after presenting the research data that there is strong evidence tying mandatory celibacy to the sexual abuse of children by Roman Catholic priests. Haggett observes from this study:

> A demonstrable link exists between mandatory celibacy and clergy sexual abuse. Sexual abuse by Roman Catholic clergy is different from sexual abuse by other populations in almost every aspect of the victim/perpetrator profiles and characteristics, differences that can only be seen by segregating respective demographics and other specifics from general population abuse.[49]

In 2002, Dr. Timothy J. Dailey, and the Washington D.C. based Family Research Council, carried out a research study that confirmed what police and psychiatrists have known for quite some time: That a definite link exists between male homosexuality and pedophilia. Dailey's report published as *Homosexuality and Child Sexual Abuse* "shows that while homosexual men make up less than the three percent of the adult male population, they commit a disproportionate number (one third or more) of child sexual molestations."[50] Dailey's report was subsequently sent to parents, youth groups, school administrators, Catholic bishops, and religious organizations. Secular psychiatrists, who advocate normalizing homosexuality, would reject such findings; however, it has long been established that such a link does exist.

As we turn to the multiple sexual abuse cases involving Roman Catholic priests, one thing is plainly clear: the majority of these sex abusers are homosexuals, while the minority is made up of bisexuals and heterosexuals. Moreover, there are more reported cases on file of sexual abuse committed by Roman Catholic priests, than those involving clergy from denominations where ministers are allowed to marry. The frequency of these ongoing, horrid acts is so numerous within the Catholic Church that multiple support groups and organizations have been established to reach out to victims of priestly abuse and also to force the Pope and the clergy under him to answer for their massive cover up of these perverted atrocities.[51]

---

[48] See Louise Haggett, *The Bingo Report* (Freeport, Maine: CSRI Books, 2005).

[49] http://rentapriest.blogspot.com/search?q=the+bingo+report

[50] "Study Shows Link Between Homosexuality and Pedophilia" from the September 2002 edition of The Interim (http://www.theinterim.com/2002/sept/02study.html).

[51] The oldest and most active of these support groups is SNAP (Survivors Network of those Abused by Priests)

The numerous law suites filed by the abuse victims against the various dioceses in America indicate the seriousness and veracity of this issue. A brief review of following pedophilia scandals in the U.S. will show any objective observer that this is a pervasive and continuous problem within the Catholic Church. This becomes even more disturbing when it is discovered that in each sexual abuse case the pedophile priest was conveniently transferred by his superiors (who knew all along he was a sex abuser!) to another parish—where he molested even more children. Instead of being defrocked from the priesthood and turned over to law enforcement authorities for prosecution, the molesters were allowed to remain priests for some time. The scandal was ignored, or simply covered up by the bishop of the diocese with full complicity from the Vatican. Rome continued to protect these guilty pedophiles instead of protecting the innocent lives of children who were severely ruined and damaged by them. Such unconscionable behavior is criminal, intolerable, and totally inexcusable for a religious institution that boastfully claims that it is Christ's one true church on Earth. Rome's damnable actions, particularly with the ongoing sexual abuse scandals of her priests, undeniably demonstrate otherwise!

Certainly the most famous sexual abuse case was the scandal that rocked the Archdiocese of Boston for the past decade. Amid accusations of sexual misconduct against a number of priests, it was revealed that there was a deliberate cover-up by Cardinal Bernard Law that allowed these deviant priests to continue to rape and molest innocent children. Such crimes could have been prevented if Cardinal Law had acted quickly and decisively in dealing with his wayward priests. Two particular priests under the Cardinal's supervision, Paul Shanley and John Geoghan, were predatory wolves in priest's clothing. While still a priest, Shanley was a member of the North American Man/Boy Love Association (NAMBLA), which is an organization that advocates the legalization of sexual relations between adult males and underage boys! Shanley and fellow priest John J. White were co-owners of a bed and breakfast establishment that catered to gay clientele. Shanley was convicted and found guilty in February 2005 of statutory rape of a minor, and was later accused of additional sexual violations against other under age boys.

For over thirty years, another Boston area priest, John Geoghan, was accused of sexual abuse by more than 130 people! Since then, a more recent settlement involving 552 sexual abuse victims in the Boston area resulted in a payout of 84 million dollars, a similar dollar amount was paid by the Diocese of Covington, Kentucky in its settlement of 360 sexual abuse claims back in 2006. Additionally, official church documents of the Boston diocese revealed Cardinal Law's extensive and continual role in covering up for the pedophile activities of his priests. He repeatedly moved Paul Shanley and John Geoghan from parish to parish, despite knowing full well repeated allegations of pedophilia and sexual misconduct were made against the two priests. When Cardinal Law was put under oath in a court of law, he refused to answer directly about why he knowingly condoned and allowed these pedophile priests to continue in their sexual misconduct by moving them from parish to parish. His pathetic answer for this unforgivable exercise was that he simply failed to keep proper records. The Cardinal also often resorted to "selective amnesia" when he failed to recall pertinent facts in the case. Law was eventually forced to resign and Pope John Paul II reappointed him to the Vatican without any discipline or punishment for his gross and willful negligence in the Boston Archdiocese sex scandal.[52]

---

established in 1989. The founders of this organization were surviving victims of sexual abuse perpetrated by Catholic priests. They can be contacted on the web at www.snapnetwork.org. Voice of the Faithful is another advocacy group founded in 2002 by lay Catholics who were instrumental in bringing the sex scandals of the Boston diocese to light. It currently has 25,000 members.

[52]   For a full documentation of the sex abuse crisis in the Archdiocese of Boston see the Pulitzer Prize price winning

On the West Coast, there were two disturbing sexual abuse cases that rocked the Archdiocese of Los Angeles within the last decade. The first of the two most prominent law suites involved sexual abuse victim Rita Milla who was a teenager at the time she was molested by several priests. Milla was repeatedly molested by a Catholic priest Santiago Tamayo. Later, this same morally reprobate priest forced this poor, hapless victim to have sex with seven other priests until she got pregnant. Upon learning of this, the priests intimidated her into to keeping this scandal a secret. They sent her to the Philippines where she came close to death while giving birth. Milla later recalled, "I almost died protecting them." It was at this point she went to the Archdiocese of Los Angeles to seek help from her terrible plight. Her complaint of sexual abuse fell on deaf ears. When the diocese failed to appropriately act in her defense, Milla was left with no choice but to sue. Tamayo fled to the Philippians, but racked with guilt, the priest later returned to America and made a full confession. He produced letters irrefutably showing that his superiors knew he was in the Philippians and even paid him to remain there to avoid further scandal and embarrassment to the Los Angeles Diocese. One letter from the diocese requested that he "not reveal that you are being paid by the Los Angeles archdiocese unless requested to under oath."

However, contrary to his claim under oath, the Cardinal was fully aware of Tamayo's situation. His staff had sent a letter earlier to Tamayo offering him more money—in effect bribing him to keep quiet. This was done in an effort to avoid any potential lawsuits that would "only open a wound and further hurt anyone concerned, including the archdiocese." Later, a lawsuit filed in 1998 by Rita Milla and other sexual abuse victims of Father Tamayo went to trial and the jury ruled that Cardinal Mahony and the archdiocese were liable for what happened to Rita Milla and the other victims and awarded the plaintiffs $30 million dollars for various damages and injury. When the attorney for the plaintiffs questioned the Cardinal about his prior knowledge of Father Tamayo and his gang of raping priests, Mahony equivocated and tap danced around the questions, and denied having any previous knowledge of the affairs.

The jurors felt, however, that he was simply lying about what happened and sought to cover it up to save the soiled reputation of the Church and its priests. But the prevaricating Mahony belied his sham denial, and did indeed know of this lothario priest when he publicly defrocked Tamayo, not for the sex abuse he committed against a female minor, but for getting married! In the aftermath of this settlement, Cardinal Mahony had the lying audacity to tell a news reporter that he has a "zero tolerance policy" toward abusive priests. He went on to say that the number one priority for the diocese was to care for the victims and "make sure all children and young people are safe and we don't have a repetition of this."[53] Mahony's apologetic tone and resolve now rings hollow and sounds utterly mendacious; just a few years later in July 2007, his own Archdiocese of Los Angeles shelled out an astounding 650 million dollars to settle over 500 lawsuits involving sexual abuse cases involving priests![54] One pedophile priest under Cardinal Mahony's supervision, named in this specific law suite, was Oliver O' Grady, a habitual pedophiliac who raped children in every parish he was assigned to. In 1993, O' Grady was convicted and sentenced to fourteen years in prison for "lewd and lascivious acts" repeatedly committed over a 12-year period against two minors, the brothers John and James Howard from 1979 to 1991.

---

book, *Betrayal: The Crisis in the Catholic Church* compiled and written by *The Boston Globe* newspaper staff published by Back Bay Books in 2003. Information can also be accessed at *The Boston Globe* web site: *The Boston Globe Spotlight Investigation: Abuse in the Catholic Church* at http://www.boston.com/globe/spotlight/abuse/

[53] *CBS News*, April 23, 2002 at www.cbsnews.com/stories/2002/23/eveningnews/main/507039.shtml.

[54] *Los Angeles Times* July 17, 2007.

All during this time, O' Grady was transferred from parish to parish molesting children—including a nine month old baby—with Cardinal Mahony's full knowledge of the crimes. O' Grady later admitted under oath during a 2005 video deposition that he molested twenty-five children in northern California. Amy Berg's award winning 2006 documentary *Deliver Us From Evil* gives a harrowing and chilling account of O'Grady's compulsive sexual abuse of the victims and their families, along with personal interviews of O'Grady himself. The film convincingly shows how Cardinal Mahony did in fact have detailed knowledge about the sexual abuses of Oliver O'Grady, despite the Cardinal's claims to the contrary; in a video taped deposition given in 2004, he had previously stated he did not know O'Grady was a serial child molester. In one of the interviews from the documentary, O' Grady produced letters of correspondence between himself and Cardinal Mahony which showed the Cardinal not only knew of the allegations of child abuse made against O'Grady, but also transferred him to other parishes to escape a potential legal and media backlash. Earlier in 1984, Mahony and the diocese shut down a police investigation in Stockton, California after accusations of child molestation were made against O'Grady. The investigation was halted after officials from the diocese promised to remove the priest from any further contact with children. Instead, he was reassigned to a parish in San Andreas, about fifty miles away from Stockton, where he molested more children! Mahony, in accordance with Vatican policy, made repeated attempts to impede and short circuit investigations of sexual abuse. The Cardinal went so far as to make an appeal to the Supreme Court of the United States to prevent any access to Church documents which reveal the full extent of the Church's knowledge and systematic plot to cover up numerous scandals involving Catholic priests.

Several Roman Catholic dioceses have been forced to file for bankruptcy, due to the sheer volume of law suites filed by sexual abuse victims against the many priests who violated them. In February of 2007, the San Diego diocese attempted to file bankruptcy to postpone paying out an enormous sum of money to the victims. However, in September 7, 2007, the diocese did agree to pay the sum of nearly 200 million dollars to settle 144 claims of sexual abuse committed by the clergy.[55] To illustrate how pervasive the problem of pedophilia exists in its priesthood, the Roman Catholic Bishops of the United States had released a report in 2005 stating there was 783 clergy sex abuse cases filed against the Catholic Church, most of which date back decades in whose cumulative settlement cost totaled to an astounding 464 million dollars!

These are just some of the many sexual abuse cases of the Catholic Church. This does not even take into consideration the cases involving child-molesting priests throughout the world in other countries like Australia, Austria, Belgium, Brazil, Britain, Canada, Croatia, the Czech Republic, France, Germany, Ireland, Italy, Mexico, the Netherlands, the Philippines, Poland, and Spain. The unremitting frequency of sexual abuse among the Roman Catholic clergy throughout the world obviously dispels the fantasy of Roman Catholic apologists who, in their vain and silly attempts to both defend the unnatural imposition of celibacy and deny any connection between this and sexual immorality, continue to claim that the problem of sexual abuse among priests is but sporadic and limited to a few isolated incidents.

There is compelling evidence that the Roman Catholic Church's insistence that her priests and monks must take a vow of lifelong celibacy is a major contributing factor in the sexual immorality of her clergy. The numbers and the statistics makes this a crisis of epidemic proportions that will not go away until the Vatican honestly addresses the issue of mandatory celibacy from a biblical perspective. In doing so, they will see that they follow an unhealthy, devilish tradition which has helped spawn every type of sexual perversion that

---

[55]   *The New York Times* September 7, 2007. There is also the 2009 BBC documentary as well, going into further detail of this scandal.

has soiled and pervaded its clergy for nearly ten centuries! In each of these legal cases, including the many other ones not mentioned here, Rome was eventually forced to reach financial settlements with the sexual abuse victims only after those victims gained a voice to be heard from the media, advocacy groups, law enforcement agencies, and the courts. These groups in turn exerted great pressure on the Roman Catholic Church to publicly admit the recurring problems of child molestation and sexual immorality, and to take full responsibility for them. Historically, it has been the official policy of the Vatican to cover up the aberrant sexual behavior of her priests, while imposing a code of strict secrecy on all members of the clergy who have direct knowledge of any sexually aberrant priest. This code of secrecy is justified by an official Vatican policy entitled "The Pontifical Secret" and is enforced by the Holy See on every member of the clergy who participates in an official investigation into allegations of sexual abuse of minors by a priest.[56]

The procedure for carrying out this vile cover up and obstruction of justice to protect guilty priests from secular prosecution is found in another confidential church document entitled, ***Crimen Sollicitationis*** released by the Vatican in 1962. The document was approved and sanctioned for ecclesiastical polity by Pope John XXIII. The document instructs how an ecclesiastical tribunal is to proceed when a priest has violated the confessional for sexual purposes, and also what to do when a parishioner (a minor or adult) has been sexually violated by a member of the clergy. The document was discretely circulated to every bishop and every major religious superior in the world, who were instructed to keep the document hidden away in the diocesan secret archives, never to be published or commented upon. Subsequently, in the decades that followed, priests throughout the world were molesting children and getting away with it because their superiors quickly transferred the priests out of the parish to escape potential arrest and conviction.

This systematic cover up can be directly traced back to this 1962 Vatican document, the contents of which clearly reveal what was to be done to a priest found guilty of sexual misconduct of any kind. Bishops are instructed to pursue the sexual abuse cases of priests "in the most secretive way" and "are to observe the strictest secrecy" by all involved—including the alleged victim. An oath of professed silence under pain of excommunication was taken by those members of the clergy involved in the proceedings Once the case has been adjudicated, all parties are to be "restrained by a perpetual silence" from ever disclosing the facts of the case itself.

Those who broke this silence were subject to automatic excommunication from the Church. The document then goes on to instruct how the offending priest was to be expeditiously transferred "to another assignment." The ***Crimen Sollicitationis*** document is a manual for deception, subterfuge, and the most shameless cover up contrived in the modern day. It basically provides protection for pedophile priests and threatens to punish those with excommunication who would make the matter known to the proper authorities outside the Catholic Church. In 2003, forty-one years after this diabolical document was drafted and secretly implemented by the Vatican, the Pope's deplorable secret was discovered and exposed by CBS news correspondent, Vince Gonzalez, who was able to obtain a copy of the document for his expose on the sexual abuse scandals in the Catholic Church.[57] When this document is read in its entirety, the reader will see it is clear blueprint for

---

[56]   Thomas P. Doyle, A.W.R. Sipe, and Patrick J. Wall, *Sex, Priests, and Secret Codes: The Catholic Church's 2,000-Year Paper Trail of Sexual Abuse* (Los Angeles: Volt Press), 52, 339-340.

[57]   *CBS News* August 6, 2003 "Sex Crimes: Cover –up by Vatican?" There is also the 2006 BBC documentary, *Sex, Crimes, and the Vatican* filmed by Colm O'Gorman who was raped by a Catholic priest in the diocese of Ferns in County Wexford in Ireland when he was 14 years old. O' Gorman documents how Cardinal Ratzinger, who later became Pope Benedict XVI, used The ***Crimen Sollicitationis*** document for twenty years before he became Pope Benedict XVI to silence allegations of sexual abuse by priests.

deception and cover up. The victim's rights and welfare are largely neglected while the sex-abusing priest is afforded protection and relocation to avoid bringing any shame and embarrassment to the Catholic Church. This helps maintain the masquerade of moral and sexual purity exhibited by the priesthood. This unlawful and terribly immoral policy was reinforced in May 2001, when Cardinal Joseph Ratzinger, the prefect of the Congregation for the Doctrine of the Faith (formerly known as the Holy Office of the Inquisition!), who later became Pope Benedict XVI, sent a letter to all Catholic bishops admonishing them that any investigation carried out by the Church concerning claims of pedophilia were subject to the "Pontifical Secret" and were not to be reported to law enforcement until such investigations were completed. Failure to comply would lead to excommunication.

A January 11, 2011, Associated Press release disclosed a letter written in 1997 from the Vatican to Ireland's bishops, warning them not to report all suspected child-abuse cases to police. The newly released document was obtained by Irish broadcasters RTE and provided to the Associated Press. The official letter marked "strictly confidential" exposes how the Vatican rejected a 1996 Irish church effort to help police identify pedophile priests following the first wave of publicly disclosed lawsuits. Archbishop Luciano Storero, the late Pope John Paul II's diplomat to Ireland, signed the Vatican letter. In 1996, Irish church leaders, to their credit, published a "groundbreaking document" detailing their collective determination to immediately report all sexual abuse cases to police. But Storero's response was to say the Irish church's policy was not recognized by the Vatican, and further warned that priests who are captured or reported to police risk having their "in-house punishments" overturned by the Congregation for the Clergy, which happened in the case of repeated offender, Father Brenan Smyth, who raped and molested more than 100 children after his case was overturned by a Vatican court! Victim's groups believe this document to be "the smoking gun" needed to prove the Vatican enforced a policy of cover-up and deception, ordering bishops repeatedly not to turn pedophile priests over to law enforcement, and thus thwarting any kind of justice for victims (see "Vatican warned Irish bishops not to report abuse" January 18, 2011 by Shawn Pogatchnik with Associated Press at http://www.bishop-accountability.org/news2011/01_02/2011_01_18_Pogatchnik_VaticanWarned.htm). Currently, as of this writing the Vatican's child-protection policies remain in legal limbo. In attempt to save face, the Vatican's website "advises bishops worldwide to report crimes to police"—albeit in a legal non-binding way. However, such advice is omitted, at the time of this writing, from the official, legal advice provided by the Congregation for the Doctrine of the Faith, which still continues to uphold and practice the secrecy of canon law in these matters.

The demand for this imposed secrecy was in clear violation of current laws of the United States and most of Europe! The heinous part to all this is that there is no concern for the victims of these predatory priests; but only an attempt to protect the soiled reputation of the Catholic Church by way of secrecy and cover up. The just and fitting punishment that God will mete out to these pernicious priests, who have defiled innocent children and brought them great harm, is solemnly foretold by Jesus in Mark 9:42: ***"But whoever causes one of these little ones who believe in Me to stumble, it would be better for him if a millstone were hung around his neck, and he were thrown into the sea."*** The fate of being drowned in the sea with a heavy millstone would be a far more preferably destiny for these clerical wretches, than to cause one small innocent child to stumble and be ruined for life through sexual abuse by a priest of Rome claiming to be the representative of Jesus Christ. It is no coincidence that when you examine how the Vatican systematically dealt with sexually abusive priests in the last forty years, the manner and calculated method mirrors exactly what is prescribed in the ***Crimen Sollicitationis*** document.

The Irish priest Brenan Smyth was investigated, and when found out; he was quickly reassigned to another parish where he continued to molest more children. In some cases, the Church transferred him over and over again to various places, knowing full well the priest's personal history of sexual crimes against children and adults. The Vatican's inexcusable cover up for their unspeakable depravity has recently cost the Catholic Church two to three billion dollars, (and counting) in legal settlements with the victims (Louise Haggett, "The Bingo Report: Mandatory Celibacy and Clergy Sexual Abuse," pages 189-190). Only God knows how many more victims were sexually abused by priests; the figures to date reflect only cases that have gone public and do not include the many more that remain covered up by the Vatican.

The claim that the doctrine of enforced celibacy is the central cause of the sexual abuse scandals of the Catholic clergy is empirically confirmed by the dramatic increase in the numbers of scandals that have occurred after celibacy became a requirement for priests in the eleventh century. Pope Gregory VII first imposed this mandatory requirement of celibacy when his first Lenten Synod convened in March of 1074 A.D.[58] Here, Gregory VII decreed that there was to be an immediate separation between priests and their spouses, and the imperious pope took measures to see that this decree was rigidly enforced. Priestly celibacy became official church policy when ratified by the Second Lateran Council in 1139 A.D. under the supervision of Pope Innocent II. From that point on, all Roman Catholic priests had to be celibate. Though there were rightful protestations coming from those priests who were already married at the time, Gregory VII took the extreme and unprecedented measure of authorizing the laity to withdraw their obedience from all priests and clergy who did not abide by the decree on celibacy. The real reason for why the Papacy came to this decision was borne out of material and monetary concerns, rather than for any biblical or pastoral reason. Married priests, upon their death, would naturally bequeath their property and financial estate to their wives and children. This in effect left the papal church without any material assets to show for in the future.

The enforcement of celibacy then became very profitable and lucrative for the Church. Without a wife and children to inherit his possessions, the priest's property and money went to Rome by default. This showed a clear mercenary motive behind Rome's arbitrary enforcement of priestly celibacy, as the huge estates, land holdings, and financial largesse of the Vatican expanded immensely due to this unbiblical doctrine being forced upon the clergy. The innumerable sex scandals and perversions that have been rife among Rome's Popes and priests for the last one thousand years, are due, primarily, to the inhuman and callous demand for mandatory celibacy since the eleventh century. The New Testament advises that it is better to marry than to burn with sexual passion (1 Corinthians 7:9). Rome's flagrant disregard of this prudent prescription, and her obstinate refusal to allow its priests the valid option to take a wife, is the chief source for so much sexual immorality going on within the clergy. Until Rome admits that her call for mandatory celibacy is a clear violation of the New Testament Scripture, her clergy will continue to be scandalized with pedophilia, adultery, fornication, concubinage, and homosexuality.

After being ordained to the sacramental ministry of the Catholic Church, priests are conferred with the honorific title of *Father*, and are to be addressed as such by the Catholic faithful. This is in direct contradiction and violation of Jesus' commandment to His disciples forbidding any man on Earth to be called "father" in the spiritual and religious sense of the word. ***Do not call anyone on earth your father, for One is your Father, He who is in heaven"*** (Matthew 23:9). This prohibition certainly does not forbid a child from calling his

---

[58]   Henry C. Lea, *History of Sacerdotal Celibacy in the Christian Church* (Kessinger: 1932), 190. Lea's fine scholarly work is an historical review and analysis of the effects and results that have negatively accrued from enforced celibacy in the Catholic Church.

biological male parent "father" because Christ made use of this paternal designation Himself throughout the Gospels (Matthew 15:4; 19:5; Luke 15:11-31). Calling no man your father obviously has a different meaning than this. Roman Catholic apologists are quick to deny that this is a prohibition against assigning divine titles to a man by presenting a flurry of passages from both the Old and New Testaments where the term "father" is used as supposed proof texts to justify the practice of addressing the Catholic priest as "Father." But a closer examination of these passages reveals that Rome's justification for violating the Lord's commandment in Matthew 23:9 results from a failure to make a critical distinction between the various meanings and uses for the word "father."

This is most evident when Catholic apologists make an allusion to what Paul said to the Corinthian Church where the Apostle calls his converts his *children* and he their *father* through the ministry of the Gospel. *"For though you might have ten thousand instructors in Christ, yet you do not have many fathers; for in Christ Jesus I have begotten you through the Gospel"* (1 Corinthians 4:15). Catholic defenders use this text to say that Paul claims for himself the spiritual title of "father" in the same manner a Roman Catholic priest does. This is simply not true. Paul is using the analogy of a family in terms of a father caring for his children. The Apostle's converts became spiritually born again through his Gospel message.[59] In that sense, Paul *fathered* their conversion through the Gospel he preached to them, which they believed for salvation and spiritual rebirth. Therefore, Paul was not demanding that all Christian ministers be called "father."

Furthermore, Paul was not claiming an ecclesiastical title for himself, but rather he was stating a fact about his relationship with the Christians at Corinth. If a person begot me to the Christian faith through trust in Jesus Christ the term "father" could then exclusively apply to that person in saying of him, "You are my father in the faith and gave birth to me through your Gospel message". But to turn that into an ecclesiastical title to be universally applied to a group of celibate priests from the Roman Catholic Church, who did not spiritually beget the person in question, even though they may belong to the same church and arguably do not have the right Gospel in the first place, is a total misuse and misappropriation of the term "father."[60]

Catholic apologists are simply taking 1 Corinthians 4:15 out of context when misusing the text to claim their priests are to be called "father." The inspired writers of the New Testament Peter, Paul, James, and Jude never referred to themselves with the religious title of "father", nor did they require Christians to call them by that title. They humbly called themselves *"servants"* (slaves) of the Lord Jesus Christ (Romans 1:1; Titus 1:1; James 1:1; II Peter 1:1, et al). The word father can have several meanings in Scripture besides the designation of a biological male parent or grandparent. None of them properly fit the Roman Catholic understanding of father in the titular sense. Father can denote a male figure that is the founder of a people or nation. Abraham is often called the *father* of the Jewish people, and the spiritual patriarch for those who follow the Judeo-Christian faith (Luke 16:24; John 9:56; Romans 4:16-17). The plural use of *fathers* can be collectively used to mean the founding patriarchs of a society, the ancestors of a nation, a race or people, and the eldest men of a community (see Exodus 13:5; Deuteronomy 1:8; Psalm 78:5; John 6:31 Acts 7:2, 9,

---

[59]   You find the same use of this analogy in the Epistles of John where he classifies the different stages of believers from the new (children) to the maturing (young men), and finally the fully mature believer (fathers). See 1 John 2:1, 13-14. Every Christian church will have these three types of believers. John thus addresses his epistle to Christians of all spiritual maturity levels. He is not giving license for calling a Christian leader by the official title of "Father."

[60]   I am partially indebted to the astute observations of Dr. James White, here, in his stimulating debate with Jesuit priest, Father Mitchell Pacwa (see *The Great Debate 2003: "Is the Roman Catholic Priesthood Biblical and Ancient?"* #553 Video Disc #2). In a similar fashion, we have Elisha addressing Elijah with the term "father" because Elijah personally took care of him and appointed him heir to his prophetic office (see 2 Kings 2:12)

32; 22:1). The biblical meaning for fathers here does not square with the clerical priests' presumptuous title of "father", but has a similar meaning when Americans speak of "the Founding Fathers" of our country. The phrase refers to those men who helped frame and draft the Constitution of the United States from its beginning. Thomas Jefferson was a founding father but historians do not formally call him "Father" Jefferson. In the early history of Christianity, there were the Church Fathers who helped formulate the building blocks of Christian theology. But we do not formally and individually call them "Father".

In the context of Matthew 23, Jesus is warning His disciples not to be like the Pharisees by arrogating to themselves formal religious or spiritual titles like "father" that belong to God alone. When examining Scriptures in their proper context, no verse is found where the word "father" is used that gives a blanket endorsement for conferring on a servant of God or minister of Christ the formal religious title of "father."

Jesus' prohibition in Matthew 23:9 not only applies to the Pharisees, but also includes anyone demanding to be addressed by the title of "father." Hence, the Catholic priest is in the direct cross hairs of Christ's prohibition, and that is all there is to that! Addressing priests of Rome by this title is to commit rank blasphemy against the first Person of the Trinity—God, the Father. Scripture warns us not to think of men above what is written (Romans 12:3; 1 Corinthians 4:6). Catholic apologists wrongly claim that the command of Matthew 23:9 is used as a hyperbole, and not to be followed. However, the statement does not have the characteristics of a hyperbole.

Hyperbole is often used in Scripture to shockingly to describe a radical or impossible thing to do, in exaggerated terms. Jesus deliberately uses hyperbole to stress that it would be more likely for a camel to pass through the miniscule eye of a sewing needle than for the rich to enter into heaven by trusting in wealth instead of the Savior—an impossible thing to do (Matthew 19:23-26). The commandment of Matthew 23:9 is not strange or radical, but is possible to obey without extreme difficulty; therefore it cannot be interpreted as hyperbole. It is not a strange or radical command, which is typical of the hyperbole. The command is clear, straightforward, and no amount of strained circumlocution from Roman Catholic apologists changes this fact.

Finally, there is the issue of the clerical dress of the Roman Catholic priest. Again, one looks in vain in the New Testament to find this queer practice of a priestly class wearing a distinctive black dress to symbolize their elevation over the laity and common people. The Roman clerical collar is another invention of the Catholic institution to signify the priest has the power to dispense the seven sacraments of the Roman Catholic Church. The practice of wearing special garments or vestments such as those worn by the Levitical priesthood passed away with the abolishment of the Old Covenant economy. The sanctified garment, which will be worn by saints (all genuine believers in Christ), in heaven at the Marriage Supper of the Lamb, is neither black nor reserved for an esoteric "clergy" but is a pristine and dazzling white robe of incorruptibility. Christ will personally adorn each member of the Church with this glorified garment that is a symbol of His imputed righteousness (Revelation 3:5; 19:7-8). The Roman Catholic priesthood is a pathetic, ineffective imitation of what Christ gloriously offers in the New Covenant gift of redemption—which He alone purchased in the supreme role of our great High Priest. Every simple believer is destined to reign with Him forever on Earth as priests and kings of the Most High God (Revelation 1:6; 5:10).

CHAPTER 10

THE MASS AND THE SACRAMENTS, PART 1

The sacrifice of the Mass and the sacraments are the warp and woof of Roman Catholic salvation. The Mass is the crown jewel, the sum and summit of the seven sacraments dispensed by the Roman Catholic priesthood. The ritual of the Mass is a distinctive feature of Roman Catholicism and is the most important of the sacraments. The Catholic Church maintains the Mass is a primary channel of saving grace conveyed through the Eucharist (communion wafer and wine). In brief, the Catholic Church explains the Mass to consist in the following act allegedly performed by the priest:

> The Mass is the unbloody reenactment of the sacrifice of Calvary. Through the consecration of the bread and wine into the body and blood of Christ, the Mass perpetuates the sacrifice of the Cross by offering to God the same victim that was immolated in Calvary for the redemption of man. In the Mass the priest speaks not in his own name, but as the ambassador of Jesus Christ, speaking the very words that Christ uttered at the Last Supper. Thus Jesus Christ is both the High Priest and the Victim in the sacrifice of the Mass and in the sacrifice of the Cross, and the ends for which both sacrifices were offered are identical.
>
> The manner in which the sacrifices are offered is alone different: on the Cross Christ really shed His Blood and was really slain; in the Mass, however, there is no real shedding of blood, no real death; but the separate consecration of the bread and of the wine symbolizes His death upon the Cross. The Mass is the renewal and perpetuation of the sacrifice of the Cross in the sense that it offers anew to God the Victim of Calvary and thus commemorates the sacrifice of the Cross, reenacts it symbolically and mystically, and applies the fruits of Christ's death upon the Cross to individual human souls. All the efficacy of the Mass is derived, therefore, from the sacrifice of Calvary.[1]

---

[1]   John A. O'Brien, *The Faith of Millions* (Huntington, Indiana: Our Sunday Visitor, 1974), 304.

Because participation in the Mass is vital for obtaining eternal salvation in Roman Catholic soteriology (doctrine of salvation), every Catholic is required by the Code of Canon Law to attend Mass every Sunday and on special feast days throughout the year (see *The Code of Canon Law*, **Can. 1246** and **Can. 1247** and the *Catechism of the Catholic Church* **[1389, 2042,** and **2181]**). A willful failure to comply and participate in the Mass by the Roman Catholic is to commit a "mortal sin" in the eyes of the Church and can jeopardize one's salvation (*Catechism of the Catholic Church* **[2181]**). Official Roman Catholic dogma teaches that the Lord Jesus Christ instituted the perpetual sacrifice He offered on the cross in the Mass when He celebrated the Last Supper on the night of His betrayal: When He declared that the Passover bread was His body and the Paschal wine was His blood, Christ miraculously changed them into His literal and physical flesh and blood under the appearances of bread and wine for the disciples to eat and drink. This is what is called the *Eucharist* in Roman Catholic theology.[2] Other terms used for the Eucharist are "the Blessed Sacrament", "the Host", and "Holy Communion". The *Catechism of the Catholic Church* claims that Christ instituted the perpetual sacrifice of Himself in the Eucharist at the Last Supper, which is to be continued by the priest's ongoing performance of the Mass (*Catechism of the Catholic Church* **[1382]**). The Mass is a "continuation" of Christ's sacrifice on the cross.

The Catholic Church teaches that at "the Last Supper", on the night He was betrayed, our Savior instituted the Eucharistic sacrifice of His body and blood. This He did in order to perpetuate the sacrifice of the cross throughout the ages until He should come again.[3] The Second Vatican Council decreed "*that in the Mass the priest represents Christ and the continual sacrifice of the cross* that is made present in the Church whenever the priest, who represents Christ our Lord, does what Christ himself did and commanded his disciples to do in memory of himself." (Emphasis added.) The idea therefore is that Christ instituted the first Mass at the Last Supper when He took bread and the cup of wine, gave thanks, broke the bread and gave to his disciples saying: "Take, eat and drink; this is my Body, this is the cup of my Blood. Do this in memory of me."[4] At that moment, the bread and wine became the actual body and blood of Jesus Christ. Rome claims that it was here that Jesus commissioned the disciples and their successors to be priests with the power and authority to do the same thing when performing the Mass (*Catechism of the Catholic Church* **[610-611, 1337]**). Further elaborating on this claim, the Council of Trent (whose decisions are still binding on all Roman Catholics to this day) claims that the Mass is a propitiatory sacrifice of Christ offered in an "unbloody manner" on the altars of Roman Catholic churches which has equal efficacy and power to forgive sin for the dead, the living, and those being purified in purgatory as did the bloody sacrifice Christ offered on the Cross two-thousand years ago! During the twenty-second session, Trent presumptuously declared to this effect:

> And inasmuch as in this divine sacrifice which is celebrated in the Mass is contained and immolated in an unbloody manner the same Christ who once offered Himself in a bloody manner on the altar of the cross, the holy council teaches that this is truly propitiatory and has this effect, that if we, contrite and penitent, with sincere heart and upright faith,

---

[2] The Eucharist in Catholic theology comes from the Greek word *eucharistein* (meaning, "thanksgiving") based on the word usage in Luke 22:19. The "Eucharist" is defined by Rome to be "the true Body and Blood of Jesus Christ who is really substantially present under the appearances of bread and wine, in order to offer himself in the sacrifice of the Mass and to be received as spiritual food in Holy Communion. It is called Eucharist, or 'thanksgiving,' because at its institution at the Last Supper Christ 'gave thanks,' and by this fact it is the supreme object and act of Christian gratitude to God" (John A. Hardon, *Pocket Catholic Dictionary*, pages 132-133).

[3] *Catechism of the Catholic Church*, 368 **[1324]**.

[4] Austin Flannery, *Vatican Council II*, 174.

with fear and reverence, draw nigh to God, we obtain mercy and find grace in seasonable aid. For, appeased by this sacrifice, the Lord grants the grace and gift of penitence and pardons even the gravest crimes and sins. For the victim is one and the same, the same now offering by the ministry of priests who then offered Himself on the cross, the manner alone of offering being different. The fruits of the bloody sacrifice, it is well understood, are received most abundantly through this unbloody one, so far is the latter derogating in any way from the former. Wherefore, according to the tradition of the Apostles, it is rightly offered not only for the sins, punishments, satisfactions and other necessities of the faithful who are living, but also for those departed in Christ but not yet fully purified.[5]

In the Mass, "the sacrifice of the cross is perpetuated", since in the Eucharist the bread and wine is literally transformed into the flesh, blood, soul, and divinity of Jesus Christ (see the *Catechism of the Catholic Church* [1413]). Therefore the Eucharist literally becomes the Lord Jesus Christ, Almighty God, under the appearance of bread and wine, after a Catholic priest performs the act of consecration during the liturgy of the Eucharist by repeating the words of institution Jesus spoke when saying, **"This is My body...this is My blood"**. This is the high point in the Mass. Once consecrated to this end, the Eucharist must be adored and worshipped as God!

> In the most blessed sacrament of the Eucharist the body and blood, together with the soul and divinity, of our Lord Jesus Christ and, therefore, the whole Christ is truly, really, and substantially contained. In the liturgy of the Mass we express our faith in the real presence of Christ by genuflecting or bowing deeply as a sign of adoration of the Lord. The Church knows that the Lord comes even now in his Eucharist and that he is there in our midst.[6]

The Mass is not merely a symbol for Christ's once-for-all sacrifice, but the literal and physical continuation of it. The Documents of Vatican II formally define it in the following way:

> For in the sacrifice of the Mass Our Lord is immolated when "he begins to be present sacramentally as the spiritual food of the faithful under the appearances of bread and wine." It was for this purpose that Christ entrusted this sacrifice to the Church, that the faithful might share in it both spiritually, by faith and charity, and sacramentally, through the banquet of Holy Communion. Participation in the Lord's Supper is always communion with Christ offering himself for us as a sacrifice to the Father.[7]

"Immolated" means more than just a symbolic re-presentation of the death of Jesus in the Mass; it is an actual sacrifice for sin. The word "immolate" means to offer or kill as a sacrifice. Every time the priest performs the Mass he is thus offering up the physical body and blood of Christ to be a propitiatory sacrifice for sin in which the wrath of God is appeased and the sins of the penitent are expiated. *The St. Joseph Baltimore*

---

5   *The Canons and Decrees of the Council of Trent*, 146. The *Catechism of the Catholic Church* upholds this definition at Trent when asserting, "As sacrifice, the Eucharist is also offered in reparation for the sins of the living and the dead and to obtain spiritual or temporal benefits from God, 395 **[1414]**.

6   *Catechism of the Catholic Church*, 383, 385 **[1374, 1378]**.

7   Austin Flannery, *Vatican II Council*, 102-103.

Catechism (No. 2)—a standard text used for the training and instruction of Roman Catholic children at the Junior High level—states that the sacrifice of the Mass continues the selfsame sacrifice that Christ offered on the cross almost two-thousand years ago:

> The Mass *continues* the Sacrifice of the cross. Each time Mass is offered *the Sacrifice of Christ is repeated.* A new sacrifice is not offered, but by divine power, one and the same sacrifice is *repeated*...In the Mass Christ continues to offer Himself to the Father as He did on the Cross.[8]

Christ is portrayed in Roman Catholic theology to be the perpetual "victim" in the sacrifice of the Mass.[9] The Catholic Church claims that in the Mass the Lord Jesus Christ leaves His throne of glory in heaven to humbly obey the command of the priest by coming to Earth and personally indwelling the bread and wine at the Mass to be sacrificed on the altars of Roman Catholic churches all over the world. When the priest lifts the communion bread and the chalice of wine up during the *consecration* part of the Mass, the *Sanctus bell* is rung by the altar boy to signify that the elements of the bread and wine have now been magically transformed into the literal body, blood, soul, and divinity of the Lord Jesus Christ. The Eucharist is the same human and divine Jesus who was born of the Virgin Mary, lived, died, was resurrected and ascended to heaven only to descend again and again into the communion wafer of the Catholic Mass. The priest in this sense is a God-maker, in that he is able to "call into being the body and blood of the Lord Jesus Christ" during the Mass, and he therefore recreates the birth, life, and sacrifice of Jesus Christ. With the Vatican's formal seal of approval, given with the *Nihil Obstat* and *Imprimatur*, Roman Catholic priest and author Martin von Cochem, quoting from Pope Leo I and Hildegard, makes the following shocking but unverifiable claim:

> Every day we may be present at this happy birth, every day our eyes may behold it, if we will but go to Mass. For then it is in very deed renewed, and by it the work of our salvation is carried on...At the moment when in the Mass the bread and wine are changed into the Body and Blood of Christ, the circumstances of His incarnation and birth and mirrored before us as clearly as when these mysteries were accomplished by the Son of God when

---

[8] Bennet Kelley, *The New Saint Joseph Baltimore Catechism* (New York: Catholic Book Publishing Co., 1969), 171. Rome has contradicted itself here when their apologists and bishops use double talk to disclaim the teaching that the priest does repeat the sacrifice of Christ over and over again in the Mass. A statement from the U.S. Catholic Bishops states that the Eucharist, who is Jesus, "does not sacrifice himself again and again. Rather, by the power of the Holy Spirit his one eternal sacrifice is made present once again, re-presented, so that we may share in it" (The Real Presence of Jesus Christ in the Sacrament of the Eucharist: A Statement of the U.S. Catholic Bishops given at its June 2001 General Meeting).

[9] One Catholic priest, with the official approval of the Roman Catholic episcopate, actually calls Christ "the eternal victim" who offers Himself up through the Roman Catholic priest during the "sacrifice" of the Mass (see John Laux, *Mass and the Sacraments: A Course in Religion*, Book II [Rockford IL: Tan, 1990], 59). The efficacy of the Mass to remove sin is the same as when Christ died on the cross two thousand years ago and shed His blood to remove sin—only the manner and method have changed, for the *Catechism of the Catholic Church* states: The sacrifice of Christ and the sacrifice of the Eucharist are one single sacrifice: The Victim is one and the same: the same now offers through the ministry of the priest, who then offered himself on the cross; only the manner of offering is different." "In this divine sacrifice which is celebrated in the Mass, the same Christ who offered himself once in a bloody manner on the altar of the cross is contained and is offered in an unbloody manner" (page 381 **[1367]**).

162

He was on earth. This testimony has been confirmed by the Church; she bears witness to the truth that the birth of Christ is renewed and re-presented afresh in the sight of heaven, just as when it took place more than 1900 years ago. In what manner and by whose agency Christ is born in Holy Mass St. Jerome tells us in these words: "The priest calls Christ into being by his consecrated lips," that is to say, Christ is born into the world at the bidding of the priest when his lips utter the words of Consecration....And if we really believe this, we shall adore the divine child at Holy Mass with the same reverence and affection as did those who were privileged to behold Him with their bodily eyes. (Martin von Cochem, *The Incredible Catholic Mass* [Rockford, IL: Tan, 1997, pages 90-91]).

The act of the Mass causes Christ, in all the fullness of His deity and humanity, to exist and be contained in a piece of bread and cup of wine. Rome actually teaches that this piece of consecrated bread literally becomes God incarnate at the moment the priest performs the act of *consecration* during the Mass! Christ is therefore really, substantially, and wholly present in the Eucharist. This is what is meant when Roman Catholic theologians refer to "the real presence" of Christ—that Christ is *literally* and *physically* contained in the communion elements of the bread and wine. Rome holds that even the smallest crumb of the Host and tiniest drop of wine contain the fullness of Christ's body and blood, and would include His deity and humanity in every part (see *Catechism of the Catholic Church*, [1377]). Through this astounding act, the wonder of all wonders and the miracle of all miracles is performed when the creature creates his Creator on the Roman Catholic altar of the Mass.[10] Roman Catholic priest and author John A. O'Brien explains how this supposedly happens in his popular book *The Faith of Millions*:

When the priest pronounces the tremendous words of consecration, he reaches up into the heavens, brings Christ down from His throne, and places Him upon our altar to be offered up again as the victim for the sins of man. It is a power greater than the monarchs and emperors: it is greater than that of saints and angels, greater than that of Seraphim and Cherubim. Indeed it is greater even than the power of the Virgin Mary. While the Blessed Virgin was the human agency by which Christ became incarnate a single time, the priest brings Christ down from heaven, and renders Him present on our altar as the eternal victim for the sins of man—not once but a thousand times! The priest speaks and lo! Christ, the eternal and omnipotent God, bows his head in humble obedience to the priest's command.[11]

Thousands of times each day, the Lord Jesus Christ is called down from heaven to Earth by the verbal fiat of a Roman Catholic priest to inhabit a piece of bread and cup of wine, to serve as a perpetual sacrifice

---

[10] Angelic Doctor of the Roman Catholic Church, Alphonsus de Liguori, in his book *Dignity and Duties of the Priest or Selva*, makes the following blasphemous claim: "Hence priests are called the parents of Jesus Christ... for they are the active cause by which He is made to exist really in the consecrated Host. Thus the priest may, in a certain manner, be called the creator of his Creator, since by saying the words of consecration, he creates, as it were, Jesus in the Sacrament, by giving Him a Sacramental existence, and produces Him as a victim to be offered to the eternal Father. As in creating the world it was sufficient for God to have said, Let it be made, and it was created—He spoke, and they were made—so it is sufficient for the priest to say, 'Hoc est corpus meum,' and behold the bread is no longer bread, but the body of Jesus Christ" (see http://www.fisheaters.com/holyorders3.html).

[11] *The Faith of Millions*, 255-256.

for sin and object of worship to faithful Catholics, who believe they are literally eating Christ's flesh and drinking His blood during the ritual of the Mass. The theological term for the alleged transformation of the entire substance of the bread and wine of the Eucharist into the actual body and blood of Jesus Christ is called *transubstantiation*.[12] Though the word *transubstantiation* was not used until the twelfth century, the idea of such a transmutation was first made public and widely circulated in the Catholic Church in the ninth century by the monk Paschasius Radbertus in his written work *The Body and Blood of the Lord* (c. 790 –865 A.D.). Radbertus is also now believed to have been the mastermind behind the *Pseudo-Isidorean Decretals* giving historical justification for the Papacy's absolute powers to make its fraudulent claims. The word "transubstantiation" simply means a change of one substance into another. Here the term is used to describe when the bread and wine of the Catholic Mass is changed into the flesh and blood of Christ. Radbertus' expostulation on the concept of transubstantiation gained wide acceptance within the Roman Catholic institution and became the standard work and definition on the subject, leading the Church to formally adopt it as official Roman Catholic dogma during the Fourth Lateran Council in 1215 A.D.

Radbertus postulated that what was created in the words of institution was the very body and blood of Jesus Christ; though the color and taste of bread and wine outwardly remain the same, the inward substance of each was changed. The bread and wine thus remain so by outward appearance (*accidents*) but the inward essence (*substance*) of both elements, after the priest speaks the words of Eucharistic institution, are changed into the flesh and blood of Jesus Christ![13] Even though the bread and wine still outwardly look like bread and wine after the words of institution are spoken, they have, nonetheless, been wholly converted into the body and blood of the Lord Jesus Christ. Seven hundred years after Radbertus, the Council of Trent made transubstantiation a normative and mandatory belief of the Catholic Church when declaring:

> But since Christ our Redeemer declared that to be truly His own body which He offered under the form of bread, it has, therefore, always been a firm belief in the Church of God, and this holy council now declares it anew, that by consecration of the bread and wine a change is brought about of the whole substance of the bread into the substance of the body of Christ our Lord, and of the whole substance of the wine into the substance of His blood. This change the holy Catholic Church properly and appropriately calls *transubstantiation* (Emphasis added).[14]

During the Mass, when the priest says the words of institution, he solemnly bows before the bread and wine to signify that he is now worshipping these elements as God Almighty! After consecration, the Eucharist is placed in an ornate metallic or wooden box called the tabernacle, which stands behind the Roman Catholic altar.[15] Whenever Catholics enter into the sanctuary of a church they must genuflect and bow down to this

---

[12]   The word *transubstantiation* was first used in the twelfth century by Magister Roland, who later became Pope Alexander III (1100/1105-1180 A.D.).

[13]   Paschasius Radbertus in Jaroslav Pelikan's *The Growth of Medieval Theology (600-1300): The Christian Tradition: A History of the Development of Doctrine, Volume 3* (Chicago: The University of Chicago Press, 1978), 76.

[14]   *The Canons and Decrees of the Council of Trent*, 75.

[15]   The tabernacle is an unbreakable container or receptacle in the church in which the Eucharistic bread is reserved. The box is secure and stationary and its door is locked with a key. The tabernacle is placed in a prominent location usually in an elevated position behind the altar in the sanctuary of a Catholic church (see Richard P. McBrien's *Encyclopedia of Catholicism*, 1241).

piece of bread stored in the Tabernacle to show their worship and reverence for the fact that the Creator of the Universe in the Person of the Lord Jesus Christ is literally, physically, and fully present in the consecrated pieces of bread that are in the tabernacle. Rome therefore commands, exhorts, and expects Catholics to pray, adore, and worship the Eucharist that is able to perform the same miracles Jesus performed when He walked this earth two thousand years ago. A refusal to worship the Eucharist as God is to incur the damnation of Rome! The Vatican thus declared at the Council of Trent that:

> If anyone says that in the holy sacrament of the Eucharist, Christ, the only begotten Son of God, is not to be adored with the worship of *latria*, also outwardly manifested, and is consequently neither to be venerated with a special festive solemnity, nor to be solemnly borne about in procession according to the laudable and universal rite and custom of holy Church, or is not to be set publicly before the people to be adored and that the adorers thereof are idolaters, let him be anathema (see *The Canons and Decrees of the Council of Trent*, page 80).

The Catechism of the Catholic Church enjoins all Roman Catholics to participate in the Eucharistic worship of Jesus in the communion bread whether in the tabernacle or on the altar.[16] When the Eucharist is not consumed or eaten, the Lord Jesus is believed to be living day and night in the tabernacle under the species of bread waiting to perform acts of love and healing, and to receive acts of worship! A popular Catholic tract entitled *The Blessed Sacrament: God With Us* exultingly proclaims to all Roman Catholics that:

> Jesus dwells continually in our midst in the Blessed Sacrament. Day and night He abides among us under the lowly species of bread, in the narrow Tabernacles of our churches. Here He is not only our infinitely great God, but also our merciful Savior and our most faithful friend. The same miracles He wrought for the corporally sick during His earthly life, He performs in our days from the Tabernacle for those spiritually ill. He gives sight to the **"blind"** by granting them light to see the evil of sin, the value of things eternal, the value of Crosses and sufferings, the value of resignation to the will of God. He gives power of movement to the **"lame"** by prompting their sluggish will to resolve and act for His love alone. He raises the "dead" to life by calling souls from the death of sin to the life of grace...Jesus is present in the Blessed Sacrament with His Divinity and Humanity, His soul and body, His flesh and blood. *Through His Real Presence, the Tabernacle becomes the treasury of all riches, for it contains Jesus, the fountain of all grace, with the infinite plenitude of His divine treasures. There He holds them ever in readiness for us; He calls and invites us to come and take them. His presence is the life of the Church, the life, the joy and delight of every loving soul* (Emphasis added).[17]

---

[16]   *Catechism of the Catholic Church*, 385-386 **[1378-1380]**.

[17]   Prepared by the Benedictine Covenant of Perpetual Adoration, *The Blessed Sacrament: God With Us* (Rockford, Il: Tan Books, 2000), 10,12. This tract goes on to say on the back cover that the consecrated bread of the Mass *"includes all the immensity of Christ's love that is contained in the mysteries of His life on earth—His incarnation, His life and labors, His Passion and Death. We lay hold of all these treasures through the Blessed Sacrament. And thus, before the Tabernacle we can receive eternal and inexpressibly precious graces and favors"* (Emphasis added).

To facilitate the worship of the "Blessed Eucharist" the communion wafer is placed in a *monstrance* and carried in solemn procession or set upon the altar. The monstrance is a vessel made of gold or silver that contains the consecrated Host in the middle, around which is a sunburst design to highlight where the wafer is affixed by a circular piece of glass. The monstrance is placed on a Roman Catholic altar where Catholics are to acknowledge, pray, worship, and adore the wafer to be the Lord Jesus Christ. To underscore the seriousness with which this is firmly believed in Roman Catholicism, a person has only to go into a Catholic bookstore and see that a considerable number of prayer books are devoted to the worship of the Eucharist. These prayers are actually addressed to the communion wafer. One such prayer offered to the Eucharistic bread makes the following confession:

> All thanksgiving be to You, Jesus, for continuing to empty Yourself in the humility of the Sacrament, taking the form of the Sacred Host, appearing before us in the likeness of bread, obediently accepting a state even more humble than humanity to nourish us always in the Eucharist with the fullness of Divinity.[18]

There are religious orders and societies that are exclusively devoted to the worship of the communion wafer. The Missionaries of the Blessed Sacrament, The Congregation of the Blessed Sacrament, and The Sisters of the Blessed Sacrament are some of these religious orders that engage in the perpetual worship of the Eucharist, twenty-four hours a day, seven days a week! By the condemnatory decrees of the awful Council of Trent, Rome has pronounced condemnation on anyone who rejects and denies that the Mass is a real and effective sacrifice of Christ to remove sins, and on those who further say that the worship of the Eucharist is idolatry, in that the Eucharist is not the real body, blood, soul, and divinity of the Lord Jesus Christ. Canons one and two of the Thirteenth Session say:

> If anyone denies that in the sacrament of the most Holy Eucharist are contained truly, really, and substantially the body and blood together with the soul and divinity of our Lord Jesus Christ, and consequently the whole Christ, but says that He is in it only as in a sign, or figure or force, let him be anathema. If anyone says that in the sacred and holy sacrament of the Eucharist the substance of the bread and wine remains conjointly with the body and blood of our Lord Jesus Christ, and denies that wonderful and singular change of the whole substance of the bread into the body and the whole substance of the wine into the blood, the appearances only of bread and wine remaining, which change the Catholic Church most aptly calls transubstantiation, let him be anathema.[19]

---

[18] Vincent Martin Lucia, *Come to Me in the Blessed Sacrament* (Plattsburgh, New York: MBS, 2000), 13. In this same prayer book the author has Jesus saying that His love keeps Him a prisoner in the tabernacle for twenty centuries, day and night, veiled under the species of bread and concealed in the small white host (page 150). Apparently, the author forgot the biblical truth that the immensity and fullness of God, whether seen through Father, Son, or Holy Spirit, cannot be contained within any part of creation, in a temple, or a piece of bread in a Roman Catholic tabernacle made by human hands. ***"Behold heaven and the heaven of heavens cannot contain you." "Thus says the Lord: Heaven is My throne and earth is My footstool, where is the house that you will build Me? And where is the place of My rest? For all those things My hand has made"*** (1 Kings 8:27; Isaiah 66:1-2).

[19] *The Canons and Decrees of the Council of Trent*, 79

Canon Three of the Twenty-Second Session says:

> If anyone says that the sacrifice of the Mass is one only of praise and thanksgiving; or that it is a mere commemoration of the sacrifice consummated on the cross but not a propitiatory one, or that it profits him only who receives, and ought not to be offered for the living and the dead, for sins, punishments, satisfactions, and other necessities, let him be anathema.[20]

Rome has never revoked any of these anathemas, and they are still in force today. The atonement of Jesus Christ is the core of the Gospel. Thus, if you have a false and incorrect understanding of it, you do not have the true Gospel. This is the essential problem of the Roman Catholic Mass. Rome claims the Eucharistic sacrifice of the Mass is the same sacrifice of the cross Jesus instituted during Passover the night before His death. The words of Jesus at the Last Supper were not intended to be taken in a literal cannibalistic manner, requiring the disciples to eat his flesh and drink His blood (Matthew 26:26-28; Luke 22:17-20; Mark 14:22-25). The Lord often spoke in parables, metaphors, and similes to vividly convey some truth about His Person and work (Matthew 13:34-35). Such assertions about Christ's flesh and blood corresponding to the bread and wine do not necessarily mean that these terms are to be understood as literal, any more than when the Lord made other direct assertions about Himself, such as *"I am the door"* (John 10:9), and *"I am the true vine"* (John 15:1). Roman Catholics do not believe that Jesus meant that He was literally a door or a vine either when making these statements. They know He was speaking in metaphors and figures of speech. Indeed, right after the Last Supper was celebrated, Jesus told the disciples that His teachings and the words He spoke to them up to that point in time were given in figurative language. *"These things I have spoken to you in figurative language"* (John 16:25).

Again, Jesus said this after the Passover meal was finished, and after the words of institution were said; what He said about the cup of wine and bread were therefore figurative of His broken body and shed blood, and were not intended by Him to be a literal presentation! These figurative things were what Jesus taught during the Passover meal, in which He instituted the Lord's Supper, when declaring the Passover bread and wine to be His body and blood. In John 14:31, and the events following in chapters fifteen and sixteen, obviously indicate Jesus was on His way to Gethsemane when He told the disciples that the words He spoke to them before, during, and immediately after the Passover meal were figurative. That would most certainly include the traditional passages in the synoptic Gospels concerning the body and blood of Jesus Christ, which Roman Catholicism traditionally uses to justify the transubstantiation of the Mass. The words Jesus spoke about the bread and wine being His body and blood were figurative expressions for the New Covenant and of the Messiah's imminent death on the cross for the salvation of man. They were not intended to be *literal*, but *symbolic* representations of a literal reality and truth. The biblical context in which the words, "Take, eat; this is My body," and "drink, for this is My blood," were given in order to demonstrate, quite obviously, that despite their vivid and straightforward delivery, they are to be symbolically understood.

After Jesus spoke the words of supposed "consecration" recorded in Matthew 26:26-28 and Mark 14:22-25 to inaugurate the Mass, whereby the bread and wine were allegedly transformed into His body and blood, He still referred to the cup of wine as *"the fruit of the vine"*—thus indicating it still remained wine after He had symbolically alluded to it representing His blood, that was shed the next day to ratify the New Covenant. Christ said, *"Assuredly, I say to you, I will no longer __drink of the fruit of the vine__ until that day when I*

---

20   Ibid., 149.

drink it new in the kingdom of God (Mark 14:25). Observe that Jesus did not claim the cup of the Last Supper to literally be His blood. He did not say, "I will no longer drink of the cup of My blood", but rather He would no longer drink from "*the fruit of the vine.*" The Lord's phrase denotes by its clear identification that He did not mean the cup of wine literally became His blood, but rather was symbolic of it.

The cup Jesus held in His hands was wine before and after He instituted the Lord's Supper. This inconvenient truth makes it all the more obvious that Jesus intended His words to be taken in a figurative and symbolic sense, and thus rules out the possibility that His words were to be understood literally, in the fashion Roman Catholicism unconvincingly attempts to prove when claiming the Mass and the doctrine of transubstantiation are validated by the words of Jesus. The New Testament views Jesus to be the Passover lamb that was slain for the sins of the world (John 1:29; 1 Corinthians 5:7). The disciples and the early church knew, of course, that He was not literally a Passover lamb but that the Paschal lamb and all the Old Testament animal sacrifices were exemplified, foreshadowed, and fulfilled in the death of Jesus the Messiah. The Passover lamb was symbolic of this powerful truth in the same manner the cup of wine and bread served at Passover was figurative extensions of Christ's broken body and shed blood. In view of this:

> The Scriptures clearly explain that "For indeed Christ our Passover was sacrificed for us" (1 Corinthians 5:7). When John the Baptist saw Jesus he proclaimed: "Behold! The Lamb of God who takes away the sin of the world!" (John 1:29). Jesus fulfilled each and every Old Testament type that pointed to the coming Messiah. This included the Passover Lamb. During the Last Supper, Jesus was declaring that He would die in our place. All who repented of their sins and placed their trust in Him would be delivered from the bondage of sin and death.

> Of course during the Last Supper Jesus did not become a literal lamb, nor did the bread become His literal body. To the Jewish believers in attendance it would have been clear that Jesus Himself was to be the sacrifice for their sins. Jesus would fulfill the Jewish prophecy that the Messiah would bear our sins in His own body (Isaiah 53:12; 1 Peter 2:24). It would be His body that would be killed and His blood that would be shed for our sins. The Old Testament's sacrifices and offerings—which foreshadowed Christ—would be fulfilled in the Son of God. No longer would there be any need to offer sacrifices for our sins. God Himself would once and for all atone for all sins. This is what Jesus meant when He referred to the Passover elements as His body and blood.[21]

The whole idea that Jesus was literally meaning the bread was His physical body and the wine His actual blood defies logic, the physical reality of the situation, and most importantly, Scripture itself. It is obvious from these three areas that Jesus did not intend that His words were to be taken literally by His disciples, or anyone else for that matter. To adopt a literal view that the bread and wine actually became the body and blood of Jesus when He said, "This is My body" and "This is My blood" simply contradicts the basic laws of physics—one of which states a material object may not occupy two different places at the same time and the corollary to this is the law that no two physical objects may occupy the same place at the same time. If Jesus meant that the elements of bread and wine literally became His body, blood, soul, and divinity, when

---

[21] Roger Oakland and Jim Tetlow, *Another Jesus?* (Santa Ana California: Understand the Times, 2004), 63-64.

saying the words of consecration, He would have to physically exist and be present in two places at the same time—This is a physical impossibility.

The Gospel accounts of the Last Supper in no way collectively indicate that the disciples believed the bread and wine were literally changed into the flesh and blood of Christ. This is mainly because the Lord Jesus was still physically present with the disciples after He spoke the words of institution! Nor do we read in the Gospel accounts that the disciples ever explicitly acknowledged and worshipped the elements of the bread and wine to be the actual body and blood of Jesus Christ, wherein the fullness of His deity is contained. Nowhere in the apostolic writings of the New Testament are Christians required or told to worship the Eucharistic elements of the bread and wine as Jesus Christ!

Furthermore, to believe that Jesus recreated Himself through the act of spontaneous transubstantiation to exist in the bread and wine of the Last Supper, would logically entail that God created Himself in another object, when by definition God is eternal (Psalm 90:2; John 1:3; 8:58; Colossians 1:16-17), has therefore always existed, and the fullness of His deity can never be created or indwelt in an object, thing, or person other than in Himself and the incarnate Person of Jesus Christ. Transubstantiation is a practical denial of the unique quality and expression of the Incarnation. The Incarnation is borrowed from the word "incarnate", which means to indwell or inhabit a human body, and is the biblical doctrine central to Christianity. It teaches the eternal God, in the Second Person of the Trinity, became a flesh-and-blood human being in the Person of Jesus of Nazareth. He was both God and man with two distinct natures (divine and human) united in one person.

The Gospel of John describes the Incarnation as the eternal Word Who was with God, and was God, yet "became flesh" in the human body of Jesus (John 1:1, 14). Christian theologians call the uniting of two natures (divine and human) in the person of Christ the *Hypostatic Union*. The Hypostatic Union allows for the perfectly equal and simultaneous sharing of both a human nature and a divine nature in the Person of Jesus Christ. This union allowed Jesus Christ to be both God and man at the same time. Each of the natures are distinct, and this means the divine attributes are not transferred to the human nature so that the divine becomes limited and confined to one place, and nor does the human become infinite without spatial limitations. After the incarnation, Christ became the God-Man forever.

Once born of the Virgin Mary, Jesus will always have a human body through which His divinity is revealed. When one looks at Jesus, he or she literally sees the invisible God made visible in human form (John 14:9; Hebrews 1:3). When God became a man in the person of Jesus, He voluntarily confined Himself to a physical body that was naturally limited by space and time. Once Jesus was born of a human mother, God the Son has always physically inhabited one exclusive human male body (with the exception of when Jesus' dead body was in a sealed tomb for three days) and will exclusively do so throughout eternity with a resurrection body. To then say that Christ physically re-incarnates Himself in the bread and wine each time a Roman Catholic Mass is said by a priest is to repudiate the unique and unrepeatable one-time event of the Incarnation that occurred when God, for *one time* and *all time*, became a man.

The Word of God teaches this event and miracle is unrepeatable and will never happen again. God the Father prepared *one body at one time* in history for God the Son to exclusively inhabit. ***"Therefore, when He came into the world, He said: 'Sacrifice and offering You did not desire, but a body You have prepared for Me. In burnt offerings and sacrifices for sin You had no pleasure. Then I said, 'Behold, I have come—In the volume of the book it is written of Me—to do Your will, O God'"*** (Hebrews 10:5-7). God prepared a *body*, not the Eucharistic bread of the Roman Catholic Mass, for the incarnation of the God-Man Jesus Christ! Transubstantiation contradicts the biblical orthodox view of the Incarnation here in that it requires multiple incarnations over against the single, one-time-for-all Incarnation of the Lord Jesus Christ! Evangelical theologian Norman Geisler demonstrates the inconsistency with logic and Scripture that transubstantiation leads to, for those who adopt a literalistic interpretation of Jesus' statements about His body and blood with regard to the bread and wine of Communion. Geisler inductively concludes:

> Jesus could not have been speaking physically in this case, because ever since the Incarnation He has always been a human being and has always dwelt continuously in a human body (except when He was in the grave). *If the bread and the wine He held in His hands were actually His literal body and blood, then He would have been incarnated in two different places at the same time.* One physical body cannot be in two different locations at the same time, so despite Catholic protests to the contrary, transubstantiation (logically) involves two bodies and two incarnations of Christ, which is contrary to the orthodox doctrine of *the* Incarnation.[22]

The physical characteristic of humanity is inherently expressed through a human body. The physical manifestation of Christ's humanity cannot, therefore, be divorced and separated from His human body when He walked this earth or when He now resides in heaven. Catholicism's insistence that the physical body of Christ is ubiquitous (present everywhere) on the altars of Roman Catholic churches throughout the world is to erase and blend together the two distinct natures of Christ, and thereby nullify the Hypostatic Union of the Incarnation. When theologians speak of the omnipresence of Christ this refers to His spiritual presence, not His physical presence. Scripture teaches that God is Spirit (John 4:24). Through God's Spirit, the three Persons of the Godhead are spiritually present everywhere (Psalm 139:7-16), and since Christ is God, He is also spiritually omnipresent (Matthew 28:20; John 1:48). But His physical, bodily presence is confined to one location at one time. Currently, Christ's bodily presence is seated at the right hand of God the Father (Romans 8:34; Hebrews 1:3). The disciples naturally understood Jesus' words, "This is My body and blood," with regard to the bread and wine of Passover, to be figurative signs of His impending crucifixion. The disciples knew these words were not literal for the obvious and tangible reason that the physical body of Christ remained in the room with His blood still coursing through His veins. If transubstantiation were true in this instance, Christ would be holding His own body, blood, soul, and deity (His entire being) in His hands. This interpretation is silly and nonsensical, and makes about as much sense as if a man were to pluck his eyes out and hold them in his hands, just to see the front of his face!

When Christ used the word "is" (*estin* in the Greek) in Luke 22:19-20 to define the symbolic elements for the New Covenant, He was employing what is called an equative verb in Aramaic that indicates *representation*, not *identification* (see Darrell L. Bock's *Luke 9:51-24:53 Baker Exegetical Commentary of the New Testament*, Grand Rapids: Baker Book House, 1996, pages 1724-1725). The Aramaic-speaking disciples of Jesus would thus naturally understand His words concerning the bread and wine to be powerful symbols of the Messiah's body and blood. Catholic apologists continually rail at the Protestant "Fundamentalists" for refusing to take Jesus' words, "This is My body," and "This is My blood", as literal, while they interpret the rest of Scripture literally. This accusation is based on the common misunderstanding that Evangelicals take every word of the Bible literally. The rash charge of hypocrisy is leveled at this perceived inconsistency when it comes to Christ's words said over the "Eucharist." But this accusation must be turned back on the defenders of Romanism over a question dealing with Christ's statement in Luke 22:20: ***"Likewise He also***

---

[22]   Norman Geisler, *Systematic Theology*, Vol. 4 (Minneapolis: Bethany House, 2005), 157-158.

took the cup after supper, saying, This cup is the new covenant in My blood, which is shed for you." If the wine and bread literally becomes Christ's flesh and blood, why not believe the cup Jesus held in His hands was also literally transubstantiated into the New Covenant? Indeed, if Jesus meant the wine literally became His blood in Matthew 26:28 and Mark 14:24 according to Catholic belief, why then do they freely admit the cup mentioned in Luke 22:20 and 1 Corinthians 11:25 is symbolic? Rome's literal understanding of the first phrase "this is My body" upon which the doctrine of transubstantiation is built crumbles over this interpretive inconsistency.

The real issue concerns what is the proper interpretation of the Scripture that should be applied here by the student of the Bible. Evangelicals hold to the historical-grammatical method of interpretation, which seeks to explain and interpret the original sense of the Bible according to the normal customary usages of its language. This method of interpretation was prevalent in first-century Israel among the rabbis and their students, and was the method Jesus and His disciples used for explaining the Scriptures. Holy Scripture must be taken according to its plain, ordinary sense and appropriately interpreted within proper context. When this fundamental principle of biblical hermeneutics is applied to the bread and wine of the Last Supper, there are sound reasons for not taking Christ's words about His body and blood to mean they were literally present in the bread and wine. The context of the words of Jesus, and the insuperable difficulties associated with it, if one were to assign a literal meaning to them, make it impossible to take the words literally, and it justifies interpreting His words in no other way but figuratively. Those difficulties that render unacceptable and quite absurd the veracity of the Roman Catholic view of transubstantiation are physical, conceptual, and biblical in nature. The last point the author will demonstrate in the forthcoming pages. Millard J. Erickson provides an excellent overview here on this critical point from the Evangelical perspective:

> Since it is our general practice to interpret Scripture literally, we must be prepared to offer justification if we interpret these words in any other way. In this particular case it so happens that there are certain considerations which do in fact argue against literal interpretation. First, if we take "This is my body" and "This is my blood" literally, an absurdity results. If Jesus meant that the bread and wine were at that moment in the upper room actually his body and his blood, he was asserting that his flesh and blood were in two places simultaneously, since his corporeal form was right there beside the elements. To believe that Jesus was in two places at once is something of a denial of the incarnation, which limited his physical human nature to one location.
>
> Second, there are conceptual difficulties for those who declare that Christ has been bodily present in the subsequent occurrences of the Lord's Supper. While the preceding paragraph introduced the problem of how Christ's flesh and blood could have been in two places simultaneously, here we face the problem of how two substances (e.g., flesh and bread) can be in the same place simultaneously (the Lutheran conception) or of how a particular substance (e.g., blood) can exist without any of its customary characteristics (the Catholic view). While those who hold to a physical presence offer explanations of their view, their cases rest upon a type of metaphysic which seems very strange to twentieth century minds, and indeed appears to us to be untenable.[23]

---

[23] Millard J. Erickson, *Christian Theology* (Grand Rapids: Baker, 1992), 1121. Transubstantiation unwittingly divinizes the human nature of Jesus by imputing the attribute of virtual omnipresence to the Eucharist when the bread and

The sacrifice of the Mass cannot be a continuation of Christ's sacrifice on the cross that was instituted by Jesus at the Last Supper because it is out of sequence in place and time with the actual crucifixion event. The Mass is an *anachronism* because Jesus celebrated the Passover *before* He was crucified and Scripture informs us that Christ's sacrifice for sin could not be truly efficacious until He physically died (Hebrews 9:16-17). But the so-called Mass came first and is therefore out of place and time with the crucifixion, if the former is an expiatory continuation of the latter. The claim of the Mass to be a genuine sacrifice of Christ is anachronistic in that it does not follow a proper time sequence and is incongruous with cause and effect. The Law of God required that Christ must suffer, die, and shed His blood, first, for a true sacrifice for sin to be made. The Mass cannot be an extension of Christ's sacrifice for sin when the only true and final sacrifice He offered on the cross was not yet made. A principle law of causality states that no cause is greater than its effect. This law is contradicted if the Mass Christ supposedly inaugurated before His death occurred prior to His crucifixion on Calvary. The Mass could not logically or sequentially be the continuation and re-presentation of the cross after the event if the Mass already occurred before in point of time. If the Mass potentially had the same power to forgive and pay for sin in the same way the Cross did, why would Jesus have to die in the first place if He could effectively and essentially offer the same sacrifice through the "unbloody sacrifice" of the Mass?

The crucifixion on Golgotha would then be practically unnecessary and superfluous if this were the case. If the Lord's Supper were a redemptive sacrifice the Lord Jesus would have plainly said so. In point of fact, Christ never once alluded to the Last Supper to be an out-and-out "unbloody sacrifice" of Himself. Not once in the New Testament is the Lord's Supper called the "Mass." The Mass is just another unbiblical invention of Rome to justify her works-system of salvation, and to keep her poor adherents in spiritual bondage to their sacramental rites, instead of trusting alone in the Person and finished sacrifice of Jesus Christ on the cross for salvation. In Luke 22:19, Jesus gives the reason why the Church is to celebrate Communion. ***"And He took bread, gave thanks and broke it, and gave it to them, saying, This is My body given for you; do this in remembrance of Me"***. We see plainly here that when Jesus instituted the ordinance of the Lord's Supper He said, "Do this in *remembrance* of Me." He did not say, "Do this for a sacrifice of Me", or, "Do this as a re-presentation of My sacrifice", or yet, "This do for a continuation of My sacrifice." Christ asked to be *remembered*, not *sacrificed*! The Last Supper is a memorial meal, a commemorative celebration, not a propitiatory sacrifice, that looks back to the cross where the Lord Jesus gave His body to death and shed His blood to ratify the New Covenant and bring final redemption for His people. The word Jesus used for *"remembrance"* in the Greek text of Luke 22:19 is *anamnesis* (ανάμνησις). The word means to remember and recall to mind a particular event or person.[24] With regard to the disciples in the context of Luke chapter twenty-two, they were to partake of the bread as an act of remembrance and reverence, with the thought that the Passover matzo (the unleavened bread used for the Passover meal) was a symbol for the broken body of

---

wine become the human body and blood of Christ on the altars of Roman Catholic churches throughout different parts of the world at exactly the same time. There arises from this a disturbing confusion between Christ's deity and His humanity. Evangelical author Eric Svendsen lays out the obvious problem here when correctly observing: "This confuses Christ's deity (which is omnipresent) with Christ's humanity (which is not omnipresent). The only way Christ could be in the bread and wine is through His deity; i.e., spiritually. Just as Christ in His physical body cannot be in more than one place at a time, so also if the Eucharistic bread becomes the actual body of Christ, then it can be in no more than one particular location at a time" *Evangelical Answers*, page 177.

[24]   *BAGD*, 58.

the Lord Jesus, and stood for a commemorative meal celebrating His death for the salvation of mankind. The same reason was given to Israel when God commanded them to celebrate Passover.

The Passover meal was to be celebrated for a memorial to symbolically commemorate the miracle of the Exodus when God delivered the Jewish people from the slavery of Egypt by the shed blood of the lamb. The Jewish people were commanded by God to celebrate this meal throughout their generations *for a memorial of redemption* (see Exodus 12:14). The Passover meal was not the Passover sacrifice of the lamb itself but a type and symbol for it. It was with exactly the same figurative meaning and understanding that the Lord Jesus, when celebrating Passover on the night before His death, borrowed from the same premise to institute the Lord's Supper. For just as the Passover meal was a symbolic commemoration of Israel's exodus from Egypt, so too was the Last Supper instituted by Christ, for the Church, to be a powerful, perpetual, and symbolic reminder of the Lord's death for the redemption of His people.[25] Moreover, if the Roman Catholic belief that Christ was commanding His disciples to literally eat His flesh and drink His blood were true, it would violate the prohibition in the Law of Moses forbidding Torah-observant Jews, like Jesus and His disciples, from drinking blood of any kind (Genesis 9:4; Leviticus 3:17; 17:14). To drink blood of any kind within the community of Israel was so serious a transgression that it incurred the extreme displeasure of Yahweh and brought immediate excommunication from the people of God! ***"Moreover you shall not eat any blood in any of your dwellings...whoever eats any blood, that person shall be cut off from his people"*** (Leviticus 7:26-27). This law was not the opinion of Moses, but a command spoken directly from God (Leviticus 7:22).

Jesus never would have condoned or instructed His Jewish disciples, who were mindful of this law, to flagrantly disobey a direct commandment of God. To require the drinking of blood would have violated God's Law. Jesus explicitly stated in Matthew 5:17 He did not come to ***"destroy"*** the Mosaic Law but to confirm and fulfill all its requirements. To then require that the disciples drink His blood at the Last Supper, would have undoubtedly violated and transgressed that very divine Law and made Jesus a lawbreaker, and one who contradicts His own teaching. Christ upheld the Old Testament teaching of not to physically eat or drink blood of any kind. Several years later, after Christ left the earth, Peter, a Torah-observant Jew, confessed to the Lord that he never ate or drank anything deemed non-kosher in Acts 10:14: ***"But Peter said, Not so, Lord! For I have never eaten anything common or unclean."***

If Peter believed he had eaten and drunk the flesh and blood of Christ in the Mass, then his claim of keeping kosher would not be true. One of the main decisions ratified by the Apostles at the Jerusalem Council reaffirmed the Old Testament prohibition against eating things with blood, and then applied it to Gentile Christians (Acts 15:29). A prohibition of this nature does not make sense if the Church were in fact drinking

---

[25] Bible commentator Paul Barnett agrees, with the following cogent observation about why Jesus instituted the Lord's Supper for the Church to celebrate: "But Jesus' actions and words were not merely prospective, to explain to the twelve that night the meaning and significance of what would happen the next day. Rather, what Jesus did and said was to be repeated into the future as a way of bringing *him* to the 'memory' of his people. This matches exactly the Lord's institution of the Passover meal in Egypt. The Lord instructed Moses and Aaron that it was to be 'a day of *remembrance* for you. You shall celebrate it as a festival to the Lord' (Exod. 12:14, NRSV). By the actions, the words, and the eating and drinking at the dinner of the Lord, the new covenant people 'call to mind' the death of their Lord on their behalf. Jesus intended his people corporately to 'remember' him, which they do when they eat his 'dinner' together. Jesus offered his sacrifice on the cross for his people once. He achieved an eternal salvation by this never-to-be-repeated act (see Heb. 9:26-10:10). There can be no re-offering of that sacrifice, but only the 'remembrance' of it." Paul Barnett, *1 Corinthians: Holiness and Hope of A Rescued People* (Ross-shire, Great Britain: Christian Focus, 2000), 216.

Christ's blood at the Mass during this time. If that were the case, the Apostles would have contradicted one of the main decisions they drafted at the Jerusalem Council which was convened and inspired by the Holy Spirit (Acts 15:28). To somehow imagine that Christ would require that Christians break the Old Testament commandment not to drink blood, or the New Testament commandment not to drink blood, is to sin against Scripture and the Person of Jesus Christ. The Roman Catholic Mass is therefore unscriptural on these grounds, and is in direct contradiction of both the Old Testament and the New Testament. Paul uses *anamnesis* (remembrance) twice in 1 Corinthians 11:23-25 when repeating Christ's words for celebrating the Lord's Supper: *For I received from the Lord that which I also delivered to you: that the Lord Jesus on the same night in which He was betrayed took bread; and when He had given thanks, He broke it and said, "Take, eat; this is My body which is broken for you; <u>do this in remembrance of Me</u>." In the same manner He also took the cup after supper, saying, "This cup is the new covenant in My blood. <u>This do, as often as you drink it, in remembrance of Me</u>"* (Emphasis mine).

In the same way the Lord Jesus intended, Paul also tells the church at Corinth that the Lord's Supper is celebrated to remember and proclaim that Christ died for the Church. Such a reverent and affectionate recollection for what Christ did in His death is to be proclaimed through the celebration of the Lord's Supper. Here would have been a propitious opportunity for the Apostle to tell the church about those critical elements necessary for salvation bound up in the Roman Catholic Mass as traditionally defined by Roman Catholicism for the Lord's Supper. Paul makes no mention of Christ being the perpetual victim in the Mass. There is no mention of a priesthood transubstantiating the bread and wine into the flesh and blood of Christ. Nor is there any mention that the Lord's Supper is an "unbloody sacrifice" that is a continuation of Christ's sacrifice on the cross. There is no patent declaration or doctrine in the New Testament that the bread and wine become the actual body, blood, soul, and divinity of Jesus Christ which must be worshipped and adored. There is no teaching elaborated in the Scripture asserting that the memorial meal of the Lord's Supper is in fact an expiatory sacrifice and a sacrament of Christ's continued sacrifice through which God's saving grace is conveyed.

There is no New Testament teaching that says the commemorative value of the Lord's Supper is equal with, and has the same power to forgive sin as, the death of Christ on the cross. In the end, Paul makes no mention of the Roman Catholic Mass at all in 1 Corinthians 11:24-25. Roman Catholic apologists beg to differ and offer their interpretation, which, not surprisingly, supports the doctrine of the Mass. But again, when the Bible reader carefully studies the context of First Corinthians eleven, he or she will see that the chapter does not support the so-called 'sacrifice' of the Mass. "Not so fast", comes the predictable reply of the Roman Catholic theologian and apologist. They appeal to what Paul goes on to say, particularly in verses twenty-seven and twenty-nine, and from there allege that he validates transubstantiation in the Lord's Supper when issuing the following warning: *"Therefore whoever eats this bread or drinks this cup of the Lord in an unworthy manner will be guilty of the body and blood of the Lord...For he who eats and drinks in an unworthy manner eats and drinks judgment to himself, not discerning the Lord's body"* (1 Corinthians 11:27, 29). From a *prima facie* reading of these verses, the Roman Catholic argues that Paul obviously teaches here that a person cannot be "guilty of the body and blood of the Lord", unless the bread and wine of the Lord's Supper were actually and literally the flesh and blood of Jesus Christ through the supernatural act of transubstantiation. Catholic apologist Patrick Madrid thinks this assumption provides an inescapable conclusion supporting the doctrine of transubstantiation:

If the Eucharist were merely a symbol, as many Protestants claim, then a Christian who received the Eucharist unworthily could not be guilty of such a sin. But if the Eucharist really is the body and blood of Christ under the appearances of the bread and wine, as the Catholic Church teaches, then one would in fact be committing a grave sacrilege by receiving it while in the state of mortal sin or in believing what the Church teaches about the Real Presence.[26]

But reading the context of First Corinthians 11:26-28 reveals that Madrid's arguments are false and flat wrong, and that the passage does not support in any way the Catholic claim that "the Real Presence" of Jesus' flesh and blood is contained in the bread and wine of Communion. Three times in these verses Paul calls the Eucharist "bread" and not the flesh of Christ. Indeed, the Lord already said the blessing over the bread and wine, which would have been the words of institution in the Mass. The bread and wine still remained such after this, and Paul explicitly acknowledges the same in 1 Corinthians 11:26-28. A clear statement of this nature clearly evinces that no fundamental change of transubstantiation had taken place! Paul says when the Christian eats and drinks in an unworthy manner he is still eating bread and drinking from the cup of wine. They remain, and are understood to be, bread and wine every time the Lord's Supper is celebrated. Furthermore, Christ could not be physically contained or present in the bread and wine of the Roman Catholic Mass, due to the fact that the Lord's Supper "proclaims" Christ's death until He physically returns which would obviously imply the Lord's physical absence during the entire church age, when the meal is celebrated. Paul writes in 1 Corinthians 11:26: ***"For as often as you eat this bread and drink this cup, you proclaim the Lord's death till He comes."*** If Christ were physically present in the elements of the bread and wine during the Mass, then waiting for His physical return would be meaningless and contradicted here. Jesus told the disciples He would not come again for the Church until after He finished preparing living accommodations for them in heaven, which He affectionately called His "Father's House" (John 14:1-4).

Many Christians call this event the Rapture, at which time Christ will bodily return in the air to *physically* and *personally* reunite with the Church (See 1 Corinthians 15:51-57; 1 Thessalonians 4:14-18). But during the interval of the present age, the Lord Jesus would be physically absent from the earth. He never said that He would bodily return, in a physical manner, prior to the Rapture or His second coming to Earth. Because of Christ's physical absence from the earth, He desires that His Church ardently remember Him through the powerful, symbolic reminders of the bread and wine in the Lord's Supper, which point back to the perfect and final sacrifice of Christ for sin. The Church is to celebrate this memorial meal until Jesus comes again to consummate the meal in person with the Church at the Wedding Supper of the Lamb (Luke 22:16; Revelation 19:7-10). Until that time, the New Testament categorically teaches Christ will be physically absent from the earth while in heaven. He cannot therefore be physically present in the sacrament of the Mass (Matthew 23:39; 26:11; Luke 5:34-35; John 14-17)! Christ is spiritually present with the Church when they come together to celebrate the Lord's Supper, to proclaim in reverent retrospection the fact Christ's death saves sinners. Hence, since spiritual communion is the goal, Christ's bodily presence is unnecessary.

Ordinary bread and wine can serve as adequate reminders for Christians as they gather to "proclaim the Lord's death until He comes" (1 Corinthians 11:26). "Then they will not need symbols, for they shall have Him!"[27] Indeed, the Greek word for "guilty" (ενοχος, *enochos*) is an adjective which is a legal term

---

26   Patrick Madrid, *Where Is That in the Bible?*, 114.

27   McCarthy, *The Gospel According to Rome*, 138.

used to express liability for sinning against the Lord in some way, or to be held liable for His death. To be "guilty" of the body and blood of the Lord is to misuse and take advantage of the circumstances and the Eucharistic elements surrounding the celebration of the Lord's Supper and miss the point of the meal, which is to *proclaim* salvation through Christ's death on the cross; it is "proclaimed" in the bread saying and the cup saying. The profanation of the Lord's Supper by the Corinthians placed them under the same liability as those responsible for Christ's death in the first place. Hence, to be guilty of the body and blood of Christ means to be liable or morally responsible for His death, by treating the symbols of it in the bread and wine in a disrespectful and contemptible manner.

> What Paul has done here seems clear. Taking the two elements of the Supper, the bread and cup, he has expressed the Corinthians' "guilt" in terms of what the bread and cup *signify*, the Lord's body and blood. But what he intends by this is less obvious. The adjective "guilty" is a technical legal term to express liability. In genitive constructions such as this one, it can denote either the person sinned against or the crime itself. In this case, therefore, it can mean either "guilty of sinning against the Lord" in some way, or "to be held liable for his death," which the body and blood *represent*.... More likely, therefore, the "guilt" Paul has in mind is that of the crime itself. *His point is that those who carry on at the Lord's Table as the Corinthians are doing have missed the point of the meal, which is to proclaim salvation through Christ's death, signified in the bread and cup and proclaimed" in the bread saying and cup saying.* To "profane" the meal as they are doing is to place themselves under the same liability as those responsible for that death in the first place. Thus, to be "guilty of his body and blood" means to be liable for his death (see Gordon Fee, *The First Epistle to the Corinthians*, pages 560-561, emphasis mine).

Transubstantiation never enters the picture here, and is nowhere mentioned being the issue or problems with the Lord's Supper that is addressed by Paul in 1 Corinthians 11. Paul points out what these problems were in 1 Corinthians 11:17-22, and in verses 33 and 34. What these verses reveal is that the Corinthian Christians had a flippant and contemptible disregard for the Lord's Supper and a disturbing lack of respect for each other, particularly when they gathered around the Lord's Table to celebrate Communion. They came to this table with acute divisions among themselves and used the Lord's Supper for a place of gluttony and drunkenness, while at the same time depriving others from partaking in the sacred meal. To conduct oneself in this way was to behave "in an unworthy manner" and reflected an utter failure to reverently recognize the sacred symbols of the bread and wine that memorialized the death of Christ through His broken body and shed blood.

The Corinthians' shameful behavior at the Lord's Table indicated that they were treating the Lord's Supper just like any other profane or common meal. Paul warns and admonishes them, in light of this unfortunate circumstance, to examine their attitude and motives for celebrating the Lord's Supper, lest by their misconduct they receive chastisement by the Lord, as some already did with being sick and suffering premature death. Paul strictly charged the Corinthians to correct their misbehavior with a proper appreciation for what the elements of the Lord's Supper represent. To then bring these various, sinful practices to the Lord's Table, without the slightest moral compunction, was "a failure to recognize practically the symbolism of the elements, and hence the treatment of the supper as a common meal."[28] The Lord's Supper was supposed

---

[28] Robert Duncan Culver, *Systematic Theology* (Ross-shire, Great Britain: Christian Focus, 2005), 1001.

to be the worshipful recollection of the supreme selfless act of Christ's death on behalf of others. But the Corinthians had turned the memorial of redemptive selflessness into an experience of shocking selfishness. After considering the aforementioned explanation, schooled Roman Catholics would point to what Paul wrote in 1 Corinthians 11:29 about "not discerning the Lord's body" and exclaim that the Apostle sacramentally understood the bread of the Lord's Supper to literally be the physical body of Christ, and plainly said so here. Does this phrase, in fact, corroborate the transubstantiation of the Mass?

The key exegetical issue centers on how to interpret "the Lord's body." The earliest and most reliable Greek manuscripts within the context of First Corinthians eleven strongly suggest the meaning of "body" is the New Testament Church, which is also referred to as "the body of Christ" throughout the Pauline *corpus* (Romans 12:4-5; 1 Corinthians 10:16-17; 12:12-27; Ephesians 4:15-16; Colossians 1:18; 3:15). The earliest and best Greek New Testament manuscripts omit the phrase "of the Lord." So what Paul probably originally wrote read, "Recognize the body."[29] But if otherwise, the context of the living situation (*sitz im leben*) in Corinth reasonably argues that Paul was speaking about how the Corinthian Christians were failing to recognize the church as the body of Christ by mistreating its individual members—a fact borne out most prominently when they came to celebrate the Lord's Supper together.[30] This is especially underscored by the fact Paul had earlier reminded them, through a play on words asserted in 1 Corinthians 10:16-17, that the Church, though consisting of many members, is metaphorically considered to be *one bread* and *one body*. This unity is best exemplified when the church corporately participates in the Lord's Supper. Here, they are witnessing to their unity with the crucified Christ who died for them. Failure to recognize this, and the careless approach with which the Corinthian Christians were celebrating the Lord's Supper, was a serious problem not because of what the bread and wine *was* but what they *represent*.

Both Paul and the church at Corinth did not understand the Lord's Supper to be an altar where the sacrifice of Christ was taking place, according to the idea of the Roman Catholic Mass, but a fellowship meal in which by it they could look back with adoration on the once-for-all singular sacrifice Christ made for them. Through this commemorative celebration, Christians are allowed to corporately and individually realize and practically reflect on the saving benefits Christ's death brings to their lives. In this way, to participate in the Lord's broken body and shed blood, symbolically represented by the bread and wine, afforded the church the opportunity to share in the provisions and benefits of the New Covenant. The cumulative case of the historical context of Israel, the pagan meal of eating a deity, and the grammar and the language of 1 Corinthians 10:16-17 and 11:17-34 simply do not allow for the idea and understanding that in the Lord's Supper Christians were actually eating Christ's flesh and drinking His blood.

> Neither the language and grammar nor the example of Israel nor the examples from pagan meals allow such a meaning. The "fellowship", therefore, was most likely a celebration of their common life in Christ, based on the new covenant in his blood that had previously bound them together in union with Christ by his Spirit. But while their "fellowship" was one with another, its basis and focus were in Christ, his death and resurrection; they were

---

[29] Bruce M. Metzger, *A Textual Commentary on The Greek New Testament*, 2nd Edition (New York: American Bible Society, 1994), 496.

[30] In conclusion, failure to discern the body of the Lord is "to fundamentally misunderstand the nature of the Christian community and act in ways which undermine its vitality, its life and witness. It is that which stands under God's judgment, for to do harm to Christ's body is to oppose the purposes of God for which the Lord's body was broken and His life's blood was poured out" See Walter Kaiser, *Hard Sayings of the Bible*, 610.

thus together in his presence, where as host at his table he shared anew with them the benefits of the atonement…Paul's concern, of course, is that the drinking of this cup is for believers "sharing in the blood of Christ." As noted above, there is little evidence that the food of sacred meals was understood to be an eating of the deity. Since, therefore, the cup is specifically interpreted by the Lord (cf. Mark 14:24), and continued to be understood in the early church (1 Cor. 11:25), as "my blood of the new covenant," this language almost certainly refers to their sharing in the provisions and benefits of that covenant. This also means that they did not consider their table to be an altar where sacrifice was taking place, but a fellowship meal where in the presence of the Spirit they were by faith looking back to the singular sacrifice that had been made and were thus realizing again its benefits in their lives. In this way they shared "in the blood of Christ."[31]

In the First Epistle to the Corinthians, there is no mention of the Lord's Supper being a propitiatory sacrifice, or that participation in it was necessary for salvation. Neither does Paul explicitly describe that the elements of bread and wine are transubstantiated into the literal body and blood of Christ. Hence, Rome's use of a proof text for the Mass and transubstantiation here, upon closer exegetical examination, is found to be entirely untrue and grossly inaccurate. Paul told the Corinthians that the celebration of the Lord's Supper served to proclaim, in a sermonic picture, the Lord's death. He did not say it was an expiatory sacrifice for sin, or a continuation of Christ's sacrifice, but a *proclamation* of that sacrifice for sin already once made! In First Corinthians 11:24-29 the Apostle Paul discusses the events surrounding the institution of the Lord's Supper and its meaning and practical application for the Church. There is no mention of sacrifice, worship, or salvation in the Eucharist in the mold of Roman Catholicism. The alcoholic content of the Eucharistic wine still remained after it was allegedly changed into the blood of Christ. We know this because Paul had rebuked the church for using this wine to get drunk (1 Corinthians 11:21). Now if transubstantiation took place, the wine would have lost its alcoholic content after it was supposedly changed into the blood of Christ. The fact alcohol was still present for the Corinthians to get intoxicated with indisputably proves that no transubstantiation took place or was even considered.

If the Eucharistic wine had been Christ's blood, through and through, the Corinthians could not have been intoxicated with it. Today, if a person were to drink enough Eucharistic wine used in the Mass, he, too, would become intoxicated because no real change has actually taken place. Wine is wine and blood is blood! The Catholic cannot come back and try to say that the wine partially became the blood of Christ, when his Church insists that the wine is thoroughly changed into the blood of Christ after the process of transubstantiation is complete. From the New Testament example of 1 Corinthians 11:21, the Roman Catholic cannot reasonably maintain that the wine truly becomes the blood of Christ and still retains its alcoholic content. If it does, then it is not truly the blood of Christ, and transubstantiation altogether collapses in on itself.

The Catholic Church has gone to great lengths to explain just how transubstantiation takes place in order to give it some semblance of coherency. In doing this, they borrowed heavily from the physics of the pagan Greek philosopher Aristotle (384-322 B.C.), who lived three hundred years before Christ. Aristotle is still required reading by the Catholic Church for seminary candidates entering the priesthood. Aristotle explained in his work *Physics* that a physical object is made up of two elements—**substance** and **accident**.

---

[31]   Gordon Fee, *The First Epistle to the Corinthians* (Grand Rapids: Eerdmans, 1987), 467-468.

The accident is the outward appearance of an object that the eye sees; the **substance** is the inward essence or core of that object which remains invisible to the eye.[32] Aristotle maintained that an object could appear like one thing on the outside and yet have a completely different essence on the inside. Thus, in modern parlance, a cat could theoretically look like a human being on the outside but still have a feline nature on the inside, making it really a cat! So though it may look like a man, act like a man, and walk like a man on the outside (the accidents), it still remains a cat on the inside (the substance). Such are the absurd possibilities in Aristotle's world of physics.

Thomas Aquinas struggled and wrestled with the physics of transubstantiation and how he could apply the physics of Aristotle to best explain the absurdity of transubstantiation. Aquinas devoted a notable amount of space to this subject in his massive theological tome *The Summa Theologica*.[33] Aquinas applied the Aristotelian concept of accident and substance to explain the transubstantiation of the bread and wine into the body and blood of Christ during the Mass. Thomas postulated in this way that after the priest spoke the words of consecration, the bread and wine were immediately changed into the body and blood of Christ. Though the outward appearances of the Eucharist still appeared to look and even taste like bread and wine, they really were in their inward essences the flesh and blood of Jesus Christ through and through! From this postulation, Rome teaches that when the priest pronounces the words of institution during the consecration of the Mass, the elements cease to be really bread and wine and literally become the flesh and blood of Jesus Christ, though they still outwardly appear to be bread and wine. With the discoveries of modern science and physics, the ancient physics of Aristotle have proven to be false and totally unscientific. They are obsolete, and are no longer accepted as true science. Modern physics now knows that physical objects are made up of protons, neutrons, and electrons—the building blocks for material substances. This particular field of modern science is called Quantum Physics. Yet in spite of this, the Catholic Church still appeals to the antiquated physics of Aristotle to explain and get beyond the absurdity and illogicality of transubstantiation. Even though this is contrary to reason, contrary to Scripture, and contrary to the empirical senses, Rome stubbornly continues to uphold and defend this ludicrous concept. To believe in a miracle of the transubstantiation kind is to embrace what is deceiving to the senses of sight, touch, and taste, for what looks, tastes, and feels like bread and wine really is the human flesh and blood of Jesus Christ.

No modern physicist worth his salt would accept or resort to the outdated, disproven and illogical physics of Aristotle. It is scientifically impossible that if the substance, shape, color, flavor, odor, and texture of the bread and wine remain the same, the bread and wine are somehow mysteriously changed into the body and blood of Christ during the Mass. When the Catholic partakes in these Eucharistic elements, they do not taste like flesh and blood but what they really are—bread and wine! That is because all empirical proof and tactile sense supports the fact no change of any kind occurs. To explain away the obvious to intelligent-minded and sensible Catholics, Rome insists that the faithful must believe this by faith to be a miracle, which appears to be contrary to reason and sense. It is deemed an inscrutable miracle, "a mystery of faith" transcending any normal observance or perception by the physical senses, that is unable to be fully explained and understood.

The claim of transubstantiation does not fit the normative definition of a miracle presented in the Bible. A biblical miracle occurs, or is performed in the realm of observable phenomena, whereby the ordinary course of events is suspended or superseded by a supernatural demonstration that is perceptible to the physical senses and is empirically verified in the historical setting (Exodus 4:1-9, 30-31; 1 Kings 18:17-39; Matthew

---

32   Aristotle, *The Basic Works of Aristotle* (New York: The Modern Library Classics, 2001), 236-252.

33   Thomas Aquinas, *The Summa Theologica* Volume 2 (New York: Benziger Brothers, 1947), 2434-2479.

11:2-8; John 2:11; 5:36; 6:30; 11:40-42; Acts 2:22; 10:38; 13:6-12). The miracle is performed by God to elicit faith in both the observer and recipient of the miracle (Luke 4:9-12; Matthew 12:38-42). The Bible records no miracle of transubstantiation where something was subtly changed or altered into something different in shape and substance, and still retained the same outward appearance after said transformation occured.[34]

With transubstantiation, there are no visible, outward phenomena routinely observed to physically verify that the bread and wine have indeed been changed into human flesh and blood. Catholics are taught, in this regard, not to trust their senses when the elements of the Eucharist appear outwardly the same after the words of institution are spoken by the priest at Mass. This invisible, physically unverifiable 'miracle' cannot be a miracle because it is an "empirically unknowable event in the empirical world." The lack of established, verifiable evidence for the miraculous in the Mass undoubtedly shows it is no miracle at all. Evangelical scholars Norman Geisler and Ralph Mackenzie make two formidable and salient points on this matter for why this is so:

> *The Mass shows no evidence of the miraculous.* The Roman Catholic response to the foregoing arguments is that the Mass is a miracle and, therefore, appealing to the normal, natural way of observing things is irrelevant. Miracles are not normal occurrences. This strategy, however, will not work, since the Mass shows absolutely no evidence of being a miracle.
>
> First, using the same kind of reasoning to try to justify an invisible material substance miraculously replacing the empirically obvious signs of bread and wine, one could justify the belief in Santa Claus at Christmas or a little invisible gremlin moving the hands on one's watch. Transubstantiation is literally not sensible, even though its object is a sensible (i.e., physical) body. Philosophically, it is an empirically unknowable event in the empirical world, and theologically, it is a matter of pure faith. Catholics must simply believe what the

---

[34]   Everett F. Harrison, *Baker's Dictionary of Theology* (Grand Rapids: Baker), 356. Dave Hunt in his highly controversial, yet historically accurate book, *A Woman Rides the Beast*, shows from both the Old and New Testaments there is no occurrence of this kind whenever a miracle of God takes place. Rome's miracle of transubstantiation, whereby the bread and wine of the Mass inwardly transmute into the body and blood of Christ, yet still retains the outward appearances of bread and wine, is a foreign concept to the miracles of the Bible. Hunt specifically illustrates this by pointing out: "There is no such 'miracle' in the Bible. The opening of the Red Sea so that the Israelites could walk through it on dry land was a feat that both Jews and Egyptians observed and that both understood had occurred by God's power. Suppose it had been a 'transubstantiation kind of miracle'—the Red Sea 'opened' under the appearance of remaining closed and the Israelites had 'walked' across dry land 'under the appearance' of having to swim across. Suppose Christ healed a blind man 'under the appearance' of his not being able to see, or raised the dead 'under the appearance' of lifelessness. Such suppositions are ludicrous, yet that is exactly the nature of the 'transubstantiation miracle.' Let's take the miracle of the water turned to wine at Cana of Galilee. When the governor of the feast tasted it he exclaimed to the groom, 'Thou hast kept the good [best] wine until now' (John 2:10). Suppose instead he had said, 'This isn't *wine*, it's *water!*' The servants reply sincerely, 'No, sir, it's *wine*.' The governor's voice rises in anger: 'Don't mock me! It looks like water, it tastes like water, it *is* water!' The servants insist, 'Sir, it is *wine*. Jesus miraculously turned water into wine *under the appearance of it remaining water*.' There is no such 'miracle' in the Bible, and for Rome to make such a claim is a lame attempt to cover obvious fraud" (page 386-387).

teaching Magisterium tells them, namely, that the host is really Jesus' body, even though their senses tell them otherwise.

Second, if the Mass is a miracle, then virtually any natural empirical event could also be a miracle, since miracles could be happening without any empirical evidence they were. This is like a physical resurrection without an empty tomb. If this is true, then nothing is a miracle. Hence, claiming that the Mass is a miracle undermines the very nature of miracles themselves, at least as special events with apologetic value (Authors' emphasis).[35]

Surely, after reading the above quotation, some devout proponents of the Mass will appeal to documented cases of "Eucharistic miracles" where the elements of the bread and wine actually exhibited traits of flesh and blood after the act of consecration.[36] There are even video presentations on YouTube showing a Host placed into a Monstrance slowly turning into a fleshly red color. Whether these are credible miracles or not is highly debatable. The occurrence of miracles does not, by themselves, validate that they come from God or legitimize a message or person being sent by God. The Lord warns His people against following a miracle worker if that "sign" or "wonder" should cause them to embrace a message or follow a person that would lead them away from the Lord and His Word. The people of God are to reject and not listen to or follow these deceivers (Deuteronomy 13:1-3). The evil magicians of Pharaoh were able to duplicate some of the miracles God wrought through the hand of Moses (see Exodus 7:11-13, 22; 8:7). Jesus foretold that there will be many people at the Great White Throne Judgment who will have worked miracles and prophesied in His name yet did not personally "know" Him. Christ will condemn them to eternal fire for being "workers of iniquity" (Matthew 7:21-23). Jesus also prophesied that many false Christs and false prophets would perform miraculous signs and wonders to draw followers away from the true Messiah to follow after falsehood and deception (Matthew 24:24).

The Anti-Christ and his global propaganda minister, the False Prophet, will perform miracles by the power of Satan to seduce and deceive the whole world into following them (2 Thessalonians 2:9-10; Revelation 13:11-15). Scripture points out in these passages that the ability to work a miracle does not automatically mean such miracles, and the person performing them, are from God or His Son Jesus Christ. The overriding criterion of whether a messenger and a miracle are from God is not to be solely determined by the ability to supernaturally perform a miracle, but rather is based and certified on if the messenger or miracle is in agreement with the Word of God. Does what he teaches and does confirm and point people to God's revelation found in the Scriptures? Obviously, the alleged miracles of the Eucharist are not biblical, and turn people away from the Christ of Scripture to believe and embrace that an inanimate piece of bread is Almighty God in the Person of Jesus Christ, and is to, therefore, be adored, kissed, and bowed down to in worship.

This is an act of explicit idolatry and is a blatant violation of the Second Commandment forbidding the worship of any man-made object or image as God. ***"You shall have no other gods before Me. You shall not make for yourself a graven image—any likeness of anything that is in heaven above, or that is in the***

---

[35] Norman Geisler and Ralph Mackenzie, *Roman Catholics and Evangelicals*, 265.

[36] One such popular book from the Catholic perspective, written to defend the miraculous nature of transubstantiation, gives a chronological presentation from the eighth century to the present of alleged miracles that occurred with the Eucharist. See Joan Carroll Cruz's *Eucharistic Miracles* (Rockford, Il: Tan Books, 1987). Not once does the author allude to the Scriptures to authenticate these miracles of the Eucharist, since they are not based on the Bible, but on the mystical experiences of the Catholic devotees to the Mass.

earth beneath, or that is in the water under the earth. You shall not bow to them…" (Exodus 20:3-5).[37] All idolatry is the false worship of God. An idol is simply a thing or object used to visibly represent the invisible God, to replace Him in His physical absence. Christians, under the authority of the New Testament, are exhorted to remove idols from their lives (Acts 15:20; 1 Corinthians 10:14). **"Little children, keep yourselves from idols" (1 John 5:21).** Eucharistic worship is a manifestation of idolatry in the Catholic Church, which really says that Rome is not satisfied with worshipping the invisible God in Spirit and in truth. So out of the carnal and fallen human nature, there arises a hunger for the need to worship the tangible and physical—a typical trait of the idolatrous inclination.

Catholic theologians have created a visible representation of God based on a clever, insidious twisting of Christ's words spoken at the Last Supper. Christ said, "Take and eat", not "worship and adore", when speaking of the bread and wine at the Lord's Table. Rome teaches her people to look to a physical thing, like the Host of the Mass, for power, and to worship it as almighty God. This is nothing less than idolatry! The worship of created matter comes from an ancient pagan belief that an idol has power, or is the embodiment of a god that must be worshipped. That idol also has the power to give life. With the example of the idolatry found in the Mass, the Eucharist is the divine Christ that imparts eternal life to those who eat or ingest the Host. But God is not a piece of bread, and any attempt to make Him into that is gross idolatry and falls under the harsh condemnation of God. Scripture bears witness of this in the book of Isaiah. There, the Holy Spirit speaks through that prophet to expose the idolatrous practice of baking bread and making it into a God, which is a clear foreshadowing of the idolatry of the Roman Catholic Mass and the worship and adoration of the Eucharist. **"Then it shall be for a man to burn, for he will take some of it and warm himself; Yes, he kindles it and bakes bread. Indeed he makes a god and worships it"** (Isaiah 44:15).

Roman Catholic worshippers of "the Blessed Eucharist" are guilty of doing this very thing when attending Mass to worship the wafer god—a thing anticipated and condemned long ago by God's Word from the prophet Isaiah![38] In the New Testament, the worship of a man-made "Consecrated Host" falls under the idolatrous practice described in Romans 1:25, where Paul explains that idolaters exchanged the truth of God for *a lie* and worshipped and served created things rather than the Creator. The idolatrous lie of transubstantiation is that the Eucharistic piece of bread contains the fullness of eternal deity and becomes Jesus Christ to be worshipped, prayed to, and adored. This is exactly where the deception and folly of idolatry lies: It creates a false image of God, whether called Christ or by another name, which is inadequate

---

[37]   The Roman Catholic Church conveniently sidesteps the second commandment that prohibits the worship of idols or graven images (man-made objects) by simply deleting it from their Catechisms, thus effectively allowing them to use images like the Eucharist for worship of the divine. To compensate for this, Rome deceptively divides the tenth commandment into two, making it the ninth and tenth commandments. A deceptive practice of this nature is done to allow for the use of images and relics in their worship without giving the appearance that Roman Catholics are breaking the second commandment when worshipping the elements of the Eucharist.

[38]   Bible commentator F.C. Jennings makes the same application of Isaiah's ancient words here to the modern-day worship of the Roman Catholic Mass. He comments: "The poor papist…worships a piece of bread, before which all prostrate themselves at the sound of what they term the 'sacring bell'—could idolatry be grosser? Nor indeed is *any* object needed, for the light of later revelation shining into every heart finds there is a never-ending hunger, and calls even that longing *'covetousness, which is idolatry!'* Who can claim freedom from it? If we are not satisfied with God in Christ, we too are idolaters", *Studies in Isaiah* (Neptune, New Jersey: Loizeaux Brothers, 1982), 522. And that is the core problem with Catholics and the Mass. They are simply not satisfied with the Christ of Scripture alone and, out of this dissatisfaction, have created another Christ from a physical object of bread to be worshipped and adored.

to His deity and unworthy of His majesty. The greatest sin of idolatry lies in the fact that it is slander and libel against the Person, nature, and character of the one true God. Idolatry is a misrepresentation of these things. To brazenly proclaim that a wafer becomes the eternal Creator, Jesus Christ the second Person of the Trinity, is a slanderous and blasphemous representation that is absolutely foreign to the Christ of Scripture.

The only visible embodiment of God in all His fullness is exclusively found in the human person and body of Jesus Christ (John 1:1-2, 14; Hebrews 1:1-3; Colossians 2:9). He is not found or subsumed in any other thing, person, or inanimate object like the Communion Host. To make such a claim is blasphemous idolatry and nothing less! God is infinite and invisible. He is omnipotent and omnipresent. God is a living Spirit (John 4:24), and to therefore say He becomes a piece of bread in the Roman Catholic Mass is to deny the above attributes—the essential characteristics of His divine being. The wafer god of Roman Catholicism makes the infinite God finite, the invisible God visible, the omnipotent God impotent, the all-present God local and limited, the living God dead, the spiritual God material, the sovereign God subordinate and under the control of the human creature, and the incorruptible Christ corruptible. In short, the wafer god of Roman Catholicism makes the God of the Bible the exact opposite of what He really is! What the Psalmist said about idols in Psalm 115 is equally true of the idolatrous wafer gods of the Roman Catholic Mass. They are truly lifeless and devoid of the divine presence and being. *"They have mouths, but do not speak; eyes they have, but they do not see. They have ears, but they do not hear. Noses they have, but do not smell. They have hands, but they do not handle. Feet they have, but they do not walk; nor do they mutter through their throat. Those who make them are like them. So is everyone who trusts in them"* (Psalm 115:5-8).

What the Psalmist wrote here about the mute and lifeless idols of his day certainly applies to the deified Eucharist of Catholicism. The Eucharistic Christ lacks the sentient qualities of human beings—the wafer turned into the human and divine Christ cannot think or talk; it cannot see or hear, nor can it walk, nor is it able to express those attributes peculiar to the Godhead. That means the communion wafer of the Mass, if truly God, must display the classical attributes of deity—omniscience, omnipresence, and omnipotence! It does not even possess intelligence or reason in this debased condition either. The wafer god of the Mass is what the Bible calls a "graven image", which is a phrase for an idol, or something that is specifically made or fabricated by the hands of men to be worshipped as a deity or visibly representing this deity.

Throughout the Bible, God unsparingly condemns the practice of making graven images for the purpose of idolatry. God will not accept any worship of an idol purporting to represent Him in any way that is made by the work of human hands. This, by definition from Scripture, is an idol. The Catholic appeal to worship the Lord Jesus Christ in the fabricated, man-made image of the Eucharistic Host is an idolatrous practice based on religious tradition without any biblical mandate. God has pronounced a curse on anyone who makes a graven image to represent His deity to be worshipped. *"Cursed is the one who makes a carved or molded image, an abomination to the Lord, the work of the hands of the craftsman, and sets in up in secret"* (Deuteronomy 27:15).

The Catholic Church is guilty of doing this very thing. Whenever the liturgy of the Mass is said the worshippers of the Eucharist acknowledge that the communion bread of the unbloody sacrifice of the Mass is "made with human hands", and by virtue of that admission, fall under the condemnation of offering a graven image up to be worshipped as God. Every time the elements of the Eucharist are offered up on the altar during the Mass, the priest recites the following prayer: "Blessed are you, Lord, God of all creation.

Through your goodness we have this bread to offer, which earth has given and *human hands have made*. It will become for us the bread of life" (Emphasis mine).[39]

God would never deign to grant such an idolatrous request made from the liturgy of the Catholic Church, because it is an egregious violation of the very thing God's Word forbids, namely, that God can in some way be contained, represented, and worshipped in any object made by human hands, and that said object can be contained or housed in a temple, house, or building of human construction. To affirm this is to sanction the sin of idolatry—a thing abominable in the eyes of God (Deuteronomy 18:9; Ezekiel 8:5-19). The immensity of God is above the confining limits and restraints of human artifice and fabricated sanctuaries. The Apostle Paul reiterated this fundamental biblical truth to the Athenian Greeks who regularly built elaborate temples for their Grecian gods to dwell in. He corrected this false worship and idolatrous practice by emphatically stating that God is neither housed in man-made temples, nor is He to be worshipped there. ***"God, who made the world and everything in it, since He is Lord of heaven and earth, does not dwell in temples made with hands. Nor is He worshiped with men's hands, as though He needed anything, since He gives to all life, breath, and all things"*** (Acts 17:24-25).

The idea that the Lord Jesus Christ can now be contained within a man-made piece of bread affixed to a monstrance, or placed within a tabernacle in Roman Catholic Churches throughout the world, diametrically opposes and openly defies the prohibition in Scripture against making the eternal God into an idol to be housed in fabricated temples made by human hands. The Lord Jesus Christ currently sits at the right hand of God the Father in heaven; and in no way quietly and dutifully returns to Earth at the request of a Catholic priest reciting Mass to personally indwell the communion host to be carried about in worship and stored in the small container of the tabernacle. The real Christ of Scripture is not there! For ***"Christ has not entered the holy places made with hands...<u>but into heaven itself, now to appear in the presence of God for us"</u>*** (Hebrews 9:24).

The communion wafer is made with human hands, and the Eucharistic tabernacle is a "holy place" also made by human hands that the Catholic Church says is the house for the Eucharistic Jesus to dwell in! The Catholic Church would have their faithful believe that this is a present reality going on in their churches and tabernacles throughout the world. This, in spite of the fact that God has clearly said in Scripture, He does not permanently dwell in man-made temples or fabricated objects made for idolatrous worship. Rome teaches otherwise with the Eucharist, the Monstrance, and the tabernacle, and therefore places itself squarely against the Word of God. In this present age, under the economy of the New Covenant, Christ is not contained in a piece of bread, nor does He enter into a holy place that human hands have made. He has entered into heaven itself and physically remains there until the end of the present age. He will not physically return to Earth until the Second Coming.

In Matthew 24 Jesus warned and foretold that before His return, certain signs and events would characterize the end-times of the present age. One of those distinct signs of the last days would be people claiming that Christ had returned, and through this false claim, deceive many in the end. Jesus warned: ***"Take heed that no one deceives you. For many will come in My name, saying, 'I am Christ,' and will deceive many"*** (Matthew 24:4-5). Christ's exhortation to "take heed" means that His followers are to pay close attention and be on the alert for those who will come claiming that Christ has physically returned to Earth. The Lord further stated that great signs and wonders would accompany these appearances of "false Christs". Jesus then describes the particular way these counterfeit Christs try to appear, and contrasts that with how

---

[39]   Alfred McBride, *Celebrating the Mass* (Huntington, Indiana: Our Sunday Visitor, 1999), 33.

He would personally return to Earth at the end of the present age. *"Then if anyone says to you, 'Look, here is the Christ!' or 'There!' do not believe it. For false Christs and false prophets will rise and show great signs and wonders to deceive, if possible, even the elect. See, I have told you beforehand. Therefore if they say to you, 'Look, He is in the desert!' do not go out; or 'Look, He is in the inner rooms!' do not believe it. For as the lightning comes from the east and flashes to the west, so also will the coming of the Son of Man be" (Matthew 24:23-27).*

In verse 23 of Matthew 24, Jesus informs us that throughout the present age the peddlers of these false Christs will claim that their 'messiah' is hidden away and found in a hidden room or secret chamber. The Lord Jesus disavows this spurious claim by telling His followers not to believe it. The original Greek word for "inner rooms" is *tameion* (ταμειον), and it's meaning provides an enlightening feature that demonstrates how this prophecy is being uniquely fulfilled with the Eucharistic Christ housed in the Roman Catholic tabernacles. The word can mean a "store chamber," "private room", "inner chamber", or a "closet".[40] *Strong's Exhaustive Concordance of the Bible* offers this explanation for *tameion* in the following entry:

> Tameion (tam-ion); neuter contraction of a presumed derivative of tamias (a dispenser or distributer; akin to temno, to cut); a dispensary or magazine, i.e. a chamber on the ground-floor or interior of an Oriental house (generally used for storage or privacy), a spot for retirement.[41]

When the Roman Catholic priest stores the wafers of the Mass in the tabernacle and says that Christ is literally found there, the words of Jesus spoken in Matthew 24:23 are literally being fulfilled during the course of the present age! The Lord Jesus warned His followers in advance, so that when this occurred Christians could know and realize they were living in the period of time just before the return of the true Christ to Earth. Rome's idolatrous teaching that the communion wafer literally becomes the Lord Jesus Christ at the Mass, to be worshipped and stored in the private chamber of a tabernacle, is the promotion and proclamation of "another Christ". The Eucharistic 'Christ' of Roman Catholicism is unquestionably false and counterfeit, according to the prophecy and description Jesus gave about false Christs in Matthew twenty-four.

If Rome was correct in absurdly claiming Jesus expected His disciples and the Church to eat His flesh and drink His blood, He would be asking them to become cannibals and vampires, no less! Undaunted by this ghoulish prospect, associated with transubstantiation, Roman Catholic defenders are quick to point to the words of Jesus spoken in John chapter six about "eating His flesh" and "drinking His blood" for justification of this belief. *The Catechism of the Catholic Church* dogmatically points to what Jesus taught in John 6 as a proof text that His followers must literally eat His flesh and drink His blood within the context of the Roman Catholic Mass to have salvation and eternal life.[42] In this chapter Jesus gives the famous "Bread of

---

[40] W.E. Vine, *An Expository Dictionary of New Testament Words*, 171.

[41] *Biblesoft's New Exhaustive Strong's Numbers and Concordance with Expanded Greek-Hebrew Dictionary* quoted in *Another Jesus*, 20.

[42] *Catechism of the Catholic Church*, 372 [**1336, 1338**], 393 [**1406**]. The Council of Trent arrogantly pronounces Rome's condemnation on all those who would rightly condemn worship of the Eucharist as idolatry. Canon six of the thirteenth session of that council states: If anyone says that in the holy sacrament of Eucharist, Christ, the only begotten Son of God, is not to be adored with the worship of *latria*, also outwardly manifested, and is consequently neither to be venerated with a special festive solemnity, nor to be solemnly borne about in procession according to the laudable and universal rite and custom of holy Church, or is not to be set publicly before the people to be

185

life" discourse that was prompted by His miracle of multiplying the loaves and fishes to feed the multitude of five thousand people.

"So when they were filled, He said to His disciples, "Gather up the fragments that remain, so that nothing is lost." Therefore they gathered them up, and filled twelve baskets with the fragments of the five barley loaves which were left over by those who had eaten. Then those men, when they had seen the sign that Jesus did, said, "This is truly the Prophet who is to come into the world." Therefore when Jesus perceived that they were about to come and take Him by force to make Him king, He departed again to the mountain by Himself alone. Now when evening came, His disciples went down to the sea, got into the boat, and went over the sea toward Capernaum. And it was already dark, and Jesus had not come to them. Then the sea arose because a great wind was blowing. So when they had rowed about three or four miles, they saw Jesus walking on the sea and drawing near the boat; and they were afraid. But He said to them, "It is I; do not be afraid." Then they willingly received Him into the boat, and immediately the boat was at the land where they were going. On the following day, when the people who were standing on the other side of the sea saw that there was no other boat there, except that one which His disciples had entered, and that Jesus had not entered the boat with His disciples, but His disciples had gone away alone—however, other boats came from Tiberias, near the place where they ate bread after the Lord had given thanks—when the people therefore saw that Jesus was not there, nor His disciples, they also got into boats and came to Capernaum, seeking Jesus. And when they found Him on the other side of the sea, they said to Him, "Rabbi, when did You come here?"

Jesus answered them and said, "Most assuredly, I say to you, you seek Me, not because you saw the signs, but because you ate of the loaves and were filled. Do not labor for the food which perishes, but for the food which endures to everlasting life, which the Son of Man will give you, because God the Father has set His seal on Him."

Then they said to Him, "What shall we do, that we may work the works of God?"

Jesus answered and said to them, "This is the work of God, that you believe in Him whom He sent." Therefore they said to Him, "What sign will You perform then, that we may see it and believe You? What work will You do? Our fathers ate the manna in the desert; as it is written, 'He gave them bread from heaven to eat.'" Then Jesus said to them, "Most assuredly, I say to you, Moses did not give you the bread from heaven, but My Father gives you the true bread from heaven. For the bread of God is He who comes down from heaven and gives life to the world." Then they said to Him, "Lord, give us this bread always." And Jesus said to them, "I am the bread of life. He who comes to Me shall never hunger, and he who believes in Me shall never thirst. But I said to you that you have seen Me and yet do not believe. All that the Father gives Me will come to Me, and the one who comes to Me I will by no means cast out. For I have come down from heaven, not to do My own will, but the will of Him who sent Me. This is the will of the Father who sent Me, that of all He has given Me I should lose nothing, but should raise it up at the last day. And this is the will of Him who sent Me, that everyone who sees the Son and believes in Him may have everlasting life; and I will raise him up at the last day."

The Jews then complained about Him, because He said, "I am the bread which came down from heaven." And they said, "Is not this Jesus, the son of Joseph, whose father and mother we know? How is it then that He says, 'I have come down from heaven'?"

---

adored *and that the adorers thereof are idolaters, let him be anathema* (Schroeder, *Canons and Decrees of the Council of Trent*, 80).

Jesus therefore answered and said to them, "Do not murmur among yourselves. No one can come to Me unless the Father who sent Me draws him; and I will raise him up at the last day. It is written in the prophets, 'And they shall all be taught by God.' Therefore everyone who has heard and learned from the Father comes to Me. Not that anyone has seen the Father, except He who is from God; He has seen the Father. Most assuredly, I say to you, he who believes in Me has everlasting life. I am the bread of life. Your fathers ate the manna in the wilderness, and are dead. This is the bread which comes down from heaven, that one may eat of it and not die. I am the living bread which came down from heaven. If anyone eats of this bread, he will live forever; and the bread that I shall give is My flesh, which I shall give for the life of the world." The Jews therefore quarreled among themselves, saying, "How can this Man give us His flesh to eat?" Then Jesus said to them, "Most assuredly, I say to you, unless you eat the flesh of the Son of Man and drink His blood, you have no life in you. Whoever eats My flesh and drinks My blood has eternal life, and I will raise him up at the last day. For My flesh is food indeed, and My blood is drink indeed. He who eats My flesh and drinks My blood abides in Me, and I in him. As the living Father sent Me, and I live because of the Father, so he who feeds on Me will live because of Me. This is the bread which came down from heaven—not as your fathers ate the manna, and are dead. He who eats this bread will live forever" (John 6:12-58).

In these verses, particularly verses 51-58, the Roman Catholic Church teaches that Jesus is giving a promise of the Eucharist requiring His followers to literally eat His flesh and drink His blood. Rome goes on to claim that Christ fulfilled this promise at the institution of the Mass at the Last Supper which occurred a full year after the events of John 6.

> Christ did not institute the Holy Eucharist without preparing His disciples for so marvelous a gift; a whole year before His death He had promised to give them His flesh to eat and His blood to drink. It was the day after the miraculous multiplication of the loaves. By this miracle He had given proof of His almighty power, and the following night He had proved to His disciples that He was superior to the laws of nature by walking upon the sea. The crowds had followed Him to the other side of the lake and looked to Him for further signs. In reply He spoke to them in the Capharnaum synagogue a discourse in which He clearly manifested His intention of instituting the Holy Eucharist. Taking up the suggestion of the Jews that He should give them bread from heaven as Moses did, He announced to them that He would give them a more excellent Bread still, a living bread, the true Bread of Life that cometh down from heaven, of which the manna was but a figure. And when the Jews begged Him: "Lord, give us always this bread," He said to them: *"I am the Bread of Life*: he that cometh to Me shall not hunger, and he that believeth in Me shall never thirst. I am the Living Bread which came down from Heaven." He then went on to tell them in the most unmistakable terms that He would give Himself as the food of men: "The Bread that I will give is My Flesh for the life of the world." The Jews took scandal at these words and asked: "how can this man give us His Flesh to eat?" But Jesus said to them: "Amen, amen, I say unto you: except you eat the Flesh of the Son of Man, and drink His blood, you shall not have life in you. He that eateth My Flesh and drinketh My blood hath everlasting life, and I will raise him up at the last day. *For My flesh is meat indeed, and My Blood is drink indeed.* He that eateth My flesh, and drinketh My blood, abideth in Me and I in Him. As the living Father hath sent Me, and I live by the Father, so he that eateth Me, the same also

shall live by Me. This is the Bread that came down from Heaven. Not as your fathers did eat manna, and are dead; he that eateth this Bread shall live forever."[43]

Do the words of Jesus recorded in John chapter six endorse the Roman Catholic doctrine that Christians are to literally eat the flesh and drink the blood of Christ offered under the appearance of the bread and wine at the Mass? An extended study and analysis of these verses will prove the answer to be an emphatic no! John chapter six opens with Jesus performing the miracle of the multiplication of five barley loaves and two fishes to feed five thousand people. The overwhelming response from the crowd who witnessed this miracle of provision was to acknowledge that Jesus was the preeminent Prophet foretold to come by Moses in Deuteronomy 18:15-18 and forcibly take Jesus to make Him their King. Jesus knew their motive for doing this was primarily to fill a carnal and material need without giving due consideration for the greater need of spiritual salvation. Consequently, the Lord wisely withdrew Himself from the overzealous crowds to a private place in the hills of Northern Galilee to avoid this untimely coronation that was solely based on satisfying the carnal appetites of the physical body. The crowd reasoned from this miracle that Jesus, like their forefather Moses who provided the manna for Israel during their forty-year journey in the desert, would also provide them physical bread so they would not experience hunger or lack of food ever again. The people wanted Jesus to fill their stomachs with physical bread and were not interested in the spiritual dynamic of Christ's Person, work, and ministry.

In verse twenty-six Jesus exposes their crass and selfish motives to be just this. ***"Jesus answered them and said, 'Most assuredly, I say to you, you seek Me, not because you saw the signs, but because you ate of the loaves and were filled'"*** (John 6:26). The crowds were therefore not seeking Jesus because of the miracles He performed, but only because their appetites were filled with the loaves and fishes He multiplied. After verse twenty-six, which serves as the catalyst and primary reason for what follows in verse twenty-seven to the end of chapter six, Jesus develops a parallel and contrast between physical bread (i.e., the manna from heaven) and the Spiritual Bread that He alone is and gives. This theme frames the context for John six and resonates throughout the Bread of Life discourse.[44] The Lord Jesus intended the quality of this Bread to be spiritually understood in a metaphorical or symbolic manner, in contrast to it being misunderstood in terms of just physical bread, whether in the form of the manna from heaven or other types of bread like the Eucharist.

Such a contrast is crucial to remember when seeking to correctly interpret John 6. Verses 27, 29, 35, 40, 47, 63, and 68 collectively provide the key of interpretation to unlock the true meaning of the chapter. These verses will reveal that Jesus intended His words about eating His flesh and drinking His blood to be interpreted figuratively, not literally, like the Roman Catholic Church would have us to believe. The command Jesus gave His audience in verse twenty-seven sets the tone for the contrast He makes between physical bread and the Spiritual Bread that is recurrent throughout John six. ***"Do not labor for the food which perishes,***

---

[43]   Laux, *Mass and the Sacraments*, 38-39.

[44]   Bible commentator, J. Carl Laney, observes that in verse 27, "Jesus at this point began to develop a contrast that would be amplified throughout the discourse. Physical food quickly spoils. The spiritual food, which the Messiah ("Son of Man") has authority to provide, issues in eternal life. *No contrast of this nature between the physical and the spiritual, and the natural and supernatural that Jesus establishes in John six, would exist if the Savior really meant that He would be physically contained in a piece of bread like the Catholic Eucharist.*" J. Carl Laney, *Moody Gospel John Commentary* (Chicago: Moody Press, 1992), 126. Such a dichotomous analogy would be senseless for Jesus to make with His audience, whose main concern was acquiring physical bread and food to sustain their physical life, if He were talking about His personal indwelling of the Eucharistic bread (Emphasis mine).

but for the food which endures to everlasting life, which the Son of Man will give you because God the Father has set His seal on Him" (John 6:27).

That statement expressing the distinction between physical food that perishes and the eternal food which lasts forever, which only the Messiah can give, forms the basis for taking Jesus' words about eating His flesh and drinking His blood figuratively instead of literally. From Christ's simple and profound words here, we learn that any meal, food, or edible product, especially exemplified by physical bread, will perish, no doubt due to, among other things, its physical, biodegradable qualities. But the spiritual food that Jesus Christ gives, which is altogether different from its physical counterpart, is imperishable, lasts forever, and is therefore not subject to decay or the ruin of time. Catholic apologists attempt to nullify this obvious contrast and distinction given in the context of John 6:27-58 when they say, in effect, that the bread Jesus spoke of in terms of His flesh is literally contained in the physical bread of a transubstantiated Eucharist and would therefore be no more materially different than manna or any other kind of physical bread with respect to being subject to mold and decay. Nor does it help these desperate Romanists to insist, according to their Canon Law (without any biblical warrant or justification from Scripture), that once decay and spoilage appears in the communion wafer, which is supposedly transmuted into the flesh and blood of Christ, the Savior immediately leaves the species of bread and wine. The point is they have already placed Him in bread that is potentially perishable and in so doing contradict, in principle, what our Lord taught about Himself in John six being the imperishable bread from heaven in contrast to any physical bread or food that is perishable (see John 6:27, 58)!

Jesus exhorts His hearers not to work for perishable food, like what they ate when the Lord multiplied the loaves and fishes, but to seek after spiritual food that issues into eternal life that He alone, the Son of Man, can give to them. It is not about physical things—having all the food you can eat, or the material blessings one can accumulate from God. Jesus can give the soul spiritual food that endures and produces eternal life. The food Jesus was talking about here was not bread and wine but bread and fish; no wine is mentioned, and this, right away, would preclude a Eucharistic context that Romanists seek to impose on the discourse of John six. Here the transition is made in verse twenty-seven from the physical to the spiritual—a critical element to correctly interpret the content of John chapter six that Roman Catholic Bible defenders of the Eucharist commonly overlook. Jesus is trying to move His audience into a spiritual direction away from the physical, whereby they were to focus instead on the Person of Christ as the spiritual food which produces eternal life, in contrast to material bread that is perishable, and at best can only temporarily sustain physical life. The focus of this imperishable food is Jesus Christ, the dispenser of eternal life, not the Eucharist of the Roman Catholic Mass. And so with reference to the audience of Jesus' day and the readers today of John six,

> ...Jesus exhorts them by taking things into a spiritual direction, telling people to work not for perishable food, but for food that lasts for eternal life, which the "Son of Man" will give them. *In their original context, Jesus' words refer not to the Eucharist...but to Jesus' identity as God's messenger...and the blessing of eternal life available through him* (Emphasis mine).[45]

The mention of labor by Jesus prompted the crowds to ask Him in verse twenty-eight what particular work they needed to do that was necessary to earn God's approval and have eternal life. *"Then they said to Him, What shall we do, that we may work the works of God?"* His answer given in verse twenty-nine is the

---

[45]   Andreas J. Kostenberger, *John: Baker Exegetical Commentary On the New Testament* (Grand Rapids: Baker Book House, 2004), 207.

warp of woof of salvation and the only means by which it is received. It is simple faith and belief in the Lord Jesus Christ alone for eternal life that qualifies as the "work" of God, which He requires from humanity. The Galilean crowd thought in terms of performing good *works* (plural) to win the approval of God and thereby earn eternal life. If they did these stipulated works, they believed God would then give them this imperishable food that brings eternal life. Jesus corrected this false notion of salvation by works by informing the crowd that there is only one *work* (singular) that God requires for man to receive eternal life from Him—believe that Jesus is the Messiah sent by God to give the world eternal life. *"Jesus answered and said to them, This is the work of God, that you believe in Him whom He sent"* (John 6:29).

The word "believe", with reference to Jesus as the exclusive object of that faith and belief, is mentioned four times in John 6:35-47 and figures prominently in this chapter and throughout the Gospel of John. For John, believing in Jesus is to wholeheartedly trust that He is Savior and Lord, the Author and Giver of eternal life. Whenever Jesus mentions that belief in Him saves the soul, there is no work, act, or deed added to that saving faith; it is belief alone in Christ that brings eternal life. Jesus' statement in verse twenty-nine, that belief in Him is the only 'work' or requirement for salvation is a fundamental truth of the Gospel repeated throughout the Gospel of John (e.g., see John 1:12; 3:16; 7:38; 11:25-26). Thus the 'work' of God is to simply believe on the Lord Jesus Christ to have eternal life. Salvation is not attained by doing some physical act or participating in a religious ritual like the Roman Catholic Mass. And this is precisely where Rome is guilty of denying the true Gospel and of offering a counterfeit Gospel in its place—when they demand the requirement of eating and drinking the flesh and blood of Jesus Christ in the Mass as an added necessity for receiving salvation and eternal life. Faith in the risen Christ apart, or separate, from the sacrament of the Mass cannot save the soul in the eyes of the Roman Catholic Church, especially since that same Church "affirms that for believers the sacraments of the New Covenant are *necessary for salvation*."[46] Rome's insistence one must believe and also participate in the sacrament of the Mass for salvation is a blasphemous addition to and blatant contradiction of Jesus' own spoken words in John 6:29 and other key passages in the Gospel of John, which categorically state that belief in Jesus alone is sufficient for salvation! This is one of the reasons why Jesus must have been using metaphorical language when speaking about eating His flesh and drinking His blood in John six; otherwise you have an irresolute contradiction in the Word of God between salvation by faith in Christ alone and salvation by faith plus the added requirement of the sacramental ritual of the Mass.

Failing to grasp the spiritual significance behind Jesus' miracle of the multiplication of the loaves and fishes, the crowd from the synagogue now demands another miracle from Jesus as proof to further authenticate His unique claims of being the Messiah, the Son of Man, whom God has approved, sent, and ordained as the One who gives food that brings eternal life. *Therefore they said to Him, "What sign will You perform then, that we may see it and believe You? What work will you do? Our fathers ate the manna in the desert; as it is written, 'He gave them bread from heaven to eat'"* (John 6:30-31). The people qualify this request for a miracle by recalling the events of Exodus 16:4-35 where Moses, as they supposed, had miraculously fed Israel with manna from heaven for forty years. The challenge behind this request from the crowd was to see if Jesus could equal or excel the miraculous provision of Moses that lasted for forty years. Jesus had only fed them once; Moses had fed Israel with manna that fell from heaven for a period of forty years; Jesus had merely multiplied the few loaves in His hands; Moses had enough manna to feed hundreds of thousands every day. From this, they were thinking that if Jesus' authority were equal to or greater than Moses', then He would do the same or better. The crowd's challenge to Jesus, borne out of skepticism and

---

46   *Catechism of the Catholic Church*, 319 **[1129]**.

unbelief, was motivated by a desire for the physical and material need of the pallet and stomach. They assumed the imperishable food that brings eternal life Christ spoke about in verse 27, was similar in kind to the physical, but perishable, manna from heaven.[47]

The focus of the crowd's faith was dependent on what physical act Jesus could perform for them in the here and now. Such a shallow and transitory faith was not interested in the invisible, spiritual, and transcendent realities of eternal nourishment in Christ. The theological descendants of this Galilean crowd exist in the Romanists of today, who also wrongly insist on taking and understanding Jesus' words about spiritual food and bread to be merely literal, physical, and tangible when they dogmatically proclaim that the spiritual bread Jesus is teaching about is a piece of transubstantiated bread. And by doing this, they, much like their Galilean ancestors before them, fail to spiritually comprehend the true meaning of what it really means to eat the flesh and drink the blood of Jesus Christ, as we shall discover in the following pages.

The Lord Jesus corrects the crowd's erroneous assumption that Moses provided the manna in the desert. Christ tells them that it was God the Father, not Moses, who provided the manna from heaven. God is the only One who can and has provided the *"true"* bread from heaven. This spiritual bread is not to be identified with physical bread of any type, which, by the way, would practically exclude the Eucharist, but is none other than the Lord Jesus Christ who came down from heaven to give eternal life to the world. ***"Then Jesus said to them, 'Most assuredly, I say to you, Moses did not give you bread from heaven, but My Father gives you the true bread from heaven. For the bread of God is He who comes down from heaven and gives life to the world'"*** (John 6:32-33). The words of Christ here are revealing, to the extent that they again differ from the Roman Catholic interpretation that Jesus is talking about the Eucharistic bread of the Mass. From Christ's words, here, we learn the following: First, Jesus said this bread came down out of heaven (literally in the Greek text the preposition εκ is used to mean "out of") from God Himself. This is the first mention that Jesus is the bread from heaven and the emphasis is on the present reality of Jesus standing before the Galilean crowd and offering Himself for their salvation and eternal life. The institution of the Lord's Supper in the future is not the focus of John chapter six. The focus is on the Messiah standing in front of them whom they saw for themselves. This bread from God is *spiritual* and eternal bread, whose origin is heavenly and does not come from *this world*, or have its origin in the physical or earthly domain. It cannot therefore be physical bread made from the earth.

When Rome thus claims that this bread points to the Eucharist, they deny the heavenly origin of this bread because the Eucharist comes from wheat that is planted in the ground and therefore comes from the earth; it does not first and directly come from heaven, as Jesus points out in verse 33 and repeatedly throughout the narrative of John six (see also verses 41, 50-51, 58). Second, the bread of God is spoken of in terms of a male person when Jesus uses the third person, masculine singular pronoun "He". The bread of God is God the Son who came from heaven to give eternal life to the world. He did not come from the earth but already existed in heaven when He came to Earth. The Eucharist is physical and comes from the earth; its wheaten content comes from grain planted in the ground, and by virtue of this, it cannot be the spiritual bread that comes from heaven. This is another major reason why Christ meant His words to be taken figuratively and not literally—because this spiritual bread originally came from heaven and does not originate from the earth as with the man-made Eucharist!

---

[47]   The Jews' request for the replication of manna from heaven by the hand of Jesus reflected a rabbinic belief of the first century that the Messiah, the end-time Redeemer, will bring down manna again from heaven to feed Israel (see 2 Baruch 29:8 of the *Pseudepigrapha* written around 100 A.D.).

In verse 34, the crowd's response, at once, reflects that they did still not understand Jesus' use of bread in a spiritual way, but rather in a mundane and fleshly way of satisfying physical appetite. Jesus then plainly states that He is the Bread of Life Who gives eternal life to the individual recipient. ***"Then they said to Him, 'Lord, give us this bread always.' And Jesus said to them, 'I am the bread of life. He who comes to Me shall never hunger, and he who believes in Me shall never thirst'*** (John 6:34-35). The words Jesus spoke in verse 35 in reference to hungering and thirsting unequivocally establish the symbolic meaning for eating Christ's flesh and drinking His blood in a spiritual sense mentioned in verses 53-56. "Coming" to Christ and "believing" in Him will become "eating" His flesh and "drinking" His blood in verse 54. They are one and the same, and denote the spiritual act of committing one's life to Christ in faith and trust. When done, the believer discovers that Christ alone spiritually satisfies the hunger of the human heart and the thirst of the human soul. Coming to Christ, and believing on Him, are really interchangeable terms with eating and drinking. Hence, to come to and believe in Jesus Christ is to spiritually eat and drink of Him in a metaphorical manner. Jesus uses these terms to mean the same thing.

It is clear from John 6:35 that Jesus intended His words of "eating" and "drinking" to mean we are to come to Him and believe in Him. That fact sets the meaning for eating and drinking His flesh and blood in verses 53-56. The Gospel of John equates the two as one. We find the same exact metaphorical and spiritual meaning used for drinking in John chapter 4, when Jesus told the Samaritan woman that He had spiritual water to give, so that whoever drinks of it would never thirst again (John 4:14). Jesus uses the same metaphor in John 7 to convey the same spiritual truth, through the analogy of drinking water to represent belief in Him that brings the refreshing experience of salvation to quench a person's spiritual thirst (John 7:37-38). For Jesus, drinking is to believe in Him and to believe is to drink of Him, the same with the spiritual act of eating too. Thus, the spiritual meaning held for drinking the water of Christ in John chapter four is likewise maintained in John chapter six for symbolically drinking the blood of Jesus.

Since the Roman Catholic Church teaches from John 6 that Catholics are to literally ingest the flesh of Christ and drink His blood, why not take the words of Jesus in John 4 about drinking the water in the same way, just like the Samaritan woman wrongly interpreted Him to mean in John 4:15. She took His words to literally mean physical water instead of spiritual water as He meant. Furthermore, Jesus said in John 4:14 that anyone who does drink of this spiritual water will have a fountain in him springing up into eternal life. Obviously, Jesus did not mean that if we physically drink water served by Him, we would never physically thirst or die, and we'd have a water fountain shoot up in the air out of our mouths! Even Roman Catholic scholars know that Jesus' words to the woman of Samaria were obviously figurative in meaning to denote a spiritual reality about salvation and permanent satisfaction in Jesus Christ. Rome's unwarranted shift—its interpretive inconsistency from the spiritual meaning in John four to the crudely literal and physical meaning in John six—shows an inharmonious and faulty exegesis and a conspicuous disregard for the context of the chapter, as well as the broader context of John's Gospel where spiritual drinking from Christ is the same as to believe in Him. Former Catholic Mike Gendron compares the events of John four to the events of John six and rightly concludes after listing their close similarities: "The Roman Catholic Church displays its inconsistent teaching by taking the words of Jesus literally in John 6 but not in John 4. Ask them why they must eat and drink His flesh and blood for eternal life but do not have to drink His water" ("Proclaiming the Gospel", April-June, 2007, Vol. 16 No. 2)

This inconsistency is due to the fact that they are using a pretense for the sacrament of the Mass and transubstantiation, and are constantly seeking to force these unbiblical doctrines into any biblical context that could appear to justify and agree with them. One of the first rules for interpreting the Bible correctly is to

discover and **determine** the context. The context of a passage or chapter in the Bible will determine whether the meaning is figurative, metaphorical, or literal. This is no less true with the Gospel of John, and particularly with the sixth chapter. The Gospel of John contains seven great "I AM" statements that Jesus confessed about Himself. The "I AM" statements reveal a certain aspect of Christ's ministry and divine Person that are all personified in metaphorical language to represent who Jesus is and what He can do. The first of these seven great statements is found in John 6:35 where Jesus says, "I Am the Bread of Life" to represent the spiritual reality that He is the true and lasting sustenance for spiritual life. The other six "I AM" statements are: *"I Am the Light of the World"* (John 8:12); *"I Am the Door"* (John 10:9); *"I am the Good Shepherd"* (John 10:11-14); *"I Am the Resurrection and the Life"* (John 11:25); *"I Am the Way, the Truth and the Life"* (John 14:6); and *"I Am the True Vine"* (John 15:1). It is obvious in each of these statements, Jesus was using metaphors to illustrate fundamental truths about Himself—that includes the Bread of Life metaphor in John 6:35. All seven statements are metaphors, and that certainly includes the Bread of Life affirmation!

Surely, when Jesus said, "I Am the Light of the World or "I Am the Door", He did not really mean that He was literally a light or a door, but rather these were metaphors to underscore that He illumines the mind to reveal the true nature and character of God and is the door by which we have access to and fellowship with Him. Metaphors used in the Bible are usually employed with "to be" verbs such as "is", "are", and "am" or comparative words such as "like" and "as." And these features are present throughout the narrative of John six to plainly indicate that the language of Jesus in the Bread of Life Discourse is to be understood in a metaphorical/spiritual manner, rather than in a literal/physical way. When a person comes to Christ and believes in Him, he or she will, in effect, eat from the Person of Jesus Christ, and as the Bread of Life, He will permanently satisfy the spiritual hunger and appetite of the soul. That does not mean, however, the believer will not hunger and thirst for the presence and power of Christ, but that such hunger and thirst will always be satisfied and not go unfed by the Lord. Jesus' identification of Himself as the Bread of Life is a metaphor He uses to illustrate and teach that just as physical bread is necessary to sustain the natural life, so too, in a much greater and more effective way, is the Lord Jesus Christ necessary spiritual sustenance for eternal life.

In John 6:35 Jesus says He is that bread who gives life to one and all; and those who come to Christ with personal faith will "never" thirst or hunger again. The Greek word for "never", ou me (οὐ μή), is a double negative used to emphasize the utter impossibility of something occurring opposite of what is being affirmed.[48] Hence, when the sinner places his personal trust in Christ he will be permanently satisfied and will never grow thirsty or hungry again. Of course, Jesus was not literally saying that if a person believes on Him he or she would never physically hunger or thirst again. Everyone knows that eating physical bread and food cannot permanently satisfy hunger for the rest of this life, nor can drinking a physical drink permanently quench the physical thirst for the rest of this earthly life. But when the Catholic maintains that the bread and wine is the actual flesh and blood of Christ to be eaten and drunk, he must also take the words of verse 35 to be literal as well. So when Christ said "I Am the Bread of Life," and Catholics believe they are literally eating His flesh and drinking His blood in the Eucharist, they should never physically hunger or thirst again once they have done so for the first time. When a Roman Catholic receives the Host (communion bread) and cup of wine, he should never have to eat or drink again! But of course they do, and further prove so when they repeatedly eat and drink food and continually partake of the bread and wine in the Mass.

---

[48]   The emphatic negation of οὐ μή is the strongest way to deny or negate something in the Greek. See Daniel B. Wallace, *Greek Grammar: Beyond the Basics* (Grand Rapids: Zondervan, 1996), 468.

Rome belies this crude, literalistic interpretation, when through its Canon Law and Catechisms, it demands its faithful adherents must continually eat the flesh and drink the blood of Christ offered through the Mass. If Jesus' words about bread in John 6:35 were indeed to be taken literally, a Catholic should only have to eat this bread once so that he will never physically hunger or thirst again! Obviously this does not happen, because Christ was speaking *spiritually* here to *metaphorically* illustrate by comparison and contrast that He, as the Spiritual "Bread of Life", gives eternal life and sustains our spiritual life when received by faith in the same manner, but on a lower level, that the ingestion of physical bread perpetuates physical life. Jesus uses the imagery of bread because the people sought Him out for more bread after He fed them with the miracle of the multiplied loaves and fishes. For Catholic theologians to then say that the bread of John six means the Eucharist of the Lord's Supper simply does not agree with this historical context and does not fit the interpretation for "bread" in this particular chapter. The Lord's Supper is not even mentioned or explicitly referred to once in John six. The events of this chapter happened a full year before Christ inaugurated the Lord's Supper from the Passover meal! To thus read the Eucharist and the Roman Catholic Mass here is anachronistic and nothing better.

Christ's image of hunger and thirst anticipates the eating and drinking of verses 53-56, and the hungry and thirsty soul that comes and believes in Jesus does, by these two distinct acts, spiritually eat and drink, respectively, from the nourishing life of Christ, the Bread of Life. Therefore, the *coming* and *believing* in Jesus will become the *eating* and *drinking* of verse 53. The state of not hungering or thirsting is equated by the Lord and directly correlates with those who *come* to and *believe* in Christ.[49] Those definitions are *spiritual* and *symbolic* in meaning, rather than *earthly* or *physical,* and retain that same meaning throughout the rest of John six. To favor Rome's crass, literalistic interpretation reduces the text to an absurd cannibalism that is incoherent in meaning, contradictory of the symbolic premise laid out in verse 35, and implausible with the norms of everyday reality. Every person who comes to Christ does physically hunger, and every person that believes in the Savior does physically thirst afterwards; this obviously proves that the terms of "eating" and "drinking" Christ's flesh and blood are not physical but spiritual in their meaning! Eating and drinking, we learn throughout the narrative of John six, consist in the acts of *coming* to Christ and *believing* on Him.

Rome ignores, or conveniently overlooks the symbolic meaning of eating/drinking for coming to and believing on Jesus, when stressing that the actions of eating and drinking the flesh and blood of Christ (as believed to occur in the Mass), mentioned in verse 54, stand by themselves in the text, with no prior equivalent given by symbol or metaphor in the preceding verses. The learned comments of Bible scholar D.A. Carson, in his fine commentary on the Gospel of John, should remind the Catholic: It is the person who *comes* to

---

[49] To spiritually eat of Jesus Christ is to come to Him without reserve, and to drink of Christ is to believe and trust Him. Both actions of coming to and believing in Christ are equivalent to eating and drinking, and are slightly different in meaning. To "come" to Christ is to repent and change one's course of direction in life from the self and refocus it on the glorious Person of Christ. To "believe" in Him is to accept what God has testified about His Son Jesus Christ in the Scriptures, and that what He accomplished in His death and resurrection is sufficient alone for the salvation of the sinner. "There is, no doubt, a shade of difference between 'believing on' Christ and 'Coming to' Him. To 'believe on' Christ is to receive God's testimony concerning His Son, and to rest on Him alone for salvation. To 'come to' Him—which is really the effect of the former—is for the heart to go out to Him in loving confidence. The two acts are carefully distinguished in Heb. 11:6: 'without faith it is impossible to please him: for he that cometh to God must believe that he is: and that he is a rewarder of them that diligently seek him." Arthur Pink, *Exposition of the Gospel of John* (Grand Rapids: Zondervan, 1975), 327-328. Thus, when one *comes* to Christ he comes in faith to believe in Him.

Christ and *believes* in Him that does not hunger or thirst, and so the metaphorical language found throughout John 6 takes on a more intense and graphic language of *"eating"* and *"drinking"* in verses 53-56, with the meaning of the metaphors having already been defined and established in verses 27-35.

> The essentially symbolic nature of "bread of life" and related expression in this discourse is disclosed by the mingling of metaphorical and non-metaphorical elements. **Jesus is the bread of life, but it is the person who *comes* to him who does not hunger, not the person who *eats* him; similarly, it is the person who *believes* in him who does not thirst, not the person who drinks him. Thus, when the language becomes more rigorously metaphorical in vv. 49ff., and we read of eating Jesus' flesh and drinking His blood, the meaning of the metaphors has already been established** (Emphasis mine).[50]

In verses 36 through 40, Jesus rebukes the crowd for their lack of true faith. Even when they were given the inestimable privilege of seeing the Messiah for themselves, the people still refused to believe. In view of their inexcusable unbelief, Jesus points out to His audience that a person can only believe in Him when God the Father sovereignly exerts His power to elect those who are chosen to believe, and He will demonstrate this power by enabling people to come in faith to Christ. And everyone who comes in faith will be received by the Father and never be rejected. Jesus then repeats that He came from heaven, sent by God to do His will on Earth. His will is that all who believe in Jesus the Son will not be lost, but rather raised to immortal life in the resurrection. The Galilean audience grumbled and complained among themselves at these astounding claims. As their ancestors complained before Moses in the wilderness after being miraculously fed by the manna from heaven, the audience of John six likewise grumbled about Jesus affirming His heavenly origin and God being His Father who sent Him to Earth to accomplish His will. They ignored the proof of the miracle of the multiplied loaves and fishes as proof of Christ's heavenly Messiahship and His unique Sonship to God as His Father. On the surface, their objections appeared reasonable, because they knew Jesus' earthly parents were Mary and Joseph.

The crowd was not, however, privy to the truths, made known through divine revelation, of the Virgin birth and the Incarnation. Jesus existed as God in eternity past and became God incarnate in time and history when conceived by the power of the Holy Spirit in the womb of Mary. Joseph, therefore, was not His biological father. The Lord Jesus chides the people for their unnecessary murmuring and reminds them again how no one can accept Him unless God, first, sovereignly draws them to the Savior. Those who learn from God and eat and drink of His teaching will come to Jesus in faith (John 6:41-46). In verses 47 and following, Jesus again uses the Bread of Life metaphor for Himself as the object of faith bringing eternal life to the person who believes. ***"Most assuredly, I say to you, he who believes in Me has everlasting life. I am the bread of life. Your fathers ate the manna in the wilderness, and are dead. This is the bread which comes down from heaven, that one may eat of it and not die. I am the living bread which came down from heaven. If anyone eats of this bread, he will live forever; and the bread that I shall give is My flesh, which I shall give for the life of the world"*** (John 6:47-51).

Verse 47 reiterates that simple belief and trust in the Person and teachings of Jesus Christ bring everlasting life to the believer. This is the third time in John six that belief is required for receiving eternal life from Jesus Christ. Belief in Christ is the necessary act for salvation. Jesus again, here, equates the "eating"

---

[50]   D.A. Carson, *The Gospel According to John* (Grand Rapids: Eerdmans, 1991), 290-291.

and "drinking" of Him to "believing" in Him for eternal life. Nowhere in the Bread of Life discourse did Jesus say "believe" and then "eat My flesh and drink My blood" as two separate requirements for salvation, which would be the case if the Roman Catholic's sacramental understanding of these verses were true. The only requirement Jesus demands is to *believe* in Him, of which He later extrapolates into the symbolic acts of eating and drinking His flesh and blood in the last part of the discourse. That Jesus is not saying He is literal, physical bread to be eaten is further made evident in verses 48-50, where Jesus again reminded His audience that the Israelites ate the manna forty years in the desert and still died, even after they ate it. But those who eat of the Bread of Life He offers, will never die.

Surely if the Romanist's interpretation of John 6:50-51, which requires a Catholic to physically eat and drink the flesh and blood of Christ in the Eucharist, were literally true, no Roman Catholic would suffer death once the bread and wine of the Mass is eaten and drunk. The fact that death, the great leveler of all, has come to every person participating in the Mass of the Roman Catholic Church proves the literalist interpretation of Rome to be patently wrong and totally absurd. This is another unimpeachable reason why the Lord was obviously speaking figuratively and spiritually all throughout John chapter six.[51] Jesus was simply using the figure of bread, the common food of that day, to point out the contrast between that physical bread, typified by the manna, that when eaten a person still dies, and Christ, the Spiritual Bread, Who, when received by faith, brings spiritual life forever. Catholic teachers are using the wrong analogy of the Lord's Supper for John six when the Lord Jesus refers to the Old Testament miracle of the manna coming down from heaven.

If John had the Lord's Supper in view, when recording the events of chapter six, the correct and more appropriate analogy would have been the Passover meal, not the manna from heaven. The words Jesus spoke in verses 47-58 are preceded and followed by the analogy of the manna from heaven. The word *"flesh"* that Jesus uses in verse 51 to say that He gives His life for the salvation of the world is *sarx* (σάρξ). In the Greek New Testament, *sarx* is normally associated with the Incarnation of Christ or His redemptive death for sinners (See George R. Beasley-Murray, *Word Biblical Commentary: John* Second Edition, Nashville: Thomas Nelson, page 94, 1999). The term *"flesh and blood"* is a Hebrew idiom of the New Testament referring to the whole person, not to the Eucharistic elements of bread and wine (Matthew 16:17; 1 Corinthians 15:50; Galatians 1:16; Ephesians 6:12; Hebrews 2:14). The word *"flesh"* and the phrase *"flesh and blood"* are not used in the New Testament with reference to Holy Communion or the Lord's Supper. The word customarily found in the New Testament Communion texts is *"body"*, not *"flesh."* John reveals to the reader that the preincarnate Word of God became "flesh" (John 1:14). Jesus shared the same flesh and blood life with all physical humanity when He became a man (Hebrews 2:14-15). Christ's physical death in the *"flesh"* was God's judicial sentence of condemnation on all evil done in the human body (Romans 8:3).

Moreover, the sacrificial meaning is further reinforced by the use of the Greek preposition "for" *hyper* (υπερ) in the second clause of John 6:51, where Jesus says He would give His flesh *for* the life of world. The preposition *for* is repeatedly used in the Gospel of John to underscore the sacrificial nature of Christ's death for the redemption of mankind from the ruin and condemnation of sin (see John 10:11, 15; 11:51-52; 15:13; 17:19; 18:14). The sacrificial context is more in keeping with John six and the rest of this Gospel than the Eucharistic connotation Rome says it must mean. The Roman Catholic belief that a person must repeatedly attend Mass to eat and drink the flesh and blood of Christ to continually remain in a state of grace is baldly

---

[51] Moreover: "If Christ is speaking physically of His body and blood in John 6, then those who eat of Him will never physically die. But all of the apostles themselves are dead. If He did not mean that eating Him would prevent physical death, then neither did He refer to physically eating Him. He is obviously speaking spiritually *all through that chapter*, as elsewhere" (Dave Hunt, *A Woman Rides the Beast*, 380).

contradicted by the use of the Greek Aorist tense for "eat" *phage* (φάγη) and drink (πιητε) in verses 51, 53, and 54, which denotes a once-for-all action or decision—done or made one time which is not repeated.[52] The words for "eat" and "drink" in these verses are used in this way to mean a once-for-all act. Jesus was not, therefore, speaking of continually eating and drinking His flesh and blood, all the time. He was speaking of the act of faith that is done once with ongoing results lasting forever. So to eat of Him once, is to continue eating from Him forever. So even if the Catholic apologist were correct in asserting one has to literally eat and drink Christ's flesh and blood, you would only have to do it one time to have eternal life. The person who comes to Christ must come to Him only once to receive eternal salvation.

Anyone who personally appropriates Him in the act of faith receives the Savior once for all time, and thereby will never spiritually die or hunger again. Indeed, the word "believe" is used in the aorist tense all throughout the New Testament and the Gospel of John to signify a one-time act exhibiting the exercise of faith and trust in Jesus Christ that, once done, results in salvation. When the Samaritan woman brought the people of the village to hear Jesus, John 4:39-41 states, ***"And from that city many of the Samaritans believed in Him…and many more believed because of His word."*** "Believe" in this text is in the aorist tense. When the Philippian jailer asked Paul and Silas, "What must I do to be saved?" Their answer was: ***"Believe in the Lord Jesus, and you shall be saved"*** (Acts 16:31). The word "believe" here is also in the aorist tense and means that a person is to believe only once in Jesus to receive salvation—it does not say one must continually believe to be saved; and this fact alone strikes down the Roman Catholic belief that a person must continually partake in the sacrament of the Eucharist to remain in a state of grace in order to retain an open-ended, conditional salvation![53]

The Jews therefore quarreled among themselves, saying, "How can this Man give us His flesh to eat?" Then Jesus said to them, "Most assuredly, I say to you, unless you eat the flesh of the Son of Man and drink His blood, you have no life in you. Whoever eats My flesh and drinks My blood has eternal life, and I will raise him up at the last day. For My flesh is food indeed, and My blood is drink indeed. He who eats My flesh and drinks My blood abides in Me, and I in him. As the living Father sent Me, and I live because of the Father, so he who feeds on Me will live because of Me. This is the bread which came down from heaven—not as your fathers ate the manna, and are dead. He who eats this bread will live forever" (John 6:52-58).

The Jewish audience began to quibble among themselves over how Christ could physically give His flesh to eat for the life of the world. Such a cannibalistic suggestion in their minds rendered the words of Jesus about eating His flesh to be horrendous and absurd. That is because they failed to understand them correctly in a figurative way, opting, like their Roman Catholic counterparts, to assign a crude, cannibalistic meaning to them. Jesus' response was to be even more graphic and pointed in verse 53 when telling the crowd it was necessary, indeed, to eat His flesh and drink His blood to have eternal life. Such life-giving ingestion will also ensure those who eat of Christ have eternal life and will experience the resurrection from the dead and

---

[52]   Eugene Van Ness Goetchius, *The Language of the New Testament* (New York: Charles Scribner's Sons, 1965), 175. When a word is used in the aorist tense it occurs only one time; it is not a repeated action. The aorist tense indicates an action performed in past time.

[53]   The Greek verb "believe" occurs nine times before and after verses 52-58 in John six. Such faith is exclusively used to mean belief in the Person of Christ and is even inseparably identified with "faith in God, who has sent the Son." Of the ninety occurrences of the Greek verb "believe" (επίστευεν) found in the Gospel of John, none refer to a sacrament like the Eucharist or the Mass! Markus Barth, *Rediscovering the Lord's Supper* (Eugene, OR: Wipf and Stock Publishers, 1988), 81-82.

live forever with the Lord. Catholic apologists traditionally argue that the Greek word *trogo* (τρώγω), used in the present tense to mean "chew or "chewing" *trogein* (τρώγειν) is listed four times in verses 54, 56, 57, and 58 to indicate an ongoing act of chewing and gnawing. The word is more intense and graphic than just eating and must be taken literally here in John six. This particular usage, they go on to deduce, argues for the necessity of accepting a literal interpretation of eating the flesh and drinking the blood of Christ in the Eucharist.[54] This section is part of the distinct pericope of John 6:52-58 Catholic theologians typically point to as the proof text for their Eucharistic understanding of these verses that demands one must physically eat the flesh and drink the blood of Christ in the Eucharist for salvation.

This assumption is a mere conjecture and an unqualified inference on the part of the defenders of Catholicism. *Trogo* is a synonym for the aorist tense of "eat" (*phage* found in verses 51, 53, and 54), and is therefore interchangeable with *phage* to mean the same thing. *Trogo* is the more common Greek word used in the New Testament for the present tense act of eating; of the two words, *trogo* is the more graphic and vivid description. John's alternation between "eat" (φάγη) and "chew" (τρώγω) reflects the stylistic variety of the writer and expresses the various ways Jesus was metaphorically expressing that belief in Him was required for eternal life. To eat, one must chew, and to chew, one must eat. This is a matter of common sense, as reflected in John's alternate use between "eat" and "chew"; there is no contextual indication or validation that the meaning of the Eucharist is intended here. The crowd misunderstood Jesus' words of eating His flesh and drinking His blood when they erroneously interpreted a spiritual truth, He spoke, in a carnal and cannibalistic way. Hence, they were offended at this. Jesus already stated to His Jewish audience in John six that God required them to believe in Him as the Messiah whom God sent to give the world eternal life (verses 29, 35, 40, 47).

Jesus merely reaffirms the same in verses 53-58 with the more emphatic, graphic, and vivid language of chewing His flesh and drinking His blood. Jesus already defined what eating and drinking entailed in verse 35—it is coming to Him and believing in His Person. This meaning is the same and holds to the same equivalent of eating and drinking in John 6:53-58. The vivid imagery of eating, chewing, and drinking in no way automatically means a Christian has to literally eat Christ's flesh and drink His blood, like the Catholic is required to do in the Mass. Such terms of eating and drinking are Hebraic idioms Jesus used to serve as spiritual equivalents to coming to and believing in Him as the Messiah of Israel. Being a good Rabbi, Jesus was following, here, the standard teaching methods of the Rabbis of his day.[55]

---

54   Ludwig Ott, *Fundamentals of Catholic Dogma*, 374.

55   In the Talmud tract, *b. Sanhedrin 99a*, even the Rabbis speak figuratively of "eating the Messiah" to symbolically represent the act of fully receiving Him for who He is and what He has done that will bring full satisfaction to the soul (*Commentary On the New Testament Use of the Old Testament*, 450). On this point, famed Hebraic scholar J.B. Lightfoot notes the following, with reference to Jesus' words of eating His flesh and drinking His blood in John six, "There is mention, even amongst the Talmudists themselves, of eating the Messiah. Rabh saith, 'משית עתידדין לארשי דאכלי שני *Israel shall eat the years of Messiah*.' [The Gloss is ᵏ, "The plenty and satiety that shall be in the days of the Messiah shall belong to the Israelites."] Rabh Joseph saith, 'True, indeed: but who shall eat thereof? חילק וביליק כלי לה *shall Chillek and Billek* [two judges in Sodom] *eat of it?*' We must accept against that of R. Hillel, who saith, 'אלוהו בימי חזקיה אין משיח להם לשראל שכבר *Messiah is not likely to come to Israel, for they have already devoured him in the days of Hezekiah*'...Behold, here is mention of eating the Messiah, and none quarrel the phraseology. They excepted against Hillel, indeed, that he should say that the Messiah was so eaten in the days of Hezekiah, that He was not likely to appear again in Israel; but they made no scruple of the scheme, and manner of speech at all. For they plainly enough understood what was meant by *eating the Messiah*; that is, that in the days of Hezekiah they so much partook of the Messiah, they received him so greedily, embraced him so gladly, and in

The graphic intensity which Jesus' words carry in John 6:53-58 in no way arbitrarily means He wanted us to understand them literally, any more than we are to take His words of a camel going through the eye of a sewing needle as being physically possible (Matthew 19:24). Jesus called the Pharisees "whitewashed tombs" and "serpents" (Matthew 23:27, 33). Does this mean they were physically transmuted into snakes and graves? Are we to take these words to be literally true since they are strong and graphic metaphors? Roman Catholic Bible scholars certainly do not, because they are obvious similes and metaphors. Vivid phrases and graphic metaphors that are employed by Christ in Scripture are not necessarily reason enough to affirm they must have a literal and physical meaning. The same equally holds true for Christ's idiomatic meaning behind the eating and drinking imagery in John six. From their context, such ingestion language is to be understood spiritually and symbolically, especially since the Lord frequently and cryptically spoke in parables, graphic symbols, and picturesque metaphors (Matthew 13:10-11). The act of "eating" and drinking" was a common idiom and metaphor in the Hebrew Scriptures, which became a part of Jewish thought throughout the history of the Old and New Testaments.

The acts of *"eating"* and *"drinking"* were symbols frequently used in the Old Testament for personally experiencing and appropriating the words and blessings Yahweh has lavishly and freely given to His prophets and people. The Psalmist invites everyone to come, *"Taste and see that the Lord is good"* (Psalm 34:8). Later in Psalm 119, He exults in the sweet influence that God's Word brings to the hungry soul who spiritually ingests it. *"How sweet are Your words to my taste, sweeter than honey to my mouth"* (Psalm 119:103). Speaking on behalf of the Lord, Isaiah the Prophet beckons the sinner to come, *drink and eat* from the refreshing and nourishing realities of salvation in Isaiah 55:1: *"Ho! Everyone who thirsts, Come to the waters; and you who have no money, come, buy and <u>eat</u>. Yes, come, buy wine and milk, without money and without price."* The prophets were commanded by God to fully assimilate and absorb His word within their souls, hearts, and minds by "eating" its life-giving content. The prophet Jeremiah joyfully declared of this: *"Your words were found, and I ate them; and Your word was to me the joy and rejoicing of my heart"* (Jeremiah 15:16). God told Ezekiel to "eat" the scroll of judgments that were decreed against disobedient Israel so that the prophet would be thoroughly immersed with the revelation God had given Him. *"Son of man, <u>eat</u> what you find; eat this scroll, and go, speak to the house of Israel." So I opened my mouth, and He caused me to eat that scroll. And He said to me, "Son of man, feed your belly, and fill your stomach with this scroll that I give you." So I ate, and it was in my mouth like honey in sweetness* (Ezekiel 3:1-3).

In the New Testament, the same Hebraic idioms of "eating" and "drinking" are also utilized to signify the operation of the mind and the reception of the soul in understanding and applying the basic principles

---

a manner devoured him, that they must look for him no more in the ages to come…But the expression seems very harsh, when he speaks of 'eating his flesh' and 'drinking his blood.' He tells us therefore, that these things must be taken in a spiritual sense…But what sense did they take it in that they did understand it? Not in a sacramental sense surely, unless they were then instructed in the death and passion of our Savior; for the sacrament hath a relation to his death: but it sufficiently appears elsewhere that they knew or expected nothing of that…But to partake of the Messiah truly is to partake of himself, his pure nature, his righteousness, his spirit; and to live and grow and receive nourishment from that participation of him. Things which the Jewish schools heard little of, did not believe, did not think; but things which our blessed Saviour expresseth lively and comprehensively enough, by that of eating his flesh and drinking his blood" (John Lightfoot, *Commentary on the New Testament From the Talmud and Hebraica*, Vol. 3 Peabody, MA: Hendrickson, 1995), 308-309. Bible scholar E.W. Bullinger points out that the ancient Hebrew language used the verbs of *eating* and *drinking* to denote the operation of the mind in receiving, understanding, and applying doctrine or instruction of any kind (Bullinger, *Figures of Speech Used in the Bible*, 826).

of God's Word. Paul says that Christ was the "spiritual" Rock from which the Israelites drank and ate for nourishment while sojourning in the desert forty years. ***"All <u>ate</u> the same spiritual food, and <u>drank</u> the same spiritual drink. For they drank of that spiritual Rock that followed them, and that Rock was Christ"*** (1 Corinthians 10:3-4). Peter exhorts those new in the Christian faith to drink in the ***"pure milk of the word"*** for spiritual growth and maturity (1 Peter 2:2). The writer of Hebrews warns his readers who ***"<u>tasted</u> the heavenly gift"*** not to neglect the salvation of the New Covenant by reverting back to the inferior sacrificial system of the Old Covenant (Hebrews 6:4). The Apostle John was told in the Apocalypse by the angel of the Lord to "eat" the contents of the prophecies that comprised this biblical revelation. He did so, and exclaimed, ***"Then I took the little book out of the angel's hand and ate it, and it was as sweet as honey in my mouth. But when I had eaten it, my stomach became bitter"*** (Revelation 10:10).

Following His Old Testament predecessors, Jesus makes the same practical use of these Hebrew eating idioms throughout John chapter six to convey the indispensable truth that one must fully receive His life-giving death, pictured through His flesh and blood phraseology, to receive eternal life, and thereby have that spiritual life forever maintained by nourishing on the Son of God, who gave His life to give life to all who believe in Him. Indeed, every language in the world has these same eating idioms; the English language is no exception. When someone exclaims, "I could eat a horse", he or she does not mean they would actually eat a thoroughbred. The phrase simply means: "I am very hungry." When I say that "you will have to eat your words", I do not mean that somehow you will have to materially eat those words, but that you will retract what you previously said and apologize for it. To say he is "eating his heart out" for his ex-job does not mean he is literally eating his heart, which has been just ripped out of his chest, but that the person ardently wishes he could go back to work at his ex-job.

Jesus was a Torah-observant Jew and would, therefore, never have commanded or expected His Jewish disciples and countrymen to violate the Law of God concerning the dietary laws of the Old Testament (*Kashrut*) with respect to committing an act of overt cannibalism, such as eating and drinking human flesh and blood that Catholics wistfully do (so they think) when participating in the Mass. If Christ meant for His Jewish followers to understand His words in John 6:52-58 to be literal, then He would be commanding them to violate what the Word of God clearly forbids in both the Old and New Testaments! The Torah expressly forbids the eating of flesh with blood in any way. In Leviticus 17:10-12, 14, the Lord commanded: ***"And whatever man of the house of Israel, or of the strangers who dwell among you, who <u>eats any blood</u>, I will set My face against that person <u>who eats blood</u>, and will cut him off from among his people. For the life of the flesh is in the blood, and I have given it to you upon the altar to make atonement for your souls; for it is the blood that makes atonement for the soul. Therefore I said to the children of Israel, No one among you <u>shall eat blood</u>, nor shall any stranger who dwells among you eat blood.... for it is the life of all flesh. Its blood sustains its life. Therefore I said to the children of Israel, <u>You shall not eat the blood of any flesh</u>, for the life of all flesh is its blood. <u>Whoever eats it shall be cut off</u>"*** (see also Leviticus 7:26-27). This prohibition was likewise upheld by Jewish Christians for the Church in the New Testament. Acts 15:20 authoritatively decreed from the Jerusalem Council: ***"But that we write to them, that they abstain from pollutions of idols, and from fornication, and from things strangled, <u>and from blood.</u>"***

If Roman Catholic transubstantiation were correct when declaring Jesus Christ requires we have to physically eat His flesh and drink His blood in John chapter six, then He would be commanding the Jewish people to violate what the word of God has unequivocally prohibited in both the Old and New Testaments! So then, is it breaking the sacred command of Torah (the Word of God) to symbolically require a person to eat flesh and drink blood, which is forbidden by the Word of God? No, not at all; for in Numbers 23:24 it is prophesied by God through Balaam that Israel's military defeat of their enemies will be so thorough and complete that they will symbolically drink up their blood until there is no trace of them left. ***"Behold, the people shall rise up as a great lion, and lift up himself as a young lion: he shall not lie down until he eat of the prey, and <u>drink the blood</u> of the slain"*** (Numbers 23:24). The God of Israel was being figurative here to describe Israel's defeat of their enemies without literally violating the Law of Moses by physically drinking blood. We should not then condemn the Lord's words as promoting cannibalism since they are acceptable on the basis that such words are only figurative in meaning. In this same vein, therefore, Jesus also figuratively gave His flesh and blood to His disciples for all time to consume by the act of faith for the impartation of eternal life. When the Lord Jesus commands in the present tense that a person must "eat" and "drink" of Him in verses 54-58, He is speaking to those physically present at that time; and so by this fact does not lend credence to the Roman Catholic doctrine of transubstantiation—that one has to, *hereafter*, continually eat and drink Christ's flesh and blood in the bread and wine of the Roman Catholic Eucharist for salvation.

By using the present tense in these aforementioned verses in John six, Jesus was speaking to the audience from the synagogue of Capernaum and made the requirement for them to obey and believe Him at that time. If Jesus were expecting His commands of eating His flesh and drinking His blood to be taken literally at that moment in time, He would have to be killed and His blood shed for them to cannibalistically eat and drink of Him for them to have salvation and eternal life! However, if Jesus intended His words of "eating" and "drinking" to be understood figuratively to mean the crowd was to partake of Him by faith, just as the human body partakes of food through eating and drinking to sustain physical life, then this was something they could do immediately at that time. The Lord's Supper would not be instituted until a full year after the events of John six had occurred; and so Christ's audience in John six would not have even remotely understood this Eucharistic requirement and obeyed it under the ritual of the Roman Catholic Mass, which was not available to them at that time. This is why, among other obvious reasons stated in this chapter, Jesus' words of eating and drinking are to be taken in a **metaphorical** way of **believing** in Him, rather than literally eating or drinking Him.

The "flesh" of Christ is indicative of His Person, and His "blood" refers to His life poured out for sinners on the Cross (Leviticus 17:14). Jesus is saying that to spiritually eat and drink His flesh and blood is to personally assimilate and appropriate His Person and life-saving death to have eternal life. Christ's words of "eat" and "drink" are, of course, not advocating cannibalism. The words mean that a person must spiritually receive Jesus Christ into His life to have Eternal life. He must consume, absorb, drink in, partake, and digest the saving death of the Messiah to have spiritual life and an ongoing, continuous relationship with God.

Catholic apologists go on and say that Jesus never rebukes or corrects His Jewish audience for understanding His words to mean that they had to eat His flesh and drink His blood in a physical and cannibalistic way. Thus, the silence of Jesus here unimpeachably confirms their literal understanding of His words about eating His flesh and drinking His blood.[56] Surely, if they were wrong or misunderstood Christ's words, the Romanist so reasons, Jesus would have undoubtedly corrected the Jewish crowd on this point. Such an argument from silence is not a good one, when considering the Lord Jesus often spoke in metaphors and parables, and when misunderstood for speaking in a literal or physical way by His audience, He did not *always* bother to correct them. In John 2:15-21, after Jesus drove the corrupt moneychangers from the Temple,

---

[56]   Keating, *Catholicism and Fundamentalism*, 233. Former Baptist minister, now current Catholic apologist, Tim Staples, also argues that Jesus must have expected His audience to really eat His flesh and drink His blood as Rome teaches because Christ lost many disciples as a result of this teaching, but still did not run after those disciples saying, "Stop, I didn't mean it literally!" (See http://members.aol.com/chasklu/religion/private/truth5.html.)

He was challenged by the religious authorities to perform a miraculous sign to authenticate His Messianic authority in the face of what they perceived was a brazen and unwarranted act. Jesus said to them, *"Destroy this temple, and in three days I will raise it up"* (John 2:19).

The Jewish leaders heard this and naturally assumed Jesus was talking about the second temple King Herod was building in their day. Not once in John chapter 2 did Jesus correct their misunderstanding based on a crass literalism. They wrongly thought Jesus was saying He would destroy the Temple in Jerusalem and rebuild it in three days. Indeed, some three years later or so, when Jesus stood on trial for His life, this accusation was brought up again and Jesus did not correct their misunderstanding, even when He knew He was actually talking about the physical resurrection of His body from the dead that would take place three days later (Matthew 26:61-63)! With this, Johannine scholar Edwin Blum correctly observes:

> Jesus' hearers must have been shocked and puzzled by His enigmatic words. But the puzzle is unlocked by understanding that Jesus was speaking of His making atonement by His death and giving life to those who personally appropriate Him (cf. John 6:63). Faith in Christ's death brings **eternal life** (cf. vv. 40, 47, 50-51) and (later) bodily resurrection (cf. vv. 39-40, 44).[57]

Jesus deliberately couched divine truths in dark sayings, riddles, and opaque parables to conceal vital truths about the kingdom of God from those who were inveterately opposed to Him, while simultaneously provoking those who listened to Him with an open heart to press in and discover the transforming principles of God's kingdom which came from His words and teaching (see Matthew 13:13-16). This proved to be the weeding out process to separate true believers from those who were spurious. We find the same discriminatory process used by Jesus again in John six. The majority of the Jewish audience was repulsed by the very idea of eating Jesus' flesh and drinking His blood. They could not get past the physical aspect of this to see Jesus was talking about a spiritual appropriation of His life and death under the terms of His "flesh" and "blood", and that God alone sovereignly chose those who have been predestined to come to the Savior. They could not grasp this because they were following Jesus for carnal motives. And so they were *offended* when *He spoke a spiritual truth in a physical way*. They could not get beyond the tangible and fleshly, to arrive at the ethereal and eternal reality of salvation by faith in the Son of God, which takes place within the hidden confines of the human heart, mind, will, and soul.

Furthermore, Jesus disabuses them for wrongly interpreting His words of eating and drinking His flesh and blood in a crude and physical manner when predicting His ascension to heaven—a supernatural feat that would preclude them from eating and drinking from Him in any physical manner, simply because He would no longer be on Earth. How could they possibly do this if He were to ascend back to heaven? The point of Christ predicting His ascension in verse 62 to this skeptical crowd is that when they witness or hear of this event, they will then know that His demand of eating His flesh and drinking His blood is a purely spiritual exercise, since He will no longer be physically present among them. Hence, His words were not to be taken in a literal, physical, and cannibalistic sense, but rather in a symbolic and spiritual way of receiving Him by faith, in trust and dependence on His bodily death on the cross for eternal life (John 6:62).

The Roman Catholic faces a further dilemma with a literal interpretation of eating and drinking Christ's flesh and blood when it is affirmed that the "eating" and "drinking" in John 6:53-54, and the "believing"

---

[57]   *The Bible Knowledge Commentary*, 297.

mentioned in verse 40, produce the same result of eternal life. If both are literally true, then what happens to the person who does believe in Christ, but does not eat the flesh and drink the blood of Christ in the Roman Catholic Eucharist? Moreover, if Christ meant His words literally here, what happens to the person who only eats the Eucharist but does not drink from the communion cup; or if he drinks from the communion cup but does not eat the Host? This would be especially problematic for the Catholic laity who was prohibited from drinking the communion cup for centuries, before Vatican II rescinded this prohibition. This dilemma is not solved or mollified with Rome's expeditious attempt through its Councils and Canon law to teach that ingestion of the Eucharistic Host (the bread) is sufficient alone for salvation when Jesus required in John 6:53-56 that a person must both *eat* and *drink* from Him to have eternal life![58] The only reasonable and sound way to harmonize these contradictions, which Rome has unwittingly created when insisting the acts of eating and drinking must be literal, is to interpret the words of John 6:53-56 as figurative in meaning. If these verses were interpreted literally, they would blatantly contradict and oppose numerous Scripture passages which plainly state, in no uncertain terms, that salvation and justification before God are given on the basis of grace alone conveyed through faith alone in Jesus Christ alone (John 3:16; Acts 4:12; Ephesians 2:8-9, Titus 3:5-7, et al)![59]

Catholic apologists typically point to the words of John 6:55, where Jesus says: "For My flesh is *real* food indeed, and My blood is *real* drink indeed" to argue that the Greek word for "real" *alethes* (ἀληθης) used in this verse must have been used by Jesus to point out the literal reality of the bread and wine really and truly being His flesh and blood in the Eucharist.[60] Such an interpretation, if valid, would undermine and remove the clear analogy of contrast Jesus continually maintains in John six between physical bread, like the manna, that can only sustain biological life, and the spiritual bread that He represents in His life and death, that *truly* gives eternal life to those who *believe* in Him. The word *alethes* is used to mean what is true as opposed to what is false. The Lord's point in this verse is not to justify transubstantiation, when the communion bread and wine are changed into His flesh and blood, but to emphasize that just as real physical life on Earth comes directly from eating and drinking food and water, so too *true* spiritual life that endures forever and exists on a higher plane than the material and physical comes directly from eating and drinking from the Person of Jesus Christ. One must personally receive Christ and trust that He alone has the ability to give salvation and the abundance of unending, spiritual life.

To come, believe, and see, and be drawn by the Father to Jesus (John 6:29, 40, 47) is the same spiritual and symbolic equivalent of eating and drinking from Christ. In the course of the Bread of Life Discourse, Jesus comes down to His audience's level of physical hunger and thirst, in the attempt to bring them up to His level of stressing the necessity of receiving eternal life through Him, which can alone permanently satisfy the thirst and hunger of the human soul. Reformed apologist James White clarifies this more precisely when observing that in John six,

> Jesus decides to come down to their level in an attempt to bring them up to His. He moves on with the metaphor, already firmly established, of eating=believing. The only way to eternal life is through union with the Son of man. This involves a vital faith relationship with Him, symbolized here by the eating of His flesh and the drinking of His blood. To

---

[58] *The Canons and Decrees of the Council of Trent*, 134. The Council of Trent further contradicts the words of Christ by anathematizing anyone who says the Faithful must receive both the bread and wine of the Eucharist together (page 135). Jesus required both the act of eating and drinking together; He did not separate the one from the other!

[59] Mike Gendron, "Eat My Flesh and Drink My Blood "(page 2 of 6), at www.reachingcatholics.org/eatdrink.html

[60] John Salza, *The Biblical Basis for The Catholic Faith*, 100.

make the equation complete, Jesus places "eating My flesh and drinking My blood" in the exact same position as: (1) hearing His word and believing on Him who sent Jesus (John 5:24); (2) being drawn by the Father (6:44); (3) looking to the Son and believing (6:40); or (4) simply believing (6:47). The result is the same in each case—eternal life, or being raised up at the last day. Taken all together, we have a clear indication of Jesus' usage of the metaphor of "eating His flesh and drinking His blood" in John 6. Consequently, the Roman Catholic interpretation of this passage is left without a foundation. Jesus is obviously not speaking of a Sacrament of the Eucharist supposedly established years later. His referring to His body and blood paralleled clearly with belief in the Son and the drawing of the Father. *Consistency of interpretation must lead to the rejection of a sacramental interpretation of this passage. The literal meaning, given the parallelism already firmly established in this passage, has to refer to the union of the believer by faith with Jesus Christ, not a participation in the Roman Catholic Mass* (Emphasis mine).[61]

If we were to follow the Roman Catholic's sacramental interpretation of John 6:52-58, then verse 57 of this pericope would naturally have to mean the same. When Jesus said in this verse, *"As the living Father has sent Me, and I live by the Father, so He who feeds on Me will live because of Me"*, the comparative use of "as" establishes a direct parallel between how the Son lives by the Father and how the Christian lives by the life-giving power of the Son. If Roman Catholicism is right when it teaches Jesus demands believers must *literally* eat His flesh, then this direct parallel would equally demand that Jesus had to literally eat the Father to live, in that Christians are to live off Him in the same exact way the Son lives off the Father. Jesus, of course, does not subsist on the Father by physically eating Him. He lives His life in complete dependence upon the Father just as the physical body is sustained and depends on physical food for life. Christ's analogy of eating and drinking means the same. As biological life is completely dependent on material food for physical life, so is spiritual and eternal life given and dependent on partaking in Christ by faith.[62]

To leave no room for doubt, in John 6:63, Jesus makes it quite clear to His Jewish audience how His words about eating His flesh and drinking His blood were spiritual in meaning, when He unequivocally declared: *"It is the Spirit who gives life; the flesh profits nothing. The words that I speak to you are spirit, and they are life."* Jesus is saying to them that His words of eating and drinking must be interpreted in a spiritual manner, and are not to be understood in a physical way that would entail cannibalism; for the consumption of human flesh cannot impart eternal life nor can it make a man spiritually alive. Former Protestants, now full blown 'converted' Roman Catholic apologists Marcus Grodi and Scott Hahn, were discussing the meaning of "flesh" in John 6:63 on the television program *The Journey Home*—a talk show of ex-"Protestants" that is regularly aired on the Catholic television network EWTN. Hahn presumptuously claimed Jesus was really saying that all human flesh profits nothing, except for His own resurrected flesh, which does, indeed, spiritually profit the Roman Catholic when eating and drinking Christ's literal flesh and blood contained in the Eucharist. Hahn asserts:

> In John 6 when Jesus says "eat my flesh" and "drink my blood" and "I'll raise you up," and then He goes on to say that the flesh availeth nothing, it's the Spirit that gives life,

---

61   James R. White, *The Roman Catholic Controversy*, 172-173.
62   See the e-mail article: "Why John 6:47-58 Does Not Refer to the Lord's Supper" at http://www.geocities.ws/baptistsite/John6.html.

His point is not to negate what He had previously said. When He says the flesh availeth nothing, He doesn't say, "*My* flesh availeth nothing," He's speaking about *the* flesh, that is, *our* flesh. And so when He says "My flesh is food indeed, My blood is drink indeed, he who eats My flesh and drinks My blood abides in Me, and I in him," what He's going on to say in verse 63 is—what makes His flesh so different than our flesh? Our flesh which is so weak, His flesh which is so strong—it's the Spirit. The flesh availeth nothing, it's the Spirit that gives life, but the Spirit uses the instrument of Christ's flesh and blood to give us this divine life, so that He abides in us and we abide in Him precisely through this flesh which communicates nothing less than the Holy Spirit.[63]

Jesus gives no such qualifying exception of this kind in John 6:63 when He says "the flesh"; such a collective term in Scripture denotes all corporeal humanity without exception (Isaiah 40:5-6; Matthew 16:17; 24:22; 1 Corinthians 1:29). If Jesus had meant *our flesh*, as Hahn contends, Christ would have pointedly said "your flesh", in contrast to His flesh; but Jesus did not say that! Hahn and Grodi are simply approaching the Scripture with their own presuppostional bias towards Roman Catholicism, and are therefore reading this Catholic understanding of the Mass into John 6:63 that is clearly not there. Even Marcus Grodi admits this when telling his guest, Scott Hahn, on the same program, that when reading through the Bible it is important to "read it through Catholic eyes."

Moreover, Hahn flatly contradicts Christ's teaching in this verse when he proclaims that it is the Eucharist that gives divine life and communicates the Holy Spirit to the believer. Jesus said it was His *"words"* that do these things, and nothing else. The Holy Spirit is not given through the Eucharist, but rather, Scripture teaches He is a gift given by faith in Jesus Christ, which comes from the Father sent through His Son (John 14:26; 15:26-27; 16:7; Galatians 4:6). This is what theologians call "the Procession of the Holy Spirit"; this biblical doctrine describes the eternal relationship between the Holy Spirit and the other two Persons of the Godhead. He proceeds from them eternally without diminishing, diluting, or changing God's nature. He does not proceed or emanate from any physical object or religious act of man. The Spirit thus proceeds from the Father and the Son and no other thing or person. The New Testament simply does not support the Roman Catholic doctrine here, as peddled by Grodi and Hahn, that the Holy Spirit is given and communicated through the ritual of the Mass.

When the Holy Spirit was poured out and given on the Day of Pentecost, the Apostles were most likely gathered in the Temple at Jerusalem for prayer, not celebrating the Eucharist (Acts 2:1-9). They celebrated the Lord's Supper, if you assume the phrase "breaking bread" means Holy Communion, *after* the Holy Spirit had already been poured out (Acts 2:42, 46). One looks in vain throughout the New Testament to find the Holy Spirit given and communicated to believers by partaking in the Mass. Once again, Roman Catholics assert one thing and Scripture teaches the opposite! In the book of Acts we also learn that the Holy Spirit is given through the preaching of the Gospel to those who believe it. For it was while Peter was preaching to Cornelius and his household that the Holy Spirit "fell upon all those who heard *the word,*" thus indicating the Spirit is given at the moment of believing the Gospel (Acts 10:44). The Holy Spirit was also conveyed through the laying on of apostolic hands (Acts 8:17-18; 19:6).

The New Testament does not support the Roman Catholic teaching that the Holy Spirit is given through the eating of a piece of bread and the drinking of a cup of wine allegedly transubstantiated into Christ's flesh

---

63   *The Journey Home*, August 18, 2008.

and blood, respectively. Neither does Scripture espouse the belief or idea that salvation can be achieved by an experiential encounter with the human flesh of Jesus Christ, whether it be in the bizarre cannibalistic rite of the Mass, or the mere acknowledgement Jesus exists in a human body. After his conversion, the Apostle Paul no longer evaluated Christ according to the flesh, and so speaks for all Christians in this case when writing, ***"Therefore, from now on we regard no one according to the flesh. Even though <u>we have known Christ according to the flesh, yet now we know Him thus no longer"</u>*** (2 Corinthians 5:16).

On this basis alone, Paul would not have held to, or validly recognized, the Roman Catholic requirement that a person must literally eat the human flesh of Jesus Christ to truly know Him and have salvation. Rome foolishly thinks they discern Christ in the flesh invisibly present within a piece of bread that has to be eaten and worshipped as God, when it is the Spirit of God and the divinely inspired words of Christ, instead, which truly bring eternal life to the hungry and thirsty soul who *believes* in Him. When Christ states that the flesh alone does not achieve what God wants to do—namely, give salvific life to the world, He includes all human flesh, even His own flesh apart from the Word and the life giving Spirit; as George Beasley-Murray observed about the meaning of Jesus' words in John 6:63:

> The flesh alone, even of the Son of Man, does not achieve the end which God has purposed, namely of giving life to the world (= "profits nothing"). Just as the Incarnation of the Son of God is not to be abstracted from its end in crucifixion-resurrection for the life of the world, so both are bound up with the sending of the Spirit for the union of God and man in Christ in the kingdom of God...The words of Jesus in the discourse are "Spirit and life"—for those who receive them in faith, since they who accept them and believe in the Son receive the Spirit and the life of which he speaks.[64]

In the end, the audience of John six utterly failed to grasp this, and ended up leaving Christ and was offended over this teaching because they misunderstood His words in a carnal and physical way. Jesus is essentially telling them, and all who think like them, as does Rome: "Do not misunderstand my teaching in terms of physical eating and drinking, because the physical constitution of the human body cannot produce the spiritual reality of eternal life. Only My words empowered by the Spirit of God have the spiritual and supernatural power to give this life to those who accept and believe in them."

When someone comes to Christ and believes in Him and communes with Him, that person eats and drinks into his life the works and words of Jesus Christ. The whole Bread of Life Discourse of John six is given within a spiritual and figurative context. By taking these verses out context, the Roman Catholic Church falls into the same literalist error the Galilean crowd of John six did when giving a *physical* interpretation to a *spiritual* truth.

Christ's categorical repudiation of the physical flesh—an object subject to spoilage and decay—producing spiritual life most certainly includes the 'Eucharistic Jesus' of the Roman Catholic Mass. It is only by the power of the Holy Sprit of God applied through the Word of God, taught in the words of Jesus here and throughout Scripture, that can give the abundance of eternal life to those who receive it with a believing soul, heart, and mind (Psalm 119:50, 92-93; Romans 8:11; Ephesians 2:1-5). In John 6:63, this life is given through the words of Jesus Christ applied by the power of the Holy Spirit. There is no mention of it being mediated through Roman Catholic priests or the Eucharist transubstantiated into the flesh and blood of Christ. So when

---

[64]   George R. Beasley-Murray, *John*, 96.

Jesus speaks to them about eating and drinking from Him as the Bread of life, He is not speaking literally, but in a figurative way to illustrate a spiritual truth. Such phraseology is used for a symbolic expression of faith. Through this faith the believer digests, assimilates, and appropriates the saving life of Jesus Christ into his life so, in the end, the Son of God's life becomes the very life of the believer. This life brings us into a living union with Christ so we can continually fellowship (continuously eat and drink) with the Savior. This is a direct and personal relationship with Jesus Christ that cannot be substituted with the mere physical acts and objects of the sacraments.

The crowds were offended by their crass misunderstanding of Jesus' words about eating and drinking His flesh and blood, and that only God can draw a person to Him for salvation. Repulsed, they turned back from following Jesus because of unbelief, leaving only the Apostles remaining with Him. (John 6:64-67). When Jesus then pointedly asked the Apostles if they wanted to leave Him also, Peter immediately answered on behalf of the other Apostles: ***"Lord, to whom shall we go? You have the words of eternal life. Also we have come to believe and know that You are the Messiah, the Son of the living God"*** (John 6:68-69). Peter's answer shows that he and his fellow Apostles correctly understood it was *belief* in the *words* of Jesus Christ and faith in Him as Lord and Messiah, and that eternal life is received and given by God. They proved by this confession they understood and remembered what Jesus had just said in verse 63—that it is not the flesh, but the Spirit of God, acting through the spoken words of Christ, which bring eternal life to the believing soul. They rightly grasped, unlike the disaffected crowds departing in unbelief, that to eat and drink from Christ is to believe in Jesus, the divine *Lord* and *Messiah*. Peter had no understanding or thought that Jesus' words were referring to the Roman Catholic Mass and the Eucharist, where the bread and wine are changed into the flesh and blood of Christ. If that were the case, Peter would have then said to Jesus, "Lord, to whom shall we go? You have the *flesh and blood to eat and drink* that gives eternal life." No, the Apostle wisely knew eternal life is found through believing in Jesus Christ and His spoken word, not in physically eating His flesh and drinking His blood!

If the "Blessed Sacrament" contains the full humanity of Jesus Christ through and through, that means Catholics would consume and eat all that would entail. Each time when Catholics eat the Host, they are eating every bodily part of Jesus Christ—His hair, eyes, ears, fingernails, toenails, and dare I say His lower extremities as well. This is not sacrilegious to point out, however, since Rome actually believes the communion wafer transubstantiates into the physical body of Jesus Christ to be eaten and consumed. Rome's emphasis on the eating of the Eucharist for salvation flies in the face of what Paul declared in Romans 14:17, where it is emphatically stated that entrance and living in the Kingdom of God does not consist in the act of *eating* and *drinking* of food and drink: ***"For the kingdom of God is not eating and drinking, but righteousness and peace and joy in the Holy Spirit."*** Undoubtedly, if salvation for Paul consisted in continually eating and drinking Christ's flesh and blood after the ritual of the Mass, He would have plainly stated it here and would certainly not have shunned the act of eating and drinking in any way as being an essential part of God's kingdom.

If the glorified and risen Christ truly resides in the wafer of the Roman Catholic Mass, He would have to go through the normal process of digestion, whose end results in defecation, an utterly blasphemous thought to even entertain. But Rome forces us to this conclusion with their idolatrous concept of the "Blessed Sacrament." To evade this horrendous end, the Catholic Church has resorted to a desperate expediency by conveniently teaching the "real presence" of Christ in the Eucharist lasts only for "fifteen to twenty minutes" and then "disappears" once assimilated into the digestive system.[65] The Word of God spoken from the lips of Jesus, however, dispels this outlandish notion when proclaiming in Matthew 15:17 that all foods (even the Eucharist), without exception, go through the mouth, enter the stomach, and are processed and eliminated from the other end of the body: ***"Do you not yet understand that whatever enters the mouth goes into the stomach and is eliminated?"*** The essential problem at the heart of the Roman Catholic Eucharist is the temporary presence of Jesus that stays until the communion bread is digested. If you were a Roman Catholic, Jesus would be only temporarily inside of you once you ingested the wafer. He would leave after the bread was digested. If you choose to celebrate Mass once a week, then Jesus could only be physically present inside of you for fifteen to twenty minutes a week.

The New Testament knows no such arcane doctrine as this. Christ promised His *spiritual* presence would always be with the Church during His *physical* absence in the present age. He promised, ***"Lo, I am with you always, even to the end of the age"*** (Matthew 28:20). In John 14:16-18, Jesus promised He would also be present in His people through the Holy Spirit who would come and personally indwell every born-again Christian. And once the Holy Spirit comes to live within the Christian, He will stay with the believer forever, not a mere fifteen or twenty minutes in an idolatrous piece of bread reputed to be the Almighty God! ***"And I will pray the Father, and He will give another Helper, that He may abide <u>with you forever</u>—the Spirit of truth, whom the world cannot receive, because it neither sees Him nor knows Him; but you know Him, for He dwells with you and will be in you. I will not leave you orphans; I will come to you"*** (John 14:16-18).

The Bible tells us God will be with His people, and Christ will be in the Church through the Holy Spirit who personally indwells every Christian for time and eternity. This indwelling is established by a personal relationship with God when abiding faith in Christ is shown (John 15:1-5). This indwelling of God's Spirit is not given or mediated through a transubstantiated piece of bread, but is communicated directly from God to the believer upon repentance and faith in Jesus Christ (Acts 2:38-39; 3:19; 5:31-32). Celebrating the Lord's Supper is a memorial reflection honoring what Jesus accomplished in His death for the salvation of mankind. In all of the New Testament passages dealing with the presence and indwelling of Jesus Christ in the Christian believer, not one single verse teaches that the impartation of the Holy Spirit is conveyed, contained, and communicated by eating and drinking the deified bread and wine of the Mass.

Christians, both individually and corporately, are viewed in Scripture as the temple of God in whom His Spirit resides. ***"Do you not know that you are the temple of God and that the Spirit of God dwells in you?"*** (1 Corinthians 3:16; 6:19-20). Jesus never taught He was going to physically return to Earth in the form of the Catholic Eucharist stored in a tabernacle receptacle. The Bible is clear that the Holy Spirit's presence in the Church (the people of God, not a church building or cathedral) makes them *the* living temple of God on Earth. Though Christ is *physically absent* from the Church, He is *spiritually present* within the Church—there is no other person or object where this holy residency occurs. The whole idea of the Roman Catholic wafer god is the product of a mind fixed on idolatry to which no sanction or accommodation is given in Holy Scripture. On the contrary, Scripture condemns, in no uncertain terms, any doctrine or act of idolatry.

Tragically, those who turn to idols for worship, as Catholics do when turning to "the Blessed Sacrament" encased in a monstrance for worship, forsake God's mercy for the empty lies of a worthless idol. ***"Those who regard worthless idols forsake their own mercy"*** (Jonah 2:8). Scripture seems to indicate that the resurrection body of Jesus Christ was without blood and so could not be transmuted into the bread and wine of the Mass. When the risen Christ appeared to the disciples on the evening of His resurrection, they were

---

[65]   Thomas L. Kinkead, *Baltimore Catechism No.4*, (E-Book #14554) Question #245, January 1, 2005.

terrified and assumed they were seeing a disembodied spirit or ghost. To dispel this mistaken notion and to verify He was alive in a resurrected body, Jesus said, ***"Why are you troubled? And why do doubts arise in your hearts? Behold My hands and My feet, that it is I myself. Handle Me and see, <u>for a spirit does not have flesh and bones as you see I have</u>"*** (Luke 24:38-39). The resurrection body of Christ, you will notice here, consists of *flesh* and *bones*, but no mention of *blood* is made. The circulation of blood sustains all mortal flesh; it is the life of physical flesh—***"For the life of the flesh is in the blood…for it is the blood that makes an atonement for the soul"*** (Leviticus 17:11).

All of Christ's blood was shed and poured out on the cross for man's salvation. Christ now has a resurrected, glorified body that lives forever in heaven seated at God's right hand. Christ's resurrection body is immortal and contains no blood because His body is directly sustained and lives by the eternal Spirit of God according to ***"the power of an endless life"*** (Hebrews 7:16). So then, Christ's resurrection body cannot be a sacrifice or re-sacrificed in the Mass for this very reason, nor is the bread and wine of the Eucharist the pre-crucified body of Jesus either, since it would be impossible and unscriptural for Him to revert back to a non-glorified bodily state to be subject to death or sacrifice once again. For, ***"Christ, having been raised from the dead, dies no more. Death no longer has dominion over Him. For the death that He died, He died to sin once for all; but the life that He lives, He lives to God"*** (Romans 6:9-10). Further, if Roman Catholics were actually chewing on the flesh and bones of Christ in the Eucharistic bread, they would in effect be breaking and crushing His bones, and in the process nullifying the prophetic fulfillment of Exodus 12:46 and John 19:36, where it is predicted that none of the bones of the Messiah ***"shall be broken"*** in His sacrificial death. This is impossible because ***"the Scripture cannot be broken"*** (John 10:35). On this alone, the "unbloody sacrifice" of Christ in the Catholic Mass is invalid!

The presence of *Celiac disease* among Catholics eating the Host is another embarrassing fact proving the inner wheat content of the communion wafer has not really been changed into the flesh of Jesus Christ. Celiac disease is an autoimmune disorder of the small intestine that occurs in people who have an allergic reaction to any food product that is eaten with a gluten protein found in wheat. Common symptoms of this genetic disease are diarrhea, extreme weight loss, chronic fatigue, distended stomach, and mouth ulcers. Roman Catholic canon law requires the communion bread used in the Mass must be made out of wheat.[66] Roman Catholics who have Celiac disease endanger their health every time they eat the communion wafer of the Mass, since it is made of wheat grain that contains the gluten protein! But if transubstantiation were true and the inward substance of the bread changed into the very flesh of Jesus Christ, the presence of this harmful protein would be supernaturally removed by this transformation! The Roman Catholic could then eat the wafer without fearing the physical symptoms of Celiac disease, if this change of inward substance actually occurred. Before the medical community had diagnosed this disease, Catholics with Celiac disease were suffering these symptoms every time they ate the Eucharist.

This uncomfortable fact irrefutably verifies by repeated experience that no actual change of the inward substance of the Eucharist miraculously occurs. For if they were really eating the flesh of Christ in the Eucharist, there would have been no allergic reaction to the wheat because, though the outward appearance looked like bread, the inward substance would have been changed into Christ's flesh. To avoid this obvious embarrassment, the Congregation for the Doctrine of the Faith expeditiously convened a special council in the year 2002, to approve wafers with low gluten content. Such an admission here shows a tacit denial that

---

[66]   **Canon 924 §2** states, "The bread must be wheaten only, and recently made, so that there is no danger of corruption" (*The Code of Canon Law*, 169).

the inward substance of wheat has really been miraculously changed into the flesh of Christ as the Roman Catholic doctrine of transubstantiation demands. Science has undeniably verified that no such supernatural change of transubstantiation takes place in the Eucharist, since Catholics with Celiac disease still display the same symptoms when eating the consecrated Host after it has been allegedly changed into the flesh of Jesus Christ! Some Catholic Celiac sufferers have requested permission to use rice wafers instead, in order to avoid the painful consequences of eating a wheaten Host, which has allegedly changed its substance after transubstantiation is performed; such petitions have always been denied by Rome. As with most everything, Rome says one thing in their belief system and yet acts in the very opposite way. Transubstantiation in the Mass is a clear example of this inconsistency.

CHAPTER 11

THE MASS AND THE
SACRAMENTS, PART 2

The New Testament book of Hebrews has much to say on the nature, power, and extent of Christ's sacrificial death for mankind. The inspired author of this profoundly instructive book devotes more space to the New Covenant death of Jesus Christ than any other book or author of the New Testament canon. For argument's sake, let us assume the writer of Hebrews was a Roman Catholic and the sacrifice of the Mass was a paramount feature of the continuation and reenactment of Jesus' death on the cross, given over and over again in an "unbloody manner." If this premise were true, then here would be the best place for the writer of Hebrews to give a clear, detailed teaching and careful instructions about how, where, and in what specific way the priest is to conduct the ongoing sacrifice of Christ in the Mass.

When the reader goes to the book of Hebrews, he or she will find no such thing. If the animal sacrifices of the Old Testament required careful and scrupulous observance, as the Bible reader quickly discovers from reading extended portions of the Torah in Exodus and Leviticus, he or she would also find the same meticulous detail in much greater measure for carrying out the Mass in the New Testament, especially since the New Covenant sacrifice of Messiah is infinitely superior in scope—for it is God Himself in the flesh being sacrificed.[1] No such detail is even remotely found in the New Testament Scriptures. Indeed, what

---

[1]   A select citation culled from Exodus and Leviticus will sufficiently prove this salient point: **In Exodus chapters 25 through 30, and in Leviticus chapters 1 through 9, the LORD gave Moses meticulous, detailed instructions on how to construct the tabernacle, create priestly garments, and perform holy sacrifices. Here are some examples:**

Exodus 25:8-10: *"And let them make me a sanctuary; that I may dwell among them. According to all that I shew thee, after the pattern of the tabernacle, and the pattern of all the instruments thereof, even so shall ye make it. And they shall make an ark of shittim wood: two cubits and a half shall be the length thereof, and a cubit and a half the breadth thereof, and a cubit and a half the height thereof."*

Exodus: 26:1-2: *"Moreover thou shalt make the tabernacle with ten curtains of fine twined linen, and blue, and purple, and scarlet: with cherubims of cunning work shalt thou make them. The length of one curtain shall be*

Hebrews has to teach and reveal about the sacrifice of Jesus Christ goes in the very opposite direction of what

---

eight and twenty cubits, and the breadth of one curtain four cubits: and every one of the curtains shall have one measure."

Exodus 27:18-19: *"The length of the court shall be an hundred cubits, and the breadth fifty every where, and the height five cubits of fine twined linen, and their sockets of brass. All the vessels of the tabernacle in all the service thereof, and all the pins thereof, and all the pins of the court, shall be brass."*

Exodus 28:6-8: *"And they shall make the ephod of gold, of blue, and of purple, of scarlet, and fine twined linen, with cunning work. It shall have the two shoulder pieces thereof joined at the two edges thereof; and so it shall be joined together. And the curious girdle of the ephod, which is upon it, shall be of the same, according to the work thereof; even of gold, of blue, and purple, and scarlet, and fine twined linen."*

Exodus 29:11-12: *"And thou shalt kill the bullock before the LORD, by the door of the tabernacle of the congregation. And thou shalt take of the blood of the bullock, and put it upon the horns of the altar with thy finger, and pour all the blood beside the bottom of the altar."*

Exodus 30:1-3: *"And thou shalt make an altar to burn incense upon: of shittim wood shalt thou make it. A cubit shall be the length thereof, and a cubit the breadth thereof; foursquare shall it be: and two cubits shall be the height thereof: the horns thereof shall be of the same. And thou shalt overlay it with pure gold, the top thereof, and the sides thereof round about, and the horns thereof; and thou shalt make unto it a crown of gold round about."*

Leviticus 1:14-17: *"And if the burnt sacrifice for his offering to the LORD be of fowls, then he shall bring his offering of turtledoves, or of young pigeons. And the priest shall bring it unto the altar, and wring off his head, and burn it on the altar; and the blood thereof shall be wrung out at the side of the altar. And he shall pluck away his crop with his feathers, and cast it beside the altar on the east part, by the place of the ashes: And he shall cleave it with the wings thereof, but shall not divide it asunder: and the priest shall burn it upon the altar, upon the wood that is upon the fire: it is a burnt sacrifice, an offering made by fire, of a sweet savor unto the LORD."*

Leviticus 2:1-3: *"And when any will offer a meat offering unto the LORD, his offering shall be of fine flour; and he shall pour oil upon it, and put frankincense thereon: And he shall bring it to Aaron's sons the priests: and he shall take thereout his handful of the flour thereof, and of the oil thereof, with all the frankincense thereof; and the priest shall burn the memorial of it upon the altar, to be an offering made by fire, of a sweet savor unto the LORD: And the remnant of the meat offering shall be Aaron's and his sons': it is a thing most holy of the offerings of the LORD made by fire."*

Leviticus: 4:24-25: *"And he shall lay his hand upon the head of the goat, and kill it in the place where they kill the burnt offering before the LORD: it is a sin offering. And the priest shall take of the blood of the sin offering with his finger, and put it upon the horns of the altar of burnt offering, and shall put out his blood at the bottom of the altar of burnt offering."* (All quotations here are from the Authorized Version of the Bible). The above examples are just a few of the many detailed instructions that are contained in the books of Exodus and Leviticus. The intent of this is to show that if God required this type of attention to detail in the **Old Testament** regarding sacrifices and priestly ministry, why are there no instructions in the New Testament regarding the "on-going sacrifice of **Calvary**" as claimed to occur in the Roman Catholic Mass? The answer is obvious: Believers in the New Testament are not required to "re-present" the sacrifice of Calvary, but are called to celebrate the **Lord's Supper** in an act of remembrance. If the opposite were true—if believers were called upon to perform a sacrifice, as in the sacrifice of the Mass—the Lord surely would have laid out details similar to those in Exodus and Leviticus.

is claimed to occur in the Roman Catholic Mass. A closer examination of this point overwhelmingly proves this so. One of the great themes of Hebrews is that Jesus Christ has inaugurated the everlasting realities of the New Covenant with His "once for all" perfect sacrifice, which has permanently replaced the inferior and repetitious animal sacrifices that were characteristic of the Old Covenant. The concept and meaning of the ongoing sacrifice of the Mass is also refuted by these fundamental truths in the book of Hebrews.

A simple comparative study between what the Bible teaches in the book of Hebrews about the sacrificial death of Jesus Christ and the claims of the Mass readily demonstrates the Roman Catholic doctrine to be false, blasphemous, heretical, and therefore completely unbiblical. The Mass, examined in this light, is a practical denial of the finality and full efficacy of Christ's single atoning sacrifice He offered one time only on the cross two thousand years ago—a sacrifice that never can be continued or repeated. The Mass cannot be a legitimate propitiatory sacrifice for sin in the eyes of God because no sacrificial blood is shed. The Word of God requires the blood of the innocent victim must be shed for the remission of sin to take place. The reason for this is given in Leviticus 17:11: *"For the life of the flesh is in the blood: and I have given it to you upon the altar to make an atonement for your souls; for it is the blood that makes atonement for the soul."* This shedding of blood was a necessary requirement in both the Old Testament and the New Testament for an efficacious sacrifice to truly remit sin and give forgiveness to the sinner.

This is precisely the point the writer of Hebrews makes when discussing the sacrifice of Jesus Christ. *"And according to the law almost all things are purified with blood, and without shedding of blood there is no remission"* (Hebrews 9:22). Under the Old Covenant, forgiveness of sin could not be given until the blood of the animal acting as an innocent, substitutionary sacrifice was shed on the altar (Exodus 29:12; Leviticus 4:7, 18, 25). In the New Covenant, the blood of Christ was shed on Calvary to forgive and remit all sin for all time. The fact Catholic theology calls the Mass an "unbloody sacrifice" (see *Catechism of the Catholic Church*, page 381, **[1367]**) flies in the face of the biblical requirement and definition for what qualifies as an acceptable expiatory sacrifice as stipulated by God in the Torah.[2] The whole idea of an unbloody sacrifice is an oxymoron. The Bible says blood must be shed for the remission of sins to be made.

The concept of the "unbloody sacrifice" of the Mass is a blatant contradiction of what the New Testament teaches about the atonement of Jesus Christ, in that Scripture requires and affirms that His shed blood on the cross was the redemption price by which all sin has been expiated. On this qualified ground from Scripture, the death of Christ on the cross, where His blood was shed, and the alleged 'sacrifice' of Christ in the Mass, where no blood is shed, claim two entirely different acts and sacrifices, that based upon this antipodal difference cannot be one and the same! The shedding of blood signified that a life was given and an effective sacrifice was made. According to God's law, this had to be done if atonement was to be accepted. The Bible speaks of no "unbloody sacrifice" that can remove sin. If there is no shedding of blood, no remission of sins can be made. The Mass in the form of an "unbloody sacrifice" cannot be a legitimate sacrifice since no blood is being shed; it is therefore a blasphemous counterfeit of the true sacrifice of Jesus Christ.

After all, what is being sacrificed in an unbloody manner is not an animal, or meat but is GOD HIMSELF; and this sacrifice infinitely exceeds those previous sacrifices in the Old Testament in terms of value. The author is personally indebted to researcher David Violente for these critical observations.

2   The sole exception the Law of Moses made to this law was to accommodate the poor who could not afford to buy a lamb, goat, dove, or pigeon for sacrifice. The poor were allowed to bring one-tenth of an ephah of fine flour instead to substitute for an animal sacrifice (see Leviticus 5:11-13). This was clearly an exception and not the norm under the economy of the Old Covenant.

The performance of the Mass does not have the power to remove sin, because no blood is actually being shed! Another criterion for a genuine biblical sacrifice is: that the one being offered or sacrificed has to suffer and die in order that expiation for sin can be applied to the sinner. Forgiveness under the Old Testament was thus ratified by the death of the particular animal being sacrificed. This was demanded throughout the Torah, most especially and frequently in the book of Leviticus. Likewise in the New Testament, the only way for the New Covenant to go into effect, granting a full pardon for sins, was for Jesus, the Mediator of the New Covenant, to suffer and die. Using an analogy from the legal profession, the writer of Hebrews likens the New Covenant to a will and last testament. He points out that just as the death of the testator (the person who had the will drawn up) must occur first for the will to go into effect, so too was it necessary for the death of Jesus Christ, the author and benefactor of the New Covenant, to occur first in order for the benefits of the New Testament to be put into effect upon its beneficiaries. This was vouchsafed by the shedding of Christ's blood on the cross when He died. Christ's death therefore put into effect the spiritual benefits of the New Testament for the beneficiaries He died for. *"For when there is a testament there must also of necessity be the death of the testator. For a testament is in force after men are dead, since it has no power at all while the testator lives"* (Hebrews 9:16-17). Jesus Christ had to die and shed His blood only once to bring final salvation from sin.

Without the Messiah's death you could not have the benefits of the New Covenant (eternal life, redemption, regeneration, justification, sanctification, and glorification) put into force. *"And for this reason He is the Mediator of the new covenant, by means of death, for the redemption of the transgressions under the first covenant, that those who are called may receive the promise of the eternal inheritance"* (Hebrews 9:15). This truth, by itself, places the Roman Catholic in an insoluble dilemma from the Word of God concerning the sacrifice of the Mass. The Catholic Church teaches that Christ does not die over and over again in the sacrifice of the Mass (see "Is the Mass a True Sacrifice," *This Rock,* Volume 14, Number 7, September 2003*);* yet this sacrifice is supposedly the same one Christ offered on the cross, and therefore has the same power to remove sin. But, as we have already noted from the book of Hebrews, Christ must die first and His blood must be shed for it to be truly an efficacious sacrifice that God requires and demands as stipulated in His Word. The fact the Mass fulfills neither of these two biblical qualifications obviously shows it to be a counterfeit sacrifice that stands in diametric opposition to the Word of God.

The idea that the Mass is the continuation of Christ's sacrifice on the cross two thousand years ago goes contrary to and explicitly denies the clear, repeated assertion in the book of Hebrews declaring that Christ's sacrifice for our sins was a *one-time event*, and such an act of atonement comprised *one single* sacrifice for all time, requiring the death and the shedding of blood from that sacrifice. Since the Mass fails to qualify in these two areas, it cannot ever be considered by the Bible-believing Christian to be a propitiatory sacrifice for sin offered through the Person of Jesus Christ!

The New Testament emphatically states, eight times, that Christ's sacrifice happened only once: six times in the book of Hebrews, one time in the book of Romans, and once in 1 Peter (see Romans 6:10; Hebrews 7:27; 9:26, 28; 10:10, 12, 14; 1 Peter 3:18). One of the recurring themes in the book of Hebrews is that Jesus' sacrifice was a <u>one-time act</u> offered on Calvary. Once, one time, once for all, and one are all terms interchangeably used in Hebrews to mean Christ's sacrifice on the cross was final, unrepeatable, finished, and a unique one-time redemptive event in the history of the world. These terms of finality are *res ipsa loquitur*—that is, they speak for themselves and are straightforward enough in their unanimous meaning of unrepeated singularity and finality to require no explanation. Once means an act is done one time and no longer continued after it occurs! The idea of *once* sacrificed or *one* sacrifice naturally rules out the possibility of repetition or continuity. The Word of God unequivocally refutes the ridiculous Roman Catholic teaching that Christ's sacrifice continues or is perpetuated in the Mass. Scripture clearly teaches that Christ's sacrificial act on the cross was a *one-time* sacrifice offered up *once for all* by one single individual—the Lord Jesus Christ. This sacrifice is not offered by flawed and sinful mortal man, such as the Roman Catholic priests! By that definition and fact alone, this perfect one-time sacrifice of Christ cannot be <u>repeated,</u> <u>continued,</u> or <u>reenacted,</u> nor can it be offered up by anyone else.

Furthermore, Hebrews 7:13 states that Christ, being the sole Mediator of the New Covenant, shares the altar with no man. Messiah alone offered His once-for-all sacrifice on the altar of Calvary! ***"For the one of whom these things are spoken belonged to another tribe, <u>from which no one has ever served at the altar.</u>"*** This was written after the death of Christ, and therefore prohibits any person from serving at this sacrificial altar—not before, and certainly not after His sacrifice was made two thousand years ago. The Catholic belief that their priests officiate at the same altar as Christ is a different "Christ" and a different "sacrifice" than the one found in the Bible. The book of Hebrews repeatedly declares Christ's atoning sacrifice for sin was a **ONE-TIME EVENT!** ***"For Christ has not entered the holy places made with hands, which are copies of the true, but into heaven itself, now to appear in the presence of God for us; not that he should offer Himself often, as the high priest enters the Most Holy Place every year with blood of another—He then would have had to suffer often since the foundation of the world; but now, <u>once</u> at the end of the ages, He has appeared to put away sin by the sacrifice of Himself. And it is appointed for men to die once, but after this the judgment, so Christ was offered <u>once</u> to bear the sins of many"*** (Hebrews 9:24-28).

Notice throughout this passage the sacrificial act of Christ's death for the removal of sin is spoken of in the past tense, to obviously indicate Christ has already died *once* in the past to remove sin; and *once* this offering was accomplished He no longer offers His life for a sacrifice. The permanency of such an act leaves no room for the foreign idea of Christ's sacrifice from the cross continuing on in the Mass. The word "once" in the Greek text conveys the meaning of a one-time completed action which would negate any repeated action in the future, so much so that the following can be affirmed about the author of Hebrews: "The author does not even consider the possibility of a second sacrifice of Christ in the future; he probably expects the time of waiting to be short…the single sacrifice of Christ… avail[ed] for all sin, past as well as present and future."[3] The New Testament Greek word for "once-for-all" is *ephapax* (ἐφάπαξ) and means, in relationship to the sacrifice of Jesus Christ, a one-time completed action that does not continue.[4] This word is used in Hebrews 7:27 in conjunction with the word "offered" in the aorist tense to especially show that Christ offered (one time in the past, not many times over like in the Mass) Himself a sacrifice for sin once for all on Calvary

---

[3]   Paul Ellingworth, *The Epistle to the Hebrews* (Grand Rapids: Eerdmans, 1993), 484.

[4]   Amazingly, Roman Catholic apologist John Salza engages in outright dishonesty when he states the word "once-for-all" actually means "perpetual", not "over and done with" (*The Biblical Basis for the Catholic Faith*, 94-95). He is claiming the exact opposite of what is true here in the desperate attempt to defend the perpetuity of Christ's sacrifice in the Mass. Every time the word "once-for-all" is used in the New Testament and the book of Hebrews it means what it says—a one-time sacrifice that is not repeated or continued in any way because of its perfect accomplishment the one time it was offered—unlike the imperfect sacrifices of the Old Covenant which needed to be repeated daily and even annually on Yom Kippur, the Day of Atonement (Hebrews 10:10-14, 18). Salza, apparently, sees no problem with his cognitive dissonance here when believing in a completely contradictory meaning for the biblical phrase of "once-for-all", whose use in Scripture means one time and no more! If once-for-all did mean "perpetual", as it does in Salza's confusing and contradictory world of Catholicism, then why not equally accept the absurd paradoxes of *flaming* snow balls and *square* circles!

to show such a one-time sacrificial death was a completed event in history. The daily offerings of the Mass stand in direct opposition to the fact Christ's sacrifice was a perfect one-time offering, and by virtue of that fact, does not need to be continued or repeated on a daily basis, as the animal sacrifices offered by the priests under the Old Covenant were. ***"For such a High Priest was fitting for us, who is holy, harmless, undefiled, separate from sinners, and has become higher than the heavens; who does <u>not need daily, as those high priests, to offer up sacrifices</u>, first for His own sins and then for the people's, for this He did <u>once for all when He offered up Himself"</u>*** (Hebrews 7:26-27).

In Romans 6:11, Paul uses the word *ephapax* to reinforce the very same meaning, and to affirm that Jesus can never die again because His sacrifice for sin was done once for all when He died and rose from the dead. Therefore, this one-time offering for sin in the past completely destroys the whole Roman Catholic idea that Christ continually offers up the sacrifice of the cross each time the Mass is recited and its elements distributed. For Paul, if Jesus were to be sacrificed again, He would have to also die once more; and this would be simply impossible and unthinkable for the One who has risen from the dead and conquered death never to die again: ***"knowing that Christ, having been raised from the dead, dies no more. Death no longer has dominion over Him. For the death that He died, He died to sin once for all; but the life that He lives, He lives to God"*** (Romans 6:9-10). Author and former Roman Catholic Bill Webster points out why this is critically important when refuting the great error of the Mass, when he writes about the significance of the phrase *once for all*:

> There is an important Greek word which is used to describe both the death and sacrifice of Christ: *ephapax*, which means 'once-for-all'. In Romans 6:9-10 Paul clearly states Christ can never die again because his death was 'once-for-all'. The author of Hebrews insists that Christ cannot be sacrificed daily, that his body is offered 'once-for-all' and that because this once-for-all sacrifice has brought complete forgiveness of sin there is no longer any requirement for an offering or sacrifice for sin. All that the animal sacrifices and human priesthood signified in the Old Testament, Christ has fulfilled. Consequently, God has abolished the priesthood and all sacrifices.[5]

That Jesus is the final "once-for-all" sacrifice for sin automatically prohibits the repetitious or continuous offering of His body for sacrifice any time in the future. This truth is further reinforced by the central message in the book of Hebrews that the sacrifices of the Old Testament were imperfect and unable to permanently "put away" sin, whereas Christ's one singular sacrifice of the New Covenant was perfect and has permanently removed sin. And because this happened on the cross, once for all time, the need for a repeated sacrifice(s) has ended. Hence, in light of this, Hebrews 10:18 declares: ***"Now where there is remission of these, there is no longer an offering for sin."*** For the writer of Hebrews a repeated sacrifice denotes imperfection. The repetition of sacrifice exhibits the inherent inability to perfect those by whom it is offered. Repetition implies imperfection, and since Christ's one-time sacrifice for sins was perfect there is no more need for a repeated sacrifice. ***"By that will we have been sanctified through the offering of the body of Jesus Christ <u>once for all</u>. And every priest stands ministering daily and offering repeatedly the same sacrifices, which can never take away sins. But this Man, after he had offered <u>one sacrifice</u> for sins forever, sat down at the right***

---

[5]   William Webster, *The Church of Rome at the Bar of History*, 128.

hand of God, from that time waiting till His enemies are made His footstool. For by one offering he has perfected forever those who are being sanctified" (Hebrews 10:10-14).

Roman Catholic defenders of the Mass generally respond to this by saying the sacrifices spoken of in Hebrews apply only to the animal sacrifices of the Old Covenant and do not therefore apply to the continuity of Christ's sacrifice in the Mass. While it is true that the historic context of Hebrews does first point to the Levitical priests and the sacrifices they offered under the economy of the Old Covenant, the practical application from this can still universally apply to any sacrificial system, as in the case of "the perpetual sacrifice of the Mass," which seeks to add, continue, or repeat the final, one-time sacrifice of Jesus Christ for sins that was offered "once for all." To continue with expiatory sacrifices for sin, whether under the sacrificial system of Old Testament Judaism or Roman Catholicism, is to be guilty of a *fundamental repudiation* of the one final, unrepeatable sacrifice Jesus offered once on the cross—a sacrifice that is finished and complete! The New Testament repeatedly tells us Christ offered Himself once as the final sacrifice for all sins and, by that consummate accomplishment, further eliminated any need for repetition or continuation of His sacrifice, or any other for that matter. Rome's distortion of the Lord's Supper into a continuation of Christ's sacrifice in the Mass is not only unbiblical but also anti-biblical, and a blasphemous denial of Christ's one-time final sacrifice for sins which can never be continued or offered again. Former Roman Catholic priest Alexander Carson came to this same life-changing conclusion while reading the New Testament book of Hebrews when still a Catholic Priest performing the sacrifice of the Mass:

> On a Sunday night in July 1972, I began to read the Book of Hebrews in the New Testament. This letter exalts Jesus, His priesthood, and sacrifice over all the Old Covenant or Testament. This is some of what I read: *"Who needeth not daily, as those high priests, to offer up sacrifices, first for his own sins, and then for the people's: for this he did once, when he offered up himself"* (Hebrews 7:27). This startled me, and I began to feel very uneasy. I understood for the first time that Jesus' sacrifice was a one-time sacrificial offering at Calvary, in itself effectual to reconcile me to God and believing repentants of all ages. I saw at this time that the "Holy Sacrifice of the Mass" offered by me and thousands of other Catholic priests daily throughout the world, was a fallacy and completely irrelevant. If the "sacrifice" I daily offered as a priest was meaningless, then my "Priesthood," which existed for the purpose of offering that "sacrifice", was likewise without meaning or basis. These realizations were soon clearly confirmed as I continued to read in Hebrews Chapter 10: *"But this man (Jesus) after he had offered one sacrifice for sins for ever, sat down on the right hand of God; From henceforth expecting till his enemies be made his footstool. For by one offering he hath perfected for ever them that are sanctified"* (Hebrews 10:12-14). *"Now where remission of these is, there is no more offering for sin"* (v. 18). That night *the Roman Catholic Church lost credibility to me, for it had taught as truth what was clearly contrary to the Scriptures.* I then chose the Scriptures as my standard of truth, no longer accepting the "Magisterium" or teaching authority of the Catholic Church as my standard. In my letter of resignation from the Catholic Church and ministry, I said to the bishop that I was leaving the priesthood because *I could no longer offer the Mass, as it was contrary to the word of God and to my conscience* (Emphasis mine).[6]

---

[6]   Alexander Carson in *Far From Rome Near to God*, compiled by Richard Bennett (a former Dominican Catholic

To say the sacrifice of Christ must be continued, or repeated, is to debase it and fundamentally deny the unrepeatable nature of its perfect accomplishment. As touched on earlier, another important truth in Hebrews is that the repetition of Old Testament sacrifices admits to their imperfection (Hebrews 10:1-3). What is repeated is imperfect, and a thing's continuation implies that it is not consummated or completed. Rome's belief that the Mass is the very continuation of Christ's sacrifice on the cross deduces from the perspective of Scripture, that His sacrifice is imperfect, open-ended, and therefore not completed and finished. No other conclusion is possible. Undeterred by this biblical argument against the continuity of Christ's sacrifice in the Mass, Catholic apologists (such as Robert Sungenis) counter by confidently pointing to Hebrews 9:23 and argue that the phrase *"better sacrifices"* within the context of the New Covenant obviously points to the ongoing sacrifice of Christ continuously renewed or re-presented in the Mass. ***"Therefore it was necessary that the copies of the things in the heavens should be purified with these, but the heavenly things themselves with better sacrifices than these"*** (Hebrews 9:23).

From this, it is affirmed by the defenders of Rome, that the "better sacrifices" refer to the plural aspect of Christ's single sacrifice on the cross uniquely continued and re-presented each time the Roman Catholic priest performs the Mass on Earth, and when Christ appears before the Father in heaven.[7] Great difficulty has been attached to this seemingly strange use of the plural for the singular sacrifice of Christ. Indeed, this is the only place in the New Testament where Christ's once, final, and non-repetitive sacrifice for sins is spoken of in terms of plurality.

The use of sacrifices in Hebrews 9:23 for the single one-time sacrifice of Christ does not validate or prove the legitimacy of the Mass—for that would immediately contradict what the author of Hebrews has repeatedly asserted about the sacrificial death of Christ being a one-time event, which need not be continued or repeated over and over again, as the sacrifices of the Old Covenant were—due to their inability to fully and finally expiate sin. The *better sacrifices* of Hebrews 9:23 is a literary *enallage*, where the plural is used in exchange for the singular to indicate that the single and superlative sacrifice of Jesus Christ on the cross completes, concludes, and fulfills all the multiple sacrifices offered under the Old Covenant—which collectively prefigured the one final, perfect sacrifice of the Cross.[8] Jesus does not continue this sacrifice on Earth through the Catholic Priest, nor in heaven where He is currently seated at the right hand of God after His sacrifice for sin was already finished on Golgotha (Psalm 110:1; Hebrews 1:3; 10:12). Astute Bible commentator A.W. Pink gives an accurate meaning for the phrase "better sacrifices" used in Hebrews 9:23 when articulating that:

> It is the use of the plural number here in connection with the sacrifice of Christ which has occasioned difficulty to some. It is a figure of speech known as an "enallage," the plural being put for the singular by way of emphasis. It is so expressed because the great sacrifice not only confirmed the signification, virtue, and benefits of all others, but exceeded in dignity, design and efficacy all others.[9]

---

priest) and Martin Buckingham (Lafayette, Indiana: Associated Publishers & Authors, Inc., 1994), 199-200.

[7] Video of the debate: "Is the Roman Catholic Mass A Propitiatory Sacrifice?" conducted between James White and Robert Sungenis. This unedited debate is available from Alpha and Omega Ministries, P.O. Box 37106 Phoenix, Arizona 85069. See also Sungenis' book, *Not By Bread Alone* (Santa Barbara, California: Queenship Publishing Company, 2000), 80-93.

[8] John Owens, *Hebrews Volume 6*, 376; E.W. Bullinger, *Figures of Speech Used in the Bible*, 490

[9] A.W. Pink, *Exposition of Hebrews*, 519.

All the varied sacrifices required under the Mosaic Law were comprehended and answered in Christ's great and final sacrifice. This explanation is by no means a casuistic attempt to evade a proof text arguing in favor of the perpetual sacrifice of the Mass, but is a reasonable conclusion reached by many a careful Bible exegete and expositor well familiar with the varied figures of speech used in the Bible; Hebrews 9:23 is no exception here. Another possible meaning for why the plural "sacrifices" is used, with reference to the New Covenant sacrifice of Jesus Christ, is that the Jewish author was using what is called in Hebrew "the plural of intensity", which, by the way, is also found in Isaiah 53:9 to describe the sufferings and death of the Messiah. The Hebrew text from that passage literally reads: *"And he made his grave with the wicked, and with the rich in his deaths"*. We know that Jesus fulfilled this prophecy in His death when a wealthy member of the Sanhedrin, Joseph of Arimathea, had the Lord buried in his own tomb (Matthew 27:57-60).

The plural noun "deaths" cannot mean that Jesus died many times over, but denotes in Hebrew the extremely violent and intense nature of the death the Servant-Messiah would experience, as prophesied in Isaiah 53; this is one of the common ways the plural of intensity in Hebrew grammar functions. Plural nouns in the Hebrew Scriptures can also express majesty, supremacy, preeminent rank, magnitude, and excellence.[10] So it is more than reasonable to assume that the Jewish writer of Hebrews, familiar with this particular usage for a plural noun in Hebrew, likewise used this same concept in the Greek text of Hebrews 9:23 to describe the plurality of benefits, accomplishments, and excellencies that alone are bestowed through the preeminent sacrifice Jesus Christ offered on the cross for the ratification of the New Covenant, by which all the other sacrifices offered under the Old Covenant are replaced and subsumed. The *"better sacrifices"* of Hebrews 9:23 are not referring to the multiple times Jesus is continually offering Himself up in the sacrifice of the Mass, but speaks of the intensely bloody and violent manner Jesus offered that once, non- iterative sacrifice and the supreme place it permanently obtained above all other sacrifices for sin. The word "better" is frequently used in the epistle of Hebrews to signify the supreme and final benefits of the New Covenant that endure forever. The one final sacrifice of Christ, which is infinitely "better" than the animal sacrifices of the Old Covenant, is no different in this regard.

The Catholic Church further teaches that, while Mass is only *performed* on Earth by a priest officiating in an earthly sanctuary, it is actually, at the same time, *offered* by Jesus Christ Himself in the heavenly sanctuary. There, he appears before God to continue the same sacrifice He made on the cross until the end of time.[11] In the Mass, Christ offers His propitiatory sacrifice on the cross to the Father. To justify this position, Catholic apologists routinely point to Hebrews 9:12 to say that Jesus is presently offering His blood through the sacrifice of the Mass in an unbloody manner. Yet even in this verse, Rome's interpretation is disproven by the once-for-all nature of Christ's unrepeated sacrifice on Calvary. *"But Christ came as High Priest of the good things to come, with the greater and more perfect tabernacle not made with hands, that is not of this creation. Not with the blood of goats and calves, but with His own blood He entered the Most Holy Place once for all, having obtained eternal redemption"* (Hebrews 9:11-12).

These verses do not teach, in any conceivable way, the idea that Jesus Christ is perpetually presenting Himself for a continuation or re-presentation of His sacrifice in the presence of God every time a Catholic

---

[10] "Plural nouns are extremely common in the Hebrew Scriptures. They are not just used to denote numerical plurality, but also to emphasize a particular meaning of the noun. In Hebrew, plural nouns express majesty, rank, excellence, magnitude, and intensity. In Isa. 53:9, 'death' is a plural of intensity used by the writer to indicate that the death mentioned was a particularly violent one." D.R. McConnell, *A Different Gospel* (Peabody, Mass: Hendrickson, 1988), 128.

[11] *Catechism of the Catholic Church*, 387 **[1383]**.

priest performs the Mass. This is a wrong understanding of what the author of Hebrews was saying here. In order to ascertain the real meaning of Hebrews 9:11-12, one must determine when it was that Jesus entered into the heavenly sanctuary by the merits of His sacrificial blood.

The answer, derived from the life and ministry of Jesus, dispels any idea He is somehow continually offering himself to God in heaven as an "unbloody sacrifice" whenever the Mass is said on Earth. The event described in Hebrews 9:11-12 immediately occurred after Jesus triumphantly proclaimed that His sacrifice on the cross for sin was finished (John 19:30). He then surrendered His soul into the direct care and hands of God, His Father (Luke 23:46). Such closely connected acts are totally in keeping with the typical order of how the Old Testament priest carried the blood of sacrifice into the Holy of holies to make propitiation before God. Once this was done, the priest left the Holy place to appear before the people waiting outside and declare that God had accepted this sacrifice. Christ's formal presentation of His sacrifice was a once-for-all action that transpired in heaven the moment He dismissed His soul into the presence of God in the heavenly sanctuary. The tearing of the veil in the Temple of Jerusalem at the very moment of Jesus' sacrificial death denoted His entrance into heaven and the presence of God by way of His blood that was poured out on the cross, which now allows sinners direct access to the Father through the Messiah's reconciliatory death (Matthew 27:51; Hebrews 10:19-20). The *resurrection* and *ascension* were the proof and vindication by God that He *publicly* and *historically* accepted His Son's one-time sacrifice.

> In pouring out His blood on the cross and surrendering His spirit into the hands of the Father, Christ expiated sin, and at that very moment the veil of the temple was rent, to denote His entrance into the presence of God. No sooner had He expired, than He entered Heaven, claiming it for Himself and His seed. His resurrection testified to the fact that God *had* accepted His sacrifice, that justice had been fully satisfied, and that He was now entitled to the reward of His resurrection...That Christ did enter heaven at death is clear from His words to the thief (Luke 23:43); 2 Cor. 12:2, 4 places "paradise" in the third heaven. In every other passage where the term "once" occurs concerning the atoning work of Christ, it is always used contrastively with the *frequent* repetitions of the O.T. sacrifices: see Heb 7:27; 9:25, 26; 10:11, 12.[12]

---

[12] A.W. Pink, *Exposition of Hebrews*, 490-491. The late Pope John Paul II, in his book *Crossing the Threshold of Hope*, deliberately changes the wording of Hebrews 9:12 to make it appear that Christ continues His sacrifice in heaven through the Mass as celebrated by the Catholic priest on earth. The Pope writes: "The Church is the instrument of man's salvation. It both contains and continually draws upon the mystery of Christ's redemptive sacrifice. Through the shedding of His own blood, Jesus Christ *constantly enters* into God's sanctuary thus obtaining eternal redemption' (cf. Hebrews 9:12)." See Pope John Paul II, *Crossing the Threshold of Hope* (New York: Knopf, 1995), 146. This change of tense by the Pope flies in the face of what is originally written in Hebrews 9:12, where the word is *entered,* and is used in the aorist tense in the Greek, indicating a one-time past event. Where the Pope says, "constantly *enters*", the writer of Hebrews says Christ "*entered* the holy place once for all, having obtained eternal redemption." Notice how the Pope omits the phrase "once for all" and inserts the present tense, *enters*, in the text to replace the past accomplishment of Christ's sacrifice for a completed redemption, and give support for the ongoing practice of the Mass. The Pope is actually guilty here of altering and changing the Word of God to make it mean the exact opposite of what is claimed by the writer of Hebrews. Those who seek to alter or change the written Word of God will suffer the severest of judgments, and this includes any Pope who has done this (as demonstrated above) on so vital a subject as salvation (Deuteronomy 4:2-3; Proverbs 30:6). The reason for the deliberate alteration of Hebrews 9:12 by Pope John Paul II is to uphold the Mass, where salvation is not finished

Christ's presentation of His sacrifice before God occurred *only once,* in contrast to the repetitious sacrifices of the Old Testament, and therefore completely rules out His sacrifice being frequently continued, as is believed to occur in the Roman Catholic Mass. The recurrent use of "once" with respect to Christ's sacrifice by the writer of Hebrews inarguably proves this to be the case. No further sacrifice or presentation thereof is required. The New Testament consistently reveals throughout its pages that the present ministry of Christ, Who is seated at God's right hand, is one of *intercession, not sacrifice* (Luke 22:69; Romans 8:34; Ephesians 1:20-21; Colossians 3:1). Five times in the book of Hebrews Christ is described as "seated", or as having "sit" or "sat down" at the right hand of God (Hebrews 1:3,13; 8:1; 10:12; 12:2). His sitting down took place after His sacrifice was accomplished for the complete purification of our sins, and therefore signifies that such a sacrifice is never to be repeated or continued again! The act of sitting speaks of Christ's final accomplishment and cessation of all His sacrificial activities *"when He had by Himself purged our sins, sat down at the right hand of the Majesty on high"* (Hebrews 1:3). The fact Christ "sat down" after He accomplished His sacrifice for sin offered once, for all time, stands in stark contrast to the procedure the priests conducted when offering sacrifices under the Old Testament economy. There were no seats or chairs provided in the Tabernacle or Temple where sacrifices took place for the priests to rest and cease from sacrificial activity.

The reason for this omission was that the priest's sacrifices were to be offered over and over again. His job of sacrifice was never finished. It had to be repeated all the time and necessitated constant standing. But when the Lord Jesus offered His sacrifice of the New Covenant, He triumphantly proclaimed from the cross, *"It is finished"* (John 19:30). This statement in the Greek text (*tetelestai*) was a standard phrase used in the commercial world of the first century to mean a financial debt was "paid in full." *Tetelestai* is the perfect passive indicative of *telo* (τελω) and means "finish", "bring to an end", or to "complete" something.[13] When Jesus proclaimed *tetelestai*, and then died on the cross, He was announcing that His redemptive sacrifice for the elect was complete and that it brought an end to the whole system of sacrifices made for sin. Jesus did not say of His sacrifice on the cross, *"It shall be continued"*, as would be required if the Mass were truly continuing Jesus' sacrifice on the cross.

The death of Christ for the sacrifice and payment for our sins is a finished transaction two thousand years ago securing the redemption of lost sinners with the total expiation of all sin. To argue for the necessity of the Roman Catholic Mass today in the face of such vital truths is to deny this by adding such superfluous subtraction. To argue the Mass somehow continues Christ's one and only sacrifice on the cross given 2,000 years ago, is to say, that it is not sufficient by itself, without perpetuity or continuality, to fully redeem and

---

with the completed sacrifice of Christ's death on the cross but continues on in the Mass. "Now why would the Pope change the Scriptures? Why would he want Catholics to think the Bible teaches Christ "constantly enters into God's sanctuary thus obtaining eternal redemption" instead of what it actually teaches, that Christ "entered the holy place once for all, having obtained eternal redemption"? Because Rome holds that salvation is an ongoing process. The Church must continually represent Christ as a victim in the Sacrifice of the Mass for our salvation. With each offering, some 120 million times per year, the Church says, "the work of our redemption is continually carried out" (James G. McCarthy, *Talking with Catholic Friends and Family* (Eugene, Oregon: Harvest House, 2005), 104. This in spite of the fact that the writer of Hebrews states in the very verse in question here that salvation is an accomplished fact. Realizing that Hebrews 9:12 teaches this, the Pope simply altered the passage to fit his premise that the Mass is biblical and the sacrifice of Christ must continue on. This was no accidental slip of the pen or unintentional alteration, but a premeditated calculation to change the Word of God to agree with the unbiblical concept of the Mass.

13   J. Carl Laney, *John,* 350.

purge the lost from their sins. The work of our redemption is not being carried out in the Mass. The crucified and risen Savior completed it on the cross two thousand years ago. Jesus said it is finished! A person does not keep working on what has already been accomplished at the cross, the forgiveness of sins. On these grounds alone, the Roman Catholic Mass should be uncompromisingly rejected by the Bible-believing Christian as a dangerous and harmful counterfeit that renounces the finished work of Calvary by maintaining it must be continued, when Christ stated emphatically that *"It is finished."* To say Christ's sacrifice for sin must be continued in the Mass, is to make Him out to be a liar, and is to further disparage the authority of the Scriptures on this matter!

Defenders of Catholicism think that Christ's present intercession, as High Priest in heaven, is one of presenting His sacrifice to God every time Mass is celebrated. The mistaken assumption here is to presumptuously think that intercession is the same in Scripture as sacrifice. Intercession is part of prayer for someone, and this is what Christ is now doing in heaven for the Church! Hebrews 7:25-27 makes the distinction between intercession and sacrifice when it says that Jesus *"always lives to intercede for us"*. For this reason, the inspired writer of Hebrews then goes on to explain, this intercession does not entail sacrifice of any kind, when the one-time sacrifice of Christ put an end to the need for any daily sacrifices. *"Therefore He is able to save completely those who come to God through Him, because He always lives to intercede for them. Such a high Priest meets our need—one who is holy, blameless, pure, set apart from sinners, exalted above the heavens. Unlike the other, he does not need to offer sacrifices day after day, first for his own sins, and then for the sins of the people. He sacrificed for their sins once for all when He offered Himself"* (Hebrews 7:25-27). Intercession does not mean continuing a sacrificial act. Christians are commanded to *intercede* for the governing authorities that rule over them (1 Timothy 2:1-2). Christ's present intercession for us primarily involves sending His Holy Spirit to indwell us and the receiving and answering of our prayers which He presents before God (John 14:13-17; 16:1-10, 23-24). No sacrifice of Christ is required in this present ministry of intercession. Rome's apologists will seek to deflect such criticisms by appealing to Hebrews 13:10 where it states: *"We have an altar from which those who serve the tabernacle have no right to eat."* Catholics take hold of the word *altar* in this verse to claim this speaks of the altar where Mass is celebrated. The use of *altar* naturally lends itself to the place of sacrifice, the Roman Catholic reasons, and thus this is where Rome's priests continually offer the sacrifice of Christ in the Mass.

Such an interpretation is groundless in the face of what the writer of Hebrews has already said up to this point: that Jesus Christ in His Person, office, and sacrificial work is the fulfillment and antitype of all the types foreshadowed in the Tabernacle. The once-for-all sacrifice of Christ has put an end to the animal sacrifices of Old Testament Judaism, and those priests have no right to continue with these sacrificial offerings, seeing that they have come to an end by the cross. Hebrews 13:15 further makes it plain that the Christian's "altar" is a spiritual one, and that the "sacrifice" we are to offer is a spiritual one. The altar of Hebrews 13:10 is not the Roman Catholic altar of the Mass, but is a metonymy—a spiritual symbol for the sacrifice of Calvary where the Son of God made the supreme sacrifice for sin. It is to this historic *altar* sinners must go to receive forgiveness and pardon, and where the Christian receives continual cleansing for sin after he has believed (1 John 1:9). The author of Hebrews makes no connection between the *altar* of Hebrews 13:10 and the Eucharist of the Mass; the two are not equated here. Roman Catholic apologists simply *invent* such a connection for the justification of their ongoing sacrifice of the Mass, which is a direct insult and practical negation of the cross' finality and unrepeatable perfection. Bible commentator A.W. Pink further elaborates on the consequences of that deceitful fabrication:

"We have an altar". Most fearfully has this clause been perverted by those who have given it a meaning and put it to a use wholly foreign to the design of the Spirit in the passage from which it is taken. Deceived by the mere sound of words, the affirmation has been boldly made that not only did the Israelites in O.T. times have a literal and material altar, but that "we," Christians also "have," by Divine appointment, "an altar" that is a material one of wood and stone and hence the "altar" and "high altar" in many "protestant churches." But an altar calls for *a sacrifice*, and hence the invention of "the Mass" or "unbloody sacrifice of the flesh and blood of Christ" offered by the priests.... "We have an altar," namely, Christ, and He is the only altar God *owns*, and the only one which must be recognized by us. For almost nineteen centuries—since God employed the Romans to destroy Jerusalem—the Jews have been without an altar, and are so to this day. For Romanists to invent an altar, and make it both the foundation and centre of their entire idolatrous system, is the height of presumption, and a fearful insult to Christ and the sufficiency of His sacrifice. If those "which serve the tabernacle"—they who continued officiating in Jerusalem in the days when the apostle wrote this epistle—had "no right" to "eat" of the Christian's altar, that is enjoy and derive benefit from the person and sacrifice of Christ, then how much less have the Pope and his satellites any title to the benefits of Christ while they so wickedly usurp His place and prerogative.[14]

The whole tenor of the epistle of Hebrews is a reverberating death knell to the whole conception of the Mass. With His sacrifice complete, never to be continued or repeated again, the Lord Jesus has sat down at the right hand of God to signify His sacrificial work is finished (Hebrews 1:3; 8:1; 10:12; 12:2). The finality of Christ's sacrifice, which contradicts the idea of renewal and continuity of that sacrifice in the Mass, is further highlighted and underscored by the contrast between the continuing and repetitious sacrifices of the Old Testament and the single, one-time sacrifice of Christ in the New Testament (Hebrews 9:12). After this perfect and unrepeatable sacrifice was offered, Jesus entered into the presence of God to intercede on behalf of the redeemed—not to continue His sacrifice, but rather as One whose sacrifice was already offered and accepted (Hebrews 4:14-16). Only by death and the shedding of blood is a biblical sacrifice effective for the redemption of the sinner. Hence, Christ had to die with the shedding of His blood so that His sacrifice can expiate sin. These two qualifications rule out an unbloody sacrifice of the risen Christ in the celebration of the Mass for the simple fact that no death or shedding of blood occurs! And such a reoccurrence is impossible because the finality of "once for all" is drawn from one death, which is derived from the one time death and sacrifice Christ offered on the cross that is in no way, or by no method, repeated, continued or re-presented again! For by His *one single sacrifice*, Christ has perfected for all time those who are sanctified (Hebrews 10:12, 14). The doctrine of the Mass must be rejected on the biblical grounds that it implies an insufficiency and imperfection of Christ's death on the cross, in that it must be continued today and therefore lacks the perfect sufficiency to save the sinner by its once-for-all accomplishment two thousand years ago.[15]

Another supposed proof text from Scripture that Rome has traditionally used to support the sacrifice of the Mass is Malachi 1:11: ***"For from the rising of the sun, even to its going down, My name shall be great among the Gentiles. In every place incense shall be offered in My name, and a pure offering. For***

---

14   A.W. Pink, *Exposition of Hebrews*, 1173, 1180.
15   Richard Knolls, *Roman Catholicism: Issues & Evidences*, 125.

My name shall be great among the nations, says the Lord of hosts." The Catholic Church believes that the celebration of the Mass is the fulfillment of Malachi 1:11. For, the sacrifices of the Mass are offered "in every place" throughout the world in Catholic churches and sanctuaries and are, therefore, in perfect keeping with Malachi's prophecy.[16] The New American Bible translation (NAB) that is used by the Catholic Church translates "incense" to mean "sacrifice" to give extra credence to the doctrine of the Mass. A closer examination of the Hebrew text suggests otherwise. The Hebrew word in question derives from a verb that means, "smoke is made to raise" (*muqtar*), as in the case with incense being burned before the altar. The word clearly means "incense", not an atoning sacrifice that would be the case if Christ's sacrifice in the Mass were meant.[17] The Septuagint (the ancient Greek translation of the Old Testament), which predates the birth of Christ some 270 years, uses the word "incense"—a Hebrew word not normally used for sacrifice in the Old Testament. The "pure offering" does not necessarily mean a sacrifice for sin, but is usually associated with the voluntary grain offering that Jewish worshippers of Yahweh gave to Him out of thanksgiving and gratitude (see Leviticus 6:14-23).

These sacrifices are foretold to occur "in every place." Literally, this phrase should read "from every place", to indicate that the *Goyim* (the Gentiles) will actually come from every place and nation of the world to offer worship before the reigning Messiah in Jerusalem, during the future millennial kingdom where a rebuilt temple will stand and incense and memorial sacrifices will be offered in formal worship to the Messiah-King (Ezekiel 40-47).[18] Contextually, then, the prophecy of Malachi 1:11 is not a prophecy about the Mass, but is a prediction about what worship will be like during the time following the second coming of Christ in the millennial kingdom. The conditions of universal submission and worship of Israel's Messiah in this Messianic prophecy cannot be happening now in any way, for the simple and disturbing fact that the world does not formally acknowledge and worship Jesus Christ as the one true God, but instead curses His name and rebels against His authority everywhere one looks. The millennial/futurist interpretation and timeframe for the fulfillment of this prophecy is the most consistent and likely meaning of Malachi 1:11, and in no way accommodates or lends any legitimacy to the errant interpretation that it somehow supports the Mass.

> Instead, we must appreciate here the presence of eschatological messianic universalism, that is. The common Old Testament doctrine that the true God would one *future* day reign over all peoples, who would have no choice but to acknowledge his sovereignty…. Such a view is the consistent outlook of the prophets (Isa. 2:2-4; 11:10-12; 42:1-9; 45:1-3, 15, 22-23; Jer. 3:17; Mic. 4:1-2; Zeph. 3:8-9; Hag. 2:7; Zech. 8:20-23; 14:16; compare the oracles against foreign nations throughout the prophetic books) and is also widely represented elsewhere in Scripture (e.g., Exod 9:16; Pss. 22:28 [27]; 95-99). *Since it is entirely within the grammatical boundaries of the language of this verse to consider that it points to the future rather than to the present, there is every reason to regard the verse as a prediction rather than as a description of current events, as a future contrast to a present reality* (Emphasis mine).[19]

Catholic apologists typically point to the 'sacrifice' of bread and wine the Old Testament priest Melchizedek offered on behalf of Abraham in Genesis 14:18, as an archetype prefiguring Christ offering

---

[16]   *Catechism of the Catholic Church*, 697 **[2643]**.

[17]   Andrew E. Hill, *Malachi* (New York: Doubleday, 1998), 188.

[18]   Charles Feinberg, *The Minor Prophets* (Chicago: Moody Press, 1990), 253.

[19]   Douglas Stuart, *Malachi* in The *Minor Prophets*, Thomas Edward McComiskey, ed., (Grand Rapids, MI: Baker), 1306.

Himself in the sacrifice of the Mass: ***"Then Melchizedek king of Salem brought out bread and wine; he was the priest of God Most High."*** From this incident, the Catholic Church formally interprets the bread and wine of Melchizedek to mean the following: "This sacrifice can only refer to the proffering of His body and blood (referring to Jesus Christ) under the forms of bread and wine at the Last Supper and in the Holy Mass."[20] A closer examination of Genesis 14:17-20, however, reveals that the text in no way supports the concept of the Catholic Mass, but has an entirely different meaning. In this chapter we read that after Abraham and his army had defeated the armies of King Chedorlaomer, the Patriarch was met by Melchizedek, priest of the Most High God, who gave them food and wine. This generous act was not a sacrifice of any kind, but was done to feed the hungry and thirsty soldiers of Abraham's army. The provision of "bread and wine", though at times a luxuriant, daily provision in the Ancient Near East (Judges 19:19; Ecclesiastes 10:19; Lamentations 2:12), was also a form of refreshment for returning soldiers after war (Judges 8:5; 2 Samuel 16:1-2). Melchizedek greeted these battle-weary soldiers with food (bread) and drinks (wine) and then gave his priestly blessing over Abraham for a well-fought victory. Melchizedek is a type of Christ, not in a sacrificial manner, but by the fact that His birth and death were not recorded and thus has the appearance of being eternal. It is in this sense, Hebrews 7:3 tells us, that the earthly Melchizedek, in his dual role of both king and priest, serves as a type and prophetic foreshadow of the immortal Christ who is both King and Priest forever.

The Mass, the Eucharist, and Holy Communion are essential components in the Roman Catholic sacramental system of salvation. The Sacraments, of which these form a part, play an indispensable role in the religious life of every Roman Catholic. The Sacraments are officially seven in number: Baptism, Holy Eucharist, Confirmation, Penance, Holy Orders, Matrimony, and Anointing of the Sick. The Sacraments cover the whole life of the practicing Catholic from birth, childhood, adulthood, marriage, to death. Indeed, the Sacraments and the participation in them are deemed necessary for salvation according to the official teaching of the Roman Catholic Church. These seven sacraments, they say, were originally founded and instituted by Jesus Christ. According to the Council of Trent, anyone who should dare disagree on this, and the required number of the Sacraments, receives Rome's imperious condemnation. During the seventh session of the Council of Trent, it was decreed in Canons one and four, respectively, that:

> Canon 1. If anyone says that the sacraments of the New Law were not all instituted by our Lord Jesus Christ, or that there are no more or less than seven, namely baptism, confirmation, Eucharist, penance, extreme unction, order and matrimony, or that any one of these seven is not truly and intrinsically a sacrament, let him be anathema. Canon 4. If anyone says that the sacraments of the New Law are not necessary for salvation but are superfluous, and that without them or without the desire of them men obtain from God through faith alone the grace of justification, though all are not necessary for each one, let him be anathema.[21]

Trent's scathing anathema would include most of the non-Roman Catholic Christian world, since most of them believe there are less than seven sacraments. Such an anathema has never been formally repealed or rescinded by Rome, since it is considered an infallible pronouncement of both Pope and Council. The most recent *Catechism of the Catholic Church* issued in 1994 reaffirms the necessary belief of salvation by the

---

[20]   Ludwig Ott, *Fundamentals of Catholic Dogma*, 403; *Catechism of the Catholic Church*, 371**[1333]**, 376 **[1350]**, 429-430 **[1544]**.

[21]   *The Canons and Decrees of the Council of Trent*, 51-52.

sacraments when baldly stating: "The Church affirms that for believers the sacraments are *necessary for salvation*."[22] Furthermore, it is also claimed these seven sacraments, given by Jesus Christ, administered through the officiating priest, have the supernatural ability to confer saving grace upon the one receiving the sacrament, provided the person receiving them has the right disposition and attitude. The sacraments are not only the channels of saving grace for salvation, but also impart *sanctifying grace* and *actual grace* to keep one in an acceptable state and fellowship with God.[23] Catholic priest Lawrence Lovasik astonishingly claims that if one does not receive the seven sacraments of Rome, he or she cannot be saved or receive the grace of God giving eternal life.

> THE SEVEN SACRAMENTS ARE THE NECCESARY MEANS ESTABLISHED BY CHRIST THROUGH WHICH HIS REDEEMING, LIFE-GIVING, SANCTIFYING GRACE IS IMPARTED TO INDIVIDUALS' SOULS. You must centre your life upon the sacraments established by Christ if you want to save your soul. ... *The sacraments are the source of your real life, the divine life that will unite you with God in this world and in eternity. ... Without them your soul must die.* IF YOU DON'T RECEIVE THE SACRAMENTS AT ALL, YOU DON'T RECEIVE GRACE. If you don't receive them properly, that is, if you receive them seldom and with little devotion, you receive less grace (Emphasis mine).[24]

Catholic dogma further teaches that these seven sacraments are simply outward signs instituted by Christ to give grace.[25] As such, they impart divine grace by the dynamic principle of *ex opere operato*, which is a Latin phrase meaning, "from the work done", or from "the work having been worked." Catholicism basically defines this process, as applied to the sacraments, to mean, "that as long as the ritual was validly performed (the correct material gestures with prescribed words pronounced by a proper minister with the proper intention), the sacramental reality would be conferred on a recipient who had the intention of receiving it."[26] The infusion of *sanctifying grace* through the administration of the sacraments initially ensures the salvation of the initiate or infant at water baptism. This saving grace is continued and sustained in the life of the Catholic so long as the person does not fall into "mortal sin", which, in effect, has the power to remove such grace from the soul.[27] To continue and be sustained in this state of saving grace, one must continually partake of the Sacraments through which grace is communicated to the properly disposed recipient. The

---

[22] *Catechism of the Catholic Church*, 319 **[1129]**.

[23] Austin Flannery, *Vatican Council II*, 20. The Catholic teaching of the sacraments being "channels of grace" conveys the idea that the seven ordained sacraments act as conduits or avenues, if you will, through which God's saving grace exclusively flows from the reservoir of Christ's suffering and death. See John A. O'Brien, *The Faith of Millions*, 143-144.

[24] Lawrence Lovasik, *The Eucharist in Catholic Life*, (New York: Macmillan, 1960), 14-15. Catholic theologian Ludwig Ott further explains the dependence of the sacraments in the Catholic's life from birth to death when elaborating: "The supernatural life is generated by baptism; brought to growth by confirmation; nourished by the Eucharist; cured from the diseases of sin and from the weakness arising from Penance and Extreme Unction. By the two social sacraments of Holy Orders and Matrimony the congregation of the Church is guided, and spiritually and corporally preserved and increased" (*Fundamentals of Catholic Dogma*, 339).

[25] *The New Saint Joseph Baltimore Catechism*, 144.

[26] Thomas Bokenkotter, *Dynamic Catholicism: A Historical Catechism*, 178.

[27] *Catechism of the Catholic Church*, 539 **[2000-2004]**; 508 **[1861]**; 277 **[978]**.

impartation of *actual grace*, once a sacrament is properly received, provides temporary, supernatural intervention by God to enlighten the mind and empower the will to perform supernatural acts that eventually "lead to heaven." Actual grace, by way of the sacraments, is a "transient divine assistance" to enable the dutiful Roman Catholic to "obtain, retain, or grow in supernatural grace and the life of God."[28] In other words, the Roman Catholic sacraments provide salvation and sanctification so that one can get to heaven and achieve the optimum state of Christian spirituality in this life.

These sacraments are not automatic, but are effective, only insofar, the individual receiving them, "must cooperate with heavenly grace" through the active participation of receiving the sacraments as the channels of grace. This active cooperation between the Catholic and God results in the performance of "good works", manifested in such things as obedience to the commandments of God and the Church, and acts of charity and self-denial with the performance of moral virtue. The conclusive result, according to the belief of Roman Catholicism, earns a reward from God. These acts of cooperation collectively then merit and obtain "eternal life."[29] While nominally affirming that no one can initially earn this saving grace, Rome paradoxically teaches that once received we can merit "for ourselves and for others all the graces needed *to attain eternal life* as well as necessary temporal goods" (emphasis mine).[30] This salvation leading to eternal life can only fully be received through the sacraments that are properly given by the Roman Catholic priesthood. Moreover, Rome further claims that during the present age of the Church, Jesus Christ "manifests", "makes present", and "communicates" His work of salvation through the liturgy and the sacraments in what is termed "the sacramental economy."[31] With the passage of the conciliar decisions of the Vatican II Council, Rome has, however, slightly amended their view to now express that any rite of water baptism performed in non-Catholic churches among "separated brethren" (from Rome) brings them "into a certain, though imperfect communion with the Catholic Church."[32] This sacrament, at least, then, gives any non-Catholic the hope of salvation and at once shows how the sacrament(s) are essential and indispensable to the Catholic model of salvation.

The arbitrary designation of seven sacraments is neither found nor listed in Scripture, or, for that matter, in the theological writings of the Early Church Fathers. Indeed, even according to the *Catholic Dictionary*, such a sevenfold enumeration of the sacraments was virtually unknown for the first twelve centuries of the Christian Church![33] The word *sacrament* is not found in the New Testament when referring to water baptism, the Lord's Supper, marriage, and the anointing of the sick. Nor are these symbols and acts of expressions of faith ever said by Jesus, the Apostles or the writers of the New Testament to actually confer saving or sanctifying grace to the Christian believer. The English word "sacrament" comes from the Latin word *sacramentum*, which is a compound word derived from *sacro* and *āre*, and means to make sacred, dedicate to gods or sacred uses. In ancient times, the word referred to a pledge of money by two parties that occurred in a sacred place.

In ancient Rome various gods were invoked when swearing a solemn oath. But it is used peculiarly to denote a military oath by which soldiers bound themselves by a certain rite and prescribed words to the state and the magistrate, that they would strenuously perform what the emperor had commanded and would

---

28   John A. Hardon, *Pocket Catholic Dictionary*, 8.

29   *Catechism of the Catholic Church*, 541**[2006, 2008]**.

30   Ibid., 545 **[2027]**.

31   Ibid., 304 **[1076]**.

32   Austin Flannery, *Vatican II*, 487.

33   The enumeration of seven sacraments was unknown for "nearly twelve centuries of church history", Addis and Arnold, *Catholic Dictionary*, 734.

not desert the military standard. The post-apostolic church employed the term to signify any sacred rite or mysterious doctrine. "Hence everywhere in the [church] fathers you will find the sacrament of the Trinity, of the incarnation, and of faith, and in general the whole Christian religion comes under this name. In the Latin Vulgate, the word is used to translate the word 'mystery' (Greek for *mysterion*) in a number of passages (e.g., Eph. 1:9; 3:9; 5:32; Col. 1:27; 1 Tim. 3:16; Rev. 1:20; 17:7), *even though the word mystery is never used to describe baptism or the Lord's Supper* (Emphasis mine)."[34]

None of the leading authorities in the Church from Justin Martyr in the second century A.D. to Radbertus in the eighth century knew, taught, or arbitrarily established a sevenfold sacramental system, which at once shows that Rome's apologists cannot legitimately demonstrate that the Church Fathers individually or collectively counted seven sacraments, neither more nor less. Most of them, however, did acknowledge only Baptism and the Lord's Supper to be the proper sacraments of the New Testament Church. Catholic scholar Thomas Bokenkotter even concedes that the number of the sacraments varied from two to five, and even to thirty during the first eleven centuries of Church history![35] A careful search of the Ante-Nicene and Post-Nicene Church Fathers will show this to be an incontrovertible fact, leading the great Church historian Martin Chemnitz to rightly conclude when examining Rome's historical claim of seven sacraments:

> We have shown, however, that it is wrong for them to maintain that there are seven (neither more nor fewer) sacraments to be counted in the New Testament. *For in all of antiquity there is not found a single testimony concerning the sevenfold number of sacraments, and that neither fewer nor more are to be counted.* And those who everywhere boast about the consensus and the voice of antiquity are not able to produce one witness (Emphasis mine).[36]

Such a glaring absence in the New Testament canon, and in the first thousand years of Church history, of there being seven enumerated sacraments is a further indictment that Roman Catholicism's demand for these seven sacraments as necessary for salvation is artificial, man-made, and without proper biblical warrant. Such an historical omission is problematic for Roman Catholics who lived prior to the Council of Trent, and did not yet know that they had to receive the sevenfold sacramental system for salvation. Are we then to suppose they are all damned, in the words of Trent, since they did not know or were not aware that these seven sacraments impart salvation and must be received before death? Those who, therefore, did not receive or acknowledge these seven sacraments for the first eleven hundred years of Church history would thereby be condemned by that Council's ridiculous and revisionist doctrine, which the Catholic Church still defends and teaches to the present day! The idea of seven sacraments was first proposed and taught by twelfth-century theologian Peter Lombard (1100-1164) in his *Book of Sentences,* and then formally affirmed over three hundred years later by the Council of Florence in 1439. So that means the Savior of the world allowed a total of fourteen centuries to pass from the inception of the Christian Church before the means of salvation, via the seven sacraments, was fully revealed and available to mankind! Utter nonsense!

Catholic apologists will typically resort to a convoluted, circular reasoning here, by saying that the theologians of earlier times did not know the mind of the Church on this matter of seven sacraments, and so the different numbers of the sacraments were thus offered even though there were always seven among the lot. And since the Traditions of the Church were still developing within the mind of the Church, those who

---

34   http://www.reformedonline.com/uploads/1/5/0/3/15030584/chapter_1_sacraments.pdf.

35   Thomas Bokenkotter, *Dynamic Catholicism*, 177.

36   Martin Chemnitz, *Examination of the Council of Trent, Part 2*, 35.

lived prior to the twelfth century would have, nevertheless, agreed with the stipulation of seven sacraments had they known the mind of the Church. The absurdity of this notion is that it would be saying, in effect, that you do not believe something, but since you agree with the mind of the Church, you really believe it—even though you did not know what it is you believe.

The whole idea of *ex opere operato* is more akin to the pagan rites of alchemical magic, mysticism, and Gnosticism, than what is found in the Word of God when speaking about the purpose and function of the two sacraments or ordinances (Baptism and the Lord's Supper) of the Christian Church. Like the dynamic theory of magic, once the Catholic Priest performs the prescribed act or gesture with the proper verbal confession or incantation following it, he has the inherent power to generate and release the power of divine grace from the material objects (e.g., water, bread, wine, and anointing oil) and instruments used in the ritual performance of these sacraments. New Testament and Classical scholar Ronald Nash points out the pagan origin of Rome's unbiblical *ex opere operato* in contrast to the biblical nature of the sacraments when revealing:

> The phrase *ex opere operato* describes the pagan belief that their sacraments had the power to give the individual the benefits of immorality in a mechanical way without his undergoing any moral or spiritual transformation. This certainly was not Paul's view, either of salvation or of the operation of the Christian sacraments.

In the New Testament picture, the sacraments were:

> Considered to be primarily *dona data*, namely blessings conveyed to those who by nature were unfit to participate in the new order inaugurated by the person and work of Jesus Christ. Pagan sacraments, on the contrary, conveyed their benefits *ex opere operato*.[37]

Even Catholic supporters of the magical powers of the seven sacraments admit the unbiblical idea of *ex opere operato* comes straight from the pagan world of Gnosticism and was adopted into a spurious form of Christianity, which eventually formed into Roman Catholicism! A Roman Catholic website called *Our Lady's Warriors*, devoted to the worship of the Virgin Mary, makes the stunning admission:

> The second great component of Gnostic thought is magic, properly so called, i.e. the power *ex opere operato* of weird names, sounds, gestures, and actions, as also the mixture of elements to produce effects totally disproportionate to the cause. These magic formulae, which caused laughter and disgust to outsiders, are not a later and accidental corruption, but an essential part of Gnosticism, for they are found in all forms of Christian Gnosticism and likewise in Mandaeism. No Gnosis was essentially complete without the knowledge of the formulae, which, once pronounced, were the undoing of the higher hostile powers. . . When Gnosticism came in touch with Christianity, which must have happened almost immediately on its appearance, Gnosticism threw herself with strange rapidity into Christian forms of thought, borrowed its nomenclature, acknowledged Jesus as Saviour of the world, simulated its sacraments, pretended to be an esoteric revelation of Christ and His Apostles, flooded the world with apocryphal Gospels, and Acts, and Apocalypses, to substantiate its claim. As Christianity grew within and without the Roman Empire, Gnosticism spread

---

[37]   Ronald Nash, *Christianity and the Hellenic World*, (Grand Rapids: Zondervan, 1984), 153.

as a fungus at its root, and claimed to be the only true form of Christianity, unfit, indeed, for the vulgar crowd, but set apart for the gifted and the elect. So rank was its poisonous growth that there seemed danger of its stifling Christianity altogether, and the earliest Fathers devoted their energies to uprooting it.[38]

The fact of the matter is this: the whole sacramental salvation system of Roman Catholicism, when examined by the incisive light of Scripture, is exposed to be utterly false and strikingly absent therein, in the face of the fact that the New Testament sets forth clearly that salvation is given through faith alone as a gift of God's unmerited grace, exclusively offered through the finished work of Jesus Christ alone to those believing in Him (Ephesians 2:8-9; Titus 3:5)! The Bible further teaches that this free gift of salvation does not depend on any meritorious, good work (moral, religious, or humanitarian in nature), nor any religious ceremony, ritual, or law we must do in order to obtain, sustain, or keep God's salvation of grace, once it is given to the repentant believer in Jesus Christ. The merit system of Rome's sacramental salvation is therefore excluded by this New Testament reality (Galatians 2:16; 3:11).

The Sacraments of Rome are not necessary to receive God's saving grace! The one and only channel through which this saving grace flows is faith alone in Jesus Christ, who has *"saved us, and called us with a holy calling, not according to our works, but according to His own purpose and grace which was granted us in Christ Jesus from all eternity"* (2Timothy 1:9). The sacraments of Rome are not necessary for salvation because salvation involves a personal trust and relationship with the Savior—not an endless repetition of rituals and priest craft to earn or aquire God's favor and forgiveness. The New Testament reality of salvation exclusively involves faith in Christ alone (John 3:16; Acts 16:31), not an ongoing infusion of grace mediated through the sacraments. Indeed, one looks in vain in the pages of Holy Scripture to find seven sacraments enumerated and pointed out as necessary for the constant source and regular supply of divine grace.

God's grace, whether it be for full and final salvation or sanctification, is not communicated, channeled, or given thorough the sacraments of Rome, but comes directly through the Lord Jesus Christ to those who simply believe in Him. It comes by no other person or thing—be they priest, pope, or a sacramental rite. *"And of His fullness we have all received, and grace for grace. For the law was given through Moses, but grace and truth came through Jesus Christ"* (John 1:16-17). The grace for salvation and eternal life, which are free, comes as a direct result of believing in the Savior and the Word of Scripture given, concerning God the Father sending His Son to save the sinner. *"Most assuredly, I say to you, he who hears My word and believes in Him who sent Me has everlasting life, and shall not come into judgment, but has passed from death into life"* (John 5:24). Jesus said that belief in Him is the sole "work" from God one must do to have this eternal life. *"This is the work of God, that you believe in Him whom He sent. Most assuredly, I say to you, he who believes in Me has everlasting life"* (John 6:29, 47). Jesus never mentions the need for sacraments and the like here in the Gospel of John or anywhere else in all of the New Testament! Faith is the only requirement for salvation: the New Testament forthrightly teaches salvation is by faith in Jesus Christ alone, and not a sacramental system He supposedly grants and empowers the Roman Catholic priests to dispense!

In reality, the whole sevenfold sacramental scheme by Rome has allowed the Catholic hierarchy to establish a spiritual monopoly on the grace of God so that a lifelong control over the people may be maintained and enforced, with the intended design that obedient Catholics must come to the priests if their souls are to be redeemed by the sacraments, instead of *going directly* to Jesus Christ for the free gift of

---

[38] http://www.ourladyswarriors.org/dissent/defgnost.htm

salvation. And so Catholics fearfully remain under the spiritual bondage and control of Rome and her so-called grace-infusing sacraments from the cradle to the grave. The travesty of this is seen in the fact that the focus of salvation is taken off the Lord Jesus Christ and placed upon the priest and sacraments of Rome, resulting in dependence upon these rites and rituals instead of trusting solely in the finished work of Christ's cross, from where saving grace issues alone.

Rome's insistence upon the dependence on sacraments for salvation is a denial of the New Testament principle of *solo Christo*, which proclaims that it is in the Person and saving act of Jesus Christ *alone* that the beginning and completion of salvation is revealed, offered, and finalized—without any addition or subtraction. The justified rejection of the sacramental salvation system of Roman Catholicism by the Protestant Reformers of the sixteenth century was based squarely on this scriptural principle. Putting one's faith and hope in the grace-infusing sacraments of Rome is, essentially, a misplaced trust in the unbiblical principle of *Sola Ecclesia Romanus*—that only the Church of Rome has the means for granting and issuing salvation, through life-saving sacraments allegedly given them by Christ. And so this sadly leads the Catholic world to mistakenly and tragically rely on the sacramental rituals of Rome for eternal life, which cannot truly save in the end, when all they need to do is to put their trust in the Person of Jesus Christ alone for the salvation offered by God to all sinners, as a once-for-all free gift. Indeed, biblical apologist Ron Rhodes expresses this fundamental biblical truth quite well when he writes:

> We will look in vain for references to seven sacraments that are needed for a regular supply of grace. Indeed, God's grace is given to us not through ritualistic ceremonies, but comes straight from God to all who believe in the Person of Jesus Christ: "Therefore having been justified by faith, we have peace with God through our Lord Jesus Christ, through whom also we have obtained our introduction by faith *into this grace in which we stand*; and we exult in hope of the glory of God" (Romans 5:1-2, emphasis added).
>
> Eternal life, according to Scripture, cannot be earned. Verse after verse in Scripture indicates that eternal life is a free gift that comes as a result of believing the Savior, Jesus Christ. Jesus said: "Truly, Truly, I say to you, he who believes *has* eternal life" (John 6:47; emphasis added). "The *free gift of God* is eternal life in Jesus Christ our Lord" (Romans 6:23, emphasis added). "I will give to the one who thirsts from the spring of water of life *without cost*" (Revelation 21:6, emphasis added).
>
> Not through rites, but *through Christ alone* we have peace with God (Romans 5:1-2). Our salvation is available as a once-for-all free gift resulting from faith in Christ (Ephesians 2:8-9). As Ephesians 2:18 puts it, through Jesus we have "access in one Spirit to the Father." Indeed, "there is one God, and one mediator also between God and men, the man Christ Jesus (1 Timothy 2:5). We need no priests to mediate between us and God.[39]

Salvation is not in a sacrament but belief in Jesus Christ. For, ***"neither is there salvation in any other, for there is no other name under heaven given among men whereby we must be saved"*** (Acts 4:12). Roman Catholic sacramental salvation is contrary to the united testimony of the New Testament that believing in Jesus Christ saves sinners once—fully and finally! The Gospel of John is replete with this truth—a Gospel

---

39   Ron Rhodes, *Reasoning from the Scriptures with Catholics*, 181-182.

written specifically for the purpose that people may believe in Jesus Christ and have eternal life (John 20:31). In the first twelve chapters of John's Gospel, we witness how Jesus' ministry and teachings strongly emphasize that salvation and eternal life are received by faith in Jesus Christ alone! One of the key words in these chapters is *believe* (see John 1:12; 3:16-18, 36; 5:24; 6:28-29; 7:38-39; 8:24; 9:35-38; 11:25-26; 12:36-37). When you read all these verses, it becomes quickly evident they collectively teach that salvation is obtained by faith or belief in Jesus Christ alone. There is no mention of a sacrament being required! Sacramental salvation is contrary to the examples of salvation given in the historical narratives of the book of Acts (Acts 4:12; 10:43; 11:16-18; 14:27; 15:9-11; 16:30-31). In all these instances, the people who were saved in the early church were saved once for all by believing in Jesus alone, without any sacraments being required or needed for a process of salvation to begin!

Salvation by sacraments flies in the face of what Paul teaches in the book of Romans about salvation by God's grace alone. Salvation is the power of God for everyone who *believes* that Jesus is Lord and confesses that God has raised Him from the dead; those who exercise this kind of faith shall be saved (Romans 1:16; Romans 10:9-10). Paul makes no mention for the need of sacraments for salvation here, but rather belief in the Lord Jesus Christ alone. In fact, Paul further affirms in Romans 3:21-24; 4:4-6; 11:6 that salvation by grace cannot be mixed with works, since works prior to salvation—salvation *by* works—and works combined with salvation—salvation *with* works—are utter impossibilities. This is because grace, by definition, is unmerited favor. Therefore, if the sinner is saved by grace, performing works for it cannot save him; and if saved by works, then it cannot be by grace, or a mixture of the two, as Roman Catholic sacramental salvation teaches! Grace and works are mutually exclusive of each other when it comes to salvation. Sacramental salvation is not part of the Gospel that saves as defined in 1 Corinthians 15:1-3. In these verses, the Apostle Paul lays out the specific contents of what that saving Gospel includes; it is faith in the death, burial, and resurrection of Jesus Christ. Nothing more! Paul's definition of what the Gospel is in 1 Corinthians 15 does not mention one single sacrament of Rome!

The great theme in the book of Galatians is that salvation is given by God's grace alone to the one who believes in Christ, apart from any works of merit or religious ceremony (Galatians 2:16; 3:11). To then claim, like Rome, that a believer in Christ must receive the sacraments for saving grace, in addition to "initial" faith in Jesus, is clearly to distort the Gospel after the same manner the Judaizers in Galatia were also doing when they claimed that, while salvation was received by faith in Jesus Christ, works were also necessary to sustain and keep that salvation. When Rome talks about salvation being a combination of grace and the works of the sacraments, it is not a final and sure salvation through personal faith in Jesus Christ. It is a gospel of faith plus works proclaimed and practiced, under the guise of grace. This, by New Testament definition, is "another gospel" and a stark contradiction to what Paul taught in Galatians about salvation being a free gift of God that is received by faith alone, apart and separate from any requirement of performing religious works or keeping the law. Any gospel that mixes grace with a law of works (whether Judaism or Roman Catholicism) for salvation, justification, and sanctification is "another gospel" (2 Corinthians 11:4; Gal 1:6) and, at the same time, a perversion of the one true Gospel of grace expounded in the New Testament. While Rome has historically, albeit nominally, proclaimed that salvation is a free gift of God's grace, they, nevertheless, have practically denied such when making the sacraments necessary and determinative to salvation. Hence,

> If it is asserted that Christ's work is dependent upon the actions of humankind, and that God has simply made a way of salvation available that is still dependent upon works (whether these be penances, baptism, whatever), this is "works salvation." Works are

a necessary part of this kind of doctrine, and it is this that Protestants say is in direct contradiction to the Word of God. It is not necessary that God's grace or mercy be absent in salvation for a teaching to be branded "works-salvation." The key issue is whether those works are necessary and determinative to salvation.[40]

Good works performed by the saved Christian come after he has received salvation, and are therefore a result of salvation, for it is the power of God's Spirit which produced these works as an outflow and result of the salvation experience. Rome's sacramental salvation is totally contrary to the biblical model of salvation, which plainly states salvation is a free gift of God's grace, and that works follow as the evidence and product of that salvation (James 2:14-26). Pastor David Cloud could have not set this forth more accurately when he writes:

> This is true Bible salvation. Eternal life, forgiveness of sin, righteousness, and the Holy Spirit are received when an individual acknowledges his sinfulness, repents of his sin and trusts Jesus Christ as Lord and Savior. It is only after this that a person can do any work to please God. Works and ceremonies, such as baptism and the Lord's Supper, in themselves have nothing to do with forgiveness of sin, eternal life, the new birth, or becoming a child of God. Rather, obedience to God follows salvation as naturally as living follows one's natural birth. First we must receive new life through personal faith in Jesus Christ as Lord and Savior. Then, having life, the regenerated believer serves his Master.[41]

Thus, if the Roman Catholic person is trusting in works, merits, baptism, the Eucharist, confirmation, the last rites, sacraments, wearing the scapular, papal indulgences, and anything else besides or plus Jesus Christ, and not in Christ alone for complete and full salvation, he or she has embraced a counterfeit, unbiblical salvation that cannot save in this life or in the life to come! The New Testament teaches that there are only two rites or ordinances instituted by Christ for observance in the Church. These are baptism and the Lord's Supper. With regard to baptism, the Lord Jesus commanded the Church in the Great Commission to go into the entire world and make disciples of all nations, baptizing them in the name of the Father, Son, and Holy Spirit (Matthew 28:19). When celebrating Passover on the eve before His crucifixion, Jesus established the Lord's Supper to be celebrated in remembrance of His death for the salvation of sinners (Luke 22:19). Instead of actually conferring saving grace, these two ordinances of the Church serve as signs and symbols that bear witness to the power of that salvation already given to the believer in Christ as portrayed in His death (represented in the Lord's Supper) and resurrection (represented in water baptism). These two ordinances of the Church serve a pedagogic function in that they both enlighten and edify the born-again Christian about the spiritual realities of walking with Jesus Christ. They do not contain a magical, or mysterious, intrinsic power to automatically impart saving grace by themselves, but present fundamental truths about the person and power of the Messiah in a visual, tangible and sensible way.

Ideally, these ordinances serve as badges of a profession of faith, or signs of one already saved as a member of the Christian Church. They establish a visible difference between members of the church and the unbeliever enmeshed in the ungodly world-system. Whenever a person was saved in the New Testament,

---

[40]   James R. White, *The Roman Catholic Controversy*, 131.

[41]   David Cloud, "What the Roman Catholic Church Teaches About Salvation." See www.wayoflife.org/database/ rccandsalvation.html

baptism and the Lord's Supper were given after the person was saved, as testimony to the person coming to faith in Jesus Christ. The sacraments were thus administered after the person became Christian and not before, and therefore cannot be the efficacious cause for salvation, as the Roman Catholic scheme of the sacraments is said to create. Suffice it to say here that all the New Testament examples, particularly the ones given in the book of Acts, of individuals baptized and partaking in the Lord's Supper had already professed belief in Jesus Christ, and were saved *prior* to receiving these "sacraments". They were not eligible to receive them until the salvation experience had already occurred.

The sacraments are therefore immaterial to the impartation of salvation itself; they were not administered to produce this salvation, nor were they given concomitant to maintain or sustain that salvation. For, both the reception and maintenance of salvation, is by the immediate power of God alone in those ***"who are kept by the power of God through faith for salvation ready to be revealed in the last time"*** (1 Peter 1:5). The New Testament pattern was that these sacraments of baptism and the Lord's Supper were received *after* salvation already took place, and not *before*. In the following pages, a thorough examination of the remaining sacraments from a biblical perspective will demonstrate this fact more closely (especially with regard to baptism), as we previously did with the Lord's Supper (for the same treatment on the Lord's Supper see chapter 10 and 11, respectively).

The Sacrament of Baptism.

Water baptism in the Roman Catholic sacramental system is defined as that sacrament which produces the spiritual rebirth of the infant or adult who is undergoing baptism by the priest. It is the first of the seven sacraments in order and importance. The watery effect of Roman Catholic baptism supposedly removes the stain of original sin the sinner inherits from the guilt of Adam. It also simultaneously blots out all sins committed before baptism as well as all punishment for sin.[42] The sacrament of baptism has the inherent power to cleanse all sin from the professing person who is properly baptized by the Catholic priest.[43] The *Catechism of the Catholic Church* confesses the following belief on baptism:

> When we made our first profession of faith while receiving the holy baptism *that cleansed us*, the forgiveness we received then was so full and complete that there remained in us absolutely nothing left to efface, neither original sin nor offenses committed by our own will, nor was there left any penalty to suffer in order to expiate them.[44]

Baptism in the Catholic Church is the crucial sacrament that actually produces spiritual rebirth by which one becomes born again and cleansed from all sins as Rome interprets Jesus to mean in John 3:5, when stating one must be born of "water and the Spirit" to enter into God's kingdom. Thus, in the sacramental system of Rome, baptism is a necessary act for salvation. For, "Baptism is *necessary for the salvation of all men* because Christ has said "unless a man be born again of water and the spirit, he cannot enter into the kingdom of God"

---

[42] *Catechism of the Catholic Church*, 353 **[1263]**; John Laux, *Mass and the Sacraments*, 15; John A. O'Brien, *The Faith of Millions*, 152

[43] In cases of an emergency or an extenuating circumstance, where a priest or deacon is not present or cannot be found, Roman Catholic teaching does allow for any person, even a non-Catholic or a heretic, to perform baptism provided it is done validly in the way the Catholic Church requires.

[44] *Catechism of the Catholic Church*, 277 **[978]**.

(emphasis mine).[45] Rome has decreed baptism is not only a necessary act for salvation, but is also needed for entry into heaven. On these two points, The *Catechism of the Catholic Church* emphatically affirms,

> The Lord himself affirms that baptism is *necessary for salvation*. He also commands his disciples to proclaim the Gospel to all nations and to baptize them. Baptism is necessary for salvation for those to whom the Gospel has been proclaimed and who have had the possibility of asking for this sacrament. *The Church does not know of any means other than Baptism that assures entry into eternal beatitude*; this is why she takes care not to neglect the mission she has received from the Lord to see that all who can be baptized are "reborn of water and the Spirit." *God has bound salvation to the sacrament of Baptism, but He himself is not bound by His sacraments.*[46]

Furthermore, to reinforce such a teaching, the Council of Trent, with its many draconian decrees, forthrightly cursed anyone who would disagree with the notion that baptism is a necessity for salvation: "If anyone says baptism is optional, that is, not necessary for salvation, let him be anathema!"[47] Rome also claims such a baptism provides "initial justification" for the sinner that is continued by the ongoing infusion of grace given through the sacraments. "Justification is conferred in baptism, the sacrament of faith. It conforms us to the righteousness of God, who makes us inwardly just by the power of his mercy." So vital then is baptism to the Church of Rome that it is performed on infants as soon as possible after birth.[48] This practice is called "infant baptism." Historically, Rome has taught that if the infant dies before the rite of baptism is performed, that baby's eternal destiny hangs in doubt since it is by the waters of baptism the infant's inherited sins are washed and removed!

In the eyes of the Catholic Church, those babies who fail to get baptized "can only hope God, in His mercy, has made another way of salvation for children who have died without baptism."[49] From the Medieval period, the Catholic Church has taught that all unbaptized babies go to a place called Limbo when they die. The official teaching, as expressed in the Councils of Florence and Trent, categorically declared that the limbo of infants (*limbus infantium*) is the "permanent state of those who die without baptism, and for whom the want of baptism has not been supplied in some other way, *cannot enter heaven*" (Emphasis mine, *Pocket Catholic Dictionary*, 229). Over the years, limbo has become more and more odious to the public at large, due to the fact that such a place has negative connotations of being a place forever bereft of the beatific presence of God, reserved for practically innocent infants, who neither attained the knowledge of good or evil, nor had the volitional ability to choose to accept or reject Christ as Savior; and cannot of their own choosing be baptized or not—even though, as we shall shortly discover, baptism is not a requirement for salvation! To avoid further embarrassment over the calloused concept of Limbo, the Catholic Church has recently backed off from the harsh overtones of this doctrine in recent years and has done a complete reversal over this punitive doctrine of unbaptized infants.

On April 22, 2007, the International Theological Commission, under the supervision and support of the Vatican, released a document entitled, "The Hope of Salvation for Infants Who Die Without Being Baptized".

---

45 *The New Saint Joseph Baltimore Catechism*, 153.

46 *Catechism of the Catholic Church*, 353 **[1257]**.

47 H.J. Schroeder, *The Canons and Decrees of the Council of Trent*, 53.

48 *The New Saint Joseph Baltimore Catechism*, 154.

49 *Catechism of the Catholic Church*, 350 **[1250]**; 353 **[1261]**

The Vatican document conveniently concluded that, now, unbaptized infants who die will in fact be saved and enjoy the beatific vision."[50] In April 2007, Pope Benedict XVI authorized the official publication of this document to be considered "consonant" with the Church's teaching.[51] This in spite of the fact that for well over five hundred years, limbo was traditionally taught and defined by most officials of the Catholic Church to be a place of damnation for unbaptized infants separated from the presence of God! A good question to ask now of Rome is, what about all those millions of unbaptized babies who died before the Vatican had this change of heart? Where are they now, since, prior to this time, Catholic teaching permanently consigned these poor unwashed infants to a place of banishment from heaven and the presence of God Himself?

But when the serious student of Holy Scripture turns to its pages to learn the truth about the purpose and reason for baptism in the Christina's life, he or she will find a completely different picture than the one errantly drawn by Roman Catholicism. To familiarize oneself with the idea of New Testament baptism, you must first determine the context, meaning, and usage for the word "baptism." There are two basic words in the Greek text that are used for the act and concept of baptism: (1) bapto (βαπτω) and (2) baptizo (βαπτιξω). Both words do not always bear the same meaning. Bapto can mean the act of dipping, submersion or immersion, whereas baptizo can mean an ontological change in identity by any means—for example, when a garment is dyed and changed into another color.[52] So, when the word "baptize" or "baptism" is used in the New Testament, it usually can mean the act of immersing into water as a profession of faith in the saving death, burial, and resurrection of Jesus Christ, or the believers' union and identification with the Savior. Again, context will assuredly determine which meaning is intended, or if both are meant at the same time. Thus, it would be a mistake to automatically assume that when the word "baptism" or "baptize" is mentioned in the New Testament, water baptism must automatically be meant every time.

First and foremost, water baptism in the New Testament is not *salvific* (it does not produce salvation as Rome claims), but it is a visible, outward sign or symbol signifying the Christian's *identification* and *union* by faith with the Savior, Jesus Christ, in His death, burial, and resurrection. This is the intended meaning of what Paul says in Romans 6:3-4. ***"Do you not know that as many of us were baptized into Christ Jesus were baptized into His death? Therefore we were buried with Him through baptism into death, that just as Christ was raised from the dead by the glory of the Father, even so we also should walk in newness of life."*** Upon closer inspection of this passage, Paul means more than just a saving union with Jesus Christ, via the rite of water baptism. When the sinner comes to faith in the Lord Jesus Christ, he or she is covered and immersed under the influence of Christ's saving act for them, of which water baptism is merely an outward sign that visually pictures this prior act of trust in Jesus Christ for salvation. Hence, baptism is not the antecedent cause of salvation, as Rome falsely assumes with their doctrine of baptismal regeneration when claiming Romans 6:3-5 teaches that such a saving union is created or "brought" about through the actual rite of water baptism.[53] Paul's use of baptism in Romans 6:3-5 does not mention water anywhere, and therefore can conceivably convey the greater idea of identification with Christ in His death and resurrection for the sinner's salvation, without necessarily pointing to the idea of the rite or act of water baptism!

Also upon closer observation, the baptism of Romans 6:3-5 actually argues for the superior reality of the Holy Spirit baptism of the believer in Christ uniting and identifying the Christian with the Savior in His death, burial, and resurrection. Water baptism is not the cause or means of this spiritual identification, but is

[50] www.catholicculture.org/culture/library/view.cfm?id=7529&CFID=30313445&CFTOKEN=72202961
[51] *New York Times* (April 20, 2007) "Vatican commission: Limbo reflects 'restrictive view of salvation'"
[52] Gerhard Kittel, *Theological Dictionary of the New Testament*, Vol. 1, 529-530.
[53] *Catechism of the Catholic Church*, 179 **[628]**; 345 **[1227]**.

the outward, external symbol of the greater reality of Spirit baptism. Since the superior reality of the Holy Spirit baptism in Christ is greater than its inferior sign in water baptism, and the former is far more frequently mentioned in the New Testament canon than the latter, it would be erroneous to give precedence and greater emphasis to the inferior over the superior, and the symbol greater priority over the substance in Romans 6. Moreover, if Paul means a water and ritual baptism in Romans 6, he would have clearly included the term "water" as the descriptive modifier to baptism, which he does not. Consequently, the Apostle would have written Romans 6:3-4, if water baptism were the productive means of salvation and union with Jesus Christ, to read: *"As many of us were immersed (baptized) into water in Christ were immersed into water into His death. Therefore we are buried with Him by immersing in water into His death."* The meaning of spiritual baptism in Christ, rather than water baptism, fits the context of Romans six better, when one realizes that "a *baptism* into water (not taking out) is impossible; a *baptism* into Christ (*not taking out*) is the very demand of salvation."[54]

Baptism scholar Dr. James Dale, who wrote the definitive study on the word, use, and practice of baptism in the classical Greek, Jewish, and early Christian period of the church, gives a detailed treatment of this very issue in his four-volume work, "ΒΑΠΤΙΖΩ". In volume four, Dale gives a detailed analysis of the New Testament use of the word "baptism" and what it means most of the time, especially as it is found in relationship to its contextual meaning in Romans 6:2-4. The key to understanding the nature of what Paul means here by reference to baptism is tied up with the Greek preposition eis (εἰς), which means "into", and its integral relation to "baptism." It is simply what the text of Romans 6:3-4 says it is: a *baptism into Christ* (into His death and resurrection), not a *baptism into water*; water baptism does symbolize such a union or identification, but does not produce this saving union with Christ. To merely assume that Romans 6:3-4 is speaking about the ritual of water baptism is to force that idea into the text when it clearly speaks of a baptism into Christ, not a baptism of water! From the simple rule of letting the words of Scripture speak in context for themselves, Dale logically concludes:

> That this baptism is real, by the Spirit, and not ritual, by water, is further conclusively shown by the fact that εἰς with its regimen related to βαπτιξω declares definitely and finally the baptism and the nature of baptism.... If these things be true, then, when in the statement of any baptism εἰς and its regimen appears, the baptism is thereby definitely and absolutely declared, and all further inquiry is concluded. In the passage before us the baptism spoken of is declared to be *"into* Christ" and (its equivalent) *"into* death;" and this it must be for all with whom the word of God expressly declared is the end of all controversy. And as we can only be made partakers of the blessings which belong to Christ and his death, by the grace and power of the Holy Ghost, this baptism can only be the real and regenerative baptism of the Divine Spirit.[55]

If Paul does allude to water baptism in Romans 6, it is clear from his use of the word *"likeness"* in verse 5, that it obviously conveys a symbolic comparison between the figure and the reality it represents.[56] So with

---

[54]   James W. Dale, *Christic Baptism and Patristic Baptism* (Phillipsburg, NJ: P&R Publishing, 1995), 242.

[55]   Ibid., 244-245.

[56]   The Greek word for "likeness" (ομοίωμα) used in Romans 6:5 customarily means "a likeness but not an identity between that which is represented and reality". The word, then, is utilized in terms of a comparison with something not identical with the thing, act, or person being compared (Thomas R. Schreiner, *Romans*, 313). So too with water

this clearly in mind, Paul is basically saying baptism, by water immersion, is symbolic of that union and identification with the Lord Jesus when the Holy Spirit baptizes the believer into Christ, and the newness of life is thus received which results from regeneration through the redemptive events of the Savior's death, burial, and resurrection. If, for the sake of argument, Paul is describing water baptism in Romans 6 as a symbol representing the spiritual union of Christ and the believer, then Christ's death becomes our death and His resurrection becomes our resurrection. Water Baptism is the symbol for these spiritual realities and no more! It does serve as an effective picture of Christ's death, burial, and resurrection for us, which is the very essence of the Gospel message (1 Corinthian 15:1-4). Former Catholic, William Webster, correctly expresses what Paul probably meant in Romans six when alluding to what baptism really signifies:

> Here in Romans 6 Paul refers not just to baptism with water, but also to the spiritual reality which underlies the sign of water baptism—the identification with Christ that takes place when an individual is baptised by the Holy Spirit into Christ and the newness of life that results from regeneration. He is not merely describing water baptism here, for the whole point of this chapter is that those who are baptised, which is what water baptism signifies, are freed from sin and they walk in newness of life as slaves of righteousness (Rom. 6:4, 17-18). But again, this is not something which is effected through water baptism; it is a supernatural work of the Holy Spirit in the heart of man or woman.[57]

Paul means exactly the same thing when writing in Colossians 2:12: ***"Buried with Him in baptism, in which you also were raised with Him through faith in the working of God, who raised Him from the dead."*** Notice from this passage it is *through faith in the working of God*, not the sacrament of baptism, as Rome would have all Catholics believe, that the believer is brought into saving union with Jesus Christ, in His death and resurrection. Indeed, in many instances where baptism is mentioned in the New Testament, both the Roman Catholic Church and the Alexander Campbell movement of the 1800's, the latter of which later became the Protestant "Church of Christ" denomination, share the same conviction that such passages teach in their collective force that water baptism is essential for salvation, and in the efficacy of "baptismal regeneration"—the remission of sins being accomplished through the waters of baptism performed by an ordained minister of the Church. The deceptive doctrine of baptismal salvation originated with the Roman Catholic Church, and is now being promulgated in the same fashion with the Campbellite "Church of Christ." And both appeal to the same passages of Scripture, which they, of course, take out of context to support their unbiblical idea of baptismal regeneration.

The Catholic apologist's traditional appeal to the "water" of John 3:5 to argue that Jesus demanded water baptism for spiritual rebirth does not in any way validate Rome's sacramental understanding of baptism for salvation. A closer and thorough examination of the verse in question with other related Scripture passages makes this obvious. Yet, in fact, a great many Bible commentators and professing Christians have thought, along with the Roman Catholic Church, that Jesus' words "born of water" in John 3:5 mean baptism. They do not mean this at all! In historical context, John chapter three takes place when a prominent leader of the Pharisees—a man by the name of Nicodemus—comes to Jesus by night to inquire more about this compelling

---

baptism: It is the symbol that is likened to the believer's spiritual union with Jesus in His death and resurrection for them. Baptism is not identical or the cause of this saving union, as Rome falsely claims, but is symbolic of this redemptive reality entered into by faith.

[57] William Webster, *Salvation, the Bible, and Roman Catholicism*, 79.

Rabbi and learn if He were really the Messiah of Israel sent by God. Jesus responds in John 3:3-6 with the following teaching about the necessity of spiritual rebirth for entrance into the kingdom of God: ***"Jesus answered and said to him, 'Truly, truly, I say to you, unless one is born again, he cannot see the kingdom of God.' Nicodemus said to Him, 'How can a man be born when he is old? Can he enter a second time into his mother's womb and be born?' Jesus answered, 'Truly, truly, I say to you, unless one is born of water and the Spirit, he cannot enter the kingdom of God. That which is born of the flesh is flesh, and that which is born of the Spirit is spirit.'***

In order to find the correct meaning for "water" in John 3:5, we must go back to the phrase "born again" that Jesus used in verse 3, when telling Nicodemus that no one could "see the kingdom of God" without being "born again." The Greek word for "again" is *anothen* (ανωθεν) and can either mean "again" or "above." In John 3:4, Nicodemus evidently understood this term to mean "again", and assumed Jesus was inconceivably talking about a physical rebirth entailing the impossible task of a full-grown, adult man laboriously attempting to re-enter his mother's womb. In verse five, Jesus corrects this misunderstanding by indicating that the supernatural, spiritual rebirth He spoke of was from "above", by the regenerating power of God's Holy Spirit. This is indicated by the fact that Jesus differentiates between physical birth and spiritual rebirth as two mutually exclusive and antipodal realities, when declaring in verse six, ***"that which is born of the flesh is flesh, and that which is born of the Spirit is spirit."*** In other words, human procreation can only reproduce a physical person and no more! It cannot in any way produce a spiritual rebirth. And so, only the regenerating power of the Holy Spirit can produce and bring forth a spiritual rebirth directly from God above! The point being made here is: Like generates like, so flesh gives birth to flesh, and the Spirit gives birth to that which is spiritual. Hence, natural, human birth produces people who belong to the earthly, physical family of humankind, but not to the children of God. Only the Holy Spirit gives birth to spirit.

Spiritual rebirth, in the sense Jesus means, excludes any human, physical, and fleshly act, which also encompasses any other physical element of the earthly, like water, generating a spiritual rebirth. The use of "water" belonging to the physical realm of the material earth, where all flesh lives, must therefore have an entirely different meaning that would automatically rule out any physical or fleshly application to mankind, which the rite of Roman Catholic baptism naturally involves. This is further underscored by the fact physical birth, wind, and water, mentioned, in John three are simple analogies Jesus ingeniously borrows from the natural world to illustrate the real source (God' Spirit), power (God's Word), and effects (cleansing and transformation) of the new birth. The phrase ***"born of water and the Spirit"*** in John 3:5 is used in the same way. So in keeping with the tenor of Jesus' teaching here, nothing in this world can generate the power of spiritual rebirth; flesh can produce only flesh. Although, things in nature, like water, wind, and physical birth, are symbols to picture and describe how spiritual rebirth from God occurs, and the particular effects it has on the person who believes in Jesus Christ for salvation. Even in the beginning of John's Gospel, the reader is told that the power of spiritual rebirth, whereby the believer in Christ becomes a child of God, is not an act that can be exercised by human act of will, or physical generation, or performance of any kind—the act of sacramental baptism included— but is a supernatural, sovereign act of God alone, bestowed upon those who *believe* in Jesus Christ. Those who are baptized do so by an act of their own will. The new birth is altogether different from this; it is an act of God! Those who receive the Savior in this way experience spiritual birth. ***"But as many as received Him, to them He gave the right to become children of God, <u>to those who believe in His name: who were born, not of blood, nor of the will of the flesh, nor of the will of man, but of God"</u>*** (John 1:12-13). So then, "born of water" in John 3:5 cannot mean the physical rite of baptism as the agent for spiritual rebirth; it must mean something else.

Other uses of "water" in the Gospel of John, the New Testament, and even the Old Testament confirm this to be the case. Water in these instances is often a recurring symbol used for the Gospel of salvation or the Word of God. In John 4:10-14, Jesus told the woman of Samaria that ***"whoever drinks of the water that I shall give him shall never thirst; but the water that I shall give him shall be in him a well of water springing up into eternal life."*** That Jesus means the "water" here in a metaphorical sense, and not a literal way, is made evident when He contrasts the two in verse 13: ***"Jesus answered and said to her, 'whoever drinks of this (physical) water will thirst again.'"*** This "living water" of verse ten was not literal water, but is an emblem for the "gift of God", alluded to in the same verse, given to those who come in faith to Jesus as the Messiah and Author of eternal life. We encounter such a symbolic use of water again in John 7:37-39: ***"On the last day, that great day of the feast, Jesus stood and cried out, saying, 'If anyone thirsts, let him come to me and drink. He who believes in Me, as the Scripture has said, "out of his heart will flow rivers of living water."' But this He spoke concerning the Spirit, whom those believing in Him would receive; for the Holy Spirit was not yet given, because Jesus was not yet glorified."*** Clearly here, again, "water" is not to be understood literally, but in a figurative sense to symbolize the impartation of the Holy Spirit, where the source of eternal life and real spiritual living are found. On the eve of His crucifixion, Jesus washed all of the disciples' feet to illustrate His ability to spiritually cleanse them from sin, and His continuing ability to cleanse through the gracious work of sanctification. After Jesus completed this teaching, He then pronounced the following to the disciples in John 15:3, ***"You are already clean because of the word which I have spoken to you."***

The Apostle John repeatedly uses the metaphor of water for the cleansing power of the Word of God and the refreshing presence of the Holy Spirit in his Gospel and the book of Revelation (Rev 7:17; 21:6; 22:1, 17). Obviously, John's metaphoric use of "water" gives us sufficient justification for understanding the word "water" in John 3:5 in a figurative manner to mean the Word of God and its power to cleanse the sinner through the regenerating work of the Holy Spirit. Paul uses the same metaphorical meaning for water (tying it in with the regenerating work and power of the Holy Spirit) when writing that Jesus saves us through ***"the washing of regeneration and renewing of the Holy Spirit"*** in Titus 3:5. Water in Scripture is a metaphor for God's Word, the Bible (Psalm 119:9; John 13:5 with 15:3; Ephesians 5:26). The New Testament Church is spiritually cleansed, not by the magical waters of Roman Catholic baptism, but by the ***"washing of the water by the Word"*** according to Ephesians 5:26. This washing or cleansing by God's Word is done so that Christ Jesus ***"might present her to Himself a glorious church, not having spot or wrinkle or any such thing, but that she should be holy and without blemish"*** (Ephesians 5:27). If the rite of water baptism were the primary means of this spiritual cleansing, Paul would have certainly mentioned it in this context. He does not because it is the *Word of God* that serves as a primary cleansing agent for sin, of which baptism is an outward symbol. The two instruments, or supernatural agencies, the Lord uses to produce the spiritual rebirth are the Holy Spirit and the divine Word. Jesus was, therefore, using water as an emblem or symbol to represent the Word of God, by which people are cleansed and born again.

The Word of God brings about the reality of the new birth. James 1:18 informs us, ***"Of His own will He begat us by"*** (Baptism? No, but by) ***the Word of truth."*** Again, the Apostle Peter writes, ***"being born again, not of corruptible seed*** (or any other physical element of the earth, like water) ***but of incorruptible, through the word of God, which lives and abides forever"*** (1 Peter 1:23). Jesus' use of the term "born of water and the Spirit" from the perspective of the New Testament precisely corresponds with the two elements involved in the sinner's spiritual rebirth— (1) the Word of God, symbolized by water in this instance, and (2) the Holy Spirit. As a senior teacher of Israel, the well-trained Pharisee and practicing Jew that Nicodemus was, being quite familiar with the Old Testament, the Hebrew Scriptures, Nicodemus would probably have associated "water" and the "Spirit" with the collective promises of the Old Testament that God was going to *pour* out His Spirit upon all Israel, so that the nation would be renewed, purified, and washed from sin by the cleansing powers of the Holy Spirit, just as water removes dirt and filth. In this vein, Ezekiel 36:25-26 and Isaiah 44:3 would immediately come to Nicodemus's mind. Both passages of Scripture connect the *metaphor* of water with the Spirit together in the acts of sprinkling and pouring out to convey the combined work of cleansing from impurity and renewal from spiritual death that will occur when God's Spirit is poured out like clean and living water. *"Then I will sprinkle <u>clean water</u> on you, and you shall be clean; I will cleanse you from all your filthiness and from all your idols. I will give you a new heart and put a new spirit within you; I will take the heart of stone out of your flesh and give you a heart of flesh"* (Ezekiel 36:25-26). And in Isaiah 44:3, God says this giving of the Spirit can be compared to the generous pouring out of water to the thirsty. *"For I will <u>pour water</u> on him who is thirsty and floods on the dry ground. I will <u>pour</u> My Spirit on your descendants, and My blessing on your offspring"* (see also Isaiah 55:1; Joel 2:28-29).

That Nicodemus should have been readily familiar with the spiritually symbolic meaning of water in the Old Testament—a meaning that uniformly conveys the idea of purifying and the washing away from the pollution of sin—is further indicated by Jesus' mild censure in John 3:10 (*"Are you the teacher of Israel, and do not know these things?"*) over this Pharisee's apparent lack of knowledge concerning the renewal, rebirth, and regeneration by the Spirit of God, symbolized by the allusion to "water". This washing takes place by the power of the Spirit. From this historical context of first-century Israel in which John three unfolds, New Testament linguist scholar James Dale is right to conclude:

> This language of the Savior must, therefore, be interpreted under the ruling fact that it was addressed to *a Jew* on whom the use of ritual water was obligatory and efficacious for the removal of ceremonial impurity; and to a *Pharisee* living under the ministry of John, whose preaching, that the higher and essential purification of the Spirit was necessary in order to welcome the Messiah and to enter into the kingdom of God, he most probably rejected.[58]

Jesus, furthermore, would not have been talking about Christian baptism for the simple fact Nicodemus could not have remotely understood such a reference when such a rite or "sacrament" did not yet exist, because the Christian Church was not yet born! If Baptismal regeneration were true, as Rome believes John 3:5 teaches, then such people as Nicodemus, John the Baptist, Mary, Joseph, and all the Old Testament saints could not have been saved either, since the requirement for salvation was water baptism. Secondly, if baptism is necessary for salvation, then all the unbaptized believers in the present age are damned and eternally lost because they failed to be dipped or immersed in water. This would leave the repentant thief on the cross, who was not baptized, in a terrible situation and make the promise of Jesus to him about joining the Savior in Paradise an outright lie (Luke 23:43)! Nor was Christ teaching baptism was necessary for salvation in John 3:5, because this would contradict every passage in the Bible where the reader is plainly informed that salvation is a gift of God's unmerited grace, not of works, or anything the sinner does to earn it (e.g., John 3:16; Romans 10:9-10; Ephesians 2:8-9). This free gift is received by belief in Jesus the Messiah for salvation, even as John chapter three teaches throughout its verses (John 3:16, 18, 36)! That is exactly the point John makes in his Gospel.

---

[58] James W. Dale, *Christic Baptism and Patristic Baptism*, 364-365.

In John 3:14-18, Jesus tells us how to experience the new birth—it comes by simply *believing* in Him. Surely, if Jesus meant to teach water baptism was necessary for salvation in John 3:5, He would have baptized every single person who came to Him in faith. All four Gospel accounts record no such obvious activity. Indeed, we are told the opposite in John 4:2, that Jesus *did not baptize* any one. This would be quite disturbing and troubling, if John 3:5 had Jesus teaching water baptism was necessary for salvation, and then the very Author of that salvation, did not Himself baptize anybody! In addition to this, John uses the phrase "born of God" in his first Epistle four times (1 John 3:9; 4:7; 5:1, 4) to indicate the new birth produces a sinless nature; a godly love for fellow Christians and one's neighbor; and a supernatural ability to overcome a world hostile to Christ and His faithful followers. 1 John 5:1 declares, ***"Whoever believes that Jesus is the Christ is born of God,"***; and in that same epistle, where the new birth is frequently mentioned with attendant evidences, water baptism is never mentioned as the cause or agent that brings about this spiritual rebirth. It is *belief* in Jesus the Messiah, and nothing else, which brings about the new birth!

John 3:5 can also be legitimately translated from the Greek to read: ***"born of water, even of the Spirit."*** The Greek word kai (και) usually translated to mean "and", can also grammatically function in what Greek New Testament scholars call the "ascensive" use.[59] In this use, it does not introduce an additional element (e.g., the added necessity of water baptism for salvation), but heightens the meaning of the previous element. The ascensive use is where kai is often translated "even." If so, this would mean Jesus was teaching Nicodemus that the new birth by the Spirit of God is like water which can cleanse and renew with life the one who was once defiled and spiritually dead. If Jesus had meant the act of water baptism here, as Roman Catholicism demands, He would have said: "Unless one is born of water baptism and the Spirit, he cannot enter into the kingdom of God." He, of course, did not say this, and Rome's faulty interpretation that water baptism is meant in John 3:5 is nothing more than a clever inference from the word "water", which apparently ignores how the symbol for water, representing the Holy Spirit, is repeatedly employed throughout both the Old and New Testaments of the Bible. The following observation made about the meaning of "water" in John 3:5 rightly summarizes the probable meaning and intent that lays behind the phrase "born of water and the Spirit":

> The word "*and*" (kai) can also be translated "even." The way it is translated here is left up to the translator. In light of the rest of Scripture, it probably should be translated "even." This would mean that water with all of its cleansing power is a symbol of the Holy Spirit: "No one can enter the Kingdom of God unless he is born of water and the Spirit." A strong argument for this is in the very next verse. The new birth is spiritual, apart from any natural phenomenon. It has nothing to do with any physical substance, including water. It is not of the flesh, not any material thing. It is of the Spirit (cp. Ro. 8:11; Eph. 2:1).

> Is it possible that *water* means "baptism" here? When John was writing the gospel, he and the readers of his gospel would have known what was meant by *Christian baptism*. However, when Jesus was speaking to Nicodemus, there was no such thing as Christian baptism. It is unlikely that Jesus would say something that Nicodemus could not grasp and understand. Jesus was not one to confuse him, but to lead him to be born again. There was no way Nicodemus could be baptized in order to be born again—not then—for Christian baptism had not yet been instituted (*John: The Preacher's Outline & Sermon Bible*, 53).

---

[59]   BAGD lists for the ascensive use: Matthew 5:46; 10:30; Mark 1:27; 4:41; Luke 10:17; Acts 5:39; 22:28; 1 Corinthians 2:10; 2 Corinthians 1:8; Galatians 2:17; Ephesians 5:12

If Jesus demanded water baptism for salvation, as proposed by Rome, why then did He forgive and save people in His ministry without the requirement of baptismal regeneration? The woman of disrepute in Luke 7:47-50 was personally saved and forgiven by Jesus without going through the rite of water baptism. *"Therefore I say to you, her sins, which are many, are forgiven, for she loved much. But to whom little is forgiven, the same loves little." Then He Said to her, "Your sins are forgiven…Your faith has saved you"* (Luke 7:47-48, 50). Notice here that Jesus forgave the woman and declared she was saved by faith. Christ forgave and saved her without baptism! The blind man of Luke 18:35-43 was saved in the same way when Jesus told him, *"Receive your sight; your faith has saved you"* (Luke 18:42). The man's salvation was received immediately upon his faith in Jesus without any demand for baptism.

But in the face of this fact, Roman Catholic apologists, like John Salza, will object to this by pointing out what Jesus said in Mark 16:16:

> He commanded the apostles to baptize (see Mt 28:19). He would not have been giving His apostles instructions to perform an insignificant ritual at this climactic event. Jesus also said, "He who believes and is baptized will be saved" (Mk 16:16). Jesus is teaching that, for adults, believing is not enough to be saved. They must also be baptized.[60]

If Salza is correct here, then we have an insuperable problem and a patent contradiction in which one portion of Scripture allegedly teaches that baptism is necessary for salvation, whereas other portions solely require faith in Jesus Christ. Which is right? We know, both from logic and the basic principles of biblical hermeneutics, that contradictory propositions cannot both be true; one of them must be false. In this case, faith alone in Christ is sufficient enough for complete salvation, as opposed to water baptism being an added requirement to faith for a person to be saved. A careful consideration of Mark 16:16 will demonstrate that the former is true, and that the latter is not what the passage in question means or teaches; for if it did, then we have an obvious contradiction in God's Word! In Mark 16:16, Jesus is not teaching that those *who failed to be baptized* are condemned; but those who *do not believe*. He stated: *"He who believes and is baptized will be saved; but he who does not believe will be condemned."* A superficial reading of this verse could lead a person to hastily conclude that the unbeliever must be baptized to be saved. But another fundamental principle of Bible interpretation is that more difficult passages are cleared up and interpreted in light of easier passages to understand. Since it has been established from Scripture that salvation always occurs when a person believes in Jesus Christ prior to baptism, Mark 16:16 confirms and compliments this general truth of the New Testament.

It is clear from this verse that *unbelief* is the basis for God's condemnation, not a failure to be baptized. Jesus plainly says, *"He who does not believe will be condemned,"* not "he who does not believe *and is not baptized* will be condemned."[61] Note also that belief in Christ for salvation must come first, before baptism, in Jesus' estimation—*"He that believes and is baptized."* The earnest believer will be saved, and will consequently be baptized in obedience to Christ's command of discipleship. Hence, the rejection of the Gospel for salvation by the unbeliever would subsequently include the rejection of baptism that follows it. So then, "there was no need to say anything about baptism, since their definite refusal of the message would

---

[60]   John Salza, *The Biblical Basis for the Catholic Faith*, 70. See also the *Catechism of the Catholic Church*, 277 **[977]**, 352 **[1257]**.

[61]   Norman L. Geisler and Ron Rhodes, *Correcting the Cults* (Grand Rapids: Baker Book House, 1997), 141.

involve a refusal to make a confession of faith in baptism."[62] In other words, what is meant here is that if a person really does believe and is saved, he or she will obey God and be baptized. He or she will not, therefore, be baptized in order to be saved, but will be baptized because they are already saved by believing in Christ. Although one can be baptized and condemned because he did not believe, a person who truly believes is not condemned whether baptized or not; for, *"he who believes in Him is not condemned"* (John 3:18).

Another New Testament passage the Roman Catholic Church points to in defense of baptismal salvation is Acts 2:38. After giving his powerful sermon on the day of Pentecost, Peter is asked by the Jewish audience: *"What shall we do?"* (Acts 2:37). Peter responds by saying in verse 38: *"Repent, and let every one of you be baptized in the name of Jesus Christ for the remission of sins; and you shall receive the gift of the Holy Spirit."* A surface reading of this passage by Roman Catholic scholars is trumped about to dogmatically claim Peter (and, for that matter, the New Testament) clearly demands the act of water baptism for salvation and the removal of sin.[63] Thus, baptism *for* the remission of sin, actually means that the water of baptism has the power to wash away or fully remit one's sins. What Acts 2:38 really means hinges on the interpretation of "for", which is the Greek preposition *eis* (εἰς). The Authorized Version of Acts 2:38 is misleading and inaccurate when it translates Peter saying, *"be baptized...for the remission of sins."* Their translation of this verse does make it appear Peter is, indeed, confirming that baptism is the means or cause by which the remission of sins occurs, and baptismal regeneration is necessary for salvation.

The translators, however, failed to see or consider that *eis* (for) is used in a variety of ways in the New Testament to mean different things in the Greek. Upon closer inspection of Acts 2:38, and the events surrounding the meaning of Peter's command to be baptized, it becomes reasonably clear what this really means within the immediate context of Acts, and the broader context of the New Testament. In Greek, the preposition *eis*, "for", can be used to mean either (1) "with a view to" or (2) "because of."[64] In Matthew 3:11, John baptized sinners *because of* (*eis*) their repentance, or in Matthew 12:41 the people repented *because of* (*eis*) the preaching of Jonah. In these cases *eis* means "because of." So Acts 2:38 could have Peter saying water baptism was to be done "because of" or "in view of the fact" the people had already repented and were saved. Remission of sins, then, called for the act of baptism, resulting in a view moving toward baptism, and fostered the very occasion for it. Peter called for his audience to first repent of their unbelief and believe in Jesus is the Messiah of Israel, and then, following this, asked them to be baptized. Acts 2:38 would then more likely read: *"Repent, and let every one of you be baptized in the name of Jesus Christ because of the remission of sins."* This alternate meaning exposes the misguided interpretation of Roman Catholicism that has Peter declaring baptism is necessary for salvation to be false—especially in light of the fact the New Testament teaches everywhere that sins are forgiven as a result of faith in Christ. Baptized *for the remission of sins*

> ...does not mean in order that sins might be remitted, for everywhere in the New Testament sins are forgiven as a result of faith in Christ, not as a result of baptism. It means be baptized because of the remission of sins. The Greek preposition *eis*, for, has this meaning "because of" not only here but also in such a passage as Matthew 12:41 where the meaning can only be "they repented because of [not in order to] the preaching of Jonah." Repentance brought

---

[62]   D. Edmond Hiebert, *The Gospel of Mark* (Greenville, SC: Bob Jones University Press, 1994), 484.

[63]   Ludwig Ott, *Fundamentals of Catholic Dogma*, 355.

[64]   C.F.D. Moule, *An Idiom-Book of New Testament Greek*, 2nd ed. (Cambridge: Cambridge University Press, 1960).

the remission of sins for this Pentecostal crowd, and because of the remission of sins they were asked to be baptized.[65]

The New Testament order for salvation is repentance, faith, and then water baptism. The rite of baptism does not precede the forgiveness of sins. Indeed, salvation by faith in Jesus Christ alone, apart from baptism, existed before and after the birth of the Church on Pentecost—the precise pattern found throughout the book of Acts. The order throughout the book is hearing the Word, repentance from sin, and belief in Jesus Christ for salvation, followed after with the act of baptism (See Acts 2:41; Acts 8:12-13, 36-38; 9:18; 10:47-48; 16:14-15, 31-33; 18:8; 19:4-5). This fact of first belief, and then baptism, is what the term "Believer's Baptism" means—a term we will come back to later on and further explain relative to infant baptism. Peter taught this in Acts 10:34-43, where Cornelius and his household believed in Christ and received the Holy Spirit before they were baptized! Paul did likewise when declaring that belief in Christ is the basis for salvation with baptism following after, once the act of believing in Jesus for salvation was exercised (Acts 13:38-39; Acts 16:30-31; Romans 10:9-10; Galatians 2:16; Ephesians 2:8-9). The Apostles did not demand baptism as a prerequisite for salvation. What Peter exclaimed in Acts two was for the people to repent, and after their sins were forgiven be baptized as evidence for this. Christians are supposed to be baptized immediately after they are saved—this was the method regularly practiced in the book of Acts. People *were* saved and *then* baptized on the same day. Peter expected his audience to do the same in Acts two. To reverse this order, and make salvation dependent on baptism, as Roman Catholicism does, is to teach salvation by works, and is to introduce the foreign, heretical element of 'another gospel' into the Scripture to replace the only true Gospel of the New Testament—salvation by faith alone in Jesus Christ apart from any kind of works performed! For this reason alone,

> Acts 2:38 should not be used to teach salvation by baptism. If baptism is essential for salvation, it seems strange that Peter said nothing about baptism in his other sermons (Acts 3:12-26; 5:29-32; 10:34-43). In fact, the people in the home of Cornelius received the Holy Spirit *before they were baptized* (Acts 10:44-48)! Since believers are commanded to be baptized, it is important that we have a clean conscience by obeying (1 Peter 3:21). But we must not think that baptism is a part of salvation. If so, then nobody in Hebrews 11 was saved, because none of them was ever baptized.[66]

When Jesus commissioned the Church to preach *"repentance and remission of sins"* in Luke 24: 46-47, He did not mention the need of water baptism as the cause or necessary antecedent for remission and forgiveness of sins. Instead, He said to them, ***"Thus it is written, and thus it was necessary for the Christ to suffer and to rise from the dead the third day, and <u>that repentance and remission of sins should be preached in His name</u> to all nations, beginning at Jerusalem"*** (Luke 24:46-47). Certainly if the Roman Catholic sacramental understanding of baptism were a fundamental necessity for salvation and the forgiveness of sins, Jesus would naturally have included such an act in Luke 24:46-47, especially if baptism were a requirement for the forgiveness of sins. He simply would not have omitted it. But we learn from this passage that forgiveness is given when the believing sinner expresses repentance, which naturally involves

---

[65] Charles Ryrie, *The Acts of the Apostles* (Chicago: Moody Press, 1961), 24.

[66] Warren Wiersbe, *The Wiersbe Bible Commentary*, The New Testament (Colorado Spring: David C. Cook Publishers, 2007), 328.

faith, in the proclaimed death and resurrection of Jesus Christ. Verses 46-47 tell us that this opportunity for salvation offered among the nations is to be presented through the communication of preaching in Christ's "name" alone about His death and resurrection—the two basic elements that make up the Gospel (1Corinthians 15:1-4).

Preaching the Gospel is the established way ordained by God for salvation to be exclusively given, without any reference to water baptism, or any other of the sacraments of Rome! Receiving the Gospel is the sole means by which God has ordained the sinner to be saved. For, *"it pleased God through the foolishness of the message preached to save those who believe"* (1 Corinthians 1:21)—not those saved who are baptized! There is no mention of the sacrament of baptism being demanded or required for salvation in Luke 24:46-47 by the Lord Jesus Christ! Instead, the content of the Great Commission calls on the Church to preach that repentance and remission of sins are offered in the crucified and risen Messiah, nothing else!

Nor can the pertinacious Catholic apologist try and point to the Great Commission in Matthew 28:18-20, where baptism is specifically mentioned, as justification for baptismal salvation. Baptism there is not mentioned in connection with salvation *per se,* but is commanded in relationship to Christian discipleship—a disciple in the New Testament is one who is already saved and has committed himself to follow Jesus, beginning with baptism. Believe, and then be baptized, to become a disciple is the order the Great Commission in Matthew 28 follows. Salvation comes before baptism and Christian discipleship, and such an ordered sequence is properly reflected in the Great Commission of Matthew 28:18-20.

The baptism of the Apostle Paul in Acts 22:16 is yet another passage the Roman Catholic Church will usually point to when affirming that baptism forgives sins.[67] In Acts 22, Paul is recalling his personal encounter with and conversion to Jesus Christ on the road to Damascus before a crowd of Jews in Jerusalem outside the Temple. In verse 16, he describes what happened after he came to faith in Jesus the Messiah. After arriving into Damascus, Ananias came to Paul and related to him what Jesus told him about Paul's ministry and commission from the Lord. Paul was then commanded by the Lord through the instructions of Ananias to *"arise and be baptized, and wash away your sins, calling on the name of the Lord"* (Acts 22:16). Catholic apologist Patrick Madrid appeals to this incident in Paul's salvation as proof that the Catholic teaching on the nature of baptism and its effect of washing away sin is true.[68]

But Paul had already experienced salvation when he was personally confronted, touched, and commissioned by the risen Christ on the road to Damascus three days earlier before the events with Ananias and baptism transpired (Acts 9:9-17; 26:15-18; Galatians 1:12;). Christ already called Paul a "chosen vessel" before he was baptized (Acts 9:15). Ananias called him "brother Saul" to indicate Paul was already a brother in Christ when he met him in the house of Judas and therefore a Christian before his baptism was performed (Acts 9:10-17). Paul received and was filled with the Holy Spirit before his baptism in water. And Romans 8:9 declares that only one who is saved has the Holy Spirit. So the aforementioned facts about Paul's salvation make it quite obvious he was already saved and forgiven *before* he was baptized. The Greek text of Acts 22:16, where the verbs "be baptized" (βαπτισαι) and "wash away" (απόλουσαι) occur, are both in the aorist imperative tense and are commands, while "arise" (αναστας) and "calling" (ἐπικαλεσάμενος) are participle verbs in the aorist tense.[69] Taking all this into consideration, based on the grammatical construction of the original Greek text, the passage can literally be translated to read: *"Having arisen be baptized, and have*

---

[67]   *Catechism of the Catholic Church*, 342 **[1213]**.

[68]   Patrick Madrid, *150 Bible Verses Every Catholic Should Know* (Cincinnati: Servant Books, 2008), 77.

[69]   Nathan Han, *A Parsing Guide to the Greek New Testament*, 282.

your sins washed (by) calling on the name of the Lord." [70] It was by the calling on the name of the Lord, that Saul's sins would be washed away.

The washing away of sins is directly associated with calling on the name of the Lord, not with baptism. This is exactly what the Bible teaches (See Isaiah 55:1; Jeremiah 33:3; Joel 2:32; Acts 2:21), and it is what Paul also taught and wrote in Romans 10:13—*"Whoever calls upon the name of the Lord will be saved".* The forgiveness of sins in Paul's case, and in the case of all believers, occurs when they call upon the Lord for salvation; the waters of baptism do not magically produce it. The baptism of Paul was a figurative gesture that pictures what had occurred in his inner life—his soul and heart were transformed and the guilt of his sin washed away by the forgiveness of Christ. Baptism is "a picture of God's inner work of washing away sin" (1 Corinthians 6:11; 1 Peter 3:21).[71] In the whole Lucan *corpus*, incorporating the Gospel of Luke and the Book of Acts, Luke never mentions baptism as a necessary act for receiving the forgiveness of sins, but rather he writes that repentance and faith must come first, with the command of baptism following after salvation and forgiveness have already been received. New Testament scholar James Dunn reiterates this critical distinction when observing:

> Luke never mentions water-baptism by itself as the condition of our means to receive forgiveness; he mentions it only in connection with some other attitude (repentance— Luke 3:3; Acts 2:38) or act (calling on his name—Acts 22:16). But whereas water-baptism is never spoken of as the sole prerequisite to receiving forgiveness, Luke on a number of occasions speaks of repentance or faith as the sole prerequisite (Luke 5:20; 24:47; Acts 3:19; 5:31; 10:43; 13:38; 26:18 c.f., 4:4; 9:35, 42; 11:21; 13:48; 14:1; 16:31; 17:12, 34). In other words, water baptism is neither the sole preliminary nor in itself an essential preliminary to receiving forgiveness...Finally we may note that in Acts Christians are called 'those who call upon the name of the Lord,' but never 'the baptized.' The essential characteristic of the Christian and that which matters on the human side is in the last analysis faith and not water baptism.[72]

If, indeed, water baptism were an essential prerequisite for salvation and the cleansing away of sin, then Paul's ministry to Jew and Gentile would have been continuously punctuated with the demand and preliminary act of water baptism, from those willing to believe the Gospel for salvation, by no less than the Apostle himself. And yet, in contrast to that assumption, Paul proclaimed the following in 1 Corinthians 1:17: *"For Christ did not send me to baptize, but to preach the Gospel."* In this passage, Paul makes a clear distinction and difference between *baptism* and the *Gospel*. And since it is belief in the Gospel of Christ that saves (Acts 16:31), baptism cannot be an added necessity for salvation. Three basic things are learned from this admission which strikes at the heart of the Roman Catholic doctrine of baptismal salvation. (1) Water baptism is not considered essential for receiving salvation, but is exclusively offered through the message of the Gospel. (2) Water Baptism is a subordinate feature of the Gospel that saves. It is an important mark of discipleship, not salvation, as Paul so indicated in the practice of his ministry. Hence for Paul, baptism was *subsequent*, *consequent*, and *dependent* upon the preaching of the Gospel. Paul was saying in 1 Corinthians 1:17: "My mission is to preach the Gospel, first and foremost, not to administer the rite of water baptism."

---

[70]   William Macdonald, *Believer's Bible Commentary*, The New Testament, 469.

[71]   John Walvoord and Roy B. Zuck, *The Bible Knowledge Commentary*, The New Testament, 418.

[72]   James Dunn, *Baptism in the Holy Spirit* (Philadelphia: Westminster Press, 1970), 96-98.

Apparently, then, Paul was not following Rome's prescribed sacrament of baptism for salvation here! (3) If baptism is the doorway into salvation and entrance into the Church, as Roman Catholic theology claims, why did not Paul include it in his evangelistic ministry? The answer is that it was not part and parcel of salvation to begin with, just as the New Testament teaches throughout!

Paul's commission, given by Jesus Christ, to preach the Gospel to the Jews and mostly to the Gentile world was very specific as to purpose and function. If baptism was essential for salvation, it is quite reasonable then to assume that such an evangelistic commission would certainly include the sacrament of baptism and its mention from the outset by Jesus Christ, Who personally called and commissioned Paul to the apostolic ministry. Paul's evangelistic commission by Christ is recounted three times in the book of Acts, and not once does the Lord tell Paul to baptize converts for salvation (Acts 9:5-17; 22:6-16; 26:12-18). In Acts 26:16-18, Paul relates what the risen Christ told him concerning this evangelistic commission. It was: *"To open their eyes, in order to turn them from darkness to light, and from the power of Satan to God, that they may receive forgiveness of sins and an inheritance among those who are sanctified by faith in Me."* Observe here that the Lord Jesus makes no mention of water baptism in what Paul was to do and say. Paul was to enlighten the Jew and the Gentile with the Gospel ("to open their eyes") and bring conviction of sin through repentance and turning away from sin and satanic power, to embrace the one true God ("to turn them from darkness to light, and from the power of Satan to God").

The forgiveness of sins was to be received through faith in the Lord Jesus Christ, which would set these individuals apart as Christian believers (forgiveness of sins and an inheritance among those who are sanctified by faith in Me).[73] Here we have the whole Gospel message Paul was to preach, and yet water baptism is not mentioned at all being integral to the Gospel of salvation! From then on, Paul preached this Gospel far and wide throughout most of Europe and the Middle East without a demand for baptism as a preliminary requirement for salvation. By doing this, Paul does not neglect or diminish the responsibility or the divine institution of baptism. It should be the first act the Christian convert does immediately after his salvation. If water baptism produced salvation, it would have figured prominently in Paul's New Testament epistles. He denies it ever being a necessary act for salvation by virtue of affirming that exclusive faith in Jesus Christ is the supreme act for salvation, apart from human work or merit before and after salvation is received (Acts 13:39; 15:9; 16:31; Romans 3:21-28; 4:5; 5:1; 9:30; 10:9; Galatians 2:16; 3:11, 24; Ephesians 2:8; Philippians 3:9).

But in spite of all this, the Roman Catholic sacramentalist will confidently point to Peter's teaching about baptism in 1 Peter 3:21 giving clear proof text that water baptism does indeed save.[74] In this passage, the Apostle uses the Old Testament example of Noah and his family's escape from the worldwide flood by finding refuge in the Ark as a type of Christian baptism, which serves as the "antitype." *"When once the Divine longsuffering waited in the days of Noah, while the ark was being prepared, in which a few, that is, eight souls, were saved through water. There is also an antitype which now saves us—baptism (not the removal of the filth of the flesh, but the answer of a good conscience toward God), through the resurrection of Jesus Christ"* (1 Peter 3:20-21). Peter is simply saying that the salvation of Noah and his family from the judgment of the flood prefigures New Testament salvation, which is symbolically pictured by Christian baptism, which "now saves us" through the resurrection of Jesus Christ. Before the reader draws a hasty conclusion that Peter is teaching baptismal regeneration, he must carefully weigh the context and specific

---

73   James W. Dale, *Christic Baptism and Patristic Baptism*, 327.

74   This is exactly what Roman Catholic priest John R. Waiss does in his debate with evangelical Christian James McCarthy in the book, *Letters Between A Catholic and an Evangelical* (page 206).

use of how water baptism is being meant here. Using Noah's ark as a typological background, in which eight people were saved from the flood, Peter tells his audience in verse 21 that it is *the resurrection of Jesus Christ*, symbolized by the waters of baptism, which actually saves the Christian.

This meaning is further strengthened by the fact Peter declares baptism to be a symbol or antitype corresponding to salvation through the resurrection of Jesus Christ—of which Noah's deliverance from the flood serves as a prophetic type. The Greek word for "type", "symbol" (or "symbolize" in some English translations), and "antitype" used in 1 Peter 3:21 is *antitupos* (ἀντίτυπος). The word carries the exact idea of correspondence between the form and the reality it points to.[75] An antitype is an earthly picture or pattern of a greater spiritual reality. In this case, Peter is illustrating that the eight souls, who remained in the ark unharmed, are analogous to the Christian experience of salvation for those who are united, joined, and immersed in Jesus Christ, symbolized by the act of water baptism; an act and gesture that pictures the resurrection of Christ by which salvation and safety from judgment is experienced. In this respect, Christian baptism symbolizes the salvation of the risen Christ, which brought the faithful deliverance from God's judgment, just as in a similar fashion the Lord brought Noah deliverance by way of refuge in the ark, which in turn brought he and his family safety and salvation from the deadly waters of the flood. And so the waters of baptism are like the waters of judgment that inundated the earth in Noah's day. As Noah was saved by seeking refuge in the Ark floating safely through the waters of judgment, so, also, the Christian believer is saved today by resting in Jesus Christ, whose death, burial, and resurrection saves the believer from God's judgment as well—which is best symbolized in the act of baptism. Ergo: "We are saved by that of which baptism speaks—the death, burial and resurrection of Christ!"[76]

Further inspection of Peter's typological use of the historical event of Noah's flood in the Genesis account with Christian baptism demonstrably proves Peter is not equating baptism with salvation as one and the same thing. That Peter was not saying the act of water baptism literally saves a person is further confirmed and pointed out by his explanatory disclaimer that baptism does not effect or produce *"the removal of the filth of the flesh."* To make sure his words are not so misunderstood as to teach that the rite of water baptism magically cleanses one from the filth of outward or moral defilement, Peter is saying it is the antitypical baptism, which points to ultimate deliverance from death "through the resurrection of Jesus Christ," that saves and is therefore symbolized in the act of Christian baptism! Peter's words in verse 21 are a reminder to his readers and the church for all ages that the act of water baptism does not have the ability or spiritual power to wash away the corruptibility or moral filthiness of sinful flesh; it merely typifies, by the outward act, the inward spiritual reality baptism represents—the believer's union with Jesus in His death, burial, and resurrection, which brings escape from divine judgment, as Noah's Ark did from the deadly waters of the worldwide flood. To paraphrase what Peter is saying would go something like this: *"Antitypical baptism now saves you, not the outward rite or physical ceremony of water baptism itself, but the inward spiritual reality which baptism represents."* [77] The baptismal antitype, which now saves the New Testament believer, refers

---

[75]   BAGD, 76. Bible commentator John MacArthur's comments are helpful here: Peter used **corresponding to that**, a phrase containing the word *antitupon*, which means "copy," "counterpoint," or "figure pointing to" to make the transition to the salvation in Christ. That word yielded the theological term *antitype*, which in the New Testament describes an earthly expression of a heavenly reality—a symbol or analogy of a spiritual truth (cf. John 3:14-16; Heb. 4:1-10; 8:2, 5). The preservation in the ark of those who believed God is "analogous to the salvation believers have in Christ." John MacArthur, *The MacArthur New Testament Commentary* (Chicago: Moody Press, 2004), 217.

[76]   Hugh Pyle, *"The Truth About the Church of Christ",* 42.

[77]   Bo Reicke, *The Disobedient Spirits and Christian Baptism* (Eugene: Wipf & Stock Publishers, 2005), 149-172;

to Christian baptism by full immersion into water to be symbolically united in Christ's baptism to the cross, and our identification with Him in it, and our burial and rising from death with Him.

There are at least eight reasons from Scripture why 1 Peter 3:21 does not teach that undergoing the physical rite of water baptism saves a person: **(1)** It would mean that water instead of the shed blood of Jesus Christ on the cross was the primary agent for the cleansing and remission of sins, when Scripture so clearly teaches that the blood of Jesus Christ, alone, cleanses from all sin (Matthew 26:28; Ephesians 1:7; Hebrews 9:14; 1 Peter 1:18-19; 1 John 1:7). **(2)** Water would become the agent of salvation instead of Jesus the Savior. Christ's death for the salvation of sinners would be useless in and of itself if one could merely be baptized in water for salvation. **(3)** Baptism by itself does not produce the radical moral transformation of character that spiritual rebirth in Christ can. History has shown that people are regularly baptized all the time and continue to live in the same ungodly manner as they did before being baptized. **(4)** The complete work Christ accomplished on the cross for man's salvation was not sufficient enough if baptism had to be added later. Thus Jesus' statement ***"It is finished"*** would be untrue, leaving salvation unfinished because baptism had to be added later. **(5)** The repentant thief on the cross was not baptized, and yet Jesus assured him he would be in paradise with the Lord after death. **(6)** Jesus did not go around personally baptizing people for salvation during His ministry on Earth (John 4:1-2); rather, He called on people to repent of their sins and believe in Him for salvation (Matthew 4:17; John 3:16-18). **(7)** New Testament baptism is associated and connected to death and burial with Jesus Christ, not with spiritual birth or the impartation of eternal life (Romans 6:4; Colossians 2:12).

(8) Finally, there are around 150 passages in the New Testament which teach salvation is received by faith alone in the Lord Jesus Christ. Peter would not have gone against or contradicted this preponderant testimony by teaching water baptism was necessary for salvation in one single verse, particularly when he taught elsewhere (even in the very same epistle) that faith in Jesus Christ results in the salvation of the soul (1 Peter 1:9).

Peter states in verse twenty-one the real purpose of baptism is the "appeal" or "answer" of a good conscience toward God.[78] The believer makes the pledge that He will now follow Jesus Christ as His obedient disciple united with the Lord in His death, burial, and resurrection. Baptism is an appropriate symbol of this reality for a public confession and act upon the one baptized openly declaring he or she now trusts in Jesus Christ for the forgiveness of sins with a pledge or an appeal to have a clear conscience now, cleansed from all guilt, condemnation, and accusation, that provides a good answer before God. The good conscience, which comes with baptism, is achieved when the believer is obedient to the command of Christ to be baptized (Matthew 28:18-20); any Christian who deliberately refuses to be baptized after faith in Jesus Christ is expressed is living in deliberate disobedience to the Lord's command. To have a good conscience would entail the person to then be baptized.

The obedient response of baptism is for the obtainment of this good conscience before God; it does not remove the stain of original sin as Roman Catholic teaching claims. But this baptism shows to all, the believer's desire to repent and believe in the death and resurrection of Jesus Christ for salvation, and from that faith, unite with Him in a new life of obedience and fellowship, starting with the public act of water baptism. The act of baptism is the believer's symbolic answer of "yes" to God's offer of salvation exclusively given

---

Wayne Grudem *1Peter* in the Tyndale New Testament Commentaries (Grand Rapids: Inter-Varsity Press, 1989), 163.

[78] The Greek noun "pledge" (eperotema) occurs only once here in the New Testament and carries with it the idea or meaning of a question given in a legal proceeding with the anticipation of an answer given by the one queried. See D. Edmond Hiebert *1 Peter* (Winona Lake, Indiana: BHM Books, 2002), 249

and made effective by the resurrection of Jesus Christ. Water baptism is simply the consequence of saying, "yes" to that salvation. Both the King James and the New King James translations accurately preserve this meaning of pledge, or the answer of baptism to the believer's reception of Christ's salvation for him or her. The overriding meaning of what 1 Peter 3:20-21 is saying does not lend any credence to the Roman Catholic belief that water baptism saves. On the contrary, it promotes the very opposite:

> Peter's categorical assertion that baptism "saves you" has been misinterpreted; but the statement is not unparalleled in the New Testament (cf. Rom. 6:3-5; Gal. 3:27; Col. 2:12). The material waters of Christian baptism are not the outward instrument that produces an inner spiritual regeneration; baptism is an act of obedience that bears witness to the inner union by faith with Christ the Savior. Peter, like Paul, assumed that in true Christian baptism, the outward sign and inner reality are kept together; the rite without the inner reality is useless, just as the dollar sign on a check is valueless apart from the monetary reality in the bank...In view of that question-and-answer usage of the noun, the translation in the KJV, "the answer of a good conscience toward God," is quite acceptable. That translation makes it clear that the believer's acceptance of baptism is his answer to the Spirit's questions that stir his conscience and result in his conversion. His answer is given out of a good conscience, a conscience purified by the blood of Christ and assured of personal acceptance with God. His baptism is his answer to the work of God in his heart, bearing witness before the world to what God has done for him.[79]

Infant baptism is nowhere mentioned or practiced in Scripture. A thorough review of the relevant New Testament passages will at once reveal infant baptism was not practiced or taught by Jesus, the Apostles, or the early church of the first century. Evidence for it is simply not found! Not once did Jesus and the Apostles demand or practice infant baptism, just as Bible teacher John MacArthur correctly points out:

> Infant baptism is not in Scripture, and against that statement, there is no evidence—there is no refuting of that statement. Scripture nowhere advocates infant baptism. It nowhere mentions infant baptism. It doesn't exist in the Bible; there is no example of it, there is no comment on it, it's not there. It is therefore impossible to prove that infant baptism is valid, from the New Testament. It's not possible to support it from the New Testament or for that matter, from the Old Testament.[80]

Nonetheless, the defenders of Rome ignore this indisputable fact and try to justify the practice of infant baptism on the basis of Scripture by way of inference, invention, or vague implication.[81] The incident in the

---

[79] Ibid., 248, 250.

[80] John MacArthur, "A Scriptural Critique of Infant Baptism," at http://www.gty.org/products/audio-lessons/80-194, 3. It should also be pointed out that several Protestant denominations also practice infant baptism. The Eastern Orthodox, Lutheran, Anglican, Methodist, Reformed, and Presbyterian Churches include belief in infant baptism in their creedal statements and confessions of faith.

[81] Even Catholic priest and apologist John A. O'Brien, while attempting to defend the practice of infant baptism, candidly admits, "There is no explicit mention of the baptizing of infants in the New Testament" (John A. O'Brien, *The Faith of Millions*, 155).

Synoptic Gospels, recorded in Luke 18:15-17; Matthew 19:13-15; and Mark 10:13-16, where Jesus bids the infant children to come to Him, is considered by Catholic theologians to be a proof text for Jesus' endorsement of infant baptism. Of the three citations, the one in Luke 18 is preferred since the word "infants" is used for the children who were bidden to come at the request of Jesus. *"Then they also brought infants to Him that He might touch them; but when the disciples saw it, they rebuked them. But Jesus called them to Him and said, "Let the little children come to Me, and do not forbid them; for of such is the kingdom of God. Assuredly, I say to you, whoever does not receive the kingdom of God as little child will by no means enter it"* (Luke 18:15-17). After pejoratively chastising "Fundamentalists" for dismissing infant baptism on the grounds of misunderstanding such Catholic alleged "proof" texts like Luke 18:15-16, the website answer forum, *Catholic Answers*, presumes to take Luke 18:15-16 to mean Jesus was endorsing an infant's entrance into the Kingdom of God by way of baptism.

> Now Fundamentalists say this event does not apply to young children or infants since it implies the children to which Christ was referring were able to approach him on their own. (Older translations have, "suffer the little children to come unto me," which seems to suggest they could do so under their own power.) Fundamentalists conclude the passage refers only to children old enough to walk, and presumably, capable of sinning. But the text in Luke 18:15 says, "Now they were bringing even *infants* to him"…The Greek word *brepha* means "infants"—children who are quite unable to approach Christ on their own and who could not possibly make a conscious decision to "accept Jesus as their personal Lord and Savior." And that is precisely the problem. Fundamentalists refuse to permit the baptism of infants and young children, because they are not yet capable of making such a conscious act. But notice what Jesus said: "to such as these [referring to the infants and children who had been brought to him by their mothers] belongs the kingdom of heaven." The Lord did not require them to make a conscious decision. He says that they are precisely the kind of people who can come to him and receive the kingdom. So on what basis, Fundamentalists should be asked, can infants and young children be excluded from the sacrament of baptism? If Jesus said, "let them come unto me," who are we to say "no," and withhold baptism from them?[82]

The problem and issue here is not whether infants are able to come to Christ or not, based upon their inability to make a decision for receiving the "sacrament" of baptism, but, rather, is baptism even mentioned at all in Luke 18:15-16? Catholics are simply *begging the question* here when they assume the passage under debate is explicitly or inferentially talking about infant baptism, when in fact it is completely absent from the text! The issue here is a child's unhindered accessibility to Jesus for His blessing and prayer. The mothers of the infant children came to Jesus for this express purpose, and He did exactly that, and no more. The same accounts given in Matthew 19:15 and Mark 10:16, also, clearly indicate the same meaning. *"And He took them up in His arms, laid hands on them, and blessed them"* (Mark 10:16). The Jewish parents were simply bringing their infants for Jesus so that He could *"lay hands on them and pray"* (Matthew 19:13). No response, or request, for baptism was made or given by either party (the parents or Jesus).

---

[82]   See http://www.catholic.com/library/Infant_Baptism.asp "Infant Baptism", 1-2.

Additionally, the claim that the Greek word brephos (βρέφος) exclusively means infants is contradicted by its use in 2 Timothy 3:15, where it refers to children beyond the toddler stage who are old enough to intelligently hear the Holy Scriptures read to them for their understanding—as was the case with Timothy, when his mother taught him the Scriptures at a young age.[83] But whether the children brought to Jesus were infants or older children beyond the infant stage, or a combination of both, in Luke 18:15-17 is immaterial, because the subject of the passage deals with the blessing and prayer of Jesus said over children. It, furthermore, in no way deals with the subject of infant baptism for salvation by the very fact this rite is not even remotely addressed or named in the passage. And that is all there is to that! Nor did these infants need to be baptized, because Jesus was to go on and say that they are of, or in, the kingdom of heaven. No mention of their being consigned to an imaginary "limbo" is conjured up here by Him for these little ones!

Another of Rome's unwarranted inferences for infant baptism is supposedly deduced from the words of Peter spoken in Acts 2:39: ***"For the promise (of salvation and the outpouring of God's Spirit) is to you and your children, and to all who are afar off, as many as the Lord our God will call."*** It is claimed here when Peter offered salvation through the act of baptism that such a promise is for infants, since the Greek word for children (*teknon*) can include infants; hence infants should be baptized for salvation.[84] Though the Greek word for children can mean literal offspring, it can also take on a meaning for posterity or descendants down through the generations. The meaning here is not babies but descendants, which is found elsewhere in the book of Acts and the New Testament (Acts 13:33; Galatians 4:28; 1 John 2:18, 28). What Peter meant by *children* was that the promise of the Spirit and salvation in Christ were not only good for the men standing before Peter on the day of Pentecost, but also for their descendants and posterity to come after them, near and far! This meaning is made all the more evident when Peter tells the same crowd in Jerusalem to repent and seek to be baptized. Such requests for a decision followed by an act of commitment to discipleship would surely exclude those, like infants, who are too young and therefore incapable of being able to understand and make a conscious decision to be baptized out of repentance and faith. Certainly, there could have been children on that day old enough to understand what Peter was saying who were eligible for salvation once they deliberately and consciously believed in Jesus Christ for salvation.

For it would be highly unlikely that the three thousand present on that day were childless adults! Once repentance and faith were shown, they too could be baptized along with their believing parents. Indeed, this is further reinforced by what transpires in Acts 2:41-42, where we are told that the audience, consisting of the three thousand souls, ***"gladly received the word"***, were then baptized, and steadfastly continued in the doctrine of the apostles ***"fellowshipping, in the breaking of bread, and in prayer."*** All of those acts necessitate an ability to understand the Gospel Peter preaches and the conviction and will power to act in faith—something infants are too young to do! These historical and exegetical factors make it impossible for Rome, or anyone else, to reasonably adduce that infant baptism is being commanded and practiced in Acts 2:39.

> It is sometimes adduced that Peter's exhortation to baptism on the day of Pentecost included children. After saying "Repent, and be baptized every one of you," he adds, "For the promise is unto you, and to your children" (Ac 2:38-39). But the prior command to repent surely excludes those incapable of faith. "Children" is a reference to their posterity, to

---

[83] Darrel Bock, *Luke 9:51-24:53*, 1469.
[84] John Salza, *The Biblical Basis For the Catholic Faith*, 72.

whom the opportunity of salvation certainly belonged, but the avenue of obtaining it was through repentance, even as it was for their parents.[85]

The *promise* offered to both parents and children was *not* baptism but *the promise of the coming Holy Spirit* who would indwell believers in Jesus Christ. The Lord Jesus had promised to pour this out on His followers; a very thing Peter said was foretold and partially fulfilled in their midst with the prophecy of Joel 2:28-32, which the Apostle quotes and alludes to in Acts 2:17-21.

> What is the meaning of the word *promise?* Luke, who reports Peter's words, refrains from providing details. The definite article preceding the noun *promise* seems to indicate that Peter has the specific promise of Joel 2:28-32, which was fulfilled on the day of Pentecost. Before his ascension Jesus tells the apostles, "Do not leave Jerusalem, but wait for the promise my father made, of which you heard me speak" (1:4; see also Luke 24:49). And the exalted Christ pours out the promised Holy Spirit he received from God the Father (Acts 2:33).[86]

Another line of argument for the Roman Catholic practice of infant baptism is taken from the cluster of New Testament passages in the book of Acts and 1 Corinthians where the reader is informed that whole *households* where *baptized* (Acts 10:44-48; 16:14-15; 30-34; 18:8; 1 Corinthians 1:16). Roman Catholics typically assume that such *household baptisms* surely included the baptizing of infants.[87] Their thinking goes along the lines that if you have households where families live, you must have babies there, and since the New Testament says the members of these households were baptized, it stands to reason, then, that babies were present in these homes and were also baptized by the Apostles—from whence we have the justification for the practice of infant baptism in the Church. The first household baptism occurred with the house of Cornelius in Acts 10:44-48.

The events that unfolded here make it obvious that *only believers* were baptized. While Peter was still preaching the Gospel to Cornelius and his household, the Acts narrative says, "They heard the Word… believed it and…the Holy Spirit fell upon them… they spoke with other tongues magnifying God…and they were baptized." *All* the persons in Cornelius' household heard, they *all* believed and the Spirit came on *all*, and they were *all* baptized. The acts of hearing, praising God, and believing in Jesus Christ followed by water baptism are gestures of believing adults and those old enough to willfully exhibit these volitional abilities and responsibilities, which immediately rules out infants, who are simply not old enough to have such capacities or capabilities. The members of Cornelius' household were adult members, and perhaps children old enough to hear and understand the Gospel, who gathered for this momentous occasion. Infants are not listed as being present. For Romanists to insist otherwise is reading something into the text that is not there in the desperate attempt to defend a practice that is not endorsed or found in the New Testament.

Next we read in Acts 16:14-15 about a certain woman named Lydia, who believed in the Gospel Paul and his companions preached. Afterwards, ***"she and her household were baptized."*** Again, no mention is

---

85 Robert L. Saucy, *The Church in God's Program* (Chicago: Moody Press, 1972), 199.

86 Simon J. Kistemaker, *Acts* (Grand Rapids: Baker, 1990), 106-107.

87 Paul Flanagan and Robert Schihl, "Baptism: Initiation and Regeneration," at http://www.catholicapologetics.org/ap060200.htm#ap060201; Bishop James C. Gibbons, *The Faith of Our Fathers* (Baltimore: John Murphy, 1891), 308.

made here of infants being present in the home. Lydia was probably not married since she said *"come to my house"* indicating she had no husband in the home at the time. As a seller of purple items, her household would consist of servants and workers to help her with this enterprise. They also believed Paul's message of the Gospel and were baptized along with Lydia in their newfound faith. Even though we do not read this in the text, it is safe to deduce they did believe in accordance with Christ's explicit commandment to believe and be baptized (Mark 16:16). This was the clear pattern in the book of Acts, and there is no good reason to believe it was not followed here with Lydia and her household. The scriptural pattern of *believe and then be baptized* is further evinced in the same chapter of Acts with the baptism of the Philippian jailer and his household. After witnessing the miraculous earthquake that freed Paul and Silas from jail, the Philippian jailer asked them, *"Sirs, what must I do to be saved?"* Their response is given in Acts 16:31-34: *"So they said, 'Believe on the Lord Jesus Christ, and you will be saved, you and your household.' Then they spoke the word of the Lord to him and to all who were in his house. And he took them the same hour of the night and washed their stripes. And immediately he and all his family were baptized. Now when he had brought them into his house, he set food before them; and he rejoiced, having believed in God with all his household."*

It is evident here that no infants or babies were baptized in the Philippian jailer's household by the fact that all who were in this household *heard* the Word of God spoken to them by Paul and Silas and *believed* it. Having believed, they all were baptized based upon their confession of faith in Jesus Christ. All of them were clearly old enough to understand, believe, and then undergo baptism, leaving no doubt there were no babies or infants in the mix. And so, the Roman Catholic proof text for infant baptism inaccurately based on the household baptism of Acts 16:30-34, quickly disappears in the face of such irrefutable facts! Babies cannot believe, rejoice, and express a desire to be baptized as the Philippian jailer and his household did accordingly in Acts 16. Paul's answer to the Philippian jailer about how one could be saved also reveals that it is faith or belief in Jesus Christ alone that saves the person. The Apostle did not say <u>"Be baptized and you will be saved"</u> or <u>"Believe and be baptized and you will be saved"</u> but instead *"Believe on the Lord Jesus Christ, and you will be saved."* The Roman Catholic doctrine teaching baptism is necessary for salvation falls apart on this transparent answer the Scripture provides in Acts 16:31 for how salvation is given and received. The same situation holds exactly true with the household of Crispus in Acts 18:8-9. He believed on the Lord with his entire household. Obviously, if he had children in the home, they were old enough to understand the Gospel message and be baptized as a result of their profession of faith, and any child old enough to believe in the Gospel for salvation is also old enough to be baptized. Again, there is no explicit mention of infants being present in the home. Nor can infant baptism be applied by Catholics in 1 Corinthians 1:16 concerning the household of Stephanas which Paul had baptized.

Paul later goes on to say that those in this same household were old enough to be called "the first fruits of Achaia" and they *"devoted themselves to the ministry of the saints"* (1 Corinthians 16:15). If infants were in the home of Stephanas, how in the world could they have the ability to be old enough to actively be devoted to serving the saints? The cluster of New Testament passages dealing with *household* baptisms speak loudly and often against the practice of infant baptism—which is quite the opposite of what Romanists claim they teach. For, all the occupants in the household passages heard and were taught the Word of God. Once they believed in the Gospel message, they were baptized, *after* they experienced salvation. This agrees with the established pattern of the New Testament, where people were taught the Word, the Gospel was presented to them, they heard with open hearts, believed and were subsequently baptized. The people in question, or infants, were not baptized for salvation in any of these instances of household salvation. To reiterate, what we, and more importantly what the Scriptures, teach on this point is undeniable, wherein "the evidence of New

Testament examples of baptisms, including those of households where indication is given of the occupants, shows a consistent pattern of hearing the Word, belief, and then baptism."[88]

Rome's erroneous practice of infant baptism chiefly lies in their desire to hastily conclude that whenever the word "household" is used in the New Testament with reference to baptism, it must automatically mean every member of the family including infants. The burden of proof falls on the Roman Catholic to demonstrate infants were baptized here, when in fact each instance indicates otherwise. Based on this biblical evidence, the conclusion of Christian apologist Moisés Pinedo is most appropriate here when it comes to the Catholic teaching that household baptisms must necessarily include the baptism of infants, based on a superficial understanding of "household":

> Although at first glance this argument may seem valid, it is actually an assumption lacking biblical support. First, it is hasty to conclude that when the Bible writers referred to the "household" of someone, they always included every member of the family. Second, there is no biblical evidence that those households included babies or young children. Since there is no way to prove that there were babies in the households in question, nor that the word "household" necessarily included babies, these passages do not endorse infant baptism.[89]

To further the cause of infant baptism, the Roman Catholic Church teaches that circumcision of a Jewish male infant on the eighth day prefigures the New Testament baptism of an infant entering the Catholic Church. Their reasoning goes on to say that just as circumcision brought salvation to an eight-day-old Jewish child under the Old Covenant once the circumcision was performed, so too, when the infant is baptized within the Catholic Church, he or she becomes saved under the New Covenant.[90] An appeal to what Paul wrote in Colossians 2:11-12 is used to make such a connection. ***"In Him you were also circumcised with the circumcision made without hands, by putting off the body of the sins of the flesh, by the circumcision of Christ, buried with Him in baptism, in which you also were raised with Him through faith in the working of God, who raised Him from the dead"*** (Colossians 2:11-12). But one looks in vain in the Old Testament to find a passage that flatly says circumcision saves. If that were really the case, then only Jewish males could be saved, since they were the only ones required to be circumcised. Jewish women could not be saved under such a strict, exclusionary economy! On the contrary, the Scripture constantly affirms the act of circumcision did not save anyone or grant spiritual regeneration. Justification or salvation from God exists apart from rituals, ordinances and religious rites, whether circumcision or water baptism (see Romans 3:29; 4:9-12; Galatians 6:14-15). Circumcision was a physical sign that the newly born Jewish child had become a member of the nation of Israel and the physical descendant of Abraham, and therefore, a participant in the blessings of the covenant God made with Abraham and his descendants. The sign and seal of the physical perpetuity of this covenant was circumcision (Genesis 17:9-14).

Entrance into the New Covenant is not gained by a rite, ceremony, or religious act, but is for all people—men, women, and children—who voluntarily profess their belief in the Lord Jesus Christ, that He died on the cross for their sins and rose again from the dead to give them eternal life (John 1:11-12; 3:16; Romans 10:9-10; Acts 16:31). Circumcision did not involve the conscious decision of the infant, whereas in New Testament salvation, the recipient is aware and conscious of making the act of faith or belief for salvation. Circumcision

---

[88]   Robert Saucy, *The Church in God's Program*, 202.

[89]   Moisés Pinedo, "Infant Baptism" at http://www.apologeticspress.org/articles/240120.

[90]   *Catechism of the Catholic Church*, 148 **[527]**.

was for Jews only; baptism is for every believer in Christ, whether Jew or Gentile; male or female; free or slave (Galatians 3:28). Jesus did not mention baptism as a parallel and replacement for circumcision. Nor did the Apostles at the Council of Jerusalem consider baptism as a replacement for circumcision. If Rome is right, and circumcision was only a type of baptism, why did Paul have Timothy circumcised (Acts 16:3)? Surely an act of such a nature could have been explained away on the grounds water baptism had replaced circumcision and was no longer necessary. Obviously Paul did not share the Roman Catholic belief about baptism taking the place of circumcision. The circumcision of Colossians 2:11-12 is a supernatural work of God's Spirit *"made without hands"* within the heart of the transformed believer in Christ, which Paul goes on to correctly say follows the believer's faith with baptism—they are two different things. Baptism is a deliberate act of obedience by the believer every time it is performed. This would rule out infants who are simply too young to possess this kind of decision making capacity. And so:

> A Christian circumcision is 'made without hands', therefore it cannot be water baptism. It implies faith, and a putting off of the old carnal nature; therefore it cannot be predicated of infants . . . All the teaching of this passage is in favour of our doctrine, that a soul must be conscious of regeneration before it can ask the privilege of following Christ in His baptism . . . Baptism avowedly sets forth truths in which infants can have no conscious participation. It implies in its recipients faith, repentance, the answer of a good conscience, deliberate acceptance of Christ as Savior and as an Exemplar of life.[91]

While Colossians 2:11-12 does liken circumcision to baptism; it does not say the former has been replaced by the latter with the idea of infant baptism. The passage is using circumcision to describe God's work of salvation, not the practice of infant baptism. Circumcision is mentioned some forty-four times in the New Testament, and in each case it is never used in connection with water baptism. Not bothered in the least by these irrefutable observations from Scripture, Romanists will still, nonetheless, teach that the faith of the infant's parents stands in proxy for the child, and through this surrogate faith salvation is conferred through the rite of baptism on the child by the Catholic priest. Catholic apologists appeal to instances of this nature in the biblical examples of certain events in the Old and New Testaments. God spared the firstborn of Israel on the basis of the parent's faith in the blood of the lamb placed on the lintels and doorposts of the Israelite homes (Exodus 12:24-28). Jesus cast the demon spirit out of a young boy at the request of his father (Mark 9:22-25). The paralytic was healed and forgiven based on the faith of his friends who lowered him down through the roof to be healed by Jesus (Luke 5:17-26). Jesus heals the centurion's servant based on the centurion's faith (Matthew 8:5-13). The collective argument here is that if God saved and healed people on the basis of other people's faith in lieu of another, than He can also grant salvation when an infant is baptized based on the faith of the parents.[92]

The Passover example covered all the firstborns' sins whether young or old, including adults, children, or infants. If the blood was on the doorposts, all that were in the home were spared from death regardless of age. This was a deliverance from physical death, not eternal salvation and the impartation of eternal life. The same meaning can be applied to the examples of the New Testament healings of both the centurion's servant and the father's son who was a demoniac. Yet a closer examination reveals that these miracles brought physical healing and deliverance, not eternal salvation. The New Testament requirement to receive the latter

---

[91]   T.G. Rooke, *The Doctrine and History of Christian Baptism* (London: Alexander & Shepheard, 1894), pp. 42-45.

[92]   John Salza, *The Biblical Basis for the Catholic Faith*, 71; Patrick Madrid, *Where Is That In Scripture?*, 102

is personal and individual faith by each person. Yes, but what about the paralytic whom Jesus healed? His salvation was accomplished when Jesus told him his sins were forgiven. The faith Jesus saw was not only from the paralytic's friends but also from the paralytic himself. In order for the man to be forgiven and healed he had to personally believe in what the Lord commanded him to do.

The Lord commanded him, *"I say to you, arise, take up your bed, and go to your house"* (Luke 5:24). Here, Jesus required the man to personally prove his faith in Him to heal him by doing this act. Luke 5:25 records that the man obeyed this request and thus demonstrated his belief in the ability of Jesus to forgive and heal! *"Immediately he rose up before them, took up what he had been lying on, and departed to his own house, glorifying God."* Clearly by this act the man was not healed by someone else's faith, but by *his own* personal faith in the word of Jesus. There was no proxy salvation here due to his friends' collective faith. They helped him to get to Jesus, but the man was saved and healed when he *personally* demonstrated his faith by obeying Jesus' command to arise and walk home.

Truth to tell, there is no set pattern given in Scripture by way of example, or incident, of anyone being saved because he or she was part of a family or a believing group of people who were exercising faith on behalf of that person. Scripture knows of no salvation imparted through ritual, baptism, or through the faith of another. The Bible does not teach proxy salvation, as it would have to if the Roman Catholic doctrine of salvation by infant baptism were true. In contrast to this belief, the Bible says salvation is received through the act of personal faith and belief in Jesus Christ (John 3:16; Acts 15:8-11; 16:30-31; Ephesians 2:8-10; 2 Timothy 3:15). One becomes a child of God when he believes in Jesus Christ (John 1:12). Christ invites each person to individually come to Him for salvation (Matthew 11:28-30). Justification and peace with God are given through personal faith in Jesus Christ (Romans 5:1). The Holy Spirit is given by faith and is not dispensed or imparted by water baptism. The clear and consistent example from the New Testament is the practice of *credo-baptism* (i.e., baptism is performed after the person confesses belief in Jesus Christ), instead of *paedo-baptism* (baptism performed on infants or babies), which is nowhere found in the pages of the New Testament. Biblical baptism is called Believer's baptism. The Bible reiterates baptism is to be only performed on those who have already believed in the Lord Jesus Christ as their personal Lord and Savior (see Acts 2:41; 8:12, 36-37; 10:43-44, 47). The Scriptural standard is that baptism comes after believing in Jesus for salvation.

The danger of the unscriptural practice of infant baptism, as sanctioned and performed by the Catholic Church, can easily and dangerously lull both parents and their children into a false sense of security by thinking water baptism alone provides the basis of salvation, when millions of these deceived souls have not truly been born again through personal faith in Jesus Christ. Rome's teaching of baptism being necessary for salvation, can naturally lead Roman Catholics to trust in their own baptism and their membership in the Catholic Church instead of placing exclusive trust in the crucified and risen Christ alone. Millions of unsaved souls are lost sitting in Roman Catholic churches all over the world because such a misplaced trust in the sacrament of baptism is relied upon for their salvation. It is precisely here that infant baptism robs a child of the opportunity of later knowing and understanding the Gospel message when he is old enough to express faith, followed with personal obedience to Christ's command to be baptized, and have unbounded joy in experiencing salvation and the decision to follow the Lord Jesus Christ.

Infant baptism draws people away from trusting in the atonement of Christ alone, to trust instead in a religious ceremony of man-made tradition. From this, Roman Catholic infant baptism and its Protestant versions, for that matter, lead unsaved church members to wrongly think they can substitute baptism for repentance, faith, and spiritual rebirth, and thereby replace the biblical prescription of salvation for mere ceremony and Roman Catholic sacramentalism. Seeing there is no direct or implicit command, example, or implied request for infant baptism in one single verse of the Bible, Catholic apologists will predictably appeal to an argument from silence, stating in effect: since there may be no explicit mention of infant baptism in the New Testament, it does not by this silence prohibit its practice from being followed. So the lack of prohibition in Scripture would not necessarily disallow infant baptism. But this argument is presumptuous and fallacious because it suggests that where the Bible does not prohibit something it then automatically means it must be permissible. The Bible does not prohibit the baptism of unborn "fetuses" or the baptism of dead people, or the baptism of animals; should we not then make these official practices of the Christian Church? No, of course not.

The same thus applies to the unscriptural doctrine of infant baptism for salvation; especially when the established practice and pattern in the New Testament is *believer's baptism* and nothing more—the person believed, and then was baptized following his profession of faith in Jesus Christ. Scripture mercifully does teach that when an infant dies, whether baptized or not, he or she goes to heaven to be in the joyous presence of the Lord (2 Samuel 12:23; Matthew 19:14; John 1:29; Romans 5:15-21). Infant baptism, from a biblical perspective, is not needed or required, since the atonement of Christ covers for infant souls who could not, and were therefore unable to, believe, through no fault of their own. The baptism of infants was simply not practiced in the apostolic church of the first century. Infant baptism arose and was intermittently practiced at the end of the second century A.D. In fact, Tertullian, the early church father of that time (150-230), wrote a whole theological treatise entitled *On Baptism*, disapproving of such a practice. He suggested that the baptism of infants should be properly deferred until they are old enough to exercise faith, and understand the significance of baptism.[93] In the third century, Origen proclaimed infant baptism was a universal practice stretching back to apostolic times. But such a claim lacks documented evidence and ignores the fact that many other church fathers disagreed and debated over the validity of its practice in the early church during the first two-and-a-half centuries of its existence.[94]

The *Catechism of the Catholic Church* even admits infant baptism is derived from the "tradition of the Church" and that it became an "explicit practice from the second century on."[95] Rome admits here that the doctrine of infant baptism is not based on Scripture, but mere religious tradition which arose well over two hundred years after the New Testament was completed. Even Roman Catholic scholar Thomas Bokenkotter admits the practice of infant baptism is not valid and lacks support from Scripture, creating a large mass of inert, in-name-only Christians, who have not undergone genuine conversion, and who lack understanding on what it really means to be a Christian; no doubt because they have reduced salvation to the reductionist act of water baptism!

> Theologically, the grounds for insisting on infant baptism no longer seem valid. Scriptural study no longer supports the necessity of infant baptism, while historical studies show that in the early Church, adult baptism was the norm and was performed with no sense of urgency. Often the catechumen had to wait years before being baptized. Moreover, the practice of making infant baptism the norm has helped to create the situation of a

---

93 Alexander Roberts and James Donaldson, *The Ante-Nicene Fathers* (Grand Rapids: Eerdmans, 1951), Vol. III, Tertullian, *On Baptism,* p.678.

94 Joachim Jeremias, *Infant Baptism in the First Four Centuries* (Philadelphia: Westminster, 1962), 66, 86; Robert L. Saucy, *The Church in God's Program*, 203.

95 *Catechism of the Catholic Church*, 351 **[1252]**.

Church composed formally of a large, inert mass of nominal Christians who have little understanding of what it means to be a member of a Christian community.[96]

To follow Rome's lead and believe the waters of baptism actually possess the ability to save and remove sin, with the proper form of words spoken over the person baptized by the officiating priest, is an insidious form of idolatry and nothing more. To trust in sacramental water at this point is no better than the uncivilized pagan trusting in idols made and carved from wood or stone! Water is no different. True biblical faith is spiritual and solely rests in the Person and work of the crucified and risen Christ—nothing more, nothing less (John 3:14-16; 4:24); it does not look to any visible, material object or rite for its saving content (Hebrews 11:1). To escape the parochial notion that if one is not baptized in the Roman Catholic Church he cannot be saved, Catholicism came up with the idea of *baptism of desire* and *baptism of blood*. Sadly, this was developed early on, based upon some of the writings of the early church fathers who entertained the unscriptural doctrine of salvation by baptismal regeneration. *Baptism of desire* occurs when the person seeking to undergo water baptism is prevented from doing so due to premature death or some prohibitive circumstance. *Baptism of blood* applies to those whose blood is shed in martyrdom for the Catholic faith before they were baptized.[97] Such an act, the Catholic Church claims, is meritorious for salvation.[98] Again, the Roman Catholic addition of these two kinds of 'baptisms', if true, would add human work or achievement as part of salvation, when Scripture itself demands belief alone in Jesus Christ as the sufficient means whereby one is saved. Needless to say, this is why the so-called *baptism of desire* and *baptism of blood* are totally absent from Scripture. The next sacrament in Rome's sacramental system of salvation is *Confirmation*.

The Sacrament of Confirmation.

The sacrament of Confirmation is administered after the sacrament of baptism is performed. For those who were baptized in infancy, Confirmation is usually performed when the child is around seven to twelve years of age. For adult converts, it can be performed anytime after the initial rite of baptism has been performed. Confirmation is the sacrament through which the Holy Spirit comes to the Catholic recipient in "a special way" to enable him to profess, grow, and be strengthened in the Roman Catholic faith.[99] *The Catechism of the Catholic Church* states, "Confirmation perfects Baptismal grace: it is the sacrament which gives the Holy Spirit in order to root us more deeply in the divine filiation, incorporate us more firmly into Christ, strengthen our bond with the [Roman Catholic] Church."[100] The Sacrament of Confirmation is officially and formally conferred when a bishop extends or lays his hands over the one to be confirmed. He then anoints the candidate's forehead with anointing oil (Chrism) making the sign of the cross, and then speaks the following: "Be sealed with the gift of the Holy Spirit. I sign you with the sign of the cross and I confirm you with the chrism of salvation, in the name of the Father, and of the Son, and of the Holy Spirit."

The sacrament of Confirmation supposedly imprints an indelible mark or character on the Catholic initiate so it cannot be repeated.[101] Reception of this sacrament, which brings the Holy Spirit and His gifts

---

96   Thomas Bokenkotter, *Dynamic Catholicism*, 196.

97   *Catechism of the Catholic Church*, 352-353 **[1258-1260]**, 357 **[1281]**.

98   John A. O'Brien, *The Faith of Millions*, 155.

99   *The New Saint Joseph Baltimore Catechism,* 157.

100   *Catechism of the Catholic Church,* 367**[1316]**; *The New Saint Joseph Baltimore Catechism*, 158.

101   Ludwig Ott, *Fundamentals of Catholic Dogma*, 366.

to the one confirmed, is formally completed when the bishop lightly taps the person's cheek to signal the Holy Spirit has come upon the individual being "confirmed." The sacrament of Confirmation thus allows the Catholic to receive the fullness of the Holy Spirit and His various gifts by the laying on of hands of a Roman Catholic bishop. When biblically challenged on this claim for the presence of the sacrament of Confirmation in Scripture, the Roman Catholic Church will point to the events of Acts 8:14-17, Acts 19:1-6 and the doctrine of laying on of hands mentioned in Hebrews 6:2 as proof for the practice.[102] However, when it comes to Rome's facile "proof texts", closer inspection and scrutiny reveal an altogether different meaning than the one Rome advocates. The sacrament of Confirmation is no different, as we will see. In Acts 8 we read that after the preaching of Philip the Evangelist in Samaria, with many Samaritans believing in the Gospel, the Apostles Peter and John came from Jerusalem and laid hands on them, and they received the Holy Spirit (Acts 8:1-5, 14-17).

In this act, Catholics believe, the sacrament of Confirmation is instituted. Roman Catholic theologians teach from the events of Acts 8:14-17 that just as the Apostles, Peter and John, confirmed the Samaritan believers by laying their hands on them to receive the Holy Spirit, so does the Roman Catholic clergy through its bishops, as successors to the Apostles, have the same power today to confer the Holy Spirit on the faithful through the sacrament of Confirmation.[103] In Acts 19:1-6, when Paul learns that the Ephesians believed in Jesus, but were not baptized, he both baptizes them and lays hands on them and the Holy Spirit came upon them as a result. Again, Catholic theologians and spokesmen take this to obviously mean here the Apostle was performing the sacrament of Confirmation to give them the Holy Spirit. The whole ritualistic idea of using a physical sacrament like Confirmation to confer and seal the believer with the presence, power, and protection of the Holy Spirit has no support or uniform presence in Scripture. The so-called sacrament of Confirmation is, simply, in the words of ex-Catholic priest Richard Bennett, "a deceitful tradition in conflict with the Lord's written Word."[104] To regulate and reduce the coming and indwelling of the Holy Spirit to the rote and ritual of Confirmation under the control of the sacramental system of "the (Roman Catholic) Church" goes against the very nature of the operation of the Holy Spirit explained by Jesus and as manifested and demonstrated in the early church!

The Holy Spirit is independently sovereign in His operation; He cannot be controlled or subdued by man to perform in a predictable pattern of a ritual contrivance such as Confirmation. To illustrate this basic spiritual truth, the Lord Jesus likened the Spirit's operation—His coming and going among men—to the independent motion and power of the wind. ***"The wind blows where it wishes, and you hear the sound of it, but cannot tell where it comes from and where it goes. So is everyone who is born of the Spirit"*** (John 3:8). Like the wind, which cannot be harnessed or contained, so too is the Holy Spirit's advent, descent, and indwelling among the Church; He is sovereign in action beyond man's control. The Spirit, like the wind, goes where He pleases, when He pleases, and blows upon those whom He chooses. Rome's creation of the sacramental system, with the sacrament of Confirmation, which attempts to rigidly systematize, narrow down, and manipulate where, when, and how the Holy Spirit goes and acts, reduces in a restrictive fashion the diverse manner and spontaneous operation with which God's Spirit moves among people. His ministry and power cannot, by the very nature of the case, be confined to a ritual act, or exclusively narrowed down

102 John Salza, *The Biblical Basis for the Catholic Faith*, 109-110.
103 L.S. Thorton, *Confirmation: Its Place in the Baptismal Mystery* (London: Dacre, 1954), 73; Heinreich J.D. Denzinger, *The Sources of Catholic Dogma*, trans. Roy J. Deferrari (St. Louis and London: B. Herder Book Co., 1957), 165.
104 Richard M. Bennett, "Salvation and the Sacraments" at www.bereanbeacon.org.

through a denominational organization or clerical body. Rome's idea of Confirmation is patently guilty of this very thing when claiming that its bishops, or their designated proxies, have the exclusive right to dispense the Holy Spirit to those who submit to their ritualistic exercise of empty gesture and impotent religiosity. Would to God the Romanist advocates of Confirmation heed the timely words of Bible teacher G. Campbell Morgan when he appropriately admonishes:

> We must be careful not to create a system that does not hold good in all cases. If we say there must be some human intermediation, then why not in the case of Cornelius? The moment we become mystified in the presence of the operations of the Spirit, we have reached the heart of truth. "The wind bloweth where it will, and thou hearest the voice thereof, but knowest not whence it cometh, and whither it goeth." The moment in which any theologian, or school of theology, attempts to systematize the method of the coming of the Spirit into human lives, in that moment they are excluding a score of His operations, and including only one… "The wind bloweth where it will;" and this is the supreme glory of the Christian Church. Its life and its power is not that of organization or ministry, but that of the indwelling Spirit.[105]

A quick review of how the Holy Spirit came upon believers in the book of Acts immediately reveals He came upon people in different ways, and not in the prescribed and predictable way the sacrament of Confirmation outlines. When the Holy Spirit was poured out on the day of Pentecost, it was done without the formal laying on of hands and the anointing of oil that would be prescribed by the rite of Roman Catholic Confirmation (See Acts 2). Ananias, who, from what we can tell, was neither an Apostle or a bishop, laid hands on the Apostle Paul, who was then filled with the Holy Spirit—no anointing or tapping on the cheek by a bishop of Rome occurred here (Acts 9:17). In Acts chapter ten, we are told the Holy Spirit fell upon Cornelius and his household while the Apostle Peter was still speaking the Word of God (Acts 10:44-45). Again, Peter, as the alleged first Pope and bishop of the Church, did not lay hands on them, tap them on the cheek, and pronounce to them the Holy Spirit has come.

These three divergent ways the Holy Spirit was given in Acts 2, 9, and 10 immediately raise the question, why was the Holy Spirit given through the laying on of apostolic hands in Acts 8:14-17 and 19:1-6? There were several practical reasons for this particular operation—none of which justify the practice or validate the Roman Catholic idea of Confirmation: (1) Although the Holy Spirit normally arrives, baptizes, indwells, and seals at the moment repentance and faith in Christ are shown, Peter and John's arrival to lay hands on the Samaritan believers *confirmed* Philip's evangelistic preaching to be God-ordained through the New Testament Church, and further validated it as authentic in the eyes of the Jerusalem Church. (2) It further validated Philip's ministry to the Samaritans by the coming of the Holy Spirit, which is a sign of the coming Messianic kingdom (Jeremiah 31:31-34; Ezekiel 36:23-27; Joel 2:28-32; Matthew 3:11). (3) The sending of the Holy Spirit, in this instance, by the laying on of hands by the Apostles, was an effective way to accept and unite Jewish believers with their brethren in Samaria to help heal the rift and animosity that existed between Jews and Samaritans. For, up until this time, Jews had no dealings with Samaritans (John 4:9); and so when the Apostles came to lay hands on the Samaritan believers it was to show that God accepts all who truly believe in Jesus Christ, regardless of race or any other background, as equal members into the fellowship of

---

[105]   G. Campbell Morgan, *The Acts of the Apostles*, 206.

the church and family of God. (4) Such a gesture assured the new Christians of Samaria that God loved and favored them no less than the Jewish Christians of Jerusalem.

The situation in Acts 19:1-6 is an occurrence where those in Ephesus were prepared to receive the Messiah when He came through John the Baptist's ministry. Hence, they were disciples of John, who knew about Jesus without as of yet receiving the Holy Spirit from Him. They were ignorant of His coming at Pentecost, so God sent the Apostle Paul to instruct them to believe in the One coming after John—namely, Jesus. When they believed and underwent Christian baptism, Paul placed his hands on them and the Holy Spirit came on all of them. This was done, not to establish or confer some magical rite of Confirmation, but simply to publicly demonstrate that Jesus Christ was saving and welcoming Gentiles in the same fashion on an equal plane in the same way He had done with the Jewish people who had believed in Jesus. This was formally sealed and done at the hands of one of Christ's Apostles—Paul, whom the Lord personally chose. When Paul laid hands on these twelve Ephesian believers, he did not use a "Chrism" or a liturgical recitation, as Catholics bishops are required to do, when supposedly conferring the Holy Spirit to a candidate for this sacrament. From the four instances where the Holy Spirit is given and poured out in the book of Acts (Acts 2:1-4; 8:11-17; 10:44-47; 19:1-6), it is revealed that the outpouring of the Holy Spirit is complex, diverse, and that He is free to flow and move as He deems necessary—a reality that goes against Rome's entrenched doctrine that the Holy Spirit is conferred in only one way, through the routine and fixed ritual of Confirmation. Thus, an honest reading of the Luke-Acts narrative obviously rules out such a parochial mentality concerning the giving and sending of the Holy Spirit, by God through Jesus Christ, to the believer.

> The complex record of the gift of the Holy Spirit in Luke-Acts rebukes all attempts to formulate a monolithic doctrine of the means by which the Holy Spirit is conferred. All must admit that "Nowhere is it claimed in Acts that baptism of itself, or the laying on of hands as such or even a combination of them both, confers or can confer the Spirit." Rather, in these narratives, "the freedom of the Spirit is strongly emphasized." Luke's primary concern is with the fact of the gift of the Spirit and not with any real or imagined means through which the Holy Spirit is conferred.[106]

The mention of the "doctrine of the laying on of hands" in Hebrews 6:2 alludes not to the Catholic sacrament of Confirmation—the laying on of hands here is not explicitly identified with that! What the writer of Hebrews means by the laying on of hands is found in the Old Testament practice of this on the Day of Atonement. This would make perfect sense, because the writer's audience consisted of Jews, who were well acquainted with the rites and ordinances of the Old Covenant priesthood and animal sacrifices. On the Day of Atonement, the High Priest would lay his hands on the head of a live goat and confess all the iniquities of Israel over it. That goat would then bear the sins of Israel as it was lead away into the wilderness (Leviticus 16:21). One of the dominant themes of the book of Hebrews deals with how the once-for-all final sacrifice of Jesus the Messiah replaced and put an end to the Old Covenant animal sacrifices, best epitomized on the Day of Atonement, of which the latter fulfilled the former. So, naturally, the Hebrew audience would associate the laying on of hands with the primary role it played on the most solemn day of the year in the religious calendar of Judaism. Astute Bible commentator A.W. Pink expresses most aptly this very point when explaining,

---

[106]   Roger Stronstad, *The Charismatic Theology of St. Luke* (Peabody, Mass: Hendrickson, 1984), 70; J.H.E. Hull, *The Holy Spirit in the Acts of the Apostles* (London: Lutterworth Press, 1967), 90; Eduard Schweizer, "πνευμα," *TDNT*, Vol. VI, 414.

"And of laying on of hands." The key which unlocks *the real meaning* of this expression is to be found in the O.T., to which each and all of the six things here mentioned by the apostle look back. Necessarily so, for the apostle is here making mention of those things which characterized Judaism, which the Hebrews, upon their profession of their personal faith in Christ, had "left." The "laying on of hands" to which the apostle refers is described in Lev. 16:21, "And Aaron shall lay both his hands upon the head of the live goat, and confess over him all the iniquities of the children of Israel, and all their transgressions in all their sins, putting them on the head of the goat, and shall send him away by the hand of a fit man into the wilderness." This was an essential part of the ritual on the annual Day of Atonement. Of this the Hebrews would naturally think when the apostle here makes mention "doctrine (teaching) . . . of laying on of hands."[107]

With the exception of Acts 8:17 and 19:6, the context of Acts and the rest of the New Testament does not teach the church must have a sacrament of confirmation or that the Holy Spirit is poured out, given, and received by the laying of hands on the believer. Nor does Scripture use these two exceptional cases as a command or teaching for it to be a normative practice and doctrine of the Christian life; although the practice of laying on of hands can be used for ordination and prayer among the members of the church by fellow believers and leaders of the congregation or to impart some spiritual gift for the ministry (Mark 16:18; Acts 6:6; 13:3; 1 Timothy 4:14). The instructions Jesus gave the Apostles to receive the Holy Spirit are given in Luke 11:9; it included the acts of asking, seeking, and knocking (petitioning). No mention of a sacrament of Confirmation is made here, nor a "bishop" from the Church needed to tap the cheek of the one receiving the Holy Spirit! A recurrent theme in New Testament Scripture informs the Bible believer the Holy Spirit was sent, and is given, directly by Jesus alone to every believer, once trust in Him is truly exercised. The Spirit is not given by the church or its clergy, but is sent by God the Father through the Son, Jesus Christ *alone* (John 14:16-18, 26; 15:26-27; 16:7, 13-15; Matthew 3:11; Acts 1:5).

Furthermore, *contra* the Roman Catholic teaching on Confirmation, The New Testament Scriptures reveal it is through hearing, understanding, and responding with faith to the Gospel that a person is baptized, filled, and sealed by the Holy Spirit and joined to Christ and His Church. This sealing of the Christian by the Holy Spirit is guaranteed by the faithfulness and power of the risen Christ to keep every born-again Christian safe and preserved until the completion of our redemption with the resurrection/translation of our bodies when the Lord Jesus Christ returns at the Rapture of the Church (Romans 8:23; 1 Corinthians 15:51-53; Ephesians 4:30). Ephesians 1:13 further makes it clear that once the believer trusts in Jesus after hearing and believing the Gospel of salvation, he or she is sealed with the Holy Spirit of promise. The Word of God teaches this act of sealing is a sovereign act of God the Father who sends the Holy Spirit to indwell and thereby seal the believer in Jesus Christ to preserve, protect, and keep him safe until the redemption of his body—which completes the work of salvation. The sealing of the believer by the Holy Spirit accomplishes several things—none of which are associated with a so-called rite of Confirmation! Again, no bishop performing a sacrament of Confirmation ever enters the picture here—which is a pure invention from the traditions of men, and not from the authoritative Word of God. The sealing of the Holy Spirit signifies Christ's ownership of the redeemed (2 Timothy 2:19); approval and approbation from God (John 6:27); vindication and validation for

---

107   Arthur Pink, *Exposition of Hebrews*, 282.

the believer's faith (1 Corinthians 9:2); the guarantee of the completion of our salvation with the redemption and glorification of our bodies from the inherit corruption sin and death breed (Romans 8:20-23).

In the meantime, no true believer in Jesus sealed by the Holy Spirit will be lost or perish because of this permanent sealing (John 17:11-12). The real motive for Rome's creation of the Sacrament of Confirmation is to strengthen and tighten the cords of control over the unsuspecting soul who unwisely puts trust in the Roman Catholic sacraments for salvation. *The Catechism of the Catholic Church* states: "For by the sacrament of Confirmation, [the baptized] are more perfectly bound to the Church and are enriched with a special strength of the Holy Spirit."[108] But God does not want anyone to be bound to the sacramental system of the Roman Catholic Church, especially when Jesus came to free people from every bondage—even spiritual bondage to a religious system like Rome's (see John 8:36; Galatians 5:1). When the Holy Spirit is present, poured out, given, and received, He brings liberty and freedom not servile dependence on some religious ceremony or sacramental system—*"Now the Lord is the Spirit; and where the Spirit of the Lord is, there is liberty"* (2 Corinthians 3:17). The real history of Confirmation does not go back to the Bible, but emerged from the slow formation of church tradition within the Roman Catholic system covering a span of eight hundred years. It eventually grew out of the rite of baptism, where the act of anointing oil was used, and was not formally accepted as a distinct sacrament itself until the twelfth century, with the writings of Thomas Aquinas (1225-1274 A.D.).[109] The Church in the East has never accepted or separated Baptism and Confirmation from each other as two different sacraments. Confirmation is not in the New Testament simply because it is a man-made tradition of Roman Catholicism.

Even established Roman Catholic scholar Richard P. McBrien honestly admits the following in his mammoth tome, *Catholicism*: "Confirmation, as distinct from baptism, had no basis in Sacred Scripture precisely because it was only in the Middle Ages that a specific theology of Confirmation was developed in order to justify, *after the fact*, the now autonomous rite carried out only by the bishop."[110] Confirmation is really just another unnecessary link in the convoluted chain of Roman Catholic sacramental salvation. Roman Catholic Confirmation simply lacks the warrant of Scripture and the command of Jesus Christ therein to demand it must be a normative practice of the New Testament. So, it rests on an empty claim without the authority of God's Word behind it.

The Sacrament of Penance

The sacrament of Penance, also variously called the sacrament of conversion, confession, forgiveness, and reconciliation, is the act of forgiveness of sins given by the priest to the Catholic after baptism is granted. Forgiveness or absolution is given once confession is made, contrition is expressed, and the act of penance prescribed by the priest is performed. The *Catechism of the Catholic Church* thus defines this sacrament in the following ways:

---

[108] *Catechism of the Catholic Church*, 358 **[1285]**.

[109] Thomas Bokenkotter in *Dynamic Catholicism* writes, "The emergence of confirmation as a distinct sacrament in the Western church was a very slow process, covering a span of some eight hundred years—if we take as our starting point the structure of the Roman initiation rite as described in documents of the sixth century and as our terminal point the fully developed theology of confirmation as a separate sacrament found in the work of Thomas Aquinas" (Page 191).

[110] Richard P. McBrien, *Catholicism*, 817.

It is called the *sacrament of conversion* because it makes sacramentally present Jesus' call to conversion, the first step in returning to the Father from whom one has strayed by sin. It is called the *sacrament of Penance*, since it consecrates the Christian sinner's personal and ecclesial steps of conversion, penance, and satisfaction. It is called the sacrament of confession, since the disclosure or confession of sins to a priest is an essential element of this sacrament. In a profound sense it is also a "confession"—acknowledgment and praise— of the holiness of God and of his mercy toward sinful man. It is called the sacrament of forgiveness, since by the priest's sacramental absolution God grants the penitent "pardon and peace." It is called the sacrament of Reconciliation, because it imparts to the sinner the love of God who reconciles: "Be reconciled to God." He who lives by God's merciful love is ready to respond to the Lord's call: "Go; first be reconciled to your brother."[111]

Forgiveness for the Catholic primarily comes through the priest who acts in the place of Jesus Christ to grant absolution for both venial and mortal sins. Roman Catholic theology divides sin into these two categories. Venial sin is defined by Rome as "an offence against God which does not deprive the sinner of sanctifying grace." It is called venial (from *venia*, meaning pardon) and consists of "daily sins" or "light sins" or "lesser sins."[112] Examples of small sins like these would be: laziness, telling little white lies, lack of generosity and love in the small things. Venial sin cannot keep one out of heaven, but could require a person to spend a specific amount of time in purgatory after death. Mortal sin occurs when a person commits a grave sin with full knowledge and free consent of the will. The nature of mortal sin involves a willful turning away from God to pursue a course of abject wickedness. The act of mortal sins kills or brings about the death of supernatural grace imparted in the soul at baptism and precludes one from entrance into heaven. Mortal sins are so named because they bring a loss and termination of God's sanctifying or justifying grace in the Roman Catholic. Murder, adultery, hatred of neighbor, renouncing the Catholic faith, and idolatry are typical examples of mortal sin. If a Catholic should die in a state of mortal sin, he or she will go to hell for all eternity. The only way mortal sin can be forgiven by God is for the priest to perform the act of absolution and for the sacrament of Penance to be administered to the person willing to return to the Church to receive it.[113]

The performance of "penance" must follow the act of confession if absolution from sin given by the priest is to take place. The official Roman Catholic teaching plainly affirms,

"Absolution takes away sin, but it does not remedy all the disorders sin has caused. Raised up from sin, *the sinner must still recover his full spiritual health by doing something more to make amends for the sin: he must 'make satisfaction for' or 'expiate' his sins. This satisfaction is also called 'penance'* (Emphasis mine)."[114] The act of penance the confessor must do to obtain forgiveness from God, through the priest, depends on the degree and the severity of the sin committed. Whatever penance is given it must correspond "as far as possible with the gravity and nature of the sins committed."[115] Rome has deemed the sacrament of Penance, like baptism, necessary for salvation. For,

---

[111]   *Catechism of the Catholic Church*, 396-397 **[1423-1424]**.

[112]   John A. Hardon, *Pocket Catholic Dictionary*, 449.

[113]   Matthias Premm, *Dogmatic Theology for the Laity*, (Rockford, Ill: Tan Books, 1982), 373. See also http://www. ewtn.com/expert/answers/mortal_versus_venial.htm.

[114]   *Catechism of the Catholic Church*, 407 **[1459]**.

[115]   Ibid., **[1460]**.

It is through the sacrament of Penance that the baptized can be reconciled with God and with the Church ...This sacrament of Penance <u>is necessary for salvation</u> for those who have fallen after Baptism, just as Baptism is necessary for salvation for those who have not yet been reborn.[116]

Rome's blasphemous Council of Trent repeatedly condemns any and all who would deny that forgiveness from God must come through a Catholic priest administering the sacrament of Penance. Canon 29 reads:

If anyone says that he who has fallen after baptism cannot by the grace of God rise again, or that he can indeed recover again the lost justice but by faith alone without the sacrament of penance, contrary to what the holy Roman and Universal Church, instructed by Christ the Lord and His Apostles, has hitherto professed, observed and taught, let him be anathema.[117]

Typically, the sacrament of Penance begins when the Catholic enters into the confessional—a small enclosed booth containing at least two small compartments, one for the priest and the other for the confessor, separated by a small sliding screen that the priest sits behind during the act of confession. Once inside, the priest opens the opaque screen giving the cue for the kneeling Catholic to address the priest in the following way: "Bless me, Father, for I have sinned. It has been one week since my last confession (here the confessor states how long it has been since he or she made confession—days, weeks, or years). I said my penance and received Holy Communion" (or "received Holy Communion and said my penance," whatever the case may be). The penitent continues, saying, "I confess to Almighty God and to you, Father, that I..." Here, the dutiful Catholic confesses all his sins, especially mortal sins, since his last confession; this includes the type and number as nearly as the person can remember. Once done, the Confession ends with the penitent saying to the priest, "For these and all the other sins of my past life I am heartily sorry and ask pardon of God and penance of you, Father." At this point the priest will give his advice, counsel, or admonition. After this he will then prescribe the specific acts of penance necessary for the absolution of sin. The more serious the sin, the more serious the penance required and the lesser will correspondingly require a lesser act of penance.

This could entail doing a certain number of acts or religious exercises like restitution, public apology, making pilgrimage to a Catholic shrine, or reciting prayers like the Rosary, the "Hail Mary" and "Our Father" a certain number of times. At this point, the priest will raise his right hand making the sign of the cross upon the Catholic penitent and speak the prayer of priestly absolution over him, which goes something like this: God, the Father of mercies, through the death and resurrection of His Son, has reconciled the world to himself and sent the Holy Spirit among us for the forgiveness of sins; through the ministry of the Church may God give you pardon and peace, and I absolve you from your sins in the name of the Father, and of the Son, and of the Holy Spirit."[118] When the priest begins to pronounce the word of absolution, the absolved is to then say the *Act of Contrition*:

"O My God, I am heartily sorry for having offended Thee, and I detest all my sins because I dread the loss of heaven and the pains of hell, but most of all, because they offend Thee, my God, Who art all good and deserving of all my love. I firmly resolve, with the help of Thy grace, to confess my sins, to do penance and to amend my life. Amen." After the priest grants absolution, he will tell the person, "Go in peace and

---

[116]   Ibid, 278 **[980]**.

[117]   *The Canons and Decrees of the Council of Trent*, 45-46, 102-103.

[118]   *The Essential Catholic Handbook: A Summary of Beliefs, Practices, and Prayers* (Liguori, MO: Liguori, 1997), 52-53

sin no more." Then the Catholic says in return, "Thank you, Father." Once out of the confessional, penance must be done so that forgiveness from God can be obtained.[119]

The Roman Catholic priest wields tremendous power with his ability to grant forgiveness of sin through the sacrament of Penance. Without this sacrament, the Roman Catholic has no hope of heaven or from escaping the eternal fires of hell. Thus, the Catholic's participation is vital, because it is by this penance he does before the absolving priest that expiation and satisfaction for sin is made. Catholics are taught penance actually "merits" the grace of God for the forgiveness of sins. With the approval of the Magisterium, Jesuit priest John Hardon confirms this when stating, "Penance means repentance or satisfaction for sin ... Penance is also necessary because we must expiate and make reparation for the punishment which is due for our sins ... Satisfaction is remedial by meriting grace from God."[120]

And yet, the sacrament of Penance is still not efficacious enough to remove all punishment for sins because the temporal punishment due for them can still remain after death and will have to be satisfied by staying in purgatory for a period of time. So in the end, the Roman Catholic cannot know with certainty before, after, or at the point of death if all his sins are expiated or forgiven! The Catholic Church demands that a Catholic must go to Confession at least once a year beginning at the young age of seven. According to the Code of Canon Law, "All the faithful who have reached the age of discretion are bound faithfully to confess their grave sins at least once a year."[121] Canon Law further affirms the priest, in his role of giving absolution for sin, acts as more than just a sympathetic listener; he is in fact acting in the place of God and Jesus Christ with real power to cleanse and forgive sin, in the divine role of both "judge" and "healer", who can both dispense "divine justice" and "divine mercy", so that he actually contributes to the salvation of souls! Paragraph One in Canon 978 states: "In hearing confessions the priest is to remember that he is at once both judge and healer, and that he is constituted by God as a minister of both divine justice and divine mercy, so that he may contribute to the honor of God and the salvation of souls."[122] The nature of confession

---

[119] *Confession: Its Fruitful Practice* (Rockford, Ill: Tan Books, 2000), 73-74.

[120] John A. Hardon S.J., *The Question and Answer Catholic Catechism* (Garden City: Image, 1981), Questions 1318, 1320, 1390, 1392, 1395, 1400. Father Mitchell Pacwa is quick to speak out of both sides of his mouth here when affirming that while no one can earn or merit salvation, or entry into heaven through the sacrament of Penance, the Catholic can, nevertheless, share by the act of Penance in the merits of Christ to that end because he or she is a member of His mystical body in union with Him (see Pacwa's book, *Go in Peace* (West Chester, PA: Ascension Press, 2007, 28-29.) Again, nowhere in the New Testament do we find such distorted and convoluted thinking. A believer becomes a member in the body of Christ's Church after salvation and baptism in the Holy Spirit are already experienced and received (1 Corinthians 12:12-14). The Word of God unequivocally views grace and merit as mutually exclusive realities so that grace, by its very nature, is unmerited through and through, whereas merit is based solely on the ability to work or earn something (see Romans 11:6). To then think the Christian can somehow merit the unmerited riches of Christ for our salvation through the sacramental act or work of Penance is to flatly contradict Scripture and nothing more (see Ephesians 2:8-9; Titus 3:5—where salvation is a free gift from God from beginning to end and is not conferred by any human work or effort). This is the essential problem with Roman Catholicism—they blend salvation by grace together with works to propose a contradictory system where a person can *de facto* merit grace by the act of sharing in the merits of Jesus Christ through the sacraments! The focus then inevitably turns on the individual receiving the Sacrament from the priest.

[121] *The Code of Canon Law*, 178.

[122] Ibid., 177.

to a priest is *auricular*, that is, it is to be normally spoken or whispered to the priest, who then must hear it with the ear to grant proper absolution.[123]

Roman Catholic theology has constructed a seven-step plan to receive forgiveness of God through a priest. One, then, must do each of these seven acts, works, or steps to be forgiven! The seven-step process to receive this are: (1) Examination of conscience—involves an internal audit of the mind about past actions that were sinful. (2) Contrition—the deep regret or remorse over sin and the firm resolve to sin no more. One Catholic website states if you are willing to confess all of your sins and do penance and resolve to sin no more, then your sins will be forgiven (see http://www.fisheaters.com/penance.html, page 4 of 15). (3) Confessing your sins to God through the priest. This is self-explanatory. (4) Penance—the performance done as required by the priest for forgiveness. (5) Act of contrition—consists in reciting the traditional prayer called "Act of Contrition" to the priest in the confessional box. (6) Absolution—is granted by the priest once he hears your confession. (7) Penance. To do penance means you are to carry out the priest's instructions necessary for the forgiveness of sins. Once this seven-step process is done, the Catholic is forgiven until he or she commits a sinful act again; then the process must be repeated over and over if forgiveness is to be maintained. Pages 3-8 of the aforementioned website gives a full explanation of this work-oriented effort to earn God's forgiveness.

Does the Bible endorse and demand a believer must confess to a priest and receive the sacrament of penance to be forgiven by God? Of course not! The evidence from God's Word undeniably shows confession of sin must be made directly to God in order to receive His forgiveness of sin and salvation. King David confessed his sins of adultery and murder directly to God alone and received forgiveness in the end. No priest of that day was required to be present and hear such a confession! Psalm 51 is David's personal confession to God asking Him alone to pardon and cleanse him from all of his sins. *"Have mercy upon me, O God, according to your loving-kindness; according to the multitude of Your tender mercies, blot out my transgressions. Wash me thoroughly from my iniquity. And cleanse me from my sin"* (Psalm 51:1-2). Likewise, what David confessed in Psalm 32:5 epitomizes what true biblical confession and divine forgiveness really constitutes. *"I acknowledged my sin to You, and my iniquity I have not hidden. I said, I will confess my transgressions to the Lord, and You forgave the iniquity of my sin."* All throughout the seven penitential Psalms, we see the Psalmist making a confession of sin to God alone and receiving forgiveness from Him, without any human intermediary having to stand between the confessor and a forgiving God (see Psalms 6, 32, 38, 51, 102, 130, and 143). King Solomon's prayer of dedication of the first Temple asked for God's forgiveness whenever the nation repented and confessed their sins directly to Him (1 Kings 8:30-50).

Solomon's prayer underscores how true confession to God is to be made and how forgiveness is received. When Israel turned to God *exclusively*, confessed their sins to Him *directly*, the Lord would then hear from heaven and immediately forgive His repentant people. *"When Your people Israel are defeated before an enemy because they have sinned against You and when they turn back to You and confess Your name, and pray and make supplication to You in this temple, then hear in heaven, and forgive the sin of Your people Israel, and bring them back to the land which You gave to their fathers"* (1 Kings 8:33-34). Here, in the very Temple, before the presence of all its priests, Solomon does not state Israel had to first go to the priests and confess their sins to receive God's forgiveness. Though national Israel, as a whole, did receive corporate forgiveness on the Day of Atonement through the sacrificial rite of the High Priest, we see people

---

[123]   There are now exceptions to this rule. Now in some quarters Catholics can write down, mail, e-mail, or call into a parish to receive absolution from a priest if they cannot do so in person for one reason or another.

were individually encouraged to approach God personally in prayer to confess their sins to Him for individual forgiveness throughout the Old Testament period.

Israel was exhorted to go directly to God in prayer in order to receive forgiveness from Him alone. Daniel's confession of his sin and the sins of his people was direct and personal. Again, no attempt was made by the prophet to find a priest while in exile to confess his sins so God could officially grant pardon (see Daniel 9:3-19). Nehemiah's prayer for himself and Israel was a confession of sin directly offered to God (Nehemiah 1:4-11). Ezra, a priest himself, encouraged Israel to make a direct confession to God. *"Now therefore, make confession to the Lord God of your fathers, and do His will."* (Ezra 10:11; see also 9:5-10). Surely if confession of sin must be made to a priest, Ezra would have been the first to insist on such a practice from those confessing their sins!

If the Catholic apologist objects to these points on the basis such realities belonged to the Old Testament economy alone, we are quick to respond by pointing out the same truth of confessing one's sins to God directly for His forgiveness is even more pronounced in the New Testament, when it comes to the complete absolution of sins through the final atonement of Jesus Christ. People throughout Jesus' ministry in Israel came directly to Him to receive forgiveness from God. An unidentified woman (church tradition says it was Mary of Magdala) knelt at Jesus' feet seeking His pardon and forgiveness of her many sins. The Lord, seeing her repentance, declared to her, *"Your sins are forgiven . . . Your faith has saved you. Go in peace"* (Luke 7:36-50). No mention here by the Lord of Mary having to go first to a priest appointed by God or Christ. She came directly to a forgiving Jesus without any intermediary. The paralytic brought to Christ, was not only miraculously healed, but had his sins directly forgiven by the Lord: *"Son, your sins are forgiven you"* (Mark 2:5). One of the object lessons here is that a person must come straightway to Jesus Christ alone with unhindered access to receive forgiveness of sins from Him! Notice: the universal New Testament salvation truth evident in these two instances from the Gospels, both the woman and the paralytic, were forgiven by coming to Jesus directly and by placing faith in Him alone.

No requirement for a sevenfold sacramental step of Penance was mentioned, announced, or demanded. They simply came to Jesus as Lord and Savior and believed in Him for God's forgiveness. The repentant thief on the cross was forgiven and welcomed into heaven by Jesus because he acknowledged his sin and the authority of Jesus as Lord and King to pardon this thief for all his crimes (see Luke 23:39-43). In the Great Invitation of Matthew 11:28-30, Jesus invites all people to come to Him for the redemptive relief from the heavy burden and guilt of sin. In Him, is exclusively found the rest and relief of forgiveness of all sin. *"Come to Me"*, Jesus says, not to the Church or her alleged priests and their sacraments, but come directly to Jesus whom we now go to through the avenue of repentance, faith and prayer! Again the Romanist could object here and maintain these aforementioned events occurred before Jesus instituted the Church, the papacy, and the priesthood; therefore it does not apply to the current church age inaugurated at Pentecost in Acts chapter two.

The writer of Hebrews eagerly encourages every New Testament believer to go by himself "boldly to the throne of grace" to find divine aid, comfort, and forgiveness from God in time of need, without the aid of a sacrament or Catholic priest. For at this throne of divine mercy, stands the supreme High Priest, Jesus Christ, to meet and succor us without the aid or intervention of any other! *"For we do not have a High Priest who cannot sympathize with our weaknesses, but was in all points tempted as we are, yet without sin. Let us therefore come boldly to the throne of grace, that we may obtain mercy and find grace to help in time of need"* (Hebrews 4:15-16). Now, here, does the Scripture direct us to go into a confessional box to obtain forgiveness of sin from God through a priest of Rome? Certainly not! We are, rather, directed to the sinless Savior, Jesus Christ for that—our one and only heavenly High Priest! Christians are not only to go before

Jesus in this manner but also to approach God through Him as our legal advocate and defense attorney, and on that sure foundation confess our sins to Him who has forgiven us and cleansed us from all sin. This is what 1 John 1:7-9 and 2:1-2 counsels the believer in Christ to do. *"If we confess our sins, He is faithful and just to forgive us our sins and to cleanse us from all unrighteousness . . . My little children, these things I write to you, so that you may not sin. And if anyone sins, we have an advocate with the Father, Jesus Christ the righteous. And He Himself is the propitiation for our sins"* (1 John 1:9, 2:1-2). These two passages from the first epistle of John tell every Christian that we need to confess our sins to God and not to a priest! The practice of confession of sins to God is an ongoing act by the Christian, as evidenced by the Greek word for confess which is in the present tense in 1 John 1:9.

The word "confess" conveys the idea of agreement, where the believer agrees with God about committing sin or wrong and the ongoing need of cleansing and forgiveness offered by the blood of Jesus Christ (See Fritz Rienecker and Cleon Rogers, *Linguistic Key to the Greek New Testament,* page 786). We learn from 1 John 1:9, that not only does confession of sin by the sinner to God bring salvation to the person who believes in Jesus Christ for cleansing, but also that the confessing of sin by the saved believer is also mandated to restore and continue fellowship with God—even after the salvation issue has already been permanently settled when faith in Jesus Christ was exercised in the past. Should the Christian refuse confession of sin, he or she will be disciplined by God, even suffering a premature death if fellowship is not restored by confession of sin and repentance towards the Lord (1 Corinthians 11:30; Hebrews 12:4-11; 1 John 5:16).

The Christian's salvation is not in question here, since once saving faith in Jesus is exercised the person cannot perish; but fellowship with the Savior can be disrupted by unconfessed sin. Scripture does advise we should confess our sins one to another, not in order to have forgiveness with God, but rather to achieve reconciliation and reparation of fellowship and restored relationship with other Christians who have been sinned against and alienated by those wrongs committed. *"Confess your trespasses to one another, and pray for one another, that you may be healed"* (James 5:16). And note further, James says we are to make this confession *"to one another"*; this undoubtedly means a mutual and reciprocal confession which bars a unilateral confession a person would have to make before a priest, or else a priest would also have to make a confession to the one who also just confessed to him, if James 5:16 is to be honestly used as a proof text by Catholic apologists for the sacrament of confession. It is here where they will use this verse to incorrectly teach a person must confess his sins to a priest and no more, while conveniently ignoring the reciprocal nature of this confession!

The atoning advocacy of Jesus Christ, Who now stands in the presence of God for the Christian who sins, is the sole basis for full pardon and absolution for those sins. It does not come through a ritual or a sacrament of absolution performed by some priest. Absolution of sin comes from nothing else but the eternal efficacy of Christ's propitiatory sacrifice, which saves, forgives, and keeps those saved and forgiven, who accept His sacrifice as the means whereby all of this has been accomplished. So, when the Christian sins, he or she can avail themselves of this fount of continual cleansing, each time they go to God in prayer and confess their sins to Him alone, so that fellowship with the Lord can continue on in the ongoing cleansing power of Christ's shed blood. Scripture nowhere demands one must perform some penitential work or merit in the form of "penance" to receive God's forgiveness. All one is required to do is believe on the Lord Jesus Christ, crucified and risen, through Whom forgiveness of sins is proclaimed and given. Forgiveness, remission, and cleansing of sin in the biblical context has absolutely no affinity or similarity with the Roman Catholic sacrament of penance. God's forgiveness directly comes from Christ's saving death and shed blood the moment a repentant sinner trusts in Him alone. ***"Therefore let it be known to you, brethren, <u>that through this Man is preached to you the forgiveness of sins</u>"*** (Acts 13:38).

Biblical forgiveness is full and absolute when confession of belief in Christ is made and extends to all sins committed prior to and after the person is saved (See Jeremiah 31:34; Colossians 2:13). The forgiveness of God through Jesus Christ is not extended or judicially mediated through priests, a system of sacraments, or the Church itself, but evangelically declared by the Church for the unbeliever to hear the Gospel message and believe, to receive salvation for the forgiveness of sins (Matthew 26:28; Luke 24:47; Acts 2:38; 5:31; 26:18). Former Roman Catholic priest Richard Knolls makes an important observation when pointing out: "In Scripture, forgiveness, remission, cleansing, purging and removal of sins are terms used interchangeably. When employed in respect to God's relation with man they indicate that which is entire and final (Acts 3:19; 13:39; Colossians 1:14; 2:13; 1 John 1:7; Hebrews 10:17-18). See *Roman Catholicism: Issues & Evidences*, page 153.

The whole idea of confessing to a priest for absolution of sin is simply not found or taught in the New Testament. In the Old Testament dispensation, the Israelite had to approach God through Levitical priests who offered animal sacrifices to God on behalf of the people. So, the High Priest and the priests officiating with him did act as mediators between God and His people Israel. But all of this permanently changed with the coming of the New Covenant economy, consisting in the atonement of Jesus Christ for the complete forgiveness of sins. With this finally accomplished, there is now no longer a need for a Christian to approach a priest as some absolving mediator, because the New Testament informs us that all believers are now priests. All Christians are called a ***"holy priesthood"*** and a ***"royal priesthood"*** in 1 Peter 2:5-9; and in Revelation 1:6 and 5:10, the Church is also referred to as a ***"kingdom of priests"*** without any mention that this same priesthood has the actual power to forgive sins! Indeed, in both passages from Revelation, the redeemed Church makes the unanimous confession that Jesus Christ alone has washed, redeemed, and forgiven this spiritual priesthood of all believers by His shed blood. So if the Roman Catholic, celibate priests and their sacrament of Penance were crucial for the forgiveness of sin, and the retaining of salvation, why is there no mention of this here or in 1 Peter 2:5-9? The answer is there is no such concept or reality found in the New Testament at all!

Furthermore, there is no longer any need of a mediating priesthood as a go-between because all believers have unhindered access into the presence of God once the veil of the temple was torn in two upon the atoning death of Jesus, which showed to all the wall of division and separation between God and Man was forever removed and eliminated (Matthew 27:51). The tearing of the veil, which typified the human body of Jesus Christ (Hebrews 10:20), signifies a new and living way has been established for God to forgive sinners and allow them into His presence without any further need for a sacrifice or priesthood other than Christ's own. Now, anyone who repents and believes in the crucified and risen Christ for the forgiveness of sins can approach God directly, without the use or need of a human mediator or priesthood. Every Christian can therefore go to God directly and immediately, because Jesus' sacrificial death for us in the role of our great High Priest and only Mediator between God and us has successfully opened the way (See Hebrews 4:14-15; 10:21; 1 Timothy 2:5). Hence, there is no more need for an absolving priesthood dispensing conditional forgiveness that we find in Rome's priests and in the sacramental works system of confession and penance they pedal among their undiscerning parishioners.

The Roman Catholic assertion her priests have the actual power to bestow forgiveness on the sinner is dead wrong for the simple fact the Scriptures repeatedly teach us forgiveness comes from God alone! Never once did He confer this divine prerogative to man. Psalm 130:4-8 declares forgiveness of sins and redemption from all iniquities comes from God, and no other. God ever stands ready to forgive openly and completely those who call on Him with repentance and faith. *"For You, Lord, are good, and ready to forgive, and abundant in mercy to all those who call upon You"* (Psalm 86:5). He does not station Himself behind a priest in the secrecy and darkness of some confessional box to forgive when someone fulfills the works requirement of Rome's sacramental system. The sinner must ask and seek God for this forgiveness—Who alone has the authority and power to grant full pardon unto salvation. The Psalmist realized this indispensable truth when praying to God, *"Look on my affliction and my pain, and forgive all my sins"* (Psalm 25:18). When we sin, Scripture advises we go to God, asking Him simply, *"O Lord God, forgive, I pray!"* (Amos 7:2). Rome says Jesus instituted the sacrament of Penance through which the Roman Catholic priest stands between God and the penitent with the authority to forgive sin. And yet we clearly are told in Matthew 6:9-12 of how Jesus commanded His disciples to pray to God the Father in heaven, asking Him to forgive us our debts (sins) as we have forgiven others. If Roman Catholicism were correct here, Jesus would have said, "Go to the priests in My Church and confess to them and God will forgive you through them. No such absurdity exists in the Word of God. It is God Himself, and no other, who forgives all the sinner's iniquities (Psalm 103:3).

When Jesus claimed the power to forgive sins as Almighty God, the people and religious leaders surrounding him rightly exclaimed, *"Who can forgive sins but God alone?"* (Mark 2:7). Jesus responded by affirming He did have the power to forgive sins and demonstrated and proved this divine authority by healing and thus forgiving the paralytic man. He did not dispute what the scribes said about God alone having the power to forgive sins; they were right on that point. Jesus possessed the power and authority to forgive sins because He is God! And so Catholics do well to learn from the obvious lesson here when they try to defend the priest's actual power to forgive sins on behalf of God: the only man who can forgive a person's sins on behalf of God is His Son Jesus Christ, and no other.

> The religious leaders were correct in their statement that only God can forgive sins (Exodus 34:6-7; Psalm 103:3; Isaiah 43:25; Daniel 9:9); the priests merely declared people ritually clean. They also rightly understood that Jesus was claiming to be God. But in labeling Jesus' claim to forgive sins as blasphemous, the religious leaders showed they did not understand that Jesus was *God*. Jesus had God's power and authority to heal bodies and forgive sins. Forgiveness of sins was a sign that the messianic age had come (Isaiah 40:2; Joel 2:32; Micah 7:18-19; Zechariah 13:1) . . . The Son of Man has the delegated authority of God the Father to forgive sins. The teachers asked, "Who can forgive sins but God alone?" and the answer is, **"No human except one delegated that authority by God himself. And the Son of Man has that authority"** (Grant Osborne, *Life Application Bible Commentary: Mark* [Wheaton: Tyndale, 1994], pages 50-52).

The chief 'proof' text from the Bible the Roman Catholic Church appeals to for justification of the Sacrament of Confession and the priest's power to actually forgive sin is John 20:19-23 (particularly verses 22-23): *"Then, the same day at evening, being the first day of the week, when the doors were shut where the disciples were assembled for fear of the Jews, Jesus came and stood in the midst, and said to them, 'Peace be with you.' When He had said this, He showed them His hands and His side. Then the disciples were glad when they saw the Lord. So Jesus said to them again, 'Peace to you! As the Father has sent Me, I also send you.' And when He had said this, He breathed on them, and said to them, "Receive the Holy*

Spirit. *If you forgive the sins of any, they are forgiven them; if you retain the sins of any, they are retained.*"
Catholic priest John A. O'Brien speaks for Rome's traditional interpretation of John 20:21-23 when stating,

> It is to be observed also that Christ gave them power not merely to announce that sins were forgiven but actually to forgive them—"whose sins *you* shall forgive, they are forgiven them." If the authority of the Apostles were restricted to the declaration, "God pardons you," they would then require a special revelation in each case to make the pronouncement valid. Furthermore, the power conferred is a *judicial* one. They are not told to forgive or to retain indiscriminately but judicially, according as the sinner deserves. This obviously requires the specific acknowledgment or confession of sin. Lastly, it is to be noted that their authority is not restricted to any particular kind of sins, but extends to all without exception. Would it be possible to express in a clearer or more unmistakable manner the conferring upon the Apostles of this power of pardoning than in the plain language and in the solemn manner used by Christ? The divine Master, it would seem, wished to eliminate for all time the possibility of any misconstruction of His meaning by reiterating in the plainest and most literal terms what He has already stated to them in the beautiful rich metaphor of the Aramaic tongue. How is it possible for any Christian who professes to believe in the truth of Christ's teachings to escape the conclusion that He conferred upon His Church the selfsame power of forgiving sins which He Himself possessed?[124]

This alleged transference of power from Jesus to the Apostles to actually and literally forgive sin was not limited only to them but is passed on to, and is perpetuated through, their successors—the Roman Catholic clergy of Popes, bishops, and priests who now possess such power to forgive the sins of those who confess to them. Those who do not avail themselves of the forgiveness offered by God through the Catholic priest cannot therefore be forgiven. The popular *Baltimore Catechism* proclaims:

> The priest has the power to forgive sins from Jesus Christ, who said to His Apostles and to their successors in the priesthood: "Receive the Holy Spirit; whose sins you shall forgive, they are forgiven them; and whose sins you shall retain, they are retained." Only God can forgive sins. But He can decide for Himself how He wants to do it. And the way He has decided upon is to use priests as His instruments. We can truly say that Christ forgives sins, using the lips and hands of the priest, or we can say that the priest forgives sins by the power Christ gives him.[125]

The Catholic Encyclopedia assumes such a sacramental meaning is obvious for John 20:23 supposedly because,

> Christ here reiterates in the plainest terms—"sins", "forgive", "retain"—what He had previously stated in figurative language, "bind" and "loose", so that this text specifies and distinctly applies to sin the power of loosing and binding (a reference to Matthew 16:19). He prefaces this grant of power by declaring that the mission of the Apostles is similar

---

[124]   John A. O'Brien, *The Faith of Millions*, 169-170.
[125]   *The New Saint Joseph Baltimore Catechism*, 185.

to that which He had received from the Father and which He had fulfilled: "As the Father hath sent me". Now it is beyond doubt that He came into the world to destroy sin and that on various occasions He explicitly forgave sin (Matthew 9:2-8; Luke 5:20; 7:47; Revelation 1:5), hence the forgiving of sin is to be included in the mission of the Apostles. Christ not only declared that sins were forgiven, but really and actually forgave them; hence, the Apostles are empowered not merely to announce to the sinner that his sins are forgiven but to grant him forgiveness—"whose sins you shall forgive". If their power were limited to the declaration "God pardons you", they would need a special revelation in each case to make the declaration valid. The power is twofold—to forgive or to retain, i.e., the Apostles are not told to grant or withhold forgiveness nondiscriminately; they must act judicially, forgiving or retaining according as the sinner deserves. The exercise of this power in either form (forgiving or retaining) is not restricted: no distinction is made or even suggested between one kind of sin and another, or between one class of sinners and all the rest: Christ simply says "whose *sins*." The sentence pronounced by the Apostles (remission or retention) is also God's sentence—"they are forgiven" … "they are retained."[126]

Does John 20:23 indeed teach Jesus gave the authority to forgive sins to the Roman Catholic Church and her select priesthood? No, in no way, because, as we have already shown from Scripture, it is God Who alone has power and authority to forgive sin (Isaiah 43:25; 44:22; Jeremiah 50:20; Luke 5:21), and so to change such an immutable truth by claiming Rome's priests now have this special prerogative is to contradict Scripture and, at the same time, usurp God's exclusive right and supreme authority to grant pardon and forgiveness for any and every sin committed! The key to arriving at the proper interpretation of John 20:23 is found in the translation of the Greek text and how the grammar is actually employed in the verse. The phrases Jesus spoke "are forgiven" and "are retained," are spoken in the perfect tense. The verse would then literally read: ***"If you forgive the sins of any, they are already forgiven them; if you retain the sins of any, they are already retained."***

Anyone familiar with Greek grammar here will know the perfect tense normally expresses a past action completed with ongoing results. Therefore the forgiveness or the retainment of sins has already occurred prior to the disciples' ability to declare this to be so. The perfect tenses used in John 20:23 are in the passive voice and at once show it is God who is acting alone, either to forgive or retain the sins of the one being acted upon.[127]Jesus is giving the authority for the disciple to affirm or deny this is the case, where God has already determined the results of either action. John 20:23 simply means the Sprit-filled and -empowered Church is given the authority from God to pronounce or declare the forgiveness of sins—which is now accomplished and offered through the death and resurrection of Jesus Christ upon all who receive this—and the judgment and condemnation on those whose sins will not be forgiven because they reject Christ's offer of salvation through His saving death on the cross. Simply put, the Church is to proclaim the forgiveness of sins on those who repent and believe the Gospel, and the retention of sins on those who do not believe it.

Throughout the pages of the New Testament, God's forgiveness of sin and the redemptive benefits of Christ's suffering and death are formally and exclusively offered through the preaching of the Gospel—and 1 Corinthians 15:1-4 defines the Gospel to be that ***"Christ died for our sins according to the Scriptures, and***

---

[126]   *Catholic Encyclopedia*: The Sacrament of Penance (http://www.newadvent.org/cathen/11618c.htm).
[127]   D.A. Carson, *The Gospel According to John,* 655.

that He was buried, and that He rose again the third day according to the Scriptures." Paul goes on to tell his Corinthian audience it is by this very Gospel one stands right with God and is saved from the penalty of sin. No mention is given for a sacrament of penance when it comes to salvation from sin and with it God's forgiveness. The Apostle clearly states this all comes through the preaching of the Gospel (1 Corinthians 15:1). And this is exactly what Jesus meant when He commissioned the Church with the mission of John 20:23. He gave them the authority to preach the Gospel so that forgiveness of sins from God could be offered. It is *not a judicial power* to forgive sins that is given here by Christ to His Church but, rather, *a declaratory power* to proclaim sins are now forgiven by Him to those who repent of sin and believe in Him—and conversely, the authority to declare sins are retained or remain unforgiven on those who refuse repentance and remain in unbelief towards the Gospel![128] Leon Morris' comments here, made about the real meaning of John 20:23 over and against the sacramental meaning from Roman Catholicism, are quite enlightening:

> Those who refer the words to the ministry usually concentrate on the power of absolution. They think of the Christian priest as a man with God-given authority *to declare* to men that their sins are forgiven. It ought not to be overlooked that the power to declare sins forgiven is on all fours with the power to declare them retained. I do not think that this verse teaches that any individual Christian minister has the God-given authority to say to a sinner, "I refuse to forgive your sins. They are retained." But unless this can be said, the words about forgiveness cannot be said. The one goes with the other.
>
> It should also be borne in mind that, according to the best text, the verbs "are forgiven" and "are retained" are in the perfect tense. The meaning of this is that the Spirit-filled church can pronounce with authority that the sins of such and such men have been forgiven or have been retained. If the church is really acting under the leadership of the Spirit it will be found that her pronouncements on this matter do but reveal what has already been determined in heaven.[129]

Even Roman Catholic scholar Richard P. McBrien concedes that the text of John 20:22-23, "by itself," does not prove Jesus instituted the Roman Catholic sacrament of Penance, when admitting:

> The text to which Catholic doctrine has traditionally appealed in asserting the sacramentality and divine origin of Penance is John 20:22-23, which records one of Jesus' post resurrection appearances: "Receive the Holy Spirit. If you forgive the sins of any, they are forgiven them; if you retain the sins of any, they are retained" (see also Matthew 16:19; 18:18). <u>By itself, the text does not "prove" that Jesus instituted the sacrament of Penance as we know it</u>

---

[128] William Barclay captures what the text of John 20:23 really means when he comments: "This sentence does not mean that the power to forgive sins was ever entrusted to any man or to any men; it means that the power to proclaim that forgiveness was so entrusted; and it means that the power to warn that that forgiveness is not open to the impenitent was also entrusted to them. This sentence lays down the duty of the Church to convey forgiveness to the penitent in heart, and to warn the impenitent that they are forfeiting the mercy of God" (quoted in *The Gospel According to John* by Leon Morris, page 848).

[129] Leon Morris, *The Gospel According to John*, 849.

today or that he conferred the power to forgive sins only on the Apostles, their successors, and their chosen delegates (*Catholicism*, page 836).

What Jesus does give to the Church, and to each Christian individually, is the privilege and authority to declare or proclaim the basis upon which the forgiveness of sins by God is given or withheld. And by letting Scripture interpret Scripture, we discover this commission was carried out and understood by the Apostles and disciples to consist of the proclamation of the Gospel to the world—and whoever receives it will have their sins forgiven, and whoever rejects this Gospel will not have their sins forgiven—by essentially having these retained against them for the day of judgment. This is exactly what the Apostles did, taught, and wrote in the New Testament. And this is precisely how Peter understood the commission of John 20:23 when he told the Jewish nation to repent and receive the remission of sins offered in the name of Jesus Christ (see Acts 2:28; 3; 4:10-12). The Apostle further confirmed to Gentiles that this forgiveness was offered, "that, through His name (i.e., Jesus Christ), whoever believes in Him will receive remission of sins" (Acts 10:43). The Apostle Paul similarly declared the same thing when exclaiming, *"Therefore let it be known to you, brethren, that through this Man is preached to you the forgiveness of sins"* (Acts 13:38).

It is by faith in Jesus Christ that God pardons, remits, and forgives the sinner—not by going through a sacramental ritual of confessing to a priest (John 3:16; Romans 5:1; Galatians 2:16; 3:11; Titus 3:5; 1 Peter 1:9, 18-19). The whole idea of the Apostles and disciples setting up confessional boxes, or going around and expecting their converts to privately confess their sins to them, so that they could personally grant absolution and give acts of penance to do is never once done or practiced in all of the New Testament!

> The scriptural reality is that there is not a single verse in the New Testament (including John 20:23) that instructs us to confess our sins to some priest. Nor do we see a single example in the Book of Acts or any other biblical book of anyone making confession to a priest (or disciple). Confession is to be made to God alone (Psalm 32:5; Nehemiah 1:4-11; Daniel 9:3-19; Ezra 9:5-15).[130]

The commission Jesus gave in John 20:23 is the same event recounted in Luke 24:46-48 and holds the same meaning—the disciples were to go into the world and proclaim that the forgiveness of sins is offered in the name of Jesus Christ—the very thing the Apostles did throughout the Book of Acts. Jesus' words at once show He was not instituting a sacrament of penance for the church, and thus ordaining priests to hear confession and grant absolution, but that He was simply ordaining preachers of the Gospel. This group Jesus spoke to and commissioned was not just the twelve Apostles, but all those who were present; for John and Luke mention other disciples were present with the eleven Apostles and were included in the commission Christ gave as recorded in both John 20 and Luke 24! Such a fact then clearly indicates all Christian disciples of Jesus are to carry out the mission of proclaiming forgiveness of sins through belief in that Gospel they are to proclaim. The mission and message is given to the Holy Spirit-empowered church as a whole—no select priesthood is marked out or signified here. The Lord has entrusted you and me, as born-again followers of Jesus Christ, with the evangelical authority to preach the Gospel of salvation, whereby the forgiveness of God is offered through faith in Jesus Christ to those who repent and believe, but is withheld to those who do not believe. Thus, the focus of John 20:23 is not on *Roman Catholic sacramentalism* but on *Christian evangelism*—the preaching of the Gospel, and nothing more:

---

[130]   Ron Rhodes, *Reasoning from the Scriptures with Catholics*, 223

There is no doubt from the context that the reference is to forgiving sins, or withholding forgiveness. But though this sounds stern and harsh, it is simply the result of the preaching of the gospel, which either brings men to repent as they hear of the ready and costly forgiveness of God, or leaves them unresponsive to the offer of forgiveness which is the gospel, and so they are left in their sins.[131]

Since the New Testament doctrine and historical practice (as we discovered earlier in chapter nine) teaches the priesthood of all believers, the commission of John 20:23 is given to every born-again believer in Jesus Christ, and consists in the act of preaching the verdict heaven has already made—forgiveness of sins through the shed blood of Jesus Christ for those who believe, and the retention of sins bringing condemnation on those who do not believe the Gospel message of salvation. So this Gospel-preaching ministry will produce two results: the remission of sins to those who believe the Gospel of Jesus Christ, and the punitive retainment of sins leading to condemnation on those who reject its saving message. The same idea of remission and retainment through the proclamation of the Gospel is exactly what Paul describes in 2 Corinthians 2:14-16. *"Now thanks be to God who always leads us in triumph in Christ, and through us diffuses the fragrance of His knowledge in every place. For we are to God the fragrance of Christ among those who are being saved* (whose sins are remitted because they believe in Christ) *and among those who are perishing* (whose sins are still retained against them for their unbelief)*. To the one we are the aroma of death leading to death, and to the other the aroma of life leading to life."* This is precisely the pattern we find throughout the New Testament Scriptures. This is the ministry of Gospel preaching and reconciliation, which was practiced by all Christians in the early church. Nowhere was it restricted or limited to the Apostles or a priestly class in the form of a Roman Catholic hierarchy.

There is not one single instance where Jesus conferred to His disciples the actual and judicial power to forgive sins based upon their discerning ability of a person's willingness to perform certain acts of penance to earn God's forgiveness given through a church or ecclesiastical clergy. Stephen, a deacon in the Apostolic church, boldly proclaimed to the unbelieving elders of Israel God's displeasure with them over rejecting the coming of Jesus the Messiah—their sins were thus retained (Acts 7:51-52). The first martyr of the Christian church was not a priest or ranking cleric of a select clergy! Philip, another deacon in the early church, actively preached the Gospel of the forgiveness of sins through Jesus Christ to the Samaritans, the Ethiopian eunuch, and all the cities leading to Caesarea (Acts 8:5-7, 26-40). Paul informs all the Christians in Corinth that God has committed to each one of them a ministry of reconciliation (2 Corinthians 5:18-21). Paul defines what this ministry is; it is not some sacrament of Penance dispensed in a confessional box, but is in fact the proclamation of the Gospel, *"that is, that God was in Christ reconciling the world to Himself, not imputing their trespasses to them, and has committed to us the word of reconciliation. Now then, we are ambassadors for Christ, as though God were pleading through us: we implore you on Christ's behalf, be reconciled to God. For He made Him who knew no sin to be sin for us, that we might become the righteousness of God in Him."* (2 Corinthians 5:19-21)

Here, we see from Scripture that the message of reconciliation with God given to the church consists in proclaiming that Christ's sinless substitutionary death for sinners reconciles them to a forgiving God. It is not found in a sacrament where people must confess their sins to priests inside a private booth. True biblical reconciliation comes through faith in Christ's vicarious death for sinners, and no more! Every member of

---

[131]   John Marsh, *The Gospel of John* (New York: Penguin, 1968), 641-642.

Christ's church has been entrusted with proclaiming the full remission of sins on those accepting Christ's expiatory death for them. Even former Roman Catholic priest Joseph Zacchello eventually came to this conclusion when realizing that Rome's exclusive claim for her priests' power of remitting sins, by a form of absolution in the tribunal of confession, was empty and without biblical support or justification:

> Christ was then commissioning His apostles to preach the Gospel to every creature. His own mission entailed great suffering; so would theirs. His mission, which was then accomplished, was to save men and "take away the sins of the world." They were now being sent to make that salvation known, to preach about forgiveness of sins obtained by Christ. Christ sent His apostles to preach that sins are forgiven to those who believe in Him. Thus the words: "Whose sins you shall forgive, they are forgiven them, etc." This means whose sins you are the means of forgiving by your preaching of the Gospel, they will be forgiven; and whose sins you retain, they will be retained; for the Gospel, while it is the "cause of life" to some, is the "cause of death" to others. The Gospel is a message to all nations and carries a responsibility to those who refuse to accept it. All ministers and all Christians have the power of remitting sins by preaching of Christ, by making known to unbelievers the price of salvation paid by Christ. "Through Him forgiveness of sins is proclaimed to you" (Acts 13:38) . . . Only the priests of Rome claim the power of remitting sins by a form of absolution in the tribunal of confession. The apostles never practiced this but preached forgiveness of sins and salvation through faith in Christ. "Believe and be saved" is the motto of the New Testament.[132]

In John 20:23 we have Jesus giving the Apostles and the other disciples (and by extension all of the Church) the Spirit-filled power of declaring God's terms for granting forgiveness of sins to those who believe in Jesus, and the verdict of sins which remain unforgiven on those who don't believe in Jesus. So, when the sinner accepts the forgiveness of sins offered through the New Covenant death of Jesus the Messiah, the Christian can authoritatively say to the person who believes in Jesus: "Your sins are forgiven you"; and conversely if a person rejects the atoning death of Jesus, the Christian preacher can then say by the authority of Scripture, "Your sins are not forgiven."

> Proclaiming the forgiveness of sins was the prominent feature of the apostolic preaching in the Book of Acts. Jesus was giving the Apostles (and by extension, the church) the privilege of announcing heaven's terms on how a person can receive forgiveness. If one believes in Jesus, then a Christian has the right to announce his forgiveness. If a person rejects Jesus' sacrifice, then a Christian can announce that that person is not forgiven.[133]

---

[132]   Joseph Zacchello, *Secrets of Romanism*, 102-103.

[133]   John Walvoord and Roy Zuck, *The Bible Knowledge Commentary* (New Testament), 343. Furthermore, ex-Catholic priest Clark Butterfield is absolutely correct when he points out that no one in the New Testament period or following after, during the beginning centuries of the early church, interpreted John 20:20-23 in their writings to mean a person had to confess his sins to a priest and receive absolution from him: "Immediately after the New Testament years and in the beginning centuries of church history, no Christian writer has left a record that the text of John 20:21-23 was used to support a concept of confessing sins to a clergyman and receiving absolution from him. Nor is there a record that the Church in general claimed the power to personally forgive sins through confession to

As we discovered in previous pages about the Mass, the New Testament unanimously teaches that the shed blood of Jesus Christ on the cross accomplishes the removal and full remission of sins. Forgiveness of sins by the death of Jesus is the essential truth of the New Covenant (Jeremiah 31:31-34; Matthew 26:28). Penal satisfaction with God rests in the blood of Christ alone. But with the Roman Catholic sacrament of Penance, absolution alone is not enough to fully and completely absolve the Catholic from his sins; even with the death of Jesus Christ included, the confessing Catholic must "recover his full spiritual health by doing something more to make amends for the sin; he must 'make satisfaction for' or 'expiate' his sins. This satisfaction is also called 'penance'." This satisfaction for sins imposed upon the penitent is not only required as a "safeguard for the new life and as a remedy to weakness, but also as a vindicatory punishment for former sins" (see *Catechism of the Catholic Church* [1459], and also the Council of Trent, Session 14, Chapter 8). The Roman Catholic system requires prayer, fasting, saying the rosary, and forms of bodily mortification like the flagellation of self (more common here in the Middle Ages for monks and priests) as the standard acts of penance to expiate sin; and those sins that *still* require expiation or punishment must await the soul's temporary consignment in purgatory, until all this is done and the Catholic soul is ready to be released for entrance into heaven.

Of all Rome's egregious heresies, this has to be one of the most blasphemous, simply because it practically reduces and diminishes the complete and perfect efficacy of Christ's atoning death to fully expiate all sin into something which has to be renewed, reset, and propped up over and over again by works of penance, until sin is committed once more and that forgiveness is lost, only to have the sacramental process begin all over again. For Rome to insist the sinner must still pay the "temporal" punishment for his sins is to essentially admit the blood of Christ is not powerful enough to permanently, completely, and irreversibly remit all sin and to satisfactorily propitiate the divine punishment for them here and now the moment saving faith in the Cross of Christ is exercised. To add anything else to this, whether it be sacraments, performing penance, confession to a priest, and so on, is to emphatically teach God requires more than just faith in the atoning death of Jesus Christ for the salvation of the sinner; and this in effect makes the observant Roman Catholic, receiving the sacraments from the priest, to be his own savior! To perform penance in order to expiate your sins is to not put full trust in the power of Christ's blood to permanently and completely remove sin the moment faith in Jesus Christ is made! Such an errant doctrine is contrary to the biblical truth that sinners are totally cleansed from all sin here, now, and forever after by the blood of Jesus Christ the moment they believe in Him—and not because of human suffering or some penitential acts we must do as a meritorious condition for receiving the forgiveness of God.

The Bible resoundingly teaches God set forth Jesus Christ to serve *"as a propitiation by His blood, through faith, to demonstrate His righteousness"* (Romans 3:25). Propitiation simply means to fully satisfy the wrath of God for the punishment of sin. The result brings a full expiation of sin by the forgiveness of God demonstrated on the repentant sinner, followed by a total cancelation of the punishment due those sins because Christ Jesus, in His death, vicariously endured the totality of God's wrath for all sins in the sinner's place as His sinless, righteous substitute. Since Jesus bore the full punishment due our sins, there is no more punishment which remains whether temporal or eternal for the Christian's sins (Romans 8:1)! Christ took them all and bore the collective punishment for them Himself when dying on the cross for our sins! And so

---

a presbyter or elder. The Church did not consider its presbyters (also known as bishops or 'overseers') to be priests in any sense. At that period it was the proud boast of Christians to the pagan world that they had neither altar nor sacrifice and therefore no priest" (*Night Journey from Rome*, Chino California: Chick Publications, 1982), 108-109.

it is because God, not the Roman Catholic Church with their confessional boxes and their priests waiting to grant penance, sent His Son to be the propitiation for our sins (1 John 2:2) that we are now cleansed from all sin, and thereby fully delivered from the righteous wrath of God now, and yet to come (see 1 Thessalonians 1:10; 5:9). God's Word promises that those who do accept the propitiatory death of Jesus for their sins will never come under the condemnation of God and the punishment that comes with it (John 3:18; Romans 8:1-2, 34; 1 Thessalonians 1:10; 5:9). By this fact alone, there is no longer any type of lingering punishment from God on those whose sins have been expiated and removed by the crucified Christ.

A January 27, 2010, press release from the *Times* in the United Kingdom revealed that the late Pope John Paul II habitually whipped himself as an "act of penance" in remorse for his sins and an attempt "to feel closer to God." Several witnesses give testimony to this sad and disturbing fact. Monsignor Slawomir Oder, who is at the time of this writing, was in charge of the canonization process looking to declare the late Pope a saint, says the Polish-born Pope performed self-flagellation when a bishop in Krakow and continued to do so in the Vatican after being elected Pope in 1978. The Monsignor goes on to recount how the Pope believed self-flagellation was "an instrument of Christian perfection emulating the sufferings of Christ." Self-flagellation has been practiced among the Roman Catholic clergy since the medieval period, and is done with the belief it brings merit and forgiveness from God as an act of Penance.[134] Pope John Paul II continued with this practice and belief. Another witness to this unbiblical practice comes from Sister Tobiana Sobotka—a Polish nun who worked for John Paul in his Vatican apartment and at the papal summer residence at Castel Gandolfo. When relating to this pope's practice of regular self-flagellation, she states: "We would hear it—we were in the next room at Castel Gandolfo. You could hear the sound of the blows when he would flagellate himself. He did it when he was still capable of moving on his own."[135]

The account of Pope John Paul's self-flagellation for penance is simply tragic because Christ died for all of our sins. In fact, Isaiah 53:5 foretold the Messiah would vicariously bear the punishment for the sinner by undergoing flagellation Himself, when saying *"And by His stripes we are healed."* This was accurately fulfilled when the Romans whipped Jesus as He was bearing God's chastisement for our sins (John 19:1 with 1Peter 2:24). Had the late Pope John Paul II realized this great salvation truth, he would not have vainly sought to flagellate himself. Had he understood the Gospel correctly, John Paul would have rested in the vicarious sufferings of Jesus as the perfect payment for his sins. Whipping yourself in remorse for your sins, like the late Pope evidently did, is not necessary, needed, meritorious, or required by the Lord and His Word, nor anything of the sort, to get closer to God or satisfy His righteous justice against sin. What we see in this shocking story about the Pope's self flagellation is a larger reflection of Roman Catholicism's bankrupt theology, defective Soteriology, and total ignorance coming from a lack of correctly understanding what the Gospel really is, how it is truly applied to the sinner's life, and how this salvation is given and received.

The Pope's unbiblical justification for the practice of the sacrament of Penance through flagellation was to supposedly "emulate the sufferings of Christ."[136] Yet we know from Scripture the Christian does not

---

[134] Some of the more famous self-flagellants in the Catholic Church were St. Francis of Assisi, St. Teresa of Avilia, St. Ignatius Loyola, Thomas More, and Mother Teresa.

[135] *The Times*, January 27, 2010, online edition, http://www.timesonline.co.uk/tol/comment/faith/article7003976.

[136] Roman Catholic belief teaches from what Paul says in Colossians 1:24 that a person can suffer for Christ and gain merit, favor, and forgiveness with God for oneself and others as an act of penance or even "atonement" (see Ludwig Ott, *Fundamentals of Catholic Dogma*, page 317). *"I now rejoice in my sufferings for you, and fill up in my flesh what is lacking in the afflictions of Christ, for the sake of His body, which is the church."* Catholic teaching takes the phrase *"and fill up in my flesh what is lacking in the afflictions of Christ"* to mean any Catholic who dies in

need to do that! Jesus has already given us a commemorative way by which the church can remember the sufferings and death the Savior endured for our sins; it is in the ordinance of the Lord's Supper (Luke 22:19; 1 Corinthians 11:23-26). Unlike the Roman Catholic sacrament of Penance, the Bible states the forgiven sinner in Christ does not have to pay for one single sin, since Jesus already paid the full price for us on the cross (Romans 3:25-28; 5:8-21; Colossians 1:20-23).

The whole idea of sacramental penance, whether it be in the acts of self-flagellation, reciting the rosary, saying an "Our Father" or a "Hail Mary", etc, takes away from the once-for-all sacrifice of Christ for our sins in propitiation (full satisfaction) of God's wrath won for us by the atonement Jesus made on the cross (see Hebrews 7:11-27). Hebrews chapter 7 makes it quite clear Jesus' sacrifice for all sin was a "once-for-all" sacrifice. In light of this, there is no more required sacrificial act or rite to appease God's punishment for sin since Jesus bore the full brunt of them on the cross. Catholic penance, however, is the opposite, and at once supplants and depreciates this accomplishment! The idea one must do penance to pay for one's sins and contribute to his own salvation, or remain in a state of grace and justification, is not found in the Scriptures. The Bible does demand "repentance" which is quite different from the idea of 'penance'. Roman Catholic apologists typically counter this claim by pointing out Bible passages in the Roman Catholic Douay-Rheims version of the Bible (based upon Jerome's Latin Vulgate) which do command penance. No other credible translation of the Bible translates "repent" to mean or read, "Do penance."

In several passages where "repent" is meant from the Greek text, Rome has inserted the word penance in its place! Several quotations from the Roman Catholic Douay-Rheims version demonstrate this: ***"And in those days cometh John the Baptist preaching in the desert of Judea. And saying: <u>do penance</u>: for the kingdom of heaven is at hand"*** (Matthew 3:1-2). Jesus said in Luke 13:5: ***"No, I say to you: but unless you shall <u>do penance</u>, you shall all likewise perish." "But Peter said to them: <u>do penance</u>, and be baptized"*** (Acts 2:38). ***"And God indeed having winked at the times of this ignorance, now declareth unto men, that all should every where <u>do penance</u>"*** (Acts 17:30).

But when we turn to the Greek text of the New Testament, we find the more accurate and correct word that belongs in these passages is "repent" instead of "penance." Repentance is not the same as penance. The New Testament Greek word for "repent" (*metanoeo*) is found where the substituted word "penance" is found

---

an imperfect state must still pay the temporal consequences for their venial sins in purgatory or can partially do so now by performing acts of penance that call for bodily suffering. Yet, what Paul was actually saying in Colossians 1:24 was not this! The context and wording of this passage make this obvious. Paul refers to the suffering he was going though for the sake of the Church and the ministry of proclaiming the Gospel, which we learn from his other letters and in the book of Acts, was inflicted upon him wherever he went. Since Christ is now in heaven, He no longer physically suffers on Earth for the Church. So in that sense, He does lack, or remains absent from, this kind of suffering which was experienced by Paul and now by other Christians who suffer for Jesus. The suffering and atonement Christ accomplished on the cross is more than sufficient to make **perfect forever** all who believe in the Gospel (Hebrews 10:10-14). In a mystical sort of way, Christ does suffer through His body, the Church, when they are persecuted on Earth. He told Saul of Tarsus as much when saying to him from heaven, ***"Saul, Saul, why are you persecuting Me?"*** when he was persecuting and killing Christians (Acts 8:1-3; 9:1-5). But in no way does Scripture teach a Christian can suffer to atone for his or another's sins, procure God's forgiveness, or add to the perfect merit of Christ's death to achieve salvation in any way; as it is written in Psalm 49:7, ***"None of them can by any means redeem his brother, nor give to God a ransom for him"***. Such an idea assigned to the Roman Catholic sacrament of Penance would logically mean Christ's death on the cross is insufficient at a certain point to completely save and forgive sinners. If true, this would be a blasphemous notion that contradicts many other New Testament passages (e.g., John 17:4; 19:30; Hebrews 1:1-3; 10:14).

in all the aforementioned Scripture passages. [137] *Strong's Exhaustive Concordance of the Bible* formally defines *metanoeo* to mean: change one's mind (i.e. to repent); to change one's mind for better; heartily to amend with abhorrence of one's past sins. The word "repent" occurs thirty-four times in the New Testament. Vine's Complete Expository Dictionary of Old and New Testament Words defines *metanoeo* (μετανοιω) thus:

> 1. Metanoeo (3340), lit., "to perceive afterwards" (meta, "after," implying "change," noeo, "to perceive"; nous, "the mind, the seat of moral reflection"), in contrast to *pronoeo*, "to perceive beforehand," hence signifies "to change one's mind or purpose," always, in the NT, involving a change for the better, an amendment, and always, except in Luke 17:3, 4, of "repentance" from sin. The word is found in the Synoptic Gospels (in Luke, nine times), in Acts five times, in the Apocalypse twelve times, eight in the messages to the churches.[138]

Biblical repentance is entirely different from the Roman Catholic concept of Penance. Repentance is a change of the heart and mind that results from the conviction of sin by the Holy Spirit for unbelief toward Jesus Christ (John 16:7-9). Penance is focused on what the person must do for absolution as instructed by the priest. Repentance is the fruit of turning to Jesus in faith for salvation. It is not a work or prerequisite for salvation but granted by the goodness of a merciful God (Matthew 3:8; 4:17; Romans 2:4). Penance is a work created by the traditions of men and is imposed by the priest on the Catholic wanting reconciliation with the Church. Repentance comes from the heart and is a sovereign work of the Holy Spirit, causing the sinner to turn from sin and embrace the Lord Jesus Christ as Savior. Penance is an outward ritual prescribed by Rome's priests, controlled by a certain few, making them arbiters of God's forgiveness. God wants people to repent not so they can be punished for their sins later on if they fail to recount them one by one to a priest of Rome, but to receive full pardon and forgiveness through Jesus Christ, Who bore the punishment for those sins on the cross. It is freely offered to everyone who believes (Isaiah 55:1). Penance is a counterfeit repentance and should be abandoned for real repentance turning one to trust in Jesus Christ alone for the forgiveness of sins.

> Penance is a wholly different thing from gospel repentance. Penance is an outward act. Repentance is of the heart. Penance is imposed by a Roman priest. Repentance is the sovereign work of the Holy Spirit. What God desires in the sinner is not a punishment of oneself for sins, but a change of heart, a real forsaking of sin, shown by a new life of obedience to God's commands. In short, penance is a counterfeit repentance. It is the work of man on his body; true repentance is the work of God in the soul. The divine Word commands, "Rend your heart and not your garments" (Joel 2:13). Penance is "rending the garments," an outward form without inward reality. But what God demands is not acts of penance, but repentance, which means turning from sin. "Let the wicked forsake his way, and the unrighteous man his thoughts; and let him return to the Lord, and He will have mercy upon him: for He will abundantly pardon" (Isa. 55:7).[139]

---

[137] The modern Roman Catholic translations of the Bible finally acknowledged this error and replaced the incorrect rendering "do penance" with the correct word "repent" for metanoeo in all the NT passages.

[138] W.E. Vine, *An Expository Dictionary of Biblical Words*, 951-952.

[139] Mark Edward Sohmer, *The Gospel of Rome: Part 8: Penance*. See http://www.sohmer.net/GoR/07-penance.php

Rome's insistence on the necessity of the Sacraments for salvation, in this case the Sacrament of penance, is a circumvention of the free gift of salvation from beginning to end. The need of doing penance by the Pope and the millions of Catholics who follow him sadly exhibits a level of uncertainty, on their collective part, about the finality and assurance of salvation, and a lack of understanding about the true biblical Gospel that proclaims the free and full pardon of sin by simple faith in the death and resurrection of Jesus Christ (Hebrews 9:1-15). Reciting a "Hail Mary", the rosary, or the more extreme example of flagellating oneself for penance are "dead works" which cannot save the person in the biblical sense from the punishment of sin.

Performing acts of penance to earn God's forgiveness, taught by Roman Catholicism, is not sanctioned or found in Scripture, and it utterly betrays a lack of faith, and a lack of trust in the finished work of the cross by which God *fully* and *freely* pardons, expiates, and forgives the sins of those who believe Christ's death is the propitiatory sacrifice for all sin. To those honest seeking Catholics wanting assurance of salvation, Christ and His Word do not want you to be in despair over this, or be uncertain regarding your salvation. He alone accomplished this for you on the cross and offers it to you as a free gift from start to finish. The Lord calls for a repentance from the "dead works" of Rome's sacramental system (Hebrews 6:1; 9:14) to trust in Jesus alone for the forgiveness of sins through His once-for-all sacrifice on the cross—nothing more and nothing less! On Good Friday, Jesus died for the sins of the world, and as divine perfection incarnate made the perfect sacrifice to propitiate God's wrath. Christ suffered for six hours on the cross taking the punishment due for every sin upon Himself, which you and I deserved and earned by our wicked rebellion and sinfulness against God. The completion of our redemption, with the full pardon of sins, was vouchsafed for us when Jesus cried from the cross, *"It is finished."* Salvation and forgiveness from God to the believer in Christ is a done and finished work. Therefore, no further payment for sin is needed through penance or some system of meritorious suffering that Roman Catholicism demands. Thinking you can pay Jesus back by doing penance is a sign of unbelief demonstrative of a prideful unwillingness to accept that the penalty of our sins has already been paid for in full by Jesus Christ, Who bore God's punishment for all of them on the cross. To deny such a magnanimous gesture by God is an insult to Him as the Giver of a free gift to the one who thinks he or she must do additional work to keep it or add to its perfect effectiveness. At the very core of Rome's sacrament of penance is a gross belittlement of the perfect efficacy of Christ's work of expiation for all sin on the cross. Since the cross was a perfect and finished work, saving sinners who believe in Him for salvation, nothing can be added to it. For that reason every forgiven Christian can take his sins directly to the Savior and receive forgiveness from God on the basis of His shed blood alone.

This will not sit well with the Roman Catholic sacramentalist, because he believes God's forgiveness can only be administered through the sacraments as the priest properly administers them. This reduces salvation down to the claim that the only way to God and the reception of His forgiveness is by going through the priest and the sacraments of the "Church." In doing this, Rome has in effect repaired the torn veil that stood between the Holy Place and the Holy of Holies separating the sinner from God, which was rent upon the death of Christ allowing direct and free access to God (Matthew 27:51); which thereby robs the believer of this free, unhindered access to God the Father through the cross of Jesus Christ. The imposition of a priesthood and the system of sacraments for salvation are simply erecting a wall blocking direct, equal, and free access to God through the Person of Jesus Christ, Who stands ever ready to receive, forgive, and save all sinners who come to Him by faith. Rome's belief in the sacraments is nothing more than a belief in a system of salvation replacing that of a personal relationship with Jesus Christ established on trust and faith. Rome teaches her own: "Go to the sacraments for salvation and forgiveness." But the word of Christ says we are to go to Him and believe in His finished work of the cross to be saved and totally forgiven of sins (John 3:14-18;

5:24; 6:29, 47)! Jesus Christ did not come to offer a convoluted system of Roman Catholic sacraments for a probationary salvation until we inevitably fall into sin once again, only to be "rejustified" over and over again by the grace imparting sacraments, but rather, He came to offer Himself alone as the ransom for our sins (Mark 10:45) that has saved us from all sins *once for all*, *permanently*, *completely*, and *irreversibly*. Bible critic of Roman Catholicism Robert M. Zins accurately states this, and very well too, when explaining how the Roman Catholic Church has placed their system of sacraments above and before the finished work of Christ's cross, a recurring and disturbing theme in Catholic theology:

> It would be wrong enough for the Romanist to teach that a priest alone has the power to forgive sins. But they are not done! The priest has power to also prescribe suitable satisfaction for sin to the poor misguided sinner who seeks his hope in Rome. Adherents to Rome are taught that their satisfactions to God are part of their forgiveness. We ask, "Where in Scripture is our own atonement for sins the basis for forgiveness? Where is penance shackled onto the repentant sinner by either Christ or the Apostles?" At the heart of Rome's doctrine of repentance is a dreadful misunderstanding of the completed work of Jesus Christ on the cross. Christians believe that they can add nothing to the finished work of Christ. For this reason, the Christian takes his sins directly to Jesus and pleads His blood alone for forgiveness. The Christian enters into the Holy of Holies upon the blood of the Lamb and finds absolution from the Father . . . Over and over we see this same theme in the Catholic religion. Romanists are bent on delivering a system of salvation rather than the Person of Christ. If we could identify one overarching principle which separates Romanism from Christianity it would be this: Rome has concocted a religion designed to arrive at Jesus Christ, whereas Christianity is a *relationship* with the Person of Christ and not a *system* fashioned by man to get to Him! Rome says, "Christ has told us to do this and that and more of the same if you want to have a relationship with me." The Christian says, "Christ has told us to have a relationship with me." The Christian says, "Christ has told us to place all of our trust and confidence in His finished work and we shall be saved." For the Christian, Christ has not come to offer a sacramental system. On the contrary, He offers Himself. No system in the world can be substituted for the Person of Christ. It only intensifies the denial of Christ to insist that He gave to the world the Romanist religion.[140]

The division of sin into the arbitrary category of "venial" and "mortal" sins is a dangerous one not supported in Scripture. Such a twofold categorization of sin from minor to major sins can potentially and practically lead to a minimization of the severity and extreme danger of sin, leading a Catholic to perhaps believe venial sins are not bad enough to harm himself or others and to offend God. After all, whatever sin is committed can most of the time easily be cleared by going to a priest to confess and receive the sacrament of penance. The idea of an easy out like this, given the predictability of corrupt human nature, is rife with abuse. If the Catholic knows all he has to do to receive forgiveness is make a private confession to a priest, he can enjoy whatever particular venial sin he chooses to do, or blithely do it with premeditation knowing all he has to do is admit to a priest and he can escape God's condemnation for that sin. Though many Roman Catholics don't view the sacrament of penance in this way, and do take all sin very seriously, the opportunity

---

[140]   Robert M. Zins, *Romanism*, 100.

for abuse, misuse and the minimizing of the severity of sin easily results, as history has repeatedly shown with the sacrament of penance (which will be documented later in the pages below). Speaking careless words or gossiping about someone is routinely classified by the Catholic Church to be a venial sin, when the Word of God properly views this as very severe and serious—so much so that it will be the basis for a person's justification or condemnation before God! Jesus certainly understood this to be the case when properly evaluating all sin as serious enough to call down the judgment of God, when giving warning about speaking careless words in Matthew 12:36-37: ***"But I say to you that every idle word men may speak, they will give account of it in the day of judgment. For by your words you will be justified, and by your words you will be condemned."***

Even thinking the wrong things are not treated lightly or in a venial fashion by the Lord. To lustfully desire after women in one's mind may not be morally equivalent to actually committing physical adultery with her; it still needs to be eliminated, removed, and totally "cut off" from one's thought life. Failure to do so would lead to the damnation of hell! Jesus taught: ***"You have heard that it was said to those of old, 'You shall not commit adultery.' But I say to you that whoever looks at a woman to lust for her has already committed adultery with her in his heart. If your right eye causes you to sin, pluck it out and cast it from you; for it is more profitable for you that one of your members perish, than for your whole body to be cast into hell"*** (Matthew 5:27-29). The Word of God makes no categorical distinction between "mortal" and "venial" sins. Granted, while it is true not all sins are equally bad, and the Bible does make a distinction between the varying degrees of sin along with their accompanying punishment for them (Jeremiah 7:26; Luke 12:47-48; John 19:11), God's Word, nevertheless, affirms, that the consequences of sin, whether great or small, are the same in the end—separation from God bringing spiritual and physical death. ***"The soul who sins shall die"*** is the immutable verdict of Scripture in Ezekiel 18:4. In this way, all sin is mortal and produces death. The wages for all sin, individual and collective, is death, whether it be denominated small, big, minor, major, or in the Catholic's case, "venial" or "mortal." Full guilt for sin is imputed whenever God's will and His revealed Word are disobeyed for those who sin against God's law, whether it is a minor infraction or a major violation. God's Word in James 2:10 confirms this to be the case when declaring, ***"For whoever shall keep the whole law, and yet stumble in one point, he is guilty of all."*** Sin is like cancer; once it appears in one malignant cell or clusters of many in the body, if left unchecked, it will spread and produce death.

The committing of just one sin, let alone many, would be enough, then, to produce death, separation from, and the condemnation of God! Salvation from sin is salvation from all sin—venial or mortal. Deliverance from the reality of hell, the revocation of God's condemnation, and forgiveness for every sin is given through the shed blood of Christ, which has cleansed, and keeps on cleansing, the forgiven sinner. The degree and gravity of sin is not determined by it being either 'venial' or 'mortal,' but by what sin always produces by its very nature. Sin is measured by what it cost God to redeem the sinner—the death of His Son on the cross! Doing penance, the Roman Catholic could never pay the infinite price of moral perfection which God's law demands—only the perfect God-Man (the Lord Jesus Christ) could do that in the flesh on behalf of sinners both in the perfect life He lived and in the perfect death He died as payment for our sins! ***"For if when we were enemies we were reconciled to God through the death of His Son, much more, having been reconciled, we shall be saved by His life"*** (Romans 5:10). The feeble idea of penance could never accomplish this. To then say we can make penance for our sins with the sacrament of confession is a gross underestimation and profane trivialization of the tremendous cost and gravity of what sin really is in the eyes of God, and of the great cost He paid to rescue us from its deadly dominion. One could conceivably view the small act of eating the forbidden fruit by Adam and Eve in the Garden of Eden to be a minor act of disobedience—even a venial sin! However small this act was—even on a venial level—it was, nevertheless, still the clear violation of God's revealed will given to our first parents which brought God's condemnation and judgment of death upon them and all mankind (Romans 5:12-21).

Jesus taught sin is both an internal and external problem manifested by thoughts within and acts without, respectively. So if one thinks or acts in a wrong way, he or she is guilty of sin before God (Matthew 5:28; Mark 7:21-23). Sin first is conceived in the mind, then gestates, and finally is birthed by action whose end brings forth death (James 1:15). So sin, whether entertained in the mind, or acted out by the body, brings the same result regardless of its size or enormity—spiritual death. Yet, here, Catholic teaching will point to 1 John 5:16-17 as an argument for the distinction of mortal and venial sin, claiming that not all sins lead to death, while other sins do lead to death, i.e., the loss of eternal life and saving grace due to the commission of mortal sin. *"If anyone sees his brother sinning a sin which does not lead to death, he will ask, and He will give him life for those who commit sin not leading to death. There is sin leading to death. I do not say that he should pray about that. All unrighteousness is sin, and there is sin not leading to death"* (1 John 5:16-17). Jesuit priest Mitch Pacwa, speaking on behalf of the Catholic Church, believes the distinction of mortal and venial sin is taught in 1 John 5:16-17, and he therefore takes the liberty of rewording the phrase "sin leading to death" to read as "mortal sin" in an attempt to lend credence to the Roman Catholic position. Pacwa goes on to say this verse teaches a mortal sin to be a "grave violation of the divine law", and that left to itself, without the sacrament of penance applied, the person essentially dies in a state of mortal sin, loses his salvation, and forfeits the eternal life he once had![141]

Does the phrase "the sin leading to death" support the Roman Catholic idea of "mortal sin," so that when a Christian commits a grave sin of a mortal kind he or she loses eternal life and forfeits salvation, resulting in eternal death? The answer is an emphatic "no" when taken in context with the overall message of what First John and the Gospel of John teach about the *permanent nature* of salvation. Contextually, First John chapter five deals with a specific situation where a Christian in the church sees a fellow brother committing what is deemed "a sin which does not lead to death." If this is the case he is to ask God to grant life to this brother and with this request the avoidance of premature death. Yet John the Apostle indicates this situation only applies to the case of the Christian whose sin does not lead to death. John does not recommend intercession for the sin leading to death.

The key to interpreting what kind of sin is meant in 1 John 5:16 hinges on how "death" is interpreted and understood in the first epistle of John. Death for John here, and even in his Gospel, signifies the state of the unbeliever devoid of God's life, presence, and power, leaving him or her in a state of spiritual darkness (John 3:18-20; 1 John 2:9-11).

John uses the term "brother" in his first epistle to denote anyone who makes a profession of the Christian faith regardless if a true believer or not. But those who claim to be a Christian, yet show otherwise by their abiding hatred for a fellow believer, are murderers and do not have eternal "life" abiding in them (1 John 3:15). If someone claims to be a Christian, yet demonstrates a life characterized by hatred toward a brother, he clearly shows he is not a true Christian and does not have eternal life but still is walking in sin leading to spiritual death. You either have eternal life in God through belief in Jesus Christ or you do not! And any truly born-again Christian, who has received this eternal "life" from God, by definition, cannot lose it for any reason once he has received it from God. For eternal life is unending, lasting forever, and cannot be lost or terminated.

---

[141]   Mitch Pacwa, SJ., *Go in Peace*, 10.

The Roman Catholic idea that a mortal sin can terminate eternal life if a Christian commits it flies in the face of what the Scriptures teach, and contradicts the very meaning of the word "eternal" when it refers to the spiritual life given by God; for once a person receives eternal life from Christ he or she cannot ever lose it. Christians who receive eternal life have it forever; it can never be lost, nor will it expire or perish at some later point in time, the sins and moral failures of the Christian notwithstanding! Jesus promised this wonderful reality in John 10:27-29: ***"My sheep hear My voice, and I know them, and they follow Me. And I give them eternal life, and they shall never perish; neither shall anyone snatch them out of My hand. My Father, who has given them to Me, is greater than all; and no one is able to snatch them out of My Father's hand."*** Moreover, we read in John 5:24 that once someone believes in Jesus Christ for eternal life, he can never fall back into realm of spiritual death and God's judgment. He has permanently passed from death into life. ***'Truly, truly, I say to you, he who hears My word, and believes Him who sent Me, has everlasting life, and shall not come into judgment but Has passed from death into life."***

Once those who hear the word of Jesus and believe on the Father and the Son have eternal life for a permanent possession, so much so they will never lose it or be condemned—an inviolable fact the Apostle Paul powerfully confirms in Romans 8:1, 31-39. In verse 37-39, Paul says not death, nor anything in life embracing the cosmic all, which encompasses reality both in the physical and spiritual dimensions, can ever separate the true believer from the love of God shown through Jesus Christ. Any misguided and unbiblical concept of mortal sin, which Roman Catholicism says can separate the believer from the saving grace of Jesus Christ, must be included here in Paul's complete and comprehensive list of the hostile elements of life (including death itself) and their utter inability to separate the believer from the eternal life and unconquerable love given by Jesus Christ to the child of God. Returning to "the sin leading to death" of 1 John 5:16, a believer can experience premature physical death for unrepented sin but he will not revert back to the state of condemnation or spiritual death because he has already received eternal life and is, therefore, "kept by the power of God," through the faithfulness of Christ, to remain saved for all time (1 Peter 1:5). In this regard, the true believer cannot sin leading to a spiritual and eternal death which Scripture says is only reserved for the unbeliever, whether he claims a profession of Christian faith or not. So in this established light, the sin leading not to spiritual/eternal death is applicable only for the believer, whereas the sin leading to spiritual/eternal death is exclusively applicable to the unbeliever. Hence we agree then with the keen observation of Bible commentator Colin G. Kruse when he writes:

> A better approach is to examine who it is in 1 John that the author sees committing sins which do and do not lead to death. It is the 'brother' whose sin is not unto death for whom the readers are urged to pray. This suggests that the sin that does not lead to death is most likely that of the believer. If this is the case, then the sin that does lead to death is most likely that of the unbeliever. Within the overall context of 1 John, where the secessionists are now regarded as unbelievers, even antichrists, the sin that leads to death is probably the sin of the secessionists, in particular their denial that Jesus is the Christ come in the flesh and that his death is necessary for salvation. This explanation has the advantage of relating the matter of sins that lead and do not lead to death to the central issues being addressed by the letter.[142]

---

[142]   Colin G. Kruse, *The Letters of John* (Grand Rapids: Eerdmans, 2000), 194.

Of all the proposed meanings for the Johannine phrase, "the sin leading to death", as it relates to the bona fide Christian, is not an argument for the validity of mortal sin and the loss of saving grace, but rather applies to those deceivers and antichrists who have not experienced true spiritual rebirth and are hence not "born of God", and are further living a life incompatible with being a born-again child of God, while at the same time falsely professing a faith in Jesus Christ. Conversely, then, a true Christian born again by the Holy Spirit of God cannot commit a sin leading to eternal death, because once faith in Jesus Christ is made, the saved person permanently passes from the domain of spiritual death into the realm of eternal life, so that he or she cannot ever fall back into a perishable state of spiritual death, as the Savior promised in John 5:24. For when the believer receives eternal life in Jesus Christ, it is just that—a life with Him that never ends. So if Rome were right with their idea of mortal sin, eternal life as defined by Jesus Christ, would not truly be everlasting, since it could be terminated whenever a believer commits a sin and thus forfeits saving grace, only to be renewed all over again with the Sacrament of Confession. Scripture simply does not teach this when it comes to every true born-again believer in Jesus Christ who has received eternal life from Him the moment faith in the Lord Jesus is exercised.

The warning of John, then, about committing a sin which "leads to death" must, of necessity, apply to those who claimed to be believers but by their sinful lifestyle and heretical beliefs denied basic truths about Jesus Christ (namely, His deity and incarnation), and thus showed they were really in spiritual darkness; and, in the words of the Apostle John, demonstrated they did not belong to the believing Christian community. *"They went out from us, but they were not of us; for if they had been of us, they would have continued with us; but they went out that they might be made manifest, that none of them were of us"* (1 John 2:19). Catholic apologists cannot therefore legitimately use 1 John 5:16-17 to teach the distinction of mortal and venial sins and the loss of saving grace when a believer supposedly commits a mortal sin, because the passage in question is dealing with counterfeit Christians and not real Christians at all. The observations of what 1 John 5:16-17 really addresses here by former Catholic William Webster are quite appropriate to quote when making this important point:

> Thus a Christian cannot commit a sin unto death in the sense of eternal death. In these verses John is talking about those who, though they may have professed Christ, have never genuinely experienced new birth. In fact, one reason for his letter is to warn true believers against those who were deceivers and false teachers. They claimed to be Christians but their lives were inconsistent with their profession. They walked in darkness (1:6); they did not keep the commandments of God (2:3-4); they loved the world (2:15-17); they lived in unrighteousness and sin (3:4-10); they did not love (3:14-19); and they denied basic truths about the person of Jesus Christ (2:22-23; 4:2-3; 5:1). These men knew the truth, but they had either completely rejected it or gone into apostasy or embraced a life-style of open and deliberate sin. It is probably to these that John is referring when he speaks of certain individuals committing 'sin unto death' . . . Thus John is not dealing with genuine Christians in this passage at all, but with those who are counterfeits, or are false teachers. It is impossible for a Christian to commit a mortal sin in the way in which the Roman Catholic Church suggests, for true believers can never lose eternal life, and will not live in sin or apostatize from the faith. The truth is that, ultimately, there is no distinction such as mortal and venial sin made in the Bible. All sin in God's eyes is mortal and condemns to hell. The consequences in the human realm for certain kinds of sin will differ but the

ultimate consequences are the same for all sin—eternal death: 'The wages of sin is death' (Rom. 6:23); 'The person who sins will die' (Ezek. 18:20).[143]

Another disturbing feature associated with the Sacrament of Confession is what Catholic theologians call the "seal of confession." The seal of confession, or what is also termed "the seal of the confessional," is defined in the Roman Catholic Code of Canon Law to be "inviolable," which therefore makes it "absolutely wrong for a confessor in any way to betray the penitent, for any reason whatsoever, whether by word or in any other fashion."[144] Canon Law demands this inviolate secrecy of the confessional is to be upheld and maintained even if the one confessing is the worst of criminals, whether his criminality was in the past or continues in the present. Shockingly, this prohibition remains in force, even if such harmful behavior on behalf of the one confessing to the priest is harming and hurting others. Once again, Canon Law states: "The confessor is wholly forbidden to use knowledge acquired in confession to the detriment of the penitent, even when all danger of disclosure is excluded" (Can. 998, pages 177-178). Any priest, who for sake of the law or the safety of the public does expose the person in question, will suffer excommunication and be defrocked! The Fourth Lateran Council (1215) imposes the strictest punishment for any priest who dares violate the secrecy of the confessional, when harshly declaring:

> Let the priest absolutely beware that he does not by word or sign or by any manner whatever in any way betray the sinner: but if he should happen to need wiser counsel let him cautiously seek the same without any mention of the person. For whoever shall dare to reveal a sin disclosed to him in the tribunal of penance we decree that he shall be not only deposed from the priestly office but that he shall also be sent into the confinement of a monastery to do perpetual penance.[145]

What has inevitably happened under the *de facto* immunity and protection of the seal of the confessional is the harboring of the criminal and lawbreaker and his escape from due justice. History is replete in the Catholic Church with such scandalous consequences the so-called seal of confession brings in providing anonymity to the wrongdoer who has victimized the innocent and vulnerable. The current scandal of pedophile priests is a prime example of this dangerous and harmful doctrine and practice. Recently, the confidentiality of the confessional had provided protection for one pedophile priest, which proved to be a considerable impediment to the proper prosecution and punishment of this evil predatory monster hiding behind the sham confidentiality of the confessional! The case in question involved a certain priest who engaged in sexual misconduct with a twelve-year-old child who came to him for confession! The priest went on to molest two hundred other young boys. To make matters worse, the confidentiality aspect of the confessional was used by the Vatican as a tactic to avoid bad publicity and allowed this perverted priest to continue on with his heinous behavior and horrible offenses against the innocent. The seal of the confessional allowed for this to happen!

Another example, where the seal of the confessional subverted justice, allowing the innocent to be unfairly punished occurred several years ago in the Bronx, New York, when a priest learned through a confessor that two men on trial for murder were both innocent. The confessor secretly admitted to the

---

[143] William Webster, *Salvation, the Bible, and Roman Catholicism*, 46-47.
[144] *The Code of Canon Law*, Can. 983, 177.
[145] http://en.wikipedia.org/wiki/Seal_of_the_Confessional.

priest he was guilty of the murder. Rather than go immediately to the authorities with this knowledge, that would have found the two men not guilty, the priest waited for twelve years after the confessor died, while the two men were imprisoned during this time period. Clearly, the whole idea of the secrecy and seal of the confessional followed by this priest permitted the guilty murderer to escape the justice of the courts, and innocent men to be falsely accused and found guilty for a crime they did not commit. In Germany, a priest knew of his confessor's sexual rape and brutal murder of three eleven-year-old boys before he was caught some four years later. The travesty here is those later crimes could have been easily prevented had the priest alerted the police once the criminal made his identity known in the confessional. Instead, what we have here in all these cases is the Catholic Church's blind and inexcusable devotion to the confidentiality and anonymity of confession which permits both priest and parishioner to get away with wrongdoing and criminality at its worse depths and escape exposure, prosecution, and punishment.[146]

Though one can understand the need for the sinner's opportunity to unburden his soul, when it threatens or harms his person or others, there are and should be practical and reasonable grounds for waiving the confidentiality seal when another life is threatened or harmed. Although the priest is required to strongly encourage and urge the penitent to turn himself in if he has violated state or federal law, the priest cannot inform or report serious criminal conduct to law enforcement agencies. Here is another example of Rome's blind allegiance and intransigent adherence to the letter of the law of their false doctrine above and beyond doing what is just, right, and one's moral duty in the eyes of God to serve and love our fellow man. To know a person is committing a grave injustice, and to let it continue in order to uphold an unbiblical doctrine like the seal of confidentiality because a church body forbids exposure, is to sin against God and one's fellow man, which results in failing to do good—and failure to do good in this way, the Bible says, is sin. *"Therefore, to him who knows to do good and does not do it, to him it is sin"* (James 4:17).

To then simply let child molestation and murder of the innocent go on unabated and unpunished with other assorted evils (as in the aforementioned cases) because the priest cannot divulge the identity of the evildoer (to keep the seal of confession intact) is indeed an infraction of God's law and therefore a sin of the highest degree in the manner of James 4:17! Well did our Lord prophesy of such hypocrites, here, when thundering: *"Woe to you, scribes and Pharisees, hypocrites! For you . . . have neglected the weightier matters of the law: justice and mercy and faith. These you ought to have done, without leaving the others undone. Blind guides, who strain out a gnat and swallow a camel!"* (Matthew 23:23-24) And this is precisely what Rome does with its practice of upholding the seal of confession at all costs, to the extent the guilty are afforded protection and escape, while the innocent are denied justice and protection because the letter of a man-made tradition must be maintained at all terrible costs, while all the while the law of God's justice and righteous retribution is continually subverted under the veil of secrecy afforded by the confessional!

Sexual scandal between priest and female confessor has been another ongoing problem created by the secretive nature of the confessional. This is shockingly facilitated by the fact that in the past, particularly before Vatican II, priests were 'legally' required by Roman Catholic Canon Law to go into very graphic sexual detail with female penitents about the sordid contents of their sexual sins. Unless such a foul interrogation of mind-polluting questions was conducted, and the particular sin revealed and confessed in all its pornographic detail, forgiveness could not be granted. Former priest Charles Chiniquy, in his famous book, *The Priest,*

---

[146] The above examples from real life experiences come from an excellent article analyzing the legal and moral ramifications of the secrecy of the confessional written by Ronald Goldfarb in The National Law Journal at http://www.bishop-accountability.org/news2010/03_04/2010_04_09_Goldfarb_SecretsOf.htm

the Woman, and the Confessional, historically recounts many of the scandals, abuses, and sexual sins which have resulted in the unbiblical practices of the confessional. Near the end of his book, the former priest goes on to give extracted quotations from the various official books and manuals to be used by the priest listing the salacious questions in Latin that were to be asked. Having taken four years of Latin myself in Roman Catholic school, once I translated these questions asked by the priest of the woman in question, I quickly and repulsively discovered the content of these intrusive questions was so horribly vulgar and terribly obscene that a person of common decency cannot and would not repeat their pornographic contents in public, much less in the published domain.[147] Chiniquy painstakingly recalls the agonizing and shameful experience of doing this very thing himself when soliciting, as a single celibate man, the foul details of the sexual sins of female parishioners who were humiliated by the false guilt and casuistic sophistries imposed and used by Rome to force them into divulging what should have inviolably remained a personal matter between the repentant sinner and God:

> Perhaps the world has never seen a more terrible desperate, solemn struggle than the one which is going on in the soul of a poor trembling young woman, who, at the feet of that man, has to decide whether or not she will open her lips on those things which the infallible voice of God, united to the no less infallible voice of her womanly honor and self-respect, tell her never to reveal to any man! The history of that secret, fierce, desperate, and deadly struggle has never yet, so far as I know, been fully given. It would draw the tears of admiration and compassion of the whole world, if it could be written with its simple, sublime, and terrible realities.

> How many times have I wept as a child when some noble-hearted and intelligent young girl, or some respectable married woman, yielding to the sophisms with which I, or some other confessor, had persuaded them to give up their self-respect, and their womanly dignity, to speak with me on matters on which a decent woman would never say a word with a man . . . But alas! I had soon to reproach myself, and regret these short instances of my wavering faith in the infallible voice of my Church; I had soon to silence the voice of my conscience, which was telling me, "Is it not a shame that you, an unmarried man, dare to speak on these matters with a woman? Do you not blush to put such questions to a young girl? Where is your self-respect? Where is your fear of God? Do you not promote the ruin of that girl by forcing her to speak with a man in such matters?

> I was compelled by all the Popes, the moral theologians, and the Councils of Rome, to believe that this warning voice of my merciful God was the voice of Satan; I had to believe in spite of my own conscience and intelligence, that it was good, nay, necessary, to put those polluting, damning questions. My infallible Church was mercilessly forcing me to oblige those poor, trembling, weeping, desolate girls and women, to swim with me and all her priests in those waters of Sodom and Gomorrah, under the pretext that their self-will

---

[147] Charles Chiniquy, *The Priest, the Woman, and the Confessional* (Chino, CA: *Chick Publications*, No date given), 141-143.

would be broken down, their fear of sin and humility increased, and that they would be
purified by our absolutions.[148]

The real, underlying reason for the Catholic Church's use of the confessional is the potential power it holds and has wielded down through the centuries of its existence. Indeed, the confessional has proven to be a powerful means of control, oppression, and intimidation by the Catholic clergy. Along with the power of self-preservation, the power of procreation and the strong desire to form an intimate, sexual bond with the opposite sex is one of the strongest desires of human beings. The force of this desire overrides every other desire for the good and propagation of the species. To therefore deny or suppress these desires in an unnatural way from legitimate expression (within the covenant of marriage) is to inflame and agitate those desires to seek expression and fulfillment, and will in the end cause the person to seek gratification by unnatural means since the God-ordained biblical form of legitimate expression is denied.

Placing a single celibate male in the secret confines of the confessional to repeatedly hear the sexual details of women is courting disaster, which has led to countless sexual scandals within the Roman Catholic Church! To review such scandals here would take considerable space—several volumes—and requires a separate study altogether. These shocking abuses, born from the clandestine meetings between a celibate priest and female penitents, are part of the historical record of the Roman Catholic Church.[149] The perils of penance between a male and female in private were already being felt by the fourth century, so much so that the first Council of Toledo in 398 prohibited any familiarity between the virgins dedicated to God and their confessors. Already by the early fifth century, the twisted practice of "confession" was so rife with sexual misconduct that in 428, Pope Celestine found it necessary to impose strict punishment on all priests who seduced their female confessants to fornicate.

In 1560, Pope Pius IV issued a papal Bull ordering all girls and married women to appear before the Inquisition to denounce and reveal all their father confessors who had seduced them into sexual sin. The turnout of female victims was so great over the next few months, the whole enterprise was soon afterwards given up by the Holy Inquisition because the sheer number of deflowered women made it virtually impossible to punish all the guilty confessors. This failure was typical of all other unsuccessful efforts by the Popes and priests of Rome to curtail the sexual scandal of the confessional:

> The daily abominations, which are the result of auricular confession, are so horrible and so well known by the Popes, the bishops, and the priests, that several times public attempts have been made to diminish them by punishing the guilty priests; but all these commendable efforts failed.
>
> One of the most remarkable of those efforts was made by Pius IV about the year 1560. A Bull was published by him, by which all the girls and married women, who had been seduced into sins by their confessors, were ordered to denounce them; and a certain number of high church officers of the Holy Inquisition were authorized to take the depositions of the fallen penitents. The thing was, at first, tried at Seville, one of the principle cities

---

[148]   Ibid., 16-17.

[149]   Otto Von Corvin dedicates an entire chapter in his book to these sordid sexual scandals between female confessants and the priest who hears the lewd details of their torrid confessions (*Scandals in the Roman Catholic Church*, Salt Lake City: Merkur Publishing, 2003, pages 347-386).

in Spain. When the edict was first published, the number of women who felt bound in conscience to go and depose against their father confessors was so great, that though there were thirty notaries, and as many inquisitors, to take the depositions, they were unable to do the work in the appointed time. Thirty days more were given, but the inquisitors were so overwhelmed with the numberless depositions, that another period of time of the same length was given. But this, again, was found insufficient. At the end, it was found that the number of priests who had destroyed the purity of their penitents was so great that it was impossible to punish them all. The inquest was given up, and the guilty confessors remained unpunished. Several attempts of the same nature have been tried by other Popes, but with about the same success.

But if those honest attempts on the part of some well meaning Popes, to punish the confessors who destroy the purity of the penitents, have failed to touch the guilty parties, they are, in the good providence of God, infallible witnesses to tell the world that auricular confession is nothing else than a snare to the confessor and his dupes. Yes, those Bulls of the Popes are an irrefragable testimony that auricular confession is the most powerful invention of the devil to corrupt the heart, pollute the body, and damn the soul of the priest and female penitent (Charles Chiniquy, *The Priest, the Woman, and the Confessional*, 43)!

The secret seal of the confessional not only invited sexual immorality on a grand scale, but was also a means of political and personal blackmail, control, and an insidious way to find out the hidden sins, scandals and plans of kings, rulers, and prominent people through which silent control or blackmail by the church could then be established. To this end, the practice of auricular confession helped Rome to acquire and achieve a strong domination over the political affairs of men (especially in Europe and for well over 1,000 years) for centuries! Indeed, the sacrament of confession has been called the "eyes" of the Church by which it sees and knows everything for the twin purposes of control and seduction. Undoubtedly, then,

With the help of auricular confession the Roman Catholic Church rules the world without any great expense and complaints. And there is no question about the high value of confession. Even the heretic Marnix of St. Aldegonde already mentioned, 300 years ago, that if the confession were taken away from the Church it would be the same as cutting out its eyes. He expresses it with the following words: "...without a doubt the auricular confession is worth a pair of eyes. Because the Church needs one eye to find out all about the secrets and hidden plans of the kings and rulers of this world, through which the Church came into possession of all governments and dignitaries in a peaceful manner. And the Church requires the other eye to look at and touch the bosom of young girls and distressed women to determine and learn their secrets. And then they impose a loving kind of penance which will comfort their frightened conscience and will also noticeably ease the burdens on their hearts. Oh, how often have these holy clerics and monks given distressed and infertile women such good advice during their auricular confession that it did not take long before they became very happy mothers. And from that time on they developed the same kind of fervent love for their father confessors as they had for their own husbands"...The

Auricular confession is just like purgatory and other similar clever inventions, and it is one
of the many means through which the Roman Church acquired control over humankind.[150]

The exercise of control through the use of the confessional was adroitly used by the Jesuit order to further
the Vatican's political agenda and strengthen its power among the nations. Often times the father confessor of
a European monarch or political ruler was a Jesuit priest! With this key role, the Jesuit order devised certain
rules that allowed for lying, murder, lechery, perjury, and political assassination in order to advance the cause
of the church and maintain control over ruler and citizen through the exploitation of the seal of confession.[151]
Anyone familiar with church history will readily see the whole idea of the sacrament of confession with its
secretive "seal" and the use of the confessional box has absolutely no basis in Scripture whatsoever, nor do we
see evidence of its practice in the early church for its first four hundred years of existence! Expert historian
on the practice of auricular confession Henry Charles Lea documents this when he writes:

> Of course, in the early centuries, when the only form of penitential confession recognized
> by the Church was public, there could be no injunction of secrecy. If evidence of this
> be wanted it can be found in the early codes prescribing the functions of the priesthood
> and the penalties imposed for derelictions—the canons Hippolytus and the Apostolic
> Constitutions, the so-called Canons of the Apostles and the canonical epistles of Gregory of
> Nyssa and Basil the Great, the penitential decrees of such councils as those of Elivira, Nicea
> and Ancyra and the collections of the African Church. All these together form a tolerable
> extensive body of canon law, representing the doctrine and practice of the different churches
> up to the close of the fourth century, and had there been any duty incumbent on priests to
> listen to the confessions of sinners and to veil them in impenetrable silence, there would
> unquestionably have been some allusion to it and some penalty prescribed for its violation.
> The absolute ignorance of any such duties manifested by all these lawgivers is sufficient
> evidence of their non-existence (*A History of Auricular Confession and Indulgences in the
> Latin Church Part One*, page 415-416).

The practice of private confession came after the practice of public confession was beginning to be
abandoned in the church, and was gradually introduced in the sixth century, mainly through the influence
of Celtic monk missionaries "who brought this form of private penance with them to the European continent
in the sixth and seventh centuries."[152] The private confession of Penance did not originate with Jesus and His
apostolic band and therefore was not sanctioned by the New Testament, but was *invented* later by medieval
Romanists of the seventh century, as the *Catechism of the Catholic Church* startlingly reveals when admitting
the following:

> Over the centuries the concrete form in which the Church has exercised this power received
> from the Lord has varied considerably. During the first centuries the reconciliation of

---

[150] Ibid., 347-348.
[151] Otto Von Corvin provides a few examples taken from extracts of Jesuit manuals where certain rules are prescribed
to circumvent moral laws in which any morally sensible person would find offensive and quite appalling (see
Scandals in the Roman Catholic Church, pages 348-351).
[152] Thomas Bokenkotter, *Dynamic Catholicism*, 224.

Christians who had committed particularly grave sins after their baptism (for example, idolatry, murder, or adultery) was tried to a very rigorous discipline, according to which penitents had to do public penance for their sins, often for years before receiving reconciliation. To this "order of penitents" (which concerned only certain grave sins), one was only rarely admitted and in certain regions only once in a lifetime. During the seventh century, Irish missionaries, inspired by the Eastern monastic tradition, took to continental Europe the 'private' practice of penance, which does not require public and prolonged completion of penitential works before reconciliation with the Church. From that time on, the sacrament has been performed in secret between penitent and priest. This new practice envisioned the possibility of repetition and so opened the way to a regular frequenting of this sacrament. It allowed the forgiveness of grave sins and venial sins to be integrated into one sacramental celebration. In its main lines this is the form of penance that the Church has practiced down to our day.[153]

Here the Catholic Church freely admits today that private confession was not instituted until a full seven hundred years after Christ and the New Testament Church was established; and yet Rome's Council of Trent hypocritically curses anyone who rejects that secret confession is necessary for salvation and furthermore denies Christ established it from the beginning:

If anyone denies that sacramental confession was instituted by divine law or is necessary for salvation by divine law; or says that the manner of confessing secretly to a priest alone, which the Catholic church has always observed from the beginning and still observes, is at variance with the institution and command of Christ and is a human contrivance, let him be anathema.[154]

The whole idea of a private confessional box was another man-made invention of Roman Catholicism that has no support or point of origin found in the New Testament! For well over 1,200 years, ministers of the Church heard confessions in a public setting, which was to eventually prove too embarrassing to both confessant and father confessor over time. To remedy this problem, the private confessional box was invented during the Counter Reformation period (1545-1648) with the decree of the Council of Valencia in 1565, where it was mandated confessional boxes should be set up, especially for the hearing of confessions from women. In the same year, Charles Borromeo (1538-1584) ordered such a rudimentary structure to be placed between priest and penitent; a decade later he demanded confessionals should be placed in all the Churches of Milan. Church historian Henry Charles Lea gives a concrete account of this development in his massive tome on the history of auricular confession in the Roman Catholic Church, demonstrating at once that its invention came well after the New Testament period and was therefore not instituted by the Lord Jesus Christ or His Apostles!

It seems strange that it was not until the Counter Reformation had commenced that the simple and useful device of the confessional was introduced—a box in which the confessor sits, with a grille in the side, through which the kneeling penitent can pour the story of his sins into his ghostly father's ear without either seeing the face of the other. The first

[153] *Catechism of the Catholic Church*, 403, **[1447]**.
[154] *The Canons and Decrees of the Council of Trent*, 102-103.

allusion I have met to this contrivance is in the council of Valencia, in 1565, where it is ordered to be erected in churches for the hearing of confessions, especially of women. In this same year we find S. Charles Borromeo prescribing the use of a rudimentary form of confessional—a seat with a partition (*tabella*) to separate the priest from the penitent. Eleven years afterwards, in 1576, he orders confessionals placed in all churches of the province of Milan and he alludes to their use in his instructions to confessors. The innovation was so manifest an improvement that its use spread rapidly. In 1579, the council Cosenza adopted it; in 1585, that of Aix; in 1590, that of Toulouse; in 1607, that of Mechlin; and in 1609, that of Narbonne. Some resistance was apparently expected on the part of the priests, for there are occasional threats of punishment for disobedience, and at Mechlin, where three months were allowed for compliance with the order, no one was permitted subsequently to hear a confession in any other way, except in case of necessity or by special licence from the Ordinary. The Roman Ritual of 1614 orders the use of the confessional in all churches, and prescribes its position in an open and conspicuous place. Yet, in 1630, Alphonso di Leone repeats the old injunctions that confessor and penitent shall not face or touch each other, and alludes to confessionals only as a device used in many dioceses, showing that as yet they were by no means universal. Indeed, as late as 1709 the Spanish Inquisition found it necessary to issue an edict ordering priests to hear confessions in the body of the church and not in cells or chapels. *Yet in spite of the introduction of confessionals the necessity is felt of constant watchfulness to prevent abuses, and the modern councils, like those of old, are untiring in their admonitions of the precautions to be observed for the prevention of scandals* (Emphasis mine).[155]

So the real reason for these "confessional boxes" was to avoid further scandal. But privatizing public confession, by surreptitious use of the confessional box, ironically, only served to inflame and enhance these sexual abuses to greater frequency and intensity, as subsequent history has shown. For as long as the celibate priesthood exists, and young attractive women must secretly confess to these sexually starved clerics, and as long as Rome refuses to change on this point instead of following the Word of God accordingly, the trouble of solicitation to sexual sin will be inevitable and shamefully continue on. Again, Henry Charles Lea chronicles the very same thing when pointing out:

The power of the confessional, one of the most effective instrumentalities invented… for enslaving the human mind, was peculiarly liable to abuse in sexual matters. No one can be familiar with the hideous suggestiveness of the penitentials without recognizing how frequent must be the temptations arising between confessor and penitent, while their respective relations render seduction comparatively easy, and unspeakably atrocious. To deprive such relations of danger requires the confessor to be gifted with rare purity and holiness, and when these functions were confided to men such as those who composed the sacerdotal body as we have seen it throughout the Middle Ages, the result was inevitable… It was inevitable that this trouble should continue…throughout the whole history of a celibate priesthood. So constantly was "solicitation"—*solicitatio ad turpiae*, as it came to

---

[155]   Henry Charles Lea, *A History of Auricular Confession and Indulgences in the Latin Church, Part One* (White Fish, MT: Kessinger Publishing, 2004), 395-396.

be technically called—borne in mind that the medieval canonists recognized that a parish priest known to be addicted to it forfeited his jurisdiction over his female penitents... St. Bonaventura, indeed, declares that there are few parish priests free from this or other defects that should incapacitate them... As the Council of Trent assumed that God would not deny the gift of chastity to a celibate priesthood, it could scarce refer to such a matter [as solicitation] and it adopted no provisions to lessen evil. About that time, however, a preventative effort was commenced by the invitation of the confessional. Hitherto the priest had heard confessions in the open, with the penitent at his knees or seated by his side, which gave ample opportunity for temptation and solicitation. To remedy this the confessional was gradually evolved—a box in which the confessor sits, while the penitent outside pours the tale of his sin through a grille, neither being visible to the other. The earliest allusion to such a contrivance... occurs... in 1547... the Roman Ritual of 1614 prescribes its employment in all churches. The command was obeyed but slackly, [due to] the pronounced opposition of the priesthood, who objected to this seclusion from their penitents... Mechanical devices, however, went but a little way to cure an evil so widespread and so persistent... The crime was secret and known only to the confessor and penitent, and the latter, whether she yielded or not, was deterred [from complaining] by the notoriety which accompanied it...to say nothing of the dangerous enmity which she would excite. Strictly speaking, such matters were not covered by the seal of the confessional, but she could scarce know this in the face of assertions freely made to the contrary. The spiritual courts, moreover, which held exclusive jurisdiction, were not...disposed to treat the offender harshly and ...would... reject accusations which could not be supported by witnesses.... Then beyond all else was the ever-present dread of scandals... Thus the crime, though particularly heinous, was almost assured of impunity.[156]

Roman Catholic history embarrassingly reveals the confessional box was a late invention occurring around the Counter-Reformation period, hitherto unknown to Jesus and the early history of the Christian Church. It was partly devised as an expeditious attempt to curtail the increasing occurrence of sexual immorality, decrease seductive solicitations to that end, and widen the Church's public and private control over her unwitting followers. Yet the creation of the confessional box only intensified and cloaked this deviant behavior which goes on today with the misguided fabrication of confession made in the confessional box of Roman Catholicism's manipulative and deceitful doing. Though Catholics often say they experience great psychological relief in the unburdening of their guilt-ridden soul before a priest, there is no settled peace and firm repose in the fact God has forgiven all sins by way of Christ's atonement on the cross. As a former Catholic, I felt temporary relief and momentary comfort from this fleeting sacrament, only to be hounded with guilt and fear of the judgment of God later on for sins I committed after coming out of the confessional. It wasn't until I embraced the promise of God's Word and the full, final, and infinite forgiveness at Calvary that I had a peace and rest in the Savior, knowing He died for all my sins and thereby secured pardon for all time so that no sin will ever be brought up again to accuse or condemn me, because the crucified Christ has made full payment, which is secured and holds fast for the span of all time—never needing a renewal or revision by any imaginary sacrament of penance!

---

156   Henry Charles Lea, *History of Sacerdotal Celibacy in the Catholic Church*, 496-500.

For it is on this glorious basis the born-again believer can triumphantly proclaim with the Apostle Paul: *"Who shall bring a charge against God's elect? It is God who justifies* (not Rome with its ongoing and inefficient sacrament of penance, which at most can only falsely offer the Catholic temporary psychological relief!). *Who is he who condemns? It is Christ who died, and furthermore is also risen, who is even at the right hand of God, who also makes intercession for us* (so any need of a priest on Earth mediating forgiveness through the confessional is totally unnecessary and not required here!). *Who shall separate us from the love of Christ? Shall tribulation, or distress, or persecution, famine, or nakedness, or peril, or sword... For I am persuaded that neither death nor life, nor angels nor principalities nor powers, nor things present nor things to come, nor height nor depth, nor any other created thing, shall be able to separate us from the love of God which is in Christ Jesus our Lord"* (Romans 8:33-39).

So this all-inclusive list would certainly include all sins the believer commits after salvation, whether "mortal" or otherwise. For if, as Rome dogmatically pontificates, mortal sin committed after conversion to Christ could separate the Christian from the saving grace of God, then the promise of Romans 8:33-39 is an outright lie, and is thus null and void! And herein is the stark contrast of the sacrament of penance contrasted with the cross of Jesus Christ made most evident in bold relief: the sacrament of penance makes one beholden to a man-made religious system, producing bondage to it; whereas the cross of Christ makes one a child of God, forever freed from the bondage of all sin; the sacrament of penance binds the conscience to fixate on sin; the cross of Christ releases us from the guilt of sin to bask in His righteousness; the sacrament of penance instills fear and looming condemnation for the uncertain Catholic; the cross of Christ gives comfort with the assurance of full, final pardon for those who look to Him for salvation; and finally, the sacrament of penance implies the atonement of Christ is not sufficient of itself to accomplish a full, irreversible pardon and acquittal of guilt the moment the act of faith in Jesus is made; but the cross of Christ guarantees a full, final, and irrevocable pardon once faith is made in the crucified and risen Messiah Who has victoriously proclaimed, *"It is finished,"* with respect to forgiveness of sins by His perfect sacrifice. The Catholic belief that one must go to a priest (acting in the role of a mediator between God and man) to be forgiven by God is a practical denial and obvious repudiation of 1 Timothy 2:5, where God's Word unequivocally proclaims that Jesus Christ, our great and supreme High Priest, serves as the *one* sole Mediator between God and man, Who now grants full and final pardon and forgiveness from God on the basis of faith in Christ's propitiatory death. *"For there is one God and <u>one Mediator</u> between God and men, the Man Christ Jesus"* (1 Timothy 2:5).

Without a doubt, the sacrament of penance is nothing more than a tradition of man—a fabrication of a manipulative clergy with no support from Scripture or historical warrant from the early church fathers. Certainly, if this sacrament were critically important to salvation, it would have a prominent place in these two fundamental areas. It does not, which at once shows it to be a mere invention of the ever-evolving religion of Roman Catholicism. To conclude our section on penance, the sacrament is best found and summed up in the words of ex-Catholic priest Clark Butterfield:

> If Christ instituted a Sacrament of Penance, I want it to be clearly and unequivocally presented in the New Testament. I want it to be proclaimed lucidly by the Church fathers of the first centuries. I want it to be witnessed to constantly and consistently by believing Christians of the ages. I want it to be reaffirmed by the Reformation leaders! But the Roman rite of compulsory confession lacks any such continuity. It is a tradition of man.[157]

---

[157] Clark Butterfield, *Night Journey From Rome*, 112-113.

The Sacrament of Extreme Unction or Anointing of the Sick

This 'sacrament' was specifically known prior to Vatican II as "extreme unction" and afterwards as "the anointing of the sick." It can also be referred to in its more solemn connotation as "the last rites" because it is the last sacrament to be received by the Catholic Church. The original meaning of the phrase "extreme unction" probably refers to "the unction of those in *extremis*", i.e. of the dying, especially those who were at the point of death, or were dying.[158] The Catholic Church also calls it extreme unction because it is the last of the sacraments to be received by the Roman Catholic administered by the priest. This sacrament is now more popularly called the anointing of the sick, in which "the sick by the anointing with holy oil and the prayers of the priest, receive spiritual aid and even physical invigoration when such is conducive to their salvation. This was once called Extreme Unction because it is administered to persons who are in extreme or grave danger of death, and is usually the last of the holy anointings administered by the Church. The first anointing is received in Baptism, and the second in Confirmation."[159]

The sacrament of extreme unction has the power to forgive sin and impart the grace of God for the salvation of the soul and the healing of the body. The particular effects of this sacrament infuse and increase saving/sanctifying grace to the ill and dying; preparation for entrance into heaven by "the remission of our venial sins and the cleansing of our souls from the remains of sins"; and health to the sick body and strength for the soul against temptation.[160] In the Catholic Church today, anyone physically or mentally ill, aged and infirm, or about to receive surgery can receive this sacrament of healing. The sacrament is no longer exclusively reserved for the dying. Only a priest can administer this sacrament. For, "every priest, but only a priest, can validly administer the anointing of the sick."[161] As with the other sacraments, the sacrament of extreme unction was instituted by Jesus Christ, conferred on to His Apostles, and was then passed from them and perpetuated through the Roman Catholic priesthood.[162] Catholic apologist John Salza speaks for the Catholic Church here when confidently affirming:

> Jesus instituted the sacrament of the anointing of the sick (also called "Extreme Unction") to commend those who are seriously ill to God, so that He may raise them up and save them. The sacrament is given to those who are in danger of death by anointing them on the forehead and hands with blessed oil, accompanied by readings from Scripture. Only priests (not deacons) can administer this sacrament *because the sacrament also brings about the forgiveness of sins* (Emphasis mine).[163]

Once again, the Council of Trent, in its many bombastic and blasphemous anathemas, outright condemns any and all who dare disagree or contradict the idea that the sacrament of extreme unction has the power to

---

[158] "Extreme Unction." *The Catholic Encyclopedia*, Vol. 5. New York: Robert Appleton Company, 1909. 11 Dec. 2010 http://www.newadvent.org/cathen/05716a.htm, page 1 of 26.

[159] John A. O'Brian, *The Faith of Millions*, 260-261.

[160] See Ludwig Ott, *Fundamentals of Catholic Dogma*, 448-449; *The New Saint Joseph Baltimore Catechism*, 209-210.

[161] *The Code of Canon Law* **Can. 1003**, 180: "Only priests (presbyters and bishops) can give the sacrament of the Anointing of the Sick, using oil blessed by the bishop, or if necessary by the celebrating presbyter himself" (*Catechism of the Catholic Church*, 425) **[1530]**.

[162] *The Canons and Decrees of the Council of Trent*, 99.

[163] *The Biblical Basis for the Catholic Faith*, 125.

forgive sins and produce saving grace. "If anyone says that the anointing of the sick neither confers any grace nor remits sins nor comforts the sick, but that it has already ceased, as if it had been a healing grace only in olden days, let him be anathema" (Council of Trent, fourteenth session, Canon 2). The customary words the priest says following the administration of the sacrament of extreme anointing are: "By this holy unction and his own most gracious mercy, may the Lord pardon you whatever sin you have committed by (sight, hearing, smell, taste and speech, touch, ability to walk)". In addition to the completion of this sacrament, the sick and dying are further encouraged to ask and receive from the priest "the Apostolic Blessing," which is a complete pardon for sins and from the punishment of sins if the recipient is properly disposed. When offered, the priest will then pronounce the following declaration: "By the Faculty which the Apostolic See has given me, I grant you a plenary indulgence for the remission of all your sins, and I bless you. In the Name of the Father and the Son and the Holy Sprit. Amen."[164]

The gravity and extreme importance of receiving last rites for the spiritual welfare and salvation of the Roman Catholic is so serious, Catholics are strongly encouraged to carry cards in their wallets, or wear medals around their necks, that contain the words, "I am Catholic; call a priest," sometimes with the priest's phone number/pager number listed on the card or medal. These cards are meant to help ensure that in an emergency, a doctor, nurse, EMT, policeman, etc., will call a priest to administer extreme unction to the Catholic in need. So great is the need of last rites in the sacramental system of Roman Catholic salvation that the Catholic dares not risk dying and departing this life without it, lest he or she jeopardize the salvation of the soul and forfeit going to heaven. The anointing of the sick is usually received with the two other sacraments of Penance and the Eucharist; all three collectively make up what is called "the last rites" of the Catholic Church. All three are necessary to complete "the earthly pilgrimage" and prepare the Roman Catholic for entrance into "the heavenly homeland," passing over from death to life, from the world to the father."[165] The anointing of the sick can sometimes serve in place of the sacrament of penance whenever the Catholic is too sick and therefore unable to perform contrition and confession to receive absolution through the confessional. Not only does the sacrament of the anointing of the sick impart saving grace to the recipient, it also creates a union with the passion of Christ so the sick or dying person in a certain way... "Is consecrated to bear fruit by configuration to the Savior's redemptive Passion. Suffering, a consequence of original sin, acquires a new meaning; it becomes a participation in the saving work of Jesus" (Emphasis mine).[166]

Roman Catholic teaching, as particularly codified in the Council of Trent, typically points to Mark 6:13 and James 5:14-15 as biblical proof for the doctrine and practice of the sacrament of extreme unction (see *The Canons and Decrees of the Council of Trent fourteenth Session*, Chapter IX). The text of Mark 6:13 reads: ***"And they cast out many demons, and anointed with oil many who were sick, and healed them."*** The operative word here is the act of *anointing* with oil by the twelve Apostles who were commissioned and sent by the Lord Jesus to minister His message and power to the people of Israel. By pointing to Mark 6:13, Rome believes the institution for the sacrament of anointing the sick is found and mandated by Christ and His Apostles, who signified such by the use of anointing oil. But a closer inspection of the text reveals no such meaning or precedent for this "sacrament." Mark the evangelist tells us why Jesus sent the twelve on their evangelical mission—to demonstrate the greater power of God's kingdom in the physical realm over and against the demonic forces of Satan, to set people free from demonic possession and to bring physical

---

164   John Laux, *Mass and the Sacraments*, 118-120; "Extreme Unction" at http://fisheaters.com/unction.html.
165   *Catechism of the Catholic Church*, 424 **[1524-1525]**.
166   *Catechism of the Catholic Church*, 423 **[1521]**.

healing to those ill and sick. By reading of the same commissioning given in Matthew 10 and Luke 9:1-6 with the events of Mark chapter six, we learn these were sign miracles announcing the offer and initial arrival of the Messianic kingdom *to Israel, not the Church*, by Jesus and His apostolic representatives sent in His power and name.

The "Church" and the sacrament of "extreme unction" did not even exist at this time and would therefore be *anachronistic* to these events themselves. These things would have no meaning at all to first-century Israelites fervently expecting the coming of the Messiah and the Messianic kingdom in their day! This is especially confirmed and verified in the same commission given in Matthew 10:1-6 and Luke 9:1-6 when Jesus expressly commands them not to *"go into the way of the Gentiles"* or any city of the Samaritans but only *"to the lost sheep of Israel"* (Matthew 10:5-6). Mark 6, in conjunction with the same events narrated in Matthew 10 and Luke 9, is not historically meant for the Church, but dealt with Israel at Christ's first coming and His offer of the Messianic kingdom to them as the covenanted people of God. Keeping within this Jewish culture and context, it was quite normal and in customary practice with the way the Jewish concept *sheluchim* operated—the sending out of ambassadors for a king or country, "that is a man's representative was considered as the man himself," who were sent to fulfill a *special* commission and bring back a report[167] So the Lord's command to His disciples to heal and expel demons was directed to Israel, not to priests acting for the 'Catholic' Church dispensing a sacrament to the seriously ill and dying!

The use of anointing oil for the sick by the Apostles in Mark 6:13 is in no way an endorsement or justification for the Roman Catholic sacrament of extreme unction when the use of oil in biblical times is recalled. The administration of oil was used for a variety of reasons in biblical times. Olive oil or other kinds made of different fragrances and spices (frankincense, spikenard, and myrrh) were used for various purposes: as cosmetics (Exodus 25:6; Ruth 3:3; Luke 7:46); butter to cook food in (Numbers 11:8; Deuteronomy 7:13); as fuel for fire and light in the home and for the Menorah in the Tabernacle and Temple (Exodus 25:6; 27:20; Matthew 25:3,4,8); as symbolic for the consecration of a priest or king of Israel whom God anointed for His service (Leviticus 2:1; Numbers 4:9; Psalm 89:20; 1 Samuel 10:1; 16:13). Oil was also used for a balm to heal wounds (Luke 10:34), and to serve as a fitting *symbol* for the healing power and presence of God's Spirit. It came to symbolize the healing ministry and anointing of the Holy Spirit in the New Testament (Zechariah 4:1-6; James 5:14).[168] The use of anointing of oil in Mark 6:13 is more in keeping with the latter symbolic meaning. It was applied to represent the supernatural presence of Jesus Christ to heal the sick by the power of the Holy Spirit.

The Roman Catholic sacrament of extreme unction, with its supposed priestly absolution of sins, is simply not in view here because it is traditionally administered to the dying or to those whose death is imminent; whereas the anointing of Mark 6 takes place within the context of giving the sick a supernatural healing and a restoration back to physical life. Impending death and preparation for the afterlife, as it would relate to Rome's anointing of the sick, is nowhere found in the context of Mark 6 with the apostolic anointing of oil. "The Roman Catholic sacrament of extreme unction is not even suggested here, for that rite is administered in the expectation of impending *death*, whereas the anointing mentioned in Mark 6:13 occurs in a context of giving a person a new *lease* on life."[169] The passage in Mark 6:13 deals with physical healing and the power to exorcise demons, not the granting of a sacerdotal pardon from sins through a sacramental

---

[167] John Walvoord, Roy Zuck, *The Bible Knowledge Commentary*, 127.

[168] William Hendrickson, *The Gospel of Mark*, 231-232.

[169] Ibid., 233.

ritual. The whole issue of anointing people for the near anticipation or preparation of death is simply not found in the text as Roman Catholic teaching wrongly assumes.

> Mark himself also says (3:15): "He gave them authority to cure diseases and to cast out demons." And in Mark 6:13 nothing else is described except what the Apostles already did the first time they were sent out, namely how they healed the sick, applying the outward sign of anointing with oil. Therefore Mark does not at all say in this passage that the Apostles anointed those who were in their death struggle, in the belief that in this unction they would have the highest and firmest aid against sins, the devil, and death. Much less does he prescribe that this anointing with oil should be performed and preserved in the whole church of the New Testament at all times until the end of the world, but he is describing the gift of healing…. The evangelist says nothing either about a command of Christ or about an act of the Apostles to the effect that the oil in this unction must first be exorcised and consecrated with a set form of words…We do not read that the Apostles anointed those of whom they anticipated with good reason that they would soon die, but with their anointing they healed the sick, lest they should then and there die through that illness…Mark does not say that the purpose and effect of this unction was that through it sins would be blotted out, the wiles of the devil suppressed in those about to die, etc., but that they should with this outward sign administer the gift of bodily healing. Therefore it is plain as can be from this one comparison that Christ in Mark 6:13 neither instituted nor alluded to (as the Tridentine chapter expresses it) such an unction in order that it should be a sacrament for those who have come to the end of their lives, as the description and practice of the papalists holds. And because the Tridentine decree appeals to Mark 6, we have already shown that the papalist unction has in that passage neither institution nor command nor promise nor example so that it could be a sacrament of the New Testament, as their description has it.[170]

Even more revealing here is that Roman Catholic Bible commentators and theologians candidly admit Mark 6:13 with Matthew 10:1 and Luke 9:1-2, apart from a few patristic writers (Victor of Antioch, Theophylactus, Euthymius, Bede, and others), does not support the sacrament of extreme unction, for the following reasons: There is only present a physical and bodily healing with the act of the Apostles' anointing with oil; most who were healed did not receive Christian baptism, since the Church had not begun yet; the Apostles were not formally ordained priests; and penance, of which extreme unction is a complimentary sacrament, had not yet been instituted.[171] To read the sacrament of extreme unction or anointing of the sick into alleged proof texts like Mark 6:13 is another unwarranted leap by the Roman Catholic Church showing at once the sacrament of extreme unction cannot possibly be maintained or supported by Scripture—it is simply unbiblical and should be rightly rejected on those grounds alone!

The second New Testament passage upon which the Roman Catholic bases his need for the sacrament of extreme unction is James 5:14-15 where we read the following: ***"Is anyone among you sick? Let him call for the elders of the church, and let them pray over him, anointing him with oil in the name of the Lord. And***

---

[170] Martin Chemnitz, *Examination of the Council of Trent Part II*, 662-663.
[171] "Extreme Unction." *The Catholic Encyclopedia*. Vol. 5. New York: Robert Appleton Company, 1909. 11 Dec. 2010 http://www.newadvent.org/cathen/05716a.htm, page 3 of 26

the prayer of faith will save the sick, and the Lord will raise him up. And if he has committed sins, he will be forgiven." From this passage in James, the Catholic Church believes it is "clearly seen" that their priests have the power conferred by Christ to anoint the ill or dying with holy oil, hear the confession of sins from them, and then grant absolution with the sacrament of extreme unction. Catholic priest John Laux goes on to affirm this is exactly what James 5:14-15 means, when speaking on behalf of the Roman Catholic institution:

> That the Sacrament of Extreme Unction was instituted by Christ is clearly seen from the words of the Apostle James.... The Apostle tells us that the anointing with oil and the prayer of the priest produce grace, viz., remission of sin. But sin could not be forgiven by the anointing with oil and prayer of the priest unless Christ had willed it so. Hence Christ himself must have given this power to the anointing and the prayer, that is, He must have instituted the Sacrament of Extreme Unction. The divine institution is also indicated by the words: "In the name of the Lord": the priests anoint the sick in the name, that is, by the authority of the Lord.[172]

Catholic theology believes all the necessary elements for a grace-imparting sacrament are present here for the priest to dispense, and it is therefore a sacrament necessary to be received so as to complete and finish the salvation of the soul within the sacramental system of the Roman Catholic Church:

> In James 5, 14 et seq., all the elements of a true sacrament are mentioned: α) An outward sign of grace, consisting of anointing with oil (matter) and of the prayer of the priest over the sick person (form). β) An inner operation of grace which is definitely expressed in the forgiveness of sins, and which certainly takes place through the communication of grace. According to the context and the language in other passages (cf. James 1, 21; 2, 14; 5, 20), the saving and raising up of the sick person is at least not exclusively to be referred to the cure of the body, but also and above all to the saving of the soul from eternal destruction and to the raising-up of the soul by divine grace.[173]

The Catholic Encyclopedia agrees, while assuming the *"elders"* of James 5:14 must mean the priests of the hierarchical clergy, adding:

> The priests are to pray over the sick man, anointing him with oil. Here we have the physical elements necessary to constitute a sacrament in the strict sense: oil as remote matter, like water in baptism; and the accompanying prayer as form. This rite will therefore be a true sacrament if it has the sanction of Christ's authority, and is intended by its own operation to confer grace on the sick person, to work for his spiritual benefit.[174]

[172] John Laux, *Mass and the Sacraments*, 114.
[173] Ludwig Ott, *Fundamentals of Catholic Dogma*, 445-446.
[174] "Extreme Unction." *The Catholic Encyclopedia.* Vol. 5. New York: Robert Appleton Company, 1909. 11 Dec. 2010 http://www.newadvent.org/cathen/05716a.htm, page 4 of 26

The Council of Trent not only adheres to this sacramental interpretation of James 5:14-15 but hurls condemnation on any who would dare justifiably disagree with this forced, assumed, and erroneous interpretation:

> Can. 1. If anyone says that extreme unction is not truly and properly a sacrament instituted by Christ our Lord and announced by the blessed Apostle James, but is only a rite received from the Fathers or a human invention, let him be anathema....
>
> Can. 3. If anyone says that the rite and usage of extreme unction which the holy Roman Church observes is at variance with the statement of the blessed Apostle James, and is therefore to be changed and may without sin be despised by Christians, let him be anathema.
>
> Can. 4. If anyone says that the priests of the Church, whom blessed James exhorts to be brought to anoint the sick, are not priests who have been ordained by a bishop, but the elders in each community, and that for this reason a priest only is not the proper minister of extreme unction, let him be anathema.[175]

Does James 5:14-15 teach the sacramental meaning of Roman Catholicism? A closer examination of this New Testament passage emphatically answers: Certainly not! This is immediately made obvious in verse 14 when James counsels the sick and infirmed to call for the *"elders"* of the church, not for a *priest*; the word is in the plural here and a priest or a group of priests are not mentioned. The term *elder* is never used in reference to a priest in the New Testament. So elders and priests are two different entities and offices; and the office of the priest is not the same as the office of elders in the New Testament generally or James 5:14 specifically—for the New Testament minister is not individually called a priest but an elder, pastor, overseer, evangelist, and teacher. The *elder* was a leader chosen from among the older and more mature among the local assembly (not from a universal church at large headquartered in Rome!) to be a leader in the Christian church. The context of New Testament Scripture shows the church elder did not belong to a sacerdotal clergy or priestly class of celibate men! From this proper biblical context and meaning, D. Edmond Hiebert, explains what James really means by *"elders"* when exhorting the sick to call for *the elders of the church*:

> "The elders of the church" are obviously the leaders of the local assembly. The term elder (*presbuteros*) is a comparative form denoting one who is older than someone else (Luke 15:25); but here it is a designation of office. Like the synagogues, the early Christian churches chose their leaders from among the older and more mature members. The plural is consistent with the New Testament picture of a plurality of elders in the local church (Acts 14:23; Phil. 1:1; 1 Thess. 5:12).[176]

The Catholic interpretation further believes James 5:14-16 calls for the sacrament of penance, and the priest's power to grant forgiveness of sins, once the sick is duly anointed and then confesses his sins to the priest; for, verse 15, they claim, mandates the call for a sacramental meaning of the text: *"And the prayer of faith will save the sick, and the Lord will raise him up. And if he has committed sins, he will be forgiven.*

[175] H.J. Schroeder, *The Canons and Decrees of the Council of Trent*, 104-105.
[176] D. Edmond Hiebert, *James* (BMH: Winona Lake, IN, 1992), 294-292.

Confess your trespasses to one another, and pray for one another that you may be healed." A closer, careful, and contextual reading of James 5:14-16 yields another meaning that in no way supports the Roman Catholic interpretation of the passage! First of all, the healing of the sick does not directly come from a priest administering a sacrament whereby priest and anointing oil work together to effect saving grace. The anointing oil is symbolic of the presence of the indwelling Holy Spirit to heal and watch over the believer. Second, James tells us the purpose for the anointing is to "raise up" the sick with healing, and if the sickness is due to some sin, God's forgiveness will be granted upon confession of that sin to Him in the presence of the elders (v.15). Hence, the anointing of the sick is to promote healing and spiritual restoration, not a preparation for dying or completing the sacramental system of salvation at the end of life. Factoring these elements here makes it evident that James 5:14-16:

> …Provides no basis for the Roman Catholic Church's sacrament of extreme unction, wherein the dying is anointed with oil with the purpose of removing any remnant of sin and strengthening the soul for dying. A simple reading of the text makes it clear that the anointing with oil is to promote healing, not to ease dying.
>
> Rather than being…sacramental, the anointing is *symbolical*. Anointing in the Scriptures is usually associated with consecrating or setting apart someone for special service or attention. In this respect oil also is a symbol of the Holy Spirit, who indwells and watches over each believer (cf. 4:5). So the applying of oil to the sick is a rich symbolic act—setting the sick apart to be ministered to in a special way by the Holy Spirit. When applied by the loving hands of the elders, it is a profound vehicle for comfort and encouragement.[177]

Third, James 5:15 states it is the *object* of prayer (the Lord), and the faith placed in Him, which will heal the sick and forgive any sin. The power to heal and forgive does not reside in a priest, the anointing oil, or in a verbal formula recited by a Catholic priest, but in the supernatural power of God to do these things, received through faith by way of prayer made "in the name of the Lord." This is further confirmed in verse 16 where James says it is by "the effectual fervent prayer of a righteous man" availing much by which God hears, answers, and heals the sick and forgives them if sins have been committed. The anointing of oil with prayer is the outward expression of faith in God to heal and forgive the person in need of them. They do not produce the healing and forgiveness themselves, *per se*, but the God who answers prayers made with such faith does. This does not, however, mean God will physically heal someone every time when the instructions of James 5:14-16 are faithfully carried out. It will be generally done, but God has the first and final choice in these matters. He will always forgive sin where faith in Him and His Word are present. For in James 5:14-16, and throughout Scripture, it is *faith* in the end which brings God's healing to the sick and forgiveness to the confessing sinner.

James clearly ascribes the forgiveness of sins to "***the prayer of faith***" and not to the external sign of anointing with oil. It cannot come from or originate with a sacrament dispensed by a priest! Faith in God is the sole condition upon which the Lord's healing is given to the sick, instead of being dependent on some *ex opere operato* ability of a Roman Catholic sacrament to magically and automatically confer saving grace. One could be anointed and prayed over by the elders (and in this case a Roman Catholic priest) and still not have faith not be healed or forgiven. Faith in God is the key here in James 5:15!

---

[177]   R. Kent Hughes, *James* (Wheaton, Illinois: 1991), 256.

Believers who struggle with illness can, indeed, be confident that God will heal them in the end. But it does not require a special visit from the elders nor an anointing with oil to accomplish that. It is, as it were, part of their salvation itself, guaranteed them as a gift of grace by the Lord. James plainly envisages a much more immediate result of this special time of prayer for the sick believer.

A more fruitful approach is to focus attention on the qualification that James introduces: it is only the prayer offered in faith that brings healing. James's language here again has a point of contact with the opening section of the letter, where he insisted that the believer who asks God for wisdom "must believe and not doubt, because he who doubts is like the wave of the sea, blown and tossed by the wind" (1:6).[178]

Fourth, the confession of sins mentioned in James 5:16 is not the confession of the Roman Catholic sacrament of penance, for the simple fact the verse exhorts a mutual, voluntary confession of trespasses between elder and congregant when stating ***"confess your trespasses <u>to one another</u>"***, whereas the Catholic idea of confession is strictly *unilateral* and *arbitrary,* where the person is required to confess his sins to a priest and no more. The instruction is simple in its prescription: ordinary members of the church assembly should confess their faults to the elders or leaders of the congregation and, in equal measure, the elders should also confess their sins to their fellow Christians. The Greek word "to one another" is *allelois* (αλληλοις) and comes from the root word *allos* (αλλος), which means "another of the same kind." It is no accident James uses this word for mutual confession to refer to both an elder and a regular member of the assembly, who are equal heirs of God's grace. So James values the elders, including himself, no doubt, and the non-leadership of the Christian assembly, as equal in quality and rank, so that they could confess their sins to him and he could confess his sins to them—a far cry from the Catholic priest hearing the one-sided confession of sins by the laity and being done with it on that unilateral level alone!

If Rome were truly honest with their confession business they would conform to the real teaching of James 5:14-16, and dispense with their false interpretation calling for a unilateral confession, and instead have the priest confess his sins in mutual return to the penitent, after he or she has confessed to the priest. Ah, but doing this would rob the priest of his so-called power to forgive sins, and instead ascribe it to a greater and more authoritarian position, far above the submissive and sacramentally dependent laity! Notice here what James does *not* say. He did *not* say: *"Confess your sins to the elders,"* but rather, *"Confess your sins to one another."* Great authority and scholar on the Greek New Testament Spiros Zodhiates reinforces what has been noted above when informing us:

> Let us bear in mind here that James does not say, "Therefore, confess your sins to the elders," but "confess your sins one to another." This is very significant indeed. James is speaking to Christians in general when he says, "confess your sins one to another." If it is true that the lay people, the ordinary sinners, ought to confess their sins to the elders of the church, it ought to be equally true that the elders ought to confess their sins, not necessarily to their fellow elders, but to their brethren in Christ, their spiritual brethren.... There is something that the Holy Spirit wants to teach us through this. It is the word *allelois* which James is using here to denote "one to another," and by virtue of this word we come to the

---

[178] Douglas Moo, *The Letter of James* (Grand Rapids: Eerdmans: 2000), 244.

conclusion that James considers these elders of the same quality and rank as their healed brother over whom they prayed. He was not inferior to them, nor were they superior to him. He confessed his sins to them, and they could have confessed their sins to him. The fact that they were not sick did not mean that they were not sinners, even as his illness did not necessarily mean that he was a sinner. Thus the inescapable meaning of the verse in James is that as Christians we are all on equal footing as far as our susceptibility to sin is concerned, and confession of sin should be made by one another without distinction of rank, even between laity and priesthood. A priest, after hearing the confession of his penitent parishioner, should have the courage and the moral stamina to turn around and confess his sins to his parishioner. That is what James, the inspired Apostle, teaches.

But it is never safe to base a doctrine of such paramount importance on a single verse of Scripture. Let us look at the rest of the Bible to see whether in apostolic times there was any practice of the so-called confessional. Can we find anything in the New Testament that would indicate that there were Apostles who waited in a little room for people to come to them and confess their sins to them? The Scriptures are absolutely silent concerning this matter. Neither Peter, nor John, nor Paul in all their writings refers to people who came to them to confess their sins and whose sins they absolved. Could it be because those who were converted under their ministries became sinless? Hardly, for they constantly condemn their spiritual children for the frequency of their sins. No, there are no confessionals in the New Testament. Confession in the days of the Apostles was an incidental thing born *not* out of apostolic obligation and ordinance, but out of a voluntary compulsion of the soul of the individual. If a person did not confess his sins to Paul, it did not mean that the person was going to hell. The thief on the cross had no Apostle to confess his sin to. But he had Christ to cry to; and, praise the Lord, Christ is available to everyone! We find, then, not a single instance where any of the disciples of Christ or the Apostles invited anyone to come and confess his sins to them.[179]

God's healing of the sick and forgiveness of sins is not predicated on the Roman Catholic rite, or the priest's formulaic confession over him, but solely rests in the God who can heal and forgive. The anointing of the sick is an outward acknowledgement of both this and the expression of faith in the God who declares, ***"For I am the Lord who heals you…. Who forgives all your iniquities, Who heals all your diseases"*** (Exodus 15:26; Psalm 103:3). These are promises received by simple faith in the promises of God, Who keeps them and gives them freely directly through His Son Jesus Christ. The whole Roman Catholic idea of James or Mark establishing a sacrament of extreme unction with the power of the priest to heal and forgive sin is not in keeping with what we find in those two books of the New Testament or the entire canon of Scripture. It is another contrivance and construction of Papal Rome, whose "institution" of this sacrament is a pure invention which evolved over a long period of time during the gradual development of Roman Catholic sacramental theology. It has nothing to do with the simple prayer of faith mentioned in James 5:15 by which healing and forgiveness are graciously given by God, and so adumbrated by the anointing with oil by the church elders.

---

[179] Spiros Zodhiates, *The Book of James: Faith, Love & Hope* (Chattanooga: AMG Publishers, 1997), 672-673.

Therefore the extreme unction of the papalists is not the one of which Mark speaks, nor is it the one which James describes, whether you look at the material or the form or the action or the use, purpose, and effect. Neither has the prayer of faith of which James speaks any part in the unction of the papalists. For they pray that through this unction full remission of sins may be given, although there is no divine promise of this. And because there is no faith without a promise, therefore there can be here no prayer of faith. They also employ the invocation of the dead; because this has no command and promise from God, it cannot be a prayer of faith. Therefore it is rightly said that this extreme unction is a human invention which has neither a command from God nor a promise of grace. For what belongs to the gift of healing must not, without a special Word, be transferred to other uses. Neither were the outward miracles the instruments through which the spiritual blessings were offered and bestowed, but they only prepared the way for the Gospel, which is the ministry of the Spirit, in which faith seeks and receives grace, forgiveness, etc.

Therefore, [first], the Apostles employed the external sign of anointing with oil in the gift of healing, not because either the oil itself or the action of anointing held or brought any power and efficacy for healing (which was a miraculous thing), and much less for the remission of sins, which James ascribes to the prayer of faith—but because it was at that time customary, and known from the Old Testament, that oil symbolized supernatural and celestial gifts, therefore the employed anointing with oil in these healings was not conferred either in a human or in some magical manner, but that they were heavenly gifts by the power and working of God.[180]

The sacrament of extreme unction for the dying, as defined and practiced by the Roman Catholic priests today, was virtually unknown in the church for the first nine centuries! The earliest mention of the anointing of the sick goes back to the fifth-century letter of Pope Innocent I, who wrote to Decentius, the bishop of Gubbio. The letter discusses various points on how the anointing of the sick is to be administered by the bishop or priest to the *sick* person. Appeal is made to James 5:14 with the observation that the oil is to be blessed by the bishop and applied to the *sick* person by the bishop or priest. In the early eighth century, Bede the Venerable states in his commentary on the book of James (the earliest extant commentary we have) that it was the early practice for presbyters to anoint the *sick* with oil and pray for their healing.[181] Prior to this time, the universal Church, therefore, knew nothing of an anointing for death, nor is there anything mentioned of the anointing as a sacrament or preparation for death found anywhere in the annals of church writings for almost nine hundred years after Christ and the Apostles! Furthermore, the Catholic Church at large did not universally adopt the sacrament now known as extreme unction until the end of the twelfth century! It was formally instituted and adopted by the Catholic Church as a sacrament at the conclusion of the Council of Florence in A.D. 1439. Session eight of that council states:

The fifth sacrament is extreme unction. Its matter is olive oil blessed by a priest. This sacrament should not be given to the sick unless death is expected. The person is to be anointed on the following places: on the eyes for sight, on the ears for hearing, on the

---

180 Martin Chemnitz, *Examination of the Council of Trent Part II*, 666-668
181 Richard P. McBrien, *Catholicism*, 844.

nostrils for smell, on the mouth for taste or speech, on the hands for touch, on the feet for walking, on the loins for the pleasure that abides there. The form of this sacrament is:

Through this anointing and his most pious mercy may the Lord pardon you whatever you have done wrong by sight, and similarly for the other members. The minister of the sacrament is a priest. Its effect is to cure the mind and, in so far as it helps the soul, also the body. Blessed James the Apostle said of this sacrament: Any one of you who is sick should send for the elders of the church, and they shall pray over him and anoint him with oil in the name of the Lord. The prayer of faith will save the sick person and the Lord will raise him up again: and if he is in sins, they will be forgiven him.[182]

Up until this period, no such sacrament was required for receiving God's saving grace and forgiveness of sins. Now, after 1,400 hundred years of church history have expired, the fifth sacrament is suddenly needed to achieve the completion of sacramental salvation by the Roman Catholic hoping to make heaven, or purgatory at the least, with receiving this last sacrament before departing this life! But no such strange and foreign sacrament of "extreme unction" for salvation is found or required in the Holy Word of God. In light of this glaring absence, William Cathcart's verdict on this subject is irrefutably true, and worthy of quotation: "Such is extreme unction, one of the leading sacraments of the Church of Rome; it has no place in the Scriptures; no location among the fathers; it was never heard of until from nine to twelve hundred years after Christ. It is a MODERN INNOVATION."[183] This "sacrament", again, is just another invention of the ever-evolving religion of Roman Catholicism. Scripture tells us divine healing is found in the Messiah Jesus alone, Who was wounded for our transgression and bruised for our iniquities. And by those vicarious wounds and flagellation stripes laid on his undeserving back, we are spiritually and physically healed (See Isaiah 53:5; Matthew 8:16-17; 1 Peter 2:24). We must come to Christ alone for this, not to the Catholic Church, or any other person or religious institution for this needed healing and salvation from illness and death.

The Lord Jesus instituted two ordinances for the Church to celebrate: (1) Baptism and (2) the Lord's Supper. He did not officially institute an anointing for extreme unction. Rome's blasphemous claim this sacrament can produce a participation in the saving work of Jesus for the ailing or dying Catholic is totally contrary to the repeated teaching of Scripture wherein it is maintained the saving work of Jesus Christ is done *"by Himself"*, *"without the deeds of the law"*, *"not of yourselves, it is the gift of God"*: *"not of works, lest any man should boast,"* *"not by works of righteousness which we have done, but according to His mercy."* Christ saved us that we, by faith alone, are forgiven and permanently saved by Him (Hebrews 1:3; Romans 3:28; Ephesians 2:8-9; Titus 3:5). The prayer and anointing of James 5:14-16 is sanctioned by "the prayer of faith," not an instituted sacrament. Verse 16 summarizes the basis for God's answer to heal and forgive the one who is sick; it is by "the effectual fervent prayer of a righteous man" availing much" this is done. Yet Catholicism takes this simple truth and cleverly "weaves it into" its sacraments for salvation system which must be performed and offered by the priest. Such a deadly lie deceives the gravely ill and dying into thinking they can trust in the efficacy of this sacrament itself to save the soul—a damnable lie because it is faith in Christ alone, Scripture declares, which can only save the lost sinner from the condemnation of God.

The unbiblical idea of the sacrament of extreme unction being a participation in the saving work of Jesus Christ is an atrocious lie when Scripture teaches it was by Christ's redemptive work alone that accomplished

---

[182]   The Decrees of the Council of Florence at: http://www.dailycatholic.org/history/17ecume9.htm.

[183]   William Cathcart, *The Papal System*, 224.

salvation for sinners who cannot save themselves. Teaching the anointing of the sick produces a "participation in the saving work of Jesus" is an insidious deception encouraging the Catholic to put a false trust in his own sufferings as a necessary addition to the sufferings of Christ required to meet the conditions for salvation! It is precisely here former Catholic priest Richard Bennett rightly observes to teach this "is utterly perverse in that it holds out a false hope to trust in one's own suffering as adding some thing to that of the Lord," which is a lie of vast proportions denying the central Gospel truth in Scripture stating the work of redemption is found and obtained in what Christ Jesus suffered alone on the cross of Calvary.

When the priest performs the ritual of anointing the sick and then says, "May the Lord who frees you from sin save you and raise you up," he along with the Catholic Church, fails to see forgiveness of sins is not granted through a Church or a man to dispense, but is graciously given *directly* and *exclusively* by God alone to those who look in faith to Jesus Christ confessing their sins with repentance towards Him. To the sincere, but misguided Catholics, who think the sacrament of unction can impart or complete their salvation, we strongly and humbly urge you to turn to the compassion of the healing and forgiving Christ alone to save you Who is able to save to the uttermost all those who come to Him. To trust anyone (a priest dispensing sacraments), or anything else (the sacrament of unction), in addition to Jesus Christ alone for salvation, is to invite the curse of God's Word as given in the book of Galatians, which declares the anathema of God on every one who adds or requires that something else other than faith in Jesus Christ alone is needed for salvation. To thus demand the sacrament of extreme unction is necessary for salvation, as the Catholic Church teaches, is to therefore call down the curse of God upon themselves as given in Galatians 1:8-9.

The Sacrament of Holy Orders.

The sacrament of Holy Orders is the sixth sacrament of Rome. The Roman Catholic institution defines it this way: "Holy orders is the sacrament through which men receive the power and grace to perform the sacred duties of bishops, priests, and other ministers of the Church."[184] Holy Orders allow the priest to unite with Jesus Christ and share in His sacrificial priesthood. He is Christ's priest on Earth and his powers in this role are both sacramental and supernatural in that he is able to offer the sacrifice of the Mass and to offer forgiveness of sin through the sacrament of Penance. By the medium of Holy Orders, the priest is given these and the other five sacraments to dispense the saving grace of God to Catholics. When a male candidate is ordained through the sacrament of Holy Orders his entrance into the Roman Catholic priesthood produces three effects: First, an increase in sanctifying grace; second, sacramental grace, through which the priest has God's constant help in his sacred ministry; third, a character, lasting forever, which is a special sharing in the priesthood of Christ and which gives the priest special supernatural powers.[185]

By the ordination of holy orders both priest and bishop, Rome believes, partake in the one identical priesthood and ministry of Christ. Both priest and bishop is "Christ in person" and offer up sacrifices and dispense the sacraments of grace in His place while on the earth. The official teaching of Rome in the council documents of Vatican II claims:

> The priest offers the Holy sacrifice *in persona Christi*: this means more than offering 'in the name of' or 'in the place of Christ. *In persona* means in specific sacramental identification

---

[184] *The New Saint Joseph Baltimore Catechism*, 212.
[185] Ibid., 213.

with the 'eternal High Priest'... In fact from tradition, which is expressed especially in the liturgical rites and in the customs of both the Eastern and Western Church, it is abundantly clear that by the imposition of hands and through words of the consecration, the grace of the Holy Spirit is given, and a sacred character is impressed in such wise that bishops, in a resplendent and visible manner, take the place of Christ himself, teacher, shepherd and priest, and act as his representatives (*in eius persona*) [i.e., in His person].[186]

The method of impartation and ordination to the priesthood consist in the bishop laying hands on the candidate in accordance with what is prescribed in 2 Timothy 1:6 where Paul exhorts Timothy to rekindle the gift of God that is within you ***"through the laying on of hands."***[187] When the bishop performs the laying on of hands he then ordains the candidate into the Roman Catholic priesthood and then says: "Receive the Holy Spirit, whose sins you shall forgive they are forgiven them; and whose sins you shall retain, they are retained."

There are eight "holy" orders or offices of ministry in the Catholic institution. The first five are deemed the lowest and are ecclesiastical in origin; the higher two are considered "divine" in origin. The highest two in this clerical hierarchy is the bishop and the priest. The bishop has the greatest authority and jurisdiction, apart from the Popes and patriarchs. Bishops (the first degree of the priesthood) are granted the power to ordain men to be deacons or priests, offer all the seven sacraments of the Catholic institution, and are said to exercise all the fullness of the priesthood. The priest (the second degree of the priesthood) are commissioned to confer the powers of performing the Mass, administer the sacraments of Baptism, Communion, Penance, Extreme Unction, Matrimony, and finally, to preach, teach, counsel, and guide the parishioners.

The next degree of sacred orders is the deacon whose responsibilities include: handling the 'sacred' vessels, to give communion to the sick and the infirmed; to assist the priest and bishop in various responsibilities of the parish and diocese; to read the Scripture readings at Mass, and to help the sick, widows, and orphans. Following the deacon is the office of subdeacon whose responsibilities are to serve the deacon at Mass, to prepare the bread, wine, and "sacred" vessels for Mass and pour water into the communion wine. After the bishop, priest, deacon, and subdeacon the four lesser degrees of Holy Orders are Acolytes, Exorcists (which duty now belongs to the priest), Lectors (Readers), and Porters.[188]

Since Rome has claimed Holy Orders is a "sacrament", and defines a sacrament as an outward sign or rite able to impart saving grace, then the ordination of their priests would supposedly have the power to confer salvation upon those who receive the sacraments from those priests ordained by the Catholic bishop. Is this teaching found in Scripture? Does the Bible, the Lord Jesus Christ, and the Apostles agree with this claim made by Rome when they state the ordination of priests by a bishop is an act, which produces grace for the salvation of the soul? By this teaching are the lost saved by the ordination of priests to the Catholic Church? Is there a sacrament of holy orders with its eight offices taught in the New Testament? The New Testament declares all Christians to be priests who offer up 'spiritual' sacrifices to God (1 Peter 2:9; Revelation 1:6). None of the New Testament writers make any categorical distinction between "laity" and "clergy", nor do they set up a select company of male celibate priests to rule over the rest of a local congregation or a "Universal" Church.

---

[186]   Austin Flannery, *Vatican II: The Conciliar and Post Conciliar Documents*, Vol. II, Sec. 8, p. 74; Vol. I, Sec. 21, pp. 373-374. See also the *Catechism of the Catholic Church*, 431 **[1548]**.

[187]   *Catechism of the Catholic Church*, 444 **[1590]**.

[188]   "Holy Orders" at http://www.fisheaters.com/holyorders.html, 2-3.

The New Testament does not lists "priests" as one of the ministry offices of the church. When the Apostle Paul lists those offices in Ephesians 4:11-12, which Christ bestowed on the Church after He ascended to heaven, the office of priest is not listed among them! *"And He Himself gave some to be <u>apostles</u>, some <u>prophets</u>, some <u>evangelists</u>, and some <u>pastors</u> and <u>teachers</u>, for the equipping of the saints for the work of the ministry for the edifying for the body of Christ"* (Ephesians 4:11-12).

There are five officially listed, six if you include the office of deacon (see Acts 6), ministry of offices in Ephesians chapter four as opposed to the eight offices of Holy Orders created by the Roman Catholic Church—with the exception of bishop and deacon which are legitimate ministry offices in the New Testament Church. The list of Ephesians 4:11 is commonly referred to as the five-fold ministry of the Church. These five ministry offices are *never* called a sacrament in Scripture. Furthermore, a summary review from the Word of God of these offices will certainly show they are not defined or understood to be a hierarchy of priests given the power to dispense grace saving sacraments or reenacting Christ's sacrifice on the cross through the bread and wine of the Mass! The **Apostles** were the twelve personally chosen by Christ. The one qualification for apostleship was the person had to have been chosen by Christ and spent time with Him from His baptism in the Jordan to His ascension—a period of over three years! (Acts 1:21-22). They were also to have been personally chosen and called by Jesus, just like Paul was when He met the risen Savior on the road to Damascus and was therefore chosen by the Lord to be an Apostle as *"one born out of due time"* (Acts 9:1-8; 1 Corinthians 15:8-9; Galatians 1:1; 2:6-9).

There were others called Apostles, such as James the brother of the Lord (1 Corinthians 15:7; Galatians 1:19), Barnabus, the missionary companion of Paul (Acts 14:4, 14; 1 Corinthians 9:6); Adronicus and Junias (Romans 16:7); Silas, Apollos, and Timothy (1Thessalonians 1:1; 2:7; 1 Corinthians 4:6, 9). This second group had an apostolic ministry (which involves establishing new churches among new converts in a particular region) but did not *uniquely* occupy the office of an Apostle as the twelve and Paul did. The New Testament understanding of an Apostle was not one who was hand picked by 'Pope' Peter or the other Apostles to dispense sacraments in the role of celibate priests but, rather, one who was called and sent out by the Lord Jesus Christ and the church with the supernatural authority and commission to proclaim and take the Gospel message to the world.

Prophets were set in the church to communicate God's will for an individual Christian or a congregation and the proper course of action to take in light of a revealed message given by the prophet (Acts 11:27-30; 21:1-13). There is no indication they were functioning in a fashion similar to or the same as "priests" operating under a sacrament of "Holy Orders." **Evangelists** are missionaries, Gospel preachers who present, proclaim, and preach the Gospel wherever they go (Acts 8:4-12; 26-37; Romans 10:14-18). Not all Christians are called to be evangelists, but all Christians are expected by God to evangelize, to witness for the Lord and to do *"the work of evangelist"* by sharing the good news of salvation in Jesus Christ with the lost world (2 Timothy 2:5). **Pastors** and **teachers** are considered to be one and the same in the Greek because they are "governed by one article ("the" occurs before "pastors" but not before "teachers") and the word "and" (*kai*) differs from the other "and" (*de*) in the verse. So the reading from the Greek text would literally read "pastor-teachers."[189]

The **Pastor** is both an overseer who guides and comforts God's flock and he is a teacher in that he teaches from God's Word about who God is and the ways He prescribes for us to learn and follow. While a pastor can be a teacher in the Church, teachers are also listed as a distinct office from the pastor and are so listed in this respect in the New Testament (see Romans 12:7; 1 Peter 5:2). Observe also in Ephesians 4:12

---

[189]   John Walvoord, Roy Zuck, *The Bible Knowledge Commentary*, 635.

the intent and purpose for the ministry gifts is to prepare, equip and enable the body of believers to grow and spiritually mature into the moral image of Jesus Christ. If the sacraments of the Roman Catholic priesthood are necessary to grow in saving and sanctifying grace to this end, as Rome has long taught, why does the Apostle Paul not mention this here where it was most applicable? And with that, why is there no mention for the necessity of priests and the sacrament of Holy Orders to carry out such a need expressed and taught by Rome? The simple answer is Holy Orders, with the priesthood of Rome, are not biblical concepts found or mentioned in Scripture! When Paul discusses the various gifts of ministry in the Church in Romans 12:6-8, there is no mention of a Sacrament of Holy Orders with eight ministry offices of the Church listed. Surely if Holy Orders were preeminent above all ministry offices and functions, and also necessary to convey the sacraments of saving and sanctifying grace, Paul, and even the other writers of the New Testament, would have undoubtedly mentioned it first since it is the first and most important office for the Roman Catholic priesthood. In these verses from the book of Romans, Paul talks about the ministries of prophecy, teaching, exhortation, giving, leading, and showing mercy, but no mention is made of a sacramental priesthood.

There is no elucidation or citation of any eight offices of Holy Orders here or in any other passage or verse in all of the New Testament! Paul gives another list of ministry offices in the Church in 1 Corinthians 12:28 and, again, no sacrament of Holy Orders is listed or named. *"And God has appointed these in the church: first apostles, second prophets, third teachers, after that miracles, then gifts of healings, helps, administrations, varieties of tongues"* (1 Corinthians 12:28). Paul reiterates here the fact God has ordained and appointed certain gifts and ministries for the Church. He also ranks them according to numbered importance. When totaled, they number eight, but when combined with the other ministry offices listed elsewhere in the New Testament, the number eight is well exceeded without any mention of most of the ministry offices traditionally associated with the eight ecclesiastical offices of Rome's Holy Orders. In Acts 6:1-7, **deacons** were *mutually* appointed and chosen to the ministry by both the leaders and members of the congregation to serve and attend to the every day needs of the Christian community.

The Apostles did not set up some elaborate ordination ceremony where a Roman Catholic bishop presides and then lays hands on each one with a rehearsed gesture and proclamation making them deacons! In fact the Apostles deferred to the congregation of the local church (in Jerusalem) to seek out and decide for themselves whom among them would serve as deacons (Acts 6:3). Observe here no Apostle or bishop was singled out to ordain these seven deacons. They were not further required to first become lectors and acolytes, as Roman Catholic Canon law would require centuries later![190] By this definition, the deacons who were selected by the congregation in Acts 6 would not have qualified to hold this office since the order of "lector" and "acolyte" had yet to exist! Acts 14:23 tells how both the Apostles (Paul and Barnabus), with the disciples of the local churches, selected and appointed elders in the local church, which followed after the same pattern for the selection of deacons in Acts chapter six.

From reading the events associated with Acts 6, it is evident deacons were responsible for handling and serving the physical and material needs of the congregation (particularly with the daily aid given to neglected widows). The Greek word for deacon (*diakoneo*) means to serve others in a domestic capacity in the role of a waiter at a table (John 2:5,9), or a servant in His master's household (Matthew 22:13; John 12:26).[191] There is nothing in Scripture that would officially indicate deacons were to assist pastors and the Apostles in any

---

[190]   *The Code of Canon Law*, **Can. 1035**.
[191]   *Wycliffe Bible Dictionary*, 430.

liturgical or sacramental function; which goes contrary to the claim made by Roman Catholic teaching on "Holy Orders".

The word deacon, with reference to one who holds this ministry office in the church, occurs twice in the New Testament: Philippians 1:1 and 1 Timothy 3:8. In Philippians 1:1, Paul's gives his salutary greeting to *"the bishops and deacons"* at the church in Philippi. Paul gives the moral qualifications for the office of a deacon in 1 Timothy 3:8-13. Among the qualifications listed in these verses, there is no description of the deacon taking on any sacramental role or responsibility of helping a priest perform Mass! No, rather, God's Word in 1 Timothy 3 says deacons are to be respectful, without duplicity, modest, not greedy for money, holding the faith with moral purity, demonstrate proven character, and above all they are to have a good standing in the church with a bold and confident faith in the Lord Jesus Christ. Where in this list is there a requirement for a deacon to assist the priest with the performance of the continuance of Christ's sacrifice in the Mass? Obviously there is no requirement given because the writers of the New Testament do not teach Christ instituted a sacrificing priesthood who perpetuate His sacrifice on the cross to God and members of the church as we so thoroughly proved and demonstrated from the Scriptures in chapters nine and ten of this book.

The call to the ministry is not a uniform or predicable pattern of events played out through ritual or ceremony—contra the ordination ceremony of Rome's Holy Orders. The practice of Jesus, the Apostles, and the early church confirm this to be the case. A review of pertinent New Testament passages proves this assertion true. God's call to the ministry is both *immediate* in that He personally and directly chooses and ordains the person called, and at other times *mediate* in the sense a person's calling is confirmed as from God through the affirmation of the church. Jesus directly approached and called the twelve to follow Him and ordained them for Gospel ministry during His time on Earth and after His ascension to heaven (Matthew 10:1-23; Luke 10:1-11; John 15:16).

The New Testament pattern for ordination to the ministry is: God first calls the person into ministry and then sometime afterwards, the local church accepts and confirms this calling when giving ordination with the laying on of hands by both leadership and the people of the congregation. Paul and Barnabus were not ordained by a bishop of a diocese under the leadership of a Pope sitting in Rome (in this circumstance it would have been Peter), but the Scripture tells us they were "set apart" by the Holy Spirit prayed for, laid hands on by the church in Antioch, and sent out to preach the Gospel (Acts 13:1-5). The only two ordinances, or sacraments as some might call them, Christ introduced into the church to be celebrated by its redeemed leaders and members are: water baptism and the Lord's Supper (Matthew 28:19; Luke 22:19-20; 1 Corinthians 11:17-25). But these ordinances, in and of themselves, are meaningless if the Gospel is not first preached and then understood and believed by those who hear it from the ministers of Christ's church; for baptism and the Lord's Supper are symbols of redemption for the Gospel message itself.

The first order of business for the Church established by Jesus and His Apostles is to preach and teach the Gospel by which those who hear and believe it are saved. Neither Jesus, the Apostles, nor the early Christians of that era invoked the sacrament of Holy Orders to provide the church with a sacrificing priesthood. The preaching of the Gospel is paramount here and rises far above the administration of any sacrament. And herein is seen the error of the Roman Catholic teaching of Holy Orders when it places greater emphasis on the priest offering the alleged, ongoing sacrifice of the body and blood of Christ in the Mass, instead of preaching the Gospel and teaching God's Word above all else that is mandated by Scripture itself! Jesus Christ commands the minister of the Church to first "preach" and "teach" and then "baptize" only after a convert to the Gospel is made (Matthew 28:19-20; Mark 16:15; Acts 1:8).

The consistent testimony of Scripture spells out that Preaching the Gospel and teaching God's Word are the primary essentials for the ministry of the New Testament minister and the chief objective for ordination in the church. When Paul discusses what the ministry of the Pastor/Bishop of the Church is he declares: ***"A bishop must hold firm to the sure Word as taught, so that he may be able give instruction in sound doctrine, both to exhort and convict those who contradict"*** (Titus 1:9) All ministers of the Church are to follow Paul's admonition given to the young Pastor Timothy to: ***"Preach the Word! Be ready in season and out of season. Convince, rebuke, exhort, will all longsuffering and teaching"*** (2 Timothy 4:2). The Christian minister must be an apt teacher of God's Word (1Timothy 3:2), and must attend to regular reading and teaching of it both publicly and privately (1 Timothy 4:13). There are no instructions given here for the ministers to be ordained and anointed by a ruling bishop of that area or region with the command to distribute sacraments and present a "bloodless sacrifice of Christ" in the Mass.

Notable Roman Catholic scholars such as Raymond Brown, Bernard Cooke, and Edward Schillebeeckx have all taken issue with the simple picture portrayed in the Roman Catholic catechisms that teach Jesus ordained the twelve to be priests and to form an order of priests from the early Christian Church to be their successors. These scholars rightly say such a claim is a "rather shaky assumption", because the weight of historical evidence actually favors the view that the earliest Christian communities simply did not know, or were made aware of, any office of a priesthood in the specific mold of Roman Catholicism, but only knew and operated in various types of ministries which eventually were consolidated and became a clerical hierarchy of priests, bishops, and Popes some three centuries later.[192] Ordination to the ministry, as practiced in the New Testament church, did not center on making Eucharistic sacrifice, the sacraments, or an ordained hierarchy of clerics presiding over a "laity". Rather, as we have seen, the writers of the New Testament stress the centrality of the preaching of Gospel to the lost and the teaching of God's Word to saved members of the church for their mutual edification and spiritual maturity facilitated by the fivefold ministry of Apostles, Prophets, Evangelists, Pastors, and Teachers Christ gave the New Testament Church. In his historical study of ministry in the early church, Roman Catholic scholar, Edward Schillebeeckx, concludes from his examination:

(1) Ministry did not develop from and around the Eucharist or the liturgy, but from the apostolic building up of the community through preaching, admonition and leadership. No matter what different form it takes, ministry is concerned with the leadership of the community: ministers are pioneers, those who inspire the community and serve as models by which the whole community can identity with the gospel . . . [while] nowhere in the New Testament is an explicit connection made between the ministry of the church and presiding at the Eucharist. It is simply taken for granted that the leader of the community would normally be the one who presides at the Eucharist. (2) There is no mention in the New Testament of an essential distinction between the various members who together exercise a variety of services needed for building up the community.[193]

The idea of Holy Orders wherein a distinction between "clergy" and "laity" was made began to surface in the latter part of the third century well after the Apostles of Jesus were gone. At this time, the bishop came to be known as the *sacerdos* (the priest) elected by the people in the church; he then received formal ordination from another bishop. By the medieval period, the Roman Catholic idea of Holy Orders came to overshadow and eclipse the established officers of ministry enumerated in the New Testament.[194] The laying

---

[192] Thomas Bokenkotter, *Dynamic Catholicism*, 260.

[193] Edward Schillebeeckx, *Ministry: Leadership in the Community of Jesus Christ* (New York: Crossroad Publishing, 1981), 264.

[194] William Cathcart, *The Papal System*, 225-30; Richard McBrien, *Catholicism*, 866-870.

on of hands for ordination mentioned in 2 Timothy 1:6 was for the pastor (Timothy) in a local church setting. This was a unique impartation of a spiritual gift for ministry, which only the Apostles could impart in that day. It was not used for the ordination of celibate priests. From what we learn in the book of Acts and the Pauline epistles, the laying on of apostolic hands for the impartation of the Holy Spirit, as we saw earlier, and the giving of a spiritual gift, was confined only to the authority Christ gave the Apostles and was given to no one else. Roman Catholic bishops cannot therefore ordain priests in the same fashion—since no such authority, unique only to Christ's chosen Apostles, was ever formally conferred on their inherited successors in any of the pages of the New Testament.

The main ministry offices in the New Testament Church are bishops (overseers), pastors, and deacons. No other ministry office or holy order is named as part of the ministry duties among the local church of the apostolic period. Christian character is not automatically achieved when a bishops lays hands on a candidate for ministry, nor given with the magical impartation of a sacrament of "Holy Orders". Christian character for living and ministry are formed by the life long work of sanctification, whereby the "fruits of the Spirit" (Galatians 5:22-23) are gradually formed within the believer's life by way of suffering, testing, trials, and tribulations endured and experienced (James 1:2-4). Access to this character formation process comes by way of faith into the grace of God who uses our tribulations to produce perseverance wherein character is built and faith is strengthened and perfected (Romans 5:2-4; 1 Peter 1:6-7). No sacrament is ever introduced or named in Scripture as the principle means for this character formation and sanctifying process to live for Christ and do the ministry!

In contrast to Roman Catholic teaching, stating all laity must go through an ordained priest or bishop to acquire grace from God in the sacraments they administer, the Bible teaches no person holding a ministry office in the church, whether he be an elder, pastor, or deacon, takes the place of Jesus Christ serving as the believer's sole mediator and High Priest before God. Those ordained elders, pastors, bishops, and deacons are not superior to their Christian brothers and sisters but are equal heirs of the grace of God within the body of believers serving only one Master, One Head, One Priest, and One Mediator, *"For one is your Master even Christ and you all brethren"* (Matthew 23:8). Surely with the innumerable acts of immorality, wickedness, heresies, and moral transgressions of both the papacy and the hierarchy of Rome, the alleged apostolic succession chain passed from the Popes, to the bishops, and then on to the ordained priests, cannot be morally maintained, upheld by the authority of Scripture, or by the checkered past of the Roman church!

Indeed, history has shown the various anti-Popes, rival Popes, and other claimants to the papacy were selected by dubious persons and questionable means so that the mythical, unbroken and exemplary chain of apostolic succession was anything but unbroken or without contamination continuing from the Apostle Peter to the current pope now sitting in Vatican City. Seeing this to be the historical case, the whole foundation upon which the sacrament of Holy Orders precariously and quite presumptuously stands, falls like a tumbling house of cards being without biblical support or historical validation! Long time ardent critic of Roman Catholicism, Ian Paisley, brilliantly lays this out showing how the infamous history of Rome's hierarchy invalidates them from being part of a holy order sacrament supposedly instituted by the Lord Jesus Christ:

> The Christian ministry is an institution, but not a sacrament. Examination of the Holy Scriptures shows, that it consisted of bishops or pastors, or elders, or ministers-varied names for the same class—whose functions consisted in teaching and in rule; and of the deacons, whose special business it was to superintend the affairs of the Church with

reference to the poor, and who appear also to have been men of eminent spirituality, and who gave themselves to promote the salvation of men through the preaching of the Gospel.

This point stands intimately related to a subject of which we have in recent years heard so much Apostolic Succession. Although some branches of the Protestant Church make much of this succession, it is vain that we look to the Holy Scriptures for anything to support the assumption. There is a broad line of distinction drawn between the Apostles and all other ministers of the Gospel, so that to allege Succession is simply to practice imposition. The Apostles were men who had seen the Lord, and received a commission from his own mouth to go and publish salvation to the ends of the earth, with the promise of His presence till their work was done. We maintain that there was no succession, and nothing bearing the remotest relation to it. We call upon those that claim to be the Successors of the Apostles to produce their authority. We beg to remind them, that the Commission of the Apostles died with them, and so did the special powers, which constituted their credentials. On the subject of Holy Orders, as on every other, our watchword must be to the law and testimony. What is written? How readest thou? This is the short and the sure way to put an end to all Popish pretension on the subject of Holy Orders and Apostolic succession, whether found in Rome or in regions where better things might be expected....

Now we affirm, without fear of Scriptural contradiction, that the doctrine here set forth is wholly unsupported by the Word of God, and opposed to the whole current of inspiration. It assumes as truth what has no foundation whatever in fact. It assumes as fact a palpable absurdity.... Granting that Peter was the first Roman bishop and pope, and that the succession really commenced, enough has occurred a thousand times over to, invalidate its orders, and extinguish the fire of heaven supposed to run through the Apostolic line. In order to the continuance of the Divine authority, the spiritual power, and the sacramental efficacy, it is required that every line of the mystic chain shall be pure gold, and that not a link shall be wanting; for a single mistake, like in an arithmetical computation, will run through all that follows, rendering it null and void. *A single error will vitiate the entire line.*

To deal effectually with this point, it is needful to inquire whether the "line" can be broken; and if so, by what forces? If it cannot be broken, there is an end of argument. If according to Archdeacon Mason, (Defence of the Church of England Ministry) neither "degradation," nor "heresy," nor "schism," nor "the most extreme wickedness," nor "anything else," can divest a bishop of the power of giving trite orders, then of course the chain is strong, and all the powers of darkness cannot break it. If, according to the Puseyites, "the sacraments, not preaching, are the source of Divine grace," and if the efficacy of these is wholly "independent of the personal character of the administrator," (Tracts, Preface, 1834, No. xi.) and if it is enough that he has been episcopally ordained, then the matter is much simplified, but not strengthened; for while the utmost depravity of character, and the most impious heresy of doctrine, may, in Popish esteem, be trifling matters, yet, if a single link of the Papal chain shall be snapped, it falls asunder, and it cannot be again united. *But nothing in history is more certain than that this chain has been constantly broken, in all possible ways, at one time through the electors, at another through the elected.* For centuries the Popes were created by the authority of the emperors, and the objects of their choice were generally anti-Popes or schismatics; and Popes were often made by means still more questionable.

But the dreadful tale must not be told by Protestant lips, lest they should be charged with colouring. Let Baronius, therefore, speak, himself a cardinal, and one of the greatest of men. Referring to the ninth century, he exclaims, "Oh! What was then the face of the holy Roman Church? How filthy, when the vilest and most powerful harlots ruled in the court of Rome! By whose arbitrary sway dioceses were made and unmade, bishops were consecrated, and horrible to be mentioned, false Popes, their paramours, were thrust into the Chair of Peter, who in being numbered as Popes, serve no purpose except to fill up the catalogue of the Popes of Rome! For who can say, that persons thrust into the Popedom, without any law, by harlots of this sort, were legitimate Popes of Rome? In the elections no mention is made of the acts of the clergy, either by their choosing the Pope, at the time of his election, or their consent afterwards. All the canons were suppressed into silence-the voice of the decrees of former pontiffs was not allowed to be heard-ancient traditions were proscribed-the customs formerly practised in electing the Pope, with the sacred rites and pristine usages, were all extinguished. In this manner, lust, supported by secular power, excited to frenzy in the rage for domination, ruled in all things: (Baronius).

Time would fail to tell of Pope Sergius and his crimes; of Theodora and Marozia, and the papal profligates by whose iniquitous attentions they were signalized: of thirteen schisms in the Popedom during a century and a half, when rival Popes, each pretending to represent Peter, contended for his chair, when Popes excommunicated Popes, when Popes with Popes waged mortal war, and when both have been removed and expelled; of Pope Joan, the most abandoned of womankind, whom vengeance overtook, and whose turpitude was proclaimed in the streets of Rome at noonday; of Pope John XIII., transfixed with a dagger in the perpetration of an atrocious crime; of Alexander VI., who would have carried away the crown of sin from the men of Sodom! Teachers, Englishmen, Protestants!-Behold the UNBROKEN CHAIN OF APOSTOLICAL SUCCESSION! (Emphasis mine).[195]

So ordination and being chosen for the ministry comes from the Lord Himself who sovereignly chooses and elects those called by Him to minister and serve in His church (John 15:16,19; Galatians 1:1; 1 Timothy 1:12). The church confirms this calling with the laying on of hands, prayer, fasting, and commissioning to the ministry. This is the pattern and practice given in the New Testament and is far different procedure than the Roman Catholic idea and practice of Holy Orders. No hierarchy of monks, nuns, priests, Monsignors, Cardinals, or Popes are named in the New Testament lists of the offices and ministries of the Christian Church. These religious titles are simply man-made fabrications of Roman Catholicism.

---

[195]   Dr. Ian R.K. Paisley, "Holy Orders", pages 1,2, 3, *European Institute of Protestant Studies* at http://www.ianpaisley.org/article.asp?ArtKey=holyorders.

The Sacrament of Matrimony

The Roman Catholic Church has declared marriage has been "raised" by Jesus Christ to the "dignity of a sacrament." By this special sacrament married couples are given the grace whereby they are consecrated and strengthened in the bond of matrimonial unity.[196]

The intention of this "sacrament" is to perfect the couple's love and to strengthen their indissoluble unity. By this sacramental grace they "help one another attain holiness in their married life and in welcoming and educating their children." Christ is the source for this sacrament.[197] The sacrament of matrimony can only be shared between two baptized Catholics who are in a "state of grace" (male and female) for it to be a legitimate marriage in the eyes of the Church.[198] The non-Catholic must agree to raise the couple's prospective children in the Catholic faith and must also convert to Catholicism if the marriage is to be properly performed by a priest. Those who contract marriage before a civil authority of the State or a non-Catholic minister of religion commit a mortal sin and the "marriage" is null and void.[199]

The Catholic Church's Canon Law claims a sole and exclusive "right" to make laws and administer justice in the marriage of baptized persons so it can define and dictate the terms of acceptable marriage and what is declared an invalid marriage. These laws also stipulate under what condition a marriage can be dissolved or separation can be permitted.[200] Anyone who denies marriage is a sacrament dispensed and granted by the Catholic Church are condemned by the same in the anathema issued by the Council of Trent in the twenty-fourth session: "If anyone says that matrimony is not truly and properly one of the seven sacraments of the evangelical law, instituted by Christ the Lord, but has been devised by men in the Church and does not confer grace, let him be anathema."[201] In the past, the Catholic Church has long used the Latin Vulgate's faulty translation of Ephesians 5:32 to support the idea marriage is a sacrament when translating the verse to read: "This is a great sacrament."[202] Here Rome translates the Greek for "mystery", *mysterion* (μυστήριον) as *sacramentum*, and with that interpret marriage to be a sacrament of the church able to convey grace to those getting married. However, the word clearly is "mystery" in the Greek text, not "sacrament". The mystery consists not in a mystical impartation of divine grace to man and wife, but the mystery of the union existing between Christ and the Church, which has its earthly parallel in the marital union between husband and wife. It was not until 1941 that the Catholic Church stopped using the faulty English translation of the Vulgate and corrected the word sacrament used in Ephesians 5:32 to rightly read "mystery."

---

196   *Catechism of the Catholic Church*, 446 **[1601]**, 456 **[1638]**.

197   Ibid, 457 **[1641-1642]**.

198   The Catholic Church makes exception to this rule with the allowance of "mixed marriages" provided a dispensation is granted where both parties are required to sign a contract in the presence of two witnesses. In this contract, the non-Catholic must agree to allow the other party to practice the Catholic faith without hindrance and allow the children from the marriage to be raised and taught in the Catholic faith, and the Catholic spouse must with every effort win over the non-Catholic spouse to the Catholic faith.

199   The Code of Canon Law, **Can 1124**, 199; John Laux, *Mass and the Sacraments*, 133.

200   *Code of Canon Law*, 196-205.

201   H.J. Schroeder, *The Canons and Decrees of the Council of Trent*, 181.

202   The Latin text literally says: "Sacramentum hoc magnum est ego autem dico in Christo et in ecclesia," which translated in English means: "This is a great sacrament: but I speak in Christ and in the church."

Actually, the sacramental meaning assigned to marriage by Rome, has its origins in pagan rituals where marriage was seen as the joining of the human and divine.[203] Rome believes Christian marriage is a symbolic reenactment of Christ and the Church, and serves as a symbol for understanding marriage to be a sacrament of the Church. This meaning cannot be maintained when it is pointed out the context of Genesis 2:24, where the first marriage occurs in human history, gives no hint or indication a Christian marriage is taking place, in contrast to a secular marriage; it is the joining of a man and woman as one flesh in marriage regardless of the religious background or circumstances marriage takes place. God instituted it from the beginning as a working principle of human civilization. And with this, the text of Genesis 2 gives no indication or explicit mention God imparted spiritual grace to infuse the institution of marriage; it was to be done to insure the propagation and pro-creation of the human race in order to fulfill the creation mandate given by God to man and woman to *"Be fruitful and multiply"* (Genesis 1:28). Marriage serves as the physical vehicle to accomplish this task. Nowhere in all of Scripture does God use marriage as a direct channel or sacrament to convey His salvific grace to man. The source and fullness of all saving grace comes from the Lord Jesus Christ alone and is given to the believer directly and immediately who is saved upon receiving Him (John 1:12, 16-17). Marriage does not function in this way, nor was it designed by God from the beginning to serve this purpose.

The strategy of Rome in declaring marriage to be a sacrament is clear to the objective eye: To obtain and expand their control over everything pertaining to marriage and the family. So anything, which would fall outside of this control, is considered invalid like civil marriages by a judge or justice of the peace, or if a Protestant believer and Catholic believer should wed. Since these few examples are beyond the rule and regulation of Rome, Catholicism arbitrarily deems them unlawful since only the Roman Catholic institution can properly administer the sacrament of marriage. While the object of this chapter is not to go into a full blown treatment on the broad topic of marriage from a biblical perspective, a few pertinent observations need to be mentioned here in keeping with our topic of marriage as a sacrament. God is the author of marriage and instituted it in paradise before the fall of Adam and Eve (Genesis 2:18-25). He reaffirmed its continuity for blessing and propagation after the fall, and again after the flood (Genesis 4:1; 25-26; 9:7).

In the New Testament, the Lord Jesus Christ upholds and confirms what God had established from the beginning (Matthew 19:5-6), and even blesses marriage with His own presence when attending the marriage at Cana (John 2:1-11). Paul eloquently teaches how marriage is a beautiful and lovely picture of Christ's relationship with the Church and the unbreakable spiritual union between them (Ephesians 5:22-33). The existence of marriage had long existed before the inception of the New Testament period of history; and to postulate marriage was ordained by God and Christ, during this time to be a sacrament, is without foundation or legitimate precedent from the Word of God.

Marriage is a creation ordinance and not a Christian rite, sacrament or ceremony instituted by the Lord Jesus Christ in the New Testament. There is no teaching in Scripture, which states or teaches marriage does, in the role of a sacrament, impart saving grace producing any spiritual aid to improve the Christian's spiritual walk with the Lord or growth in sanctification. This is not the function of marriage as outlined from the biblical teaching above. The terrible irony here is seen in the fact a celibate clergy has the power to decide and dictate what qualifies as a valid marriage, what can dissolve a marriage, and how and when a marriage is annulled. The same celibate priesthood also has the audacity to instruct couples on the sexual aspect of marriage, when in theory the priests themselves have no practical experience themselves from being

---

203   Harold Hoehner, *Ephesians: An Exegetical Commentary* (Grand Rapids: Baker, 2002), 776-777.

married and therefore possessing the wisdom and life experience of a having a sex life with one's spouse! The absurd equivalent would be expecting a blind man, whose never seen before, effectively instructing a person who can see on how to really use eyesight and properly focus one's vision! And yet a priest, who is supposed to remain single, sexually abstinent, and be largely absent from the presence of women in a rectory, is supposed to give insight, advice, and counsel to married or engaged couples about the inner dynamics that make a marital relationship work? Absurd! To think a celibate clergy has the capacity and ability to instruct and control the intimate and private matters of the marriage bed is an ironic perversion and presumptuous intrusion contrary to the Word of God.

The church does not possess the arbitrary power to determine which marriage is valid or not; although the Word of God in 2 Corinthians 6:14 does warn the Christian believer against forming intimate associations with the unbeliever—and marriage would be certainly included in this prohibition. However, for Rome to state in their canon law a marriage between a Catholic (who in their eyes is considered a believer) and non-Catholic is invalid does not agree with the fact the New Testament does indeed recognize mixed marriages between a Christian and non-Christian to be a valid union in the eyes of God. Paul acknowledged this very thing with his advice given in 1 Corinthians 7:12-16. In these verses, God's Word clearly recognizes the validity of a marriage between the believer and unbeliever, and states in effect they are to remain married if both parties so choose (verses 12-13). Salvation does not alter or change the married state even if, God forbid, a Christian should marry a non-Christian. Paul goes on to say the believing spouse can exert a positive influence on the unbelieving spouse, and thereby set him or her apart (to be sanctified) for an opportunity to hear the Gospel and see it lived out by the believing spouse, which can lead to the salvation of the unbelieving wife or husband (verses 14 and 16).

Rome fails to take into account God does not view the validity of the married state based on whether one spouse or the other is Christian, in this case Roman Catholic, or not. Here is another example, of so many, where Roman Catholic tradition and the Word of God are at complete odds with each other and stand at opposite ends. For in the sight of God, a believer and unbeliever can be legitimately married as 1 Corinthians 7 obviously teaches, whereas Rome Catholic tradition says such a union is illegitimate and therefore not a true marriage which can be annulled by the Church. Once again the Christian must hold Scripture to be the supreme authority in these matters, especially when Roman Catholic teaching goes contrary and opposite of what God's Word declares to be the case. Marriage was not considered a sacrament in the church for the first five hundred years until the time of Pope Gregory in the sixth century!

There is no mention of marriage being a sacrament in the pages of God's Word; so there is not a biblical command it is to be considered a sacrament giving God's grace to those married. Marriage was not *universally* considered a sacrament until the thirteenth century and gradually developed over a long period of time. Rome formally admits:

> It is, therefore, historically certain that from the beginning of the thirteenth century the sacramental character of marriage was universally known and recognized as a dogma . . ..
> The reason why marriage was not expressly and formally included among the sacraments earlier and denial of it branded as heresy, is to be found in the historical development of the doctrine regarding the sacraments.[204]

---

[204] "Sacrament of Marriage" in http://www.newadvent.org/cathen/09707a.htm

So if Jesus has established marriage to be a sacrament of the church from the first century onward, why then did this act have to slowly develop over time until some 1,300 years later when it was finally recognized to be one of the seven sacraments of the Church? The answer is Jesus did not formally institute marriage to be a sacrament, but such belief became a tradition accepted over time as the Catholic clergy acquired more power over the people, while the knowledge of God's Word greatly diminished during the medieval period, so the average person could not learn whether this, or any other tradition of Roman Catholicism, was taught and found in the Word of God. What is absurd here with this unbiblical teaching is the fact some one hundred seventy-six Popes prior to the first pope of the thirteenth century (Pope Innocent III), along with hundreds of "fathers", "doctors" and "saints" and the eleven ecclesiastical Councils, did not know or pronounce marriage to be one of the seven sacraments necessary for salvation, nor did they learn this from the Word of God found in the teachings of Jesus and His Apostles!

The Bible teaches forthrightly and unequivocally a person is saved by faith alone in Christ's atoning death for him on the cross whereby the Savior's perfect righteousness is freely given to the believing sinner. A believer's salvation begins, continues, and ends in Jesus Christ alone and not in any ritual or sacrament of the church, whether it is baptism, the Lord's Supper, anointing of the sick, etc. Jesus is the sole source and fullness of all grace from whence all things necessary for salvation are given and found (John 1:14); it is from the Savior alone and not a church or any other person does the born-again, saved Christian receive "grace piled upon grace" (John 1:16). God did not delegate this grace to a church, or a series of physical signs performed by bishops and priests, sacerdotal gestures, or more importantly, in the administration of sacraments to be dispensed by a celibate, sacrificing priesthood. Salvation grace and justification before God is exclusively offered in the perfect and finished sacrifice of Jesus Christ, and not by way of sacraments, priests, Popes, or any ritual merchandise the Catholic Church has to offer. On this point, former Catholic priest Richard Bennett states the case quite emphatically when pointing out what Scripture has declared on this matter:

> The Roman Catholic Church's teaching of physical signs as necessary for salvation is a futile exchange of her sacraments for Him, the Lord and giver of life, and at the same time a blasphemous denial of Him and His perfect finished sacrifice. Calling "sacramental grace", "the grace of the Holy Spirit", is soul demeaning and a sacrilege against the All Holy God. What is declared in Scripture is not rituals as power sources, but rather God's righteousness in the Lord Jesus Christ. This is justification, necessary for salvation in God's plan and purpose.[205]

Salvation and the forgiveness of sins do not come through the sacraments of Rome but belief in Jesus Christ (see Romans 5:1-10). The sinner is bidden by the Savior to come directly to Him for eternal life, and no other substitute can take the place of the incomparable Christ (John 5:40). To transfer this belief to a sacramental system is to therefore forfeit true biblical salvation and *"walk after things that do not profit"* (Jeremiah 2:8). God's Word contradicts the absurd Catholic belief the sacraments are necessary for salvation and places the Roman Catholic sacramental system at direct odds with what the Bible declares to be the one and only true way to be saved. That way leads to belief and trust in Jesus Christ *alone* (John 14:6).

Salvation is not a combination of Jesus *with the sacraments*, but trust in Jesus Christ *alone* apart from any religious work or act on our part (John 1:11-12; Ephesians 2:5-9)! It is not granted by trusting in any

---

[205]   Richard Bennett, "Salvation and Sacraments", page 13.

man-made tradition, ritual, or physical object as the sacraments really are. God's Word knows nothing of Rome's blasphemous need of the sacraments for salvation, especially when God's Word states it is belief in the name of Jesus Christ, and no one else, that salvation is received and eternal life is given. ***"Nor is there salvation in any other, for there is no other name under heaven given among men by which we must be saved"*** (Acts 4:21). ***"But these are written that you may believe that Jesus is the Christ, the Son of God, and that believing you may have life in His name"*** (John 20:31). So, when the Catholic Church dogmatically says the sacraments are necessary for salvation, when God's Word teaches down the line it is faith in Christ alone that saves, Rome is in total defiance of Jesus Christ and God's Word. Rome's stubborn refusal to hear and accept this simple Gospel truth proves they are not of God. For, ***"He who is of God hears God's words; therefore you do not hear, because you are not of God"*** (John 8:47)!

The Catholic Church directs its people to look to and trust the sacraments as "channels" of grace to be eventually saved—and in their soteriological system there is no guarantee of this in the end if one dies in state of "mortal sin". But God's infallible Word instructs us to be looking unto Jesus, the Author and Finisher of our faith, as the sole object of faith and salvation, so that who ever believes in Him *will never perish* but shall have eternal (John 10:28; Hebrews 12:2). The Catholic does well to cling to Jesus alone for eternal life, if he or she truly wants to be saved. To do this, the Catholic must cease trusting in the empty and ineffective works of the Roman Catholic sacraments. As it is written in 1John 5:11: ***"And this is the testimony: that God has given us eternal life, and this life is in His Son"*** (not in the seven sacraments or channels of grace invented by the Catholic Church). Christ *alone* gives grace and eternal life, Christ *alone* saves, and Christ *alone* is the One we must trust and exclusively depend on for these things.

CHAPTER 12

PURGATORY, PAPAL INDULGENCES, AND PRAYERS FOR THE DEAD

The doctrine and belief in purgatory is another concept peculiar to Roman Catholic theology. Indeed, belief in the reality of purgatory is not an "optional" doctrine for a Catholic to believe; it is a defined doctrine Catholics must believe in.[1] Catholic theology formally defines the place of purgatory as:

> An intermediate state of purification between death and heaven that provides for the removal of remaining personal obstacles to the full enjoyment of eternal union with God. According to Catholic doctrine, such purification continues and completes the process of sanctification (or divinization) that makes intimate union with the triune God possible for persons justified and reconciled in Christ. The obstacles in view here are both venial sins, unrepented at the time of death, and any enduring dispositional consequences of the repented and forgiven serious sins committed during one's earthly life. There is no question of a reversal of the direction that one has taken in the course of earthly life. Purgatory is not an opportunity for conversion where none has transpired in earthly life. The eternal destiny of the "holy souls" is not in question. Given that individual judgment follows immediately upon death, purgatory affords an interval of final purification for erasing conditions that would prevent justified persons from enjoying full fellowship with God in the communion of saints.[2]

A more direct explanation of purgatory given in the ubiquitous *Baltimore Catechism* describes it as a place where temporary punishment for venial sins will be meted out on the Catholic soul who dies in a state of grace but was not pure enough yet to enter heaven.[3] Purgatory is a temporary place of "punishment" for those Catholics, who are considered Christians, who die in a "state of grace" but nonetheless are guilty of

---

[1]   Karl Keating, *What Catholics Really Believe*, 86.
[2]   *The Harper Collins Encyclopedia of Catholicism*, 1070.
[3]   *The New Saint Joseph Baltimore Catechism*, 249.

"venial sin," or have not fully satisfied the temporal *punishment* due their sins.[4] The word "purgatory" is derived from the Latin word *purgare*, which means to purge, cleanse, to make clean or purify—purgatory is thus a temporary place where the impurities of any remaining sin are removed from the departed soul who has died and left the body after physical death (see "Purgatory." *The Catholic Encyclopedia* Vol. 12. New York: Robert Appleton Company, 1911 http://www.newadvent.org/cathen/12575a.htm). From this etymology of cleansing, Catholic apologist, John Salza, thus reasons in his mistitled book, *The Biblical Basis for Purgatory* (which we will shortly discover later in this chapter, the Bible in no way teaches or provides any basis for the existence or doctrine of Purgatory!):

> The word "purgatory" comes from the Latin *pugare* which means to purge, purify, or make clean. The Church teaches that it is a place or condition of temporal punishment for departed souls who are destined for heaven but not completely purified from sin. Through this purgative process, spiritual contamination is removed and soul is made wholly pleasing to God so it can live forever with Him in heaven.[5]

Salza goes on to voice the Catholic Church's justification for the existence of purgatory as needed because the justice of God demands it. For,

> When we sin, we incur before God the liability of guilt and the liability of punishment. God forgives the guilt of sin through His mercy, but punishes the sinner by His justice. If God's justice demands that sin be punished, it follows that one who dies with contrition for his sins but before satisfying the full punishment for them will suffer the remaining punishment in the afterlife.[6]

The Greek word πυρόω transliterated as puroó means to burn or purify by fire.[7] The word purgatory comes from this Greek root word, and over time, came to mean the place of purgatory where imperfect souls after death are purified from remaining sins by a burning process through the purifying flames of purgatory. This naturally involves suffering. The *Baltimore Catechism* flatly states it in this way:

> God sends everyone all the sufferings they need on earth to cleanse, strengthen, and perfect their love. But most people waste their sufferings. They do not want them, complain about them, and try to escape them in every manner possible, even by committing sin. Because of this attitude, the fires of their sufferings are unable to burn away the selfishness from their love, so that it will be perfect. Then they must go to purgatory where they will have to suffer much more intensely than they would have if they had accepted the sufferings of earth. Their love is purified in purgatory, but it does not only purify our love, but makes it grow. In purgatory, God's cleansing fires burns away the soul's selfishness till its love

---

4 Ibid., 90.

5 John Salza, *The Biblical Basis For Purgatory* (Charlotte: Saint Benedict Press, 2009), 15-16.

6 Ibid.,15-16.

7 http://strongsnumbers.com/greek/4448.htm

becomes perfect and it is ready to fly to heaven. Its sufferings only purify love, they don't increase it.[8]

So before most Catholics can enter into heaven after death, they must first suffer and make atonement or expiation for any remaining sin left on them in the purifying fires of purgatory for an undisclosed amount of time. Only God knows the amount of time each soul must remain in purgatory until the purification process is complete. Purgatory is then Rome's final purification place and a necessary interim state in the afterlife before entrance into heaven is granted. Purgatory is not a second chance at salvation; for once there, the soul of the deceased will never revert to hell but will eventually arrive in heaven once the purification process is eventually complete with suffering in the burning flames. Shockingly, the Second Vatican Council baldly decrees God has revealed these things that accompany suffering in purgatory to complete a Catholic's salvation:

> The truth has been divinely revealed that sins are followed by punishments. God's holiness and justice inflict them. Sins must be expiated. This may be done on this earth through the sorrows, miseries and trials of this life and, above all, through death. Otherwise the expiation must be made in the next life through fire and torments or purifying punishments.... The doctrine of purgatory clearly demonstrates that even when the guilt of sin has been taken away, punishment for it or the consequences of it may remain to be expiated or cleansed. They often are. In fact, in purgatory the souls of those "who died in the charity of God and truly repentant, but who had not made satisfaction with adequate penance for their sins and omissions" are cleansed after death with punishments designed to purge away their debt. All who die in God's grace and friendship, but still imperfectly purified, are indeed assured of their eternal salvation; but after death they undergo purification, so as to achieve the holiness necessary to enter the joy of heaven.[9]

Not only does the Catholic Church believe one is purified by suffering in purgatory, but that such a redemptive process begins here on Earth and is achieved by the sufferings and trials a person experiences now! The Catholic Church in its Council of Trent declares a condemnation down upon anyone who denies the reality of purgatory and the subsequent need for the sinner's payment for sin in this world or after death in purgatory.

> If anyone says that after the reception of the grace of justification the guilt is so remitted and the debt of eternal punishment so blotted out to every repentant sinner, that no debt of temporal punishment remains to be discharged either in this world or in purgatory before the gates of heaven can be opened, let him be anathema.[10]

So by this standard, with the claim made for the existence of purgatory, the average Christian will not immediately enter into the pristine environment of heaven because he still has the presence of sin on his soul and has not been made perfect and clean enough yet to obtain entrance into paradise. Purgatory is a temporary

---

[8]   *The New Saint Joseph Baltimore Catechism*, 91.
[9]   Austin Flannery, *Vatican II Council*, 63-64; See also the *Catechism of the Catholic Church*, 291, **[1031]**; 297 **[1054]**.
[10] *The Canons and Decrees of the Council of Trent*, 46.

place of purification and punishment where the imperfect Christian must remain until full payment and restitution for all venial sins are made. Roman Catholic clergy, theologians, and apologists have historically used Scripture and the tradition of the early church fathers to validate and justify their belief in the doctrine of purgatory.[11] Does the Bible make explicit mention or allude by way of concept, a doctrine of purgatory as a place where most Christians must go at death, guilty of venial sins, to expiate for these sins by undergoing temporary punishment? ***The answer is an unequivocal no!***

The doctrine of purgatory is not biblical primarily because it is not explicitly mentioned, or the concept implicitly found or formulated in Scripture; and it, more importantly, contradicts the very teachings in Scripture concerning how and when God forgives and cleanses the sinner. Although the Catholic Church admits this doctrine is not explicitly mentioned by name in the Bible, they still maintain its reality is based on the "unwritten apostolic tradition".[12] Romanism is unable to appeal to any clear and direct references in Scripture proving the doctrine of purgatory for the simple and embarrassing fact it is not found once there! Indeed the *Catholic Dictionary* goes so far to state: "We would appeal to these general principles of Scripture, rather than to particular texts often alleged in proof of purgatory. *We doubt if they contain an explicit and direct reference to it*" (Emphasis mine).[13]

Yet Catholic Apologist, John Salza, goes so far to write purgatory is "expressly taught in Scripture" and then, as we will demonstrate later, gives a wild misreading of carefully selected "proof" texts to make sure scripture passages do teach purgatory, while at the same time committing exegetical fallacies all over the place in the dishonest and unconvincing attempt to prove from the Bible this unscriptural, man-made doctrine! Typically, this faulty exegesis is done, first and foremost, by lifting a verse out of context to force it into a meaning which conveniently agrees with the concept of purgatory, but at the same time ignores the proper context a verse is found in and upon which a correct exegesis and meaning is established! To cast aside the fundamental principle of biblical exegesis by ignoring or disregarding the general and immediate contexts of a scripture passage or verse, as Salza continually does in trying to "prove" purgatory from the Bible, is to eliminate the very key for correctly interpreting the biblical text in question.

---

[11] This is the method Catholic apologist, John Salza, attempts to use in his book, *The Biblical Basis for Purgatory*, when assuming beforehand purgatory is the "place of purifying penance where souls saved by Christ are made perfect and acceptable to spend life eternal in heaven." We will see later in this chapter, when dealing with the certain "proof" texts for purgatory, that both Salza and the Catholic Church he pathetically defends, predictably **presume** from the outset purgatory must exist and based upon that pretext cleverly read such an erroneous concept into Bible passages where, upon closer exegetical inspection, in no way directly mention purgatory or implicitly support it by concept.

[12] John Salza, *The Biblical Basis For Purgatory*, 16. In his debate with Dr. Walter Martin, Jesuit Priest, Mitchell Pacwa, honestly admits the doctrine of purgatory is not explicitly spelled out in the Scriptures when saying, "In terms of the Scriptures, you are right, we don't have a text that explicitly mentions it"; "it" meaning purgatory (See Catholicism Vs. Christianity-Topic-Purgatory on Youtube.com: http://www.youtube.com/watch?v=z8Kx_UMLHAM&NR=1). The typical Catholic response to the fact purgatory is not explicitly mentioned by name in the Scripture is usually answered by pointing out that the word "Trinity" is not also named in Scripture, but the concept clearly is; and so on this basis alone a person cannot deny the existence of purgatory. But, while it is true the term Trinity is not found once in the Bible, the concept of a plurality of three Persons in the Godhead certainly is (e.g., Genesis 1:26-27 Matthew 3:13-17); unlike purgatory where no concept of this nature is ever found in the Word of God!

[13] Addis and Arnold, *Catholic Dictionary*, 704.

By not keeping the context in view, Salza is free to arbitrarily read the meaning of purgatory into the passages where it is not found and grossly violate the text of Scripture, and the context in which they are originally given. This will become obvious in the following paragraphs as we examine the so-called "biblical basis" for purgatory with what Scripture really has to say here.

The idea the saved person who has been totally forgiven of sin by God, yet still has to expiate or suffer to make reparation or atonement for any kind of sin, is in direct contradiction of what Scripture teaches on this most important subject. Jesus declared the work of final atonement and complete pardon for all sin was "finished" and made secure for the believer when He proclaimed from the cross, *"It is finished"* (John 19:30). The phrase, "It is finished" is *tetelestai* (τετέλεσται) in New Testament Greek and comes from the root word *teleo* (τελεω) and carries the various meanings of "to end, i.e. complete, execute, conclude, discharge (a debt), accomplish, make an end, expire, fill up, finish, go over, pay, and perform.[14]

Christ's proclamation of "it is finished" from the cross was to say, in effect, all the moral debt and just punishment man's sin accrued has been paid in full by the redemptive death accomplished on the cross alone—leaving nothing undone or still left unpaid what Jesus has fully paid for sinners on their behalf. The word *tetelestai* was also written on business documents or receipts in New Testament times to legally declare that a bill had been paid in full. In the Greek-English lexicon compiled by Moulton and Milligan, we learn, the phrase *tetelestai* was a financial term in the ancient Greco-Roman period to indicate all debts have been remitted—paid in full: "The word was used in ancient times in connection with the payment of rent or poll tax. Receipts were often introduced by the Greek phrase *tetelestai,* indicating that the debt had been paid in full."[15] The Greek word is in the perfect passive indicative thus indicating a work done, accomplished, and completed in the past.

The connection between receipts and a full payment to absolve all debts, and what Christ accomplished dying on the cross, would have been quite clear to John's Greek-speaking readership; it would be unmistakable that Jesus Christ had died to pay for their sins. This enlightening meaning has direct bearing on the subject under our discussion. By Christ's declaration of "It is Finished", He was stating by this term all the punishment for our sins, and the expiation required to remove them, have been paid in full by His victorious death on the cross! Such a blessed and glorious truth of God's Gospel grace rules out and eliminates any need for the saved sinner to spend time in some imaginary purgatory to pay and be punished for any lingering sins at death, when in fact Christ already bore the punishment for all sins and paid for them in full on the cross two thousand years ago!

Isaiah 53:5, furthermore, tells us the Messiah' substitutionary death for sinners would fully assuage God's punishment for their iniquities and transgressions. ***"But He was wounded (pierced in the Hebrew) for our transgressions, He was bruised for our iniquities; the punishment (for our) of our peace was upon Him; and with His stripes we are healed."*** Here the prophet foretells the sufferings of the Messiah, which were fulfilled in the sufferings of Jesus of Nazareth, Who in His suffering and atoning death, vicariously bore the full punishment of God for our sins in our place. The result was not a partial forgiveness or having most of them removed, leaving the pardoned sinner to pay the rest of them in the punishing fires of purgatory. No, it was a full pardon given when Jesus bore God's punishment for them all! The result to the sinner is pardon and peace with God, not in suffering for an unspecific amount of time in purgatory, which the prophet Isaiah

---

14   *Strong's Exhaustive Concordance*, Entry 5055 in the *Greek Dictionary of the New Testament*, 71.
15   J.H. Moulton and G. Milligan, *The Vocabulary of the Greek New Testament* (Grand Rapids: Eerdmans, 1930). 630.

never mentions here. Full and final expiation for sin is exclusively found alone in the vicarious suffering and atoning death of Jesus the Savior.

Peace with God is accomplished on the grounds of Messiah's justifying grace declaring the sinner totally and permanently forgiven through faith in Jesus Christ and His shed blood to cleanse from all sin (Romans 5:1, 9-10). The Law of God requires the blood of the innocent victim, dying in place for the guilty, must be shed for expiation, forgiveness, and removal of sin to be accomplished (Leviticus 17:11; Hebrews 9:12-28). After this occurred, there is nothing in Scripture, which mandates the saved must then undergo a purifying process in a place called purgatory after they have died. Since there is no shedding of blood required by a just and innocent substitute in purgatory, no remission or expiation of sin can possibly be given. The New Testament, time and time again, repeatedly teaches: it is in Christ's shed blood one's sins can fully be cleansed, no one or nothing else can do this (Ephesians 1:7; Colossians 1:19-20). To claim the sinner can in any way remove or pay for those sins while suffering in the purifying fires of purgatory is a blatant denial, no less, of what God's Word says about how sin is removed. To hold to the existence of purgatory is a place for final cleansing of sin undermines the all-sufficient power of Christ's blood to remove all sin the moment the believer accepts His payment for the complete purification from those sins.

The Bible says the only way a sinner is saved and the penalty of sin removed is by relying on the mercy and grace of the Savior Jesus Christ. He has declared, ***"My grace is sufficient for you"*** (2 Corinthians 12:9). His grace is sufficient now, not in some distant nether place of purgatory, to fully cleanse, redeem, ransom, and deliver us from the penalty and power of sin! To teach the saved must still pay for their sins in purgatory, when Jesus Christ already paid for them in full when He died on the cross, is a mixture of grace plus works. Rome is quick to speak out of both sides their mouth when they protest on the grounds of saying purgatory is an extension of God's grace made available after the Cross—even though Jesus and His Apostles never mention such a place! To teach purgatory is a necessary place where the remainder of sins must be punished and removed is an outright rejection in principle, and on practical grounds, of Christ's declaration of "It is finished." Rome's false assertion of purgatory would say in contradiction to this, No, it is not finished by Christ, but must be finished by the meritorious sufferings of the sinner in purgatory.

What a pernicious lie this is in the vain attempt to undo what God in Christ has already done 2,000 years ago, when by the cleansing power of His shed blood, has washed away all sin and paid the full price for our redemption from its damning penalty now and forevermore. In the words of the great Christian hymn: "What can wash away my sins, nothing but the blood of Jesus. What can make me whole again, nothing but the blood of Jesus?" So, there is **no remission outside the blood of Jesus**, as Scripture clearly tells us in Leviticus 17:11 and Hebrews 9:22; 10:18. You cannot mix His perfect, cleansing blood with the fire of an illusionary purgatory, or any other grace denying work and invention of Romanism; for God Word tells us it is simply through faith in the blood of Jesus Christ we have complete cleansing and irreversible remission of our sins (1 John 1:7; Revelation 1:5; 5:9). Praise God, for salvation by grace through faith in the finished work of Christ!

The Catholic belief in purgatory, where we must go to atone for our remaining sins, and the things attendant to it (Indulgences, the Rosary, wearing the Scapular, prayers and Masses said and done for the dead), is a patent denial at the most basic level that Jesus' death on the cross two thousand years was sufficient by itself to pay the penalty for all our sins. Jesus was God incarnate (John 1:1,14), and by that fact, His sacrifice for sin was an infinite price paid for all sin—past, present, and future. To then limit Christ's infinite payment for our sins He secured at the cross to cover only for original sin, sins committed before conversion, and afterwards up until when mortal sin kills off saving grace, is to diminish and limit the infinite merits of the Person and work of the Lord Jesus Christ. To insist saved sinners must still pay, atone, suffer, and expiate for their sins after Christ has already suffered and atoned for all of them, is to practically admit the death of Jesus was not perfect enough, complete, and sufficient by itself to forgive and expiate all sin for all time from the very moment the sinner trusts in Christ's death to make full payment, satisfaction, and remission of all sin.

There is simply no teaching or doctrine in Scripture where it is required the dead in Christ must make atonement or expiation for sin in the afterlife after God has already removed these sins before they died! God's Word assures the believer, the second the Christian's soul leaves the body at death, he or she is immediately ushered into heaven to be in the presence of the Lord—not whisked away to a fiery place, like purgatory, to remain there for an indeterminate amount of time to suffer and make atonement for some unaccounted venial sins that still must be paid for! Indeed, God's Word reveals, for the believer to be absent from the body at death is to be in the very presence of the Lord (2 Corinthians 5:8). All Christians go immediately to heaven to be with Jesus the very second after they die (Psalm 17:15; Philippians 1:23.) There is no mention in Scripture of having to go or be confined in purgatory first. While on Earth, the believer will be disciplined by God for falling into sin and will suffer temporal consequences for it in this life—even sickness or premature death (1 Corinthians 11:30-32; Hebrews 12:6-7); but he or she, however, can in no way atone or pay for sins in this world, or in the life to come after death, since Christians have already been made perfect and complete through the perfect atonement Jesus Christ made on the cross for them. Concerning this unshakable truth of complete salvation in Christ, we have the truth of God's Word to stand on in this life, at death, and the glory beyond!

Hebrews 10:12-14 on this very point excludes and nullifies any need or existence of purgatory. ***"But this Man, after He had offered one sacrifice for sins forever, sat down at the right hand of God, from that time waiting till His enemies are made His footstool. For by one offering He has perfected forever those who are being sanctified"*** The atonement of Jesus Christ has "forever" made *perfect* those believers who are saved and set apart (sanctified) to God by Christ's once-for-all sacrifice. The sacrifice of Christ has purchased for all Christians in the past, present, and forever in the future the full pardon and expiation from the penalty of sin bringing peace with God. The word "perfect" (*teleiow*) in the Greek text of Hebrews 10:14 (τελειόω) is in the perfect tense and indicates a one time event completed in the past with ongoing results in the present and future.[16] It is a perfect act already completed and done in the past, which cannot, by virtue of its perfect accomplishment, ever be repeated, undone, improved, or renewed in the present or future, thus eliminating any additional expiation or cleansing in a contrived place like purgatory! The dative of instrument is used in Hebrews 10:14 to show how this perfection and complete absolution from sin is accomplished—by the sacrificial *offering* Jesus Christ made for sinners on the cross!

The writer of Hebrews mentions no sacrifices of the Mass, or being cleansed by the fires of purgatory, here to complete the purification process; for it has already been done by Christ on the cross alone. It is by Christ's shed blood offered on the Cross complete and total purification and expiation from sin has been accomplished, whereby the believer presently stands "*perfected*" by the once-for-all perfect sacrifice of Christ and is therefore purified forever. All suffering for atonement and God's just punishment for every sin was met and paid for by the death of Christ alone (see Hebrews 9-10), and does not wait for suffering in purgatory after the Christian has died to complete the purification process.

> Perfected forever must therefore refer to the absoluteness of the effect of Christ's work
> on the Cross: both in respect of the putting away of our guilt and defilement through His

---

[16]   Fritz Rienecker and Cleon Rogers, *Linguistic Key to the Greek New Testament*, 702.

blood; and the removal of sins from our persons forever, in His death, which separated us unto God. That work has *"perfected"* us forever, inasmuch as we are one with Christ before God, as we have seen.[17]

By way of the believer's *position* in Christ, he or she already stands complete, perfect and cleansed by what the Savior's sacrificial death on the cross for the redeemed sinner has sovereignly accomplished on its own perfect merits. Such has produced justification, redemption, and purification; altogether independent and external of our own experiences of suffering before or after salvation here, or elsewhere, in the afterlife in some fabricated place of purifying fire construed by ignorance, fear, deceit, falsehood, and base greed, quite apart from a sound and honest reading of Scripture--especially in what we find in the book of Hebrews. And herein is the champion truth of that sacred book eloquently reiterated and amplified:

> Because their salvation has been accomplished by the vicarious obedience and vicarious suffering, in life and death, by no less a person than Immanuel, because He glorified God's law by keeping it fully and enduring its curse, His people are both perfectly justified and perfectly sanctified, that is, a complete righteousness and complete fitness to worship in the temple of God is theirs, not in themselves, but through Christ their head. Their *title* to heaven is founded alone on the righteousness of Christ imputed to them. Their *fitness* is given when the Holy Spirit regenerates them. Their present *enjoyment* of the same is determined by the maintenance of communion with God day by day. Their perfect and eternal enjoyment thereof will issue from their *glorification* at the return of the Saviour

> The word "perfected" here is to be understood in a sacrificial rather than in an experimental sense. It has reference to the Christian's *right* to stand in the holy presence of God in unclouded peace. Our title so to do is as valid now as it will be when we are glorified, *for that title rests alone on the sacrificial work of our Substitute, finished on the cross. It rests on something altogether external to ourselves, altogether apart from what God's sovereign grace works in us or through us, either when we first believe or afterwards* (Emphasis mine).[18]

Another revealing passage from the book of Hebrews refuting the doctrine of purgatory is Hebrews 1:3, which says concerning the Lord Jesus Christ: ***"Who being the brightness of His glory and the express image of His person, and upholding all things by the word of His power, <u>when He had by Himself purged our sins</u>, sat down at the right hand of the Majesty on high."*** Purgatory—the place of complete cleansing from the defilement and guilt of sin—does not wait in a nether place after this life is over, as Catholicism wrongly assumes, but is found, accomplished, and finished at the foot of the cross where Christ shed His blood to cleanse and purge us from all our sins. Hebrews 1:3 tells us what Christ did—He purged us from our sins, and take notice how He did this—*by Himself.* Jesus *alone* made purification of sins, and salvation is granted upon that free and full pardon and does not, by the force of this fact, require any further cleansing or suffering by the sinner ever again! Purification from sin is not found in anyone or any place outside of the cross of Calvary. Indeed, the Greek word for purged used in Hebrew 1:3 reinforces this truth.

---

[17]   William Newell, *Hebrews Verse by Verse*, 340.

[18]   A.W. Pink, *Exposition of Hebrews*, 570.

The word in New Testament Greek is *katharismos* (καθαρισμός), and is used in the aorist middle tense in this verse. The use of the middle aorist tense at once suggests the act of purification from all sin was a completed action made by Christ Himself, and therefore looks no further for any future cleansing, since it is already an accomplished act done in the past by Jesus at the cross! Notice the sacred writer says it was ***"by Himself"*** Jesus Christ has purged and cleansed the believer from all sin; such a fact then automatically rules out any supplemental need for cleansing in the purgatorial fire, or meritorious suffering required by the Christian believer. Christ *by Himself,* and *only Himself,* without help or aid from any other, has purged and permanently cleansed the believer from all sin. After accomplishing this alone, Jesus now *sits* at the right hand of God, which at once shows perfect completion.

Scripture unanimously and repeatedly declares the purgation of sins is exclusively found and accomplished in the Lord Jesus Christ on the ground of Calvary; and Hebrews 1:3 is another example which renders the existence of the Roman Catholic doctrine of purgatory an unnecessary fiction built on a deficient and wrong understanding of what biblical justification and redemption really means (more on this later). *By Himself* means just that, and no amount of specious reasoning or clever eisegesis from Rome's apologists will change the immutable fact *it is by Jesus Christ alone* all sin is cleansed, removed, and put away, which presently allows every born-again believer to stand pure, cleansed, and fit for heaven now and forever without any further need for cleansing or punishment required in a contrived purgatory; since all of these were fully met and paid for by Christ's propitiatory death on the cross. With the two words, *by Himself,* our cleansing and purification from sin was gloriously accomplished and vouchsafed for every sinner who comes under the cleansing power of Christ's shed blood. Hebrews 1:3 encapsulates well this fundamental truth of New Testament salvation:

> The manner and power of this purification form the subject of this whole epistle. But in this short expression, "By Himself He purged our sins," all is summed up. By Himself: the Son of God, the eternal Word in humanity. Himself: the priest, who is sacrifice, yea, altar, and everything that is needed for full and real expiation and reconciliation. Here is fulfilled what was prefigured on the day of atonement, when an atonement was made for Israel, to cleanse them from all sin, that they may be clean from all their sins before the Lord (Lev. xvi. 30). Thus our great High Priest saith unto us, Ye are clean this day before God from all your sins. He is the fulfillment and reality, because He is the Son of God. "The blood of Jesus Christ His Son cleanseth us from all sin." (1 John 1:7). The church is purchased by the blood of Him who is God (Acts xx.28, with His own blood). Behold the perfection of the sacrifice in the infinite dignity of the incarnate Son! Sin is taken away. Oh what wonderful thing is this. When once you see that Jesus the Son of God died upon the cross, and purged your sins, and that because of His obedience unto death God hath exalted Him at His right hand, that, having effected by Himself this purification, He entered into heavenly glory, you have no more conscience of sin. You do not require day by day, as it were, to receive the forgiveness of your sins. You have been washed, you have been made clean, you have received full absolution and remission.[19]

---

[19]   Adolph Saphir, *The Epistle to the Hebrews, Vol. 1* (Jerusalem: Keren Ahvah Meshihit, 2003), 65-66.

Simple logic states that sin is infinite, and the reason for it being so is because God is the object of it, for He is the Person being sinned against. The act of sin is finite because a finite creature is committing it; but if this is committed against a person or object, which is infinite, it therefore requires an infinitely just satisfaction for judicial retribution to be served. Hence, none but an infinite person or being can meet these requirements from beginning to end. That is why only the Lord Jesus Christ, the infinite God Incarnate in His person can, by His sufferings and death, offer a sacrifice for sin, which has an infinite value, whereby the demands of divine justice provide infinite payment and satisfaction. To then require a finite person to suffer in purgatory for a finite amount of time as payment for sin that requires an infinite payment in return is logically incongruent and completely goes against the Gospel of Scripture concerning the all sufficiency of Christ's death to pay and wash away every single sin here and now for the world to come.

How indeed can the Gospel be considered "Good News" if those who believe it must remain in doubt and uncertainty about whether or not their sins are fully paid for, whether or not they have obtained forgiveness of sin and are saved forevermore the moment they believed in Jesus Christ for salvation—faults, failings, and sins committed after they came to faith notwithstanding. Bottom line: With purgatory looming for most Christians, and this not even a certainty either, if the believer should die in a state of "mortal sin", what hope of assurance of salvation and eternal life is given in the Roman Catholic system—none whatsoever! But the born-again believer does have assurance and a sure confidence concerning things hoped for and unseen (Hebrews 11:1). Those whom God elects to believe in Jesus Christ have eternal life (as a present and future possession they will never loose!), and will therefore never perish or fall from the Savior's protective grasp just as the Lord Jesus promised in John 10:27-28: ***"My sheep hear My voice, and I know them, and they follow me, I give them eternal life, and they will never perish, and no one will snatch them out of My hand."*** And the person who truly believes in Jesus Christ for salvation, forgiveness, and eternal life, will never lack any thing necessary for salvation or go thirsty again (John 4:14).

The Word of God was written to give assurance and certainty to believers they are saved, forgiven, have eternal life, and a home in heaven waiting for them the moment they die and leave this world after death (John 14:1-6). For, ***"These things I have written to you who believe in the name of the Son of God, that you may know that you have eternal life, and that you may believe in the name of the Son of God"*** (1 John 5:13). This wonderful promise is to assure and quiet our troubled hearts—quite another thing if purgatory with its punishing fires of an indefinite time period stood in the way between us and the close and immediate reach of heaven made accessible by way of the cross of Christ; for it would render these promises as misleading, false, delusional, and empty of reality! All in all, we quite agree with the astute Lutheran theologian C.F.W. Walther in his classic work, *Law and Gospel*, when he pegs the doctrine of purgatory as contrary to the Gospel of salvation promoting a doctrine of the Anti-Christ!

> You know the Papists teach that even godly persons do not enter heaven immediately after death. Rather, before they are allowed to see God, they supposedly must first pass through what the Papists call "purgatory." That is where they claim the dead are purified from sins for which they had not made full atonement by being tormented in fire. Even worse, the Papists teach that no one—not even a sincere Christian—can be assured in this present life that he is in a state of grace with God, that he has received forgiveness of sins and will go to heaven. Only a few, they say, are excused from this rule, namely, the holy Apostles and extraordinarily great saints, to whom God has given advance information by

revealing to them in an extraordinary manner that they will reach the heavenly goal. This is the doctrine of the Antichrist![20]

It is nothing less than a blasphemous affront to the grace of God to teach Jesus only partially removes and forgives the penalty for sin; and yet there still remains, according to Roman Catholicism's understanding, some penalty the forgiven and cleansed sinner must pay here on earth or in purgatory. The Catholic apologist cannot have it both ways here by vainly speaking out of both sides of his mouth when claiming Jesus did forgive all sin but still requires the sinner must expiate and be punished for any remaining sin in purgatory. The two ideas are mutually exclusive of each other; for if the sinner must pay for the temporal punishment of his sins here or in purgatory after death, then Jesus did not effectively pay for all of our sins at the cross. Early on, and we will examine the origin and development of this unbiblical doctrine later, purgatory was created and maintained by the Catholic Church in the attempt to address the moral question of people not considered "good" or "pure" enough to enter heaven upon death, or bad enough to go to hell. So purgatory was expediently invented and introduced to solve this moral problem where the person's sin are gradually purged from him after he suffers for the temporal sins he committed in this life.

The Roman Catholic creation of purgatory proceeds from a false assumption—that one can earn or suffer adequately (even if he is cooperating by the grace of God as Romanists deceitfully argue) to be good enough to enter into heaven. And here, once again, is found the fundamental difference between the Roman Catholic religion and the biblical Gospel. Jesus alone, by an act of God's sovereign and unmerited grace, purifies the believer from all sin by what He suffered and bore on the cross of Calvary *"Who gave Himself for us, that He might redeem us from every lawless deed and __purify__ for Himself His own special people, zealous for good works"* (Titus 2:14). If you add anything to this unilateral and sovereign work of purification accomplished by the shed blood of Jesus, then you say, in effect, Christ cannot practically do it by Himself. And such is the great blasphemy and error of Rome's purgatory! Full remission of sins resulting in complete purification from the defilement of them was legislated, executed, and finalized through Christ's punitive and redemptive death at the cross, and is not found or experienced anywhere else!

The powerful decree of Colossians 2:13-14 affirms this was done at the cross: *"And you, being dead in your trespasses and the uncircumcision of your flesh, He has made alive together with Him, __having forgiven you all trespasses, having wiped out the handwriting of requirements that was against us__, which was contrary to us. __And He has taken it out of the way, having nailed it to the cross.__"* Since "all" our sins were forgiven, taken away, and wiped out, there of necessity remains no more sin to be punished, cleansed, or removed. Thus the cross of Christ renders the need for a fabricated purgatory to be totally unnecessary and without legitimacy—period! In the Greco-Roman world "the handwriting of requirements" was an IOU or a legal receipt drawn up to be signed by the debtor stating in effect he was liable to pay the debt in full.[21] When that debt was paid in full the lender wrote, "Canceled" (usually in Latin or Greek) across the receipt and nailed it on a public post or wall for all to see the debtor was cleared of all further debt! In fact *The New American Standard Bible* captures this term of indebtedness when translating the phrase, "Handwriting of ordinances" as *"the certificate of debt."* So it was with our moral indebtedness to obey the Law perfectly and the penalty of condemnation for disobeying it. We could not obey perfectly or pay in full this debt; Jesus did both for us by His death on the cross. Now there stands no need for the sinner to pay this moral debt anymore

---

[20]   C.F.W. Walther, *Law and Gospel* (St. Louis: Concordia Publishing, 2010), 154-155.

[21]   Peter T. O'Brien, *Word Biblical Commentary #44, Colossians, Philemon* (Waco, Texas: Word, 1982), 125.

here, or in a fictional purgatory, because Jesus Christ paid for it in full by His death on the cross, removing both the penalty and the great moral debt our sins accrued.

The permanent result is: there is no more debt to be paid now, or in the next life after death. Our lives have been fully and totally cleansed by God's expiation of these sins by Christ's forgiving and cleansing blood He shed for the guilty sinner on the cross. Paul says God has wiped all our transgressions away in the form of a certificate of debt, having nailed it to Christ's cross leaving no trace or stain of them behind. The existence of purgatory is moot and eliminated since the cross has already accomplished all cleansing and payment for the punishment of sin! There is no more need for the believer's punishment and expiation for his sins now or later in purgatory since Colossians 2:13-14 tells us in two ways how Jesus "blotted" out these handwriting of ordinances against us both *universally* and *sufficiently* for every sinner when He died for us nailing them to His cross:

> But it must be observed, that this hand-writing may be said to be blotted out in two ways: first, *universally* and *sufficiently* as it respects God: because by the blood of Christ such satisfaction is made to God, that he cannot require that hand-writing of the law from any debtors, when they flee by faith to this Deliverer; but according to the order of his own justice is necessarily engaged to acquit them. Secondly, *particularly* and *efficaciously*, when, in fact, it is blotted from the conscience of all believers who lay hold on Christ by faith; according to that declaration of the Apostle, *Being justified by faith we have peace with God.* But, truly, he cannot have peace who sees himself overwhelmed with debt, and, moreover, entangled by a bond: but as soon as any one takes hold of Christ by faith, thenceforth this hand-writing is blotted out, and his conscience enjoys a blessed peace. And Paul in the most admirable manner hath provided for trembling consciences by a certain beautiful gradation. For, not content with having asserted in the foregoing verse, that *all our sins are forgiven us*; he subjoins, that *the hand-writing itself is blotted out*: but lest any one should think that it is not so blotted out, but that a new charge may be raised, he therefore adds, it is moreover *taken out of the way*; and lest it should be thought to be preserved hidden somewhere, and may be preferred against us hereafter; nay, says he, it is *nailed to his cross*, i.e., it is torn and rent in pieces by those nails wherewith Christ was affixed, and lacerated upon the cross. And, indeed, the guilt of our sins being expiated, and the condemning power of the moral law ceasing, the ceremonies must necessarily be abolished which proclaimed human guilt, and shadowed forth that expiation which was to be made: And thus *the hand-writing of ordinances is blotted out.*[22]

The very term ransom, redeem, and redemption frequently used in New Testament salvation precludes and removes the idea of any purgatory waiting beyond the grave! The word redemption, redeem, and ransom all generally convey the idea of paying a price to liberate one from slavery or bondage. New Testament words, like *redeem* and *ransom,* are words used to mean a price paid to free slaves or grant the release of hostages from captivity.[23] The word *ransom* was used by Jesus in Mark 10:45 to describe the payment of His life He would give in death to free those who are enslaved by the tyranny of sin, death, and the rule of Satan. Paul employs the same word and meaning in 1 Timothy 2:6 when saying of Jesus: ***"Who gave Himself a ransom***

---

[22]   John Davenant, *Colossians* (Carlisle, PA: Banner of Truth), 465.

[23]   Leon Morris, *The Apostolic Preaching of the Cross* (Grand Rapids: Eerdmans), 61.

for all, to be testified in due time." Thus the New Testament words like *ransom* are used in a *forensic* or *economic* way to describe the payment to be paid for the enslaved sinner to be released and freed from the condition of sin, which produces bondage and slavery, out of which a person is redeemed and set free. Christ's blood atonement on the cross is that full, final and sufficient ransom price that was paid to forever release and free man from his enslaved condition to sin and the imprisonment of hell waiting for him after death! Christ's death on the cross was the perfect payment to secure this, and by virtue of this perfect payment and satisfaction, has the power of releasing the redeemed from any penalty, punishment, or imprisonment.

Once faith is made in the expiatory death of Messiah, who made this perfect and infinite payment, the believing sinner is free from any punishment or imprisonment sin once imposed on him or her. To require and demand any further need of payment or temporal punishment by the believer in purgatory, would in theory and reality, deny the complete payment already paid in full by the atonement of Jesus Christ, and thus would render the perfect payment made as null and void. Moreover, to say the Christian must in some way atone and pay for any remaining sin in purgatory after Christ has already died and paid the price for them, is to categorically reject the ransom price has already been paid in full by the Redeemer who declared, *"It is finished"* when giving His life as the ultimate payment to pardon and free all who accept this ransom price paid vicariously on their behalf.

The compelling arguments we have provided above taken from the Bible, which unequivocally disproves the need for the existence of purgatory, rings deaf to Catholic apologists. Rather than admit these simple and clear truths from Scripture, Catholic defenders of this abominable doctrine use various exegetical fallacies to amazingly claim the Bible does teach purgatory—when in fact no such place in all of Scripture is mentioned or discussed. One such defender of this false doctrine is Roman Catholic author John Salza who attempts to marshal "proof texts" from Scripture justifying the existence and teaching of purgatory in his grossly mistitled book, *The Biblical Basis for Purgatory* –a mendacious name for a book, especially when a closer and more honest reading of Scripture obviously affirms quite the opposite—i.e., purgatory is not found by name or concept in the Bible, and so it is emphatically *unbiblical*! While space does not allow this author to give a detailed, page by page thorough refutation of Salza's fallacious book on purgatory we will, nevertheless, quote him whenever appropriate in our biblical critique of purgatory, and the Catholic "proof texts" he selectively quotes from the Bible that are twisted out of context in the desperate attempt to prove this unbiblical doctrine.

Suffice it to say: when Salza attempts to "prove" from the Bible God requires the saved sinner to suffer temporal punishment and pay for any remaining sins in purgatory, he only can cite examples where Scripture makes it evident God is disciplining the believer with sickness, difficulty, trouble in the flesh, or some other form of chastisement *in this life* and up to death itself—*but not going beyond death.*[24] So the burden of proof still squarely remains on Salza's shoulders to unambiguously prove his point from biblical passages where they collectively and transparently state the believer must undergo some form of punishment for venial sins after this life in the fiery confines of purgatory after the person has died. He cannot validly do this because there are no Bible verses where this foreign concept or idea is transparently found!

In many instances, where he dishonestly claims the person must go to purgatory and suffer for the temporal punishment of sins, is really talking about events happening to people *in this life* and *never of the believer in the afterlife*. Salza is guilty of comparing apples to oranges here by way of using a false analogy between the two as if they are the same—that what we suffer from God's discipline in this life must then

---

[24]   John Salza, *The Biblical Basis For Purgatory*, 58-74.

automatically mean we must temporarily suffer for them in the next life! Furthermore, he confuses discipline of the believer in this life with the condemnation of the unbeliever in the afterlife, and then reads into the biblical texts his own unsupported premise for purgatory and temporal punishment there, while completely ignoring the larger context where the passage is found.

For example, Salza takes Paul's statement in a 1 Corinthians 9:27 of becoming a cast away, reprobate, or disqualified to mean the Apostle was saying he could loose his salvation if he did not properly discipline himself (*The Biblical Basis For Purgatory*, page 72). Salza assumes the word "reprobate" here always means the unsaved "eternally condemned to hell", as used in the New Testament, when in fact it can also refer to someone being disqualified for a particular service. The word used for "rejected" in 1 Corinthians 9:27 is *adokimos* (αδοκιμος) and means someone or something that has been tested for service and found disapproved. The Apostle is writing of service here, not of salvation. He is not expressing fear that he may fail of salvation but of loosing his crown as a reward for His service to Christ. Besides, a true reprobate is one who cannot be saved and is incorrigible in the eyes of God like Judas, Satan, or those who will take the Mark of the Beast during the Tribulation period. Reprobates like this were never saved to begin with, so Salza's point does not apply to those who are truly saved and would not therefore be applied in this way to Paul, let alone the rest of the redeemed who are saved with an everlasting salvation which never can, by that definition, come to an end, be lost, or forfeited (Jeremiah 31:3; John 10:28-29). But a closer look at the context immediately shows here that Paul is not talking about loosing his salvation. The context under which being "disqualified" is given is used with reference to being dismissed or removed from ministry—the preaching of the Gospel that the Apostle likens to a "stewardship" (see 1 Corinthians 9:15-23 on this matter).

Moreover, a careful and critical distinction must be made here between the *prize* he was presently striving for in ministry and the *gift* given beforehand. The free gift is salvation (Ephesians 2:8-9) resulting in justification, and this gift cannot be earned by doing good works as Romans 4:1-8 tells us. The prize is the reward the saved person receives for faithfully carrying out ministry and is given for endurance and suffering for the cause of Christ in doing ministry; it is not a work for salvation but comes after salvation is irrevocably given and experienced. Incredibly, Salza even goes on to claim Paul's confession in Philippians 3:10-11, which states: ***"That I might know Him and the power of His resurrection, and the fellowship of His sufferings, being conformed to His death, if by any means, I may attain to the resurrection from dead",*** means the Apostle was unsure his salvation was guaranteed since the Greek phrase "if possible" is a conditional phrase which means Paul's salvation was not a certainty to him; and so then how can any Christian not offend God by presuming his own salvation if even the great Apostle Paul did not do so as well.[25] So Catholics, like Salza, make the assumption that every Christian must face further punishment of sin and cleansing in purgatory after this life is done, and no one can be certain of final salvation until then!

On the surface such a meaning ascribed to Paul's words in Philippians 3:11, *"if, by any means"*, would strongly indicate uncertainty or doubt over final salvation if one were ignorant of how the conditional clause in the Greek is used here. The "if" clause in the Greek can be also used as an "expression of expectation," and not always a phrase expressing doubt or uncertainty. Paul expression "if by any means" can also be used to express fervent expectation and "syntactically does not suggest that Paul harbored doubts about his sharing in this resurrection from the dead."[26] This is especially reinforced when we remember that Paul elsewhere

---

25   Ibid., 72.

26   "But ει πως (if perhaps) is "an expression of expectation." See Peter T. O'Brien, *The Epistle to the Philippians*, 412. The phrase can also be translated "in order that" instead of "if by any means" as it is in the NASB translation and this would legitimately remove any shade of doubt Paul allegedly expressing uncertainty of salvation here, as

expressed utmost confidence and assurance of both his salvation and participation in the resurrection of the redeemed (see 1Timothy 1:12; Romans 7:24-25; 8: 32-39; 2 Corinthians 5:1-8; Philippians 1:6; 3:20-21). Indeed, Paul says in 2 Corinthians 5:5-6 the believer's resurrection was a guarantee of salvation as sealed and confirmed beforehand by the indwelling of the Holy Spirit. *"Now He who has prepared us for this very thing is God, who also has given us the Spirit as a guarantee. So we are confident, knowing that we are at home in the body we are absent from the Lord."*

In light of this wonderful guarantee, the Christian can be "confident" he or she will be with the Lord immediately after death once the human spirit is absent from the body and will be given a new resurrected body when the Lord comes for the Church in the future. These facts about Paul, and the believer's guarantee and unshakable confidence of having full and final salvation here, forevermore expose Salza's reading of Paul in Philippians 3:11, as expressing doubt and lack of assurance over having salvation and a share in the resurrection, to be obviously false, wrong, and totally misleading to the unsuspecting and gullible who fail to check his deceptive interpretation out in the corrective light of Scripture!

The first likely proof text the Roman Catholic Church will cite for the doctrine of purgatory is taken from the apocryphal book of 2 Maccabees 12:39-46. Keep in mind, when Rome quotes from this text, they believe the book of Maccabees is part of the Old Testament Scriptures for the very simple fact they have included some of the apocryphal writings of the inter-Testamental period (the 400 year period between the Old and New Testament eras) to be part of the biblical canon, when the historical, doctrinal, and theological facts of all sixty-six books of the Bible, minus the seven books of the OT Apocrypha, militate against the various claims of the Roman Catholic Apocrypha. This fact will be later explored in volume two of this work dealing with Rome and the Bible. The passage in 2 Maccabees 12: 39-46 speaks about how the military leader Judas Maccabeus took a financial collection among his soldiers of two thousand silver drachmas to be sent to Jerusalem to make an atonement for the dead soldiers who had fallen in battle so "they might be freed from sin" in the afterlife:

> On the following day, since the task had now become urgent, Judas and his men went to gather up the bodies of the slain and bury them with their kinsmen in their ancestral tombs. But under the tunic of each of the dead they found amulets sacred to the idols of Jamnia, which the law forbids the Jews to wear. So it was clear to all that this was why these men were slain. They all therefore praised the ways of the Lord, the just judge who brings to light the things that are hidden. Turning to supplication, they prayed that the sinful deed might be fully blotted out. The noble Judas warned the soldiers to keep themselves free from sin, for they had seen with their own eyes what had happened because of the sin of those who had fallen. He then took up a collection among all his soldiers, amounting to two thousand silver drachmas, which he sent to Jerusalem to provide an expiatory sacrifice. In doing this he acted in a very excellent and noble way, inasmuch as he had the resurrection of the dead in view; for if he were not expecting the fallen to rise again, it would have been useless and foolish to pray for them in death. But if he did this with a view to the splendid reward that awaits those who had gone to rest in godliness, it was a holy and pious thought. Thus he made atonement for the dead that they might be freed (2 Maccabees 12:39-46).

Salza falsely claims.

So from this alleged event in 2 Maccabees, the Catholic Church finds justification for not only purgatory, but also the belief those living hear on Earth can pray and affect the release and remission of sins for the deceased in purgatory! Catholic theologians and scholars takes the verses in 2 Maccabees 12 to support the idea the dead were not in hell or heaven but in a third place, which would be purgatory—a place they would have to stay and be cleansed. Additionally, Judas sought to make a payment so a sacrifice could be made to provide atonement for the dead and prayers to be said so they could be eventually released from purgatory and enter into heaven. Therefore such a practice during the Maccabean revolt lends credence to Catholics today who can make prayers and offer good works to atone for the sins of the deceased, and thereby release them from purgatory so they too might also go to heaven.[27] To make a doctrine of purgatory out of this passage from the Apocrypha ignores vital details given here that do not agree with the rest of the canon of Scripture.

Moreover, the biblical canon, which was acknowledged by the Jewish community in Jesus' time, and later confirmed by the early church, did not recognize 2 Maccabees as part of the accepted body of Scripture, and thus had no authoritative claim over the Bible believer. Not once in the New Testament do we find Jesus or the Apostles quoting or referring to the two books of Maccabees! The passage in question is self contradictory within itself. For verse 45 states the dead soldiers could rest in godliness while all the while they died still practicing the sin of idolatry as indicated in verse 40—a sin God condemns all throughout the pages of Scripture! God's Word says those who trust in idols will forsake the mercy of God (Jonah 3: 9). Idolaters will not go to heaven and are barred from entering into God's holy presence (1 Corinthians 6:9; Revelation 21:8). And yet inexplicably, in verse 41, these same slain idolatrous soldiers are said to have "praised the ways of the Lord" while in the midst of idolatry and the worship of false gods! This is unthinkable, especially in light of the fact idolatry and worship of the one true God is mutually exclusive (see Isaiah 44:6-11; 2 Corinthians 6:16). The Bible plainly declares no man can make atonement for another man before God by *"any means"* in Psalm 49:7. This can only be provided and made available by God alone (Leviticus 17:11). The books of Maccabees were rejected by Jesus and the Apostles, the early church fathers rejected them, including Jerome the translator of the Latin Vulgate, and they are never quoted or alluded to in the New Testament or the Patristic writings either. To then dubiously build a doctrine, like purgatory, on such a precarious foundation is unsound and without any sanction or precedent from the universally accepted canon of Scripture from the time of Jesus until now, Catholic claims of the canonicity of the *Inter-Testamental-Apocrypha* notwithstanding! One searches in vain throughout the Old Testament to find the living making atoning sacrifices for the dead, or that such sacrifices made were an acceptable means of atonement before God!

If Judas the Maccabean and his army were doing this very thing, they were surely acting without a command from God outside the perimeters of the authoritative Word given in the Old Testament. Of all the various sacrifices given and described with great scrupulosity and detail in the book of Leviticus, and the rest of the Torah, there are no sacrifices or prayers made by the living for the dead given to atone for sin! The events of 2 Maccabees would also contradict the teaching of Roman Catholic doctrine concerning the soul who dies in the state of mortal sin. If one would read verses 40 through 46, he would learn that God killed these people because of idolatry. According to Catholicism, if a person dies in the state of mortal sin, which idolatry is, the person would go straight to Hell after death! Therefore, according to Catholic doctrine, Judas Maccabeus would have been wrong in suggesting that the people should "pray for the dead, that they might be loosed from sins" when in fact they died in state of "mortal sin"!

---

[27]   Ludwig Ott, *Fundamentals of Catholic Dogma*, 321-322; John O'Brien The Faith of Millions, 339-340.

If Judas Maccabaeus wanted to make a sacrifice for the dead, if indeed he did it, he did so without a command from God and without any example of the Old Testament saints. With all the detailed sacrifices meticulously listed and described in the Torah, not even one syllable is found in all of Moses about any sacrifice for the dead. Neither can any example of sacrifice for the dead be shown in the whole canonical Scripture of the Old Testament. Various formulas and many examples of pious prayers are found in the Old Testament, but concerning prayers for the dead neither a doctrine, nor a command, nor a promise, nor a form, nor any example is found in the canonical Scripture of the Old Testament. Although in the Old Testament the pious care for the funeral, the grief and mourning for the dead are described *ex professio* in many places, absolutely nothing is read about sacrifice or prayer for the dead, that they may be freed from sins.[28]

It was during the time of the Maccabees, there was a great spiritual decline and doctrinal apostasy from biblical Judaism. Hellenistic paganism was flooding the land of Israel and had already permeated certain aspects of Judaism—sacrifices and prayers for the dead are prime examples of pagan thought intruding upon the Jewish faith, inasmuch as there is not one single command, doctrine, or continual practice for this in canonical Scripture, or in the history of ancient Judaism! The anonymous writer of 2 Maccabees does not claim to write for God or as a prophet of God; indeed he says he simply provided a mediocre abridgment of another man's writings (Jason of Cyrene) on the events of the Maccabean Revolt (2 Maccabees 2:23-32).

The author then goes on to say his recounting of this story may be considered "poorly done and mediocre", and if not well documented and found to be a perfect record asks for pardon (2 Maccabees 15:23-39); hardly the type of confession from many of the writers of Scared Scripture who spoke and wrote with the certainty and authority God was speaking through them! Luke, for instance, when writing his Gospel confidently did so *"having had perfect understanding of all from the very first"* (Luke 1:3). Even First Maccabees acknowledges that there were no prophets in Israel at that time (1 Maccabees 4:46; 9:27; 14:41). Seeing this was the situation, how then could the writings of first and second Maccabees be considered sacred Scripture when it is already admitted there were no prophets at the time?

The apocryphal book of 2 Maccabees is not inspired Scripture from God Almighty and should therefore not be placed on an equal level with the Holy Scriptures as contained in all sixty-six books of the biblical canon! The Catholic Church is guilty here of adding to the Word of God by affirming a doctrine like purgatory to underscore its legitimacy. To do so can give those within the Catholic Church a false sense of security by thinking they can rest the destiny of their soul on a non-existent place and postpone the problem of sin until the next life, when in fact Christ Jesus has already fully dealt with this problem at the cross. Not deterred by the untenable claim for basing purgatory on the Apocrypha, Catholic scholars will then point to what Jesus said in Matthew 5:25-26 to support their spurious claims for the existence of Purgatory.[29]

In these two verses Jesus says: *"Agree with your adversary quickly, while you are on the way with him, lest your adversary deliver you to the judge, the judge hand you over to the officer, and you be thrown into prison. Assuredly, I say to you, you will by no means get out of there till you have paid the last penny."* In this parable of the judge and the accused, Roman Catholic advocates use these words to say the sinner will not be released from the prison of purgatory until the offender pays for his sins to God the judge, to the very last penny. Accordingly, from this forced interpretation, Roman Catholic author, John Salza then confidently affirms the following meaning for Matthew 5:25-26:

---

28 Martin Chemnitz, *Examination of the Council of Trent Part III*, 325.
29 Ludwig Ott, *Fundamentals of Catholic Dogma*, 484.

In this verse, Jesus associates "prison" with a temporary abode of "suffering" where the righteous are "tested" for a time. In Matthew's related passage (18:34), regarding the parable of the wicked servant, Jesus says that servant is delivered "to the torturers until he paid all the debt." Thus the spiritual (not literal) use of "prison" in the New Testament always refers to a place of temporal punishment for departed souls. In light of these precedents, then we can conclude that the "prison" of Matthew 5:25-26 is also a place of temporal punishment for departed souls—or, purgatory. Jesus' metaphorical use of money and debt (paying the last penny) also demonstrates that the man's stay in "prison" is temporary. On the money side, because people have only a finite amount of funds, and the purpose of the person's incarceration is to pay funds to satisfy the debt, it follows that his stay in prison is terminated when he runs out of the funds (that is when he is finished making satisfaction). Jesus' use of the last penny also indicates that, at some point, there will be nothing left to pay and thus no further detainment will be required. On the debt side, because debt in Scripture is a metaphor for sin and indebtedness is a finite condition, means that the sin (represented by the debt) is also finite. In other words, the sin being satisfied is venial and thus the punishment is temporal. This satisfaction is unnecessary in heaven and impossible in hell, which means the prisoner is in purgatory.[30]

Upon closer study of Matthew 5:25-26, it is obvious from the context Jesus is by no means talking about the state of the soul in purgatory in the afterlife; nor is He teaching here the dead person must pay for the temporal punishment for his venial sins committed in this life. The context of this brief, real life situation, borrowed from the Israel of Christ's time, takes place on Earth and deals with one's relationship with his fellow man in the everyday course of events of living in this *earthly* life! Where in these verses of Matthew 5 is there any indication this was a parable as Salza and other Roman Catholics assume when arguing for purgatory? There is none whatsoever! There is no transition from this life to the afterlife in these verses! Not only do Catholics wrongly view Matthew 5:25-26 in an allegorical/spiritual way, but so do the Protestants as well. Both *assume* Jesus is talking about some kind of punishment in the afterlife. For Catholics: it is a temporal punishment and purgation in purgatory until the Catholic pays for the last venial sin; and for Protestants it means: If a person does not make peace with God through faith in the Gospel in this life, he or she will then be cast into hell after this life. Both interpretations do not hold true to the context of the passage, but especially the Catholic interpretation used to support the existence of purgatory.

A closer examination of this pericope in Matthew 5:25-26 can allow us to understand the Lord's words *literally* for this life instead of *spiritually* in the afterlife, whether in purgatory first, or in hell in the most extreme case. First of all, the example of the debtor being escorted to prison until the last penny is paid was the legal practice of Roman law, since Jewish law did not imprison the one in debt. And since the province of Judea (Israel) was under Roman occupation during the time of Christ, this situation was a common prospect for the insolvent under Roman imperial law. So Christ warned the intractable party at fault to acknowledge the offense and seek to make some kind of remuneration and restitution before being hauled in court where the judge would adjudicate on the matter, rule in favor of the lender and have the recalcitrant debtor imprisoned until the last penny was paid to absolve the debt.

---

30   John Salza, *The Biblical Basis for Purgatory*, 101-103, 104.

The moral point of Jesus here is to for the person make peace and reconciliation with his neighbor with whom he has a grievance, lest he break fellowship with God, which can only then be repaired by mending a broken relationship with the offended party. By way of illustrating this, our Lord uses a simile from the judicial courts. The result of failing to reconcile with your aggrieved neighbor could lead to serious and costly litigation and possible damnation of hell fire in the end if such a irreconcilable attitude is expressed for God in the contempt of one's fellow man; hence, the earlier warning given by Jesus in Matthew 5:22 not to curse your brother as a worthless fool.

The spiritual or practical application is clear: Resolve differences with your brother to bring about a restored relationship with him and God or face the unpleasant consequences of a bad relationship with your fellowman and God that will cost one to pay for it in many ways while living on Earth in this life, and will not be resolved only until after the matter is settled entirely to both parties' satisfaction! Once again, we heartily concur with the sagacious insight of Lutheran theologian, Martin Chemnitz concerning the real meaning of Matthew 5:25-26:

> Therefore it is evident that purgatory cannot be proved from that passage in Matthew, but that this statement of His is wholly opposed to the purgatory of the papalists. For the literal sense speaks about court judgment in this life. The allegory, however, according to the interpretation of Christ and also of the ancients, exhorts to brotherly reconciliation while we are in this life, showing by a simile taken from court judgments that those will be condemned eternally without hope of salvation who are unwilling to seek reconciliation, or refuse to forgive an offense, but die in enmity.[31]

Jesus is warning his audience to avoid a physical prison before death while *on the way* to court and not a spiritual prison after death. Though not dealing with just the external or earthly, the lesson here is one of a spiritual and moral matter, and that is, make sure you have forgiveness in your heart and readiness to forgive and reconcile with your brother you have offended or be prepared to face the consequences which could very well lead to judicial punishment and imprisonment.

In 1 Corinthians 6:1-6, Paul echoes the same advice for believers in this life who seek to bring lawsuits against each other before a law court of unbelievers. Instead, they were also to settle the matter among themselves within the believing community, rather than bring reproach and shame to the Christian community before the gaze of the unbelieving world! There is nothing whatever in the context of Matthew 5:25-26 to allegorize the prison to mean a spiritual place in the afterlife where a person must go to be purged or temporarily punished for any remaining sins. Catholic writers like Salza, who attempt to turn Matthew 5:25-26 into a parable, analogy, or metaphor to represent the prison of purgatory after this life, where the person is confined and must pay off the rest of his sins there, completely miss the real, literal meaning of the passage and assume the existence of purgatory, and then read it into the passage in question.

Salza and his Catholic colleagues are eager to assume this is purgatory and hence beg the question by assuming it already exists because certain key terms like "prison," "judgment" and the fact "payment" must be made in full for release has to naturally mean, then, purgatory is meant. It is a simple case of reading into the text what Salza and Rome want it to already mean, because they assume purgatory exists, when in fact Scripture contradicts and teaches against this false doctrine! In typical fashion, what Rome confesses,

---

[31]   Martin Chemnitz, *Examination of the Council of Trent Part III*, 340.

that Jesus died to forgive and purify us from all sin, they *de facto* deny with the unscriptural doctrine of purgatory, which teaches we still must pay the punishment due our remaining sins in purgatory, and only after this is done will we be completely cleansed! So once again, Rome speaks out of both sides of its mouth. You cannot have it both ways here: either Christ died for all our sins paying the punishment for them on the cross, or He did not if we still have to pay for any one of them in purgatory! But, as we have said earlier, the Word of God declares Christ already died for all our sins and paid the full punishment for them and the eternal consequences, which they produced.

To then claim the believer still must pay for it in some purgatory that waits in the afterlife is to deny Christ's death *perfectly* paid for them all by His *once for all* sacrifice on the cross (Hebrews 10:14-15). Once Christ suffered and paid for all sin, there is nothing left to pay or suffer for, now that the debt has been paid in full at the cross! And contrary to Salza's reading of the idea Matthew 18:34, given within the context of the parable of the unmerciful servant, some how teaches the existence of purgatory, the context of this parable in no way supports it and affirms quite the opposite. Matthew 18:34 reads: ***"And His Master was angry, and delivered him to the tormenters until he should pay all that was due him."*** With the last clause of verse 34 dealing with the payment of all that was due, Catholics like John Salza, are quick to maintain that the unforgiving victim, by the teaching of Christ, has the ability to eventually pay and absolve his moral debt, gaining freedom and forgiveness from the hands of his tormentors once he has sufficiently suffered enough for his sin in purgatory, in this case the sin of unforgivness. Hence, temporary punishment must be endured there if the soul desires full expiation of sin "until he should pay all that was due him." Such is the erroneous understanding of Matthew 18:34 by the mislead advocates of Purgatory. But upon closer inspection, Matthew 18:34 does not teach or lend support for the existence of purgatory.

The Lord left the imprisoned servant in the state of depravation. Christ never mentioned the servant's ability to pay the gargantuan debt and thereby gain release. The only means of release could have been experienced in this life if the unforgiven servant had repented and forgiven his fellow servant, crying out to God the prayer of deliverance: ***"Bring my soul out of prison that I may praise Your name"*** (Psalm 142:7). The sinner does not have the means within himself to ever pay in full the infinite debt he owes God. Salza's claim "debt in Scripture is a metaphor for sin and indebtedness is a finite condition, means that the sin (represented by the debt) is also finite", is refuted by the opposite when the Lord said the slave in Matthew 18 owed his master ten thousand talents of Gold—which is roughly equivalent to almost 300 million dollars in U.S. currency (Matthew 18:24)! Such a vast sum is used to paradoxically illustrate by a large finite number, the infinite price of what sin costs—thus only an infinite and divine grace can absolve a debt so large and beyond man's natural or moral ability to pay ***"That which is crooked cannot be made straight: and that which is numbered cannot be numbered"*** (Ecclesiastes 1:15). And so sin is in the sum of 10,000 talents against God in that it is infinite in scope. ***"Is not your wickedness great, and your iniquity without end?"*** (Job 22:5).

The only means of paying this infinite debt is by accepting the eternal and infinite sacrifice Christ paid for sinners at the cross releasing them and giving then eternal life in return. Any finite suffering here or in purgatory can by no means pay the infinite debt our sins have accrued before God. Only the infinite sacrifice by the eternal Christ will do (Hebrews 9:12-14; 10:10-14)! To assume Matthew 5:25-26 is saying otherwise by teaching man can pay for the infinite cost of sin in any way apart or including the atoning death of Christ, in purgatory, is to deny the clear teaching of Scripture on this matter, which, rightly interpreted, teaches there is nothing left temporal or eternal to pay for the consequences of our sins. Period!

Finally, if this text is taken as a reference to purgatory it contradicts the clear teaching of Scripture that there is nothing temporal or eternal left to pay for the consequences of our sins. While Catholics acknowledge that Christ's death paid the penalty for the guilt and eternal consequences of our sins, they deny that this means there is no purgatory in which we pay for the temporal consequences of our sins . . . Christ's death on the cross was both complete and sufficient for *all our sins and all their consequences*. To say there is some suffering for sins left for us insults the once-for-all finished work of Christ (cf. Heb 10:14-15). Once Jesus suffered for our sins, there is nothing left for us to suffer, for there is "no condemnation" for those in Christ (Rom. 8:1). Indeed, even death is overcome (1 Cor. 15:54f).[32]

Lastly, John Salza claims the Greek use of "until" ἕως (*heos*), with reference to the sum, which the debtor must pay for release from prison, must mean the person will not be released from purgatory until he pays all his debt by suffering the temporal punishment for his venial sins. The time indicator is clearly meant by the use of until, and if so, "means the person will get out of the prison, after he has paid his debt."[33] This is true for the person who is in prison on Earth for a financial debt that remains outstanding as was the case with the debtor of Matthew 5:25-26 which, to repeat once again, is talking about the debtor facing *a physical prison in this life on Earth*! Salza once again arbitrarily reads purgatory in this passage based upon his hermeneutic of *eisegesis*, where he introduces an assumed concept of purgatory into the context without textual justification! The word "until" does not always assume a finite period of time. The word can be used to signify a complete period of time, or to what is already done without regard to the future course of events.[34]

A few examples from Scripture will prove this point. In Mathew 28:20, the Lord Jesus promised He would be with His Church "until" (ἕως) the end of the age. Does this mean then the omnipresent Jesus will only be with the Church up until the end of the present age only then to abandon us? God forbid! What it means is the Lord will be with the Church throughout the course of the present age! Indeed, a inflexible reading for the word "until", according to Salza, would then break the promise of God given in Hebrews 13:5 where He declares to every believer *"I will never leave you nor forsake you."* From reading Matthew 22:44, would we also assume God's Son will no longer sit and rule after His enemies are subdued when interpreting the word "until" of Psalm 110:1 this way? Of course not! If we were to read "until" for a temporary period of time in the manner proposed by Salza, then God would cease to exist when a person reached old age since Isaiah 46:4 states *"Even until your old age, I am He."* Obviously this is not so since God is everlasting in existence without beginning, without end (Psalm 90:2); *and so context must determine the meaning of the word "until"* without arbitrarily assuming it has to mean what we want it to mean to bolster an unsound interpretation of the passage in question!

Another passage in the Gospel of Matthew Catholics argue for the existence of purgatory is Matthew 12:32 where Jesus said: *"Anyone who speaks a word against the Son of Man, it will be forgiven him, but whoever speaks against the Holy Spirit, it will not be forgiven him, either in this age or in the age to come."* Catholics place heavy emphasis on forgiveness of sins not being given in this life, or the life to come as hinting there must be forgiveness of sins given in the afterlife, which "leaves open the possibility that sins

---

[32]   Norman Geisler and Ralph MacKenzie, *Roman Catholics and Evangelicals*, 337.

[33]   John Salza, *The Biblical Basis for Purgatory*, 103-104.

[34]   Jospeh Zacchello, *Secrets of Romanism*, 85.

are forgiven not only in this world but in the world to come"[35] Echoing this assumption, Catholic defender John Salza, believes the existence of purgatory is taught in Matthew 12:32 with the forgiveness of sins after this life, and therefore must then be obtained by spending time in purgatory:

The plain meaning of Jesus' words is obvious. Jesus declares that there is forgiveness both "in this age and in the age to come." If it refers to life after death, then this passage must refer to purgatory. That is because forgiveness is unnecessary in heaven and impossible in hell.[36] So Rome thus reasons the converse; that if sins cannot be forgiven *in the age to come*, then some sins can also be forgiven in the life to come. The phrase "in this age" and "the age to come" is a Hebrew idiom meaning for eternity and was a common expression used in ancient Judaism to denote the eternal span of time.[37] The term is a double age language to emphatically underscore the permanency of a situation; and in this case Jesus uses it to reinforce the fact the sin of blasphemy of the Holy Spirit will never be forgiven! Our Lord's meaning of this is further reinforced by the parallel account given in Mark 3:29: *"But he who blasphemes against the Holy Spirit never has forgiveness, but is guilty of eternal sin."* Another translation states this sin *"can never be forgiven".*[38]

Jesus' statement of "this age or in the age to come" was simply another way of saying the particular sin committed by the Pharisees will never be forgiven. Matthew 12:32 is not even speaking about a person paying for his venial sins in purgatory. Forgiveness of sins in the afterlife is not the meaning here, but quite the opposite—committing the unforgivable sin of which by definition there is no forgiveness for it! Salza and Rome use convoluted reasoning when they offer Matthew 12:32 as a proof text for non-mortal sins being forgiven in purgatory, when in fact Jesus is talking about a mortal sin, according to the Roman Catholic definition, which cannot be forgiven ever. How then, in the astute words of Norman Geisler, "can a statement about the unforgivness of a mortal sin in the next life be the basis for an argument that non-mortal sins will be forgiven then?" The two are polar opposites of one another and therefore cannot be used for proof or comparison for the doctrine of purgatory.

The age to come looks forward to the reign of Christ over the whole universe and existence when both the first and second resurrections have occurred and the wicked are judged and condemned to eternal fire (Revelation 20: 1-15). It does not lay in the afterlife, or deal with the final forgiveness of sins, but will be established when the wicked are removed from the earth and then will be completed when all the wicked are raised to judgment after the millennial reign of Christ on Earth is finished. The age to come, as defined both from the perspective of the ancient rabbis and early church fathers, was defined as the time Messiah would raise the dead and establish His rule over all the earth. It was never construed to be the intermediate state of the soul where final sins after death are purged and removed! The period for the remission of all sin occurs only in this life when the sinner repents and trusts in Christ's atoning death for the forgiveness of sins. When this is truly done, all condemnation and punishment by God for those sins are permanently removed forever! For whoever believes in the Lord Jesus Christ crucified and raised *"does not come into judgment, but has passed from death to life"* (John 5:24). The Word of God informs the reader once this life is terminated by death, judgment and nothing else will follow afterwards, not forgiveness of venial sins in a fabricated purgatory of Rome's deceived imagination! *"And it is appointed for men to die once, but after this the judgment"* (Hebrews 9:27).

35   Ludwig Ott, *Fundamentals of Catholic Dogma*, 483; Catechism of the Catholic Church, 291 **[1031]**.

36   John Salza, *The Biblical Basis of Purgatory*, 102

37   Donald A. Hagner, *Word Biblical Commentary, Matthew 1-13*, 347.

38   Curtis Vaughn, Gen, ed., *Twenty-Six Translations of the Bible* (Atlanta: Mathis Publishers, 1985), 138.

The context of Matthew 12:32 is dealing with the unforgivable sin which Jesus called the blasphemy of the Holy Spirit—a sin which cannot be forgiven now or in eternity after. The Pharisees were on the verge, if they had not already at this point, of committing the unforgivable sin when they attributed the miracle working power of Jesus to the power of Satan. This is what the words of Jesus in Matthew 12:32 are directed against, not the forgiveness of certain "non-mortal" sins in the afterlife! Blasphemy of the Holy Spirit is a unique sin; and can only occur when the observer actually sees Jesus physically in person perform a miracle and then claim He is acting by the power and authority of Satan! Obviously a sin of this severity cannot be committed today since Jesus is not physically present in the world to perform miracles! And so from this observation Dr. J. Dwight Pentecost is surely right when he says:

> It is evident that this sin of blasphemy against the Holy Spirit could only be committed while Christ was personally present on earth. The sin could only be committed when the nation was being given evidences as to the person of Christ though the miracles which He performed by the power of the Holy Spirit. The necessary circumstances do not exist today and, consequently, this same sin cannot be committed today.
>
> Christ was warning that generation in Israel that if they rejected the Father's testimony and the Spirit's testimony to His person and His work, there was to be no further evidence that could be given. Their sins would stand unforgiven and result in temporal judgment on that generation. That judgment ultimately fell in A.D. 70 when Jerusalem was destroyed. This sin, then, was not viewed as the sin of an individual but rather as the sin of the nation, and this sin brought that whole generation under divine judgment.[39]

In light of this historical situation, to read purgatory in Matthew 12:32 is a non-sequitur and in no way follows with the context of what is occurring in the situation described, which is talking exclusively about committing the unpardonable sin and not forgiveness of sins in purgatory! Following on the wrong assumption that Matthew 12:32 is talking about purgatory, John Salza in his awfully mistitled book, *The Biblical Basis of Purgatory*, goes on to Philippians 2:10 and tries to connect this passage together with Matthew 12:32 to then claim those who are "under the earth" means the Church "suffering in purgatory". This convenient and contrived connection leads him to then say that those in Matthew 12:32 who are forgiven in the age to come "are the same people who are "under the earth"—two allusions to the abode of purgatory,"[40] The three groups of rational beings, listed in Philippians 2:10, who will render submission and confess the Lordship of Jesus Christ, are three groups of specific people; and not one of them are placed or mentioned in purgatory by the Apostle Paul! "Those in heaven" are all the elect angels and the saints comprising all the redeemed of the ages. "Those on the earth" are both believers who will voluntarily submit to His authority and worship Jesus as King of Kings and Lord of Lords, and also the unbeliever who will be forced to bow the knee and acknowledge His universal authority when He comes and His angels gather the wicked out of the earth for His righteous kingdom to prevail at their removal into hell fire (Matthew 13:41-43; 25:41-46).

The third group called "those under the earth", are, no doubt, the fallen angels of Satan cast into hell "who sinned" and are now confined in "chains of darkness, to be reserved for judgment" (2 Peter 2:4). A second class belonging to this group located "under the earth" are all the unbelievers who are unredeemed and

39   J. Dwight Pentecost, *The Words and Works of Jesus Christ* (Grand Rapids: Zondervan, 1991), 207.
40   John Salza, *The Biblical Basis of Purgatory*, 106.

wait for the Great White Throne judgment and eternal punishment in the lake of fire (Revelation 20:11-13).[41] This triadic construction of existence is exactly what is portrayed by Jesus in Luke 16:19-31 where our Lord removes the veil over the afterlife to reveal there are two places every soul will go after death—either heaven or hell with the present life on Earth preceding beforehand. In this afterlife revelation there is absolutely no mention of a purgatory—only life on Earth, death, and the following consignment of the soul either in heaven or hell as depicted by the two different destines of the rich man and Lazarus, respectively. Incredibly, John Salza takes the account of the rich man and poor Lazarus as proof for the existence of purgatory when the very context goes completely against this! With his brazen claim, Salza incomprehensively entertains breaking away from the obvious meaning of hell in Luke 16 to suggest the rich man may have really went to purgatory instead!

> While the traditional interpretation is that the rich man is in the hell of the damned, it is possible that he was in purgatory. This is because he still loved his brothers, whereas those in hell no longer have love. He demonstrated love for his brothers begging Abraham to warn his five brothers of his place of torment (vv. 27-28). If the rich man was in purgatory, then purgatory would be "in the heart of the earth"—the locale of Abraham, Lazarus, and the rest of the righteous dead (cf. Mt. 12:40)[42]

If purgatory were really meant here as an anteroom to heaven why set up the obvious contrast in death the Lord Jesus reveals to his audience with Lazarus going to the paradise side of Hades—a place of perfect comfort, peace and joy which housed the righteous dead, (and was later emptied by the Lord when He rose from the dead and brought the righteous to heaven in the presence of God when He ascended and returned to the Father as John 20:17 and Ephesian 4:8-10 reveal), and the imprisoned side of Hades where the unrighteous, departed dead are kept in torment? The word *hell* used in Luke 16:23 is from the Greek word *Hades*; and was designated to mean, after the resurrection of Jesus Christ, the exclusive place where the unsaved spirits of the dead go between death and the second resurrection for punishment by God at the Great White Throne judgment (Revelation 20:15). The outstanding condition of the lost in hell is one of unending torment without relief—the very condition the departed soul of the rich man found himself in (Luke 16:23-24).

Hell is a place of eternal, fiery torment, burning, and punishment, which produces an insatiable thirst as particularly, described by the Lord Jesus and the writers of the New Testament (Matthew 13:42 18:8; 25:41; Mark 9:47; Jude 7; et al). The rich man experiences the same torment and unquenchable thirst those in hell suffer. The picture of contrast here is: those who go to paradise (heaven) like Lazarus, and those who go to hell like the rich man. Jesus uses the real life example of the rich man to picture the horrible truth there is no possibility of redemption for the damned after this life. This point is all the more reinforced when the Patriarch Abraham reminds the unsaved rich man he cannot pass from hell into heaven since there is an impassible gulf fixed between heaven and hell (Luke 16:25-26). The rich man surely knew the place he was in was not purgatory; his situation was destitute. If it had been purgatory, he would not have been worried about his brothers ending up there because they could have eventually worked there way out if it was purgatory! He knew if they wound up in where he was, they would be doomed!

---

[41]   John MacArthur, *The MacArthur New Testament Commentary: Philippians* (Chicago: Moody, 2001), 145-146; Peter T. O'Brien, *The Epistle to the Philippians*, 244-245;

[42]   John Salza, *The Biblical Basis of Purgatory*, 34-35.

This obvious fact at once eliminates the unfounded idea the rich man is in purgatory, especially when purgatory is supposedly somehow joined to heaven and made accessible only after the soul suffers enough there to be granted entrance into heaven. The "love" for his brothers the rich man supposedly showed according to Salza's warped reading, was borne more out of regret and remorse for his awful fate and not wanting to see others go there like himself—starting with his family. From our Lord's plain teaching, Luke 16:19-31 in no way was intended to teach the rich man could gain enough merit whether by God's 'grace' or by self effort, to escape and leave the torment side of Hades for Paradise! Verse 26 clinches this as the real meaning: *"And besides all this, between us and you there is a great gulf fixed, so that those who want to pass from here to you cannot, nor can those from there pass to us."*

The impassibility and permanency of each soul in the afterlife, as described in Luke 16:19-31, rules out the reality of purgatory since the spatial location of those in heaven or hell remains unchanged! The wicked rich man was to remain in hell forever while Lazarus was to enjoy heaven for all eternity, and the two could not cross over to each other due to the unbridgeable gulf existing between the two places! The sober and solemn point of this account of the afterlife given by Christ is to demonstrate, above all, that the choices we make in this life based on belief in God's Word (represented here by "Moses and the Prophets"), or a selfish, unbelieving disregard for it, will surely seal and determine our fate in the next life—a fate that is irreversibly fixed and immutably determined after death! Quite the opposite of what Salza is illegitimately entertaining—the unlikely possibility the events of Luke 16:19-31 could support the existence of purgatory when by content, meaning, and description simply do not in any way substantiate a groundless supposition as this!

Undoubtedly, if purgatory did in fact exist as a place where the struggling believer must go after death to have his remaining venial sins cleansed and paid for, Jesus would have made explicit mention of it here where the fate of every soul in the intermediate state after death is delineated, described, and given. Purgatory is not found here because it simply does not exist between heaven and hell, and is another unbiblical invention of Roman Catholicism, which has no *explicit* or *implicit* mention or affirmation of it in all of Holy Scripture! Undeterred by his fallacious proof texting for the doctrine of purgatory, John Salza further goes on to find purgatory in the parable of the testing and punishment of servants in Luke 12:47-48. He claims the servant who receives the greater offence than the other servants who committed lesser offences is a "strong allusion to purgatory."[43] For the servant who received more severe stripes of punishment, represents those who have committed mortal sin in this life and receive eternal punishment in the life to come; whereas the servant, who received fewer stripes, represents those who have only committed venial sins and receive temporal punishment in purgatory. With this template for purgatory already in place, Salza imposes the following meaning on Luke 12:47-48 based on his unjustified assumption for the existence of purgatory:

> Thus, Jesus makes a clear distinction between temporal and eternal punishments in the life to come. Those who sin mortally will receive the eternal punishment of damnation. Those who sin only venially will receive temporal punishment to make satisfaction for their sins, but will still be saved—they will not be "put with the unfaithful." Further, those who commit venial sins will be punished in proportion to their offense. Those who were ignorant of God's will are less culpable that [*sic*] those who were not, and thus, the ignorant servants will receive a "light beating," while the lazy servants will receive a "severe

---

43   Ibid., 110.

beating." In short, Jesus presents a continuum of punishment in the afterlife—either eternal or temporal—depending upon the person's deeds.[44]

A closer examination of the context of the parable in Luke 12:47-48, within the larger scope of Luke chapter twelve, reveals an altogether different meaning and application than the arcane and bizarre interpretation proposed by John Salza and the Church of Rome. The parable stresses the need for readiness and preparedness by believers for the Lord's return to Earth, and thus looks forward to the Second Coming when Christ returns and metes out judgment on those who did know His will on this matter, and those who were ignorant of His return and chose not to learn of it, even though the signs indicating it were given in advance. The prophetic setting for this situation will literally occur when the Master returns to Earth at the end of the seven-year tribulation period after the heavenly wedding with the Church in heaven is finished and done (see Luke 12:36 with Revelation 19:7-10). Thus the parable is set within the context of Christ's return to Earth and is an exhortation for those living at that time to be alert, watchful, and faithful upon His return, especially when the very hour of His return is not precisely known (Luke 12:39-40). The context for Luke 12:41-48 is an eschatological, end-time setting portraying the moral and spiritual conditions of people right before the Second Coming; it is not addressing the after-life or affirming the existence of purgatory as the context of Luke 12:35-40 clearly sets forth![45] There are three types of servants in view with regard to Luke 12:46-48.

The first is an unbeliever, a *false or wicked servant* in the guise of a believer. He professes to serve the Lord and His people, but instead, abuses them and exploits them for his own selfish gain. When the Lord returns to judge the sheep and goat nations, this false believer will be judged and condemned with the goat nations who did not serve the King and help His servants who were in danger and great need (see Matthew 25:41-46). The second class is the *negligent servant* or carless believer who will suffer loss of reward, but not lose of salvation, and will receive considerable chastisement and discipline (many stripes) here and his wasteful spending of time will be weighed and burned up as wood, hay, and stubble under the fiery evaluation of the judgment seat of Christ (Romans 2:16; 1 Corinthians 3:11-15; 2 Corinthians 5:10). The third class is the *ignorant servant* who did not bother to know the will of the Lord for his particular life. He will suffer divine discipline for failure to seek and acquire knowledge of God's will in the performance of his duty to the divine Master.[46] This servant's punishment will be less severe than the other two servants who knew the Lord's will but failed to perform it. Keep in mind these servants refer to the Jewish nation and the Gentile nations when Jesus returns to establish His kingdom on Earth. There is no post-mortem context given in Luke 12 for a justification of purgatory and temporal punishment, especially when all the while these verses are dealing with the domestic, moral, and spiritual situation of people living at the time when the Second Advent of Christ has occurred!

The outstanding moral principle here is not one of spending time in purgatory for the punishment of venial sins, but rather the great moral truth Christ sets forth for those who are here when He returns:

---

44   Ibid., 111.

45   John Phillips, *The Gospel of Luke* (Grand Rapids: Kregel, 2005), 187. Roman Catholic priest and Bible scholar, Joseph A. Fitzmyer, even admits in his two volume commentary on the Gospel of Luke that the question of this occurring after death cannot be "wholly excluded" but the main emphasis and more probable time frame here seems to be on the parousia (i.e., the Second Advent of Christ to Earth), "in light of the reference to the coming Son of Man." Joseph Fitzmyer, *The Gospel According to Luke X-XXIV* (New York: Doubleday, 1985), 987.

46   John Phillips, *The Gospel According to Luke*, 188-189.

the greater the privilege of responsibility and knowledge of God's will that is attained, the greater the responsibility expected and the greater the judgment will be if this responsibility to serve the Lord, according to the knowledge of His will, is not met. For those who know God's will and do not do it, the more severe the punishment will be, and the less severe will it be for those who did not do it through lack of preparation, or did not know because of ignorance. They will be demoted and chastised in the coming millennial kingdom of Christ. Those servants (true believers) who were watching and working for the Master until he comes proved their faithfulness in these two activities; but those who knew the will of the Master and are aware of His return but do not profess faith, as manifested in the fruits of watching and working for the Master, will suffer the same fate as the unbeliever represented by the *false servant*.

The servant who was ignorant of the will of the Master did not bother to take the time and effort to know the will of the Master concerning how to live and work for Him. He will suffer the same discipline as the negligent servant but to a lesser degree. Note: that both the second and third servants are chastised in this life at the end of the present age when Christ returns to execute His judgment on people, who have either performed His will in light of His return, or have failed to do so because of neglect or volitional ignorance. There is no mention of a temporal period of punishment in purgatory in the after life for these two types of servants. The judgment on all three types of servants (the *false (wicked), negligent, and ignorant*) takes place when the Lord returns to Earth to set things in order for His visible reign on Earth, which will involve adjudicating and rendering just punishment on those who behaved wickedly out of hypocrisy, laziness, negligence, and ignorance when it came to serving and obeying the Lord upon His return. The setting for Luke 12:35-48 is *on earth* at the return of the Lord!

Roman Catholic apologists, like John Salza, fundamentally err when it comes to using passages like Luke 12:47-48 to read the unbiblical doctrine of purgatory into the text when the context is speaking clearly about moral conditions in the world when Jesus returns to judge the wicked and establish His Kingdom on the earth. Salza and the Church of Rome commit an exegetical fallacy here when they *assume*, from the outset, the existence of purgatory and then proceed to read it's meaning into Scripture when the contextual data simply do not support this meaning. Both would have done well to remember to let the evidence of the Bible speak for itself, instead of twisting the facts of Scripture to fit their theory of purgatory arbitrarily imposed on selected Bible texts to fit a preconceived agenda to justify Roman Catholic dogma, where no validation from Scripture is possibly given.

The practical advice of Sherlock Holmes definitely applies to these defenders of Rome, who twist scripture to fit their own pet theories of purgatory, when the savvy detective postulates: " I have no data yet. It is a capital mistake to theorize before one has data. Insensibly one begins to twist facts to suit theories, instead of theories to suit fact."[47] The text of 1 Corinthians 3:10-17 and the recurrent use of fire is a prime example of how Rome misuses biblical texts like this one to twist the context to fit with their unsupported pretext for purgatory! The misinterpretation rests on the facile assumption the word "fire" repeatedly used in 1 Corinthians 3 must then mean and refer to the fire of purgatory! Before we examine the text of 1 Corinthians 3:10-17, a review of the manifold ways fire is used symbolically, metaphorically, and literally for this life and the afterlife will demonstrably prove from Scripture fire is not once used of the believer, the saved, or the godly *as means of cleansing their sins in the afterlife*, particularly in a place called purgatory. The meaning of 1 Corinthians 3:10-17 is no different in this regard.

---

[47]   Sir Arthur Conan Doyle, "A Scandal in Bohemia," in *The Complete Sherlock Holmes* (New York: Barnes & Noble, 1992), 163

Fire in the Bible can be used to mean the domestic duties of cooking food (Exodus 12:8; Isaiah 44:15-16; John 21:9), or burning refuse (Leviticus 8:17). Fire can also mean the process whereby metals were refined and dross from them burned off (Isaiah 1:25; Malachi 3:2-3). The use of fire for defeat or victory in war is also found throughout Scripture (Joshua 6:24; 8:8; 11:11; Judges 1:8; 1 Kings 9:16; Matthew 22:7; Revelation 17:16). Fire was also used for the execution of criminals within the community of Israel (Genesis 38:24; Leviticus 20:14; 21:9; Joshua 7:15). Fire was used for sacred purposes in the service and sacrifice of Yahweh the God of Israel (Leviticus 2:2; 6:9-13; 16:13). Another frequent use for fire in the Bible was to describe the presence of God and His power to purify or destroy the wicked (Genesis 15:17; 19:24 Exodus 3:2; 19:18; Daniel 7:9; Hebrews 12:29). God's wrath is also metaphorically likened to a burning and consuming fire (Psalm 97:3; Hosea 8:5; Nahum 1:6; Isaiah 33:12; Joel 2:3). The eschatological judgment God will execute at the end of the age will act as fire consuming and removing all the workers of iniquity, evildoers, and unbelievers who oppose God's reign on Earth (Malachi 4:1; Matthew 3:10; 13:41-42; 2 Thessalonians 1:7-8; Revelation 8:7-8; 13:13; 16:8). When fire is *literally* used for the afterlife it is exclusively used for hell—the place where the evildoer and the unbeliever are cast into and consigned forever and ever (Isaiah 66:24; Matthew 5:22; 13:42; 18:8-9; Revelation 20:10, 14-15).[48]

Any study and listing of fire in a Bible concordance will immediately show the various uses and meanings of fire in Scripture do not in any way support or lend meaning to fire as a place in the after life where the redeemed people of God must go to receive final purification from sins committing in the previous life on Earth! The only place fire is spiritually used in the post mortem state of the believer is in 1 Corinthians 3:10-15, where the fire is used to mean the evaluating and discerning examination of the mind of God when investigating the works of ministry every believer performs and builds on the foundation of Jesus Christ during the course of the Christian life on Earth. Paul says this investigation and examination of every Christian believer will occur at the judgment seat of Christ:

"For we are God's fellow workers; you are God's field, you are God's building according to the grace of God which was given to me, as a wise master builder I have laid the foundation, and another builds on it. But let each one take heed how he builds on it. For no other foundation can anyone lay than that which is laid, which is Jesus Christ. Now if anyone builds on this foundation with gold, silver, precious stones, wood, hay, straw, each one's work will become clear; for the day will declare it, because it will be revealed by fire; and the fire will test each one's work, of what sort it is. If anyone's work which he has built on it endures, he will receive a reward. If anyone's work is burned, he will suffer loss; but he himself will be saved, yet so through fire" (1 Corinthians 3:10-15).

The Catholic Church believes it has found here a certain proof text and warrant for the doctrine of purgatory.[49] Catholic apologist John Salza predictably follows suite and further claims 1 Corinthians 3:10-15 is speaking about the soul who is saved by the cleansing fires of purgatory where any remaining works, in this case "venial sins", are removed and he is then finally saved and pure enough to enter into heaven.[50]

---

[48] An exhaustive list of how fire is used in the Bible is provided in the following two works, which show in all the differing uses and contexts in Scripture, the Roman Catholic can in no way infer or claim fire is used in a purgatorial sense: *Dictionary of Biblical Imagery*, 286-289; *Wilson's Dictionary of Bible Types*, 182-188.

[49] *Catechism of the Catholic Church*, 291**[1031]**; Ludwig Ott, *Fundamentals of Catholic Dogma*, 483.

[50] "The man must pass through the same fire in order to be purged of the things that produced the bad works in the first place. Because the phrase "suffer loss" refers to temporal punishment, the man who passes through the fire experiences temporal punishment for the defects associated with his bad works. If there are any defects in the man's "spiritual" building (venial sin, evil inclinations, debts of punishment) the fire will consume them, just as

The *time* the events of 1 Corinthians 3:12-15 is the Judgment Seat of Christ and will take place in His immediate presence after the Rapture of the Church has occurred (1 Corinthians 4:5). The *place* of this judgment will be at the judgment seat of Christ in the air (2 Corinthians 5:10; 1 Thessalonians 4:17). No mention of a separate place like purgatory is mentioned or even referred to here! Having *a proper understanding of dispensational chronology* for this event is an essential if a proper interpretation is to be arrived at. Something Salza and the Church of Rome completely lack when attempting to interpret what 1 Corinthians 3:12-15 really means. The events of this chapter are called the Judgment seat of Christ where every saved Christian will stand before Christ to have his works of ministry done after salvation examined and evaluated so that reward, commendation, and assigned placement in the future Messianic kingdom are determined by the Lord. The **basis** of this judgment is the *believer's works, not his sins*, which have been already dealt with and removed at the Cross. The result is either reward for work done in the service and ministry of the Lord, or loss of that reward because the service was faulty in the eyes of the Lord.

Rome's interpretation of 1 Corinthians 3:10-15 is in error primarily because their understanding of salvation is deficient in that they fail to properly understand salvation is a free, unmerited gift, and with it, the complete removal and forgiveness of all sin accomplished by the death of Christ alone the moment the Gospel is believed by the sinner (John 4:10; Romans 6:23; Ephesians 2:8-9); and the fact rewards are only given to the saved for the works they have done for the Lord in terms of ministry, service, and acts of charity performed *after* salvation has been experienced (Matthew 10:42; Luke 19:17; 1 Corinthians 9:24-25; 2 Timothy 4:7-8; Revelation 2:10;22:12). Rewards are given for proper work done and are given in the future when every believer will stand before Christ after the rapture of the Church to have his works of ministry examined; whereas salvation is a present and permanent possession given freely to all those who believe.

Both Romans 14:12 and 2 Corinthians 5:10 speak of this very occurrence; of which 1 Corinthians 3:10-15 gives a detailed description of what will transpire at the judgment seat of Christ. This judgment, or more properly, evaluation and examination of each believer's ministry completed on Earth, will involve only believers as Paul indicates by the use of "we" when saying, *"we"* all must appear before the judgment seat of Christ. *"For we shall all stand before the judgment seat of Christ...So then each of us shall give account of himself to God"* (Romans 14:12). And he says again in 2 Corinthians 5:10: *"For we must appear before the judgment seat of Christ, that each one may receive the things done in the body, according to what he has done, whether good or bad."* In light of the above observation, 1 Corinthians 3:10-15 is talking about the judgment of the believer's *works* done in ministry after salvation, not his sins or the cleansing from sin because the believer's sins have already been atoned and cleansed for and are remembered no more (Hebrews 10:17).

Christ bore the judgment and punishment for all those sins at the cross (Romans 5:12-21); therefore the punishment and cleansing from sin by Christ for the believer does not wait a future time period or place for it to be completed! The works the Christian does for Christ will be judged, examined, and a reward or loss of reward will be determined based on the quality of the work performed while the Christian himself remains saved, though he suffer a lost opportunity for reward when his works have been examined by the Lord and found wanting. Verse nine defines the scope and circumference of whom this judgment applies to—all Christian ministers who are called God's *"fellow workers"*. And the following verses deal with what quality of work was done in Christian ministry, which will be judged, by the fiery gaze and determinative scrutiny

---

it consumed the defective materials (wood, hay, stubble) in the physical building" (John Salza, *The Biblical Basis for Purgatory*, 125-126).

of Jesus Christ. The judgment involved is not one of dealing with sins and the purification from them since no such terminology or concept is found in the passage under examination; the whole idea put forth by Rome that purgatory and the cleansing of sin is in view in 1 Corinthians 3:10-15 is completely unfounded and not supported by the context of the situation Paul is addressing here.

The judgment of 1 Corinthians 3:10-15 is a judgment to determine the quality of the Christian's work and ministry for Christ that is made plain by the two analogies Paul borrows from agriculture and architecture as they apply to the Christian minister and teacher who is to plant and build upon the foundation Christ has laid for the Church. First, the Christian worker is a farmer planting the seeds of God's Word in the field of the church and the world (Matthew 13:18-23; 37-38; 1 Corinthians 3:9). *"For we are God's fellow workers; you are God's field."* Second, the Christian minister is a builder or construction worker in modern day parlance, whose ministry is likened to building on the foundation Christ has laid down –which is Himself (verse 11). The content for these building materials are termed as precious imperishable items like gold, silver, precious stones or cheap, inferior perishable items like wood, hay, and straw (verse 12). By using the hermeneutical principle of comparing Scripture with Scripture, the works the Christian ministers does will be tested, examined, and closely inspected by the Spirit of God acting as fire, will prove and refine it as gold if these works of ministry and service to the Lord are done according to the principles God's Word and the teachings of Christ. This is exactly how God's Word purifies and turns works based on faith alone, which are then refined so as to reveal the workmanship of the believer to be of superior quality like gold and silver. God's Word is like a refiner's fire, which tests the quality and content of what the believer does for the Lord with his life. *"The words of the Lord are pure words, like silver tried in a furnace if the earth, purified seven times"* (Psalm 12:6).

Ministry works done on the foundation of Christ and His Word will in the end, when judged by the fire of God's Word and scrutinizing Spirit, prove to be precious in quality, just as gold, silver, and valuable gems are revealed so by the illumination of light and the refining process of fire; or on the opposite side will prove to be combustible and worthless because of the poor quality of the material used. Scripture repeatedly likens God's Word and His Spirit to the analogy of fire. For it will be by the infallible verity and standard of God's Word applied by His omniscient Spirit, which sees all, knows all, and penetrates through every thought, motive, and intent behind every act or work of the Christian's service for the Lord will be judged (Jeremiah 20:9; 23:29; Hebrews 4:12-13). The Spirit and Word of God will be the instruments of judgment resulting for the believer either loss or reward at the judgment seat of Christ. The fire of 1 Corinthians 3:1-15 is not purgatory, but is symbolic of both the Spirit of God and the standard of His Word used to adjudicate and analyze the works of every believer before the judgment seat of Jesus Christ. The fire here is not the purification or cleansing of sin because the fire, Paul writes, will test the works of the believer to determine what sort it is.

The *fire* is placed upon the *works* alone and not the *believer* himself. The fire is said to *test* the *works*, not *cleanse* the believer from *sin*! Moreover, if Paul is meaning purgatory here, and this place according to Roman Catholic tradition and teaching, is only a place where the Christian suffers punishment for temporal sins, and is completely cleansed from those sins at the same time, why is there both a loss and reward experienced? If it were purgatory, then only punishment, suffering, and final purification would occur. But no such events are remotely described or given in 1 Corinthians 3:10-15. The sole function of the fire will be to test the works of ministry performed by every Christian to determine what kind of quality it is. *The fire does not purge from sin but serves to disclose and reveal what kind of work was done*. For verse 13 states: *"Each one's work will become clear; for the Day will declare it, because it will be revealed by fire; and the fire will test each one's work of what sort it is"* (not sin or the amount of punishment required to pay for venial sin). Authors

Norman Geisler and Ron Rhodes give good and unassailable reasons why the Roman Catholic meaning of purgatory for the use of "fire" in 1 Corinthians 3:10-15 is a gross misinterpretation of Scripture, especially in light of the uniform teaching of the New Testament on the important subject of salvation and the believer's position in Christ, which, in the end, makes the demand for purgatory quite unnecessary:

> First of all, the believer is not burned in the fire, only his works are burned. The believer sees his works burn but he himself escapes the fire... If so, then it is not speaking of what has traditionally been called purgatory at all. Further, the Book of Corinthians is written to those "who have been sanctified in Christ Jesus" (1 Cor. 1:2). Since they were already positionally sanctified in Christ, they needed no further purification to give them a right standing before God. They are already "in Christ." After listing a litany of sins, including fornication, idolatry, and coveting, Paul adds, "that is what some of you were; But you were washed, you were sanctified, you were justified in the name of the Lord Jesus Christ" (1 Cor. 6:11). From this and other Scriptures (cf. 2 Cor. 5:21), it is evident that their sins were already taken care of by Christ's suffering (cf. 1 Peter 2:22-24; 3:18). And that they stood, clothed in his righteousness, perfect before God. They needed no further suffering for sins to attain such a standing, nor to get them into heaven. And the fact that God desired them to improve their practical state on earth does not diminish for one moment their absolutely perfect standing in heaven. No sudden rush of practical sanctification (in purgatory) is needed to get into heaven.

> What is more, the context reveals that the passage is not speaking about the *consequence* of sin but of *reward* for service for those who are already saved. Paul states clearly: "If what he has built [on the foundation of Christ] survives, he will receive a reward" (1 Cor. 3:14). The Greek word (*misthos*) used here refers to "a payment for work done" or a "reward" or "recompense given (mostly by God) for the moral quality of an action" (cf. 1 Cor. 9:17) (*Arndt, Greek-English Lexicon, "Mithos"*). So, the issue here is not *sin* and its punishment but *service* and its reward. Likewise, as even Catholic theologians acknowledge, the loss is clearly not of salvation, since "the person will be saved" (v. 15). Thus, the loss must be a loss of reward for not serving Christ faithfully. There is absolutely nothing here about suffering for our sins after death. Christ suffered for all our sins by His death (1 Cor. 15:3; Heb 2:9).

> In addition, the "fire" here does not purge our soul from sins; rather, it will "disclose" and "test" our "work." Verse 13 says clearly, "the work will come to light, for the Day will *disclose* it. It will be revealed with fire, and the fire [itself] will test the quality of each one's work (emphasis added). There is virtually nothing here related to purging from sin. Contrary to the Catholic claim, the aim of the cleansing here is not ontological (actual) but functional. The focus is on what "crowns" believers will receive for service (2 Tim. 4:8), not with how their character is cleansed from sin. It is simply a matter of revealing and rewarding our work for Christ (2 Cor. 5:10). This does not mean that this experience will have no impact on the believer's character. It is only to point out that the purpose is not to cleanse the soul from sins in order to make it fit for heaven. This is what Christ did on the cross for us objectively and was subjectively applied to the believer at the moment of

initial justification when he was dressed in the alien righteousness of Christ (John 19:30; Heb. 1:3; 2 Cor. 5:21).[51]

The fact this judgment is one of reward or loss bars the Roman Catholic interpretation of fire to mean purgatory, since purgatory is a place where sins are temporarily punished and the subject is cleansed, for however long it takes, from sin and then entrance into heaven is granted. So there is no loss here but only great gain! Thus no loss in a negative sense would occur in purgatory in contrast to what Paul says in 1 Corinthians 3:15 where a negative loss of reward happens. The phrase stating the person will be saved "by fire", though his poor workmanship for the Lord will be burned up, does not mean the fire itself saves him. Paul says the person will be saved not *by* fire but *through* the fire. It is here where Roman Catholic theologians seize upon the word "fire" to maintain the fire of 1 Corinthians 3:15 speaks of the purifying fire of purgatory. Though the fire will reveal some of the Christian's works were worthless in quality and will be consumed, it will, nevertheless, show he is still a believer and his salvation will remain after the judgment and evaluation of his works done for the Lord have been examined. Contra Rome's claim, the fire of 1 Corinthians 3:13-15 is *evaluatory*, not *expiatory* in nature and function.

Paul's use of fire in verse 15, as with its use throughout 1 Corinthians 3, is a metaphor for the fact the believer will be saved in the same way Amos 4:11 and Jude 22-23 talk about how the negligent believer will be saved in the end, just like a brand plucked from the fire.[52] Though his works of service will be burned up, due to the poor quality and material used, he will, nonetheless, remain saved in the end once the fire of God's presence and evaluation at the judgment seat of Christ is completed. A good example of this type of believer would be Lot. He had lived most of his life in the depraved and grossly perverse surroundings of Sodom and Gomorrah pursuing a life of selfish interest. He was still a believer in the one true God. Yahweh sent His angels to rescue Lot and his family in the nick of time right before Sodom and Gomorrah was destroyed by fire. He lost everything in this fiery conflagration from heaven but his life was, nonetheless, saved.

All throughout 1 Corinthians 3:10-15, Paul makes metaphorical and figurative use of words like foundation, builder, gold, silver, precious stones, word, hay, and stubble. So the use of fire is always to be understood as a metaphor. To take the flames literally, as Romanists do, would violate the contextual setting of the passage and move from the metaphorical to the literal without a transitional word or phrase indicating the switch from a figurative to a literal meaning. The Roman Catholic Church cannot prove the existence of purgatory from Paul's teaching in 1 Corinthians 3:10-15 because the fire, as used by the Apostle in the passage under consideration, holds an entirely different meaning than what Romanists believe it to mean. A contrast of the two will show this to be true in **bold relief**.

The purgatory fire of Roman Catholicism will not involve the direct presence of the Lord but will occur some place in the after life, separate and below heaven where Christ dwells. The fire Paul speaks of in 1 Corinthians 3:10-15 is simply a simile to mean the incisive judgment and glorious presence of Jesus Christ when every Christian will personally stand before Him to have his quality of service and ministry examined. The prophet Isaiah further bolsters this meaning of the fire as the very presence of Yahweh Himself acting in fiery force and influence at the *Parousia* of the Lord Jesus Christ when predicting the following. ***"For behold, the Lord will come with fire and...and His rebuke with flames of fire"*** (Isaiah 66:15).

---

[51]   Norman Geisler and Ron Rhodes, *Correcting the Cults*, 222-223.

[52]   Gordon Fee, *The First Epistle to the Corinthians*, 144.

The fire of purgatory will only be applied to certain individuals who still must suffer for their venial sins, while a select few will be allowed to by pass purgatory and go directly to heaven. The fire of 1 Corinthians 3:10-15 will be universally applied to all Christians without exception. The fire will test everyone's workmanship for Christ, including those who build on the foundation with gold and those who built with straw. The fire 1 Corinthians 3:10-15 is a neutral fire which will objectively test the work of the Christian builder, whereas Rome's fire of purgatory is one of torment, purification, punishment, and expiation of the sinful believer who temporarily fell short of immediate entrance into heaven after death. The whole idea of temporal punishment of the believer in the afterlife is not the focus of 1 Corinthians 3:10-15, but the potential loss or reward for excellent or poor service, respectively. Scripture informs us the temporal punishment of the Christian occurs in this present, earthly life for several reasons. This is not done for the purposes of expiation, atonement or satisfaction for sin, but for the ongoing work of progressive sanctification whereby the Christian gradually becomes morally conformed to the image of Christ through the work of the indwelling Holy Spirit (Romans 15:16; 1 Corinthians 6:11; Ephesians 4:30; 1 Thessalonians 4:7-8; 2 Thessalonians 2:13; 1 Peter 1:2).

Scripture does further speak how the believer will be chastised and disciplined *only in the present life* for indulging or failing to put off the deeds of the sinful fallen nature (the flesh), hence the need to mortify, crucify, and abstain from the sinful desires of the flesh through repentance and the cleansing blood of Christ shed at the cross (Romans 6, 7:14-25, 8; Galatians 5:16-24; Colossians 3:5-9; 1 Peter 2:11). Once death of the body occurs, so do the sinful deeds of the flesh come to a final end with no more presence, struggle, or chastisement for sin left. *"O wretched man that I am! Who shall deliver me from the body of death? I thank God—through Jesus Christ our Lord! So then with the mind I myself serve the law of God, but with the flesh the law of sin. And if Christ is in you, the body is dead because of sin, but the Spirit is life because of righteousness"* (Romans 7:24-25; 8:10) Scripture is clear that every Christian's destiny, immediately after this life has expired, is heaven, not in purgatory, an intermediary place lying somewhere between heaven and hell, where one must gradually be purified before going to heaven. *"For our citizenship is in heaven, from which we also eagerly wait for the Savior, the Lord Jesus Christ, who will transform our lowly body that it may be conformed to His glorious body, according to the working by which He is able to subdue all things to Himself"* (Philippians 3:20-21). Through the work of practical sanctification, the Bible teaches a believer's perfection, will be achieved through three stages—and none of these stages ever involves a purgatory!

The *first stage* is positional or imputed perfection which occurs when the perfect life and death of Jesus Christ are imputed by God to the believer giving him or her a perfect standing with God in which all sins are removed and cleansed the moment faith is exercised in Jesus Christ (Romans 5:9-10; Hebrews 10:14). *The second stage* of perfection is progressive and grows with the moral and spiritual maturity of the believer pursuing the will of God through trials, moral testing, and ministry flowing from the local church resulting in holiness, love, and the increasing knowledge of the grace of God given through Jesus Christ (2 Corinthians 7:1; Ephesians 1:17-21; 4:12; James 1:2-4; 1John 4:17-18). *The third stage* is ultimate perfection, an entire and permanent perfection of mind, soul, and body which cannot be attained in this life with the sin nature still present (Romans 7:15-24; Philippians 3:12; 1 Peter 1: 15-16), but awaits the resurrection and translation of the saint's body at the Rapture of the Church (1 Corinthians 15:51-58; 1 Thessalonians 4:14-18). At that time, the Church will stand before Jesus face to face in the glorified state of the resurrection knowing then and only then, that which is perfect, has come (1Corinthians 13:9-13).

The Bible universally teaches the temporal punishments or chastisement for the believer' sins takes place in this life as a form of correction and discipline from God so spiritual maturation and obedience can be accomplished (Psalm 51; Hosea 6:1-2; Hebrews 12:3-11). But Scripture does not say any where punishment, even harsher to come, awaits Christians after death in a temporary prison called purgatory. On the contrary, God's Word teaches quite the opposite: After death every believer will immediately be present with the Lord in heaven (2 Corinthians 5:5-8); they will personally be welcomed by Jesus in the Father's glorious house in heaven (John 14:1-4); they shall have final rest from all their labors on Earth (Revelation 14:13); and are with Christ in paradise free from any pain or torment forevermore (Luke 23:43; Revelation 7:15-17). Rome's fabrication of purgatory is totally without legitimate support from Scripture, and is in fact built on a fictional foundation of biblical misinterpretation.

Even when Roman Catholic scholar and theologian, Richard P. McBrien, candidly confesses, "There is, for all practical purposes, no biblical basis for the doctrine of purgatory" (*Catholicism*, page 1166), we then must look elsewhere for the real origins of the Roman Catholic doctrine of purgatory. And one does not have to look far before he finds its roots are found in ancient Greek pagan mythology and philosophy! The ancient Greeks, like the Church of Rome today, believed the departed souls who died had to face a judgment in the afterlife, and were held in detention until their worthiness for entrance into *Elysium* (heaven) was determined by the ruling gods of the underworld.[53] Plato expressed the pagan belief there was hope for the sinner after death where he would be cleansed and fit for heavenly bliss. These souls, he maintained, in *Phaedrus* 249, A, B who were to "come to judgment", could pay the full penalty for their sins and thereby earn entrance into heaven after payment for their injustice was made:

> As for the rest, once their first life is over, they come to judgment; and once judged some are condemned to go to places of punishment beneath the earth and pay the full penalty for their injustice, while the others are lifted up by justice to a place in heaven where they live in the manner the life they led in human form has earned them.[54]

This sure sounds like purgatory does it not? In light of this disturbing fact of the pagan roots of purgatory, we must conclude with Alexander Hislop in the following observation he makes on this point:

> The doctrine of purgatory is **purely pagan**, and cannot for a moment stand in the light of Scripture. For those who die in Christ no purgatory *is*, or *can* be needed; for "the blood of Jesus Christ, God's Son, cleanseth from ALL sin." If this be true, where can there be the need for any other cleansing? On the other hand, for those who die without personal union to Christ, and consequently unwashed, unjustified, unsaved, there can be no other cleansing; for, while "he that hath the Son hath life, he that hath not the Son hath *not* life," and never *can* have it. Search the Scriptures through, and it will be found that, in regard to all who "*die in their sin*," the decree of God is irreversible: "Let him that is unjust be unjust still, and let him that is filthy be filthy still." Thus the whole doctrine of purgatory is a system of pure bare-faced Pagan imposture, dishonouring to God, deluding men to live in sin with the hope of atoning for it after death, and cheating them at once out of their property and salvation (Emphasis mine).[55]

---

[53] Edith Hamilton, *Mythology* (New York: Warner Books, 1999), 40.

[54] *Plato Complete Works*, John M. Cooper, ed. (Indianapolis: Hackett Publishing Company, 1997), 248-249.

[55] Alexander Hislop, *The Two Babylons*, 169; See also Jacques Le Goff, T*he Birth of Purgatory* (Chicago: University of Chicago), 50-51.

Another effort put forth by Rome to find proof for purgatory in the New Testament is taken from the somewhat enigmatic passage of 1 Peter 3:18-19: ***"For Christ also suffered once for sins, the just for the unjust, that He might bring us to God, being put to death in the flesh but made alive by the Spirit, by whom also He went and preached to the spirits in prison"*** Roman Catholic defenders of purgatory believe the "spirits" mentioned here, refers to imprisoned sinners confined in purgatory who are not yet purified enough to enter heaven after death and so must remain in the prison of purgatory until they have been completely cleansed from sin before going to heaven. One Catholic apologetic web site interprets 1 Peter 3:18-19 to mean: "After Jesus' death he went and preached to the spirits in prison that were disobedient. Now, these prisoners were not in Heaven or Hell, where were they? These spirits are in a waiting place being purified for their disobedience, the place is called Purgatory."[56] Another Catholic web site operated by Catholic apologist, John Salza, states 1Peter 3:19 with 4:6 simply means, "Jesus preached to the spirits in the "prison." These are the righteous souls being purified [in purgatory] for the beatific vision" [entrance into heaven].[57]

The meaning of 1 Peter 3:19 has been long debated among Bible commentators. The interpretation of this verse rests on two key words and what they mean—(1) the *spirits* and (2) the *prison* where they are confined. A closer look at the passage will convincingly reveal the Apostle is not teaching the doctrine of Purgatory! First of all, when dealing with more difficult passages in Scripture, like this one, the student of Scripture will seek out other clearer passages to help interpret the more difficult ones. In light of this tried and proven principle of biblical hermeneutics, we know from the general teaching of Scripture concerning salvation and the existence of the after-life that: the believer who dies is saved from any further punishment or condemnation from sin; whereas the sinner, who dies in unbelief, is condemned already (John 3:16-18). Scripture is clear there is no second chance after death for any kind of salvation (Hebrews 9:27). After a person dies, his fate is fixed and forever sealed and will spend eternity either in heaven or hell where an impassible gulf exists between the two (Luke 16:19-31).

The shed blood of Christ and His expiatory sufferings are the sole basis for total and complete cleansing of sin in this life once faith in His atonement is shown and lasts for all eternity (Romans 3:23-26; 5:9-11, 18-21; 2 Corinthians 5:18-21; Hebrews 1:3; 2:17; 1 Peter 3:18; 1 John 2:2). With these truths, once again mentioned and established as standard truths of Scripture, the identity of the "spirits" are not referring to saved people, since they are already in heaven with their sins already forgiven and cleansed by faith in Jesus Christ they expressed while still alive on Earth. They, therefore, cannot possibly be referring to the saved company in the Church. Indeed Peter tells us the identity of these spirits when stating the specific time period wherein these spirits lived on Earth: it was during the time of Noah and the worldwide flood, as so indicated in verse 20 ***"when were formerly disobedient, when once the divine longsuffering waited in the days of Noah…"*** With such a time indicator clearly specified in 1 Peter 3:20 for when these "spirits" lived on Earth (during the ante-diluvian period), the identity of the selfsame "spirits" therefore cannot possible mean or refer to all the souls of Catholics or Christians throughout the present time who still must have the remainder of their sins cleansed in purgatory.

In addition, the identity of the spirits has also been long discussed and debated among a large group of Bible scholars, with some believing the spirits were the fallen angels (demons) who cohabitated with women in the days of Noah (Genesis 6:1-3).[58] If this meaning is correct, then we would have Jesus descending into

---

[56] **Defending the Catholic Faith** at: http://www.catholicforum.com/forums/showthread. php?20022-Defending-Purgatory

[57] **Scripture Catholic** at: http://www.scripturecatholic.com/purgatory.html.

[58] See Karen Jobes, *1 Peter*, 249-250; J. Ramsey Michaels, *Word Biblical Commentary: 1 Peter* (Waco: Word, 1988),

hell, the place of the damned, to preach to the fallen angels, or the human souls of the antediluvian period and offering them a second chance at salvation. But there is no other passage in Scripture where post-mortem conversion or salvation is taught, making this interpretation proposed for 1 Peter 3:19 most unlikely. The more probable meaning is based on what Peter mentions in 1 Peter 3:18 with verse 19. The Spirit of Christ preached through Noah the warning of imminent judgment, via the worldwide flood, upon the wicked and rebellious unbelievers of the pre-flood world, whose spirits are now confined in hell, where all the unsaved go after death to wait final judgment at the end of this age. This interpretation is bolstered by the fact Noah was called in 2 Peter 2:5 "a preacher of righteousness," who by the Holy Spirit is previously called by Peter "the Spirit of Christ" (cf., 1 Peter 1:11), Who also spoke through the prophets of the Old Testament—the same divine Spirit who preached through Noah to the ungodly and disobedient ante-diluvians who died and were, at the time of Peter's writing, imprisoned spirits in hell waiting the final judgment. It was to them the Spirit of Christ preached through Noah to warn of the coming judgment of the flood if they did not repent of their iniquity and turn to God. Noah resolutely preached to them for one hundred and twenty years before the flood came (Genesis 6:3).

In the words of 1 Peter 1:19, the Spirit of Christ "went" and "preached" through the words of Noah the need for repentance and coming to God for salvation and deliverance from the wrath to come. This fact, as mentioned by Peter, was revealed to remind the Apostle's audience how the power and Lordship of Jesus Christ reaches to the very unseen spiritual realm of the departed dead, who once lived on Earth and heard the Gospel, just as the believers of Peter's day can be confident Christ is also present in the words of the Gospel they too speak to the ungodly, calling them to repent and believe in the Gospel of Jesus Christ for salvation.

> The spirits in prison are those *who formerly did not obey* (better: 'disobeyed', since the word has a sense of active rebellion), *when God's patience waited in the days of Noah, during the building of the ark*. These phrases indicate that only human spirits can be intended, for nowhere in the Bible or in Jewish literature outside of the Bible are angels ever said to have disobeyed 'during the building of the ark'. Genesis 6:5-13 clearly emphasizes the *human* sin which provoked God to flood the earth in judgment…But why does Peter refer to 'spirits' if he has in view disobedience by humans who were not just 'spirits' but bodies as well? This is best explained by understanding the text to mean 'spirits who are now in prison' (*i.e.*, at the time Peter was writing), but who were people on earth at the time of Noah, when Christ was preaching to them…A similar expression is found a few verses later at 4:6, 'For this is why the gospel was preached even to the dead', which is best understood to mean 'the gospel was preached to those who are now dead' (but who were alive when the gospel was preached to them)…The phrase *who formerly did not obey* is better translated 'when they formerly disobeyed', this specifying that this was the time when Christ 'in spirit' preached to these people: *i.e.* '*when they formerly disobeyed* when God's patience was waiting in the days of Noah, during the building of the ark.' Peter elsewhere mentioned ideas similar to the thought that Christ 'in spirit' preached through Noah, for in 1:11 the Spirit of Christ is said to have been active in the prophets of the Old Testament era (*cf.* 1Cor. 10:4)…By saying that *Christ went and preached* rather than just saying that he 'preached', Peter suggests that Christ did not stay in heaven but 'went' to

206-212.

where people were disobeying, and there preached to them through the lips of Noah. The content of this preaching was not a message of final condemnation…or the completion of redemption…but concerned the need to repent and come to God for salvation. This is what Noah would have preached to those around him (even without extra-biblical literature we would draw this conclusion from 2 Pet. 2:4). It is the right message to preach when people are disobeying 'while God's patience is waiting' (*cf.* 2Pet. 3:9).

In the unseen 'spiritual' realm Christ preached through Noah to unbelievers around him. By saying this Peter can remind his readers of the reality of Christ's work in the unseen spiritual realm and the fact that Christ is also in them, empowering their witness and making it spiritually effective (cf. 1:8, 11 12 25: 2:4).[59]

The earliest indication of some type of belief in a purgatory appeared largely in the patristic writings of the Latin Church Fathers. The Greek Church Fathers never accepted the doctrine of purgatory along with the Papacy and Immaculate Conception. This became a point of contention between the Eastern Orthodox Church and the Roman Catholic Church for centuries! Some claim the second century *Shepherd of Hermes* (160 A.D.) contains a reference to purgatory based on 1 Peter 3:19 when the writer states Christians who have been excommunicated can still have their sins forgiven and be "granted another less honorable place after they have been chastised and fulfilled a period of punishment for their sins."[60] This statement is quite ambiguous; and to build a doctrine of purgatory on it is dubious at best since it is not specified whether this period of punishment and chastisement for sins is in this world or the next. It is hard to know what exactly is meant. As it stands, it is hardly a proof text for the notion of purgatory.

Origen was the first who *formally* proposed a purgatory like place within a universalistic context where every human being will eventually be saved (even Satan himself!) only after many of them undergo particular purification at the time judgment. But this purification will happen at the time of final judgment, and not in some intermediate place between the resurrection and judgment.[61] Roman Catholic apologist John Salza attempts to amass patristic evidence for the Roman Catholic belief in purgatory, and then assumes because church fathers like Clement of Alexandria, Tertullian, Cyprian, Gregory of Nyssa, John Chrysostom, and Augustine, espoused some form of purgatory, it then must be true and therefore worthy of belief and part of the body of Christine doctrine.[62] This assumes everything the Church Fathers taught must be automatically correct—even the unbiblical concept of purgatory! However, Scripture exhorts us to test and examine all teachings in the light of Scripture, regardless of the exalted position or rank of the highly respected person teaching doctrine (Isaiah 8:20; Acts 17:11; 1 Thessalonians 5:21; 1 John 4:1).

The Berean Christians, for instance, examined the Scriptures to see if what the great Apostle Paul taught them was backed up by the written Word of God (Acts 17:11). The inerrant Word of God must even be used to test what even the Church Fathers have to say on a subject of doctrine. Let it be pointed out here the doctrine of purgatory is no where explicitly or clearly found in the canonical writings of the Apostles in the New Testament, nor is it reiterated by the fathers, like Papias or Polycarp, who were direct followers personally taught by Christ's Apostles of the first century! Keep in mind, too, that false doctrine and apostasy had

---

[59] Wayne Grudem, *1Peter*, 159-161.

[60] *Shepherd of Hermes* at http://www.scribd.com/doc/27316849/The-Shepherd-of-Hermas, 7.

[61] Richard McBrien, *Catholicism*, 1167.

[62] John Salza, *The Biblical Basis of Purgatory*, 144-171

already permeated the Christian Church of the first century while most of the Apostles were still alive—as their warnings about false teachers propagating their false doctrines so amply testify (Acts 19:29; 1Timothy 4:1-3; 2 Timothy 3:1-9; 2 Peter 2; Jude 8-19). For where the church fathers agree with Scripture, we must give our assent, but where they part from Scripture, we must dissent and always side with the teaching of Scripture.

It is precisely here, when refuting the long held unbiblical doctrine and tradition of purgatory, we must agree with the great Reformer Martin Luther. When standing before the Diet of Worms and the Catholic antagonist John Eck, who decried Luther's stance on Scripture alone by accusing him of being arrogant to go against centuries of Church tradition and the teaches of the Fathers, Luther courageously and unflinchingly stood his ground on the supreme authority of Scripture alone stating: "Unless I am convinced by Scripture and plain reason—I do not accept the authority of Popes and Councils, for they have contradicted each other—my conscience is captive to the Word of God. I cannot and I will not recant anything, for to go against conscience is neither right nor safe." (From *Here I Stand: A Life of Martin Luther* by Roland Stanton, page 144.).

The same response and stance should also be uncompromisingly maintained when it comes to refuting the grace denying doctrine of purgatory and the feeble attempts at defending purgatory from a misreading of Scripture and appeal to the extra-biblical traditions of men by the Catholic Church, as so advanced by her servile and bloviating apologists. The false doctrine of Purgatory is an alien concept to the Word of God and began to arise, in nascent form, at the close of the first century to the beginning of the second century that did not attain mature form until it was given a formal place in the church of Rome by Pope Gregory the Great—who first systematized this unscriptural doctrine in the sixth century A.D., of which Origen and Augustine had already laid the fundamental ground work some two centuries earlier!

> But some of the elements in the patristic heritage were reworked in Gregory's thought. Two such were the doctrines of purgatory and the doctrine of the sacrifice of the Mass. Neither of these doctrines may be said to be Greek theologians; but Latin theology, as it was systematized by Gregory, gave then definitive form. The origins of the idea of purgatory may be traced to the widespread hope, expressed by Origen, that the power of the saving will of God extended beyond the limits of this earthly life, granting men a further opportunity for purification and eventual salvation after death. Augustine, while opposing himself to the speculations of Origen about the universal salvation of all men and of the devil, nevertheless believed that there were "temporary punishments after death" and that it was appropriate to pray that some of the dead be granted remission of sins. These suggestions about purgatorial fire, made tentatively and in passing, became "something that has to be believed [credendus] in Gregory. Again "it has to be believed [credendum est]" that the prayers of the faithful availed release from purgatorial fire for those who have sinned "not out of malice but out of the error of ignorance."[63]

Purgatory did not become an official doctrine of the Catholic Church until over 1,400 years after Jesus Christ in A.D. 1429 with the decree of the Council of Florence. Session six declares:

> Also, if truly penitent people die in the love of God before they have made satisfaction for acts and omissions by worthy fruits of repentance, their souls are cleansed after death

---

[63] Jaroslav Pelikan, *The Emergence of the Catholic Tradition,* Volume 1 *(100-600),* 355.

by cleansing pains; and the suffrages of the living faithful avail them in giving relief from such pains, that is, sacrifices of masses, prayers, almsgiving and other acts of devotion which have been customarily performed by some of the faithful for others of the faithful in accordance with the church's ordinances.[64]

Like with so many of Roman Catholic traditional doctrines, purgatory originated and developed well after Christ and the Apostles; and did not finally emerge until over a thousand years later when so much of the Church had already, at that time, departed far from sound biblical doctrine! Indeed, preeminent Medievalist French scholar, Jacques Le Goff, in his enlightening book, *The Birth of Purgatory*, validly documents how even the doctrine and the word *purgatory* did not appear and become a fixed feature of Roman Catholic theology before the late twelfth century. In fact the Latin word for purgatory (*purgatorium*) did not even appear before then![65] In the first two hundred years of the Church, there is no mention or teaching of purgatory—thus showing it is not a doctrine founded squarely on the Scriptures, nor an apostolic teaching passed down to their immediate generation of the apostolic church fathers, but an invention and fabrication of man, which crept into the Church at the beginning of the third century when many false doctrines and heresies were already being approved and taught. Eventually, the belief in purgatory became one of them.

> For at least the first two centuries there was no mention of purgatory in the Church. In all the writings of the Apostolic Fathers, Irenaeus and Justin Martyr there is not the slightest allusion to the idea of purgatory. Rome claims that the early Church nevertheless believed in purgatory because it prayed for the dead. This was becoming a common practice by the beginning of the third century but it does not, in itself, prove that the early Church viewed deceased Christians as residing in peace and happiness and the prayers offered were for them to have a greater experience of these.[66]

Yet Catholic apologist, like John Salza, will typically point to the recorded prayers of Christians in the mid second century to prove the existence of purgatory. He gives two examples in *The Acts of Paul and Thecla* and *Abercius* to then make the unsubstantiated claim: "All Christians believe these prayers could assist the dead by helping to make satisfaction for the sins that detained them in purgatory."[67] First of all, to say "all Christians" believed in purgatory by the practice of saying prayers for the dead is a great stretch of the imagination and a gross, inaccurate overgeneralization that is no where seen or proven in the writings of the Apostles, nor in the writings of their followers in the early church.

If such unanimity existed among Christians in the early church of the first and second centuries, as designated by Salza's gratuitous use of the term "all", then surely such beliefs in purgatory and prayers for the departed souls to be released from there would have a ubiquitous presence in the writings and creeds of the early church, especially since purgatory is an important part of the salvation process in the Roman Catholic system. Put within their proper contexts, many of these prayers were for the Christian departed to enjoy the blessings of heaven more and more with greater intensity, and not for souls to be released from a

---

[64] Councel of Florence at http://www.ewtn.com/library/COUNCILS/FLORENCE.HTM

[65] Jacques Le Goff, *The Birth of Purgatory*, 362.

[66] William Webster, *The Church of Rome at the Bar of History*, 114.

[67] John Salza, *The Biblical Basis for Purgatory*, 149.

theorized purgatory. They most certainly do not, and indicate the opposite is quite true here! And so astute author, William Webster, rightfully concludes from this fact:

> The written prayers which have survived, and the evidence from the catacombs and burial inscriptions indicate that the early Church viewed deceased Christians as residing in peace and happiness and the prayers offered were for them to have a greater experience of these. As early as Tertullian, in the late second and beginning of the third century, these prayers often use the Latin term *refigerium* as a request of God on behalf of departed Christians, a term which means, 'refreshment' or 'to refresh' and came to embody the concept of heavenly happiness. So the fact that the early Church prayed for the dead does not support the teaching of purgatory for the nature of the prayers themselves indicate the Church did not view the dead as residing in a place of suffering.[68]

As we noted in the previous pages above, Christ's once for all suffering for us on the cross was sufficient alone to atone for the totality (past, present, and future) of our sins whereby a complete and total irreversible cleansing was accomplished (John 19:30; Hebrews 10:14; 1 Peter 3:18). Nor is purgatory, as Catholics theologians wrongly claim, a part of the sanctification process since Scripture informs us sanctification after salvation occurs in this life before death; and after death the believer does not wait for full purification from sin, but the glorification of the resurrected body (Romans 8:30; 1 Corinthians 3:10-13; 1 John 3:2). Sanctification, as it is described in Scripture, involves the setting apart of the believer by God for His service and ministry (1 Corinthians 1:2; Ephesians 5:27). The nature of this sanctification is to make the believer more and more holy and morally conformable to the character of Jesus Christ through His Word and divine discipline from the heavenly Father (John 15:3-3; 17:17; Hebrews 12:10; Revelation 3:19).

All in all, nowhere in the New Testament is sanctification ever described in a distinct purgatorial way where the believer must pay or atone for his sins after death, whereby he receives expiation from sin in a distinct place in the after life different from heaven or hell. Sanctification is the power of God used to decrease the presence and power of sin with the concomitant increase in holiness in the earthly life of the believer as he progresses in his walk with the Lord in the present life prior to and before death (Romans 6:19, 22; 2 Corinthians 7:1; 1 Thessalonians 4:1-7).

Throughout the three stages of salvation (past, present. and future) there is no mention in the Scripture of the saved sinner having to atone, suffer or expiate for his own sins as a condition for entrance into heaven now, or in the afterlife, which would be the case if Rome's purgatory was found and mandated by Scripture. This is because the New Testament unequivocally teaches salvation is a free gift given by God unearned by the sinner who receives it by faith. The cleansing from sin is a unilateral, sovereign act by God and is accomplished in the atoning death of Jesus Christ alone (Ezekiel 16:63; Romans 5:11-21). The sinner can no more completely cleanse himself here or in purgatory simply because of man's inherent impurity and natural, unabated inclination towards sin. For, ***"Who can bring a clean thing out of an unclean? No one!"*** (Job 14:4). To do this at all would be as impossible as expecting the Ethiopian to change the color of his skin or the leopard its spots (Jeremiah 13:23). For if the sinner could at any point, before or after his salvation, on earth or in some imagined purgatory, effectively suffer to atone for his sins and thereby make expiation of any kind, the death of Jesus Christ to cleanse from all sin from beginning to end, would of necessity, and

---

68   William Webster, *The Church of Rome at the Bar of History*, 114.

the logic of the case, be deficient and incomplete for the provision of a full, free expiation and purification from all sin (Galatians 2:21). Thus in the whole panorama and outworking of salvation, it is by Christ's death *alone* we are cleansed, purified, and saved without any effort or merit from ourselves.

> To argue, as Catholic scholars do, that purgatory is part of our experiential sanctification is to overlook two important points. First, all *experiential* sanctification occurs in this life before death (cf. 1 Cor. 3:10-13; 2 Cor. 5:10; Rev. 22:12). The only sanctification after death is *actual*. The Bible calls it glorification (Rom. 8:30; 1 John 3:2). Second, sanctification is not a process of *paying* for our sins. It is the process through which God, by his grace, *delivers* us from our sins, all for which (past, present, and future) Christ has already atoned. To be sure, salvation is not fully obtained at the moment of initial justification. Salvation comes in three stages: salvation from the *penalty* of sin (positional justification); salvation from the *power* of sin (practical sanctification); and salvation from the *presence* of sin (ultimate glorification). However, in none of these stages do *we* atone for our sins as a condition for entering heaven. Salvation is not something we "do" to obtain heaven. By Jesus' sacrificial death it is done![69]

Another attempt justifying the existence of purgatory comes from the documented experiences of the lives and legends of the saints in the Catholic Church. This is the premise used in the book, *Purgatory*, compiled by Catholic priest F.X. Schouppe.[70] The author amasses a litany of experiences, visions, and revelations from the saints and apparitions of the Virgin Mary, which are all collectively documented to produce, *a fortiori*, a compelling case for the existence of purgatory. They all recount how purgatory is allegedly a place of "excruciating suffering greater than any experienced on earth." Also those souls suffering in purgatory are periodically allowed out to visit the living on Earth to plead from the Catholic faithful in this life to say prayers, make sacrifices, and having Mass said by a priest, to reduce their time in purgatory. But, as even Scripture reveals, one's experience *alone* does not validate a claim being biblically true or not, nor does an experience determine whether it is a biblical doctrine revealed by God if the experience in any way should contradict or deny the revealed truths of Scripture (Deuteronomy 18:20-22; Isaiah 8:20; Galatians 1:8-9). That is because the Word of God defines and informs experience, not the other way around. Even the Apostle Peter placed greater value and authority on the Word of God than his own personal experience with Jesus Christ on the Mount of Transfiguration when saying Christians have a more "sure Word of prophecy which they do well to heed and observe" (see 1 Peter 1: 15-19).

The Apostle Paul disclaimed and invoked the condemnation of God on any actual angelic visitation from heaven or apostolic preaching if the supernatural experience or preaching from an angel or Apostle was in clear contradiction of the one true Gospel revealed in the inscripturated Word. He warned ***"But even if we*** (an Apostle or someone representing great authority in the church), ***or an angel from heaven, preach any other gospel to you than what we have preached to you, let him be anathema. As we have said before, so now I say again, if anyone*** (that includes alleged heavenly visions from Mary, the Saints, etc) ***preaches any other gospel to you than what you have received, let him be anathema"*** (Galatians 1:8-9). As we have amply demonstrated in the previous pages, the doctrine of the purgatory is a gross contradiction of the biblical Gospel, and any so called experiences used to corroborate it are under the curse and condemnation of God

---

[69]   Norman Geisler and Ralph MacKenzie, *Roman Catholics and Evangelicals*, 338.

[70]   F.X. Schouppe, S.J., *Purgatory Explained By the Lives and Legends of the Saints* (Charlotte: Tan Books, 1986).

because the Gospel of salvation by faith *alone*, given by God's grace *alone*, mediated and given by Christ *alone*, is displaced by bidding Catholics to look elsewhere other than Calvary *alone* for complete cleansing of sin. They are told, instead, to focus their attention on another place (purgatory) where the believer after death must suffer in fire to complete and obtain that salvation and cleansing from sin. When alleged or actual experience contradicts Scripture, we must hold to Scripture as the higher authority given by God to guide, inform, and lead us into truth amidst counterfeit claims, like purgatory, that would tempt a person to look and go elsewhere other than clinging to the cross of Christ alone for cleansing and salvation (Galatians 6:14).

The promise of salvation, with the complete forgiveness of all sins, is found in the sufferings and death of Jesus Christ alone crucified and raised from death. And this message is contained in the sufficiency of Scripture itself where it was written revealed, and made known to all who will read and believe it. For here, is the sufficiency of God's Word alone paramount and far superior above any other "revelation" outside from Scripture, church tradition, or visitation from the deceased, the Saints, or even Mary herself, especially if these experiences contradict the Gospel! "The sufficiency of Scripture is a foundational teaching of the true church that says all of our faith and practice is based solely on the Bible. *All that we believe, that we experience, that is legitimate, that is truth is found solely in the Word of God and in nothing and no one else*."[71] Purgatory simply lacks credible biblical support, and its existence would pose a threat to what Scripture has revealed on the subject of forgiveness, cleansing from all sins, and salvation in the Lord Jesus Christ. In light of this, it must, in the end, be thoroughly rejected on biblical grounds and no more.

Papal Indulgences.

Catholics are told by Rome, with the existence of Purgatory assumed, there are several ways to avoid purgatory, or at least reduce the time of punishment spent there by the acts of the Church and its faithful on Earth. The primary way has been given through the granting of indulgences allegedly given by Christ to the Church—dispensed, first and foremost, by the Papacy. The official Roman Catholic Handbook of Indulgences defines an indulgence in the following way:

> An indulgence is the remission in the eyes of God of the temporal punishment due to sins whose culpable element has already been taken away. The Christian faithful who are rightly disposed and observe the definite, prescribed conditions gain this remission through the effective assistance of the Church, which, as the minister of redemption, authoritatively distributes and applies the treasury of the expiatory works of Christ and the saints.[72]

Catholic priest John A. O'Brien gives another official definition of what an indulgence is with an extended explanation for what that entails in the Roman Catholic system of salvation:

> What is the real meaning of an indulgence? It is simply the remission of the *temporal punishment* due to sin after the sin itself has been forgiven. The one phrase in the above definition that may not be entirely clear to our non-Catholic reader is "temporal

---

[71] "Scripture Truth Verses Spiritual Experience" at http://thewordonthewordoffaithinfoblog.com/2009/03/03/scripture-truth-verses-spiritual-experience/

[72] *The Handbook of Indulgences: Norms and Grants*, (New York: Catholic Book Publishing Corp, 1991), 19. See also the *Catechism of the Catholic Church*, 432 **[1471]**.

punishment." To understand that, one must first understand that according to the Catholic Church every grievous sin has attached to it a twofold penalty—an eternal punishment which is suffered either in this world, or in purgatory, or partly both.

The guilt with its eternal punishment is always forgiven in a good confession. The temporal punishment may or may not be remitted in confession, depending upon the quality of contrition. If it is not forgiven, it may be remitted: (1) through the propitiatory efficacy of deeds of penance and virtue, and (2) through the gaining of indulgences attached by the Church to certain works of charity and piety.[73]

The word indulgence originally comes from the Latin word *indulgentia,* from *indulgeo,* (to be kind or tender); it originally meant kindness or favor. In post-classic Latin, it came to mean the remission of a tax or debt. In ancient Roman law, the term was used to express release from captivity or punishment. But in the Roman Catholic sense, in which it is here considered, an indulgence is a remission of the temporal punishment due to sin, the guilt of which has been forgiven. The Catholic can obtain an indulgence for himself in this life and for souls in purgatory, and through this indulgence, can reduce the temporal punishment due sin in this life and in the after life so less time is spent in purgatory and heaven can be gained more quickly[74]

There are two kinds of indulgences the Church offers—a Plenary indulgence and a Partial indulgence. A Plenary indulgence is a full remission of all the temporal punishment due to a person's sins so no further expiation in purgatory is required; whereas a Partial indulgence is a remission in part of the temporal punishment due one's sins. Only the Pope can grant a plenary indulgence along with any other indulgences. A priest, bishop, or other cleric can grant a partial indulgence if so empowered by the Pope.[75] The Pope supposedly derives his authority for the granting of indulgences from Jesus Christ as promised in Matthew 16:19 where the Lord gave Peter, and the other Apostles after him, the power of the keys to loose both the living here and the dead in purgatory from the temporary punishment of sins. And from this the Catholic Church believes:

> No limit is placed upon this power of loosing, "the power of the keys", as it is called; it must, therefore, extend to any and all bonds contracted by sin, including the penalty no less than the guilt. When the Church, therefore, by an indulgence, remits this penalty, her action, according to the declaration of Christ, is ratified in heaven (*The Catholic Encyclopedia.* Vol. 7. New York: Robert Appleton Company, 1910. 28 Sept. 2011 <http://www.newadvent. org/cathen/07783a.htm).

The Council of Trent haughtily condemns anyone who denies the Roman Catholic Church has the power conferred on it by Jesus Christ to actually grant and give indulgences, so either the punishment for temporal sins is partially or fully absolved in this life, and for the souls in purgatory:

---

[73]   John A. O'Brien, *The Faith of Millions,* 195-196.

[74]   Kent William. "Indulgences." *The Catholic Encyclopedia.* Vol. 7. New York: Robert Appleton Company, 1910. 27 Sept. 2011 http://www.newadvent.org/cathen/07783a.htm. The Catechism of the Catholic Church promises: "Through the indulgences the faithful can obtain the remission of temporal punishment resulting from sin for themselves and also for the souls in purgatory" (*Catechism of the Catholic Church,* page 374 **[1471]**.

[75]   "Indulgences." *The Catholic Encyclopedia.* Vol. 7.

> Since the power of granting indulgences was conferred by Christ on the Church, and she has even in the earliest times made use of that power divinely given to her, the holy council teaches and commands that the use of indulgences, most salutary to the Christian people and approved by the authority of the holy councils, is to be retained in the Church, and it condemns with anathema those who assert that they are useless or deny that there is in the church the power of granting them.[76]

To any who mistakenly believe Rome's dogmatic stance on indulgences and the arrogant, intransigent anathema attached to it, pronounced on those who deny them on biblical, moral, and historical grounds, has been rescinded will see it is also equally upheld and reaffirmed today in the 'modern' Catholic Church. Pope Paul VI issued an official decree in 1967 entitled *Indulgentiarum Doctrina* wherein he, officially speaking for the Catholic Church today, proclaims: "The Church anathematizes those who state that indulgences are useless or who deny the Church's power to grant them."[77] Only a baptized Roman Catholic in good standing with the Church (which entails being "free from all sin") can obtain an indulgence through the binding and loosing power of the Papacy and from the treasury of merit, which is under the supervision and administration of the Pope.

> An indulgence is obtained through the Church who, by virtue of the power of binding and loosing granted her by Christ Jesus, intervenes in favor of individual Christians and opens for them the treasury of merits of Christ and the Saints to obtain from the Father of mercies the remission of the temporal punishments due for their sins.[78]

The "treasury of merits" is what Rome believes to be a storehouse of merit accrued by Christ, the Virgin Mary, and all the Saints. These spiritual merits are made up of a combination of the "infinite merits of Christ", and the superabundant penances of the saints, who by offering to God a greater atonement than was required for the expiation of their own sins, were conceived of as creating a spiritual bank—a spiritual fund of satisfaction which the Church dispenses when she wills, and which she applies to those offenders who seem specially to deserve her favor."[79] Indeed Mary, the mother of Jesus, and the canonized "Saints" of the 'Church' play a indispensable role in granting expiatory merit *via* indulgences to the prospective Catholic by their collective superabundant satisfaction in their suffering and the "crosses" they bore. Asking the question of what is the "superabundant satisfaction of Mary and the Saints, Rome's official answer disturbingly add them as a co-redemptive element to the singular, redemptive sufferings of Christ when answering:

The superabundant satisfaction of the Blessed Virgin Mary and of the saints is that which they gained during their lifetime but did not need them on earth, which now the Church applies to their fellow members of the communion of saints. Mingled with the Precious Blood of Christ in the treasury of the Church are the sorrows of Mary and the suffering of the Saints as they bore their crosses after Christ.[80] The Baltimore

---

[76]   H.J. Schroeder, *The Canons and Decrees of the Council of Trent*, 253.

[77]   *The Handbook of Indulgences: Norms and Grants*, 113-114.

[78]   *Catechism of the Catholic Church*, 413 **[1478]**.

[79]   Fr. Charles M. Carty and Dr. L. Rumble, *Indulgence Quizzes To a Street Preacher* (Rockford, IL: Tan Books, 1976), 3.

[80]   *The New Saint Joseph Baltimore Catechism*, 207. The *Catechism of the Catholic Church* states the treasury of the Church includes "the prayers and good works of the Blessed Virgin Mary (which are "truly immense",

Catechism goes on to state in the same paragraph fellow Catholics "can draw on this treasury" and can "contribute" to it and help those who need an indulgence to further reduce the time spent in purgatory.

These collective good works, consisting in the sufferings and good deeds of Mary, the Saints, and Catholics deemed in good standing with Holy Mother Church, have been termed by Catholic theologians as the *supererogation* of the saints. Basically, the supererogation of the Saints works in tandem with the treasury of the Church wherein it is possible for the saints to accumulate an excess of good works, which they no longer need, but can be transferred or credited to the souls in purgatory who must still suffer and pay for the temporal punishment due their venial sins. How one goes about obtaining a *partial* indulgence for oneself, or a soul in purgatory, is achieved, according to Rome, by performing certain religious acts like devotedly using crucifixes, crosses, rosaries, scapulars, medals blessed by a Pope or bishop, pilgrimages to a holy site, visitation to certain churches, acts of abstinence, attending Mass, saying prayers, and partaking in the sacrament of penance.[81]

A plenary indulgence is earned or obtained by doing four things: (1) the exclusion of all attachment to sin, even venial sin; (2) Sacramental confession; (3) Eucharistic communion; and (4) Prayer for the Pope's intentions.[82] An excess of merits or works Mary and the Saints do not need is then placed into the treasury of the Church to be withdrawn for those in need of its benefits both for the living and the dead still confined in purgatory. The object of acquiring these merits, via the conferral of an indulgence, will serve to reduce the time and amount one has to spend in purgatory for the temporal punishment of venial sins. Shockingly, the Pope, along with the official position of the Catholic Church, believes the expiatory merits of the atonement of Jesus Christ are *mixed* and are *added* by the good works and prayers of Mary and all the saints. When these are credited from the treasury of the Church to the Catholic faithful, who fulfill the requirements for the acquisition of an indulgence, "they have also contributed to the salvation of their brothers and sisters in the unity of the Mystical Body." The treasury of the Church is thus a combination of the infinite merits of Christ mixed with the good works and prayers of Mary and the Catholic saints down through the ages. Pope Paul VI, supposedly speaking on behalf of Jesus Christ and the Catholic Church, has formally declared:

> The treasury of the Church is Christ the Redeemer himself: in him the atonement and merit
> of his redemption exist and are at work. Added to this treasure is also the vast, incalculable,
> ever increasing value in God's eyes of the prayers and good works of the Blessed Virgin
> Mary and all the saints. As they followed Christ through the power of His grace, they
> became holy and they have accomplished a work pleasing to the Father. As a result, in

---

"unfathomable" and "pristine"!), the prayers and good works of all the saints, and all those who have followed in the footsteps of Christ" who by their holy lives cooperated in saving their brothers from the confines of purgatory (page 412 **[1477]**)! Of course, in their typical semantic double talk, Rome is quick to add here that all these meritorious works offered for the souls in purgatory supposedly originate from the infinite merits of Christ (*Catechism of the Catholic Church*, page 412 **[1476]**). Strange, whenever the New Testament speaks of the redemptive merits of Jesus Christ needed alone to save the sinful soul, nothing else whatsoever, whether from Mary or the Saints, is added and specifically mentioned in Scripture as a necessary corollary or supplement for expiatiation and payment for sin. That is because the New Testament teaching on salvation, and full expiation from sin, rests squarely on the death of Jesus Christ alone—thus anything added to that, by way of the "treasury of the Church" or "supererogation" of the saints, would be an utter nullification of the biblical truth salvation and the full pardon of sins, which come with it, is done *solo Christo*—by Jesus Christ alone, and no other!

81 *The Handbook of Indulgences: Norms and Grants*, 23.

82 Ibid., 22.

working out their own salvation they have also contributed to the salvation of their brothers and sisters in the unity of the Mystical Body.[83]

This salvation, with the assistance of the benefits of indulgences from the treasury of the Church, is furthered along by human participation from the faithful following in Christ's footsteps by prayer, spiritual kindness, and penitential expiation with the effort of "*bearing their own cross in atonement for their own sins and the sins of others* and with the conviction that in the eyes of the Father of mercies *they could be of service to the salvation of their brothers and sisters*" (Emphasis mine).[84] And it was by Jesus Christ, Himself, Rome claims, who gained this treasury of indulgences and thereby "entrusted this treasury" to be in the control, and safe keeping of the Popes, deemed to be "the Successors of Saint Peter, and the Vicars of Christ on earth." The granting of these indulgences for total or partial remission of the temporal punishment due to sin is under the authority and discretion of what the Popes decide to be best.[85] So these merits or indulgences can be drawn out from the treasury Christ gained and then passed on to Peter and the Popes who distribute these to the faithful of the Roman Catholic Church. This official papal doctrine was formulated by Pope Clement VI in his Jubilee Bull *Unigenitus Dei Filius*:

> For the only-begotten Son of God ... gained a treasury to be dispensed for the well being of the faithful through St. Peter, the bearer of the keys of heaven, and his successors, Christ's vicars on earth. This treasury is to be applied with mercy to those who are repentant and have confessed, on the basis of proper and reasonable causes, in some cases for punishment due to sin. The application may be either universal or for a particular case (according to what, in the Lord the Popes decide to be best). The merits of the blessed Mother of God and all the saints...are recognized as supplementing these riches of the treasury of the Church.[86]

These indulgences reside under the authority of the Roman Catholic hierarchy and are dispensed to those who wish to reduce the amount of temporal punishment for sin spent in the confined and punishing fires of purgatory. To receive such a cherished merit, the Catholic must remain *submissive* and *dependent* upon the clerical hierarchy of the church and the papacy entrusted with the keeping and distribution of these indulgences.

> Nor must we omit that in gaining an indulgence the faithful submit themselves with docility to the lawful pastors in the Church, above all to the successor of St. Peter, the bearer of the keys of heaven. Christ himself has commanded these pastors to feed and shepherd his Church.[87]

Assuming the Bible is the inerrant and infallible Word of God, and is the final and supreme authority in matters of Christian doctrine and living, the question here must be asked: Is the concept of papal indulgences found, authorized, endorsed and practiced in the Word of God? Again, with so much of Roman Catholic

---

[83] Pope Paul VI, *Indulgentiarum Doctrina* in *The Handbook of Indulgences: Norms and Grants*, 100.

[84] Ibid., 106.

[85] Ibid., 111.

[86] Ibid., 110-111.

[87] Ibid., 115.

doctrine, the answer is a clear, resounding unequivocal no! This is true primarily because Rome derives the idea of indulgences from tradition instead of Scripture alone. The main reason for this is largely because Rome sees their tradition as equally authoritative and valid with Scripture. Their tradition is thus an equal companion and extension of divine revelation. The Catholic believes this is so; and so Scripture must agree then with Roman Catholic tradition and no contradiction will exist between the two because God is the source and origin for both. But the plain and frank reading of Scripture will obviously show the whole idea of indulgences to be not only unscriptural, but also, in direct contradiction to the Word of God and ranks as one of the greatest blasphemies contrived by the papal system!

Matthew 16:19 is certainly not a proof text or endorsement for the distribution of papal indulgences. We looked at this verse earlier in the context of the papacy and how it in now way supports this religious autocracy. The meaning, again, seen in the binding and loosing, is the power of the evangelist and church disciplinarian in the role of pastor in the local Church. This same power of binding and loosing was given to the rest of the disciples by the Lord Jesus in Matthew 18:18. For Peter, the keys of the kingdom of heaven consist in an evangelical authority given to him to open the door of salvation to the Jews on the day of Pentecost, when the Gospel was preached and the Jewish audience in Jerusalem and from the Diaspora were afforded the opportunity to accept the Gospel and become heir and citizens of God's kingdom. The same opportunity was given to the Gentiles when Peter also used this key of evangelism to open the doors of salvation to Cornelius the Roman centurion. Peter preached the Gospel to them and they responded by believing in the Lord Jesus Christ for salvation and entrance into His kingdom (see Acts 10). The keys, as they refer to Peter, the rest of the disciples, and the universal church, are nowhere said in Scripture to mean or to extend into the after life enabling them to grant the power of remission of the temporal punishment for venial sins.

Peter, first, alone received the keys, and now once the door has been opened, it remains open by the preaching of the Gospel until the end of the present age when Christ returns.

Those people who believe the Gospel, now, have their sins loosed from them and are forgiven; but those people who reject it with unbelief have their sins bound to them for condemnation and the day of judgment. This is the jurisdictional boundaries and limits of those keys when they are used for evangelical purposes and for discipline within the church. Whenever a decision is made, involving discipline in the church is decreed, permitted, and decided upon, this same decision has already been released (loosed) by heaven; and whatever decision is upheld and not permitted within the church, has already been bound in heaven. The use of the keys for the administrative acts of loosing and binding is given to all Christians in the church and is validly ratified where two or three believers come together in the name and authority of Jesus Christ. There is no mention in Matthew 16:19 and 18:18 of Popes and the clerical hierarchy under him arrogantly and presumptuously exercising power over the souls in the afterlife to be released from purgatory upon their granting of an indulgence and the works performed for its efficacy to reduce or commute one's sentence and time spent in a non-existent purgatory! That much is obvious to any honest and competent Bible exegete! Simply stated, the keys of binding and loosing found in Matthew 16:19 and 18:18 were first used by Peter and now the rest of the church "for declaring the terms under which sins are forgiven, or how a person is to be excluded from the fellowship of the local church."

In other words, the disciples as a whole have a responsibility for declaring the terms under which sins are forgiven or how a person is to be excluded from the fellowship of the local church. As parallel statements, these sayings of Jesus are the basis for entrance into or banishment from the kingdom (16:19) and the local church (18:18). Both sayings relate to forgiveness of sins…The periphrastic future tense indicates that what Peter and the disciples do in this present age has already been determined by God. The church is the instrument of God, who alone can grant forgiveness of sin or consign a person to judgment. The passive voice of "will have been bound" and " will have been loosed" and the phrase "in heaven" are Semitic circumlocutions for describing God's actions.[88]

The plain words of Matthew 16:19 in no possible way support the wild interpretation Christ is bestowing upon Peter and his successors, the Popes, the power of conferring indulgences to free souls both here and in the after life from time spent in purgatory. The acts of loosing and binding do not consist in the papal impartation of indulgences but, as biblically defined, consist in the remission or retention of sins correspondingly based on whether a person believes in the Gospel or not for the forgiveness of sins. Once a person believes in Christ for salvation and remission of sins, those sins cannot be retained ever again. When Jesus Christ forgave all our trespasses and sins (Colossians 2:13), and redeemed us from the curse of the Law (Galatians 3:13), it was done now and for all eternity. But with the Pope's treasury of indulgences, the complete remission of sins is only partial, seeing the Catholic must obtain them to achieve complete pardon and purification from venial sin in purgatory—leaving the sinner himself to pay for what Christ already has fully paid when He died on the cross. The only person in the universe, who has the keys of dominion exercising complete and absolute power over the realm of the dead, whose souls now reside in heaven or hell, is Jesus Christ alone. He reassured the Apostle John on the island of Patmos, *"I am He who lives, and was dead, and behold, I am alive forevermore, Amen. And I have the keys of Hades and of death"* (Revelation 1:18).

These keys are qualitatively different from the ones our Lord gave Peter first, and then to the rest of the New Testament Church. The keys of death and the afterlife were gained by the resurrection of Jesus Christ wherein He destroyed him that had the power of death—that is, the devil (Hebrews 2:14-15). We, who now commit ourselves in faith to the only Person who has power and authority over death, and power, also over who goes to heaven or hell (Luke 12:5), no longer have fear of what waits us after death. This is because Christ alone has used the keys of His death and resurrection to open the doors of heaven to all those who believe. The authority to conquer death, and liberate the souls under its power, reside with Jesus Christ alone and have not been conferred to any other mortal—let alone the blasphemous Popes of Rome fraudulently claiming to be the exclusive Vicars of Christ on Earth. This is made obvious by the fact the Popes are mere mortals and do not have the power of resurrection life to conquer death as Christ has. And thus in light of the great truth of Revelation 1:18:

The statement that He has the keys of hell and of death implies that He is sovereign over physical death which terminates life in this world as well as over hell (Gr., *hades*), the life after death. The Greek word *hades* commonly translated "hell" refers to the intermediate state and is to be distinguished from the lake of fire or Gehenna, which refers to the eternal state. To avoid confusion it is better to transliterate the word *hades* and to use the word *hell* as referring to the eternal state only. The confusion is in the translation. Not the original.

---

[88] Michael Wilkins, *The NIV Application Commentary: Matthew*, 620.

In His death and resurrection, Christ wrested from Satan any authority the devil may have had over death (cf. Heb. 2:14-15). In some texts the order is reversed to read, "and have the keys of death and hell." As Christ possesses the key or authority over death, no man can die apart from divine permission even though afflicted by Satan and in trial and trouble. As the One who is in authority over Hades, Christ is sovereign over the life to come.[89]

When the glorified and risen Jesus appeared before John and made this great statement of reality, then, would have been the most opportune time to tell this Apostle the Lord had conferred these keys to Peter and his papal successors—who could then exercise authority over the dead in the after life, and thereby bring their souls out of purgatory with the keys of death and hell handed to the Popes of Rome by Jesus. The reason for this expected silence here, and throughout Scripture, is no such thing occurred or exists today because Jesus alone has power over death, the dead, and reserves the right alone to exercise His power over both. When the soul dies in belief, the believer is immediately escorted to heaven (John 14:1-6; 2 Corinthians 5:8; Hebrews 12:22); and when the unbeliever dies he is immediately consigned to hell to wait for judgment at the Great White Throne when the second resurrection commences after the millennial reign of Christ is completed (Revelation 20:12-15). Nor were indulgences offered to the rich man in Hades in the true account of Luke 16:19-31. When Abraham, speaking on behalf of God, told the rich man how his brothers living still on Earth, could avoid his damnable fate, he did not inform the rich man he or they, for that matter, could obtain indulgences from the church in the future given by Christ based on the merits of Mary and the Saints. The reason for this is the rich man was not in purgatory to begin with, but *in the flames of hell*, and secondly, he was further told by Abraham the brothers already had the authority, revelation, and truths of Scripture summed up in *"Moses and the Prophets"* to give them ample warning and remedy to avoid winding up in the fires of hell in the afterlife (Luke 16:31).

To believe in indulgences, with the idea the forgiven sinner must still pay, or have another pay for the temporal punishment due his sins, is a practical admission the expiation, satisfaction, and remission paid for on the cross is simply a half measure, not complete in itself to totally make payment for our sins with the ransom price of Christ's shed blood. For if Christ's death is not enough itself to remit the whole debt of sin and atone for it in full, then God in His word becomes a blatant liar when the Lord says once He has forgiven our sins, He will remember them no more for the sake of the atoning Christ. Once the sinner accepts the full payment of sin and the punishment Christ bore and paid for them on the cross, God then fully remits them and chooses not to remember these sins anymore. He will never recall them for punishment in any sense—temporal or eternal. *"For I will be merciful to their unrighteousness, and their sins and their lawless deeds I will remember no more"* (Hebrews 8:12). Because Christ paid the punishment for all our sins, such imaginary need for indulgences, the treasury of merit from Mary, or the saints is completely unnecessary—for the crucified and risen Jesus Christ has already paid a complete and perfect ransom in full. If we say indulgences are necessary in this regard, then we are saying, in effect, Christ 's death is not sufficient, *in and of itself,* to remove all punishment due our sins for all time.

The whole absurd idea of indulgences needed to get out of purgatory with a reduction in suffering is removed by the simple biblical truth Jesus Christ took upon Himself the guilt and punishment of each and every sin for every sinner who turns in repentance and faith to Him. For *"the Lord has laid on Him the iniquity of us all,"* Isaiah 53:6 tells us. When Paul defines the Gospel as *"Christ died for our sins according*

---

[89]   John F. Walvoord, *The Revelation of Jesus Christ* (Chicago: Moody Press, 1966), 47.

to the Scriptures" in 1 Corinthians 15:3, the Apostle does not mean sins, which are only applicable to this life up to this point in time. Nay, Christ's death for us is an all encompassing work washing away all sins—past, present, and future—for His is an infinite sacrifice that cleanses from all sin eternally, so there is no need for another finite and flawed sinner, whether it be yourself or another, to offer payment or merit of any kind. But instead of accepting the comforting truth of Scripture on this wonderful point, Rome's priests, theologians and apologists would have the unsuspecting parishioner left unsure and without assurance that his sins are fully and finally forgiven. The uncertain Catholic is left depending upon Rome's vacuous sacraments and blasphemous indulgences, even though there is no remaining punishment left for the born-again Bible believer because Jesus Christ fully met and satisfied the wrath of God for them with His propitiatory death on the cross. Any and every sin are washed and removed from the trusting soul in the crucified Christ. The simple teaching of Scripture on this matter is not enough for Rome, who seeks to traffic and prosper in the abominable man-made fabrication of indulgences and atonement through "personal suffering" or the "spiritual merits" of another. The words of rebuke from a cogent web site discussion on this matter merits citing here, especially when the Catholic Church insists we can pay and expiate for our own sins through the acquisition of a plenary or temporal indulgence:

> Any future sins we commit post-conversion that we may forget to confess, are swallowed up in the cross-work of Christ. Thus imperfect, forgiven sinners enter eternity under the auspices of Christ's merits alone and have no need whatsoever to stop and get a car wash before driving on the glory to heaven...As usual, the straight forward statements from the Giver of life are simply never enough to satisfy the Catholic—who would prefer to spend their entire life speculating about things we are told nothing about in an effort to uphold their vain traditions (Colossians 2:8; 1 Peter 1:18). Examples like these prove the Scriptures are really of no interest to the Catholic since they simply don't believe God has the ability to say what He means and means what He says! What Catholics have done is eclipsed the word of God and set their tradition OVER it, forever fighting against the text with their never ending distinctions, caveats, exceptions and qualifications.[90]

The Scripture does not in all of its pages teach, indicate, or even vaguely claim there is a treasury of merit or some supererogation of Mary and the Saints being an extension of the perfect merits of Jesus Christ. The Gospel residing within every born-again Christian, with whom each believer is given and lives in, is alone the divine treasure, the beginning and end of God's saving grace. The treasury of Christ's perfect merit for our salvation is in the Gospel and does not exceed beyond it to anyone or anything else. *"But we have this treasure in earthen vessels, that the excellence of the power may be of God and not of us"* (2 Corinthians 4:7). To say there is some extra treasury of merit somewhere out there, like Rome would have its undiscerning people believe, is a satanic twisting of the Gospel of grace. It is to say, in effect, the perfect payment of Christ's cross for our sins is not enough and therefore must be combined and added with the supererogation of Mary and the Saints with the spiritual benefit of indulgences granted by the Pope and the Church.

Belief in papal indulgences is to practically admit the sufferings and death of Christ were incomplete and insufficient in making a complete expiation and payment for the punishment due the sinner. To then believe the moral merits of others, and punishment and suffering voluntarily experienced now or in purgatory, can

---

[90] The Enigma of Indulgences in Catholic/Ecumenical Discussion Form at http://catholicdiscussion.yku.com/topic/511#.To4tAXK4toN, page 2 of 16.

be ameliorated with the acquirement of indulgences for the personal remission of the punishment of our sins, is nothing less than a debasement and rank repudiation of Christ and His singular atonement for the complete expiation of sins. It is both a replacement and dilution of the one true Gospel for a counterfeit Jesus and "another gospel" (2 Corinthians 11:4). The Catholic teaching on the necessity of indulgences once again is a disturbing and sad reflection of the fact they fail to correctly understand the biblical Gospel as given and proclaimed from Holy Scripture!

To assert we can be purified through the meritorious sufferings of others, or by the obtainment of papal indulgences, in order to attain salvation, is the proclamation of a false gospel and no more! Rome cannot give its faithful members a straight answer on just how much suffering is required and how many indulgences, besides a plenary indulgence, are needed to get out of purgatory. It is because the Catholic Church doesn't even know, and cannot, therefore, give any Catholic hope or assurance of heaven in this life or in the life to come, even though Scripture promises eternal life the moment a person believes the Gospel of salvation and is welcomed into heaven immediately after death (John 3:16; 14:1-6; 1 John 5:11-12; 2 Corinthians 5:4-8; Hebrews 12:22-24). In light of this glorious Gospel truth:

> The very idea that good works need to be performed to gain an indulgence for the removal of the time being punished in purgatory, is blatantly unbiblical and illogical, for it supposes that these things accomplish what Christ's death could not. *But the gospel is that Christ was crucified. He suffered the punishment that we deserved, so that we wouldn't have to!* Then, to further assert that the excess merits of Christ AND the saints are **applied** to the indulgence seeker—by doing of these good works and/or offerings, borders on the brink of religious insanity…On top of all this, the RCC does not really know how much credit is granted for each indulgence, so it becomes a never-ending hamster wheel of sacramental absurdity. The Catholic never passes "from death unto life" as Christ promised (Jn 5:24), but is always in the process of running on the treadmill *"merit grace"* (a complete contradiction in terms) and with the expectancy of finishing the "purging" process in a place where the coals are hot. Catholics are taught not to reason these things out, but to simply accept what the church says. This is what happens when the Scriptures are swept under the rug, ignoring the word of the Lord to, *"not go above that which is written."* (1 Cor 4:6).[91]

The one obvious verse from the infallible Word of God shattering the Catholic belief we can contribute to the removal, expiation, and redemption of each others sins by any means (whether it is financial, moral, or spiritual) is Psalm 49:7-8*: "No man can by any means redeem his brother, nor give to God a ransom for him. For the redemption of their soul is costly, and it shall cease forever—that he should continue to live eternally and not see the pit."* Notice what God's Word says here—no one can redeem his neighbor **by any means**; that would include everything and everyone, and such a universal negation means man cannot save himself no matter what aid or means he seeks to use. Salvation is beyond our scope and ability. *"Who then can be saved? For with man this is impossible, but with God all things are possible"* (Matthew 19:25-26). The sobering truth of Psalm 49:7-8 would then automatically exclude the meritorious acts of Mary, the Saints and the use of indulgences since no one "by any means" can contribute or bring redemption to himself or another person. Christ did it *alone* and does not extend His saving grace to the church, the papacy or

---

91   Ibid., page 9 of 16.

anyone else, in terms of the salvation of the sinner, when He accomplished our salvation and purchased our redemption *alone* by His death on the Cross.

Man is utterly incapable and morally unqualified to contribute anything in the redemptive process now or after death, as the idea of papal indulgences would presuppose, simply because none of us are morally perfect through and through to redeem each other, nor do we possess the divine power and nature to accomplish this as Jesus Christ the God-Man did. We are all sinners, and therefore unfit to help in the salvation of another because all have sinned and continue to fall short of God's glorious standard of moral perfection (Romans 3:23). None of us possess the power or qualifications to rescue the sinner from going into the pit of hell, let alone the non-existent, temporary prison of purgatory! Only Jesus Christ, as both God and man, can do this because "He was the Son of God, His life was of infinite value and able to redeem all mankind. Having been made "in the likeness of men" (Philippians 2:7), He was capable of both representing humanity before God and physically dying (Hebrews 2:14-17). Since He was without sin, His life was an acceptable sacrifice (1 Peter 1:19; 2:22). Christ *alone,* therefore, deserves the title of Redeemer. "Worthy is the Lamb that was slain" (Revelation 5:12).[92]

Of course Catholic theologians, unfazed by these obvious biblical truths, are ready to point out the words of Paul in Colossians 1:24 to teach the Catholic faithful on Earth can, indeed, by their good works, meritorious sufferings and the obtainment of indulgences, provide expiation and atonement for the punishment of temporal sins for themselves and of those souls currently in purgatory. *"I now rejoice in my sufferings for you, and fill up in my flesh what is lacking in the afflictions of Christ, for the sake of the His body, which is the church."* Carrying the analogy of the church as the body of Christ too far, Catholic theologian Ludwig Ott, takes the Pauline phrase "what is lacking in the afflictions of Christ" and assumes it means, that, since we are the body of Christ, with He as the head, we too must suffer with Him *to fill up what is lacking in the atonement of Jesus.* Hence the need for papal indulgences:

> The effect of the atonement is the remission of temporal punishment for sin. The possibility of vicarious atonement is founded in the unity of the Mystical Body. As Christ, the Head, in His expiatory sufferings, took the place of the members, so also one member can take the place of another. The doctrine of indulgences is based on the possibility and reality of vicarious atonement...The Apostle St. Paul teaches that also the faithful can rend expiation for one another. Col 1, 24: "Who now rejoice in my suffering for you and fill up those things that are wanting of the sufferings of Christ in my flesh for His body, which is the Church."[93]

Cardinal Thomas Cajetan, an avowed arch nemesis to Reformer Martin Luther, in their dispute on the biblical and theological legitimacy for the use of papal indulgences, quoted Colossians 1:24 to justify the issuance and efficacy of them, when granted by the Popes of Rome, stating in effect:

> That it was the intention of the saints to suffer for us, the Apostle testifies when he says, I fill up those things which are wanting of the sufferings of Christ for his body which is the church. Whence it appears clearly, that the divine Providence had ordained some sufferings

---

[92] See James G. McCarthy at http://www.acts1711.com/coredeem.htm.
[93] Ludwig Ott, *Fundamentals of Catholic Dogma,* 317.

of the saints should have respect to the completion of the sufferings of Christ, for his body; and that the saints did complete this ordinance by the superabundance of their sufferings.[94]

Once again, the context in which Paul wrote Colossians 1:24 concerning his physical sufferings do not mean, in any way, the atoning sufferings of Christ for our redemption are insufficient insofar that they need to be completed or supplemented by the suffering of the saints in the Church, starting with Paul himself! Paul speaks of sufferings as a minister of the Gospel and servant of Jesus Christ in service to Him (Colossians 1:25), not someone who, by those sufferings, adds redemptive merit to what is lacking in the redemptive sufferings of Christ. If Paul were teaching this, he would have immediately contradicted Himself and the Scripture when the Apostle says right before this Christ alone is sufficient to reconcile us to God in whose shed blood we have redemption and forgiveness of sins *in actu in aeternum* (Colossians 1: 14, 19-21)! A close look at the meaning of Colossians 1:24 completely undermines and disproves the Roman Catholic teaching, which believes the suffering of the faithful, with the acquirement of indulgences added to the sufferings of Christ, are needed to remain saved and provide complete payment to satisfy the justice of God.

The word in New Testament Greek for "afflictions", from the phrase ***"what is lacking in the afflictions of Christ"*** in Colossians 1:24, is *thlipis* (θλιφις). The word literally means: to pressure, to be pressed together, or to be pressed upon; it is used forty six times in the New Testament. And in all these instances, it is not once used for the physical and redemptive sufferings of Christ *on* the cross but only used for His sufferings *before* the cross! A few citations from New Testament Scriptures will suffice to underscore this very important point. In Hebrews 2:10, we read: —***"For it was fitting for Him, for whom are all, things and by whom are all things, in bringing many sons to glory, to make the Captain of their salvation perfect through sufferings"*** (i.e., the preeminent sufferings He endured enables Him to be the leader in salvation). Hebrews 5:7-10—***"Who, in the days of His flesh, when He had offered up prayers and supplications, with vehement cries and tears to Him who able to save Him from death, and was heard because of His godly fear, though He was a Son, yet He learned obedience by the things which He suffered. And having been made perfect (He is proven to be qualified by these perfect, divine sufferings), He became the Author of eternal salvation"***

In these two passages from the New Testament book of Hebrews, we see Jesus Christ proved to be exclusively qualified to give us salvation, by the fact as the sinless Son of God, He endured our imputed sins and sufferings upon Himself without committing one single sin Himself or acting out of vengeful retaliation in thought, word, or deed. The insults, physical beatings, threats, and various abuses the Savior was unjustly exposed to constituted His bodily afflictions while He was on Earth. Now that He is raised from the dead and glorified sitting at the right hand of the Father, Jesus no longer undergoes any physical afflictions for His ministry and mission carried out in obedience to the Father. Today, those sufferings are no longer physically experienced by Jesus in the body and so what is lacking in that respect is filled up by Christians who do suffer for the sake of their faith in Christ when facing persecution, insults, and spiritual tribulations for His name's sake. And this is a second way *thlipis* is used in the New Testament—to describe the suffering and persecution the Christian goes through when preaching and living for Christ. Not one of these passages suggests or teaches the Roman Catholic idea that our suffering, or being persecuted for Jesus Christ, helps or aids in our salvation, nor do these sufferings or afflictions add to the perfect sufferings of Christ for the completion of the sinner's redemption!

---

[94] John Davenant, *Colossians*, 276.

Some selected quotes from the New Testament given below will suffice to prove this point: Acts 11:19— *"Now those who were scattered after the persecution that arose over Stephen traveled as far as Phoenicia, Cyprus, and Antioch, preaching the word to no one but the Jews only."* Romans 8:35—*"Who shall separate us from love of Christ? Shall tribulation, or distress or persecution, or famine, or nakedness, or peril, or sword?"* The anticipated answer to this question is given by Paul in verse 39—none of these sufferings, hardships, and afflictions endured for Jesus Christ will be able separate us from His love, power, or divine person. The salient point here Paul makes is Christ saves us in spite of them, not because of them. This would be especially true even if the papal indulgences of meritorious suffering were granted! Ah, but where the word "afflicted" is used again would seem to support Rome's claim as found in 2 Corinthians 1:6 where Paul seems to be saying his afflictions were for the "salvation" of the Christians at Corinth when writing:

"Now if we are afflicted, it is for your consolation and salvation, which is effective for enduring the same sufferings which we also suffer. Or if we are comforted, it is for your consolation and salvation"

Does Paul in 2 Corinthians 1:6 mean, as Rome mendaciously postulates, the sufferings of Christians can be added to the sufferings of Christ on the cross in a collaborative effort to finish your salvation? Paul did not mean this, but the circumstances wherein he was afflicted for preaching the Gospel allowed the Corinthians to believe in this Gospel proclaimed for their salvation. What the Apostle means to say in 2 Corinthians 1:6 is his afflictions came from preaching the Gospel by those who opposed it—this very same Gospel the Corinthians believed for their salvation as publicly preached from the afflicted Paul. The afflictions of Paul mentioned 2 Corinthians 1:6 came from his proclaiming the Gospel by which the Corinthians believed and were saved—so in this way Paul's afflictions in this matter helped bring that Gospel of salvation to them![95] So with this meaning here, Paul is not teaching his sufferings for the Corinthians, or anyone else, has brought or achieved salvation, nor is he claiming through cooperation with the Savior he, or anyone else, helps the Lord Jesus Christ complete this salvation.

Undoubtedly, Paul would have quickly and loudly eschewed such a heretical idea, especially when he repeatedly affirmed in his writings the sterling Gospel truth that it was by Christ's sufferings and death alone the sinner has salvation (Romans 5:12-21; 1 Corinthians 15:1-4; 2 Corinthians 5:17-21; Galatians 3:13-14; Titus 2:13-14). Again, wherever *thlipis* is found and used in the New Testament for what Christians experience for living and serving Jesus Christ, it is never used, once, in the way the Roman Catholic Church teaches when proposing Christians can suffer for other Christians and add these sufferings for what is lacking in the sufferings of Christ to complete the believer's salvation. It is used either to denote suffering in general, or the sufferings and persecutions the godly believer endures for living and serving Jesus Christ in a wicked, God hating world.[96]

---

[95] Bible commentator David Garland's insight sums this meaning up well when commenting on the enigmatic saying of Paul's afflictions somehow affecting Corinthian salvation: "We might ask, however, how does his suffering affect their salvation? If Paul had chosen to shrink from the dangers he faced and to retreat unscathed to safer places, many in the Gentile world would not have heard the saving word of the gospel. As Christ endured suffering to bring salvation to the world, Paul endured it to bring the message of salvation to the world" (David Garland, *New American Commentary: 2 Corinthians*), 67.

[96] Moulton and Geden's *Concordance to the Greek Testament* (pages 460-461), lists every New Testament entry where affliction (θλιφις) is used with both meanings; and not once is the word indicative of a meritorious suffering of one Christian for another joined with the suffering of Christ to bring about salvation here or in purgatory!

What Paul thus meant in Colossians 1:24 is not that the sufferings of Christ were lacking in terms of not being enough for salvation, but His daily sufferings in His body that were inflicted upon Him during His three year ministry on Earth were limited and ended at the cross; and those physical sufferings continue now in His mystical body of the Church as they carry out the Great Commission to go into all the world and preach the Gospel and disciple those who believe in it. So the ministry sufferings of Jesus Christ continue on in His body, the Church, as they suffer for His sake in living for Him and preaching the Gospel in a hostile world who oppose and rebel against the Lord Jesus Christ and spitefully mistreat His followers.

Paul saw himself filling up and continuing the sufferings of Christ in a *ministerial* way all throughout his ministry service to the Lord; and in no way viewed these sufferings in a *redemptive sense* adding or completing the work of salvation Christ had already completed at the cross (Philippians 3:10; 2 Timothy 3:12). The following observation made by Bible expositor John MacArthur best sums up the real meaning of Colossians 1:24 and why it cannot possibly mean what the Roman Catholic Church says it must mean:

> Roman Catholics have imagined here a reference to the suffering of Christians in purgatory. Christ's suffering, they maintain was not enough to purge us completely from our sins. Christians must make up what was lacking in Christ's suffering on their behalf by their own suffering after death. That can hardly be Paul's point, however. He has just finished demonstrating that Christ alone is sufficient to reconcile us to God (Colossians 1: 20-23). To do an about face now and teach that believers must help pay for their sins would undermine his whole argument. The New Testament is clear that Christ's sufferings need nothing added to them. In Jesus' death on the cross, the work of salvation was completed. Further, the Colossian heretics taught that human works were necessary for salvation. To teach that believer's sufferings was necessary to help expiate their sins would be to play right into the errorists' hands. The idea that Paul refers to suffering in purgatory is ruled out by both the general content of the epistle and the immediate context, as well the obvious absence of any mention of a place like purgatory in Scripture. Finally, *thlipsis* (**afflictions**) is used nowhere in the New Testament to speak of Christ's sufferings.[97]

Paul bore many afflictions and sufferings for Christ's Church, which Jesus left His followers to fulfill after His ascension for the edification, encouragement, and strengthening of the Church, showing by way of example how to face persecution for The Lord Jesus as a Christian follower. This is the real meaning behind what the Apostle writes in Colossians 1:24. Rome is therefore guilty here of the fallacy of *affirming the consequent* when the Pope affirms indulgences have the power to grant full or partial remission of the temporal punishment due sin to complete what was lacking in the sufferings of Christ, which they apparently believe about Colossians 1:24, because this is what Paul must have automatically meant and taught when penning this verse. Rome assumes that what was lacking in the sufferings of Christ must only mean His redemptive sufferings without proving this to be the case, while at the same time the universal truth of Scripture teaches it was by Christ's *complete* sufferings *alone* on the cross that salvation and the punishment due our sins was met and paid in full!

This fact alone should have told the Papists Colossians 1:24 does not support an aberrant view of salvation antithetical to the New Testament. One last observation before we move on: Anglican Bishop John Davenant

---

[97]   John MacArthur, *Colossians & Philemon* (Chicago: Moody Press, 1992), 75-76.

in his massive commentary on the book of Colossians is keen to point this very thing out in his extensive critique of Rome's misinterpretation of Colossians 1:24; even going so far as to quote Medieval Roman Catholic theologian Anslem of Canterbury for corroboration of this view within the Catholic Church itself:

> In answer to all this; I admit that the faithful do experience much chastisement at the hand of God, after he has forgiven their guilt; but I deny that the intention of these chastisements is to satisfy divine justice. Although God absolves all true penitents from all satisfaction by punishment, for the sake of Christ's death, yet he does not excuse them from all salutary and chastening visitations. There is then a fallacy in the consequence, when the Papists draw this inference—The faithful, after their sins are forgiven them, endure temporal punishments; therefore they endure them to satisfy the wrath of God.... I answer, Paul's real meaning we have already explained, viz. that he bore his many afflictions for the Church, not to expiate sins, but for its edification and confirmation in the doctrine of the Gospel. When, therefore, they argue that from the circumstance of Paul having suffered many afflictions for the Church, he did so to make satisfaction to God for the Church, their argument is absurd; for we have assigned other causes for it. But we will confirm this our interpretation by the testimony of Anselm, and then conclude. *I fill up, says he, those things, which are wanting. But to whom (or where) are they wanting? In* MY *body. For in the body of Christ, to which the Virgin gave birth, no suffering was wanting; but in my body a part of his sufferings yet remain, which I endure daily in behalf of his universal body, which is the Church. For if I ceased to teach the faithful, I should not sustain these sufferings from those who are without faith: but inasmuch as I am always endeavoring to benefit the Church, I am always forced to endure afflictions. Such is Anselm's interpretation.* From which it appears that Paul suffered those afflictions for the Church, that he might thereby continually instruct the Church, not that he might make satisfaction for the sins of its faithful members.[98]

So then because Jesus Christ suffered once in His sinless person for the salvation of the world, He now no longer suffers in this way. There is nothing lacking in the passion of Christ, so it is not necessary now, or ever, for Him to suffer in this way again, personally or by proxy in the members of His church. For the Scriptures have already spoken on this point in no uncertain terms: ***"For Christ also suffered <u>once</u> for sins, the just for the unjust, that He might bring us to God." Christ being raised from the dead will never die again; death no longer has dominion over Him. The death He died He died to sin, once for all***" (1 Peter 3:18; Romans 6:9-10). Therefore, the afflictions of the Christian saints experienced by Paul, and all those within the church who undergo suffering for ministry and living for the Lord Jesus, are the things remaining of the afflictions of Christ. They are afflictions of Gospel ministry, and not related, in any way, to the completion of redemption or the expiation of sins now or in purgatory by the acquirement of indulgences. That Paul does not mean he or any other Christian suffers for the church in the same way Christ suffered for their salvation is made evident when the Apostle rhetorically asks in 1 Corinthians 1:13***: "Was Paul crucified for you?"*** The obvious answer is no!

---

[98] John Davenant, *Colossians* (Carlisle, PA: Banner of Truth, 2005), 288, 290-291. Bishop Davenant gives a very excellent and detailed excurses on the historical understanding of Colossians 1:24 from the Roman Catholic perspective followed by a point by point biblical and logical rebuttal to this in pages 269-291 of his commentary.

Paul knew nothing of any co-redemptive sufferings of the saints with Jesus for the completion of salvation when he declared to the Corinthian Christians in 1 Corinthians 2:2: ***"For I determined not to know any thing among you, save Jesus Christ, and him crucified."*** Taking all this into consideration, what Paul writes in Colossians 1:24-25 can in no way be construed to mean he suffers with Christ and then fills up what is lacking in Christ's redemptive sufferings to complete what is needed for salvation with the addition of papal indulgences. Nay, but rather he as a "minister" of the Gospel to the world and the church, suffers with Christ in this way for the advancement of the Savior's message and work among many "afflictions."

> Therefore Paul says nothing other than this, that he, as not the least important member of the body of Christ, fulfills his measure of the afflictions which yet remain or are left over to be borne by Christ's body. For when he says, "for . . . the church," he by no means understands that he suffers for the church in the same way that the one Christ suffered for all (2 Cor. 5:14) . . . And in this passage (Col. 1:24-25) he says that he suffers for the church, not as its redeemer, but as "a minister" of the church, who dispenses and fulfills the preaching of the Gospel; and for the testimony and confirmation of its truth he suffers so many afflictions. As to the phrase "for . . . the church," Paul uses the same phrase also elsewhere, adding a certain explanation, as in 2 Cor. 1:6: "If we are afflicted, it is for your comfort and salvation," not that Paul's tribulations merited salvation for the Corinthians, but, says he, your salvation is efficacious when you endure the same sufferings. "For we know that as you share in our sufferings, you will also share in our comfort" [v. 7]. And in 2 Cor. 4:15 he says about his afflictions: "It is all for your sake," not as Christ came into the flesh and suffered for you, but he adds the explanation: "So that as grace extends to more and more people" (namely in patience, perseverance, and liberation) "it may increase thanksgiving, to the glory of God." Therefore it is manifest, both from the words and from the things themselves, that this passage of Paul offers no support at all for the fraudulent papalist indulgences.[99]

With so many of Roman Catholicism's aberrant doctrines, the doctrine of papal indulgences has no support, basis, or origin in the Scriptures, or in the early church for that matter! Even the Catholic Church, prior to the rise of the anti-bibical Council of Trent, admits to the late origin and emergence of papal indulgences! It arose around the eleventh century with the concomitant rise of the doctrine of purgatory. Both are dependent upon each other for their mutual existence, for if there is no purgatory, then a need for indulgences are no longer required! Medieval Roman Catholic canon law scholar William Durandus (1230-1296), living in the thirteenth century, frankly confesses the idea of indulgences was unknown in Scripture and conspicuously absent from the early church when admitting: "About indulgences few things can be said with certainty, because Scripture does not speak expressly about them, and also the holy fathers, Ambrose, Hilary, Jerome, Augustine, say as good as nothing about indulgences."[100] The formal sanction and affirmation of indulgences with a treasury of merit came in 1343 with the pronouncements of Pope Clement VI—over thirteen hundred years after Christ and the Apostles—who were absolutely silent on such silly and unbiblical papal propositions! This fact is honestly conceded from a Roman Catholic priest and historian, who freely admits the following:

---

99 Martin Chemnitz, *Examination of the Council of Trent Volume IV*, 175.
100 Ibid., 179.

In 1343 Pope Clement VI officially sanctioned the view that Christ and the saints had left a treasury of merits that other members of the Church could draw on for the remission of the temporal punishment due to their sins. One obtained a share in the merits by means of a Church indulgence—usually granted by the Pope in exchange for some good work, often a donation of money, performed by the recipients.[101]

The Council of Trent's spurious claim the reality of papal indulgences goes back to Christ, the Apostles, and to the earliest times of the Christian church are disproven by history, early Christian doctrine, and, most importantly, the Word of God. The issuance of papal indulgences began with the imperious and highly ambitious Pope Boniface VIII, who in 1300 declared the first jubilee and granted indulgences to pilgrims who traveled to Rome. Those who made the journey were assured by this irascible Pope, bent on the acquisition of wealth and power for himself", a full remission of all temporal punishment in Purgatory with himself as the sole proprietor and issuer of these indulgences.[102] His motive was twofold: (1) To expand papal power beyond the earthly and temporal to include the eternal, spiritual and invisible domain of the afterlife and (2) To greatly increase the financial power and intake of the church upon the backs of the gullible and unsuspecting faithful. On the latter objective, Pope Boniface VIII was so successful with this that the financial offerings of the tens of thousands of pilgrims flocking to Rome to purchase indulgences was so great in their heaping accumulations that "pilgrim offerings" had to be "scooped in with rakes" both greatly enriching and expanding the centrality of the papacy and architecturally enlarging the Roman basilicas in the process.[103]

Of course indulgences are only good and efficacious so long as purgatory supposedly exists; and since we have demonstrated in the preceding pages no such place exists on biblical authority, then indulgences are equally fictitious and unsupported by the infallible Word of God. But with Rome's unrestrained and insatiable lust for greater, absolutist power, and the ever-expanding cupidity for financial enrichment, you have, here, the real source and reason for the arbitrary creation of papal indulgences. For, it is in the midst of the medieval papacy, you, also, furthermore, have their unbridled and rapacious reach for autocratic power in the zenith of opportunistic desperation to reign supreme in this life, and even extending in the world to come!

The creative fiction of purgatory first came during the time of Augustine. And over eight hundred years later, came the blasphemous and brazen fabrication of indulgences to exert tremendous influence over the desperate, superstitious, and ignorant masses who were all too willing to pay whatever monetary price to free their dear departed loves ones from the torments spent in the fires of purgatory. So, in this format, indulgences are only good if purgatory really exists, the former is existentially dependent upon the latter; thus since purgatory is not biblically validated, then indulgences are correspondingly unnecessary and no longer needed or valid. And both rest on the pretended power of a man-made papacy God does not biblically recognize or accept.

The truth is, that Romish indulgences, such as were granted in the days of Boniface VIII, and in the time of the crusades, were dependent for all their supposed importance upon the fiction of Purgatory. The comparatively trifling penances enjoined in this life, remitted by indulgences, were looked upon as of small account. It was the pretended power of the Popes to remit hundreds or thousands of years of the tortures of purgatory, or as in the case

---

[101] Thomas Bokenkotter, *A Concise History of the Catholic Church*, 214.
[102] Richard P. McBrien *Lives of the Popes*, 230.
[103] Eamon Duffy, *Saints & Sinners*, 160.

of a person who should die immediately after receiving *plenary* indulgence, to send the soul at once to heaven, without stopping at all at these purifying, but tormenting fires—it was this that gave to indulgences all their importance, and that enables those who thus blasphemously pretended to this power over the invisible world, to wield such a tremendous influence over the ignorant and superstitious, and not only to enhance their authority, but to enrich their coffers at the expense of the deluded and terror-stricken multitude.[104]

In 1342 Pope Clement VI was the first Pope to officially proclaim a treasury of merit existed, and access to it was obtained through the purchase or acquisition of an indulgence. But salvation cannot be obtained all at once; it must be gradually acquired through the various ritualistic requirements of receiving an indulgence without so much as knowing when the Catholic has finally done enough to be saved and enter heaven. More rosaries, more Masses, more alms and candles lit for prayers of the dead must be said and done without limit, over and over again. Pope Sixtus IV officially extended the power of indulgences in 1476 to the souls in the afterlife who were consigned in purgatory. His extension was a blatant attempt at enlarging the papal treasury after he depleted it with military campaigns and enriching family members.[105] Once the full remission for the punishment of temporal sins was granted by the Church through the issuance and purchase of an indulgence, the floodgates opened for the exploitation by the Popes and his avid clerics to gain and acquire great wealth from the European masses. Many of these people were all too willing to pay for entrance to heaven for themselves and for the souls of the departed to be released from the fiery torments of purgatory.

After the papacy was installed, the shameless opportunity for the abuse of trafficking in souls began and became an exploitative means for the papacy to gain tremendous wealth while playing on the fears and desperation of the masses to avoid an unpleasant afterlife! By the time of the sixteenth century, the shameless sale of indulgences became a booming business for the Catholic Church. The massive sale and universal purchase of these indulgences would even make the most money mongering televangelist of today blush with embarrassment!

The wanton practice of the selling of indulgences was indeed the chief cause for the Reformation of the Christian Church by a lowly and humble Augustinian monk by the name of Martin Luther (1483-1546). All of this was precipitated by the covetous ambitions of one, Pope Leo X (1475-1521), who saw great profits could be made through the gratuitous sale of indulgences. Leo X renewed the sale of indulgences to dismiss his official debts incurred through extravagant living, finance military expeditions, and renovate St. Pater's Basilica.[106] Germany, at the time of Leo's pontificate, was "already reeling under the impact of a hundred papal abuses" allowing for the most horrible crimes and sins to be absolved by the church for the right price. A deacon guilty of murder could be absolved for twenty crowns. A bishop or abbot who had killed an enemy could be forgiven by the church for the price of three hundred livres. Any civil authority that protested or tried to prohibit these abominable atrocities was promptly excommunicated![107]

Leo X canvassed all of Europe with the sale and offer of indulgences. Germany, however, was one area of his most intense focus. In his papal bull *Sacrosancti salvatoris et redemptoris nostri*, issued on March 31,

---

[104] John Dowling, *The History of Romanism*, 357-358.
[105] Richard P. McBrien, *Lives of the Popes*, 265.
[106] This is the current St. Peter's Basilica standing front and center in Vatican City today. It is a structure built on the lies, superstitions, and unrestrained greed of the Roman Catholic papacy in their Gospel denying acts of selling indulgences!
[107] Peter Rosa, *Vicars of Christ*, 116.

1515, Pope Leo X granted a plenary indulgence to be sold for eight years in the German churches of Mainz, Magdeburg, and Brandenburg. This super indulgence was called *the Indulgence of Peter* because all proceeds from the sales were to fund the building of St. Peter's Square and Basilica. This purchased indulgence promised the remission of all sins, except in few cases reserved by the Pope, and gave dispensation for almost all moral offenses including adultery and theft. Anyone impeding the indulgence was threatened with the church's punishment. Priests in their parishes were expected to give long and regular sermons on how *the indulgence of Peter* was necessary for the building of Saint Peter's. Four chief "graces" were attached to those who purchased this indulgence for Rome's grandiose building project, which essentially put salvation of the soul up for sale to any and all, who could afford to purchase it with the corruptible mammon of this world. Lutheran scholar and church historian Martin Brecht elaborates on what kind of profane, mercantile salvation these four "graces" were that a person could buy from Rome for the right price:

> They were, first, the complete remission of all sins. There was no greater grace. The sinner obtained complete forgiveness and thereby the grace of God anew, and moreover remission of the punishments of sin and purgatory. The sinner as such could never earn such grace, but it was nevertheless possible under the following conditions: contrition of heart, confession or at least the intention to do so, followed by visits to seven churches in which certain prayers were to be offered...Last but not least, a monetary payment, graduated according to status and means, was to be made: kings and queens had to pay twenty-five gulden, high prelates and counts ten gulden, lesser prelates and counts six gulden, townsfolk and merchants three gulden, artisans one gulden, and others a half gulden. The indigent were to fast and pray...The second chief grace consisted of the possibility of obtaining a confessional letter which entitled one twice to receive absolution from all sins, even those reserved to the Pope, at a time of one's own discretion and in the hour of death. The third chief grace, which could also be obtained by buying a confessional letter, promised the one who obtained it and his dead relatives participation in all the church's goods, i.e., its prayers, fasts, alms, and other pious works. Like the previous grace, this could also be obtained without confession; thus even in a state of sin one could also participate in the blessings of church fellowship. Not without reason was the fourth grace especially extolled. It consisted of the remission of punishment of sins for souls in purgatory by means of the Pope's intercession when one paid for these souls. In this way one could come to the aid of the dead and at the same time contribute to the building of St. Peter's.[108]

The year was 1517, and the infamous Dominican John Tetzel was commissioned by the papacy to peddle indulgences in Germany traveling throughout the region making outlandish promises to those who bought indulgences. He was reputed to have said: "As soon as a coin in the coffer rings, the soul from purgatory springs."[109] Here we have the folly and height of Rome's blasphemies against the infinite sacrifice of Christ's

---

[108]   Martin Brecht, *Martin Luther: His Road to Reformation—1483-1521* (Minneapolis, Fortress Press: 1993), 180-182.

[109]   In thesis 55 of Tetzel's *One Hundred and Six Theses*. These "Anti-theses" were a reply to Luther's <u>Ninety-Five Theses</u> and were drawn up by Tetzel's friend and former Professor, Konrad Wimpina. Theses 55 & 56 (responding to Luther's 27th Theses) read: "For a soul to fly out, is for it to obtain the vision of God, which can be *hindered by no interruption*, therefore he errs who says that the soul *cannot fly out* before the coin can jingle in the bottom of the chest."

cross where the Son of God endured the full infinite wrath of God for our sins and thus paid for them in full with His infinite, perfect sacrifice. Christ saving death on the cross was a free act of God's sovereign, underserved grace no one else could achieve, let alone purchase with the cankered gold, silver, or fading currency used to buy an inconsequential indulgence. Mind blowing as it is, Rome still to this very hour maintains the efficacy of indulgences to remove sin—even when earned or paid for to the church—apparently forgetting in this unholy commerce *"that you were not redeemed with corruptible things, like silver or gold* (as in the purchase of indulgences with these commodities), *from your aimless conduct received by tradition from your fathers* (Here, the medieval belief and practice the purchase or acquirement of a papal indulgence can remit the guilt of any sin where only the shed blood of Jesus Christ can) *but with the precious blood of Christ, as of a lamb without blemish and without spot"* (1 Peter 1:18-19). Other blasphemous claims for the magical power of indulgences the presumptuous Tetzel made are given in the following historical account:

"Here is Rome, people should not let the salvation offered by the indulgence escape them. Have mercy upon your dead parents. Whoever has an indulgence has salvation; anything else is of no avail."[110] "Indulgences are the most precious and sublime of God's gifts." "This cross" (pointing to the red cross on the papal standard) "has as much efficacy as the cross of Jesus Christ. Draw near, and I will give you letters, duly sealed, by which even the sins you shall hereafter desire to commit shall be all forgiven you."[111] Tetzel went on to brazenly and shockingly proclaim with the full approval of Rome: "I would not exchange my privileges for those of Saint Peter in heaven, for I have saved more souls with my indulgence than he with his sermons. There is no sin so great that the indulgence cannot remit, and even if any one should (which is doubtless impossible) ravish the Holy Virgin Mother of God, let him pay—let him only pay largely, and it shall be forgiven him." Playing on the ignorance of the masses, which did not know the Gospel truths of Scripture, and would do anything to free themselves and their dead friends and relatives from the tormenting flames of purgatory, Tetzel unabashedly declared: "Even Repentance is not indispensable. But more than all this: indulgences save not the living alone—*they also save the dead.* Ye priests, ye nobles, ye tradesmen, ye wives, ye maidens, and ye young men, hearken to your departed parents and friends, who cry to you from the bottomless abyss: 'We are enduring horrible torment! A small alms would deliver us;--you can give it, and you will not'. *The very moment that the money clinks against the bottom of the chest, the soul escapes from purgatory, and flies to heaven.*"[112]

Did the Popes of Rome ever formally condemn John Tetzel's blatant and blasphemous peddling of indulgences for the reconstruction of Saint Peter's Basilica to the tune of what would cost today over 63 million American dollars—a staggering sum in the sixteenth century? Did they condemn the scandalous exploitation, abuse and misuse of indulgences by John Tetzel leading the people to believe they could literally purchase salvation from the Church of Rome? No, in fact they still defend Tetzel's unsavory practices to this very hour. One only has to look at the voluminous *Catholic Encyclopedia* and their pathetic attempt at a defense for the pervasive and profane attempt of making the free, unmerited gift of salvation a commodity for purchase which Tetzel zealously engaged in. Such egregious and shameful actions would make him a heretic in any age, whose actions violate the very lifeblood of the Gospel message where God offers a free, forever, unconditional pardon of all sins to those who *"accept repentance toward God, and faith toward*

---

[110]   Martin Brecht, *Martin Luther: His Road to Reformation—1483-152*, 182-183.

[111]   John Dowling, *A History of Romanism*, 440.

[112]   Ibid., 440, 443.

our Lord Jesus Christ" (Acts 20:21). Instead, the Catholic Encyclopedia says the moral character of John Tetzel was vindicated in all, this![113]

While some Popes have admitted there was some misuse in the matter of indulgences, they have not rejected in essence what they are supposed to accomplish in remitting the sins of the living and the dead. For instance, while Pope Paul VI nominally acknowledges there was an abuse of practice concerning indulgences, and out of a cosmetic desire to reform this abuse, he reduced the number of plenary indulgences and discontinued the previous practice of attaching a certain number of days and years to a certain task required for an indulgence. But he still upheld the practice of indulgences as a means of the church granting the exclusive right to remit sin when this divine right belongs to God alone apart from any work or effort of man. And yet one can find in *The New Saint Joseph Baltimore Catechism* a partial indulgence "hastens the healing process" so a 300 days indulgence has the healing power of 300 days and so forth (From *The New Saint Joseph Baltimore Catechism*, page 207 [Section 438])!

It was 1517 when the crass commercialism of selling papal indulgences reached its zenith and aroused the righteous ire of Martin Luther. The German reformer looked on with shame as the Pope was parasitically playing on the fears and desperation of the Catholic faithful by essentially promising remission of sins for the right monetary price followed by the prescribed act. To Luther's horror, the average person was left with the obvious impression, given by the mercenary approach of Rome and her indulgence peddlers, money paid could indeed purchase some form of forgiveness from God and thus the salvation of the soul secured in one measure or another. He saw how the selling of indulgences was a booming business and a great cash flow for the Catholic Church. Luther saliently realized, with this profane practice of the selling of indulgences, the very heart of the Gospel of grace was at stake and was being overturned and subverted by the very ones claiming to be its messengers.

The Protestant Reformation was born the moment Martin Luther set to pen and paper his powerful, iconoclastic *Ninety-five Theses*, which in its ninety-five propositions exposes the false nature and unbiblical claims the Pope makes for indulgences when claiming he has the sole right given to him by Jesus Christ to forgive any and every sin, partially or fully. The great reformer staked his life and reputation on this essential truth of the Gospel when he defiantly nailed his theses to the doors of the church in Wittenberg, Germany, and gave eloquent defense against the false accusations hurled at him during the Diet of Worms. Luther's ninety-five theses also sets forth a clear explanation and defense of the New Testament Gospel and how God truly and fully forgives the repentant sinner based on His unmerited grace that is exclusively revealed through the Gospel of salvation, which can never be earned or purchased, by the undeserving sinner! Martin Luther was also aghast at how quick and easy purchase of indulgences led to their habitual abuses by people who reasoned they could sin in the future and still fall back on an easy out by purchasing an indulgence for a license and excuse to continue on in whatever future sin, since the removal for the penalty of such was

---

[113]   Johann Tetzel," *The Catholic Encyclopedia*. Vol. 14. New York: Robert Appleton Company, 1912. 16 Jan. 2012 <http://www.newadvent.org/cathen/14539a.htm>. Never mind the fact John Tetzel was crass, greedy, and unashamedly brazen in arrogantly, with the backing and strong encouragement of the papacy, thinking the gift of God's forgiveness can in any way be bought or purchased with a price when the Word of God clearly declares otherwise through and through. The words of Simon Peter to Simon Magnus equally applies to Tetzel, the papacy, and the clerics of Rome who have the audacity in offering indulgences for sale to purchase the gift of God's salvation: ***"Your money perish with you, because you thought that the gift of God could be purchased with money!"*** (Acts 8:20).

already bought and paid for. The main point for Luther's anger and disturbance over the practice and doctrine of indulgences was focused on how there was simply no biblical basis or authority for doing this!

> He saw no scriptural authority for the buying and selling of an indulgence. He recognized that the indulgence had become a "hot" product for the church. Indulgences created a great cash flow! The practice of indulgences also encouraged people to sin. Other than having to spend a little extra money, there was no "down side" to sin. It's human nature to find the money for favorite pastimes, sinful or otherwise. In Luther's day, that equaled out to finding the money for forgiveness. Just as important to Luther was the fact that the indulgence took the focus of a Christian's life away from Christ and God's forgiveness. Forgiveness was not the product of Christ's life, death, and resurrection but rather it was a financial transaction.[114]

Throughout his ninety-five theses Luther correctly pointed out indulgences took the central "focus" off of how the death and resurrection of Jesus Christ alone procured salvation for the forgiveness of sins to the sinner and was cheaply reduced to a financial transaction where God is bought off to spare any further punishment on the purchaser of an indulgence! With regard to the Pope's supposed ability to grant indulgences for the remission of sins, Luther emphatically declared in theses number six:

> 6. The Pope cannot remit any guilt, except by declaring and showing that it has been remitted by God; or, to be sure, by remitting guilt in cases reserved to his judgment. If his right to grant remission in these cases were disregarded, the guilt would certainly remain unforgiven.[115]

On using money acquired from indulgences to build the lavish and opulent St Peter's, in theses 50-51, Luther writes the Pope should use his own money instead of fleecing the sheep of his flock leaving them destitute and wanting—both spiritually and financially.

> 50. Christians are to be taught that if the Pope knew the exactions of the indulgence preachers, he would rather that the basilica of St. Peter were burned to ashes than built up with the skin, flesh, and bones of his sheep

> 51. Christians are to be taught that the Pope would and should wish to give of his own money, even though he had to sell the basilica of St. Peter, to many of those from whom certain hawkers of indulgences cajole money.

In theses sixty-two, I believe, the *sine qua non* of Luther's devastating refutation of the unscriptural practice of papal indulgences is simply and inarguably captured when the Reformer states, "the true treasure of the church is the most holy gospel of the glory and grace of God." For nowhere else is salvation and the forgiveness of sins found. To displace the singular power of the Gospel to save sinners by claiming the papacy's dispensing of its indulgences is an extension of that saving power, or an additional requirement,

---

[114]   Carol and Roddy Smith, *The Ultimate Guide to Christian History* (Uhrich, Ohio Barbour: 2001), 282.

[115]   Martin Luther, *Luther's Ninety-five Theses*, translated by C.M. Jacobs (Philadelphia, Fortress Press: 1957), 12.

is a fraudulent claim, and the creation of a counterfeit 'gospel'. Moreover, as Luther saliently pointed out in thesis eighty-two, if the Pope supposedly has the power to grant a partial or plenary indulgence remitting sin, then why does he not freely extend this to all sincerely contrite souls without requiring any "miserable money" for such a generous act? To refrain from doing so in the past and in the present to those qualified is an inexcusable act of omission on Rome's part, and at once exposes the fact their refusal to do so shows their motives are the same as the false, greedy prophets the Apostle Peter (whom they revere as the first "Pope") castigated in 2 Peter 2:3 who ***through covetousness shall they with feigned words make merchandise of you: whose judgment now of a long time lingers not, and their damnation slumbers not.***

The result of Luther's thunderous and revolutionary ninety-five theses was the spark that ignited the much needed Reformation which led to the restoration of the simple Gospel truth of justification by faith alone in Christ alone—a fundamental Gospel truth which had been buried centuries ago by the assorted false doctrines and man-made traditions of Roman Catholicism. And it is here where the Reformation created the great divide on the issues of the centrality of the Gospel, grace, the authority of Scripture, salvation, and faith and works was drawn and defined. Luther was eventually excommunicated from Rome as a heretic because of his fearless stand for the revival and restoration of the Gospel truth which had long been supplanted and set aside by the myriad of extra biblical traditions and doctrines of Roman Catholicism and the papacy. For those Protestants inclined to believe that with the long passage of nearly five hundred years, Rome has surely changed on the subject of indulgences, they are sadly mistaken.

In the papal declaration, "Incarnations Mysterium" publicly released on January 29, 1998, Pope John Paul II announced many special Jubilee indulgences for the year 2000 in which he reaffirms the unbiblical claim the church, with its treasury of merit, has the sole power to grant the remission of the penalty attached to venial sins. In this papal decree, the Pope lays out the same works based conditions the Catholic church has historically ascribed to the granting and obtainment of indulgences—pilgrimages to Rome, the Holy Land, cathedrals, and shrines ending with reciting of the "Our father" and prayers to the "Blessed Virgin Mary." The requirements for God's full forgiveness given in the plenary indulgence can also be satisfied with works of charity—visiting the elderly and handicapped, fasting, and even abstaining from the daily "consumption" of alcohol and tobacco.[116] The Catholic clergy and apologists are careful to maintain today indulgences are not for sale or for purchase, but can be received only through an act of charity or a donation made to the Church. But, however you chose to phrase this, the one outstanding and disturbing feature remains: There is still a meritorious exchange going on regardless of the disproportionality; and with this an act, the sinner can do or achieve to merit the act of God's remission of sin, which Scripture says over and over again is impossible. For the very nature of biblical salvation, as we have found, is an unmerited act of God's mercy and saving grace towards the undeserving sinner!

While good works are an important element in the Christian life, they follow salvation and are the proof of its reality. Never in the New Testament are we told the Christian must do good works to earn or

---

[116] For the full-blown salvation by works indulgence system elucidated in *Incarnations Mysterium* go to the Vatican's official web site at http://www.vatican.va/jubilee_2000/docs/documents/hf_jp-ii_doc_30111998_bolla-jubilee_en.html. After reading Pope John Paul II's disturbing explanation for how one can work or do certain religious acts to gain full pardon of sins from God, one really wonders how he can talk of the biblical Gospel of unmerited grace and then go on to immediately deny such a divine reality when the church demands certain works to receive an indulgence that leads to the full of pardon of sin (plenary indulgence). This probably best epitomizes the ongoing cognitive dissonance of Rome and the papacy when holding two mutually exclusive ideas at the same time, which cannot and will not work in the light of what biblical salvation really is!

keep salvation before or after he or she is saved. This is where the idea of indulgences is false in that it seeks to convince Catholics they can add from the saving work of Christ the need for indulgences to bring about the forgiveness of sins. The deceptive word game here lies in Rome's clever claim they are not in fact teaching salvation by works because indulgences are simply an extension of Christ's saving work from the cross. Again, there are no passages in all of the New Testament where it is plainly stated for all to know and understand, the church has the authority to grant the power of an indulgence in collusion with Christ to give the forgiveness of sins, and reduce temporal punishment in purgatory to complete the salvation process! The belief in indulgences takes away the exclusive reality believers are forgiven, saved, and reconciled to God by the cross of Christ alone as Scripture uniformly declares. God's grace freely given in salvation is not parceled out bit-by-bit under a merit system of partial and plenary indulgences. As Paul resoundingly declares in Romans 5:10-11: *"For if while we were enemies we were reconciled to God through the death of His Son, much more, having been reconciled, we shall be saved by His life."* And this reconciliation of the forgiven sinner singularly occurred when God *"was in Christ reconciling the world to Himself, not imputing their trespasses to them, and has committed to us the word* (not the sacrament, or indulgence) *of reconciliation"* (2 Corinthians 5: 19).

The so-called need for indulgences keeps Catholic souls in bondage and servile dependence on the Catholic Church instead of trusting in the all sufficiency of Christ's shed blood alone to remit, cleanse, and remove all sin! This here is the essential problem with Roman Catholic indulgences: They negate, by way of contradictory addition, the sole sufficiency of the cross and salvation by faith *alone* in this redemptive accomplishment *alone*. Christian apologist Matt Slick sums this up well when observing:

> Christ on the cross, the very propitiation offered by the Lord in his sacrifice is usurped by the Roman Catholic Church. The power and priesthood and mediatorship of Christ is replaced by that of the Roman Catholic Church and it becomes the means by which the so-called people of God are relieved of their sin punishment. This is a blasphemous claim of Rome that detracts from the power and glory and sufficiency of the cross. All Roman Catholics should stop looking to the church as a means of salvation and/or as a means of deliverance from punishment. Instead, the Roman Catholic should look to Christ alone through faith alone for the forgiveness of his/her sins. The obvious problem with indulgences is that they negate the all-sufficiency of the cross. It was Jesus who took our punishment. He took our place so that we do not have to suffer any punishment for our sins so that we might be made right with God. We are not saying that sins do not have consequences and punishments. We are saying that being made right with God is not by our suffering, but by Christ's.[117]

Prayers for the Dead.

Another disturbing, unbiblical feature associated with both purgatory and indulgences is the whole idea of prayers for the dead. The Catholic Church calls this belief "the communion of the saints." Concerning "communion with the dead" the term means, according to the *Catechism of the Catholic Church*:

---

[117]   Matt Slick, "Indulgences" at http://www.carm.org/indulgences.

In full consciousness of this communion of the whole Mystical Body of Jesus Christ, the Church in its pilgrim members, from the very earliest days of the Christian religion, has honored with great respect the memory of the dead; and *'because it is a holy and a wholesome thought to pray for the dead that they maybe loosed from their sins' she offers her suffrages for them. Our prayer for them is capable not only of helping them, but also of making their intercession for us effective* (Emphasis mine)[118].

What is meant here is: Those living within the Catholic Church have the delegated power to release the dead souls from purgatory and reduce the amount of time spent there by intercessory prayers, indulgences, alms and other religious works. The most effective is having the Mass said for the Catholic dead. The Catholic is taught that since the church is Christ's body, and therefore exists as one body in heaven and on Earth, its members cannot be separated from each other—hence the indivisible unity of the dead and the living with the ability to pray for the dead in purgatory and affect their release from there.[119] Upon a closer inspection of this claim, we find its logic quite wanting in light of what Scripture says about the true nature of the church, death, and the spiritual reality of the living and the dead. Praying for the dead is not biblical, nor is it called for in Scripture!

While it is true the church is the spiritual body of Jesus Christ, there yet exist in the physical plane the false and the true, the visible and the invisible in the professing sphere of the church during the present age (Matthew 13:16-23, 37-43, 47-50). Furthermore, the Bible does teach there is a real separation at death and therefore a real, physical separation between living believers and dead believers. Once the soul leaves the body at death, there exists a separation between the two (James 2:26). Living believers are separated from dead believers. Paul makes this point throughout the writings of the New Testament. The dead are physically absent from the bodily, physical presence of Christians living on Earth (2 Corinthians 5:6-8). Dead Christians depart this world for heaven (not purgatory) and are physically separated, in all ways, from living believers on Earth (Philippians 1:23). But the latter are comforted, as in the case of the Thessalonian Christians, with the sure promise they will, one day, be reunited with believers who have already died when the Lord descends from heaven to resurrect and translate both the dead and the living at the Rapture of the Church—then and only until then will the church from all centuries be united and together centered around the Lord Jesus Christ (1 Thessalonians 4:14-18). In light of what the Word of God reveals here, it is simply incorrect for the Catholic Church to say there is no separation between living Christians and dead Christians!

Until the Rapture, dead believers remain separated and inaccessible to believers alive on Earth, and vice-versa. To pray for the dead also undermines the fact when one believes on Christ he or she is saved and promised immediate entrance into heaven upon death when the soul leaves the body. In Luke 16 Jesus points out there are only two places every departed soul goes to after death—heaven or hell. No souls of the faithful being consigned to purgatory are ever mentioned in Luke 16—one of the most important New Testament passages on the intermediate state of the soul in the afterlife (Luke 16:19-31; John 14:1-4; Philippians 1:23). Death is a chasm and wall of separation between the living and the dead. When recounting this fact in Luke 16, Jesus indicates there is no communication allowed or given between the living and the dead (Luke 16:27-31). We cannot agree more here with the following observation one has made based on the truth of Luke 16:19-31:

---

[118] *Catechism of the Catholic Church*, 272, **[958]**.

[119] "The Communion of Saints" in *The Catholic Encyclopedia*. New York: Robert Appleton Company. Retrieved January 30, 2012 from New Advent: http://www.newadvent.org/cathen/04171a.htm

Praying for the dead is not a biblical concept. Our praying for the dead has no bearing on someone once he or she has died. The reality is that at the point of death, one's eternal destiny is confirmed. Either he is saved through faith in Christ and in heaven where he is experiencing rest and joy in God's presence, or he is in torment in hell. The story of the rich man and Lazarus the beggar provides us with a vivid illustration of this truth. Jesus plainly used this story to teach that after death the unrighteous are eternally separated from God, that they remember their rejection of the Gospel, that they are in torment, and that their condition cannot be remedied (Luke 16:19-31).[120]

Jesus did not say the living could pray for the welfare of the dead simply because both Lazarus's and the rich man's respective fates in eternity were irreversibly fixed! After death, the fate and eternal destiny of every soul is permanently sealed on whether they believed Christ for salvation or not. The Bible speaks of two mutually exclusive places only (heaven and hell); and there is no explicit mention of anything else existing in between where the dead can move from one location (purgatory) to another (heaven) on the prayers and spiritual merits of the living praying for the dead! The Scriptures unanimously teach those who truly believe in Jesus Christ and experience the spiritual rebirth from this directly, immediately and instantly enter in to heaven upon death to be in the presence of the Lord (Psalm 17:15; Luke 23:43; Hebrews 5:8-9). So there is no need for Christians on Earth to pray for the Christian dead, since the latter are in heaven before the presence of the Lord! Hebrews 9:27 says, *"It is appointed for men once to die, and after this comes judgment,"* and by that revelation at once, closes the door decisively on any idea there is room for a change or improvement in one's spiritual condition and destiny in the afterlife following death, either by the efforts of an individual, or a group of people, praying *for* the dead or praying *to* the dead.

Prayers for the dead are therefore of no avail, because the saved are already enjoying the bliss of heaven and the presence of the Lord. Not once, in all of Scripture, does God ask or demand believers pray for the dead! It is by the prayers and intercession of our great High Priest Jesus Christ; all believers are guided, helped, and brought safely to the glories of heaven upon death. For, *"You will guide me with Your counsel, and afterward receive me into glory"* (Psalm 73:24). *"Therefore He is able to save to the uttermost those who come to God through Him since He always lives to make intercession for them"* (Hebrews 7:25). The keeping power of God guards and protects the believer to the very end and in an instant when death comes to the body, he or she is instantly brought into heaven where the risen Christ stands to welcome His beloved home. There is no fear of temporary or permanent separation at this point because the unconquerable love of Christ stays with the believer all the way through from the moment of faith and spiritual rebirth to the last breath on Earth. God safely leads the saved from earth to heaven without interruption or the help of any man.

Once in heaven, immediately after death, the believer no longer needs or requires the aid or prayers from those less fortunate still living on Earth. God leads the departed soul of the believer from earth to the glories above because of His abiding presence and faithfulness to guide and bring the redeemed from this earthly scene to the glory of His presence in heaven. So from what the Word of God reveals, contradicting the need and practice of praying for the dead, in each stage and in each way from earth directly to heaven, every believer is

Firmly and safely kept by the power of God unto full salvation! The journey is not long; the transition is often very quick. The instant that he has suffered the last pang, and wept

---

[120]   "What Does the Bible Say About Praying for the Dead?" at http://www.gotquestions.org/praying-for-the-dead.html.

the last tear, and heaved the last sigh, and looked his last look of love on earth, he is before the throne of God and the Lamb, drinking of the crystal river that flows from beneath it, and basking in the effulgence of glory that beams around it. My soul, let faith, with its far-seeing eye, look within the veil, and behold the glory into which you shall before long enter, and exclaim, in the sweet exercise of that faith, ***"You will receive me to glory."***[121]

Let no person mistakenly believe upon the unfounded man-made tradition of the Catholic Church that he can somehow pray for those who have died to secure a favorable or beneficial outcome in the afterlife for the person(s) who died. The Word of God teaches each one of us will determine where we spend eternity based upon how we respond to the Gospel of the Lord Jesus Christ in this life (John 3:16-21; 36). If prayers for the dead were a standard practice and belief for the faithful, why is there no mention of it being done and taught in all of Scripture—the apocryphal citation in 2Maccabees 12: 45 notwithstanding! In fact, wherever the dead are mentioned in the sixty-six books of the Bible, not one time is there any mention made the living are to pray for the dead souls in purgatory! When the infant son of King David died, he did not resort to praying for his son. David was a prophet of God that revealed the supernatural realities of what lies beyond death, and yet did not see the need for praying for the soul of his dead son, nor did he prescribe such a belief or practice totally foreign to the Scriptures. David's response upon learning of the death of his son was, ***"Can I bring him back again? I will go to him, but he will not return to me"*** (2 Samuel 12:22-23). Here we learn David made no attempt at prayer for the dead because He knew the immediacy of heaven and the ultimate resurrection were true for both him and his infant son (Psalm 16:10).

Since God said David was a man "after My own heart" (1 Samuel 13:14), it would stand to reason the Lord would have communicated the important truth about praying for the dead, if true, especially when David wrote all of his portions of Scripture by the inspiration of God's Spirit as He revealed to David the great things concerning His spiritual kingdom both now and in the life to come! Praying for the dead was never mentioned or prescribed in the life and ministry of Jesus, particularly when He dealt with the ugly reality of death. Take, for example, the death of his close friend Lazarus in John chapter eleven. When Jesus was told Lazarus was dead, He did not instruct His disciples or the sister of Lazarus to pray for their dead brother and friend that his soul would be released from purgatory so he could enter heaven. Jesus prayed for the living at Lazarus' tomb asking God to show them standing there His resurrection power over death (John 11:41-42). And Jesus proved this when He summoned the dead Lazarus from His tomb after being dead for four days!

The practice of saying prayers for the dead is denying, in principle, the all-sufficient accomplishment of the sacrifice of Christ! When Jesus died for our sins and opened heavens gates giving unhindered, direct access to God, it was a salvation finished and complete on the brow of Calvary (John 19:30; Hebrews 10:14). There is no more need to be freed from the penalty of sin when Jesus has already ***"freed us from our sins by His blood"*** (Revelation 1:5). It is by the prayerful intercession and once for all sacrifice of Jesus, our Great High Priest, the saved sinner is brought into the immediate presence of God in heaven when he or she dies (Luke 16:23; 23:43; John 14:1-6). In light of what has been said above, praying for the dead is absent from Scripture, contrary to what the Bible teaches, and is nowhere sanctioned, mentioned, or practiced in all of its sacred pages! Prayer in the Bible was always offered *by the living* to God for *the living on Earth*; it was never offered or said for the departed souls who already died.

---

[121] "The Believer in Glory" at http://www.gracegems.org/Winslows/w25.htm

INDEX

A.

B.

C.

Canon Law
Rule which clergy and parishioners are governed
    by, 18, 43, 104, 145, 160, 194, 268, 290, 314,
    320, 330

Catechism of the Catholic Church
Contradicts Scripture, 182, 225
Teaches one can merit eternal life, 227

Catholic Church
History of deceit and corruption, 58-70, 96-101,
    145-156
Inquisition kills millions, 67-68
Not started by Jesus, 71-72
Originated with Constantine, 7-8, 77-78
Promotes works salvation system, 1-3, 172, 190,
    230-233, 268, 272, 284, 330, 389
Rejects Justification by faith alone, 225, 233, 258
    366, 327

Christ alone
Complete salvation for the believer, 401-402,
    419-420
His salvation is finished forever, 389-393, 401
Received by faith alone, 323, 388

Church Councils
Ecumenical Councils, 30, 54-57, 96
Pope not above Councils, 53-57, 103-104

Church Fathers
Considered all major bishops to be equal, 30-38
Early on, did not universally acknowledge Rome
    and its bishop as supreme, 37, 121
No unanimous Consent on the Papacy and the
    sacraments, 23, 121, 227-229

Confession
Absent from early church, 296
Dangers of, 291-294
Developed in the sixth century and on, 295-296

No support in Scripture, 269-273, 277-281, 299
Rome says Necessary for forgiveness, 266-267
To God alone, 269-273

Confirmation (Sacrament)
Absent in New Testament, 483-485,

D.

Deacons, 133-134, 141, 313-315, 317

Donation of Constantine, 72-73

Donation of Pepin, 72-73

E.

Ecumenical Councils
Did not affirm the supremacy of the Bishop of
    Rome as Pope, 30, 53-57

Elders,
114, 133-134, 141, 305, 317

Eucharist
Another Christ, 182, 185
Central to the Mass, 159-163
Christ's real physical presence, 163
Imparts saving grace, 160-161 166
Is idolatry, 181-184
Meaning, 159-160
To be adored and worshipped as God, 164-166

F.

Faith (as taught in Scripture)
Alone sufficient for salvation, not of works, 2-3, 47,
    103, 190, 203, 230 232
Catholic Church adds works, 2, 172, 227. 269, 330,
    367, 376, 388
Rome condemns faith alone for salvation, 267, 389

G.

Grace (biblical)
Freely given by God, 230, 232-233, 268, 284, 232, 389
Not earned, 38
Through faith in Christ alone, 189-190, 197, 231, 369
Unmerited, 269, 388

Grace (Roman Catholic)
Given through the sacraments, 226
Lost by mortal sin, 266
Renewed only through the sacraments, 226-227

Gregory the Great
Eschewed the Title of "Universal Bishop", 16-17, 37

H.

Holy Orders
Not Found in Scripture or the early church, 312-313, 316, 318-319

Holy Spirit
Christ gives apart from ritual and sacrament, 265
Given by faith and belief in Jesus alone, 264-265

I.

Indulgences
Catalyst for Reformation, 386-387
Man-made by Popes, 381-382
Terrible abuses, 383-386

Infallibility
Not supported by Scripture or Church history, 84, 91-92,95-97, 109
Of Bishops, 83
Of Pope, 83
Opposed by Catholic Prelates at Vatican I, 92-93
Ratified at Vatican I Council, 92, 94,

Inquisition
Millions killed, 67-69
Started by Popes, 62-63

J.

Jesuits
And Papal Infallibility, 93

John XXII
Condemned as Anti-Christ by Catholic Church Council, 90

John XXIII
42, 154

John Paul II
86, 399, 220-221, 281, 388

Justification by faith
Biblical position, 230-231, 243
Roman Catholic View (Sacraments), 225-227

K.

Keating, Karl (Catholic Apologist)
8, 32, 144-145,

Kung, Hans
71, 86, 99

L.

Last Supper
New Testament Teaching, 167-178
Roman Catholic View, 159-167

Limbo
235-236, 253

Of all believers (biblical view), 131-132
Power to forgive sin, 265-268
Sexual scandals (homosexuality, pedophilia, etc),
    146-156

Purgatory
A place of purification, 325-328
Development, 363
First Corinthians 3:10-15, 342-357
Pagan origin, 358
Refutes the finality of the Cross, 334-335, 364-365
Second Maccabees 12:39-46, 339-341
Temporary punishment, 326-327, 335

R.

Reformation
Brought the Word of God to the people, 91
Due to papal abuses, 386-388

S.

Sacraments
Anointing of the sick, 300
Baptism, 234
Confirmation, 260
Eucharist, 159
Holy Orders, 311
Matrimony, 320
Necessary for salvation, 226-227
Penance, 265
Seven in number, 225
Two ordinances of the church, 233

Salvation
Based on Christ's death alone, 221-222, 231-232
Catholic need for sacraments, 226
Initiated by baptism, 234-235, 245
Received by faith alone apart from
Our works, 2-3, 102-103, 203, 230, 250, 310-311

Salza, John (Catholic Apologist)
On Purgatory, 326, 328, 342, 344, 345, 352
Scripture twisting, 328-329, 351

Scripture
Final authority of the believer, 6, 113-114, 118
Infallible and sufficient alone, 108
Test Roman Catholic doctrines by, 123, 144

Sin
Biblical view, 285-287
Mortal, 266
Venial, 266

T.

Tabernacle
Eucharist placed there, 164-166

Ten Commandments
181, 182

Tradition (Roman Catholic)
Often at variance with Scripture, 8, 91, 106, 117,
    145, 322, 324, 371

Transubstantiation
Allegedly based on Christ's words of institution,
    126, 167-168
False sign and wonders, 184-185
Goes against Word of God, 167-180
John chapter six, 185-207

Treasury of the Church
Adds to Christ's merits, 368-370
Cannot add to the perfect work of Christ, 373-375

Trent, Council, of
Condemns biblical truth of salvation by faith alone,
    267, 389
Belief in Papacy necessary for salvation, 11

V.

Vatican Council I
And infallibility, 83-85

Vatican Council II
87, 91, 110-111, 311-312

Vicar of Christ
Holy Spirit is the true Vicar, 10
Pope blasphemes claiming to be this, 13

W.

Word of God
Fails to support many Roman Catholic doctrines,
    14, 18, 26, 107-109, 213, 324, 331, 371
The only standard we test all things by, 113-114, 118

Works, good
Faith plus works (Catholic view), 172, 189-190, 227,
    268, 277, 340, 367-369
Works follow saving faith (Biblical view), 230, 233,
    353-354, 388